SELECTED PAPERS BY SUSAN KAVALER-ADLER

VOLUME I: DEVELOPMENTAL MOURNING, EROTIC TRANSFERENCE, AND OBJECT RELATIONS PSYCHOANALYSIS

IPBOOKS.net
International Psychoanalytic Books

International Psychoanalytic Books (IPBooks)
New York • http://www.IPBooks.net

Developmental Mourning, Erotic Transference, and Object Relations Psychoanalysis, Volume 1

Published by IPBooks, Queens, NY
Online at: www.IPBooks.net

Cover art: MindMend Media, Inc. – www.mindmedia.com

ISBN: 978-1-956864-29-8

OTHER BOOKS BY THIS AUTHOR

The Compulsion to Create: Women Writers and Their Demon Lovers. (Routledge 1993, ORI Academic Press, 2013)

The Creative Mystique: From Red Shoes Frenzy to Love and Creativity. (Routledge 1996, ORI Academic Press, 2014)

Mourning, Spirituality and Psychic Change: A New Object Relations View of Psychoanalysis. (Routledge 2003, Gradiva Award 2004)   ·

The Anatomy of Regret: From Death Instinct to Reparation and Symbolization in Vivid Case Studies. (Karnac/Routledge, 2013)

The Klein-Winnicott Dialectic: Transformative New Metapsychology and Interactive Clinical Theory (Karnac/Routledge, 2014)

Saturday Nights at Lafayette Grill: True Tales and Gossips of the New York City Argentine Tango (Mindmend Press, 2016)

About the Author

Susan Kavaler-Adler, PhD, ABPP, DLitt, NCPsyA has been a practicing clinical psychologist and psychoanalyst for over 40 years. She works with individuals, couples, and groups in psychotherapy and psychoanalysis, and she supervises psychotherapists individually and in groups. For over 35 years, Dr. Kavaler-Adler also offers consultation to those who are experiencing creative blocks or self-doubts, but who wish to write for personal healing or for writing projects. Many members of her writing group were able to overcome their writing blocks and had their memoirs or professional articles published. She has helped many in her practice to convert anxiety and depression into creative self-expression in love and work.

Dr. Kavaler-Adler is the Founder—along with the help of Dr. Robert Weinstein—of the Object Relations Institute for Psychotherapy and Psychoanalysis. She is also the Executive Director, Senior Faculty, Training Analyst, Senior Supervisor, and President of the Board for the Object Relations Institute (ORI). She created a unique curriculum that integrates theories of the British Object Relations school of psychoanalysis and the American school of Object Relations theory. She teaches about the evolution of Object Relations theory in both Britain and America, and provides clinical illustrations. She teaches the clinical theory courses on the Object Relations view of the character disorder psychopathology and on psychoanalytic phenomena (and defenses) that we observe in various psychic structures. She also leads the "Analyst as Instrument" group supervision courses offered through all trimesters of each academic year, where she employs experiential role-plays as an effective training tool.

Dr. Kavaler-Adler is acknowledged for her extensive work on the Object Relations theories, including the phenomena of love-creativity dialectic, developmental mourning, erotic transference, spirituality, surrender versus submission (in life and in Argentine tango). She has written extensively about pathological mourning in terms of the demon-lover theme and the demon-lover complex. Dr. Kavaler-Adler's theory of developmental mourning expands Melanie Klein's understanding of mourning and its relation to manic depressive states, and James Masterson's abandonment depression. She defines regret as a psychological transformation process within the context of developmental mourning, a transition from Klein's paranoid-schizoid position to the depressive position. Dr. Kavaler-Adler's demon-lover complex theory interacts with the Jungian archetypal theory of the demon-lover complex by Marion Woodman. Her theory of psychic health, known as the love-creativity dialectic, was first proposed in one of her earlier books, *The Creative Mystique: From Red Shoes Frenzy to Love and Creativity*. Some of her psychobiographical work incorporates a concept of a dialectic between the Object Relations theorists Melanie Klein and D. W. Winnicott, utilizing historical facts and psychological interpretations of their lives' events and their work, as in one of her books, *The Klein-Winnicott Dialectic: Transformative New Metapsychology and Interactive Clinical Theory.*

Susan Kavaler-Adler is a prolific author, with 6 published books and over 70 peer-reviewed articles and book chapters—on issues of psychological interest that relate to clinical practice, and particularly to issues of psychological growth, healing through mourning, resolving blocks to creativity and finding one's voice, fear of success, envy, psychic health, women's issues (such as Date Rape), fear of intimacy, and meditative psychic visualization. Being a seasoned Argentine tango dancer, Dr. Kavaler-Adler dedicated one of her books, *Saturday Nights at Lafayette Grill: True Tales & Gossips of NY City Argentine Tango Scene*, to the Argentine tango scene in NY City.

Dr. Kavaler-Adler received sixteen awards for her creative psychoanalytic writing; three nominations for the Gradiva® Award from NAAP; one Gradiva® Award—for her 2003 Routledge book, *Mourning, Spirituality, Psychic Change: A New Object Relations View of Psychoanalysis;* four Arlene R. and Lewis R. Wolberg Memorial Awards for best paper (from Postgraduate Center for Mental Health), eight book awards from NIP, and 3 book awards from Postgraduate Center for Mental Health.

She is a member of many psychoanalytic societies, including that of the Postgraduate Psychoanalytic Society, the National Institute for the Psychotherapies Professional Society, the Society for Psychoanalysis and Psychoanalytic Psychology: Division 39, APA, the National Association for the Advancement of Psychoanalysis (NAAP), and the International Forum of Psychoanalytic Education (IFPE). She is also a Fellow of the American Board and Academy of Psychoanalysis.

More information about Dr. Kavaler-Adler's practice and publications, as well as her videos on main psychoanalytic Object Relations topics, can be found on her website, www.kavaleradler.com.

To my loving husband, for all his support in all my endeavors

To all my patients who volunteered to share anonymous case material to further an understanding of therapeutic action in developmental and psychodynamic terms

To all my students and supervisees who have helped me learn as we have educational dialogues while I teach

To Dr. Inna Rozentsvit, for all her editorial skills and other support, as well as to those who work with her

To Dr. Arnold Richards, the Editor-in-Chief of the International Psychoanalytic Books (IPBooks), my publisher

To Tamar Schwartz, who is helping process these volumes for publication at IPBooks.

PERMISSIONS

SELECTED PAPERS BY SUSAN KAVALER-ADLER

VOLUME 1:
DEVELOPMENTAL MOURNING, EROTIC TRANSFERENCE, AND OBJECT RELATIONS PSYCHOANALYSIS:

All articles reprinted with the permission of the original publishers

CHAPTER 1
PIVOTAL MOMENTS OF SURRENDER TO MOURNING THE INTERNAL PARENTAL OBJECT
Originally published in 2007, *Psychoanalytic Review*, *94*(5), 763–789.

CHAPTER 2
THE BEGINNING OF HEARTACHE IN CHARACTER DISORDERS: ON THE WAY TO RELATEDNESS AND INTIMACY THROUGH PRIMAL AFFECTS AND SYMBOLIZATION
Originally published in 2017, *International Forum of Psychoanalysis, 27*(4), 207–218.

CHAPTER 3
ANATOMY OF REGRET: A DEVELOPMENTAL VIEW OF THE DEPRESSIVE POSITION AND A CRITICAL TURN TOWARD LOVE AND CREATIVITY IN THE TRANSFORMING SCHIZOID PERSONALITY
Originally published in 2004, *American Journal of Psychoanalysis, 64*(1), 39–76.

CHAPTER 4:
OBJECT RELATIONS ISSUES IN THE TREATMENT OF THE PREŒDIPAL CHARACTER
Originally published in 1993, *American Journal of Psychoanalysis, 53*(1), 19–34.

CHAPTER 5:
OPENING UP BLOCKED MOURNING IN THE Preœdipal CHARACTER
Originally published in 1995, *American Journal of Psychoanalysis, 55*(1), 74–81.

CHAPTER 6:
THE CASE OF DAVID: ON THE COUCH FOR SIXTY MINUTES, NINE YEARS OF ONCE-A-WEEK TREATMENT
Originally published in 2005, *American Journal of Psychoanalysis, 65*(2),103–134. PERMISSION GRANTED

CHAPTER 7:
"MY GRADUATION IS MY MOTHER'S FUNERAL": TRANSFORMATION FROM THE PARANOID-SCHIZOID POSITION TO THE DEPRESSIVE POSITION IN FEAR OF SUCCESS, AND THE ROLE OF THE INTERNAL SABOTEUR.
Originally published in 2006, *International Forum of Psychoanalysis, 15*(2), 117–130.

CHAPTER 8:
FROM NEUROTIC GUILT TO EXISTENTIAL GUILT AS GRIEF: THE ROAD TO INTERIORITY, AGENCY, AND COMPASSION THROUGH MOURNING; PART I
Originally published in 2006, *American Journal of Psychoanalysis, 66*(3), 239–260.

CHAPTER 9:
FROM NEUROTIC GUILT TO EXISTENTIAL GUILT AS GRIEF: THE ROAD TO INTERIORITY, AGENCY, AND COMPASSION THROUGH MOURNING; PART II
Originally published in 2006, *American Journal of Psychoanalysis, 66*(4), 333–350.

CHAPTER 10:
MOURNING AND EROTIC TRANSFERENCE
Originally published in 1992, *International Journal of Psycho-Analysis, 73*(3), 527-539.

CHAPTER 11:
LESBIAN HOMOEROTIC TRANSFERENCE IN DIALECTIC WITH DEVELOPMENTAL MOURNING: ON THE WAY TO SYMBOLISM FROM THE PROTOSYMBOLIC
Originally published in 2003, *Psychoanalytic Psychology (Division 39 journal), 20*(1), 131–152.

CHAPTER 12:
EROTIC TRANSFERENCE: A JOURNEY TO PASSION AND SYMBOLIZATION
Originally published in 2014, *MindConsiliums, 14*(1), 19–43.

CHAPTER 13:
THE THERAPEUTIC ACTION OF WORKING WITH EROTIC TRANSFERENCE: AN OBJECT RELATIONS VIEW OF CLINICAL EXPERIENCE; DIFFERENTIATING THEORY FROM CLASSICAL AND RELATIONAL VIEWPOINTS
Originally presented March 2019 at the ORI's Annual Conference on Erotic Transference.

CHAPTER 14:
AN OBJECT RELATIONS APPROACH TO DREAMS: FROM PROTOSYMBOLIC TO SYMBOLIC, IN DREAM CONTENT AND WITHIN THE THERAPEUTIC OBJECT RELATIONSHIP
Originally published in 2015, *MindConsiliums, 15*(11), 1–27.

CHAPTER 15:
NIGHTMARES AND OBJECT RELATIONS THEORY
Originally published in 1987 in Kellerman, H. (Ed.), *The Nightmares: Psychological and Biological Foundations* (pp. 33–57). Columbia University Press.

CHAPTER 16:
TREATING PATIENTS WITH JEALOUSY
Originally published as "Chapter 11: Treating patients with jealousy" in 2018, in O'Neil, M.K., & Akhtar, S. (Eds.), *Jealousy: Developmental, Cultural, and Clinical Realms*. Routledge.

CHAPTER 17:
FEAR OF INTIMACY
Originally published as the "Fear of intimacy" chapter in Akhtar (Ed.) (2014). *Fear: A Dark Shadow Across Our Lifespan* (pp. 85–121). Karnac.

CHAPTER 18:
TOLERABLE AND INTOLERABLE REGRET: CLINICAL TRANSFORMATION OF THE INTOLERABLE INTO THE TOLERABLE
Originally published in 2013, in *The Anatomy of Regret: from Death Instinct to Reparation and Symbolization Through Vivid Clinical Cases* Karnac.

CHAPTER 19:
AN OBJECT RELATIONS VIEW OF CREATIVE PROCESS AND GROUP PROCESS
Originally published in 1992, *Group, 16*(1), 47–58.

CHAPTER 20:
ANATOMY OF REGRET AND REPARATION: RESOLUTION OF TRANSFERENCE RESISTANCES THROUGH THE COMBINED USE OF A WRITING AND CREATIVE PROCESS GROUP AND A MOURNING REGRETS GROUP
Originally published in 2000, *Issues in Group Psychotherapy, Postgraduate Group Journal* 4(1).

CHAPTER 21:
THE CULTURE OF THE MOURNING GROUP IN A CULTURE THAT OFTEN FAILS TO MOURN: EVOLUTION OF THEMES OF GRIEF AND REGRET RELATED TO PSYCHIC ANOREXIA AND SELF-DEPRIVATION
Originally published in 2020, *MindConsiliums, 20*(8), 1–15.

CHAPTER 22:
COUNTERTRANSFERENCE, REGRET, AND AGGRESSION: DRAMAS AND FREE ASSOCIATIONS IN AN OBJECT RELATIONS GROUP ENVIRONMENT
Originally presented at the ORI's Annual Conference and then published in 2020, *MindConsiliums, 20*(6), 1–14.

Table of Contents

PART FOUR: OBJECT RELATIONS PSYCHOANALYSIS AND GROUP THERAPY

INTRODUCTION

My father died when I was 10. I never truly mourned until I entered psychoanalytic psychotherapy in my mid-20s, after my Ph.D. Opening to the mourning process deepened me and profoundly affected my nascent capacities to love and to create. Nothing affected my clinical work as a psychologist, dance therapist, and then a psychoanalyst more than my own mourning process, as I inhabited the center of myself through inhabiting the wounded core inside of me, where I had been scarred by the loss of my beloved father. But there was anger in the love too, very distinct from the mode of hate I felt toward a very ambivalently loved mother throughout my life. In loss, rage, and yearning, I rediscovered my internal father, and there I found so many connections to my internal world. My writing transformed from merely the intellectual plane to a heartfelt and soul-wrenching level. Then I read Melanie Klein! Then I knew Melanie Klein! Then I found a theoretical mother. Then I sorted out the helpful and not helpful in her work. Then I navigated through to my own theory, and all the British and American Object Relations theories and theorists fell into place. The integrated whole became an alive pulsing world of psychic dialectic that constantly reverberated within. Mourning became the key word and key process. Grief became the key affect. Pain within grief transformed into love within sadness. The door to my father's soul could be entered. The door to my patients' souls could be entered. Then I re-read Melanie Klein and so many derivative branches that I would teach yearly. Founding the Object Relations Institute for Psychotherapy and Psychoanalysis was part of this journey.

A Theory of Affect Development

The mourning process was first declared to be a critical clinical and developmental process by Melanie Klein (1940) in her paper on "Mourning and Its Relation to Manic Depressive States." Klein would probably never have written her paper if Freud (1917) had not written "Mourning and Melancholia." However, for Freud, mourning was a normal human process that was mainly related to loss within

1

bereavement (sometimes to disappointment). He had no idea that mourning was a developmental process that could heal trauma, as well as extend and deepen development throughout a human lifetime. He did not think of mourning as a way of re-opening a capacity to love, and of developing a capacity to love, nor did he think of mourning as a route to re-open and develop a capacity to create, nor to develop the integration of love, eroticism, and all the dissociated parts of the personality.

Then Melanie Klein (1940) came along with her own mourning process as Mrs. A. Klein wrote from many clinical perspectives about the depressive position, in which the affects of heartfelt existential guilt (as opposed to defensive cognitive guilt), as well as the grief of loss, are felt, while re-owning split-off parts of the self and one's aggression. Whereas Freud only saw aggression as an obstacle to mourning, as seen in his "melancholic" in "Mourning and Melancholia" where the unconscious hate and aggression are toward the lost loved one or lost object of attachment, Melanie Klein saw how aggression could be part and parcel of the mourning process if it was brought to a symbolic level.

Klein has personal examples of Mrs. A.'s dream fantasies, which have hostile and competitive motives toward her lost son (Hans). Conscious symbolism of the hostile fantasies allows surrender to the grief of the mourning process, once the fantasies are symbolically defined by the mourner in words. For example, Mrs. A. dreams of triumphing over her son for being alive. She dreams of contemptuous attitudes toward her son as a rival, who also represents the rival she felt in her brother and mother. All of Mrs. A.'s (Klein's) aggressive impulses are contained in psychic fantasies that can be given symbolic expression, and symbolic meaning.

In this way, Mrs. A. differs from Freud's melancholic, who represses his aggression toward the idealized lost object, which he has lost through death, just as Mrs. A. has lost her son through death. For the melancholic, the mourning process is forestalled because the hostile aggression toward the lost object of attachment has to be denied and repressed, and is then turned against the self in a way that blocks the affect expression needed for the mourning process to proceed, and for the mourning process to allow surrender to the painful grief affect. Freud only spoke about the bit-by-bit painful letting go of the lost love object, having to face the denial of the loss with each bit of tearing oneself away from the adhesive attachment to the love object—as the reality that the other no longer existed was faced again and again in the mourning process. Freud did not account for the hate within the love of the mourning process.

For Freud, the hate would have to be repressed as impulses that are turned against the self, and thus block the mourning process, as in his melancholic. But for Melanie Klein, the impulses could emerge in unconscious fantasy that is then consciously symbolized by the mourner. Of course Freud dealt with dreams. It was his royal road to the unconscious. But in the case of the mourner, he did not perceive that the making conscious of aggression toward the lost love object through associations to a dream could be a way that aggression could allow the mourning process to unfold rather than to be blocked. For him, aggression blocked mourning, and so his mourner did not go through depressive position melancholia, and his melancholic did not progress forward toward surrender. This was the painful surrender to sadness within mourning, which could eventually bring love within the pain and sadness of mourning, and consequently could open capacities for both love and creativity.

My theory of *developmental mourning* is based on numerous clinical studies that illustrate the expanded view of mourning offered to us by Melanie Klein. Each case, both of individual and group work, demonstrates how the depressive position journey contains mourning, and how the natural subjective affect journey of mourning contains the depressive position. Each case shows the interaction of guilt and loss, as regret about one's own aggression accompanies grief about the loss of the other who has become a whole object, or about the loss of relatedness due to one's own aggression toward the other. In the end, it is love that survives, and with it, the radiance of potential creativity and potential eroticism, as the self-evolution takes place through a mourning process as it is seen within its developmental dimensions. Sometimes the spiritual evolution of the developmentally advancing self is seen as well (Kavaler-Adler, 2003a).

Further self-integration and separation-individuation follow parallel avenues toward the wholeness and relatedness of the self. Here we see the interaction of British and American Object Relations theory as the self-integration of internal world split-off parts, so prominent in Kleinian and Fairbairnian theory, and the separation-individuation process so prominent in American Object Relations theory (Margaret Mahler, James Masterson, Althea Horner) essentially travel the same path. Here we see that there is no need for an ego psychological focus on functioning because the evolution of Object Relations development through developmental mourning allows for a natural evolution of all the ego functions: e.g., self-reflection, psychic dialectic, observing ego, object constancy, interiority, the capacity for concern, the growth of self-agency, autonomy and continuing growth of relatedness. To follow this course, the primal level of trauma and the earliest level of object loss need to be felt consciously and mourned with full affective experience and awareness. From there, a lifelong process of mourning later life losses can be facilitated. Within the cases seen in this volume, the primal losses and traumas mourned lead to the mourning of later losses, as self-consolidation, as well as separation-individuation, proceeds with each loss mourned.

Part I: Developmental Mourning

Each of the clinical cases in Part I crystallize around poignant moments of affective surrender to the psychic truth within each analytic patient. The psychic truth can only be encountered through facing the Medusa head of internal rage, and the depth of longing to love ones who could never allow themselves to be loved. Separation-individuation and self-integration combine to move psychic spiritual development forward. One longs to love the one who one must leave. The leaving need not be literal, but it is certainly psychic and mental. Through the leaving, one transforms and evolves. The grief-ridden journey of loss and regret allows the mournful recognition of the primal other, and the true *not me* is discovered. Authentic internalization of the potentialities of the *new* can then be realized. The analyst becomes alive as a person, not merely as a subjective object or self object. It is through a grief ridden journey of mournful recognition of the primal other that one deals with the anguish of the capacity to love, and as this is dealt with, the capacity to create in-depth emerges. One then truly initiates the expression of the inner self (activates the self), figuratively waving "good-bye" to the primal other from whom one must part.

Part II: Developmental Mourning and Erotic Transference

There have been many controversies around how to work with erotic transference, and around whether to work with it at all or to just see it as a resistance. The papers in this section illustrate an Object Relations developmental perspective on allowing the full evolution of an erotic transference to be worked with when whole self and object constellations emerge through fantasy from the internal world.

The first paper, on "Mourning and Erotic Transference" (1992a), published in the ***International Journal of Psycho-Analysis***, was seen by the editor/reviewers of the journal to offer an alternative clinical approach to erotic transference than was seen in traditional psychoanalytic work. However, it is clear that allowing the erotic transference to unfold and become a developmental experience, rather than just having its psychic conflict aspects be interpreted as resistances to remembering and insight, would be in keeping with Freud's (1915) original intrigue in "Observations on Transference Love." The developmental experience of the erotic transference organic evolution, which can be seen in certain cases, opens memories and offers insight, but it also allows for the analyst to be used as a specific kind of erotic transitional object—not only as a transference object—which allows split-off romantic, erotic and loving components of the personality to be fully consciously encountered, and thus become integrated into the personality. Certain aggressive components of the personality can also be integrated in this fashion.

Each of the clinical papers on erotic transference speaks of the use of the analyst as a transitional erotic object, but in these cases, the forward developmental evolution also interacts with an affective mourning process that furthers separation-individuation, within and beyond the oedipal stage of whole object development. Further, these clinical journeys and clinical examples also illustrate the developmental role of erotic transference in its homoerotic dimensions for both lesbian and heterosexual women. While the developmental mourning process underlies all the clinical work described here, we see that Melanie Klein's (1940) contribution to mourning joins with Freud's interest in human passion, and how it can be understood and engaged with, rather than being unconsciously acted out to no clinical purpose, which only keeps its unconscious motivations repressed.

In many cases, splitting and dissociation are more apparent than repression, also stemming back to Klein. However, it is clear in these particular cases that repression evolves following splitting when the developmental mourning process proceeds. In other cases, when the person is stuck in a paranoid-schizoid position splitting as the major personality defense (along with projective identification), developmental mourning would not proceed, as it does in the cases here. There would be eroticization of part object phenomena, rather than whole object relatedness within the erotic fantasy of the internal world, as it manifests in the psychoanalytic transference. These cases need to be focused on differently, as they are more of the "women of elemental passionateness" (Freud, 1915) type of erotic enactment that Freud believed would stymie the psychoanalytic enterprise. We would call them borderline cases today, or cases of developmental arrest.

Freud wanted to distinguish between the two types of cases, of neurotics and borderlines, so that erotic transference fantasies could join the journey of dreams to reveal unconscious motivation, when neurotic repression was operating, with the symbolization of psychic fantasy. It is in the contrasting cases of concrete demands for involvement in erotic behavior with the analyst that psychoanalytic work could not proceed. In the words of James Masterson (1981), transference acting out transpires rather than transference analysis through insight into psychic fantasy. In the case of erotic transference, the role of the analyst as an erotic transitional object can be seen to transform the transference acting out into a symbolic experience for transference analysis.

5

Part III: Other Clinical Technique Papers

The papers in this next section offer the Object Relations clinical perspective on engaging with obstacles to interpersonal relatedness and intimacy. Developmental mourning, as an organic process, weaves in and out of the themes of trauma, transference, and the internal world of psychic fantasy that are faced in the clinical process.

The first two papers enter the internal world through dreams and nightmares. The paper on dreams illustrates the developmental progression of psychic fantasy that accompanies the developmental journey of affect states from the more primal to the more refined. The paper on nightmares speaks of varying British Object Relations theories, such as those of Melanie Klein, Ronald Fairbairn, and Harry Guntrip, and goes into the psychodynamics of the nightmares. In the clinical examples, the reader can see the patient progress from the paranoid-schizoid to the depressive position in character development (even though we all go back and forth). Nightmare images first seen as the bad object mother transform naturally, through developmental mourning in treatment, into the symbolized images of the analysand's own subjective experience of aggression, which was formerly split-off and projected into the internal world mother object.

The other two papers in this section were formerly chapters within the edited books of Salman Akhtar (Akhtar, 2014; O'Neil & Akhtar, 2018), while the last paper was published in Kavaler-Adler (2013). The chapter "Treating Jealous Patients" offers a brief commentary on Shakespeare's *Othello* with the malignant narcissist Iago, showing the psychic corruption of envy in Iago to lead to the destruction of the mind of a higher level jealous character, Othello, leading to murder. It proceeds to show the split-off envy and jealousy in patients, with one example of profound split-off enactment and others of more conscious struggles with jealousy and its underlying origins in childhood trauma.

The paper on "Fear of Intimacy" engages with American and British Object Relations theorists in discussing clinical examples of the difficult journey toward the capacity for true intimacy. The American scene refers to Mahler and her writings about how the toddler's ability to "image" the mother can be lost in traumatic circumstances during the separation-individuation phases of development. This has a profound effect on disrupting intimate relations in later life. The cases refer to many fears, conflicts, and traumas.

The fifth chapter in this section looks at a very poignant case of mother-daughter reparation, following extreme alienation. The case illustrates how the daughter's movement toward containing and processing tolerable regret, through psychoanalytic Object Relations treatment, contrasts with the mother's intolerable regret. Through the daughter's newfound capacities to connect with her mother, the mother briefly owns her formerly intolerable regret, in a moment of grief and longing. Both mother and daughter had been severely traumatized, but the daughter was able to use the therapeutic Object Relationship with the analyst to support her own journey from splitting off intolerable experience to developing a capacity to tolerate formerly split-off parts of her psyche. The reader here can appreciate the vivid primal affect growth process, summarized by the term developmental mourning.

Part IV: Developmental Mourning and Object Relations Psychoanalysis in Group Therapy

Part IV moves into the area of group therapy and papers that relate to integrating themes of developmental mourning with the practice of group therapy in a variety of group formats. The chapters illustrate group work and its working through of primal conflict and trauma, and how the self-integration process emphasized by British Object Relations theory and the separation-individuation process of American psychoanalytic Object Relations theory (Mahler and others following) are both advanced in group work. It can be seen how developmental progressions in affect relatedness are focused on in the group therapy process.

The first paper was published in the EGPS *GROUP* journal (1992) and describes the interaction of growth in the creative process, specifically in the writing process, with the group therapy process. We also see here the developmental mourning process that can take place through the shared container of the creative process and the group process. A weekly psychoanalytic writing group is described that had a life of six years with the members of the group described. The paper was written after about three years of the group's life. Each member of the group had a different genre of writing, but each member's creative writing process moved into an evolving exploration of their relationship with their internal mother while discovering how the internal mother relations encouraged or inhibited their creativity. Transference feelings, fantasies, and projections within the group, and in relation to the group leader, also played a part in the insight related to the deepening development of the individual creative process.

The group and I presented our group process in papers on the creative process that were part of a Division 39 (Division of Psychoanalysis, APA) panel. We went out to celebrate afterward as a group. Gratitude was expressed after much negative transference work.

The next group paper was published in a journal of the Group Department of the former Postgraduate Center for Mental Health, ***Postgraduate Center Group Journal*** relates to the transference work that two female members did with each other within two groups. They began to have a conflict within the writing group, and then proceeded to resolve the conflict, and to understand the two mother transferences involved within the parallel work in a four-hour Mourning Regrets Group, where meditative visualization was utilized in the beginning of the group. They became emotionally close to each other through the course of the group work. They did so as they truly came to understand each other, following a lot of contempt and rejection between them. The role of the group leader in the writing group is described in dealing with one of the two women threatening to withdraw. As the two women came face to face with their hostile negative transferences, and their mutual feelings of being misunderstood, they were able to own their personal regrets in the Mourning Regrets Group, and were able to mourn the loss of the mothers that they both loved. In the end, one was able to say to the other that she could see the best part of her mother in the other woman, and they sat and joked together in the intermission of this group. They each came to respect each other's creative writing process, and each other's therapeutic work within the groups. Kleinian themes of envy and the manic defense of contempt can be seen in these two women, leading to true reparation after manic defense, and after manic reparation.

The third paper in Part IV pertains the work of the Mourning, Therapy, and Support Group, formerly called the Mourning Regrets Group. It speaks of the resistance to mourning in our society at a time when John Kennedy Junior had just died, through his own negligence, which aroused anger within the mourning process, in contrast to the form of grief at the time when John Fitzgerald Kennedy was assassinated. The paper speaks of my appearance on a T.V. show with Jesse Jackson to speak of the need to mourn in our society, and of the nature of the mourning process.

This leads into a poignant case example of a woman who reveals, within the mourning group process, her form of self-hatred, which could take the form of psychic anorexia, based on a personality defense of self-righteousness in relation to self-deprivation. Everyone in the group responded to this woman in the midst of her sharing of her rage, grief, and regret. She had evolved within her individual treatment to the point where she could share deeply, and meaningfully, with the group. As this group member shared her painful anguish, and an internalized damned-if-you-do-and-damned-if-you-don't situation, related to the character of her mother, each group member reached out to the woman who was sharing her dilemma, and sharing how it impacted her marriage and family. Each group member spoke of how they could identify with what "Sharon" was sharing. There was much empathy, and a group process of progressive insight, in this group with its four hours, with a half hour lunch break (once a month). Interpretative work about surrendering old Object Relations constellations within the internal world was shared. This followed the initial meditative visualization in the group, in which Sharon saw the color red in her meditation as symbolizing her intense primal Rage. Others could definitely relate to this, and to the burden of having to carry so much rage. Grief and love followed for all.

The fourth paper in Part IV pertains to another phase of the 29 year ongoing group for Mourning, Therapy, Trauma, and Regrets. At this juncture, I was dealing with a strong countertransference process, related to my own regret, in response to the abrupt and defensive leaving of one of the group members. In working with the other members of the group following the loss of the group member who left, the group members encounter a high pitch of aggression toward one another. Mother-daughter themes then emerge with the female members of the group. The nature of internal world enactments taking place in the group can then be understood.

All four parts of this first volume of my selected papers illustrate a developmental view of psychoanalysis. Through the theory and related case illustrations, we can see the critical role of the ego's growing capacity to tolerate grief affect and mourning process. This is shown to be the path to the evolution of the psyche, as separation-individuation and self-integration progress. The role of psychic fantasy, in interaction with memory and transference, is seen in each clinical experience of mourning as a developmental process.

PART ONE:

RESOLVING TRAUMA AND CONFLICT THROUGH DEVELOPMENTAL MOURNING INDIVIDUATION

CHAPTER 1

PIVOTAL MOMENTS OF SURRENDER TO MOURNING THE INTERNAL PARENTAL OBJECTS

Originally published in 2007, *Psychoanalytic Review*, 94(5), 763–789.

Object Relations theory articulates clinical process as an emerging developmental process, in which pathological defenses and character formations are relinquished. I describe this as "developmental mourning" (Kavaler-Adler, 1992a, 1992b, 1993a/2013, 1995, 1996/2014, 2000, 2003a, 2003b, 2004, 2005a, 2005b, 2006a, 2006b, 2006c, 2007a, 2007b). Developmental mourning is a theory that relates to the essence of therapeutic action occurring through connection to the internal self states as they progress in a natural developmental process, reaching the core affects of the mourning process. This can be designated as a letting go or surrendering process. Such an organic vantage point on psychic change and developmental growth allows psychoanalytic clinicians to avoid the mechanistic approach of ego psychology's "compromise formations" and the reductionism of equating human motivations with "drives," as in classical Freudian theory. It also avoids the too-limited thinking related to self psychology's "selfobject functions," which excludes dynamic selfobjects as they appear in remarkably dramatic, personified forms in psychic fantasy. The evolution of conscious contact and connection with psychic fantasy is an integral part of the developmental mourning process.

As an overall theory, developmental mourning integrates key aspects of both British and American Object Relations theory. With its acute affect focus, this theory speaks both to critical self-differentiation processes from the theory of separation-individuation and critical integration processes from the Kleinian theory of integrating split-off self parts (self and object within the internal world).

Pivotal moments in the mourning of parental internal objects speak to the evolution of the self within the context of an object-related environment, which often is sufficiently provided in the clinical situation for the first time. Organic flow evolves as blocks and disconnections yield to mourning. This flow becomes the flow of both self and interpersonal relations. A dialectic evolves of self and other.

No longer is the renunciation of the self required (as in borderline states) or of the whole external object (as in narcissistic states).

The following three clinical vignettes and the theory that follows are offered as a means of explicating the mourning process within psychoanalytic treatment.

Helen: The Experience of the Old Objects Dying and Opening to the New: Finding the Other

Helen had left her mother and her mother country to save herself. She recovered from physical bulimia by leaving her mother and her motherland. She then recovered from psychic bulimia in her treatment, where she revealed how she swallowed her "transferential mother" and then felt like throwing up. At the beginning of treatment, Helen felt like a metal rod had been lodged inside of her, numbing her from her neck to her feet. She suffered from an arrested psychic capacity to digest and process her experience. Consequently, she experienced others as toxic intruders, perpetrating rape, possession, and assault. Helen's fantasy descriptions of the needs of others vividly described how there were vampires in her mind, sucking her blood to quench their powerful states of psychic starvation. Helen reacted to the overwhelming needs and hunger of others as if she were being swallowed up, soon only to be spit out. She relived a primitive constellation to which she was internally wed with her mother. So when she traveled from psychic vomiting to mourning and grief in her five-session-a-week analysis, vivid changes occurred, as the analyst was used as a transitional object.

As a critical turning point and pivotal moment occurred, Helen cried tears of grief along with amazement, exclaiming, "I can't believe that nothing is happening on the outside. I feel like both my parents are dying. I want to say, 'I miss you,' 'I love you,' before they die." Helen felt the mythic event actually happening as she sobbed and sobbed out the pain of her loss and longing on my analytic couch. She knew that I was present with her.

So many times Helen had spoken of her "killer rage." She used the analysis to contain her so that she could struggle to contain the visceral effects of this primal rage. She did so as she felt attacked by others, particularly by her son, whom she had once left, only to rediscover him as he was on the cusp of adulthood. By then he was filled with revenge and retaliatory hostility. As she contained the feelings of implosive and explosive rage, Helen's pain became tolerable with the analyst's presence, her visceral pain transforming into the affect of loss.

This opening took place only as Helen consciously met her own infantile longings for maternal contact in the transference. They were longings that had been severely frustrated by the separation-individuation trauma that occurred when her "infant illness" was followed by her mother's resistance to her natural developmental separation. Now she could survive her internal rage as the analyst had survived Helen's rage. Helen spoke about feeling a love for me similar to the love she had felt for her mother when young.

With this renewed connection and loving capacity, rage transformed into grief. Grief revealed itself to be an amalgamation of loss, sadness, love, and longing that opened her to the present moment and alive affective contact with the present and external other. Her internal world came alive and with it her capacity for conscious psychic fantasy.

Helen began to see herself as a grief-stricken female figure, her head down in her hands, crying for all the "sadnesses" in her life. The old and cold self had contempt for this new, sad self that had a newfound capacity for compassion, while the old self maintained a manic omnipotent attitude of defense. The external cold (false persona) self was totally dependent on mirroring from the outside to sustain its arrogant and grandiose stance of contempt, and its aggressive power against the internal sad and compassionate self.

Consequently, Helen now spoke to the analyst of rebirth in the treatment room. She also spoke of rapprochement with her mother, who had followed her to New York. Telling me of an ecstatic bliss on Mother's Day, she said, "My mother never lost her spirit! She came to our home with food and aliveness, and I gave her flowers, cake, and spiritual tapes for her to listen to."

This all occurred after a session during which Helen reported a dream in which, "my body and my mother's body separated out from each other." As she said this, I for the first time felt different and sometimes opposite feelings to those that she was feeling in the present moment. How different this felt than those earlier times when I had felt the visceral journey of her fear inside or from the times when my lungs expanded as hers expanded. How different this was from the times when she sought communal merger, proclaiming, "I want to see through your eyes and hear through your ears. I want your vision. I want it to be mine. When I read I feel like you're writing in my mind." It was only after the pivotal point of grief, where in psychic fantasy Helen imagined her parents to be dying, and also after Helen saw herself as a woman in grief, that for the first time Helen experienced the ecstasy of her own independent vision.

She exclaimed, "Now I have the vision too. I can experience it apart from you now. I can perceive the interior vision of the internal world. I can feel it as a world being created. I see the internal world as an ocean cave today. It has a clear and tactile depth to it."

As she became separate in her internal world, affect states, and psychic fantasies, Helen experienced a femininity that had formerly been undeveloped. Former dream associations had related to being a little boy. The fluid and flowing psychic fantasy of the feminine self naturally began to speak through her. Her dreams depicted a cat jumping into a sea of feathers, and four women dressed in gold and orange gowns dancing together in a rectangle. She imagined a part of her to emerge as a girl dressed in a lapis lazuli blue blouse. She associated this blue lapis lazuli color with a spiritual part of herself. Then she associated this blue color with a blouse the analyst had worn. This association brought back an associated memory of a blue blouse her mother wore and an early life trauma. Her mother had told her of a time when Helen was ill as an infant. The doctors at the hospital had given up on treating her and had told her mother to bring her home to die.

Helen only survived when she vomited, all the way home, on a train, on her mother, who was holding her in her lap. At that critical time of bare physical survival, the bond with her mother seems to have allowed her to survive psychically by being with her and vomiting on her. It was then that her mother had worn the blue blouse. Her mother cried on herself as the baby vomited on her, fearing the doctor's threat that her baby daughter would die would come true. The blue blouse absorbed the baby's vomit commingled with her mother's tears of grief.

Stephen: Finding the Loving Core and Facing Disillusionment that Opens Memory, Symbolization, and Hope

Presented here are five pivotal moments in Stephen's treatment that illustrate a profound developmental evolution in his 10-year, once-a-week treatment. Each of these pivotal moments is characterized by a psychological surrender that took place through the phenomenology of experiencing grief affect.

Through Stephen's encounter with his internal grief, formerly unconscious rage became conscious, allowing him to articulate the differentiated anger that was directed at his various internal objects. Stephen mourned these internal objects as he defined his anger while tolerating the pain of loss. Facing formerly dissociated anger and pain allowed Stephen to open to a loving core within himself. The grief of loss opened love and longing and transformed self-alienation into a loving empathy that extended to compassion for humanity, beyond individual attachment. Ultimately, growth-promoting disillusionments were felt, as idealized fantasies and wishes were surrendered in favor of facing reality and the limitations of mortality.

Even as former defenses of detachment and dissociation were surrendered, however, Stephen retreated to a defensive denial that harkened back to a former perpetual state of self-doubt. Nevertheless, Stephen was quickly able to recover from this denial and face the actuality of his childhood pain again, as it was reenacted in relation to his wife. He recovered by receiving the analyst's interpretation of his denial with a new level of receptivity, following the critical pivotal moments of his mourning process and the developmental evolution that stemmed from it.

At first, Stephen's transferential experience of his mother caused him to distance himself from involvement in the treatment with the analyst. In the ninth year, his negative transferences were both exposed more fully. One was of the resistance to a controlling and intrusive mother, who did not respect his boundaries. The other was that of a contemptuous, sarcastic, and devaluing narcissistic father. Then, in this ninth year, Stephen surrendered to the early love that he had defended against all his life, to protect himself from the verbal slights and humiliations of his father. The pivotal moment of surrender had been paved on a road of gradual grief experiences, related to abandonment and loss in his childhood, particularly the loss of a girlfriend who left him when he was 16. During this time, Stephen's capacity to tolerate grief had expanded to allow a major pivotal mourning experience to unfold that began to transform his view of himself and the world.

At this point, Stephen responded defensively to a recommendation that he come for a second weekly session. The recommendation followed a dream in which Stephen fell under concrete. I interpreted the dream's fall under the concrete as a metaphorical analogy to his falling under the defense of repression. Stephen declared, "If the recommendation is for me to come more often, then I think I'll leave." It is at this moment that Stephen pivoted and surrendered.

Stephen's statement appeared to me, as his analyst, to be a message to the transferential mother, whom he expected to want to control him. He expected a potential intrusion on his boundaries and a lack of empathy for his subjective experience, his needs, and his developmental strivings.

On the surface, Stephen also expected from me his father's caustic, contemptuous, and demeaning judgments. He had, to some extent, identified with this rejecting father of contemptuous judgments, which made him feel nauseous as he projected them onto me in the father transference. When he re-owned these contemptuous judgments, he found that his sense of insecurity with this father related back to an even deeper insecurity with his mother. He dreamed that his mother was bathing him in a sink as an infant, when the sink dropped and smashed on the floor, along with him inside of it.

I did not say anything when Stephen proclaimed that he should leave if I recommend he come more often. I do not think he expected me to say anything, either, since Stephen also knew I was quite different from this transferential mother, who would leap in to oppose and control him, as well as from the mother who would be so detached and unattuned to him that she'd let him smash to the floor and be psychologically dropped, if not actually physically so. He had also discovered that I was different from the father who contemptuously judged him as he reclaimed his projections.

Stephen was speaking from the couch, and he went on telling me his thoughts. He began to allow his threat to leave treatment to remain merely an association in a free-association process that he had come to allow more fluid expression.

With all Stephen's emerging anger toward his parents, as well as toward parental displacements from his past, Stephen had not yet reached the loss and longing related to a core heartfelt love that housed his primal attachments and his primal desire. Following Stephen's declaration that my recommendation to come for a second session led him to think of leaving (being a distancing character, who had been leaving from the day he came), Stephen had a whole series of memories of his father having hurt, embarrassed, and humiliated him. He remembered how his father had overpowered him in a forceful handshake or had wrestled him to the ground, illustrating his own superior strength in contrast to his young son's. Stephen had also had memories of many of his father's failings, feeling ashamed of the father who could be so contemptuous and sadistic with women.

Stephen recalled a particularly shocking memory that brought nausea in lieu of cognitive judgments of his part. He recalled his father bragging that he had turned over a woman's bed, while she was on it, in order to express his disdainful revenge for her unwillingness to have sex with him. Stephen then projected onto me the nauseous disdain he felt toward his father at that shocking moment of his father's revelation. He revealed that he imagined the analyst to be thinking his father's contemptuous thoughts toward him, similar to his father's contemptuous words toward the woman whom he had dumped off her bed and onto the floor. Stephen then told me he felt nauseous. I interpreted that he was projecting onto me a judgment that he was unconsciously making, but which he had converted into a visceral reaction. Stephen then remembered the father of his own adulthood, the one who had become a debilitated and lonely alcoholic. This all had followed the father's primal abandonment of Stephen when he had left Stephen's mother, and thus left living with Stephen as well, when Stephen was just one.

Despite all of this, however, in this analytic session, after his threat to leave me, as his father had left him, Stephen did a pivotal emotional turn into grief. Right in the middle of his negative memories, Stephen suddenly opened his lungs to cry and sob out his grief at the loss of the early father whom he had loved. Through his tears, Stephen found words for the first time to describe the buried treasure of primal parental love hidden under the metaphorical concrete of defense that Stephen had visualized in his dream.

First Pivotal Moment of Transformation through Grief

Stephen's voice had a new vulnerability as he surrendered to sobbing out his loss. He cried out, "For a long time I had to deny the hostile and demeaning part of my father, but now I remember that I also loved my father. I forgot completely how he could be so loving and how I could love him." Stephen continued to sob out the anguish of a buried grief, the grief of having forgotten the father he loved. In forgetting that father, Stephen had lost his capacity to deeply love and to sustain love (beyond the infatuated response to the departure of his 16-year-old, idealized girlfriend/muse). As his love for his father returned through grief affect and its memory of the father he had loved, he regained his capacity to love, although many cycles of grief were necessary to sustain it fully.

Following this experience, Stephen surrendered to his analytic treatment in a whole new way. He began to face the loss of the girlfriend he had at 16, whom I had understood to be, in part, a displacement figure for the buried and forgotten love for his sensual, seductive, and also abandoning father. Over the next two years of treatment, Stephen faced many of the disillusionments of his life, which had stood between him and the aliveness of the present.

Stephen did not just say the words of remembering his loving father and sob out his tears. He also spoke of that critical psychic pain boundary that he was dissolving as he cried from the boundary of physical and emotional pain that allows the formerly visceral attachments to become psychic. He spoke as he cried of the "heart-ripping" pain in his guts as he opened his heart to the love for his lost but now regained (in memory) father. The initial internal-object father, who had lived half in visceral form, could now turn to the psychologically graspable level of a symbolic introject, as Stephen cried out the visceral "heart-ripping" pain.

It was after this revelation of love for his early sensual father that Stephen both allowed his idealized love object to die (expressed by the memory of his girlfriend) and then allowed his loving capacity for connection to be born in the treatment room with the analyst. This allowed the analyst to come alive for him! For the first time, Stephen spoke of the analyst as a vivid personality, with the energy and passionate enthusiasm of Mahler's (Mahler et al., 1975) toddler's "love affair with the world." This is a world newly discovered outside the initial psyche, where the old and primal objects have preoccupied him.

It is directly within the pivotal moment of remembering his loving father that Stephen's pain opened to the vision of the external. It is in this moment, as the visceral attachment fully transformed to the psychological, that Stephen could for the first time greet the analyst with the power of curiosity. Stephen expressed a new level of energy and enthusiasm as he expressed various observations of the analyst, stating:

> You're someone who likes colors. ... I know you dance. ... I wonder if you
> have children. ... I know you're the director of an institute and I know you
> write books. ... I'm realizing how different you are from my mother. ...
> You never intrude on my boundaries and you're really attuned to me in a
> way she never was. ... And you're really smart. ... It's not what you say. ...
> It's also what you don't say. ... You must really have your reactions under
> control. ... You've never mentioned it again after you recommended I come
> more often. I haven't felt pressured by you. I've been free to go or stay.

Whom did Stephen say good-bye to in order to so vividly say "hello" for the first time to the analyst, now seen as a separate other, whom Stephen could have interaction with? Whom did he let die as an internal object, besides his mother, who he so clearly distinguished from the analyst at this time, that is, the mother who he dreamed of as inadequate, bathing him in a sink that falls and shatters? Stephen repeatedly suggested that the other one he would relinquish and say "good-bye" to was his remembered girlfriend. He vividly and repeatedly described how this girlfriend had become the idealized image of his desired female. She represented the ideal contrast to the devalued and inadequate mother. She also became associated in his mind with his early father's sensual aliveness. I interpreted that the internal image of this first girlfriend served, in part, as a psychological displacement from the father.

Stephen's young girlfriend had left him abruptly, supposedly to follow her dreams. She ended up calling Stephen a year after leaving him, only to announce her ecstasy in joining a cult. This was the girlfriend of Stephen's 16th year. Stephen had said that he would always be with her in spirit, and she with him. He had agreed and complied when she left. No protests! Years later, in this analytic treatment, which according to him was the first to truly touch him, his old girlfriend was reborn as a memory, and his mourning for her loss gradually transformed her from an internal object to a symbolic, cognitively represented, introject. Consequently, for the first time, Stephen could contain impulses to act out his desire for this idealized girl—woman—mother in love affairs and sexual encounters, because now he could put into words his construction of his ideal woman from the memory (and internal object image) of his first girlfriend.

Formerly, his compulsion to act out his fantasies had seriously threatened his marriage. Stephen's search for a sensual mother, who would be like the sensual father, and for the real sensuality experienced in his teens with the early girlfriend, became an internal psychic imprint of a combined muse figure. This muse figure existed as an irresistible fantasy that stood between him and his wife, between him and the analyst, and between him and his present reality, as well as between his own identity and affiliation with peers and fellow professionals.

The other side of this psychic muse figure, who was externalized in an extramarital love affair, was the internal *demon-lover* whom Stephen projected onto his wife. Stephen had called his wife shrewish, loud, and intrusive. His wife had been his demon-lover. She was the transferential mother with whom he felt trapped, the one who became associated with an inadequate mother who would drop him by washing him in a sink that broke and fell.

How interesting that pivotal moments of mourning for the female muse figure should come just prior to, and then not long after, the heart-wrenching opening toward the pivotal love for the original objects! Stephen cried out rage toward his newly recalled girlfriend, in the midst of crying out the painful sadness of grief: "How could you leave me? How are you? How could you call me and not care about me! I exist! I'm not just here to hear about some cult you want to join (being treated as a sounding board or self object). I exist!" Then he said to me, as he let tears of sadness roll down his cheeks:

What was wrong with me? ... I must have been numb! How come I didn't ask her how she was? ... Why didn't I tell her I missed her? ... Why didn't I tell her I cared about her? ... Why didn't I tell her I wanted her to come home? ... How could I have just gone over there to Europe to talk to her about the cult later that year when her father asked me to go, without ever knowing I missed her! ... Now I remember! I remember feeling a searing pain go through me when she called and said she had joined the cult. But I didn't say anything. It was all physical. I was numb other than the physical pain. I couldn't find the words because I didn't have the feelings. It was all physical. I operated from my intellect and numbed out the emotional pain in my body!

Then, after the heart connection to his primal father opened, Stephen opened through tears of grief.

Second Pivotal Moment Culminating in Manifesting Longing within Loss, in which Holding on Leads to Surrender

Stephen cried, "I won't let you go!" to his internal love object, his beloved girlfriend. In this session, Stephen told me that he has become aware that he was still making love to his first girlfriend in his mind (un-mourned love object, still in a pathological mourning state). He realized that he never left her emotionally. Stephen told me that he felt he was betraying his girlfriend from his 16th year when he now had sex with his wife. He then erupted into the anguish of loss, crying, "I won't let go" to his lost love. It is in this very moment of holding on that Stephen began to let go!

How did opening to the psychic pain of grief affect his relationship with his wife? How did it allow him to re-find his capacity to love? Stephen cried out in the midst of his grief over his father, "Maybe I had to get to this love for my father before I could love my wife! That's what she keeps telling me, that I have problems with loving." At this point, Stephen opened to much compassion for his wife, and then for humanity at large, through reaching this heart-ripping love—pain and longing for his father. Stephen now told me that he saw and felt his wife in a whole different way.

Third Pivotal moment of Grief, Transforming his View of his Wife, as his Change in the Image of his Internal Father-Object Affects his External Object of Attachment

From the same core of grief pain Stephen had felt for his father, he cried and spoke: "My wife also has some wonderful qualities!" This was the same phrase he used in the session on his father to describe the man whom he had always remembered with anger, never with love: "He also had some wonderful qualities!" And then from this recognition of his wife he cried, "Poor her! I won't love her for herself! I keep wanting her to be the fantasy woman! I won't let her be who she is!" Then he went on to describe her. He was newly concerned about his "reactivity" with his wife. He was no longer letting himself launch critical attacks on her in his mind, no longer just seeing her critical side. Now he said he was free-associating to his impulsive reactions, rather than letting them be acted out upon his wife.

Fourth Pivotal Moment, in which Newly Felt Compassion Leads to a Newfound Compassion for Humanity

"The Israelis are being murdered and we are all feeling the burden of the grief. Not that there aren't good things, but it's really a weight!" Stephen said. As he felt for all of humanity, he felt affiliated with the world and, for the first time, felt like a real member of his own professional group, as opposed to being the excluded outsider. "I always felt like any club who included me I couldn't belong to. I felt excluded, not yet ready to be with other professionals. For the first time I feel like I belong and am one of them!" After always having said, "Why am I here?" Stephen for the first time saw hope in treatment.

Fifth Pivotal Moment, in which Psychoanalysis Becomes a Journey of Hope

With hope, Stephen was able, for the first time, to face the most profound aspects of his own developmental disillusionment. He faced the disillusionment that his wife would never turn into his fantasy woman, saying with the anguish of the grief affect, "I have to give up the fantasy that my wife is going to become a different woman with a different body." He faced the disillusionment about his continuing ambivalence. He faced the disillusionment about the men he might look to as father figures sometimes turning out to be just as disappointing as his father. He also faced the disillusionment he felt in seeing the failings of colleagues in professional groups: "People just want something for themselves on these committees."

Stephen's father had become totally cynical, condemning all with contempt. Unlike his father, Stephen listened when I stated:

> It is the ability to face the grief of your disillusionment, in realizing that there is always competition, envy, self-interest, and greed, and your new ability to contain the pain of this, which allows you to experience that there are good things too. Mutuality does exist even in the face and company of competition. The envy that spoils also can be transformed into the envy that admires and aspires to become one's better self. With compassion for your hunger, you can understand envy from within and give up your addiction to self-righteousness. You can become a different man than your father. You can let your father die peacefully, as you fulfill the compassionate joining with others in this life that he was never capable of.

After this, in the tenth year of treatment, Stephen traveled from a new stage of disillusionment in treatment to a place where his self-sabotaging dissociation process could be clearly experienced, as he created it on the couch. Stephen again faced feelings that he had long dissociated, of anger and pain, related to feeling trapped with his wife. As he felt the feelings, he had meaningful associations and memories back to his sister and his primal mother. Then, abruptly and automatically, he began a dissociation process he has begun a million times before, but this time it is in the presence of the analyst, and, therefore, it can be interpreted. It is in a session in which Stephen spoke of his tendency to give up his feeling self in order to see things from his wife's viewpoint. We discussed how this mirrors the defensive necessity of his childhood to give up his self in the face of his brother's overt raging and screaming pain. We also discussed how this giving up of his self goes further back, to his mother. Just as he was feeling the anguish of this sacrifice of self, as well as the now neutralized anger toward his wife, and his mother, that once was experienced as rage, he suddenly cut himself off and said, "Now I'm thinking that this was all just a nice story."

This is the pivotal moment of denial in mourning. It is one moment that can become an enduring pathological mourning state if not interpreted by the analyst in treatment. The holding environment is not enough! Defense (resistance) interpretation is necessary. Interpretation of regressive dissociation through splitting is necessary, as in any resistance interpretation, following the resolution of preoedipal developmental arrest.

I interpreted it to Stephen, saying:

This is the disconnect, the dissociation. Your obsessional doubt disconnects you from your internal experience and rejects all the messages that were coming from your feelings. This mechanism is what brings you back to feeling ambivalent about everything, just like when you came here. All the meaning you just described from your feelings, about giving up your self to be present for your wife, and in the past, for your brother and mother—all of whom couldn't see you or tolerate knowing about your real feelings—can be lost in a moment as you now become the agent of your own disconnection. You now dissociate automatically because when you were a child, and you were really trapped in a dependence on your mother (not just in a transference fantasy), you had to dissociate. You now have the choice to be aware of your automatic tendency to disconnect from the feeling part of yourself by devaluing your feelings as you just did when you said their message was just a 'nice story.' By being aware, you have a choice to stay connected to what your feelings tell you.

Case Summary

The case of Stephen shows how the splitting of the primal mother and father objects is resolved through a mourning process that evolves developmentally. Anger, rage, regret, and loss signify affectively alive self states that open up through the attunement of the analyst to Stephen's mourning process. This results in Stephen's re-finding a primal loving self core that can open to the new and current others in his life, particularly to his wife and analyst, but also toward others in social groups and to empathy for humanity at large. Self-integration develops along with the integration of mother and father as internal objects. Whole object images form at a symbolic level, thus creating introjects from the visceral level of internal object experience. Stephen mourns the loss of the idealized mother through memories of a displacement figure, a teenage girlfriend, who had become a fantasy woman, with goddess-and demon-lover dimensions.

Stephen further mourns the demonic aspects of the primal split object through memories of the mother who "drops" Stephen as an infant, in fantasy, and through mourning the father, who assaulted Stephen with narcissistic contempt. As Stephen re-finds the core love for the early father and the early girlfriend/mother, he develops a new psychic structure that allows for a more whole object view of his current attachment objects. This lets him to show more compassion for both his wife and himself within a difficult marriage.

The analyst's attunement to the defenses against mourning, such as devaluation and obsessional doubt, is critical to providing the holding environment in which mourning can take place in all its developmental evolutions. Understanding how conscious aggression, in the form of anger, allows for grief affect and grief experience to be reached, is essential for the analyst to provide the therapeutic environment for mourning. To allow the free expression of this anger and its avenue to grief, the analyst must interpret the pathological obstacles to mourning in the form of aggression as a defense. Both defense interpretation and empathic attunement are essential to facilitate an authentic mourning process, which unfolds developmentally (Kavaler-Adler, 2003a).

Cecilia: Pivotal Moments of Mourning the Grief of the Past

Cecilia was an artist who painted visions of her internal feeling states. She painted images of a fragmented self with a "false phallic construction" (her words) that held her together. She came to analysis with a yearning to understand her manically driven phallic self. It was a false self that rejected her feminine side and infant longings. When first on the couch, Cecilia erupted with raw pain, shedding shame-filled tears and feeling a craving for tenderness that she had formerly disowned. She had come to me for treatment because of an interest in my writings on the demon-lover theme and complex. She told me that she couldn't believe how closely I had described the way she had used a grand image of her father as an extension of herself to replace a void (later to become only a "gap") within her.

In her paintings, her father and his phallic penis incubated in her womb, or she incubated in his. They were symbiotically joined by long rope tubes or by rope hair. She began to realize that her fantasy of surviving her mother's emotional absence through being joined to a father and his phallic, armored nature was only that, a fantasy. In reality, her father was unavailable and had rejected her as much as her mother, although in childhood he had shown her physical affection, which, when internalized, gave psychic life to her phallic form of sexuality. She rode motorcycles, shot off rifles, and identified with the masculine symbolism in life. She continually compensated for the lack of a loving bond to her mother, whose femininity was extremely devalued, with a masculine identification that made her seek agency through attachment to a man. She was locked into her own phallic facades and gave vivid visual expression to this in her painting.

One day in treatment, Cecilia asked me to look at one of her paintings, which she had on slides, and I declined. Cecilia ripped into me with brutally attacking and accusatory words, words that felt like metallic bullet weapons, as she spit them out at me. She enacted a rage from the past, which she would only now come to know. The symbolic level of meaning in her accusation was harshly overshadowed by the level of visceral attack. She blasted me: "You've betrayed me! When I entered analysis with you, you said you'd let me bring in slides of paintings like I would when I was in the group. You always have let me. Why are you stopping now?"

I responded, saying that I was asking her to put her experience into words now. I said that I thought it was time and that even though I viewed her paintings in the past, I believed that to do so now would evade her conveying her experience directly to me, and consequently could evade her feeling it. She listened but remained enraged at me as she left the session. It was the last of three sessions that week.

When Cecilia returned to her analysis on Monday, she was transformed. Her demeanor was full of excitement, and direct relatedness. As if she couldn't wait to tell me a story, she began:

> I was furious after the last session, and then I started to remember a scene with my mother, when I was 11. I had totally forgotten what started my cutting off from her. I had totally forgotten the betrayal that I would never

forgive her for. I gave up on words then! They were useless to me. I would only put my feeling into images in paintings from then on!

What came back to me last week was a time when I told my mother how angry I was at her. I was 11 and she seemed very cold to me. I told her how I hated her for her coldness and for how she would come into my room and dump out my belongings from my dresser drawers. When I came home from school I was forced to clean everything up and make it neat. I hated it! Now it makes me think of how later on, when my father was on the verge of a heart attack, he lay down on his bed, and my mother screamed at him for messing the bed up. He had pulled open the sheet and blanket that were tucked in so that he could lie down. That screaming, cold, controlling and rigid mother was the same one that I hated at 11 years old. When I told my mother, at the age of 11, that I hated her for her coldness and neatness she glared at me and said: "Things will never be the same between us again!" And they never were!

After Cecilia told me all of this, she lay peacefully and quietly on the couch. At that moment, she was free from all the tension that had built up within her from the last session. She also felt all the tension that she always seemed to have carried with her, which often manifested cognitively as intense and rigid judgments against me. In this moment of psychic birth (which Cecilia would paint), with the rebirth of the inner self and its internal world's plush interiority, Cecilia could breathe easy. She found an avenue to freedom that allowed affectively alive contact between us.

Cecilia began to paint her natural developmental course as it evolved from this moment. She painted an embryo that opens into psychic birth. She painted a more integrated and human figure, where only abstract self-fragments had been in evidence in early paintings, with stick figure inchoate outlines. Then she moved from a bizarre human figure, with androgynous and ambiguous features, to a truly gendered full human female form. The woman she painted was recognizable as a female. This female had a hat with hair implied underneath. The lady also looked masculine, but she held in her hands that which Cecilia's associations described as a female's fallopian tube that had been surrendered as a former weapon. Out of the repressed rage and the critical loss behind it of mother connection, Cecilia had found a core infant self that now could grow up and speak in words. In turn, the opening of the core infant-level self allowed the feminine side of her to develop.

Nevertheless, Cecilia still evaded the lower half of the female body. I interpreted that she evaded painting an image of a woman that had female genitals since she herself had always disowned that part of her own body. In response, she recalled a memory of once entering her mother's bedroom as a latency-age girl, during the evening. She recalled smelling this strange smell as she viewed her mother in her nightgown. "The smell was yucky," she said, straight from the 11-year-old inside of her. Cecilia continued, "Now I realize my mother must have just had sex and I was smelling the smell of sex from her body. I hate anything that reminds me of smelly vaginas, including your dress with the wide skirt and flowers on it. I only like tailored clothing. I hate that stupid dress of yours! It makes me feel like laughing at you."

After many discussions like this one, Cecilia popped up from the couch one day at the end of a session and declared, "I have to go home now and paint the genitals!" She said this with some urgency, but also with some humor. When she appeared for her next session, she immediately burst out with her summarizing and concluding exclamation. Quite simply she said, "I've painted the genitals!" There was nothing more to say just then. She had absorbed and digested my interpretation and had given birth to the connection to her full female body with its newly receptive spirit. Psychic space became artistic space, and art could now be put into words.

Theoretical Discussion

Developmental mourning is a theory that integrates British and American Object Relations theory, while simultaneously relating to the acute and vivid phenomenology of the psychoanalytic clinical situation. I have explicated this theory in previous writings (Kavaler-Adler, 1992a, 1993a/2013, 1995, 1996/2014, 2000, 2003a, 2003b, 2004). The primary aspects of British and American theory that are melded in developmental mourning are those of Melanie Klein and Margaret Mahler. Melanie Klein speaks of split object parts forming whole and symbolized objects when there is conscious confronting of guilt and loss in the depressive position. Mahler's theory speaks of the developmental psychological evolution of separation-individuation (Kavaler-Adler, 1993a/2013). Both of these theories allow for the flexibility of the forward and back psychological growth that is seen though the affective cycles of the mourning process.

Klein's theory explicitly relates to the forward and back cycles of psychic experience perceived through the paranoid-schizoid and depressive positions. In extending Klein's theory, Thomas Ogden (1986) suggests that we never totally evolve from the paranoid-schizoid to the depressive position, but that we are always going back and forth between the two positions, even as we evolve forward to increasing degrees of depressive position symbolization and perception. Likewise, in my theory of developmental mourning, we are always in process as lifelong mourners who are capable of progressively and perpetually integrating ourselves through mourning, although we are also retraumatized and retriggered into areas of primary psychic injury, vulnerability, and conflict.

Such continuing self-evolution can also be related to Margaret Mahler's view of separation-individuation, even though Mahler herself spoke of this process as time-limited in specific time-fixed stages. Viewed through the lens of developmental mourning, Mahler's theory can be expanded to include cycles of separation-individuation throughout the life cycle. We psychologically evolve, moving forward and back, in the organic rhythms of the self and object connection and mourning process. Old objects are clung to and then surrendered, and new objects are opened to more fully in external connection so that new and healthy internalizations can be formed.

As my theory of developmental mourning integrates the thinking of the British Melanie Klein and the American Margaret Mahler, it also integrates the theories of Ronald Fairbairn and D.W. Winnicott (see Kavaler-Adler, 2003b), the neo Kleinians, John Steiner and Betty Joseph, Michael Balint, and John Bowlby. The case vignettes in this study illustrate aspects of each of these theories.

All the cases presented illustrate the movement toward more differentiated behavior and thought, related to Mahler's separation-individuation process. They show the painful internal object clinging, but also the eventual relief of letting go and separating from the old pathological elements of the parental objects, parental objects that have continued to exist in the psyche of the adult. Surrender follows the expression of grief affect with each analysand's idiosyncratic progression and idiosyncratic transference dimensions. Rage, anger, longing, love, and the defense of denial all are phenomenological states that evolve into self-differentiation when one can surrender to conscious awareness through the tolerance for grief affect, as the pain of grief transforms into love within loss.

All the case vignettes also illustrate the resolution of self and object splitting as idealized and devalued internal objects are confronted. Powerful psychic fantasies and memories allow for the transformation of these goddesses and demons into whole object parental figures, who are of human size and not omnipotent. The primal objects and their displacements become symbolized as introjects through mourning and memory. The limitations of the parents are faced, as are the limitations of the self. This results in disillusionment, but with disillusionment comes compassion for the merely human sized other, the now more clearly seen vulnerable and often inadequate parent. This clearly illustrates Melanie Klein's theory of self-integration in the depressive position developing out of mourning. As self/object splitting is increasingly modified, defensive dissociation and projective identification are minimized.

The phenomenon of disillusionment brings us to Ronald Fairbairn (1952), who in *Psychoanalytic Studies of the Personality* wrote of the "moral defense." This is a critical psychodynamic element in all character pathology, in which the child protects the idealized image of the parent to ward off the annihilating terror of being vulnerable to the massive negligence and abuse of the "bad" or demonic parent. Fairbairn (1952) actually spoke of "devils" in describing parents incorporated as "bad objects." In distorting the parent into an ideal and devalued or "bad" parts, the child dissociates from the sealed-off self the part that houses the split-off bad (internal object) parent.

To protect the image of the parent and the psychically contrived ideal image, the child sacrifices his or her own self-image, and assigns the label "bad" to himself or herself. Then to rationalize being bad, to protect the image of the parent, the child, and then the unconscious or dissociated child within the adult, finds some trumped up moral charge against the self to excuse the hostile, abusive, or rejecting and neglectful behavior of the "good" parent.

When this is faced in analysis, the analysand must surrender the idealized view of the parent to find his or her own true self, which is not necessarily devoid of guilt, but which is innocent of the spurious guilt defensively manufactured to protect the image of the parent.

We can distinctly see this disillusionment process happening within the overall mourning process in the case of Stephen. Stephen gave up both idealizations and demonization of his parents as he opened to the pain of remembering the early love for his father. He surrendered to the loss of this father/mother object and opened to the possibility of loving his wife in her far less than ideal form. Then he could face the conflicts involved with being with his wife.

The movement of analysands into compassion through mourning brings us back to D.W. Winnicott's (1963) original paper, "The Capacity for Concern." Stephen spoke of concern for his wife and for the Israelis. Helen spoke of the evolution of a new and compassionate self, as she surrendered to loss and love within grief, and then relinquished the old cold, judgmental, cynical, contemptuous self. This surrender to compassion, which Winnicott has described as depending on the development of concern through external validation of the self as more good than bad, also speaks to the need for a therapeutic holding environment.

As Winnicott describes, it is only within the holding environment that the capacity for concern can develop. It is also necessary to the creation of this holding environment that the analyst be attuned to all the pivotal points and overall progression of the developmental mourning process. It is within the holding environment that the analyst's presence allows the affectively alive contact for the patient's mourning process affects to open. With mourning of this developmental nature new self-other connections can be internalized and sustained. It is also within the holding environment that the therapeutic analyst-patient connection supports the analyst's resistance interpretations related to the mourning process.

Furthermore, Winnicott's theory and my developmental mourning theory are present as the analyst becomes alive to the analysand as a subjective and separate other, as opposed to just being perceived as a subjective object (Winnicott, 1971) or a selfobject (Kohut, 1977). This transformation of the analyst in the mind of the analysand is illustrated here in Stephen's case. For Helen, I became alive as she found herself separate from me. Helen traveled from living through her introjections of me as part of herself to seeing me apart from her. She discovered the unique talents of her own that were not just extensions of me.

As Helen and Stephen both opened to sealed-off and split-off parts of themselves within a loving core that was formerly defended against and dissociated, they illustrate a further evolution than that of Betty Joseph's (1989) narcissistic patients, as seen in her paper on "Psychic Pain." Joseph's patients come out of a delusional world of their own self and other phantoms into contact with those in the external world. Joseph (1989) writes about this painful unsealing of the formerly sealed-off self. She speaks of this new contact with the external other (reminiscent of Fairbairn's libidinal ego coming out into contact with external others) as a prelude to the kind of pain that is experienced when heartache is first felt, which can be seen as the Kleinian view of when compassion develops (in the depressive position).

Helen and Stephen spoke of "being cracked open at the core," and of "heart-ripping pain," respectively, rediscovering a dissociated love and loving self within them. They seem to have opened their sealed-off place, and thus accepting their need and vulnerability while relinquishing their omnipotence. In Michael Balint's (1968) terms, they seem to have created a "new beginning" as they opened to the authentic or true self (Winnicott, 1971). They not only came out of a closeted area of secret and delusional omnipotence, as Joseph (1989) speaks of, but in this visceral unsealing of a core affect self they also opened to the heartache she describes. This heartache relates to Klein's depressive position compassion for a whole object other (see the evolution of this in the literary mourning process of Charlotte Bronte in Kavaler-Adler, 1990, 1993a/2013).

In Helen's case, we also see evidence of John Steiner's (1993) idea of letting the (internal) object die, which he wrote about in his book on psychic retreats. As she cried, "I can't believe nothing's happening on the outside. I feel like both my parents are dying. I'm afraid they'll die before I can say 'I love you,' 'I miss you!'" she faced the existential death of her primal internal parental objects. In allowing them to die, Helen found herself. She found herself as a separate self (in

Mahler's terms), and as an integrated self as well (in Klein's terms). Surrendering to the longing within her conscious grief, feeling the loss of those she had pushed away, she was able now to love. She relinquished her frozen internal object, part-object forms for two whole parents, and for other whole displacement parent figures, all of whom can serve as transitional objects (Winnicott, 1971) toward the world at large.

What role does aggression play in the mourning process? For John Bowlby (1963), aggression is a natural and healthy part of the mourning process (Kavaler-Adler, 2003a), as he focuses on external object attachment and loss as critical to psychic development. The expression of anger due to separation was vividly expressed by Stephen and by Cecilia. Stephen articulated his differentiated anger toward his abandoning girlfriend. The analyst's presence as a holding object supported this for the first time. Stephen cried out in the pain of longing, making his anger evocative and vivid. He screamed, "I don't want to let you go!" Yet as in all Winnicottian paradoxes that relate to the dialectical dynamics of the separation-individuation phases of development, it is in the very moment of holding on that he began to surrender to letting go.

How true this was also for Helen and Cecilia! In the case of Cecilia, however, she held on to anger toward her mother from her eleventh year. This resulted in her defense of "giving up on words," and in hiding in artwork that denied her differentiated female nature. When she was compelled to use words, she renounced her anger and her developing feminine side could then evolve. Cecilia let die the old mother who retaliated against her for her anger. Her anger, when conscious and in the service of separation, led to letting go, feeling loss, and opening to the core loving capacity within her, which had been repressed at 11, when her repressed and dissociated rage killed both her love and her feminine mode of passion. When the origin of the rage became conscious, so did her shame about her feminine vulnerability. Then Cecilia could face painting her body on canvas. She defined her female genitals for the first time.

Attunement of the analyst to the powerful psychic change through developmental mourning also involves engagement with the aggression of the patient, as in the case of Cecilia. The analyst needs to understand how conscious aggression plays a pivotal role in the mourning process, toward recovery of memories that allow for loss and love to be felt so surrender can take place. The clinical awareness of how unconscious aggression blocks the mourning process and of how conscious aggression allows mourning to flow toward the grief of loss that reconnects us to our loving capacity allows us all to open to new relationships and to new internalizations. Both intimacy and creativity evolve from this awareness within the mourning process. This was first articulated by Melanie Klein in her papers on "Mourning and Its Relation to Manic Depressive States" (1940) and "Envy and Gratitude" (1957).

This was a major psychological finding that allowed Klein to see mourning as a critical developmental and clinical process, even though Freud had only seen mourning as limited clinical phenomena, and one which he mainly related to actual bereavement. Without Freud's (1917) paper "Mourning and Melancholia," Melanie Klein (1940) may never have written her paper, "Mourning and Its Relation to Manic Depressive States." Freud saw mourning only as an adhesive loss and letting-go process (the libido detaching its adhesive tie to the lost object), whereas Klein was able to have further insight through her own mourning process, as well as through the mourning process of those in clinical treatment with her. She was the first theorist to articulate how significant aggression became an active part of the mourning process, when transference and resistance analysis allowed this aggression to become conscious in psychic fantasy.

When the analyst is attuned to the psychotherapeutic patient who is in the process of mourning, she is open to all the aspects of psychic change defined by these theorists. In addition to aggression, she is particularly open to the depressive position of Melanie Klein, where there can be symbolization of the process, and where in the process symbolization naturally occurs. Along with symbolization comes self-reflection, insight, and the remembering of differentiated historic situations from childhood. Then hope can emerge, and the process of mourning itself can be experienced as a journey. This journey of hope is also a working through process, in which lifelong psychic loss, psychic injury, and psychic conflict all interact.

Ultimately, it is the pivotal moments of surrender to the love and longing within grief affect that allow a sustained process of self-integration and self-awareness to evolve and continue, providing the very sense of "going on being" that Winnicott (1971) first spoke of in relation to the mother-infant relationship. Within this developmental mourning journey of hope, we also find the evolution of self-agency that allows for the owning of aggression and compassion, as one transforms guilt into grief, and then into renewed love, at higher and higher levels of psychological connection.

CHAPTER 2

THE BEGINNING OF HEARTACHE IN CHARACTER DISORDERS: ON THE WAY TO RELATEDNESS AND INTIMACY THROUGH PRIMAL AFFECTS AND SYMBOLIZATION

Originally published in 2017, *International Forum of Psychoanalysis* 27(4):207–218.

The neo-Kleinian theorist Betty Joseph (1989) speaks of psychic birth and birth into relatedness to another in her paper on "psychic pain" in *Psychic Equilibrium and Psychic Change*. She speaks of a severely character-disordered woman who begins to emerge from a sealed-off schizoid state. This patient's tears are shed while demanding things from the psychoanalyst, who is not yet fully "other" but some form of subjective object (Winnicott, 1953, 1969) or selfobject (Kohut, 1977). As in Michael Balint's (1968) "malignant regression," Betty Joseph's (1989) patient cannot contain and process her own affects or needs, and is compelled to demand relief, rescue, and magic answers from the analyst. As we witness this patient's visceral pain and raw mental agony, Joseph (1989) exclaims: "The experience of psychic pain is not yet heartache—though felt often to be related to the heart—but it contains the beginnings of the capacity to feel heartache" (p. 95).

How does one get to heartache? Heartache is the subjective experience of separating from the one you love, or is grief concerning hurting the one you love. These are all the elements of Melanie Klein's (1975) depressive position, and the journey to such heartache can be seen through the theory of developmental mourning (Kavaler-Adler, 1993a/2013, 1996/2014, 2003b), which integrates aspects of British and American Object Relations theory, particularly D.W. Winnicott's theory of object survival and Melanie Klein's theory of mourning as a critical clinical and developmental process.

This paper will offer clinical examples of the road to heartache through the journey of the developmental mourning process. The journey through emptiness, rage, loss, and ultimately subjectively felt grief, to a fully human experience of mature heartache, involves the beginning of psychic regret (Kavaler-Adler, 2013). Feeling the subjectivity of the other is an outgrowth of developmental mourning, which has within it the capacity to consciously face regrets about hurting the other, and particularly the other who is a primal love object. By definition, those with character disorders are dissociated from their own core subjective self. Therefore, they are disconnected from, and unaware of, the subjectivity of the other.

In my examples of developmental mourning, the beginning of heartache is seen in relation to the first anguished perceptions of the subjectivity of the other, which also involves profound existential guilt that is felt as existential grief. My theoretical view of this developmental journey always draws on a powerful clinical dialectic between the theories of Klein and those of Winnicott (Kavaler-Adler, 2014a). This dialectic has been greatly compromised when their theories have been polarized, rather than being appreciated through clinical integration and sometimes as a developmental sequence—as my clinical examples illustrate.

Resolving Developmental Arrest Related to Primal Trauma

In successful cases of treating those with developmental arrest, the Winnicottian (1965) holding environment, combined with Bion's (1959, 1963, 1970) container function, the psychoanalyst can allow patients to express pre-symbolic or protosymbolic experience. Such protosymbolic experience occurs in character-disordered patients in conjunction with primal affects related to primal self/object loss, such as a powerful oral rage and profound levels of sadness and grief (Kavaler-Adler, 2003a, 2003b).

In Winnicott's (1969) terms, object survival is the therapeutic art of tolerating the most aversive aggression, without retaliating or abandoning, and this can be extended to tolerating and feeling the deepest and most profound levels of sadness, prior to a more differentiated whole object grief. This practice is required because the patient's rage toward the primal traumatizing mother must be expressed in the transitional world of the treatment room, with an analyst who is present emotionally as well as physically. In character-disordered patients, all the perpetual moments of annihilation and abandonment terrors, spoken of as "the unthinkable anxieties" by Winnicott (1965), and as part of an "abandonment depression" by Masterson (1976, 1981, 2000), immediately trigger affects of murderous rage. At any such moment, the analyst is seen as a separate individual from the patient's internal world mother, and is not seen as a separate person from themselves. The analyst is "It!"

The Analyst is "It!"

When we can survive the patient's primal level of rage, the patient can be encouraged to risk coming out from behind a schizoid barrier and staying in treatment. Object survival is particularly important with paranoid borderline patients, but all character-disordered patients require the externalization of rage in the treatment room, rather than turning the rage inward and projecting it out onto others within their external lives. Once rage can be safely expressed in the treatment room, the patient does not have to run away. Furthermore, the other painful affects of emptiness, void, and profound primal loss can come to be tolerated. Consequently, a full developmental mourning process can proceed with primal as well as later-level losses being experienced in the treatment room. In this way, the affects, and then the memories of the primal trauma (in which the mother was lost before the child formed a separate and integrated self), can begin to be thought and remembered.

Once the analyst's object survival allows for a progression into grief affects, and then allows for the opening of the heart and the heartache, the Kleinian (1940, 1975) theory of mourning becomes highly pertinent. In the theory of developmental mourning, I integrate the primal abandonment depression mode of mourning, described so clinically by Masterson (1976, 1981, 2000), with a later experience of object loss and of existential guilt (Kavaler-Adler, 2004, 2005b, 2013). Such losses need to be grieved in order to repair the basic blueprints for relationships that exist in the internal world. Through the grief and through analytic awareness of the old constellation of attachments that are being grieved, such internal relationships can be understood on a symbolic level. This allows for conscious symbolizing (Segal, 1957) and mentalizing (Fonagy et al., 2000) within relationships in the external world so that one can be aware of having thoughts and feelings and of becoming an "interpreting subject," in Ogden's (1986) language, on an ongoing basis. One goes from "beta" to "alpha," in Bion's language, or from the paranoid-schizoid to the depressive position in Kleinian (1940, 1946) theory. Consequently, this person is no longer solely a reactive and blaming victim who perpetually turns raging accusations outward or inward, or numbs out in a schizoid way to avoid it all. They are desperately trying to control the world in a narcissistic way, to attain the addictive drug of narcissistic mirroring, another way to avoid it all.

The Case of Linda

Linda is a case in point in illustrating how object survival in the psychoanalyst was able to lead to the successful mourning of primal mother loss. Linda's story is also an example of how addiction to an eroticized bad object can be a symptom of a demon-lover complex (Kavaler-Adler, 1986, 1993a/2013, 1996/2014). This is an Object Relations complex that evidences a developmental arrest in terms of a pathological mourning state in a character-disordered patient.

Linda came into treatment after hearing me speak about the father's effect on female development. She told me that she had been impressed that I did not use notes when I gave this talk, so there was an initial admiration. This quickly gave way, however, to a split good and bad object transference constellation, which, within two years, became predominantly bad object transference. This bad object transference, and its projective identification, arose in parallel with horrific dreams and nightmares about nuclear explosions and holocaust-level destruction of the world. The split primal object transference is evidence of someone who has not adequately separated from a symbiotic mother.

The unmourned loss of a symbiotic mother creates the character-disordered patient's abandonment depression. In the case of Linda, this was compounded by the actual loss of her mother through cancer when she was eight years old. When her mother died, Linda was left with a primitive father, who became sadistic and abusive toward her. Her attachment to this demonic father became a kind of demon-lover complex, as she hated this father yet longed for him at the same time. Linda's bad object attachment to a sadistic father became eroticized through the experience of intense disgust during her sexually developing teen years. Her father in fact molested her during her early teens. Such an attachment to a molesting and abusive bad object compounded an already split good and bad self/object psychic structure.

In the transference with me, Linda alternated between experiencing me on the one hand as a "good" symbiotic mother (who encouraged regressed and highly dependent behavior), and on the other hand as a malignant bad and eroticized father. The eroticized demon father was also operating on the level of a failed primal mother of separation, one who was assaulting Linda's developmental growth rather than supporting it. Increasingly, Linda had repressed and dissociated rage toward her father, which appeared in dreams as holocausts and nuclear explosions. In treatment, this rage began to come out in Linda's view of me as some kind of controlling parent monster. She wished to both assault me and escape from me. It was in this period of treatment that I was most required to tolerate Linda's aggression, and to survive it, in Winnicott's sense of object survival.

My externality was denied, and I could not make interpretations at this time, because Linda was not operating on a symbolic level in relation to me. She was putting her split-off bad object experience with her father into me and consequently experiencing me as a sadistic and depriving father. Any interpretations were experienced as soothing and holding gestures from a symbiotic mother, one who never engaged with her on the level of words and symbolic communications; or interpretations were experienced as attacks from a sadistic demon-lover father. The symbolic meaning of the interpretation was not perceived in either case. I had, therefore, to endure Linda's attacks. I had to attempt to my best ability to avoid being retaliatory and emotionally or literally abandoning her. In Ogden's (1992) terms, Linda had not yet developed the subjective sense of being an "I." She was still a reactive "me."

This preoedipal trauma-level enactment came to a head when Linda slammed the door in my face after one session, and then came into another session and told me that she wanted to smash the windows in my office. Finally, Linda put me to the ultimate test. She called me one day, saying she did not want to come to the session because it was raining outside. I said I would not give her an alternate session that day. She did come to her session, in a rage, saying that I obviously did not care about her having to travel on the "damn A train," nor did I care about how hard it was for her to get to my office when it was raining outside and when she was tired. Linda's gut-level rage emerged palpably that day, having formerly been dissociated and repressed, hidden behind her initial idealization and revealing itself at first through nightmares. As Linda vocalized her primal preoedipal rage, which was reactive to the demand on her to be separate enough to be responsible for her session time, I spoke to her of how her nightmare nuclear explosions were in the room right now, between her and myself, with her now having her own separate and articulate voice.

Transformation to a Higher Developmental Level: Evolution of Symbolic Capacity

I had declined to merge in with Linda like a symbiotic mother, where I would adapt to her, rather than holding her to a schedule we had both agreed upon as two separate people. If I did not maintain this separate position, I would have enabled a regressive symbiosis. Further, in terms of developmental implications for the treatment at this time, it was profoundly important that I was fully with Linda while she fired her very articulate and vociferous rage at me, without me retaliating or emotionally withdrawing. When she came into her next scheduled session, Linda was operating at a higher developmental level, one in which symbolic functioning was possible for her, for the first time.

After the session, when Linda's rage had been freely expressed, she presented to me a very rich and highly symbolic dream, which was not a nightmare. In Winnicott's (1969) terms of object survival, I had "survived" through my "good-enough" containment of retaliatory aggression and my "good-enough" sustaining of emotional, as well as physical, presence, without abandonment. One could say that we both survived, and I was not just avoiding abandonment, but also sustaining an ongoing alive affective presence, as in Winnicott's (1958) "capacity to be alone." In my separateness, I also became an external object, who could serve as a container for Linda, in the transitional space between us. I did not remain an internal part-object, so Linda's compulsion to project all her dissociated parts into me was attenuated. The symbolic meaning of dream imagery could then become conscious, through free associations and analytic interpretations.

This new dream had several scenes in it. One was of another girl wanting to have sex with her, and she had bare breasts, indicating possible homoerotic desires in the transference, but I said nothing about this then. Another scene was of her mother coming down to earth, from above, and her clutching her mother's hand and weeping profusely, trying to hold her mother back from leaving her again. Linda was able to have free associations to these parts of the dream, which was totally new for her, so it was evident that she was newly connected to her core, after the expression of her dissociated rage. The defenses against her rage no longer blocked her symbolic capacities. Now, she was able to speak about dream images as metaphors with symbolic meaning.

Interpretations

Linda's longings for her long-dead mother were self-evident as she spoke of her associations to the dream scene with her mother. However, this was another scene, in which she had delivered a pizza to me, and I had given her more money than was required for the pizza, maybe a lot more money. She also told me that I was Ronald Reagan in this dream. There was no need to discuss that because, as Ronald Reagan, I would be the demon-lover father figure, idealized and demonized, since the demon-lover father was superimposed on the primal lost object of the mother (Kavaler-Adler, 1993a/2013, 1996/2014, 2010). Because the essence of the dream scene lay in the dynamic of me giving her so much more money than she expected, I made a spontaneous interpretation that prompted her warded-off grief. I said, "Consciously you think that you are giving, and giving, and giving to me (paying me), and not getting anything back, but unconsciously you believe the opposite, that I am giving, and giving, and giving to you, and you are using me up, just like you felt you used up your mother and killed her!"

As soon as I spoke these words, Linda erupted with wails of sobbing grief affect, crying and screaming out, "It's true. It's true. I did it! I did it!" Linda had believed all her life that she had killed her mother. She realized this as soon as the words were out of her mouth. She cried for quite a bit of time. She cried the tears of grief for her dead mother and the lost symbiotic mother that she had never separated from. For the first time in Linda's life, she faced the primal grief affect and the longings and guilt that accompanied such affect. When Linda had blocked such grief affect in the past, her core self-development, self-expression, and individuated voice were blocked. Sobbing, Linda continued:

> My mother wanted to die, but she had to keep going, for me. I wouldn't let her go. She loved me so much, and I hated her. I hated her because she was so old ... and I wanted a young mother. All my friends' mothers were so young. When you get what you want, it's not really what you want. My sister-in-law was young, but when my mother died, and I was sent to live with her, I didn't want to stay. I wanted my mother! There will never be anyone like my mother. I've lost her forever! She loved me so much, more than I loved her. I've hated myself for it.

Linda's cries became sobs. The floodgates, so long barricaded, were open. Linda sobbed and sobbed, lying down and then sitting up. Her dream of holding her mother's hand and sobbing was emerging into a conscious experience in that moment with me. Her grief broke though as guilt was exposed.

She sat up, still crying. I reminded her that I had tissues next to the couch. She did not move. Then I said that she obviously did not deserve to use my tissues because she was so bad. This must have registered because Linda immediately reached out for a tissue. She would take my comfort when I acknowledged the guilt that she had harbored for so long.

Our new relational dialogue proceeded, as Linda was willing to leave the session, as opposed to when she had previously slammed the door in my face, so I would feel the loss, not her. I said that I was glad we had reached this point. Linda said, "I am too." This was a major acknowledgment for her. I then told Linda that I had wondered if she would give me a sharp verbal slap, as she had done in the past, when I made our work explicit. I said that instead, she had been able to take me in, to take in my help, and to begin to acknowledge it. I was speaking to Linda about critical new achievements that were signs of her moving into the depressive position. Linda was beginning to tolerate the vulnerability of needing and loving, and the integration of loving and hating her primal internal object and its transference representation, her analyst.

Not long after this session, Linda was able to fall asleep during another therapy session. Her sleep was quite peaceful. Her ability to relax to such a degree in my presence was quite new. Her ability to feel good enough to sleep was not a resistance but rather a new phase of trust. As Linda slept, I experienced the most harmonious and musical kinds of feelings within me. I felt tenderness from her, sensing the induction of baby feelings within my lips and fingertips. Linda was finally letting me emotionally hold her, and thus letting me feel the baby within her. As she did so, we progressed past the stage, in which she had dreamed that I would not trust her to hold my baby, which seemed to have a projection of her own fears of being held. Yet Linda could only fully surrender to being held in an unconscious state. Following this session, she returned to her distancing maneuvers, but they were less rigid.

Despite all the backlash reactions, due to her fears of closeness with me, Linda was yielding to new capacities for relatedness as they developed within her. She began to allow an exchange, a real conversation between us, rather than to lecture at me, in a monologue. Linda no longer wailed me off, or talked at me in a detached manner, on any consistent basis. One day following the session in which her mourning process had opened up, she told me that she had missed her mother again, but that it no longer hurt so much. She also let me know several months later that she was crying a lot. Linda cried with and for people now, not just in isolation. She began to feel her attachments to her friends and colleagues much more strongly.

During the session after my return from vacation, Linda read to me a letter that she had written while I was away. In this letter, she revealed a lot of hidden affection for me. This letter, like her tears, seemed to be part of her developmental mourning process. I had become an external other who she was addressing and not just a mirroring audience used to applaud her performance or an idealized mother with which she yearned to merge. Pathological mourning (in which she had remained arrested in an attachment to a symbiotic mother and a sadistic narcissistic father) was changing into true developmental mourning, seen in many different forms. The developmental mourning involved object-related grief, which could be felt. As she became capable of containing guilt, I felt able to, emotionally, hold her within the psychic state of grieving her guilt. This allowed Linda to increase her capacity to contain guilt.

Through the structural work that had been done between us, Linda had come to refine raw aggression into grief affects. This allowed Linda to contain and process her internal experience, and thus to make developmental advances in self-integration and separation-individuation. As grief became tolerable, the developmental process proceeded, in which her internal objects were transformed as she gradually formed loving connections to each of them. Her hated and loved symbiotic mother began to transform into a person she could talk to—through her engagement with me, her analyst, and through her letting go of the original silent mother. She grieved the loss prompted by her guilt toward that silent mother, as well as the loss of that mother through actual death.

The relationship between Linda and me became a real Object Relationship, in which interaction and dialogue became possible, whereas words and the symbolic communication of separate individuals had been absent with her real mother. Her internal sadistic father, who used words only as accusations and demands for submission, was being transformed as well. Linda's relationship with her still-living father significantly improved as she began to feel empathy for him.

My own subjective experience with Linda developed, as I told Linda of the tenderness I had felt as she slept peacefully through that one session. However, intersubjectivity failed, as Linda's psychic dialectic between paranoid-schizoid and depressive positions (Ogden, 1992) brought her back to the paranoid-schizoid position in the clinical moment. I can only guess that bringing to her awareness the hints of intimacy between us embarrassed her. She seemed compelled to attack me in response, and to devalue the meaning of my message. She put me down and called me egocentric for presuming to read her messages in her unconscious state. As D.W. Winnicott (1971) might say, she needed to destroy my interpretations because I was being too omnipotent by making them. Yet my experience with Linda during this salient session of tenderness, as she slept peacefully in my metaphorical arms, allowed me to reach out to her. She responded by revealing her anxieties and doubts about herself, and asked me if I thought she was a monster; this she had never been able to do before.

Linda's new capacity for relational dialogues seemed reflective of a new internal dialectic, which was evolving within her. Psychic space allows for the opening up of mourning, and mourning in turn allows for the opening up of psychic space. Linda's dialogue with me was continually being internalized so that verbal-level dialectic could be internalized where only a nonverbal mother-child dialogue had once been. The internalization of such dialectic had been allowing a more flexible psychic structure to take form. Linda began to tolerate my questions, and she began to respond with discussion, reflection, a dialogue that showed the development of capacities in relationships (all part of the depressive position), and of becoming an interpreting subject (Ogden, 1986). Linda could now receive interpretations and began to see them as varying perspectives on meaning.

Our relatedness was also gradually developing, and Linda had an appreciation of it. One day, she had told me that I had never stopped caring about her. In the past, Linda had declared many times, "You're not big on praise." My response was that she hides the best parts of herself so that I could not respond to them. But now, I was able to tell Linda that as frightened as she was of her aggression, she had been even more frightened of her tenderness. Linda listened, now allowing the space between us—for reflection, discussion, and communion, as we struggled together with her self-sabotaging tendencies to withdraw or attack.

The Beginning of Heartache in Linda

When Linda began to mourn, she cried the tears of grief for her dead mother and the lost symbiotic mother that she had never separated from. For the first time in Linda's life, she was facing the primal grief affect, and the longings and guilt that accompanied such affect. When Linda had formerly blocked such grief affect, her core self-development had also been blocked, as had her self-expression and her individuated voice.

This was the beginning of heartache for this young woman. She was bereaved, suffering her very real and traumatic loss. However, she was also feeling a combination of neurotic guilt and existential guilt that becomes grief—the grief of hurting the one you love. Linda knew, after her anguish was spent, that she did not literally kill her mother. Yet she experienced killing her mother with her very real childhood needs while her mother was in a debilitated state and dying from cancer. In her memories, Linda saw her mother cranking the handle on the old-fashioned washing machine while washing Linda's dirtied clothes several times a day. She remembered that the skin on her mother's arms was hanging down from her now-bony arms, and her emaciated body was shaking in the process. In Linda's mind, this perpetual work of taking care of her daughter's physical (and emotional) needs killed her mother. And, in Linda's unconscious fantasy, she was merged into her mother's body, in a symbiotic state, and Linda's clothes were unconsciously experienced as burdensome parts of her mother's body.

Even though it was neurotic for Linda to believe she could have protected her mother from her childhood needs, she felt the existential grief over the very real guilt about her needs having become a burden to her ill and dying mother. When she cried and screamed out, "I did it!" Linda was feeling the agony of believing that having her needs had become a crime of murder. (Note that what I call "neurotic" here is also a symbiotic and paranoid-schizoid position psychic state in which the child still feels herself to be an extension of the idealized part-object breast mother, prior to the separate "I" of the subjective self [Ogden, 1986, 1992].)

When Linda sobbed because of the loss of her mother, she also sobbed because of her feeling that she had been responsible for hurting the one she loved. This combination of loss and guilt is all part of Klein's idea of the depressive position; it is also the essence of how mourning becomes a developmental process, in terms of renewing love through loss, as heartache becomes palpable (Kavaler-Adler, 2013).

Chapter 2

When the Road to Heartache is Long

The case of Linda illustrates how object survival can allow the primitive rage that has been blocking symbolic functioning to be outwardly expressed within the therapeutic holding environment, with the analyst providing holding and containing/ processing capacities. Symbolic functioning then becomes possible as the formerly split-off affects of rage, grief, guilt, and loss become possible. The patient then becomes an interpreting subject (Ogden, 1986). This interpreting subject knows that she has interpreting thoughts and feelings in her mind rather than just being reactive as an externalizing victim at a paranoid-schizoid level. As a being and interpreting subject, one can also receive interpretations from the psychoanalyst, understanding that such interpretations have symbolic meaning.

Otto Kernberg (1975) has written about how confronting and interpreting the primal oral rage can allow for blocked symbolic level capacities to open up and resume functioning. This can be seen to be true in the case of Linda, who lost her mother at the age of eight (not one or two) and had symbolic-level potential, despite a truncated separation-individuation process in which Linda's mother never related to her in words. So, in this case, Kernberg's view holds up that the primitive splitting defenses used to ward off a conscious expression of the rage interfered with the symbolic capacities that had already been developed.

Arrested Symbolic Capacity, or Blocked Symbolic Capacity, Prior to the Transformation of Heartache

In other cases, however, the chronic mode of traumatic character-disordered mothering may arrest the road to tolerated sadness, and ultimately to the heartache of being able to love another. This failure in symbolic functioning can indicate a preoedipal developmental arrest. In such a case, Winnicott's (1963) view that the symbolic functions need to be developed through new "good-enough" internalizations seems pertinent. This developmental perspective would contrast with the defense analysis perspective of Kernberg (1975), which maintains that the symbolic capacity has been developed but is merely blocked by oral rage and the defenses of splitting, projective identification, primitive idealization, and primitive devaluation that defend against such rage, and which disrupt psychological functioning.

The clinical examples in this study are meant to illustrate how the beginning of heartache represents one perspective on understanding how affects and affect states are indicative of psychological development. The beginning of heartache

45

can chart the way to developmental advances in all ego functions, not only in symbolic functioning. As one enters the guilt and loss of the depressive position and simultaneously enters the "psychic" (conscious) regret within a developmental mourning process, advances in ego functions can be seen to develop organically. This will include the development of psychic dialectic and self-integration to allow ambivalence and consciousness of psychic conflict as opposed to splitting (Klein, 1946) as well as allowing self-reflection, observing ego, interiority (Kavaler-Adler, 2006a, 2006b, 2007b), object constancy, self-and-other differentiation, the development of a subjective self (Ogden, 1986) or true self (Winnicott, 1960), and the development of capacities to be an "interpreting" and "historical" subject (Ogden, 1986).

Entering the depressive position does not mean that the paranoid-schizoid position is totally left behind. As Ogden (1992) has written, there is a lifelong dialectic between the depressive and the paranoid-schizoid positions. The subjectivity that develops in the depressive position, which accompanies Klein's criteria of being able to love and hate the same object (and being able to tolerate ambivalence), can be decentered by regression to former and early traumatic disruptions, or regression to defensive resistances that provoke paranoid-schizoid reactivity. Then the newly acquired, through the affects of heartache, subjective "I" of the depressive position can be temporarily lost, so that the person returns to being a reactive "me," who ceases to process the symbolic meanings of things, and ceases to feel like an "I" with subjectivity and agency.

The Case of Cynthia: The Road to Heartache in the Narcissistic Character Self-Loss Tied in with Object Loss: Accepting Disillusionment on the Journey to Love and Heartache

Cynthia, a woman in her mid-40s, came into psychoanalytic treatment after some years of other kinds of therapeutic approaches. As soon as Cynthia followed my suggestion to ask a psychopharmacologist to help her to come off antidepressants (which she had been taking for over a decade), the grief affect of sadness poured out of her. Cynthia was terrified of how much sadness was inside her, and like many traumatized individuals who have warded off profound sadness for a lifetime, she had the fantasy that she could drown in endless tears of sadness, which made her scared to begin the grieving process. However, she was able to speak about these fears with me.

Cynthia cried perpetually about her losses, losses of relationships, which were tied in with losses of her true, unique, and separate self, and the loss of her own autonomous voice. She also cried about the "damned if she did or didn't" situation that she suffered at the hands of her narcissistic mother, sister, and father. In treatment, she discovered that the closed system that was operating within the external world of her actual family was also operating in her internal world. She was damned if she expressed her own opinions or attempted to separate from the family and their opinions. Her family would then blame or bully her, or run their emotional blackmail upon her. They would call her "difficult," "self-centered," "entitled," "critical," and "demanding." If she submitted and silenced herself in the presence of her family, she would feel she was annihilating her own voice and ultimately her own self, and she feared that her basic sense of self would be lost for good. This was the price of being a part of her dysfunctional family.

The only way out was for Cynthia to form relationships outside her family, where she could be heard. But even when away from her family, she was plagued internally by her attacks upon herself. This resulted from her identification with her family's beliefs about her and the accusations toward her. Beyond "identification with the aggressor" (Freud, 1936), she had formed a whole internal psychic structure that had a mission to carry out the attacks upon herself, as this was always done by her family. This self-attacking psychic structure can be related to Fairbairn's (1952) "antilibidinal ego," to Klein's internal persecutory object, to Seinfeld's (1989) "antidependent self," to Masterson's (1976) "withholding Object Relations unit," or to Kavaler-Adler's (1988a, 1989b, 2014b) demon-lover complex.

When reflexively and habitually enacting this self-sabotaging and self-condemning psychic structure, Cynthia was distancing herself from others. She projected out her persecution onto a family, which was in fact persecuting her. Expressing her rage, and also having interpretations from me about the contextual meaning of her perpetual sense of persecution, allowed Cynthia to feel the externality of the others in her family. She then began to face the grief of mourning her family and separating from their most persecutory aspects rather than perpetuating the internalization of these persecutory aspects. Consequently, Cynthia became more capable of being with her family without losing her core authentic, feeling, and thinking subjective self. She began to risk voicing her opinions, even in the face of scapegoating criticism. Gradually, she was able to confront her family members about projecting their own disowned parts onto her. Even if they could not hear her, she was less vulnerable to their defensive projections as her internal persecutions lessened.

With her new tolerance for sadness in the holding environment of treatment, Cynthia began to feel the loss of others and longed for a relationship with a man. However, she automatically attacked the image of each man she dated. In other words, she perpetually turned her self-attacks outwards at men, as was done to her by her family. In addition, Cynthia longed for men that rejected her. In doing so, she actually longed for a lost or unavailable symbiotic mother and early detached father. Those who were available and present were rejected as unconscious transference mothers of separation, who were too controlling and overwhelming to allow Cynthia her autonomy. This rejection then disrupted her own sense of "going on being" (Winnicott, 1971), which was exacerbated by a failed eroticized Oedipal father in her internal world. That provoked deprivation, as a subjective feeling of "There is no chemistry. I don't feel turned on." Cynthia mentally held onto the unavailable men, thinking obsessively about them. Again, Cynthia was in a "damned if she did or damned if she didn't" situation. Nevertheless, opening to the sadness within her, which brought forth the memories that were needed to grieve the losses of opportunities and relationships in her life, began to become her route to autonomy and creative self-expression.

However, Cynthia's transferential experience of the analyst as the mother who would not allow her autonomy caused her to regress to a defensive dissociation, and she would again split-off from her core self. Cynthia needed to keep feeling the losses she had created in order to sustain contact, even when experiencing the analyst as the controlling mother. As she articulated more about me being a controlling and aversive mother, and brought in dreams about it, we could see together how her emotional withdrawals were self-sabotaging. Through projective identification, I would actually feel like a controlling mother, as I tried to engage her in the analysis rather than capitulate to her escapes from sustained contact. I would interpret a two-year-old's experience of a mother who was intruding on her autonomy, agency, and desire. With time, Cynthia reached a "good-enough" depressive position to understand such interpretations. My relational response was to relax my countertransference tendencies of her indoctrination into the value of psychoanalytic work.

Cynthia's new developmental path was paved with disillusionment about her wish to be an "idealized perfect self" as well as with heartache about the way she had rejected and detached from all those who would accept and value her. I began to interpret the constructed "perfect self" as her defensive reaction to not having had the chance to internalize an adequate symbiotic mother. Without such adequate mother internalization, she perpetuated an oppositional battle with a mother who was unattuned to her needs for both connection and autonomy as she entered a developmental path of separation. This internalized developmental conflict and trauma caused Cynthia to close off and invest in an image of her own totally autonomous perfection and self-sufficiency. She was returning to the paranoid-schizoid position to avoid the loss of the wished-for symbiotic mother and the longed-for Oedipal father. But each time I interpreted her defenses, and she could surrender to feelings of loss, grief, and sometimes regret, she would feel more whole and sustain more depressive position relatedness, even when anger and resentment would arise.

Cynthia remembered her "first love" and driving back and forth to visit him when she was in graduate school. While Cynthia lay on the couch, tears streamed down her face. She wept the soft sadness of a vulnerable feminine self that had been developmentally arrested. These tears were of lost opportunities while holding on to a man who ultimately rejected her. She held on to her "first love" for so long that she did not date guys when in her 20s. Then, in her 40s, she yearned for younger men when they were no longer appropriate.

Cynthia rejected her own talents too and began to attack parts of herself she had believed in. This brought the pain of heartache related to the unrequited love of rejecting herself. Cynthia also cried because she could not control others. This brought back grief-laden preoedipal memories from the age of two or three years when she could say, "I want to do it myself!" Cynthia screamed with rage when she could not be self-sufficient in actions because she had already been opposed and stunted in her natural developmental need to have her own words and her own voice. Her family had always silenced her with criticism and character attacks when she dared to express her own autonomous thinking. Gradually, Cynthia had to accept the disillusionment of not being able to compensate for her early loss of autonomy with the support of a maternal connection and attunement by constructing a false, and "perfect," self-image. Giving up this false perfect self brought much sadness, as if her false self was an "other" that she had to give up and then grieve. Gradually, the road of disillusionment became tolerable as she experienced this developmental mourning process in treatment.

Cynthia then went beyond rage and pain over giving up defensive control, similar to Betty Joseph's patient, and began to enter the land of true mourning. Finally, her core true self's sadness began to connect with her heart. Cynthia could begin to feel heartache, heartache for herself, and then for others that she longed for. Her heartache was less about hurting the ones she loved than about hurting her own self. She needed to learn to love her subjective and authentic self and to mourn the losses she had been creating by self-sabotage. Cynthia was also hurting those who could potentially love her when she rejected her authentic self because it was not perfect. She would gradually face this kind of loss too, as she sustained mourning of loss, as well as the existential guilt of regret. In between times of processing loss and regret, she might regress to paranoid-schizoid reactivity, closing off the transitional space between us, as she projected her idealized or demonized self parts onto me. We began a dialogue about her idealization of me when she was devaluing herself and her devaluing or demonizing of me when she was returning to clinging to her false perfect self.

In this way, Cynthia entered the pain of loss and faced her shame, transforming the narcissistic defense system that had to adjust to her narcissistic family. From an ego psychology perspective, this would have been seen as a compromise formation between self-annihilation and annihilation of the other. Cynthia had been entrapped in this compromise. Through her Object Relations psychoanalytic treatment, she emotionally learned that she needed heart-felt sadness, or sadness with pain that we can call heartache, to emerge into a position of psychic connection with herself, and with others.

The Case of Sharon: The Beginning of Heartache through the Transforming Experience of "Psychic Regret" on the Authentic Affect Journey of Developmental Mourning

Sharon came into psychoanalytic Object Relations treatment with a fairly severe character disorder, but through the course of her analysis, she began to open up all levels of dissociated rage, loss, love, and longing for becoming fully human and related. The apex of Sharon's developmental mourning process came one day in the ninth year of treatment, when she opened her heart to loving her father again, who she had turned ice cold towards when he was still alive. Her contempt for the father had become full-blown, not only because he sat in a corner and vegetated, but also because he had never stood up to the raging Medusa-like witch/monster mother who had constantly bullied and humiliated her. Then one day, a whole other story opened up about Sharon's father. A formerly forgotten father was suddenly brought to Sharon's conscious mind.

The Beginning of Heartache: "Regrets for Daddy"

When she first came to treatment, Sharon had always portrayed her father as a passive wimp. She told me that she had received rejections for plays she had written because of her view of men as being caricatured and lifeless. Soon, however, the passive "wimp" became a withholding "bastard" and also a frustrated victim of the mental health establishment of his time. He was hospitalized once, and then came home and sat inert, forever, and Sharon hated him for this.

Then there was one crystalline session of paradoxical dramas reformulating in Sharon's mind. This session had a trenchant impact on both Sharon and me. We actually became joined by a new daddy relationship from the interior space behind the former curtains in her mind. Sharon's core connections to an early daddy were re-found like the discovery of the Rosetta stone. The self that could only survive through heart connections emerged.

This session is memorable for its dialectical poles of hate and love, spinning around a father object that had been coming increasingly to life, as part-object forms come into whole-object forms, when the self and psyche integrate. By the midpoint of the session, Sharon was recalling her hate for a father who epitomized all the forms of failing her. This left her feeling alone and in orbit in the world as if she had been a "changeling" (Sharon's word) who had been dropped arbitrarily into a family system that seemed totally detached and strangely alien to her. She felt like an alien. Sharon spoke of a rage coming awake, coming out of its sealed-off and dissociated place in her internal world. She said that this rage evoked in her a feeling of being on fire, with hot wires of hate streaming through her entire body.

Sharon recalled her father's long chaotic and incoherent letters to her at camp, feeling nauseous disdain, and suffering the thoughts of how out of touch her father was. She hated him for his letters. She hated him for his inert passive dependence on her mother and his invalid status. She hated him for his lack of any sense of agency, and also for his pleading and hurt-filled eyes, which left her guilt-ridden when he was not oblivious and totally detached. She hated him for his lack of awareness of her scapegoat status with her sadistic and martyred mother.

There was hate, hate, hate! Then suddenly something erupted from another plain as a new regret consumed her. Sharon's syncopated memory jumped forward from childhood to her adulthood as she recalled how he had written to her, asking to see her, saying it might be the last time they saw each other. With this thought, Sharon started to cry in great gulps of pain that were different from other times of silent weeping. "I knew he was going to die," she said. "I didn't believe him. I wrote him back a snide, contemptuous, and dismissive letter, saying that of course we'd see each other again! I can feel that sneer in the letter now. I was cold, detached, sadistic one then, not he, not her. I was the metallic object, the unfeeling stone. I never saw him again!" As she said this, Sharon doubly erupted in an agony of grief. She gasped to breathe as tears flooded her and wiped out the hot wires of hate that had possessed her; all bad objects possess those that cannot love.

And then a new level of memory entered the door of my consultation room that neither of us had witnessed before. Sharon remembered her early daddy that she had kept immured in the darkness of her mental closet, up until that very moment. He was a daddy that she believed now, in this very moment, had truly loved her. "I never believed that my mother loved me," she said, "but I always knew my father had loved me. I forgot all of it, the daddy who loved me, the daddy I loved." Her tears washed her eyes red. I could only see them when she got up from the couch at the end of the session. She concluded: "I was so mean. I turned my heart cold. No wonder my first marriage failed, and I almost destroyed my second marriage." As her analyst, I felt the poignancy of the moment, as Sharon's heart cried out to me with her newfound capacity to love. We had discovered her daddy. I wanted to sing as her grief washed up on the raft of her core self, embedded in a barbed wire ego that could now surrender to love and life!

When Sharon left the session that day, we both knew that change could definitely happen. "He really loved me," she repeated. "That's why you've been able to love your daughter," I said, "despite your fears that you could never love, especially a daughter." Sharon nodded her head in agreement. We had a silent moment of communion. "The part of you that knew beyond your conscious ignorance that you were loved by your daddy, found your daughter. That's why she's healthy, sociable, and self-confident. It hasn't all been your husband's doing," I said. Seeing her father as a vulnerable being allowed Sharon to dream of a vulnerable mother with hurt in her eyes. The new image of her mother, and seeing a child in her mother, allowed her to relinquish the image of her mother as a monster. In relinquishing that primal object image, Sharon was able to lessen her compulsive tendency to demonize the world through the projection of this internal primal image (Kavaler-Adler, 2013).

As Sharon had more love than hate, she could mourn, and as she mourned, she also was able to open both her internal psychic space and the transitional space between us. Then she was able to receive me as an external object. I became alive for her as an "other," and this, of course, affected how I felt in the room with her. She began to have dreams about the real me, with all my idiosyncrasies, rather than having me as a stereotyped devalued and detached part-object. I could consequently feel much more related to her. I was no longer seen as an alien other, who was numbed-out like she had felt when she had perceived herself as an alien. I no longer was seen as a detached person who was going through the motions of playing a "role of a therapist." Therefore, I could wake up emotionally from a semi-detached state, where I had first felt far away or sleepy. I was no longer in a "twinship transference" clone of her sealed-off alien, isolated, and withdrawn self.

I awoke to my subjectivity as Sharon awoke to hers as I was no longer a creation of her dissociated internal world fantasy life. I gradually came to feel my own separate feeling states. Therefore, I could make my own "separate" comment to Sharon about her capacity to love, and her having been able to love her daughter more as an "other" as she reconnected with the love for her father. However, I was also feeling Sharon's feelings. I felt her hate and rage but was no longer internalizing it because projective identification had yielded to self-expression in the new transitional space between us.

I could ultimately feel the power of her love and felt the flow of this love in our intersubjective feeling space. However, I also could feel like me, not just like I was a container for her feelings, her subjectivity, and her internal objects. And when Sharon would return to degrees of the old emotional attachment in some later sessions, I would feel the loss. She also made it clear that her heart had awoken and that love and loss were now in near reach. Once Sharon said to me that she knew she "had a heart now" because she could feel what it was like to have a broken heart.

Conclusion

The clinical practice of Winnicott's object survival allows for the most primitive affect states to be expressed within the analytic space, between the analyst and patient. When these affect states are thus contained and understood in their "in vivo" moment of acute core self experience, a developmental process unfolds that evolves into a mourning process of primal object loss. This allows for a primal birth of an autonomous and authentic self. Along with the grief of loss within a developmental mourning process, primal guilt toward the internalized parental object can be felt as a subjective sense of psychic regret. Ultimately, heartache is possible, which is the visceral self-experience of the capacity to love.

Through all the clinical examples discussed here, it is evident that even those who have significant character disorders are able to reach states of human connection on the affect level of heartache, thus reaching beyond the developmental level of the patient described by Betty Joseph (1989) in her essay on "psychic pain." All these clinical examples are clear in their focus on affects as revealing developmental process and relational capacities from the level of core true self development. Also obvious from the revelation of such clinical and developmental processes is how it becomes critical to not medicate away these affects, or their primal need states, which are attached to these affects, and which awaken the conscious mind to a need for the other. The affective experience of mourning is essential for character-disorder reparation. Heartache is the signpost to the development of the subjective experience of self, an authentic, autonomous, connected, and integrated self. This is a self with impulse, affect, cognition, and perception (Horner, 2005).

The emergence of this subjective self goes hand in hand with the evolution of intersubjectivity in transitional space, beyond internal psychic space. The expansion of internal space and transitional space evolve in parallel. The interpersonal domain that then develops is always subject to regressions. Analysands can regress to "me" rather than "I," and to the analyst (or other) as "it," rather than "you" (or "thou"). Times of relived trauma, or renewed defensive resistances to outside or inside connections, intrude on subjectivity. The analytic patient can return to the paranoid-schizoid state of being a reactive "me" rather than a subjective and responsive "I" (Ogden 1986, 1992). Then the analyst can feel like their subjectivity is temporarily lost as well.

CHAPTER 3

ANATOMY OF REGRET: A DEVELOPMENTAL VIEW OF THE DEPRESSIVE POSITION AND A CRITICAL TURN TOWARD LOVE AND CREATIVITY IN THE TRANSFORMING SCHIZOID PERSONALITY

Originally published in 2004, *American Journal of Psychoanalysis* 64(1):39–76.

Melanie Klein spoke about the depressive position capacity to tolerate guilt as well as loss in relation to a loved one as being fundamental to psychic integration (1940, 1957/1980). Klein differs from all other Object Relations theorists who only speak of object loss in relation to developmental arrest versus continuing psychic development. I follow Klein's focus on guilt and loss in the ambivalence of human relationship. However, as for Klein, guilt in relation to loss is existential guilt, not neurotic guilt. I conceptualize this dynamic as psychic regret. I have found the capacity to face regret to be pivotal in psychic change and self-integration. Psychic regret involves the conscious ability to face the grief related to existential guilt and to communicate the nature of one's guilt to oneself, and often, to another, within personal relationship. In my view, the human capacity to face regrets consciously has played a significant part in an overall critical developmental mourning process (Kavaler-Adler, 1993a/2013, 1996/2014, 2003a, 2003b) that allows for the deepening and sustaining of relationships. Such psychic regret and its integration of split-off aggressive aspects of the personality also promote the development of self-agency, self-reflection, and psychic dialectic helping to resolve conflicts over love and hate. These conflicts over love and hate can relate to external or internal relationships and to one's relationship to one's self (i.e., loving or hating the self, which relates to the present but also to the feelings and impulses toward the primary objects that have been internalized, the most basic one being related to the primal mother).

I've been writing about regret in articles and books, including *Mourning, Spirituality and Psychic Change: A New Object Relations View of Psychoanalysis*

(2003a). In the meantime, Shabad (2001) has written an important book on mourning that relates to some overlapping issues. However, Shabad views regret as related to the self and signifies remorse as an existential guilt dynamic related to another. By contrast, my view of regret is an Object Relations one in which the internal world and its internal objects are highly reflective of relations with others and vice versa, so regret toward the self-sabotage of the self also becomes seen as intimately related to the internal pathological relations with the other within the internal world. Therefore, I find remorse and regret to interweave intrapsychically, and when regret is made conscious, all differentiations can be made. In working out external Object Relations, the differentiation of self and internal other, when both are projected onto an external other, becomes highly relevant to all modes of ego development, particularly in terms of self-agency and intersubjective relatedness to the other. Facing regret is an entryway into the developmental enhancement of interiority and observing ego reflection.

For Melanie Klein, true reparation that emerges through a genuine experience of guilt and loss can be as passionate as a sexual act. From my perspective, authentic regret is a passionate experience whose grief affect level merges loss and existential guilt. The cognitive level of insight that comes with such affective experience is one of identifying and defining the differentiated nature of one's regret, as one comes on the painful awareness of hurting oneself through hurting the other. In Klein's terms, this can be worded as hurting the primal internal object through hurting external objects that serve as displacements for the primal maternal other on an unconscious level. Following from this view, to face regret is to face the capacity to change.

My clinical experience illustrates that regret is a signpost to hope if it can be consciously felt and processed. If it cannot be tolerated, it can turn to despair and reinforce prior traumatic loss and developmental arrest. I believe that the holding environment (Modell, 1975, 1976; Winnicott, 1982a, 1982b, 1982c) of the clinical situation allows for the tolerance and processing of regret. This can then lead to critical psychic change as a working through process occurs in which primal modes of regret are reexperienced and relived. The following case of an analysand, whom I will call Sharon, illustrates this. The transformation of a schizoid psychic structure, with an accompanying negative or self-devaluing narcissistic image system, can be clearly seen in her case.

The Case of Sharon

Sharon first contacted me through a letter after reading one of my books. In her letter, she said that she identified with much of what I wrote, particularly descriptions of a mother and child that seemed to relate to her and her own mother. She spoke of the mother who had no boundaries, who merged herself with her daughter, and of the daughter who consequently developed a sealed-off self, split away from contact with others. She also spoke of my demon-lover theme as having puzzled her at first, because she saw her father as an inert, depressed, and passive being, not as an active monster. However, she realized that his passivity and unavailability had left her with the impression of men as part objects rather than as whole and related beings, and that the effect of their withdrawn nature was, in fact, demonic, although not overtly so. This, she wrote, caused her to have portrayed men in her creative writing as lifeless, wimpy creatures. This resulted in getting rejection notes to several plays she had written in which she was told that her male characters did not come alive.

Sharon was not a full-time writer. Her creative writing was her dream for the future, but she worked as an accountant in a large bureaucratic firm. At the time that she first wrote to me, she was a single mother, living alone with her son, divorced for several years from an alcoholic, and was just beginning to date a new man. She was also seeing a psychotherapist once a week, someone who knew that I wrote about women writers. Knowing that Sharon was working at becoming a writer, Sharon's psychotherapist had referred Sharon to my books. From Sharon's description, this therapy seems to have been supportive, with no analytic work leading to insight and with very little emotional communication between her and her therapist. At some point in this therapy, the psychotherapist recommended that she see me for psychoanalysis, acknowledging her own limitations in not practicing psychoanalysis.

The first five years of therapy with me were rather uneventful in terms of psychic change or development. Sharon maintained a schizoid compromise. She resisted coming more than once a week, and after some initial curiosity, began to come out of a sense of pure obligation, resenting each trip to my office. She resented having to be there at all. Yet, for the most part, she kept these resentments to herself, withholding them from me as she withheld much of herself. Once she did reveal that she thought I was detached and isolated in my professional attitude. Later, she would see this as a projection of her own detachment, but at the time, she thought that I probably experienced her as a burden. She thought I was performing some perfunctory role, that I only put up with seeing her because she was paying me. She only told me this later, after her assumption had changed. She also had assumed that I would probably not want to have anything to do with her if I was not being paid on a professional basis to see her. She saw herself as boring, dull, and lacking the life energy of enthusiasm.

During these early years in treatment she remarried, had a daughter with her new husband, and often spoke of being controlled by her son's demands on her.

Although distant in manner and flat in affect, Sharon did reveal some of her internal life through dreams. Her dreams revealed how imprisoned she felt within her own psychic structure. They also revealed how cold she felt inside and how stereotypic the world seemed to her. And, they revealed a sealed-off internal state, in which her aggression was split-off and frozen in a detached and cynical attitude of contempt. In these dreams, Sharon's sense of herself showed itself as a dysfunctional and incompetent being.

One early dream was a visual vista in which Sharon stood statically like a statue on the beach, looking away from the ocean, with a lion standing on one of her shoulders. The lion seemed to symbolize her sealed-off and frozen aggression. At this early time, Sharon was unaware of her cynical and contemptuous attitude, which she enacted mentally on both others and herself. Frozen rage, personified in the figure of the lion, had become a whole dissociated part of Sharon. The lion figure could have also represented the kind of split-off, antilibidinal ego structure that Fairbairn (1952) described as characteristic of the schizoid character. At the end of this dream, Sharon had the image of a prison. She described it as if she was on the outside of it (as she was outside of life), but its image could be seen as an implication that she herself was in the prison. The further implication highlighted by her own association was that she had been placed in a prison due to some criminal activity that she related to the lion-like rage within her. In its dissociated state, her rage threatened to become criminally out of control. Freezing it was her way to keep it in check. In other words, Sharon's state of dissociation created a prison within her.

In another early dream, Sharon lived in a house where the plumbing did not function and was in a state of disrepair. Her associations led to the conclusion that the house represented Sharon's self that was not functioning right, reminiscent of Bion's (1967) "attacks on linking." Attacks on linking occur consequent to early and "cumulative trauma" (Khan, 1974). Sharon could picture the house as her self with her internal plumbing not working. She had always felt that her internal connections were not working properly. She felt disconnected in so many ways, as if the links between various parts of her were not connected. Given such psychic attacks on the linking within her psyche, Sharon had to make careful written notes to remember things, as she was very forgetful. She felt helplessly out of touch when her husband accused her of lacking empathy for what he was going through, which was also an aspect of her general disconnection.

Transference

In her state of detachment, as seen by the view of her internal disconnected plumbing in her dream, Sharon saw me as detached. This view of me transformed as soon as she changed and came to life. Nevertheless, at this time Sharon saw me as strictly professional, in a stereotypic way, as she assumed that I was indifferent to her as a human being. She had me set up as a mirror of her sense of detached obligation. Since she felt burdened with this disconnected and distant obligation, she believed that she was a burden to me that I only put up with because of professional responsibility and because I needed to earn a living. I existed as a negative mirror for her. Basically, she could only see me through projective identification, an illusive and yet static image within an overall negative image system. By only seeing me once a week, she maintained a "schizoid compromise" (Guntrip, 1969) that allowed her to keep control and maintain distance from any affect hunger or need. She was about to learn how she did this with everyone in her life.

Until later in treatment, I was experienced through projective identification as part of her self, mainly a detached part, and sometimes as a split-off grandiose self ideal. I was not a differentiated transference projection until later when I then could be seen as arrogant or biased in my views. I was never consciously seen as the sadistic and infantile mother who would scapegoat her. This transference picture was consistently placed on her husband, who gave her reason to see him that way.

The False Caretaking Self

Winnicott (1982a) has written about the false caretaking self that is used by the schizoid character, whom he called the "false self" patient. Winnicott's false self operates in the external world to ward off contacts that would feel like "impingements" or intrusions to the sealed-off vulnerable infant/child self of the schizoid character. Such a false caretaking self-structure could be seen in Sharon in the early years of her treatment. Her preoccupation with caring for her house as she would try to care for and perfect a fabricated self-structure made the "house" into an external representation of her false self-system. She tried to make her external self by preoccupying herself with cleaning, decorating, and neatness in her house. Simultaneously, in her dreams, her house revealed the secret shame-ridden child self within whose "plumbing didn't work."

When Sharon married her second husband, which occurred in her third year of treatment, she focused all her energies and interest on choosing a larger more elegant suburban home, and then on decorating, cleaning, and keeping this new home neat. Her new husband's continual messiness within this new home was a constant irritant to her that resulted in many quarrels and arguments. Sharon's husband told her that she seemed to be totally preoccupied with the house and how it looked, so much so that all the other problems with him and the children seemed secondary. Sharon's husband told her that she based her entire sense of well-being on how the house looked.

Sharon's external home seemed to represent both a false caretaking self and a false narcissistic image self. Taking care of her home, when she felt she was totally impotent in the face of depending on anyone else, seemed to be Sharon's way of maintaining a narcissistic sense of self-sufficiency. Fixing up her home was something she could master. Consequently, she became her own caretaking self in the process, while simultaneously enacting an insatiable struggle to repair her own narcissistic image in fixing the image of her home. Not until Sharon could have the profound grief experience of regret could she break the spell of the princess in the perfect house, immured against intrusion by an inanimate object that was more dependable for protection and comfort than any person had been for her (see Kavaler-Adler, 1991a, on seclusion and Emily Dickinson). The original person Sharon could not trust was her mother, who had instilled in Sharon her own blueprint of general distrust. The mother had always masked her distance with an attitude of contempt.

Looking Into the Face of Medusa: A Core Traumatic Memory and the Opening of the Sealed-Off Central Self

In her state of detachment, Sharon had described horrible incidents from her childhood in a mode of reporting, without affect and with an air of cynicism or indifference that was characterized by such phrases as "It wasn't so bad." With her internal self sealed-off, the actual traumatic impact of her childhood was kept at a safe distance as was any memory of her mother's direct impact on her. Sharon was identified with her mother as one would identify with the aggressor. But all this was both repressed and dissociated, and remained out of awareness.

In the third year of treatment, there was an incident that demonstrated her identification with the aggressor, which became a whole antilibidinal attitude (Fairbairn, 1952) of self-torment and self-attack. Sharon had decided to help her husband with some research. She went to the home of an Italian professor to interview her on a book she had written. She took her tape recorder, but once inside the professor's home, the professor began speaking so fast that Sharon did not even have time to set up the tape recorder. Sharon tried to scribble down notes, but could not keep up. She meekly pleaded with the professor, "I think I should set up the tape recorder now"; however, the professor did not stop. Sharon began to become the victim of some crazy-making thinking of her own that vividly brought her back to her mother in psychic time. Desperate to do this interview, Sharon wanted to be perceived as competent, trying to force herself into the "competence" that she felt was beyond her. As the woman chattered on, Sharon began yelling at herself, inside her head, that she should be able to understand this as the professor raced through complicated research data in English. When the professor switched to Italian (a language that Sharon did not know), Sharon's self-reprimands escalated. She yelled at herself that she should understand Italian and everything this woman was saying at this fast pace.

Following the incident with the professor, Sharon declared:

> My mother always expected me to do things I couldn't possibly do at the age I was at. So I was always being yelled at for not being able to do things. It made me believe I should be able to do things I couldn't possibly do. I was always bad. So now I yell at myself for not knowing things I couldn't possibly know. My mother could never teach me how to do anything because it would make her so mad that I didn't know how to do the thing already that she would grab it away from me in a rage and do it herself. I could never learn how to do anything from my mother. My father was just this passive inert ghost, called a saint by my mother, sitting impotently in the background. My goal in life was to not end up like him. If that was what it was like to be good rather than bad, I was better off being bad.

Sharon's reenactment of her mother's emotional control and abuse in this incident with the Italian professor triggered a memory of an early life experience with her mother. The memory suggested how a vicious cycle had begun of Sharon internalizing her mother's reproaches, outlandish expectations, and reprimands as part of an internal Fairbairnian "antilibidinal ego structure" (called "antidependent self" by Seinfeld, 1989), or in Klein's terms, a "primitive superego structure." Through this memory, Sharon could for the first time experience the horrific impact of her mother rather than keeping her memory merely as an abstract narrative told with detachment. Therefore, the memory could become an entryway into the sealed-off child self within her, which would emerge more later through a group experience. Sharon could begin to connect with the anger that had been sealed-off in the split-off area in her psyche, where it had formerly resided as a lion on her shoulder in a dream.

Core Traumatic Memory: Finding the Sealed-Off Central Self

Sharon recalled a memory of being three years old and of being left alone in a park by her mother, along with her brother (two years older), in the middle of winter. Her mother went off to shop. Sharon expected her mother to come back for her. When hours rather than minutes seemed to pass, she and her brother were freezing and terrified. Sharon did not know the way home. She could not believe that her mother had just left her there and was not coming back for her. Along with her brother, Sharon walked and walked, dragging their sled behind them. She was wet, exhausted, and continually terrified, wearing big heavy snow boots and a snowsuit. She and her brother were confused about which direction to go, and now it was getting darker. Finally, they saw their apartment building. They rang the bell of their apartment. Sharon's mother answered the door, and instead of being happy to see her and happy that she and her brother had saved themselves, her mother started to scream—particularly at her—for not staying where she had left them. Her mother seemed to go crazy, screaming and then hitting Sharon, telling her she was "bad." Something inside of Sharon died at that moment, but she did not dare think consciously that her mother was crazy (see Winnicott, 1974, on "Fear of Breakdown"). Instead of looking into the face of a Medusa mother, she tried to psychically survive by thinking she herself was bad (Fairbairn's "moral defense") and tried to figure out how to be good.

Sharon could never figure out how to be good. Although remembering such memories could have brought the reverberating shock of looking into the face of Medusa—as Sharon looked into the face of a mad mother who disowned all her craziness as a form of badness that she projected onto her child—she actually spoke of all the memories and descriptions of her mother in a most detached manner in the beginning.

After the incident with the Italian professor, however, this memory came alive in a way, and Sharon's anger came alive as she recalled her helplessness. It led to her telling the analyst about a whole stereotyped "binary system" of thought that her mother employed and that she had identified with as she was shocked to discover.

The Binary Cognitive System that Bound the Schizoid Sealed-Off Self

In her newfound anger, Sharon proclaimed:

> I still don't know how I survived it all. I must have had internal resources
> from somewhere. I couldn't learn anything from my mother directly, but

I watched her. I had to become self-sufficient or I'd end up like my father, totally dependent on my mother. My brother escaped the worst of it because he was a boy. He was less easily adaptable by my mother as an extension of her, even in her mind. As a girl, I was a patsy.

By being the bad part of my mother, my mother reinforced her view of herself as this idealized image. She could never be real. If she said she wasn't angry, she wasn't angry! The reality didn't matter. She continually created the image of who she was. To be angry was bad in her mind, so no matter how enraged she was acting, she was not angry if she believed she wasn't angry! Her denial was total. She created herself as an image every minute. And others got categorized in some totally binary system in her mind. Her mind clicked away like a high-speed computer. Everyone got put in either the good category or the bad category. She would identify with the images of the good. Meanwhile, she could have been totally out of control, ranting and raving at me, accusing me of everything under the sun. Whatever she said to me I was supposed to deserve because I was bad.

Sharon began to reveal a binary thought and image system of her own, which was shocking to her when she became aware of it. She began to tell me, as I listened and understood her anger and helplessness in her relation to her mother, that she continually lived in a world of fantasy images in which she constructed stories about those around her. These stories reinforced Sharon's view of herself as an outsider in a world in which others had exciting and adventurous lives. Like her mother, she dichotomized everyone. For Sharon, everyone became a contrast to her unworthy and dejected self, the orphan child who stood on the outside looking in, tantalized by the imagined world of others from which she was excluded. She began to discover that her fabrications about others were harshly dissonant with the actual reality of what human beings were like.

One scenario that she constructed in her mind concerned a female colleague at work. To Sharon, this woman seemed to be a princess, the center of the universe. She always saw this woman as the popular office celebrity because she seemed to be entertaining others in her office all of the time, and she seemed to be socializing with others constantly at lunch. Sharon saw this woman's world as the exact opposite of her own; she drew the black and white comparisons of her binary mental system. She imagined this woman to be in a whole other universe compared to herself in her degree of happiness and well-being in this life. Sharon's binary system had dictated to her that this colleague was perpetually wanted and adored in a world from which Sharon was excluded. Sharon labeled herself the excluded loner, never stopping to consider that she had actually turned down all lunch invitations when they were offered to her. She had chosen to remain in her office doing work, having a sandwich alone at her desk. Since Sharon did not experience herself as an agent, but felt like a victim in her passive reactive experience of things, her own decision to refuse lunch invitations was denied and dissociated.

When Sharon actually dared to test reality by speaking to her colleague in the office of social parties, she was shocked to be confronted with her female colleague's views about herself and about Sharon. Her colleague, whom we can call Linda, exclaimed that she saw herself as this weak, neurotic, and overly dependent personality who lacked the strength and fortitude to say "no" to a lunch invitation, or any invitation. She saw Sharon as being an opposite type of personality who had the strength and independence to be her own person, to be self-reliant, and to say "no." Linda saw Sharon as someone who dared to be in control of her life, in contrast to herself.

The contrast of Linda's images and stories about Sharon and herself with those of Sharon's about herself and Linda washed over Sharon, rocking the boat of her binary cognitive system. This system had been clicking away as automatically, efficiently, and defensively, as had her mother's. Sharon had psychically ingested the blueprint of the binary delusion. She was shocked when confronted with her own failed hypotheses about others. This combined with the shock of her own regret when Sharon realized that she was living in a bubble of her own stereotyped fantasies that kept her far away from others. Sharon also began to realize that she had tried to negotiate her dejected position as an outsider by judging others very critically from an attitude of contempt. This attitude, combined with her emotional unavailability and her naive idealization of certain others, kept her continually at distance from everyone and from her internal, and still highly underdeveloped, true self (Kavaler-Adler, 1992).

Realizing this, Sharon began to experience a deep mode of grief that was based on the regret that she had created her own continuing losses in life, self-sabotaging her relationships with others. Her capacity to feel a deep sense of grief, based on regret, promoted a turning point for her psychic life that became a turning point in her treatment—and a turning point in her marriage and her life. At this point, Sharon began to attend therapy twice a week and entered a four-hour monthly therapy group that I conducted. Sharon's deepening commitment allowed her to immerse herself in a natural evolution of a developmental mourning process (Kavaler-Adler, 1993a/2013, 1996/2014, 2003a, 2003b).

The Turning Point of Regret

Shocked and humbled by her regret, and now immersed in the crucible of the depressive pain of grief affect, Sharon naturally opened to new insights. These insights were combined with a new sense of self-agency and self-expression. Sharon was also beginning to develop a new sense of interiority, which allowed her to begin to know what she was feeling within. When Sharon realized that she was living in a bubble of her own stereotyped fantasies, far away from others, detached and distancing with a split-off anger in the form of hostile contempt, she first dared to confront her husband, by whom she had become increasingly intimidated (as she had been by her mother). Sharon began to realize that the system of thought she had created around her husband must be as fallacious as that she had woven around the image of Linda, waking up to the fact that she was projecting her own image system-driven hypotheses onto her husband, whose real existence may very well have eluded her.

At that time, Sharon's husband was continually enraged at her. In her state of intimidation, brought on by her own projections, Sharon did not dare find out what her husband was really angry about. Until this time of her regret, Sharon also did not dare tell her husband what she was angry at him about. She was filled with the frustration of the wall created when neither she nor her husband could listen to one another. However, until now she had no clue as to how to bypass this wall and reach real communication. Once the bulb of dissonant and informative realities went on in her mind, Sharon was able to get through to her husband. She was able to be penetrated by his communications as well. Sharon's sense of agency came alive at the point of regret, grief, and the recognition of the anger that had been obfuscated by the perpetual sealing off of her psychic image system. Sharon exclaimed to me at this point:

> Suddenly I found myself mourning for all those times in my life when I drove others away and drove happiness away. Because of things from childhood I'm repeating unhappiness over and over again. Usually I don't feel something healing come out of feeling so bad. But I did feel something come out of it. I really feel I was able to say to my husband some things I couldn't say before. I was able to describe to my husband that because I was so shamed and belittled by my mother in my childhood, if my husband is treating me in a way that feels shameful, I experience so much rage that I can't listen to him and I can't process the things he's saying. I think he finally heard that. He finally acknowledged it. He finally identified what my hostility is really about. I said to him, "If you're angry about one thing

you can't just act it out and displace it onto everything. You can't just dump all this hostility onto me!"

Sharon was amazed that her husband could actually hear her.

The External Object Situation and
Off-Target Transference in Marriage

Sharon had been married to her second husband for four years and had a second child with him. She began to realize that there was a profound alienation growing between her and her husband, which would blow up abruptly into rages. These rages were expressed overtly toward her by her husband, and were expressed internally, within herself, toward her "internal" husband. Sharon kept her side of the rage very hidden, but it would escape in a split-off behavioral form as nagging, critical comments, and contemptuous judgments that drove her husband mad. These comments and judgments hinted at a whole interior world of warfare, felt subliminally by Sharon's husband as projective identification operating between Sharon and him. Her husband began to feel like there were hidden land mines in his midst. Ultimately, he told his wife that he believed that she had all these dissociated parts of her that she was out of touch with. Sharon felt devastated when her husband told her this. However, she began to realize that he was right to some extent. She became frightened of how out of control she felt of her own internal life. She felt frightened of what might flare up at any moment from within.

Until the moment of her first major experience of regret (that began a mourning process in which grief could begin to be tolerated), Sharon could not feel, differentiate, nor articulate her feelings. All her affects seemed contaminated by explosive impulses. Her first reaction to her husband's confrontation was to be convinced that she did not deserve to be alive. In this state of terror and intimidation, she could not speak. She could hardly breathe. No wonder she had hidden and controlled her whole internal life, distancing from her rage as well as her needs, by staying at a distance from most people. She lived in a world of images, an image system, surrounded by image objects (Kavaler-Adler, 1996/2014) and her manic defenses of contempt and evaluating judgments. She had lived in psychic isolation and a detached ideation that allowed her to control herself and to indirectly control others through distancing from them. Only in her marriage was Sharon threatened with the breakdown of her controls and her whole binary image system, in which she and others were either in or out, included or excluded, good or bad, or above or below one another.

Sharon had been aware that her mother had such a binary way of categorizing everyone in which Sharon was always bad and her mother, who denied all anger even as she expressed it, was stereotypically good. However, it was a shock for Sharon to be confronted with her own similar limited and defensive way of thinking. Sharon learned that her way of thinking had sealed her off contact with others and kept her rigidly navigating in a world of extreme opposite image objects, which she used to define both herself and others. In this image world, Sharon could not see anybody's point of view but her own. Therefore, when her husband kept complaining to her that she lacked empathy, she felt helpless, paralyzed, and once more accused in a way that her mother had perpetually accused her (and in the way she mentally perpetuated such mental torture).

Although Sharon's husband was projecting much onto her, she was caught up and intimidated by the projections because she was involved in a powerful projective and projective identification operation of her own. This resulted in a total state of paralysis at times in which Sharon sank into a quagmire of confusion, proclaiming that she had no idea "who was doing what to whom."

When she became consciously angry, Sharon suddenly knew who was doing what to whom. Then she could articulate all the effects she felt her husband's rages and accusations were having on her. She could then make the connection with her internal mother's accusations, which perpetually operated inside of her from the past. Becoming aware of this allowed Sharon to understand that she had been unconsciously addressing her husband from a split-off ("manic," in Kleinian terms) defense position of contempt. She had been inhabiting the split-off mother's place in her own psyche, turning outward her own demonic antilibidinal ego force that most of the time she turned inward on herself.

Gradually, Sharon could now sense how her frozen anger had been filtered through this rarefied atmosphere of superiority and contempt. When her anger became hot and her self-agency was regained, Sharon's observing ego began to differentiate all that before seemed so confusing. Then Sharon could speak to her husband of his abusive and uncontrolled displacement of rage frustration onto her. She could also listen to her husband tell her some of the specifics of his own frustration that did relate to her and her behavior, some of which concerned her vulnerability to her ex-husband's manipulations. She could even confront her husband with his manner of relating to her as he had once related to his mother.

When Sharon's husband heard and understood her on this point, Sharon was nonplused. She was unable to believe that she could have an impact. As she did begin to comprehend this, her view of herself began to change, despite the projections that her husband would continue to impose on her. Sharon was then able to say things she could never have said to her mother. She was able to be heard in a way she had never been heard by her mother! The next shock was to find out that she had had an impact on me, her analyst, which allowed her to see me in a totally different way. Gradually, Sharon allowed herself to question her views of me, and her curiosity led her to learn that powerful transference distortions combined with the reality of her actual perceptions.

Sharon originally saw me as distant and "professional," implying that I was as detached from her as she was from others. As she opened to the grief of her regret and opened to her inner life, she found me to be different with her. She was surprised that I could now seem involved, interested, curious, excited, caring, compassionate, confrontational, and warm, as well as arrogant or opinionated. When Sharon commented on this, I could tell her that as she changed by opening up more to me, I could respond in kind, and be more involved and interested in her. Sharon heard this and began to realize that the therapeutic relationship was a relationship, not just a one-way street. She was deeply relieved to see that she could have a positive impact on another person that brought a process of mutual development and engagement for meaningful work.

Psychic Transformation through the Grief, Loss, and Insight of Regret

When her fantasy system was challenged, Sharon began to see a glimmer of reality that made her, for the first time, feel the awful pain of her loneliness, a loneliness that had existed as an emptiness when numbed out behind a frozen and split-off rage. The sad tale of her childhood loneliness was highlighted by her telling me how she lived as an outsider throughout high school and only survived emotionally by looking forward to seeing the one teacher at school who would say hello to her and would thus seem to validate he existence. The tales of her mother's emotional abuse toward her were told at this time in a detached and distant way, with an attitude of skepticism, cynicism, and disbelief. Without any feeling of connection to her mother, having had to shield herself from viewing her mother's craziness as a child, she would mildly protest, even as she revealed tales of horror, "It wasn't so bad!"

The true beginning of her change was when she first felt the grief of regret, the pain of a hidden despair emerging behind an emptiness. Prior to this, she lived in a false self with a false detachment from her past. Her false self was symbolized by her perfectionistic attachment to her house, a new suburban home that she had insisted that her husband purchase. Winnicott's caretaking false personality can be seen in her caretaking for the inanimate objects of her house at the expense of any connection to her husband or children, at least as her husband saw it. When her husband confronted her, she was defensive. When he further proclaimed, however, that she had all these hidden split-off parts that would come out to attack him like he was walking in a mind field, she was in shock.

The Inner Child Opens to Life and Contact
in the Therapy Group

Sharon's experience of regret, and the self-confrontation that followed from this experience, allowed Sharon to begin to relinquish the paranoid and manic defenses that manifested as attitudes of contempt, detachment, and a guarded cynicism toward her husband and toward herself, as well as in idealized images of others that contrasted with those seen from a position of contempt. Sharon began to get in touch with her anger, a form of healthy and differentiated anger that was not a narcissistic aggression that would lead to regret, but the opposite, a self-assertive anger growing out of the separation-individuation aspects of regret. This allowed her to know "who was doing what to whom," and thus to know what her husband's problems were separate from hers (Winnicott, 1971a). She could now appropriately confront him without allowing herself to be used as a scapegoat for his sadistic projections of blame as she had been used by her mother.

Nevertheless, as she recovered from being the victim of his sadistic attacks, related to making her own sadistic judgments of herself externalized onto him as her supreme judge, her internal locus of sadistic attack on herself intensified. Sharon's masochistic defenses of self-attack and self-accusation became prominent as she surrendered her surface level of contempt toward her husband (and others) and lessened her empowerment of her husband as the external agent of her own contempt, mixed in with his own, as judgments toward her. As Sharon began to look at herself and see her faults, she began to see herself less through images of inadequacy, which she contrasted with ideal images of others, and more as someone struggling with daily life.

However, her masochistic mode of self-attack in the midst of these struggles was another defense against mourning, particularly the mourning of losses and injuries related to early childhood trauma. After Sharon increased individual treatment to two times a week, which later would become three and then four sessions a week, she also entered a four-hour (with a break), once a month, therapy group, conducted by myself. This was her critical turning point of regret and self-reflection in contemplating her life.

Within the group, Sharon was confronted with her masochistic mode of defense in a profound group experience. Consequently, she was able to experience the emergence of a three-year-old inner child self, which has been repressed and dissociated with early trauma. Her identification with her children as a reflection of the split-off parts of her self was detected in this group experience, and by me, as her psychoanalyst within the group.

When Sharon first entered the group she expected to be hated and excluded, essentially to be treated as the bad child, as she had been treated by her mother. However, rather than turn this into a self-fulfilling prophecy, she was able to talk about her fears in the group. She was greeted by a totally different response than she anticipated. The group not only told her that she came across quite differently than the way she expected, but the people in the group also expressed admiration for her involvement with others in the group, as well as for her capacity to persist in attending the group despite the awful weight of expectations. Sharon was impressed with this and relieved. Such a confrontation with the distortions in her expectations helped Sharon to disengage from her binary image system, along with the affect level of mourning loss and regret that interacted with such cognitive learning! The disparity of judgments in her head and in reality began to give Sharon some doorway to hope.

This doorway opened increasingly wider as Sharon came into contact with the traumatic losses of the past that had left her with the internalized imprint of a victimized child. The confrontation with the perceptions of others, just as with the perceptions of her by her colleague at work, helped Sharon to surrender gradually her primitive binary system of thought, in which she had always seen others in an imagined idealized and exciting life while seeing herself as a pitiful outcast on the outside looking in.

One particular group session focused entirely on Sharon. This evolved naturally in terms of the dynamics in the group, and in terms of the focus of the group on individual mourning, along with interpersonal relationships, and what they represented. At times, the individual mourning process became the primary focus of the group. In this group session, Sharon was so overwhelmed with distress about her marriage that she let down her defense of self-sufficiency and her isolation of self and affect. She surrendered in a profoundly deep way to receiving help. Every single person in the group responded to her distress and reached out to her with empathy, identifications, confrontations of her self-defeating behavior, reality confrontations, and interpretations of her psychodynamic struggles.

At first, the group members addressed her exaggerated view of her own mistakes in decision making, which was her masochistic self-persecution based on a lifelong pattern of identification with the aggressor, currently related to her husband as the aggressor, and formerly her mother. Sharon started to emotionally open up in the group when she expressed the wish that her husband be proud of her, rather than to constantly criticize her in a harsh, punitive, and judgmental manner, similar to that of her mother in childhood. Sharon revealed the wish for a mother's love from her husband that she never got from her mother. She masochistically defended her husband's blame and punitive attacks, which had reached a paranoid level at the time of this group meeting, by identifying with her husband's judgments of her, which was what she had once done with her mother. Sharon conveyed to the group members that she saw herself as a liability in her marriage, as a partner, and as a human being. The group picked up on her masochistic defense and helped her to move into the psychic space of experiencing the three-year-old child within her, seeing her identification with her own three-year-old daughter as her route there.

Some of the group dialogue is as follows:

Alicia: "I could do you so much better on bad decisions. It sounds like you have to be the bad one so your husband can be good. You need to give me a better example of a bad decision than that you've said so far."

Sharon: "I have made bad decisions that my husband doesn't even know."

Alicia: "These mistakes are normal. These things have been blown out of proportion. I had that in a marriage. You have a professional job, a marriage, and two children to be responsible for. You are doing pretty well with all this responsibility. Your husband never gives you any credit. You say your husband can't be proud of you. I'm proud of you. You are expressing things you never could do when you came here. I'm very proud of you and I think it's pathological that your husband can't be proud of you."

Victoria: "Your unexpressed rage is what's making you think you're a horrible person. I really think it's your anger that you're not in touch with that's making you think you're such a terrible person."

Sharon: "Certainly in my family I couldn't express anger."

By connecting her masochistic self-blame with her underlying childhood rage, the group helped Sharon into a vulnerable place of feeling the three-year-old child within her (her libidinal core dominated by the antilibidinal ego or self). Her masochistic defenses, just like her paranoid and manic ones in the contempt position, had defended her against this internal traumatized child self. As she felt the empathy of the group and trusted them, something she never expected to do when she came to the group, she could enter the psychic space of the child within her by entering the image of her three-year-old daughter, moving from her identification with the projected image of her daughter, at a level of symbolic representation to the level of core feeling or affect, touching and opening the formerly sealed-off libidinal core of her self.

Sharon said to the group: "It is terrifying. My daughter is very attached to my husband. If I become aware of my anger I'm afraid we'll split up the marriage." [Sharon started to cry. There was absolute silence in the group.] "I don't think I could deal with my daughter losing her father. [Crying.] It's really terrifying!" [Her dissociated abandonment experience.]

Myself: "I'm glad you're getting to it, the depth of your grief and pain."

Sharon, crying: "My daughter is three. I don't think she could bear to separate from either one of us. She's a very extraordinary child ... [crying] I just can't do anything. It would just crack her world open." [Crying, crying, sniffling, crying, and crying. There was a deep concentrated silence in the group.]

Myself: "You're reexperiencing something you've had inside of you through your daughter. You've lost pride in yourself. Somehow you know what it's like to lose it. So your fear that for your daughter, and anticipate such loss as resulting from the break up of your home." [I asked her what thoughts were entering her mind just then.]

Sharon: "I can feel a little hope now—at least I can feel. I still feel like I want to run and run and run, as hard as I can."

Myself: "Instead of running you've been mentally pounding yourself until you make yourself unconsciously forgetful."

Diana: "I think it's important that you stay with this level of feeling, not the surface stuff. The surface stuff about bad decisions is really not the issue, even if your husband makes it your issue."

Myself: "That's how she talks to herself inside her mind—as her mother talked to her. This expresses the terror of not being perfect, the fear of losing her mother if she isn't perfect. Sharon demands of herself that she do more than she is capable of, just as her mother did. Sharon is terrified of losing her mother, but now experiences it vicariously (through projective identification) through her daughter."

Sharon: "You used a term the other day, 'infantile fear of annihilation.' That's what it is."

Myself: "Sharon, it was after the session when I spoke about the annihilation terror that you forgot a session. You annihilated me to avoid feeling this terror for yourself. I can take it." [Laughter in the group.]

Victoria: "She can take it!"

Alicia: "She can take it. She's endlessly annihilated." [Laugher throughout the group.]

Male coleader: "She deserves nothing less!" [Laughter.]

Lillian: "Cut off his head." [Laughter and then quiet.]

Sharon: "I don't understand it. You're telling me I can annihilate Susan."

Myself: "It's to annihilate the fear of annihilation and to annihilate the awareness of how profound this terror is, and annihilating the awareness that I touched you in this place, even though you didn't allow yourself to feel it emotionally."

Diana: "I understand how terrifying it would be to make a decision about your daughter."

Myself: "What were you just thinking, Sharon?"

Sharon: "I was thinking that my daughter is too little to be out there by herself."

Myself: "Hmm. Like in the park when you were three or four, when you were left behind."

Sharon: "I don't want to be separated from my daughter. [Crying.] We'd have to decide. It would be a terribly painful decision."

Myself: "When you said you were left at three in the park by your mother, all alone, you are saying you were small, three or four, like your daughter is now. You identify with her because she represents the child living within you, who has been traumatized. It sounds to me like your daughter would be left alone now, just like you were. Your daughter is three. You had to find your way home from the park at three or four."

Sharon: "My brother got me home. My mother went to the super market. I thought she wasn't coming back. I guess time was much longer to us than to her [crying] ... so we walked home ... crying. We didn't know how to get there. It was trial and error to get home. We got home this way and that. When we got home my mother started screaming at me and hitting me for leaving the place she had left us." [Crying.] [We could all sense that something died inside of Sharon at that moment. Yet she was dependent on her mother and had to blame herself to protect her mother.]

Gloria: "So you'll be able to make it home now."

Sharon: "I don't know where that is."

Myself: "That's what's so terrifying."

Gloria: "Inside of yourself. You are doing that now."

Sharon: "I'm pulling my sled behind me now. I'm pulling my two kids. I have to get them somewhere too." [Crying—sniffling, as Sharon relived the trauma of losing her mother in the catastrophe of dragging her sled home in the snow and cold when lost in the park at three years old.]

Victoria: "I think it's so good you've opened up here. You don't have to make any decisions now. You just have to stay with what you feel. This is your internal three-year-old. The more you get in touch with how you felt abandoned, by experiencing your internal three-year-old, as you continue to work through the pain, you're going to be able to figure out what to do with your marriage and children. Everything else will fall into place as you continue to get in touch with your three-year-old."

Lillian: "I think it's great that you're sharing this."

Sharon: "I have the whole group's help today! I feel very fortunate that everyone here has reached out to me and I want to thank everybody. [Crying.] I really have felt nurtured here in a way that I haven't felt for a long time. I don't just see my husband as a monster." [Responding to a comment of Lillian's.]

Diana: "I don't think it's you making the monster. I mean it's the group."

Male coleader: "At the same time, Sharon, you don't want to get comfortable taking this kind of behavior toward you."

Victoria: "And I think your husband has been financially supportive and taking care of. You've experienced these other qualities in him. I'm sure he has these qualities. But given that it's been this way for a long time and Sharon feels terrible about herself, there's a dynamic between two people."

Sharon: "He used to be empathic with me as well as to others. He used to be that way with me, but things evolved."

Diana: "I'd like to stay with this. I see your lack of self-esteem plays into this."

Sharon: "In the beginning with my husband I presented myself as a needy person, and he liked this because he was a person who liked to help. Unfortunately, it got to a place where we're using each other. Our marriage was bringing out old issues for both of us. For me, I continue to see myself as incompetent, stupid, and needy. Someone else had to make decisions for me. It backfired. He started getting resentful of this role he had chosen. He got very angry. He started wanting not to be in that role anymore. He wanted a partner and I wasn't being a partner. In hindsight, you can say, if only we had not started out that way."

Victoria: "He wanted to change the rules?"

Sharon: "He was never married before. He was 36 when we met and 38 when we married. I don't think he had any idea what his needs were. Only when we got married and had a child did he realize he had needs. I think he did change the rules—not in a malicious way. He's been getting in touch with his own needs."

Victoria: "But he couldn't talk about that."

Sharon: "No. I didn't realize the rules had been changing."

Sharon's Development after the Group Breakthrough Meeting: The Growth of Self-Agency as Regret is Worked through

Once Sharon got in touch with her inner child (Fairbairn's dissociated libidinal ego, 1952, which has been reintegrated into the central self through the emotional experience of it in therapeutic regression), she was more capable of feeling the pain of others and her husband. This allowed Sharon to use her original sense of regret to promote empathy. The result was that, despite the severe conflict between her and her husband at that time of the critical group meeting, the marriage was turning around. Meaningful communication was developing and continuing between Sharon and her husband.

For this to happen, Sharon needed to emotionally separate from her husband (to avoid actual separation), which she had done with the help of her individual treatment that had been three times a week for several years. Sharon needed to see her husband's psychological problems realistically. She needed to mourn her image of her husband as an idealized parent who would take over for her in her adult responsibilities to make decisions, and her image of him as an omniscient judge. When Sharon set her husband up to judge her, he turned demonic in her mind. In this way, Sharon lost her own judgment and gave her husband (the mother displacement) too much power. She lost her emotional center, which she began to connect to when she found her inner child in the group.

The inner child needs psychic space and interpersonal contact to grow up. It is arrested when intimidated by projected judgments. Sharon had been asking her husband to possess her through evaluating her and judging her since she had failed to have faith in herself to judge herself and trust her own intuition and competence. Sharon's capacity to face her regrets has enabled her to see all aspects of her life clearly and to have a new sense of self-agency. This newfound self-agency helped Sharon to feel a new sense of competence.

Two Treatment Sessions on Working through Regret

Two sessions in the 8th year of her treatment illustrate Sharon's intensive working with the grief of her regret, and therefore with the developmental transformations in character structure that come with working through regret. Below, I quote some of the dialogue from both sessions.

Sharon: "I realize that the last couple of weeks I've been in a very contemptuous state."

Myself: "Maybe you're becoming more aware of such a state because of our last discussion about your contempt for one of the group members. We spoke of how difficult it was to contain the feeling, which made you feel like pulling back from the group."

Sharon: "There's a woman at work, who has been coming by my office. She started to annoy me. I felt she was intrusive, coming by so often, sitting down, and chattering away. I started feeling this rage build up. I guess it was contempt. I kept thinking, 'Why is she sitting there going on and on about nothing?' I guess I was contemptuous and she must have felt it. She stopped coming by. At first I told myself that I was relieved. But then I felt badly, especially after our talk about the group and my contempt there building up secretly. I tried to make amends. I push people away by acting nasty. I think I blew it. There had been a budding friendship."

Myself: "You seem to feel regret."

Sharon: "I feel overwhelmed. I've been realizing my contempt and it feels overwhelming. I feel bad. She is the one friend I made in the office. I've been pushing her away because she chatters. Surely there's a better way of dealing with someone who likes to chatter even if I don't. She's so unlike me. She really makes contact with so many people by chattering. The results are she has many more contacts in the office and outside of it than I do. I should probably learn from her rather than getting angry. I'm wondering if I can make it up to her or is it too late?"

Myself: "Why should it be too late?"

Sharon: "Maybe she's written me off because she's realized I am really not a very fun person. I'm dour and serious, not playful the way she is. I'm always worried about something, always a problem not fun."

[Later, this view of me as the creative and fun one, with her as the dour one, came out in the transference, and could be interpreted as her projecting her idealized self and her potential self onto me.]

Myself: "You're projecting onto her your own way of making quick, black-and-white harsh judgments. She could think some of these things, but you think in condemning quick rejecting judgments, so you think she is thinking that way."

Sharon: "You're probably right. She probably just thinks I need more space and she's giving it to me. Most people don't operate like I imagine. I see that I'm contemptuous with my husband too. I see his defects and dissociate myself from him, like recently at his brother's house, so that I don't get identified with his defects. As I look at this behavior in myself it looks pretty ugly—to attack people I like just because other people might have had something negative to say to them or about them. At my husband's brother's house, I dissociated from my husband. I told little anecdotes, putting my husband down when he wasn't there. I was even dissociating myself from my husband with the T.V. repairman [her shame]. I had to tell him that I didn't watch T.V., as opposed to my husband. Only my husband would engage in such contemptible activities, I implied, to the T.V. repairman. What does he care? It's ridiculous! I'm identifying with my mother, who had contempt for those who watch T.V. I'm trying not to be the victim of her contempt by being the contemptuous one."

Myself: "You're always trying to justify yourself by putting someone down. At home, it's your husband or son. In the group it's been Lisa who you put down inside your head."

Sharon: "I wish she would leave. I hate being in this state of contempt, and it goes on automatically inside of me. It's hard not to act it out and blurt out my thoughts. It's hard and painful to sit there with it. I don't want to say, 'That's moronic. If those cats are making you sick, you get rid of the cats.'"

Myself: "Is that how your mother spoke to you?"

Sharon: "Much more biting sarcasm, always saying, 'What's wrong with you!' I don't ever speak to Lisa. She seems so passive, letting things pass over her. She doesn't want to make a choice or decision. She's indecisive. I think she's a hundred times worse than I am in my indecisiveness, which I hate in myself. It drives me crazy to listen to her, like my friend in the office. I guess I made that woman disappear. Then I'm left sitting all by myself. That's not what I want. Part of me wants that, but part of me really doesn't. [Need/Fear Dilemma] When people try to get close to me I push them away."

Myself: "There are two sides of the bind. You fear isolation, but nobody is good enough. You start seeing people's defects, think they're terrible, arid then want to discard them."

Sharon: "Yes. When I have the idea of having more social contacts, it's all in the realm of fantasy. I have a big party in my mind, but then in reality I'm pushing people away. My fantasy reflects what I wish I had, a large group of really close friends." [Sharon had felt like she had friends for a period of time in the group, at the point when she had opened and let people help her. Then, however, she built up contempt afterward, thinking sarcastically that she duped them into seeing her as a victim. She pushed them away in her mind.] "There's a reason my husband has so much involvement with family and friends. He admits he needs people and makes it a priority. For me, it's something to be ashamed of. I'm just looking at the irony of it, wishing and wishing to have friends and then feeling contempt for people. It makes me think of Groucho Marx saying: 'I wouldn't join a club that would have me as a member.'"

Myself: "Woody Allen also said that."

Sharon: "I'm sorry. Groucho said it first. Woody Allen isn't original." [Sharon showed a new capacity for play here.]

Myself: "Woody Allen was just quoting Groucho Marx and acknowledging him. Now you're having contempt for Woody Allen."

Sharon: "[Laughs.] No wonder I'm stuck! I'm in the contempt mode. It's hard to feel creative or happy when I'm busy feeling contempt. I guess I could try to make amends with this woman at work. I could ask her to have lunch with me. I could talk to her. I should do that. I can see now that I'm not just depressed. I'm feeling overwhelmed with contempt." [Fear of closeness in the schizoid, getting contaminated with contemptible defects of others.]

Myself: "It's good that you can see it. It's very important." [With Sharon, the contempt was often off-target transference—toward husband and group members. In the initial transference in treatment, she had idealized me and imagined me as being contemptuous of her. Her contempt for me came out in her anger at times, but she was able to express her anger toward me, which she was not in the beginning of treatment. Such expression modified her contempt and helped her to see another's point of view.]

Sharon: "This is very basic stuff about what I do. I have to start looking at it, but I don't like it. I don't like looking at it. I don't know how I can get rid of it."

Myself: "You are in the process of awareness that can lead to change. Talking about it and feeling bad in relation to regret is the beginning of change."

Sharon: "Talking about this makes me feel really depressed—not the fake depression of self-contempt, but real regret. [Grief.] I've let my contempt run me. I've let it take over."

Myself: "That's the big regret."

Sharon: "I've let it run rampant. The only way I know how to deal with it is to do what I did with Lisa, which is to sit on it as tightly as I can. Then I feel like I'm going to explode."

In the next session, Sharon experienced and explored another form of regret, which allowed her to feel the grief related to hurting her husband and family by repeating her victimized child position, which was related to the past with her mother. Behind the regret of her own weakness related to having been continually intimidated by a sadistic bully, who she in part creates in an abusive other, was the insight about her own repetition of the victimized reactive child who was so intimidated by the mother of her childhood who truly was a bully and who she internalized as such.

Just as in the previous session, when Sharon felt the regret about the repetition of her mother's contemptuous behavior, as in identifying with the aggressor, in this session she was feeling the other side of such repetition, the side of identifying with the victimized child self that was continually intimidated by the aggressor (sadistic) part of her mother. She went beyond a realization of her anger at her mother and the displacement of her mother in her husband and took the grief endowed responsibility for her own behavior. She spoke of "perpetuating" her own pathological (the childhood defensive stance) behavior and the pain of regret that she feels for this.

Thus, in this session, we can see another example of the painstaking road to consciousness that manifests in the working through of the depressive position. Sharon herself distinguished the grief of her regret and the realization that reparation cannot undo the past ("true reparation" versus "manic reparation" in Klein's vocabulary) from the compulsive and defensive repetition of masochistic submission and masochistic self-blame and self-contempt. She realized that she continued to create a bogeyman (an omnipotent sadistic other) in order to preserve her own powerless and hopeless child position. This position had become a powerful psychic habit, which kept Sharon in the old attachment to her childhood mother, being played out with her ex-husband and also with her current husband.

The session proceeded as follows:

Sharon: "I don't know what to talk about, which probably means I'm reluctant to talk." [Then she started to cry and continued.] "My husband blew up again. My son is in a band at school and for three years he has been renting a clarinet. My husband was set on edge when he heard I'd been paying the whole rental fee for the clarinet and that my ex-husband wasn't paying anything. He said to me that he could have bet that I would never bring this up with my ex-husband for the same reason I had never demanded real child support from my ex-husband until recently, when I went to litigation, but only after my husband challenged me on that. I had made up excuses in my own mind about paying for the clarinet, pretending it wasn't important. My husband was really tormented that I let this happen without any reason. My parents believed you don't spend money on anything. You don't spend money on clothes, vacations, or anything. In my husband's family they think it's fine to spend money on yourself-for pleasure. It took me a really long time to see how one could spend money on pleasure if you have the money. I was taught not to spend money. But when I spend money on something I don't have to spend money on it drives my husband crazy! He actually used the word 'infidelity' in describing my spending money on something rather than confronting my ex-husband with his responsibility.

... After this, I talked to my ex-husband. I couldn't get him to pay for the back money for the clarinet. He always has a story and excuse. He doesn't save a dime. I let that one thing linger on for no reason—for basically the same reason I didn't confront my ex-husband in the first place—I don't want to deal with him. It's easier to swallow it. I act like I have no power. I'm just a helpless child victim and these people all have the power. I can't deal with him! I put off dealing with my ex-husband for years, thinking he'll just lie anyway. It's the same as my not having the guts to tell my mother about the bar mitzvah arrangements for my son. I know I turned my mother into a monster, and my husband, and my ex-husband. I think I have to have ruthless monsters in my life, who have all the power—and I have no power. How to change it is another matter. I also thought that if I confront my ex-husband and upset him, I fear he'd wield his power and take my son away from me. I've seen now, with the litigation, that my ex-husband doesn't have much power. I have more. I have knowledge, articulation, and determination. He cries, whines, and manipulates—but when that fails he caves in. He's a bully and my mother's a bully. He doesn't even want my son to live with him."

Myself: "You only see now that you created this whole monster." [In the depressive position, Sharon can take this interpretation. In Thomas Ogden's (1986) words, she has become "an interpreting subject".]

Sharon: "I can see why my husband looks on this with such disdain. It did hurt our family that I didn't stand up to my ex-husband. I would let my ex-husband do whatever he wanted, and I couldn't explain why I needed to hang onto that crazy relationship with him, as if I was still married to him, instead of choosing the person I was married to. When my husband confronted me, I called my ex-husband. My husband felt so betrayed, for everything from the past with my ex-husband, which was all represented to him by my paying for the clarinet. I can understand how he felt. I just feel really bad. Why didn't I think of it? I was intimidated by my bogeyman."

Myself: "Intimidated by your own bogeyman."

Sharon: "I do it with my husband, too. You know what happened for a long time. I had no awareness of my own patterns of behavior that were driving my husband crazy. When he'd get upset it would seem to come out the blue. So I developed this image of my husband as someone crazy and irrational who could be set off at any time. So I have to pussy foot around and hide things. Now I realize he was overreacting, but he was reacting to real things that I wasn't aware of. I'm still reacting to him like he's an all-powerful intimidating bogeyman.

… If I had ever told my mother that she had anything wrong she would go crazy! With my mother there was no way of predicting her reaction and what violence might occur. I felt completely powerless. It could be anything that would drive her into a rage. I just got into the habit of walking around on eggshells. I would withdraw into trying to be so good and doing everything right. I got into the habit of being this totally hopeless victim, and you know that doesn't work in a marriage. So I guess I'm feeling a lot of regrets. I'm regretting I spent so much time being manipulated by my husband because I couldn't separate out my husband from my mother. I'm really regretting what it's done to my marriage. I don't know how much can be repaired. I know I'm changing, but I can't undo what I've done. I can't take away the hurt that that caused my husband. I can't! I'm not really feeling depressed. I'm just feeling very sad and full of regrets!

… That's about the size of it. That's how I'm feeling. I'm not saying I'm a worthless human being. I'm saying I've done a lot of damage."

Myself: "You're distinguishing the reality from your fantasy of others in your projected images. Your sadness is not depression. Depression is based on defensive warding off of feeling. Your sadness is real. It's the grief that tells you what's real. When you were saying you were worthless it was just another defense and it made you feel depressed. You're not doing that now. You're in touch with the sadness that brings insight in an organic way."

Regrets for Her Aggression in the Family of the Present

Throughout Sharon's treatment, her despair and binary system were punctured and penetrated by the grief of regret. Turning points in her mind and her life seemed to occur around these points of critical regret. A more differentiated form of anger and love opened with regret. Although a clinician often sees the capacity for regret following primitive aggression made conscious, it works the other way around as well, as this case demonstrates. The capacity for regret can open a more refined form of aggression, a newly emerging object-related anger, one most vivid in Sharon's marriage at this time, but complemented by her anger toward me in the transference. She could call me on specific things now that irked her. She became quite articulate in her review of my conduct, for example, telling me how I was arrogant toward insurance companies or her husband's former therapist or was arrogant about my views on medication. A new sense of agency, a new sense of interiority, a new budding sense of femininity, and a new sense of compassion and empathy emerged through the crucible of grief, object-related in the form of regret.

There were several sessions after the ones reported on the topic of regret when Sharon continued to actively struggle with an almost annihilating terror that turned to grief and loss concerning her view of her own damaging effects on her husband and children. In these sessions, Sharon focused on how her tendencies toward split-off contempt, symptomatic of her childhood defense system of dissociation in the service of self-protection, were triggering off fights at home, creating splits between her present husband and her son, or between her husband and herself. She would sound despairing when discussing this.

"What good does it do to be aware of it?" she would challenge me. When I suggested that her awareness could offer her the chance to choose change, she would at first sound nonplussed and a bit contemptuous of me for my lack of "concrete" help. "You always say that!" she would protest. "I feel awful! I can't undo what I've done!" I would empathize with the loss she felt and would understand that it was a horrible feeling to not only see the damage in her family that she contributed to but to also see herself as the damaging one. When she was in the paranoid-schizoid position, it had been much easier to see her mother as the source of all damage or to just see her husband's damaging ways as he erupted in rages and blamed her for everything as her mother had. Now that a mourning process had brought her into the depressive position with all the capacities to feel for the subjectivity of the other, and to feel her own agency as responsible for hurting the ones she loved, life became much more complex. Life also became more colorful, however, as affects mixed all elements of pain, loss, longing, and anger, which was so easy to turn against oneself to avoid the feeling of grief.

Sharon wondered if this wasn't just an awful exercise in pain, because she didn't see how feeling so miserable could be a sign of hope. She could see no way, at that moment, for "doing something" that would make undoing (manic reparation) possible, while the frail reality of true reparation paled by comparison in her mind! Despite her anxious and angry questioning, Sharon was open to a totally new and hopeful state of mind by the next session. She would begin by reporting how much better things were going for her and her family. She would then tell me that she was able to listen to her husband's attacks, innuendoes, and overt accusations in a totally different state of mind now.

She realized that when he was having a tantrum and using her as a scapegoat, he was just having a tantrum. It was not really about her. Sharon could see when her husband used her as a displacement for his rage. Yet sometimes she would distinguish that his overreaction was a response to something she had really done and to his interpretation of it. Sharon became much more objective about her husband's behavior. Consequently, her husband stopped attacking her as much. He started openly confiding in her. He sensed her growing sense of competence. Her husband then became less irritated by Sharon's tentative and intimidated ways, on the one hand, which made her very indecisive, and by her sarcastic and contemptuous judgments on the other hand. Once Sharon felt the grief of her regrets, she became conscious of both her self-effacing intimidation, with the secretiveness and hidden withdrawals that went with it, and of the self-righteous, self-virtuous, false self, and grandiose attacks of contempt on her husband (as her mother had assaulted her with spars of sarcasm).

Everything in her family changed because of this. Her family began to enjoy going on vacations together as a unit, having a bar mitzvah for her son as a unit, and feeling the warmth of sustained connections. For the first time, her son and her husband developed a caring relationship for each other. Then, her son began to separate from a pathological narcissistic symbiosis with his biological father, developing more mature and related relationships with both men.

Regrets for Daddy

Sharon had always portrayed her father as a passive wimp ghost in the background of her childhood and her mind. When she first came to treatment, Sharon told me that she had rejections of plays she wrote because her view of men was so caricatured and lifeless due to her (part object) view of her father. Her view of her father began to come alive and form into a more whole object picture in treatment.

The passive wimp became a withholding bastard and a frustrated victim of the mental health establishment of the time, which hospitalized him. He became a live figure on which to bestow her hate. He became the detached and obscure figure, writing her long, endless descriptions in letters. Her father's letters failed to relate to Sharon at all. They seemed like a desperate attempt to express himself, but only in the form of observations on endless and disjointed details of life. Her resentment flared up. Her criticisms broke forth from the dissociated cubicles of her mind from which they had been stored and projected.

Then there was one crystalline session of paradoxical dramas reformulating in her mind. It had a dramatic and trenchant affective impact on both of us. We became joined by a new daddy relationship from the interior space behind the former curtains in her mind. Her core connections to an early daddy were found again like the discovery of the Rosetta stone. The self that could only survive through heart connections emerged as never before.

The session is memorable for its dialectical poles of hate and love, spinning around a father object who had been coming increasingly to life, as part object forms come into whole object forms as the self and psyche integrate. By the midpoint of the session, Sharon was recalling the hate for a father who epitomized all the forms of failing her that left her feeling alone and in orbit in the world—as if she had been a "changeling" (Sharon's association) dropped arbitrarily into a family system that seemed totally detached and strangely alien to her, where she also felt like an alien. Sharon spoke of a rage coming awake from her unconscious, where it had been split-off and dissociated, a rage that made her feel like she had been on fire with hot wires of hate streaming through her entire body. Her images revived my memories of Edith Sitwell's poetry, as the British poet had spoken of being a bush of flames on fire in relation to her own father ("father-mother," as intrapsychic fantasy "demon-lover"—in Kavaler-Adler, 1993a/2013, 1996/2014). She recalled her father's letters to her at camp with a sense of nauseous disdain, suffering the thoughts of how out of touch her father was with any center of being—either hers or his. She hated him for his letters, his inert passive dependence on her mother, his invalid status, his lack of any kind of agency at all in her view, and his pleading, hurt-filled eyes that left her guilt-ridden when his eyes were not oblivious and totally detached. She hated him for his lack of awareness of her scapegoat status with an out-of-control sadistic and martyred mother.

There was hate, hate, hate! Then suddenly something erupted from another plain as a new regret consumed her. Her syncopated memory jumped forward from childhood to her adulthood, as she recalled how he had written to her, asking to see her, saying it might be the last time they saw each other. With this thought, Sharon started to cry in great gulps of pain that was different from other times of silent weeping. "He knew he was going to die," she said. "I didn't believe him. I wrote him back a snide, contemptuous, and dismissive letter, saying of course we'd see each other again! I can feel the sneer in the letter now. I was the cold, detached, sadistic one then, not he, not her. I was the metallic object, the unfeeling stone. I never saw him again." As she said this, Sharon doubly erupted in an agony of grief.

She gasped to breathe as her tears flooded her and washed out the hot wires of hate that had possessed her, as all bad objects possess those that cannot love.

A new level of memory entered the door of my consultation room, a level of memory that neither of us had witnessed before. She remembered an early daddy that she had kept immured in the darkness of her mental closet up until that very moment. He was a daddy who she now, in this very moment, believed had truly loved her. "I never believed that my mother loved me," she said, "but I always knew my father had loved me. I forgot it, all of it, the daddy who loved me, the daddy I loved." Her tears washed her eyes red, and I could only see them when she got up from the couch at the end of the session. "I was so mean. I turned my heart cold. No wonder my first marriage failed and I almost destroyed my second marriage." As her analyst, I felt the poignancy of the moment, her heart crying out to me with her newfound capacity to love. We had discovered her daddy.

I wanted to sing as her grief washed us up on the raft of her core self, embedded in a barbed wire ego that could now surrender to love and life! When she left the session that day, we both knew that change could definitely happen. "He really loved me," she repeated. "That's why you've been able to love your daughter," I said, "despite your fears that you could never love, especially a daughter." She nodded her head in agreement. We had a silent moment of communion. "The part of you that knew beyond your conscious ignorance that you were loved by your daddy found your daughter. That's why she's as healthy as you and as sociable and self-confident. It hasn't all been your husband's doing."

Seeing her father as a vulnerable being has allowed Sharon to dream of a vulnerable mother with hurt in her eyes. The new image of her mother, allowing Sharon to see the child in her mother, has allowed her to relinquish the image of her mother as a monster. In relinquishing that primal object image, she has been able to lessen her compulsive tendency to demonize the world through the projection of this internal primal image.

The Growth of Gratitude through the Feeling of Loss

As Sharon became increasingly attuned to free associative thinking, with the gradual letting go of old object ties through mourning and regret, she opened her imagination in the moment to images that emerge naturally from within. Sometimes these images were projected onto a painting in my room, which she used as a Rorschach (admittedly, in her view). Sometimes they were stimulated merely by thoughts, interpersonal events, or in some cases by other stimuli in the room that she projected onto. How different this was from the woman who first came to treatment, who could only have fantasies in nightmarish dreams!

During one session, following her grief for her father, Sharon looked at the certificates I had on the wall of my downtown Manhattan office where I had framed some of my educational certificates. She remarked quite spontaneously that she had just had the fantasy of people coming into my office to collect my things, such as my certificates, after my death. Distinctly not interpreting this as her wanting to kill me off, I listened to hear the story that followed and its affect, that of grief. She said that she felt quite sad as she envisioned this scene. She feared losing me and was aware now that it would be a great personal loss for her. I had become valuable to her, not only as a psychoanalyst but as a person she cared about, and to one she felt gratitude.

Then, as she followed her line of free association, she found that she might be imagining my death to avoid thinking about her husband's death. Then she realized that the thought had entered her mind, and the fear had entered her whole psycho-physical being that her husband could die from a heart attack from what he was taking on the following year, in terms of responsibilities in both work and fieldwork in his new graduate studies. As she thought of this, she began to think of all the things her husband did for her. She began to enumerate all these things and to feel how much she could now appreciate her husband and feel gratitude toward him. Sharon mentioned how he took care of the pool at their home, did things in the house, and how he also provided a "reality check" for her, validating what was real for her, when she still felt insecure about her perception of reality. She spoke with a great feeling of grief and longing, with a whole new sense of how awareness of losing another could heighten an awareness of love, not just love due to need, but love mixed in with need that existed for its own sake beyond the need.

Sharon followed associations as visions in her mind and spoke of how she now for the first time was seeing the end of everything in her marriage, not due to a prospective divorce, but due to the potential death of her husband. This came after she was beginning to imagine a lifetime with him and to feel a sense of their working things out together and being together. Her capacity to mourn a potential loss allowed her to feel the reality of a present love that she had never fully appreciated before. The woman with the formerly detached intellect became poetic.

During the next day's session, Sharon saw a new image in her "Rorschach painting." Instead of the usual monsters she had seen earlier on, or the princess that she had found in the painting later—as the transference changed and as her view of her self changed—she saw a metallic head. However, she not only saw the metallic head, she also experienced the projective act itself in seeing the image, the visceral transmission that can come from projective identification as opposed to a mere mental projection at a representational and symbolic level. She spoke about it in terms of feeling release of pressure as she "put the metallic head outside myself." She spoke of the metallic head as having power as well as also a rigidity that she was glad to get rid of, to get outside of her body and mind.

It was as if she was experiencing the unburdening of her primitive mind's binary system of cognitive thought in both concrete and metaphoric terms simultaneously. I felt her visible relief. I was also fascinated by her fascination with this metallic object that she saw as a face, but really as a mask, conjuring up palpable images of the false self in robot-like terms. I was reminded of other patients with schizoid (or paranoid-schizoid) character structures who had metallic objects (or part objects) to which they were adhesively attached. They had metallic objects that lived within them, in the sealed-off and split-off infant part of them as remnants of a primitive mother. The original external mother usually had a schizoid character. I was also reminded of Tustin's (1990) work on autistic children, who would cling to hard objects, who resembled the original sealed-off mother object. These children would organize around the cold hard other, rather than around a warm and yielding mother.

Then Sharon proclaimed that she believed this metal face could have the power to finish writing her children's book, which she had put aside and not returned to, despite the editorial praise and encouragement she received. She said that she herself could not do so. Interestingly enough, in the very next session, she suddenly found her own feeling of agency in relation to her book.

She wondered how this had happened. Sharon noted that in the last session she felt helpless to finish the book and saw the metallic object as an external source of creative power, not sensing any internal source of such power. How had she transformed into her own sense of self-agency, she wondered? It was clear to me. One does not truly get rid of a part of the self in projective identification. Whatever is put outside can and does return to the inside through introjective-identification. Not only did Sharon feel a new sense of agency to finish her own creative work, but she also could tell me in detail her specific plan of strategic attack on her book as well as a definite timetable that she had set up for the work. She had re-owned the power she projected outside but had left the heavy burden of the metallic object attached to this power outside herself. Her power had become more flexible and resilient, like a muscle that could work at will, without much effort, rather than like a machine she had to crank up on an assembly line.

As Sharon left my office, on the day when she imagined my certificates to be collected by those clearing up after my death, she had another vision of the certificates. After her grief and love experience in the session, she said that she "felt warmth coming off the certificates." I was amused by her indirectness, still resisting direct contact or direct gratitude in my presence. I commented that if she experienced my certificates as warm it must mean that she felt me as being warm then, which was quite different than how she had imagined me for many years. She laughed and agreed with me, enjoying that I called her on her evasion of direct acknowledgment, and thus of direct love, by interpreting her displacement and projection.

Relinquishing the "Perfect People"

How did this interact with her readiness to give up the fantasy of the "perfect people," and of the "perfect person" to which she wanted to attach herself to? She had always projected not only her power but her talents, skills, and capacities to love and create out onto her fantasy perfect people. She had imbued her imagined perfect people with all the strength, intellect, elegance, and interpersonal skills that she viewed herself as lacking. She fantasized about being attached to the perfect people, becoming an extension of them through compliance and submission. She could then imagine sharing in their perfection and escaping the inferior status that she believed had been her birthright.

The first perfect person had been her brother. He was a brilliant student who entered MIT at 16, escaping the family household. When her brother left, Sharon was decimated. She had believed that he would be her salvation since she had not trusted either of her parents. She had made up a fantasy brother who would feel as involved with her as she was with him. So when her brother left abruptly, according to a plan he had calculated long ago, she was shocked. Her fantasy of his involvement with her was totally dispelled, and the impact of the shock rocked her.

Her current and second husband would become the heir to this fantasy throne. At the initiation of her relationship with him, she believed that he had all the qualities and strengths (such as having a lot of friends and related parents) that she lacked. Therefore, her second husband became the new perfect person in her mind.

The idea of giving up the fantasy of the perfect people caused Sharon much pain. She had protected herself from the awareness of her traumatized and despairing status by investing in the fantasy of the world being inhabited with perfect people who had perfect lives. If she was the only inferior being, she could tolerate life as long as the others had everything that she lacked. Like the unconscious thinking of Fairbairn's (1952) deprived child, who thought that "it is better to be a devil in a world ruled by God than an angel in a world ruled by Satan," Sharon could have hope for survival in a world where the perfect people ruled and she could attach herself to them. Such fantasy protected her from consciously contemplating the horrors of her childhood life: as the daughter of a mother who became a witch or monster or monster in her mind, as the mother had assaulted her in continuous sadistic and scapegoating attacks, and as the daughter of a father who became a vegetable after numerous psychiatric hospitalizations.

As the delusional system came into Sharon's awareness, she was faced with her beliefs being mere fantasies. This helped her piece together the elements of her actual reality. In Ogden's words (1986), she became an "interpreting subject," one who could now tell that thoughts and feelings were thoughts and feelings, not actual events. To know a fantasy is a fantasy is a critical part of entering Klein's depressive position. The grief of regret had helped Sharon arrive in this psychic place.

Conclusion

Feeling and Mourning the Inner Child:
An Interaction with the Mourning of Regret

As Sharon located her internal traumatized child self, she was able to lessen the compulsive defensive operations that isolated her from others and that kept her vicious pathological cycles going. These pathological cycles could be referred to as repetition compulsions; they could also be seen as major defense systems that warded off her affect life. Through such defense systems, she had avoided the painful affect states related to her early abuse and abandonment. These defense systems warded off the critical affects of loss, but also the affects of rage and emptiness and void states (see Masterson, 1981, on abandonment depression affects). In one defense she was identifying with the aggressor and enacting her mother's sadistic attitudes and attacks on the other, often her husband, or was doing so in her mind if not in behavior. In another, she was identified with her mother's victimization and with her own role of victim in relation to the mother. In that position, she felt helpless and inadequate and projected all her power outside of herself into the sadistic other.

Both operations could clearly be seen to operate with her husband, but they occurred with others as well. However, when she could experience the pain of regret and the cognitive accompaniment of interpreting that which she was regretting, she was able to relinquish some of her sadism and the maternal identification that went with it. Then she was able to relinquish her masochistic self-attack in a victimized position and the maternal and paternal identifications that went with that. Bit by bit, as she spoke to me quite spontaneously about her regrets, she lessened the wish to mimic her mother's form of sadistic power, either in directing it outward as identification with the aggressor or in directing it inwards as identification with the aggressor (Fairbairn's "antilibidinal ego") in an attack on her internal child self.

However, to give up this false power, based on pathological identifications, she had to feel the traumatized child self through memory and reliving. She felt this at first in the group experience, where she first contacted the inner three-year-old through projecting the dissociated child self onto her daughter. Contacting this inner core—that which Fairbairn (1952) would call the split-off libidinal ego— was both painful and yet relieving! In feeling the three-year-old within, she felt alive in a new way, experiencing a true and authentic affect self (Winnicott, 1965), with its spontaneity. She felt both the grief of losing the old tie to her mother who punished and abandoned her by separating from her through the owning of her own experience and the longing of wishing to unite with a better mother.

Later in treatment, she would still be haunted by her expectation of punishment, which at times could seem like a wish. She would speak of looking for a punishment, deprivation, or rejection after any experience of pleasure and fulfillment. For example, after the triumphant success of her son's bar mitzvah, which she had planned and seen through, bringing the whole family together into a new world of friends and family with her, she felt anxiety. For the first time, she not only tolerated a position of being a center of attention, which in the past would have filled her with tension and made her push people away, but she actually enjoyed this position for the first time! Yet right afterward, her psychoanalytic therapy sessions were spent talking about how she was expecting "the other shoe to drop." She could create a whole new state of tension by looking for the punishment. She had never had a parental model for feeling that she could deserve either success or pleasure.

Yet, as she talked about a feared punishment that never came, for the first time, she did not create it. She spoke about a compulsion to create it instead, and also about the compulsion to pull back from a new mother, the one in her middle-aged adult life who for the first time was not rejecting her. At her son's bar mitzvah, she felt accepted by her mother. This disconcerted her. Being accepted by her mother was totally unfamiliar. Part of her wished to run back to the old bad mother who was so much a part of her old self, the one so much identified by her as herself, despite its pathological and defensive origins. To be bad, deprived, punished, rejected, attacked, and abandoned was what her familiar old self was based on. Taking the risk of the unfamiliar could at one time have felt threatening of annihilation. At this later time, she just felt "unmoored." But never was Fairbairn's view of pathology being based on clinging to the original object, when it was a bad object, be more clearly seen. Now that Sharon had felt the depressive pain and difficult affect states of regret, she could symbolize her internal experience. She could talk about the dynamics of her compulsion to return to the old self and old object in clear and articulate terms. This is how she and I experienced her gradually becoming free.

For the first time, Sharon felt that she had the power and sense of agency to finish her book. She began to actively engage with the work, for the first time in over a year. She could then predict that she could finish the book by the end of the summer. Sharon's capacity to follow through on creativity grew in conjunction with and in dialectic with her capacity to love as she reached behind her husband's defensive hostility to see his needs and frustrations (see "the love-creativity dialectic," Kavaler-Adler, 1996/2014).

Finally, Sharon's husband let down his guard and revealed all his secret fears of failure and inadequacy to her. He relinquished his use of Sharon as a scapegoat for his inadequate self as he had experienced this inadequate self through the projective processes of projective identification.

Theoretical Summary

A critical distinction between Kleinian Object Relations theory and that of other schools of Object Relations thinking (particularly in America) is that Kleinian thinking (1940) is attuned to the element of existential guilt as a factor in psychic change. By contrast, the other schools of Object Relations thinking focus on the affective element of loss alone as having developmental significance in relation to healing traumas and resolving developmental arrest.

Mahler's Object Relations theory, for example, speaks of the capacity to tolerate the grief of loss as a pivotal determinant of separation-individuation. Mahler does not speak about guilt as interacting with loss in her view of psychic change evolving from the navigation of the separation-individuation phase of development, even though she does acknowledge a range of mourning experience to be natural for separation-individuation to take place.

Margaret Mahler speaks of a mild form of depressive affect experience, which she calls "low keyedness" (Mahler et al., 1975). Such low keyedness takes place in normal and timely separation-individuation processes, where there has been the internalization of good enough mothering and mother bonding. A more intense form of grief takes place when separation-individuation has been arrested, which has been called an "abandonment depression" by Masterson (1976, 1981), who follows Mahler's theory and schema of development, particularly in pathological cases of developmental arrest. Another Object Relations theorist, from the British Middle School, Michael Balint (1968), speaks of mourning in his "basic fault" cases of preoedipal developmental arrest.

John Bowlby (1969, 1980), likewise, speaks of normal mourning for psychic development as well as psychic change. Masterson, Balint, and Bowlby, like Mahler, do not mention the pain and anguish of guilt, as an existential and affective aspect of mourning and grief. They only refer to grief in terms of object loss. Fairbairn (1952), another British Object Relations theorist, speaks of relinquishing old Object

Relations ties, in a traumatic separation process, but refers more to the exorcism of bad objects than to any mourning process. When Fairbairn uses the word "guilt" he refers to a spurious or false form of guilt that is essentially a masochistic defense of self-blame, a defense that serves to deny the demonic or "bad object" aspects of the real parent. Authentic existential guilt is never dealt with by Fairbairn.

By contrast to these Object Relations theorists, Klein (1940, 1957/1980) speaks pointedly and explicitly of existential guilt as a fundamental part of the psychic change in the depressive position. The pivotal grief experience for Klein is one in which guilt and loss interact on both affective and cognitive levels. Klein refers to the psychic change that occurs primarily due to the tolerance of loss in the service of renewed love and object connection, although she focuses these thoughts mainly on the internal world development. By emphasizing the internal world, Klein is open to the beginnings of developmental thinking about the new psychic structure internalizations that can stem from the Object Relationships of the psychoanalyst and analysand in psychoanalytic treatment sessions, as she demonstrates at the end of her famous treatise "Envy and Gratitude" (1957).

Klein speaks of her internalization of the good session and good analyst (not the idealized part object analyst, but the actual real good aspect of the analyst) as a contribution to psychic (ego) structure, although she circumscribes the analyst's Object Relationship with the analysand to that transacted through the offering of interpretations. These beginning thoughts on the developmental process are, however, less emphasized by Klein than those on the reparative efforts of the psyche in the context of compulsive and hostile psychic fantasy attacks on the primal other, who is symbolically housed in the internal world and continually displaced onto all current objects in the affectively alive external world. Consequently, Klein is quite aware of the kind of grief that involves an alchemy of loss and guilt. This interpenetration of guilt and loss can lead to self and object reparation and integration within the domain of Kleinian theory.

My Extension of Klein's Theory

In following Klein on this avenue of thought (Kavaler-Adler, 1993b)—as I find her highly relevant to the clinical situation—I use the word "regret" to refer to a combination of loss and existential guilt that evolves into critical psychic change. On an affective level, this combination of self-states has a developmental valence that is critically associated with transforming character disorder into character development. I believe that my linguistic amendment of Klein to be truly within the spirit of Klein's clinical theory, which I view as a theory that stands independent of her metapsychology of the death instinct (Kavaler-Adler, 2003a).

My clinical experience illustrates that regret is a signpost to hope if it can be consciously felt and processed. If it cannot be tolerated it can turn to despair and reinforce prior traumatic loss and developmental arrest. My view contrasts with Shabad's (2001) definition of regret as an entrenchment in despair concerning self-sabotage that is more narcissistic in nature and does not relate to hurting another. Shabad reserves the term "remorse" for transgressions against another. My view, on the other hand, speaks of the clinically observable psychic transformation that can evolve through the conscious tolerance of regret. In my view, such regret can include remorse. When regret is conscious it can be grieved on an affective level and learned from on a cognitive level. This prevents the repetition of damage we do to our relationships can be prevented in the future. The conscious processing of regret can lead to critical psychic change as a working through process occurs in which primal modes of regret are reexperienced and reworked.

OBJECT RELATIONS ISSUES IN THE TREATMENT OF THE PRECEDIPAL CHARACTER

Originally published in 1993, *American Journal of Psychoanalysis* 53(1):19–34.

Object Survival and the Transitional Object

The analyst's role as a transitional object (Winnicott, 1971) becomes particularly critical with patients whose parental objects have failed to survive as "good enough" during the stages of development when the self structure is formed through object internalization. To fulfill the functions of a transitional object, the analyst must survive the patient's infantile rage, containing the aggressive attacks. Eventually, he/she must interpret the compulsion behind the aggressive assaults in terms of reenactments of pathological transactions with the parents that prohibited an affectively alive mode of object contact.

In his paper, "The Use of the Object and Relating Through Identification," D.W. Winnicott (1969) interprets object survival as tolerating infantile rage without retaliation or abandonment. The terms of object survival can be broadened beyond such a definition, however, as the psychoanalyst is seen as a transitional object who can be used for developmental purposes. Similar to an attuned parent, the analyst as the transitional object must translate the patient's needs and fears implicit behind his/her patient's rage into an understandable form. The analyst must also continue to be available for responsive emotional contact at any juncture when rage is resolved into a state of vulnerability and self-observing reflection.

Sometimes this involves active modes of engagement on the part of the analyst or a more receptive attunement. The analyst's survival also implies confronting and interpreting Object Relations reenactments so that a compulsion to act out a perpetual battle with the "bad object" (Fairbairn, 1952)[1] can be converted into alive affect, and thus into penetrating contact in relationships in the present. This allows a developmental mourning process to proceed. Survival also means setting limits to provide the structure that can allow this process to occur.

When the analyst as a transitional object does not survive in this way, a reparative "abandonment depression" (Masterson, 1976) mourning process cannot emerge. Preoedipally traumatized patients need a dialogue with an external object to sustain awareness of the good object experience so that the painful aspect of guilt and loss, often felt as devastating regret, can be tolerated. Since such characters have not securely internalized a whole object, they need an external object acting as a transitional object to allow the dialogue that leads to mourning to evolve.

The Case of Ms. D.

Borderline and narcissistic characters fail to internalize an adequate whole object is apparent in his/her inability to remain open to affect, contact, and interpersonal dialogue. Failure is also apparent in primitive defense modes of splitting and projective identification. Mother is an idealized figure with whom the patient seeks symbiosis. Psychic symbiosis is sought in fantasy, resulting in a withdrawal into a cocoon state (Modell, 1976). Hatred toward the mother is split-off. Loving and sexual feelings toward the father are initially denied. Externalized reenactments of a demon-lover father's abusive behavior may become the manifest symptoms of failures in self-integration.

Some reconstruction of one analysand's actual parental failures can be derived from her history as it emerged in the transference. In the case of Ms. D.—a woman in the fourth year of psychoanalytic psychotherapy—her childhood mother had protected and empathically held her, but separation issues were never resolved. Ms. D.'s mother had been unable to set limits with her. Her mother never seemed to have said "no" to her. Also, her mother had been unable to engage in verbal dialogue characteristic of interpersonal connection at the level of psychic separation, as in the "sharing" at rapprochement described by Mahler, Pine, and Bergman (1975). However, the "cumulative trauma" (Khan, 1974) level of Ms. D.'s parental failure was not seemingly reached until the point of the mother's death, when Ms. D. was 10. The failure of fathering to support separation from the mother became tragic and traumatic at this point. Ms. D.'s mother died, and Ms. D. was left alone with her father, who began to continually abuse and molest her. The father's demonic behavior contributed greatly to Ms. D.'s need to defend herself through an identification with the father's own paranoid thinking and narcissistic character defense system.

Both parents failed to contain Ms. D.'s aggression and to remain available for responsive emotional contact. The mother was often too withdrawn due to her own exhaustion, and the father was not only incapable of attunement to his daughter's needs but was also extremely intrusive.

Ms. D.'s case clearly illustrates the critical role of the analyst's object survival. Her split-off and sealed-off rage had shown itself within many nightmares as holocausts and nuclear explosions. After an initial phase of idealization, it began to show itself in the transference through devaluation and withdrawal into the narcissistic cocoon state (Modell, 1976). Gradually, Ms. D.'s rage became more overt as when Ms. D. fantasized about throwing a brick through my window and smashing my plants on the floor. Provocations followed, along with devaluing sarcasm.

The height of the negative transference came at the point when I clearly set limits and said "no" in response to requests for taking a magazine from my office and for last-minute changes in session times. After a session in which Ms. D. openly exploded with her most intense rage, full of accusations and taunting threats, I said to her, "those who blame others are usually blaming themselves for something." Her fury subsided in response to my comment, and she became momentarily reflective: "What do you think I'm blaming myself for?" she asked. I thought to myself that she believed that she had killed her mother, but I didn't know how we would get to that. I responded, "we can get to it. You're in a rage now, so everything seems urgent, but we can get to it." Her urgency was obviously more powerful than her reflective capacity following my response, and on the way out, she vowed she was going to wind down treatment.

In the next session, however, Ms. D. appeared with a dream, and unlike former times, she showed herself capable of staying with her dream and producing associations. The dream was vivid and in four parts.

The first three parts became most significant. In the first part, her mother came down to her from heaven, and she grabbed her mother's hand, sobbing, "mamma, mamma!" But her mother pulled away and left her again. In the second part of the dream, she was sucking on her girlfriend's breasts, and she became turned on sexually. In the third part of the dream, there was a black boy who was delivering food to a man she identified as Ronald Reagan.

Ms. D. stayed with her associations over the course of two sessions. In the second session, she began to express some momentary sadness about her mother returning to her in the first part of the dream. When she said this, she was sitting up on the couch. I responded that if she could let me be with her in that place where she felt the sadness, we wouldn't have to be enemies. She seemed to melt. Her hardness, which was generally expressed in her body by a rigid posture of lying on the couch, changed radically. She curled up on the couch in a fetal position and indicated an openness to my reflections upon her dream, exclaiming, "Yes, I really want to know what you think. I really mean it." It was then that I could make a critical interpretation based on her associations to the third part of the dream.

Ms. D. indicated that in the third part of the dream she was the black boy and I was Ronald Reagan. She commented several times, with bewilderment, that the ratio of money I paid to the delivery boy was way off. According to Ms. D., I paid much too much for fast food, food that she associated with shit. (Fast food can be contrasted to the slow food of breastfeeding that she tried to obtain in sucking her girlfriend's breasts in the second part of the dream.) She commented that it should be the other way around too. She was the one who paid me money. And why was I paying her so much?

I then told Ms. D. that although consciously she believed that she was giving too much to me and getting nothing back, unconsciously she felt tremendously guilty because she thought I was giving and giving and giving to her and that she was taking and taking and using me up, just as she felt she used up her mother[2] and killed her!

Ms. D.'s response was powerful and immediate. She began rocking and gyrating back and forth on the couch, crying out, "It's true. It's true. I did it! I did it!" She continued, "She wanted to die, but I wouldn't let go. She stayed alive, suffering, because she didn't want to leave me." Her crying opened up into sobbing for the first time in the course of treatment. The years of repressed mourning seemed to finally emerge. She wailed like those in the most acute anguish of loss.

Ms. D. sat up, still sobbing, telling me how her mother was the only one who called her by a certain name. Sobbing, she proclaimed, "She loved me more than I ever loved her. That's why I can't forgive myself." I told her that she might like to take some of my tissues. Since she couldn't respond to my offer of comfort, I interpreted her hesitation. "You really don't deserve to take one of my tissues," I said. "You're much too bad." With no overt verbal response to me, but with an obvious inner one, she swiftly reached out for a tissue.

Dialogue Following Object Survival

In the case of Ms. D., the analyst's survival of her aggression allowed a dialogue to emerge between the patient's unconscious and conscious processes. The analyst's survival of the negative transference aggression also allowed a dialogue to open up interpersonally, within the analytic space between analyst and analysand. The internal and external dialectic processes opened up in parallel. Ms. D.'s production of a dream, and her ability to associate to that dream, allowed for the emergence of an essential element of split-off hatred toward her mother, which had been unconsciously hidden behind a maternal idealization. The opening of this repressed hatred allowed Ms. D. to consciously experience her guilt. Once conscious of this guilt, Ms. D. could begin to relinquish her intense paranoid vigilance, as her externalized projections and reenactments were gradually reduced. With her tolerance of guilt, Ms. D.'s loving connection with her mother could be consciously felt, allowing her to emotionally process, and further, to conceptualize, her grief.

An internal dialectic allowed mourning to proceed as the former psychic fantasy fusion with the mother was relinquished. Comments by the patient, such as, "She loved me more than I loved her" and "I wouldn't let her go!" were part of a guilt-laden intrapsychic conflict that had been repressed and walled off behind the internal and externalized sadomasochistic battle with the father. The opening of this dialectic allowed mourning to be processed through interpersonal dialogue. The analyst's role as a transitional object allowed object survival to open up analytic space for interpretation. Critical interpretations of repressed guilt then led to the unblocking of a capacity to mourn. This kind of block in the capacity to mourn is frequently seen in the narcissistic character.

Mourning

The depressive position mourning process (Klein, 1946) is the other critical aspect of the developmental process. However, I propose that it can only follow sufficient internalization of whole object contact and dialogue. As aggression is neutralized by the survival of the transitional object, the affect of loss, induced through separation and its frustrations, is felt with a conjunctive awareness of the good in the object. In the case of Ms. D., we can see that as guilt becomes tolerable, Ms. D. begins to be able to sustain affective contact with the analyst. Consequently, good object internalization could be realized.

As guilt was faced by Ms. D., loss could be felt and tolerated. As loss is tolerated, the analyst as a transitional whole object can be taken inside in a sustained form, and thus can be assimilated into the self. Actually, as Fairbairn (1952) has articulated, it is the entire self and other dialogue with the analyst that is internalized, but the object must be experienced as "good enough" (Winnicott, 1965) for this internalization of dialogue to take place. Once the dialogue is internalized, an internal psychic structure dialectic can enhance the capacity to mourn. Object survival and mourning become interactive and complementary aspects of internalization processed through interpersonal contact.

As can be seen in this case, mourning allows the capacity for an affectively alive interpersonal dialogue to develop. This reflects the dialectic generally gained with the mother during early infancy. In Ms. D.'s case, an early nonverbal dialogue needed to evolve into a verbal and symbolic form. In cases of structural deficits existing from the earliest stages of infancy (Mahler et al., 1975; Stern, 1985), the primary dialectic structure for interpersonal dialogue needs to be built in through the encounter with the transitional object during reparative treatment. In the case of Ms. D., however, this primary structure did seem to exist. It needed to be unblocked. This involved the dissolution of character defense mechanisms that were used to counteract infantile rage reactions, which in turn were related to a painful combination of guilt and grief.

Holding and Guilt Interpretations

Kernberg (1975) credits the interpretation of primitive aggression, particularly as derived from oral envy, as the main contribution of the analyst to promoting mourning in the narcissistic character. He deemphasizes the interpersonal environment as a container for the mourning process to take place, although he does refer to interpretive interventions that promote affect experience as providing a containing function (Kernberg, 1988).

In contrast to Kernberg, I believe that the entire interpersonal environment must be emphasized. Interpretive avenues to contact are one aspect of this environment. Since a fusion of intrapsychic structure prohibits narcissistic patients from mourning on their own, the presence of another feeling human being must be emphasized to provide the kind of "going-on-being" referred to by Winnicott (1965).

In the case of Ms. D., I needed to create an atmosphere of containment so that the critical interpretive work around repressed hatred could take place. Without this atmosphere, externalizing reenactments of the hatred would have continued, in the form of sadistic provocations and masochistic submissions. My continuing emotional responsiveness was one aspect of this containment. However, verbal comments were critical as well, both for demonstrating empathy and for moving Ms. D.'s modes of transaction to the verbal and conscious level.

Three interventions appear to have been critical. The first was my saying that, "Those who are blaming others are generally blaming themselves for something." Ms. D. was able to respond to this comment by moving from externalization and blame to an intrapsychic level of reflection. If I had said this comment in a retaliatory fashion, I might have had a totally different effect. It could have been heard as counter-blame. However, free of such retaliatory impulses, the comment could be used by Ms. D. to reflect on her own guilt.

Two other comments seem important in terms of providing holding and containment so that the psychic space necessary for internalization could be created. The first was my saying, "If you could allow me to be with you in your sadness, we wouldn't have to be enemies." I believe Ms. D.'s dramatic reaction of surrendering to her vulnerability at the point when I said this was in part a response to my acknowledgment that we had been enemies. My acknowledging this served to also acknowledge my own aggression within our interaction so that Ms. D. did not have to feel all bad. However, my reference to the possibility of a more harmonious relation between Ms. D. and myself, as a consequence of her letting me into the loving part of her, also showed Ms. D. that I could be with her in both her enemy position and beyond it. I showed her my capacity to be with her in the yearnings manifested in her sadness, but this was conveyed not only by the cognitive meaning in my words but also by the tone of tender concern and involvement with which I said this.

Another significant comment seems to be related to Ms. D.'s reluctance to take my tissues. My acknowledging her sense of her own badness, by saying she didn't deserve to take my tissues, seems to have freed Ms. D. from her own internal accusations, which had been prohibiting her from receiving anything from me. Again, my tone of voice seems to have been equally significant to the symbolic message conveyed by my words. My tone was quiet, matter-of-fact, and yet confronting. I believe that Ms. D.'s shame propensity was counterbalanced by my gentle bluntness.

Fear of Crying in the Narcissist

The narcissistic character appears to be constantly warding off a fear of engulfment in his/her own pain. Inchoate tears from decades of suppressed pain seem to pose an unconscious threat. There is a profound fear of opening the floodgates. This seems like opening a Pandora's Box of engulfing crying, in which one's own inner demons must be encountered. Yielding to tears also arouses an unconscious fear of drowning. One can fear drowning in tears that echo a loss of an object of fantasy merger and also express a terror of engulfment in the very merger wished for. Intrapsychic dialogue modifies the fear of perpetual crying by processing grief affects into conceptually understandable expressions of guilt and object loss. The narcissist's compulsion to put up a wall against contact even when crying can be gradually resolved. Interpersonal contact is necessary to transform the perpetual crying of an isolated mode of pathological mourning into a productive mode of developmental mourning in which the sharing of grief is allowed.

Blocked Mourning in the Borderline Character

The borderline character, like the narcissist, suffers from arrests in a necessary developmental mourning process, a mourning process that is all the more necessary for these characters who continually ward off the affective experience of intense preoedipal trauma. In the following case of Ms. A., similar to the case of Ms. D. just reported, the analyst's survival of aggression can be seen to be critical in opening up levels of both interpersonal and intrapsychic dialectic so that mourning might proceed. This was the overall route to self-integration and self-differentiation within developmental individuation.

Ms. A. evidenced cycles of blocked mourning. In the first phase of the cycle, she defended against her aggression with a multitude of defensive techniques, among which splitting within her self and object experience could be seen, and such splitting was reinforced by projection and projective identification. In the second phase, the expression of aggression would lead to a self-reflective dialogue, which illustrated the freeing of observing ego capacities and the consequent ability to own and experience psychic and interpersonal conflict. In the third phase, this contact would lead to the intense experience of loss, echoing extreme abandonment trauma from the preoedipal past. These three phases can be seen in the following sequence of three treatment sessions from Ms. A.'s third year of treatment.

In the first session, Ms. A. entered my office and commented that there was a bad smell in the room. She then said that she believed the smell was that of body odor from my last patient. She declared that it made her nauseous. She then told me that while in the waiting room she had thought that I was doing a role-play with this last patient and that the very idea disgusted her. She also said that this other woman patient had left her shawl out in the waiting room, and it also disgusted her because it made her think that this woman was this nauseatingly vulnerable frail thing.

I suggested to Ms. A. that she was jealous. "No," she declared, "I'm nauseous!" I suggested that she would rather feel nauseous than jealous because it felt humiliating to her to admit that she felt jealous of my other patient. It especially felt humiliating to admit it to me, I added. Ms. A. became angrily defiant, and seemingly defensive, saying that all therapists she had liked to think she was jealous. I responded that perhaps we all saw the jealousy she displayed. I also told her that it was not long ago that she went into a jealous rage about her boyfriend seeing an old girlfriend for lunch, such a rage that she pulled everything out of the medicine chest and smashed things on the ground. She remained indignant and declared that this wasn't what she wanted to talk about. She accused me of wasting her session.

Chapter 4

She wanted to talk about her relationship with this woman she worked with. She said that Ms. B. was continually abusing her, and yet she felt she couldn't do without her. I said that what we had been talking about might be related to her difficulties with Ms. B. She retorted that all therapists say that. I interpreted back to her that she always said that she needed Ms. B. to help her focus, and that her difficulty focusing on her own pertained to her disowning her feelings so that she felt blocked and fragmented. I continued that if she could own her jealous feelings, she wouldn't be split away from a part of herself and she might be more focused. She responded by shouting that she hated everyone! She said Ms. B. would think she was horrible if she knew that she hated blacks, whites, women, children, Southerners, Northerners, everyone! After screaming this at me, she seemed relieved.

I told her that she was relieved because she thought I would hate her for saying these things, but she could feel that I didn't hate her, and this helped to relieve the tremendous guilt she felt about her hatred. I also added that being able to express her hatred, rather than blocking and defending against it, could help her be in touch with herself so that she could focus on her own, without Ms. B.'s help. I said that she seemed more receptive to me at that moment and could let me be with her for the first time during that session. She seemed calm. Her eyes became open and serene.

Ms. A. came into the next session in a calm and poised manner, so different in body posture from the last session in which she had seemed hunched over herself. She talked to me about her awareness that she was holding onto illusions. She said that she kept believing that Ms. B. was supportive of her, even when she wasn't at all. We talked about two other illusions that she held onto. She told me that she had phoned her boyfriend's female friend and told her that she didn't want to make her feel uncomfortable about her having lunch with her boyfriend anymore. She spoke in a related and receptive way, allowing me to be with her and to engage in an amiable dialogue. She said that she felt more able to do her work on her own now and that she was considering how else she could earn money in order to continue coming twice a week to therapy while still doing her creative work. Following this session, she phoned to tell me that she had terminated her working relationship with Ms. B. and that it was "very hard." She sounded mournful.

During the next session, Ms. A. warded off her developing sadness by provocations and projections. She told me that her insurance was running out that month and that she couldn't continue twice a week sessions during the next month (which preceded my summer vacation). She said she expected me to give her a big argument. She knew I was going to tell her she could get money from her parents or work a hundred hours a week to pay for therapy without insurance. I told her

105

that it was she who wanted to create an argument because she didn't want to feel how sad she was about having less time with me. She started to cry and said that she was scared one session a week wouldn't be enough.

She said that she felt she was finally picking up momentum in her therapy, and that I was different twice a week than once a week. She then said she wanted me to reassure her that it was all right, that once a week was enough. When I did not reassure her, she accused me of having made her feel guilty by asking her not to put paper cups in my garbage pail in the bathroom. She said she thought she was the only one I told this to, and that I made her feel like she was dirty. I told her that she was the one who thought that she was bad and that she was projecting onto a practical situation a whole drama about herself being the "black sheep" in the family.[3] I explained that she wanted to provoke an argument with me again because the prospect of having to cut down to once a week was haunting her and that she was fighting me to fight off an intense sense of loss.

Ms. A. responded with more tears, grieving that she wanted me to reassure her so that she wouldn't feel that she was losing anything. I told her that she was trying to avoid the harsh reality that once a week was not enough contact with me and that she wanted me to participate in creating another illusion with her by reassuring her. She cried some more and said that her boyfriend could face reality better than her. With tears of anguish, she said that facing reality was really hard for her. We agreed that in the future she might be able to work at another job that had insurance for psychotherapy even though she was afraid that this would interfere with her creative work.

The Capacity to Mourn

The interaction of infant and mother during the preoedipal stages of development is prominently featured in the recent empirical infant research (Bowlby, 1980; Mahler, 1975; Stern, 1985; Spitz, 1983; Brent & Resch, 1987; Beebe & Lachman, 1988). Yet, such observation of the external behavior of mothers and infants still leaves us with the dubious task of connecting external behavior with the internal world. In our theoretical attempts to make such connections, we come upon the dilemma of deciding how much any innate imprint determines a developmental unfolding, with critical stages or sequences, and of hypothesizing how it affects the interactive dialogue seen in the behavior of any unique infant and mother dyad. It is only through such theorizing that we come to propose the nature of the internal world or psyche and to specify psychic structure formation.

For Freud, observations of oedipal-level family interactions led to his theorizing about a triadic psychic structure (id, ego, superego), which was related to a proposed developmental unfolding along the instinctual lines of oral, anal, phallic, and oedipal stages. For Margaret Mahler, a proposed symbiotic phase of development becomes a prominent feature of a theory that views internal psychic structure as forming only as separation proceeds and differentiated self and object image representations are formed, which then need degrees of integrating consolidation.

Melanie Klein's theory also has proposed a developmental sequence in which degrees of differentiation proceed along with integration, but rather than differentiation preceding and prompting integration, differentiation becomes dependent on an affective process of integration that stems from the internal mourning and the related reparative interpersonal interactions of the depressive position. Instead of the triadic dialogue of Freud, or the internalized dyadic dialogue of Mahler, Klein proposes a dialogue within the internal world, which takes place between an internal object and the person who is containing it, the latter figuratively "speaking" with the internal object at an unconscious level.

Despite the differences in all these developmental theories, there is the common denominator of an internal dialogue of proposed psychic structure personas that generally rearticulates a child-parent interaction. For Freud, the superego parent speaks with the id child through the ego. For Mahler, the parent "object representation" speaks with the child "self-representation." For Klein, the parent "internal object" speaks to the "child" in the adult through unconscious "phantasy" (Kleinian spelling). For Klein, such dialogue only comes about at the depressive position, where persecution lessens. For Mahler, it comes about at rapprochement, at the end of the separation-individuation era. For Freud, it comes about with the establishment of a secure superego at latency. Yet, for all three theorists, without such internal dialogue, externalized reenactments are the consequence, and such a consequence prohibits internal integration. Without integration proceeding, compulsive externalization is perpetuated.

Psychic Structure and the Mourning Process

Such clinical observations as those described in the case vignettes of Ms. D. and Ms. A. indicate that a psychic dialectic is necessary for mourning to take place. Further, various theorists have observed that mourning is a natural developmental process that takes place at varying stages of development, and with optimal growth, throughout life (Mahler, 1975; Loewald, 1962; Jacobson, 1964). Psychopathology can be defined in terms of the arrest or blocking of such mourning, regardless of whether intrapsychic conflict or developmental trauma and deficit are responsible. Without healthy developmental mourning, a form of pathological mourning persists, which in its mildest form—that is, when the early objects are "good enough"— merely inhibits personality growth.

In more severe forms, however, when mourning is blocked, as in the preoedipal character, the pathological mourning forms a character structure impervious to healthy interpersonal contact because malignant early internal objects are perpetually held on to, creating continuing malignant projections in external relations (see Fairbairn, 1952). The preoedipally arrested character evidences such pathology, as he/she blocks mourning due to a combination of intrapsychic conflict and developmental trauma that have obviated a fluid and mutually interactional psychic dialectic. The narcissistic character shows this in the extreme!

The psychoanalytic literature from varying theoretical perspectives illustrates the view that the narcissistic character has an intrapsychic fantasy symbiosis that manifests in a structural form. Psychic fusion is constantly referred to by theorists attempting to define the narcissist. Implicit in the conceptualization of psychic fusion is an arrest or block in healthy intrapsychic dialogue. Psychic fusion infers that differentiated self and object images, such as described by Mahler (1975), have not been formed. Self and other are felt as a diffuse combination that in its extreme is felt as a merger (Kohut, 1971). The lack of a fluid dialectic also inhibits the integration of love, aggression, and the integration of masculine and feminine aspects of the self, impeding adequate gender identity formation. In the case of Ms. D., difficulties with both phallic aggression and feminine vulnerability can be seen, as well as the interplay or dialectic between both these modes of being.

George Pollock (1975) of the Chicago School of Psychoanalysis relates dialogue to psychic structure when he suggests that it is the dialogue between two internal structures that is responsible for the dynamics of the mourning process and its ongoing developmental results, that is, differentiation and integration. George Pollock proposes an ego processing a "self" through the affects of loss, disillusionment, etc., as constituting a mourning process that he sees as fundamental to all psychic change and growth. He is assigning the ego a higher level of consciousness than the self, which might be likened to an internalized parent in the form of an ego and an infant self that is ever in infancy with fresh experience. Yet, in any case, he is proposing an internal or intrapsychic dialogue as providing the conditions for the affective mourning process to proceed and to promote structural change. I am suggesting that if there is no internal dialogue among internal persona structures, no mourning process can successfully occur.

Other theorists have also implied, through their attempts to describe the psychic structure of the narcissistic personality disorder, that internal psychic structural dialogue is necessary for mourning and its developmental consequences.

Literature on Psychic Structure Fusion in the Narcissist

The Jungian analyst, Nathan Schwartz-Salant (1982), in his book ***Narcissism and Character Transformation***—similar to self psychologist George Pollock—speaks of an ego and a self in making his point that these two structures seem fused in the narcissist's pathological state. He sees the self as a soul-like carrier of personal identity, which in normal development is mirrored by an ego formed through psychic identifications. However, in the narcissistic character, Schwartz-Salant notes that the self and ego are fused, so that the personality reflects a false persona identity rather than a genuine individuated identity. The ego in its fused state cannot become a "carrier of personal identity" (Schwartz-Salant, 1982, p. 70).

Like Schwartz-Salant, James Masterson (1981) also refers to fusion, as he adopts Margaret Mahler's theory and integrates it with Object Relations. He writes of a fusion between the self and the object in the narcissistic character that precludes differentiated self and object representations. He speaks of the failure in the deflation of the infantile grandiose self, proposing such failure at the time of the practicing period for the child who ends up with a narcissistic form of developmental arrest. The failure of deflation implies that the grandiose illusion of having the omnipotent other still inside the self is perpetuated (see Mahler, 1975). Such an illusion obviates moves toward differentiating modes of affect contact with external objects.

Tendencies to withdraw into fantasies of greatness and self-sufficiency are reinforced, warding off the interpersonal contact necessary for self and object differentiation. Failure of deflation then leads to a lack of self and object differentiation during rapprochement with a consequent failure of differentiated internalizations. Thus, the psychic structure personas are not created and cannot engage in dialogue.

Only in treatment, according to Masterson, can the primal fusion become unfused, and this depends on the ability of the narcissistic patient to go through a painful primitive form of mourning that Masterson refers to as an "abandonment depression." This can only be done with the support of the therapist who provides an external dialogue where the internal dialogue is lacking. In this way, a painful form of mourning can proceed that can pave the way for the normal developmental mourning process needed throughout life. Although Masterson only deals with the critical separation-individuation phases of preoedipal development and does not refer to any further developmental mourning process, the consolidation of differentiated self and other representations through rage, loss, and grief allows for the resumption of an internal dialogue, which, according to my view, leads to developmental mourning. Such differentiation into interacting psychic structure personas seems to be necessary for the capacity to mourn without an external other, such as the analyst. Thus, for example, it would be necessary to be able to mourn through the creative process.

Otto Kernberg (1975) also attributes fusion rather than differentiated internal dialogue to the narcissistic character. He speaks of a pathological grandiose self being formed through what he actually refers to as a "re-fusion" of self, idealized object, and idealized self. Although he, unlike Masterson (who draws on Margaret Mahler's theory of primary symbiosis), speaks of "re-fusion" and not of primary primitive fusion, the theoretical psychodynamic point is essentially the same. Whichever comes first, the chicken of primary symbiosis or the egg of symbiotic fusion following frustration, the perpetual psychodynamics of the narcissistic character are the same for both Masterson and Kernberg.

In the case of Ms. D., it can be seen that the psychic symbiosis symptomatic of a narcissistic character was due to a defensive idealization of the mother, who was lost during childhood. Fantasy symbiosis with the idealized mother served to defend the patient against the anguish of loving a mother toward whom she felt intense guilt over childhood hatred. The intensity of the guilt had made an affective remembrance of the mother unbearable, so that the necessary mourning, and its grief-laden affects, had been blocked.

Summary

It was through tolerance of Ms. D.'s infantile rage (i.e., rage against reality and its limits) that the analyst was able to open up a dialogue with the patient that could lead to a developmental mourning process. The same was true for the borderline character, Ms. A.! The interpersonal dialogue between analyst and analysand, which had both empathic and interpretive functions, allowed Ms. D. to reactivate her capacities for an intrapsychic dialectic gained during infancy. In her case, as well as in that of Ms. A., the initiation of an internal dialectic allowed for a mourning process to unfold. It is proposed that this internal dialectic is evidence of the existence of the psychic structure necessary to promote both mourning and the mutuality of interpersonal dialogue. The inability to mourn, generally seen in narcissistic and borderline characters, can be seen, therefore, not only as a failure in psychic structure formation, but also as a failure in psychic structure function that is due to intrapsychic defense.

Notes

[1] See Kavaler on the "demon-lover" (1985, 1986, 1988a, 1989b).
[2] The mother who couldn't say "no" to her.
[3] Ms. A. used the term "black sheep" within the session and often depicted herself as her family's scapegoat. She had said at some point in the session that being on her own in the present world was too complicated, and that she liked to go back to the days when mothers were mothers, fathers were fathers, and black sheep were black sheep rather than bragging rebels.

CHAPTER 5

OPENING UP BLOCKED MOURNING
IN THE PRECŒDIPAL CHARACTER

Originally published in 1995, *American Journal of Psychoanalysis* 55(1):74–81.

It has been debated in the literature whether children are able to mourn. Margaret Mahler (1975) writes of the normal separation-individuation mourning of toddlers as "low keyedness." Gorkin (1984) reports about Furman's (1964) studies, which demonstrate that children are capable of mourning once object constancy has been attained, due to the adequate internalization of good object representations. Hans Loewald (1962) writes of the oedipal stage mourning of childhood that results in superego formation. Edith Jacobson (1964) writes of the natural mourning necessary to successfully navigate through adolescence to adulthood. Wolfenstein (1966), in contrast, has maintained that when there are actual losses of loved ones, children and adolescents are not capable of mourning, resulting in pathological reenactments of abandonment and loss.

Melanie Klein (1940), in her writing on mourning and manic-depressive states, and Hanna Segal (1952, 1985), in her work on the capacity for symbol formation, have maintained that mourning is a critical clinical and developmental process to open up all cognitive processes that differentiate identity and interpersonal relations, processes that others such as Mahler might relate to separation-individuation. Thomas Ogden (1986) speaks of the capacity for depressive position mourning as a prerequisite for the development of the subjectivity of the self, and for the development of awareness of oneself being an "interpreting subject," that is, one who is continually creating his own reality by generating meanings.

In the following case, it can be seen that the opening up of blocked mourning for a parent who died in childhood was the critical avenue to transforming characterological resistances to self-integration. The split-off bad self, acted out in sadomasochistic terms with powerful projective identification processes operating, as well as the cool superiority of the manic defense as a contemptuous facade, are transformed into more mature modes of interpersonal relatedness in which the patient can verbally articulate concerns about her own aggression.

The case of Ms. R., to be presented, illustrates how the combination of the therapist's "object survival" (Winnicott, 1971), the internalization of interpersonal structures stemming from the resulting affect contact, and the mourning process that was able to evolve along with such structuralization, all combined to modify archaic aggression resulting from childhood trauma, opening up love in a newly symbolized relatedness.

The loss of a parent in childhood is severely traumatic. However, when earlier separation-individuation issues have not been resolved, the trauma is compounded. In the case of Ms. R., opening up the mourning of her mother, who died during the latency years, also served as the key to mourning the early symbiotic mother who was always there to meet the patient's physical needs, but who was generally absent emotionally, as well as never being able to say "no" or set limits with the patient.

The transference reflected a split object transference, related to a borderline splitting in self structure. This split object consisted of a negative father who failed to facilitate developmental separation and also intruded on and opposed the fusion with the idealized symbiotic mother, who was also a primary mother of symbiotic nurturance for whom the patient's yearnings had become eroticized (the erotic aspect appears in Ms. R.'s second reported dream).

The characterological reenactment took the form of yearning for the symbiotic mother, followed by enraged contempt and provocations toward the negative transferential father when attempts to merge with the transferential mother were frustrated. The negative transferential father can also be seen as a split-off negative mother, operating as an internal object at a primary object connection level. This distancing behavior, which perpetually followed the frustration of yearnings for a merger, threatened to continuously re-create disruptions in the patient's interpersonal relations. In order to transform the distancing behavior in relation to the negative father, the mourning of the symbiotic mother was necessary. The mourning of the symbiotic mother could only take place when mourning of the mother's death was contained and processed in treatment.

In line with Melanie Klein's writing on the mourning process (1940), this case demonstrates how such mourning involved the grieving of intense guilt. Unlike Freud, who noted the significance of mourning in "Mourning and Melancholia" (1917), but who only focused on the painful grieving of loss in mourning, Melanie Klein included guilt over one's aggression as a necessary part of the grieving process. Her critical paper on "Mourning and Its Relation to Manic Depressive States" (1940), and all her varied writings on aspects of the depressive position, emphasized the grieving of guilt.

This case is offered to illustrate how the sequence of aggression, guilt, and loss can be navigated by the psychoanalyst who is aware of the developmental vicissitudes of the mourning process. It illustrates how Winnicott's (1969) theory of object survival interacts with Melanie Klein's view on mourning, when mourning displays a developmental sequence, from hostile aggression to contained aggression with the acknowledgment of guilt, and then the grieving of the pain of guilt leading to the tolerance of loss.

In this case, the analyst is seen to survive the patient's most intense aggression, as aggression finally crystallizes in the transference as a hot rage, following displacements and cool characterological contempt. The rage is directed against the transferential bad (part-object) father (related to elements of a split-off inadequate early mother), and when the analyst survives it by remaining related (Winnicott, object survival, 1969), and not retaliating, the patient is able to open up to dysphoric affects, and to the accompanying depressive position capacities of free association, interpretation, and the freeing of repressed feeling states for the first time.

Surviving the aggression, the analyst is for the first time seen as an analyst, rather than as a symbiotic mother or as the disappointing and rejecting bad object father. As an outgrowth of survival of aggression, the analyst also survives the patient's moves toward separation. A working alliance is formed, and dream interpretation leads to transference interpretation, resulting in the opening up of unconscious guilt and the accompanying pain of blocked mourning. The mother's death is grieved as the patient grieves the guilt of her hatred for her beloved and lost mother. The therapeutic sequence illustrates how critical the interplay is between Winnicott's clinical capacity for object survival and for the analyst's role in providing a holding environment of Klein's developmental mourning process. Once the depressive affects of the mourning process are reached, transformations in psychic structure occur, as Thomas Ogden (1986) has so clearly outlined in *The Matrix of the Mind*. This case illustrates how the combination of object survival and mourning of depressive grief can result in the development of an interpersonal and intrapsychic dialectic.

This dialectic, in turn, develops the subjectivity of the self, and the self's capacity to generate meanings, and to know that it is generating meanings. It will be seen in the following case that the opening up of a full mourning process promoted the patient's capacities to engage in a therapeutic dialogue and to reflect on the self rather than to be reactive or provocative. The patient became capable of listening to the therapist and therefore became able to take in internalizations of an interpersonal dialectic necessary to build in psychic structure. The patient became capable of talking to the therapist symbolically rather than using words as attacks, seductions, or provocations. As Ms. R. no longer needed to ward off the pain of grief, guilt, and loss, she became able to take in that therapist on an emotional level, to express gratitude, and to function on a level of symbolic communications, where interpretations from the analyst could be received as symbolic communications.

The Case of Ms. R.

Ms. R. first entered psychoanalytic psychotherapy treatment at the age of 35. She had a brief counseling experience in the past, which dealt with her manifest relationships, without engaging with her inner life or with her transference dynamics. She yearned for something deeper than that experience, as she was later to tell me in treatment, but she was also terrified of the kind of emotional contact necessary for that to happen.

Ms. R. contacted me after hearing a lecture I delivered on "Fathers and Daughters." She was attracted both to the content of my lecture and to my mode of lecturing (i.e., spontaneously, without notes). She seemed to begin with a tentative and rather fragile "idealizing transference" (Kohut, 1971), which was a thin veil for both intense primitive yearnings for a primal symbiosis and intense paranoid fears related to these desires and the very real childhood trauma that had disrupted her prolonged symbiotic relationship with her mother. Ms. R. began twice-weekly treatment with me, which she sustained with great difficulty for four and a half years. As will be seen from the case discussion, Ms. R.'s fourth year of treatment brought a critical turning point into character transformation that stemmed from the opening up of a pathologically arrested mourning process.

Ms. R.'s early reports of her life center on the abusive behavior of her father. She was left alone with her father following her mother's death, which occurred when she was nine. Ms. R. had felt very close to her mother in a nonverbal way. Her mother generally did not talk with her, nor did she encourage her daughter to converse with her. Ms. R. seemed to yearn for a state of being with her mother in a comfortable silence, but all her developmental needs for a higher level mode of more differentiated communication were frustrated by this regressive wish. One way she had attempted, it seemed, to deal with this conflict was to idealize the silent symbiotic mother, splitting off all awareness of the mother's frustrations.

Consequently, she enacted the frustrations in an aggressively hostile and withholding silence. This was a silence that separated us, which was quite different from the silence of communion that I experienced in the later phase of treatment. The frustrations of the mother's regressive symbiosis, and the father's use of language as hostile accusatory demands for submission, were combined in this hostile mode of silence. Ms. R. seemed to be attempting to merge with her mother, despite her needs for differentiation and to be simultaneously holding back verbal communication with her father who would use anything she said against her, as she related to me in reporting (in a detached and yet arrogant way) about the father's abuse.

At the same time that Ms. R. maintained (in her idealizing defense) that she had been free to be any way she wished with her mother, she also reported contradictory memories of the mother being a frenetic worker, who was constantly preoccupied. Ms. R. described her mother as working nonstop from dawn to dusk. Her mother did constant housework, including many heavy and repetitive chores. She washed several loads of laundry a day in an old-style washing machine, having to turn a handle continuously to dry and wring out the clothes. She did extensive cooking and baking, always serving her husband his favorite treats. When she finally finished her chores, she lay down on a couch, exhausted. She always appeared exhausted to Ms. R. The year prior to Ms. R.'s ninth birthday, her mother got weaker and weaker, and her efforts to continue all her household tasks could be seen in the strain of her thinning arms as she turned the handle on the washing machine.

According to Ms. R., her mother was loved by everyone. She is reported to have never said "no" to anyone. In particular, she never said "no" to Ms. R.'s father, nor to Ms. R. herself. This suited the father quite well, for when his wife was alive he was extensively catered to. However, when Ms. R.'s mother developed cancer, she rapidly weakened over the course of a year. Her death then brought a harsh and dramatic change in Ms. R.'s own life as well as in that of her father.

The first night after her mother's death, Ms. R.'s father threw her into the shower and shouted at her, "You have to wash your hair yourself. You have no mother anymore!" Ms. R. remembered being terrified, crying, and screaming in the shower. She remembered not knowing how to wash her hair and going to bed with her hair full of soap. She remembered night after night of crying all alone in her bed. Briefly, she was allowed to live with her older brother's family. However, she ran away from her brother's house and was promptly returned to her father.

Once back with her father, Ms. R. was turned into her father's maid and cook. Her father commanded her to do all of the extensive housework that her mother used to do. If she didn't do everything perfectly, he might suddenly beat her with a mop, stick, or belt. At other times, Ms. R.'s father would just scream at her. She never knew what to expect. She lived in a constant state of terror, which was reflected in her dreams, and which was in the background of our therapy sessions at all times. One of Ms. R.'s initial means of connecting to me, as her therapist, was when I sensed how terrified she was on an ongoing basis.

As Ms. R. approached puberty and adolescence, her father began to molest her in a manner that seemed bizarre and shocking to his daughter. Her father would jump upon her in a state of sexual arousal, rubbing himself upon her, sticking his hand down her pants. Then he would jump off her as soon as he had found relief. Other frightening incidents that Ms. R. would defend against feeling by labeling them as bizarre or absurd was that of her father telling her that he would educate her by pulling his pants down and showing her what a penis was.

Ms. R. came to identify with her father's narcissistic and paranoid character as a defense against the vulnerability within herself, which was promoted by all her childhood trauma. She also reacted to treatment as though it was a "bizarre" encounter with a malevolent or "demon-lover" father (Kavaler-Adler, 1986, 1988a, 1989b), a father whose phallic aggression was experienced as omnipotent and perpetually intrusive. When she experienced treatment in any more benevolent way, it seemed prompted by the induction of a maternal transference in which she felt protected, but she remained affectively sealed-off. Her character structure reflected both a narcissistic character defense, manifested as distancing to ward off contact, as well as a borderline masochistic mother personality, who was always overworked and exhausted.

First Three Years of Treatment

During the first three years of treatment, Ms. R. underwent some significant changes in her life outside of treatment, while remaining affectively sealed-off within the treatment setting. She sought empathy for her life situation and confrontation for self-destructive acting out, such as when she became pregnant and had an abortion for the ninth time in her life, and when she refused to get a mammography because she was convinced that she already had breast cancer like her mother.

When Ms. R. decided to abort her new pregnancy, she also came to terms with her belief that she could not continue to live with the man she had been living with at the initiation of treatment. Ms. R. was repelled by the sexual needs of the man she was living with. Although reporting herself to be highly erotic in brief heterosexual encounters, Ms. R. seemed to withdraw into a state of rigid contempt when she was faced with a man's sexual needs on a continuing basis, particularly when these sexual needs were invested with powerful dependency needs. Since she, herself, was deeply ashamed of her dependency needs, she was repelled when she encountered such needs in a man.

Ms. R. also judged her boyfriend to be inferior to her in intellect and education. She had remained with him during a career change when she needed both emotional and financial support to get the education she required. During the third year of treatment, she moved out of her living situation with this man. She experienced some loneliness and began to date a man who was more narcissistic and detached than her boyfriend, and she saw herself as severely victimized when he was at first emotionally unavailable and then when he, in her words, "dumped" her.

Ms. R. also tried to turn to girlfriends for companionship, while feeling much frustration and disappointment with these women. However, over the course of therapy, she began to differentiate what she could realistically expect from each of her girlfriends. When her mourning process later opened up in treatment, she was able to verbally express affection for her girlfriends for the first time, and even though some of her friends were too narcissistic to respond to this affection, she was able to take in the response of one girlfriend who reciprocated her feelings and was ultimately able to sustain a caring relationship with this girlfriend. Up until that time, however, she remained resentful of her girlfriends, always seeing them as too demanding or as too unavailable.

During the three years of treatment, prior to the opening up of the blocked mourning, the psychoanalytic psychotherapy process reflected a vicious cycle of part-object projections onto the analyst, which could only be resolved when the sealed-off affect life was opened up during the fourth-year mourning process. These part-object projections took the form of reacting to me as a good symbiotic mother at the initial stage of the cycle, only to be disappointed as her illusion of symbiosis was shattered when we could not merge in a wordless state. Her own sealed-off hostile aggression made this impossible.

Once the illusion of symbiosis with the idealized mother was shattered, I immediately turned into the threatening narcissistic and sadistic father. As this pattern developed, it seemed like there would be one mother session, followed by one father session, and then followed by another mother session. When I attempted to reach out to Ms. R., beyond the aloofness she showed in the father sessions, I was largely unsuccessful until the mourning process began to take place. The cycle would automatically continue, in the sense of a constant reenactment of having mother, and then being left alone with father (which could also be seen as being left with the early mother who failed to provide empathic contact during moves toward individuation). When I interpreted this to Ms. R., she experienced my interpretation as a gift for which she had to keep any gratitude secret. She was very hidden in her reactions to me throughout this three-year period.

Descriptive Characteristics of Ms. R.'s Character

Ms. R. demonstrated major descriptive attributes characteristic of narcissistic personality disorders, although the borderline sadomasochistic character traits (related to the father's sadism and the mother's masochism) were evident as well. For the first few years of treatment, Ms. R. had a wall up against affective contact. She would withdraw into a state that might be described as Modell's (1976) cocoon state. Like Modell's narcissists, she would like to give the appearance of total self-sufficiency, as she would lie on the couch and declare, "I have nothing to say." Eventually, this kind of declaration changed into a more willful opposition, as she began to own her resistance, saying, "I don't want to talk."

Interpretations were generally repelled. They were not mutative at this point (see Strachey, 1934), since affect was still sealed-off, defensively blocking symbolic understanding. The following developmental, as opposed to defense interpretations, however, could be tolerated. They were felt as empathic and containing. These were interpretations about Ms. R.'s wish to "re-create a state" (Stolorow & Lachman, 1980) in which she was alone with her mother in silence, or in which she was engaged in a self-protection against an intrusive father who would use anything she said against her (in the father session).

Ms. R. spoke in a detached way. She was in a manic stance (Klein, 1940), above her feeling self, as she lectured to me on "life." She described a cold, loveless world where "God had not taken care of business." She frequently lectured to me about people and the way of the world. The only warmth in her loveless world, which she would describe, was the care she gave her patients. As an occupational therapist, she was in control. Others were dependent on her. In this realm, she could function. However, she would overextend herself as her mother had. Then she would end up feeling that her patients were ungrateful. Her patients then became characters in her cold and loveless world.

Structural Characteristics of Ms. R.'s Character

Ms. R. was withdrawn, contemptuous, and devaluing of me. This description is generally symptomatic of narcissistic character pathology, but it cites only behavioral appearance. From a structural viewpoint, Ms. R.'s detachment, and her positioning herself above both her inner self and above me,[1] can be seen as the result of an inner fusion of self and early other, which she perpetually tried to reenact with me in the transference, in which I was in the role of the omnipotent other with which she was psychically fused. This mode of primitive fusion within her internal world had never successfully been resolved into modes of interpersonal connection through the symbolic language of the separate and differentiated self, and so any free mode of mutual interaction was obviated. Ms. R., consequently, induced in me, her analyst, a sense of helpless muteness, particularly when she was most identified with her vindictive and controlling father.

At other times, she induced in me the feelings of me being the intrusive and molesting father. She then responded to me as if she was being molested and phallically raped. In the manner of a borderline mode of disconnection, Ms. R. continually disrupted the therapeutic process by forgetting. She "forgot" what happened from one session to the next. Her forgetfulness was particularly severe and felt like a profound denial promoted by the perpetual blocking of affect so that she could block feeling connections with her internal and traumatizing objects.

Ms. R. also displayed a consistent defensive mode of internal splitting. When she saw me as the bad father (or bad mother-father, given the primary level of the developmental split), she seemed incapable, at an affective level, to connect with other times when she had experienced me as the "idealized" mother (see Kernberg, 1975). She constantly tried to split-off and project the bad, explosively aggressive, and hateful part of herself. The loving part of her was not tolerable unless she was in a position of control. She cut off from loving feelings with me, "forgetting" them. She apparently felt too vulnerable to sustain them. She became acutely ashamed when she was forced to confront her need for me, as for example, whenever she saw my concern during a loving moment. Her own capacity to love emerged at times, but any acknowledgment of it caused her to withdraw back inside herself, into hiding.

Walled off in her narcissistic state of self-sufficiency, Ms. R.'s reality testing was generally more adequate than the borderline character who lacks such narcissistic defense. As she put it, she had to "pay her dues." She complied, unlike many borderline characters, with the structures of her work, and with the imposition of treatment, despite a vision of a harsh reality. She "paid her dues" by paying her treatment fees. As her internal split did not extend to pervasive fragmentation, she could sustain sufficient organization to function within the limits of reality, even though she was continually exhausted from rigid defense processes (those of continually warding off affect so that she could function and care for herself).

Ms. R. did not have the flexibility of a higher-level neurotic character. Her intense narcissistic vulnerability opposed her capacity to internalize good from another and to express gratitude so that the good might be contained. Her defensive paranoia, in the face of pressure for interpersonal engagement, was apparent. She shielded herself from conscious shame by warding me off whenever she couldn't successfully recreate a state of fusion with me as an environmental mother (Winnicott, 1971), i.e., when she couldn't create me into the externalization of an internal symbiotic mother. Meanwhile, her affect block prevented me from feeling the feelings of a symbiotic mother, which was to distinctly change once Ms. R.'s mourning process could open the doors to affect contact and connection.

Dreams

When not withdrawn into a tight and resistant silence, or lecturing to me, Ms. R. sometimes reported dreams. She generally did so in a curt and hurried manner. She often referred to her dreams as some weird foreign eruption from her psyche, which she couldn't comprehend. Her dreams were often filled with violent expulsions of one kind or another. Nuclear holocausts and military maneuvers in "end-of-the-world" scenarios gave a terrifying sense of annihilation to her dreams. However, there were also more hopeful elements in her dreams. In one dream, she was lost in the wilderness, but some magical maternal figure rescued her. In another dream, she opened up a child's toy and found rich, colorful, and wonderful things inside, which I believe related to her own hidden inner core, the core originally connected with the idealized symbiotic mother. Ms. R.'s wishes for me to prove to be this magical internal mother were an important part of her motivation for treatment. As with Modell's cocoon state narcissist, the breakdown of this wish for me to be the idealized mother resulted in intense rage, which then became the opening to contact and ultimately to grief and a primary level of object connection in the interpersonal world.

When Ms. R. reported these dreams, she was extremely self-conscious and resistant to the cultivation of an associative process. No inner dialogue emerged from within. If I asked her what her thoughts were about a dream, or what she felt within it, she responded defensively, enraged that she couldn't please me. I believe that Ms. R.'s wish to please me defended her against intense shame related to the idealized transference wishes that appeared in her dreams. Her attempts to please (and placate me) also seemed intended to defend her against intense guilt related to the extreme violent impulses that she carried with her, which were explicitly seen in the violence of her internal world as it was displayed in her dreams.

Ms. R. was too fearful about my judgments at this point in treatment to expose her thoughts. Her own internal pressure to do my bidding made her feel intensely frustrated. She would easily flare-up in a tantrum-like rage. Following this, she would attempt to undo her aggression with a pseudo-compliance, and her inability to please me by doing this would again provoke her into withdrawal or rage. Yet, her cold rages thawed over time. They began to get hotter and hotter. On rare occasions, Ms. R. would be able to talk obliquely, through aggressive provocations, about the internal maelstrom that terrified her. She would say that she wished to smash my windows and to throw all my plants down on the floor. Often, she could not conceptualize these impulses. Then she would become caught in a state of paralysis and would either fail to show for a session, would come late, would be silent, or would be unable to contain herself without distracting gestures and constant agitation. The agitated state once prompted her to "give up" and to leave in the middle of a session.

If Ms. R. expressed her rage, and could not defend against it by pulling me into a power struggle or shouting match, she would sometimes move to a different level of experience, losing her rigidly entrenched guard, and would burst into a moment of tears. One day this happened as I pointed out that she was experiencing me as an intrusive and molesting father. She burst into tears of anguish, exclaiming, "I was just a baby! Why wasn't God there?" I suspected that her wishing for God was a wish for her mother who had abandoned her to her father, but I intuited she was not ready to make this connection at that time, and any attempt on my part to interpret was warded off, never affectively penetrating her consciousness. In Modell's terms (1976), she was still in her cocoon.

One dream stands out from this period, in which mourning was still predominantly blocked. She dreamed:

> You had a baby and were surrounded by a nurse and governess while you held your baby. I asked to hold your baby. You seemed apprehensive and gave the baby to the governess instead. I ran out of the room and down into the street. Outside everything was wild and out of control. Your husband came to pick you up in a car, and a truck smashed into the car.

My attempt to request Ms. R.'s associations was met by her with comments on how crazy and weird it all seemed. She then commented that I didn't want her to hold the baby. She seemed upset by this, but could not stay with it. She just said, "You didn't trust me! That's awful! You didn't trust me!" Then, she said that I was different than her and her mother because I had a governess. She seemed compelled to divide us rather than allowing me to help her understand the dream and why she didn't see herself as ready to hold a baby (the baby inside of her?).

I suggested to Ms. R. that the car and truck smashing had to do with her internal reaction to my distrusting her in the dream. I told her that I believed that she put her reaction outside of herself because she felt she wouldn't tolerate it. When she put her upset reaction outside of her, the external world became dangerously out of control. She had trouble understanding this and was still so walled off against me affectively penetrating her that interpretations at this point proved useless. I didn't press my views on her, but I thought to myself that the baby in the dream was the part of her that wished to surrender to me and to let down her defenses. I saw the baby in the dream as the tender part of her that she felt compelled to guard against my view or touch.

The following speculations of my own on the dream are an attempt to explain Ms. R.'s psychic dilemma, in which she was compelled to block a necessary developmental mourning and healing process in order to defend against the raw primitive aggression that she carried with her from the time of her childhood trauma. I would agree with Rinsley (1988) that the perpetuation of archaic aggression was inevitable since the containment of higher-level repressive processes requires neutralized aggression, which Ms. R.'s background (the failure to have "good-enough" parenting), and its consequent reactive splitting process, prevented her from attaining.

Within the dream, Ms. R. seemed to put aspects of a nurturant mother figure— as seen in the nurse and the governess—between us, so that she might protect us both from her own aggression. Her aggression was expressed in a displaced form as a truck smashing into my husband's car. Since her aggression toward me had been so centered in the father transference, her phallic assault on my husband, through the truck, might also be interpreted as her way of killing her father off, possibly in the hope of regaining her dead preoedipal mother, who was an active and persistent presence within her internal world. By warding off her aggression, as well as by disconnecting from the baby or tender part of herself, Ms. R. lost vital aspects of herself, aspects that she would need to feel and contain in order to process the grief and loss of mourning.

Although Ms. R. appeared to be identified with the baby in her dream, the identification appeared unconscious and therefore unavailable to her. Therefore, Ms. R. could not allow contact between her more vulnerable self and the diverse mother figures in the dream, all of whom appeared to be parts of me as her transferential mother. The dream portrayed a symbiotic union between myself and the baby, which was split-off from Ms. R.'s central and conscious self, preventing any direct emotional contact and connection between her and me, which could help her contain her aggression. Consequently, there was no object-related connection to help Ms. R. go beyond her aggression to the owning and processing of grief, loss, and guilt affects, all of which were latently there in her unconscious connection to her mother, following the disruption of the symbiotic fusion with her mother that occurred with the mother's death. Without any object-related affect connection with her internal mother, due to blocked mourning, there is no psychic structure for a psychic dialectic. Ms. R. needed to gain this structure by affectively connecting with me. The following descriptions of the clinical process within the fourth year of Ms. R.'s treatment allowed this to finally happen.

Critical Treatment Developments that Allowed Mourning to Begin

The fourth year of treatment began with Ms. R. bringing to me a journal that she had written during the time that I was away on a summer vacation. She had written this journal on the days when she normally would be attending sessions with me. Her attempt to keep a sustained thread of contact with her treatment while I was away was a new development. The journal served as some form of transitional phenomenon (Winnicott, 1971), which she employed, while I, her transitional object, was away.

The journal allowed Ms. R. to refrain from acting out self-destructively as she had during past vacations.[2] The journal reflected a demand for mirroring that was partially defensive, although developmental needs for confirmation of her talents were at play as well. Her wish that I read the journal upon my return had an insistent quality to it. It seemed to reflect the mirroring transference development, as Kohut has articulated to be characteristic of the narcissist (1971). In this case, the mirroring transference emerged in reaction to separation and following the breakdown of the idealizing transference into a mode of devaluation.

However, it is also reflective of the malignant regression described by Michael Balint (1968), in which the patient's instinctual demands for the analyst to do a particular thing for him or her requires limit setting. Without this limit setting, the malignant regression cannot be transformed into the benign regression in which the patient actually experiences the internal state related to his or her urgent cravings.

When I set a limit by telling Ms. R. that I would not read her journal outside the frame of our sessions, but would maintain the boundaries (in a way that prevented her from splitting off wishes for my admiration and my presence from her own conscious experience), she got angry. I invited Ms. R. to read her journal to me within the time structure of the session when she would be present with me. This was hard for her to do, for she was forced to consciously experience the shame that she felt in displaying her own exhibitionistic desires and her wishes for my attention. Her initial angry reaction appeared to come from her self-consciousness as well as from her fear of exposure.

Nevertheless, Ms. R.'s desire for my attention won out. Despite her anger, Ms. R. read a section of her journal to me—only as much as fit into one session. I responded with interest, commenting on her abilities to articulate her observations through writing. Ms. R. had formerly revealed to me, with some disclaimers, her secret wishes to write. As she read her writing from her journal to me, she revealed her observations of others who were characters in her life. There were also brief comments about her own state of mind, and many philosophical questions about life. Ms. R. became most self-conscious when speaking about herself, and became more entertaining when she described others in her writing.

After this session, Ms. R. never mentioned the journal again, but the manifest content of all her detached thoughts and reports reflected the experience of having read to me the journal. For instance, Ms. R. recalled a time when she wrote a speech for a graduation ceremony, but she wouldn't read the speech herself. A friend consented to read it for her. While the friend read, Ms. R. listened intently to detect whether everyone was laughing "in the right spots." She was pleased that they did. When I connected their laughter with my own interest at the time she read her journal to me, she became irritable, seemingly ashamed of her demand for mirroring when it was made explicit. She reacted to her shame by attacking me. Through projection, she made me the one who wanted all the attention.

I then became the narcissistic father in the transference, as well as that part of her that wanted totally undivided attention. She demanded and accused, "Why are you always talking about yourself?" In her tone of devaluing contempt, she exclaimed, "I want to talk about things outside, about my 'real' life, not about what goes on in this sterile office that I'm stuck in with you!" I noted to myself that she was speaking to me as though I was the emotionally empty narcissistic father, inside of whose house she was perpetually imprisoned following her mother's death. Inside her father's house, she was forced into the sterile activities of cleaning, not being able to go out with her friends, and not being allowed to play. Yet the sterile prison might more aptly be related to the mother since the father was violent, shocking, and sensational.

At the earlier level of the internal mother, the transference suggested that I was the physically present but emotionally and cognitively absent mother, whose silent caretaking, without verbal communication, and without the emotional contact and mirroring related to verbal dialogue, made Ms. R. feel as a child that she was encased in a sterile environment. This negative aspect of the mother was perceived through the demonic image of the father but represented a primary split in the mother representation, which perpetuated a wish to merge with the split-off idealized mother.

During this time, Ms. R.'s anger was seething, brewing, and building. Ms. R. began to test me with provocative requests. The ends of sessions were particularly difficult for her. Not having separated from a symbiotic mother, the session limit seemed to arouse anxiety that reflected untapped rage related to separation and loss. One day, as I said it was time to go, Ms. R. demanded, "Can I borrow one of your magazines?" "No," I said, "but you can come early and read it in the waiting room." She replied that she would never sit in that waiting room. Then, with a strain of ridiculing laughter, "It's so you! No windows!" At this point, she cut me off from commenting, said her session was over, and slammed the door in my face as she left. She had turned our ending into a provocative play to have the last word. She had it. She avoided feeling any sense of loss by turning the tables on me. She took charge of ending the session after I had already ended it.

Early on the evening of her next appointed session, I received a message from Ms. R. on my answering machine, "Can I see you on Friday instead of tonight, due to the weather?" It was raining out. I noted to myself that she knew that I did not have office hours on Friday. Friday was also connected with being special because I had occasionally seen her on Friday in the past when we couldn't work out any other time due to her rotating job schedule. I called her back and let her repeat her request. I responded briefly, "I have the time reserved for you at your session time" There was a pause as she waited to get more from me. Then she said, "Okay, good-bye," and hung up. I wondered if she would be coming that night. Due to her inflamed state of desire, I thought she would come. Then, as a major part of her session time passed, I thought I was wrong. However, it turned out that Ms. R. arrived later, after having gotten stuck on the subway.

Ms. R. then lay down on the couch and demanded in an imperious manner, "Now explain to me why you wouldn't change my session time!" I noted to myself her pressure to pull me into a masochistic submission with this demand. So, I merely replied, "I told you I don't do that, but I'm interested in hearing your feelings." At that point, she seemed to let go of all the pent-up rage that she had been harboring. At the height of her negative transference, she shouted:

You won't do one little favor for me! I got stuck on the subway and I thought I would have a heart attack feeling that I had to get here. You don't care that I have to travel on the damn F train, which always breaks down. I'm abusing myself by coming here. I just want you to know that my friend and I might invest in something together, and then I won't have the money to come to therapy. I think you should know. It's torture coming here. I don't even like you. You're a classical Freudian. You charge me for all my missed sessions. I can't afford this. I'm not rich. You have all the control and I'm the slave. You're so mean! Tell me why you did that to me! Why won't you answer me?

I responded:

Your questions are accusations, not questions. However, I see that the nuclear holocausts that used to only be in your dreams are coming out in the open here. Your war is right between us now.

She cut me off, shouting:

> I'm sick of dragging myself here. You don't even appreciate how I kill myself to come when I'm so tired. You don't even care that I was trying to come. I could have just missed the session. You don't even appreciate my effort. The rain is a reality. The cold is a reality. It's not me. Why are you so mean?

Toward the end of the session, I said to her, "People who blame others are usually blaming themselves for something."

At this point, there was a pause as Ms. R. seemed to become reflective for the first time in the session. She suddenly sounded quite interested in what I had to say, and became quite related as she responded, "What do you think I'm blaming myself for?"

I thought to myself that Ms. R. was filled with guilt, blaming herself for her mother's death, feeling she had killed her mother. I didn't know how we were going to get to that from where we were. I said to Ms. R., "We can get to it. Right now everything feels urgent because you're in a rage, but it's time to go."

She mimicked me in a mocking voice, "It's time to go!" As she got up to leave, she said, "I really want to wind this down."

The next week she appeared on time for her sessions. She came in on the first day in a rather sober and related mood, saying she had a dream she wanted to tell me. She said her dream had been extremely vivid and in four parts.

The Dream that Leads to Mourning

The first part of her dream involved an image of her mother coming down to her from above. She grabbed her mother's hand and started sobbing and sobbing as her mother pulled away from her again. This part of the dream can be related not only to the loss of the mother through the mother's death but also to the emotional abandonments by the mother in her failure to support her daughter's separation and individuation process. The mother's death could replicate the earlier losses. However, the patient's associations did not focus on this.

In the second part of the dream, she was sucking on her girlfriend's breasts. She started grinding her pelvis against her friend and felt turned on. Then a man entered the room. She jumped off the bed and ran into a closet to hide. She was in the bedroom of the apartment in which she had lived with her father after her mother's death.

The third part of the dream particularly captured Ms. R.'s interest. At first, there was a man who was giving her money. Then she turned into a black boy, who was delivering fast food. Ms. R. commented on how she disliked fast food. "It was like shit!" she said. [I noted to myself that this was in contrast to the slow food of breastfeeding, the kind of feeding she desired in the earlier segment of the dream.] She also said, several times, that it was strange to her that the ratio of money was out of proportion to what was being delivered. The money seemed much too much for the food.

In the last part of the dream, there was somebody riding a bicycle, who disappeared into the distance. She said she wished she could decipher who the person was.

Associations and Interpretations

Ms. R.'s associations were more forthcoming in discussing this dream than at any time prior. She spoke of holding her mother's hand and of sobbing in the first part of the dream. She spoke of her anxiety about sucking her girlfriend's breasts, and about having sexual feelings toward a woman. However, it was the third part of the dream that was to become a prominent focus of our attention. Ms. R. kept saying how she hated fast food. The ratio of money given to this black guy was out of proportion to the value of the food. Ms. R. made it clear that she was the black guy in the dream, and I was the man giving her money for the food.

For the first time, Ms. R. stayed with a dream, and also with the subject matter of our session in which the dream was reported, overnight and between sessions. She came into her next session with more thoughts about the dream. She said that I was Ronald Reagan and she was the black guy in the third part of the dream. Again, she remarked with surprise that I, as Ronald Reagan, was giving the money to her, instead of the other way around—" And why so much money?" she asked.

As Ms. R. was still sitting up on the couch, she said that she felt sad about the part of the dream with her mother. I responded by saying that if she could let me into her sadness we wouldn't have to be enemies. The moment I said this, she seemed to melt. She lay down on the couch and curled up in a fetal position. I felt the change viscerally since Ms. R. had always laid on the couch in the most still and tense fashion in the past. My comment about finding a place together beyond the enemy position in which she had been stuck seemed to have touched her. Her reaction was shown in movement and remained unconscious.

As she opened herself emotionally, it was clear that she sensed my ability to be in a more communal place with her. She was more open to that awareness now than ever before. She began to talk about the dream again, showing continued interest in exploring it, but having no further associations.

Interpretations and Mourning

I then told Ms. R. that I had something to say about it if she wanted to hear it. In a spontaneous and enthusiastic manner that was uncharacteristic for her, she said that she really wanted to hear what I had to say. Her tone was soft, open, and friendly—quite in contrast to the resistant, cold, and silent wall that she had generally put up against me. So I plunged in. In response to her continuing puzzlement about why I (as Ronald Reagan) would be giving money to her, rather than the other way around, I said: "Consciously you see yourself as giving so much to me and not getting from me, but unconsciously it's just the opposite. Unconsciously you feel that I am giving and giving to you, and you are taking and taking and using me up, just like you felt you used up your mother and killed her!"

Instantly, Ms. R. erupted with the age-old cry of a child in guilt-laden grief and despair. Lying on the couch, she began to gyrate back and forth as she cried:

It's true. I did it! It's true! It's true! I did it! I did it! My mother wanted to die, but she had to keep going for me. I wouldn't let her go. She loved me so much and I hated her. I hated her because she was so old. I wanted a young mother. All my friends' mothers were young. When you get what you want it's not really what you want. My sister-in-law was young, but when my mother died and I was sent to live with her I didn't want to stay. I wanted my mother! You only have one mother! There will never be anyone like my mother. I've lost her forever! She loved me so much more than I loved her. I've hated myself for it.

Ms. R.'s cries became sobs. The floodgates, so long barricaded, were open. Ms. R. sobbed and sobbed, lying down and then sitting up. Her dream of holding her mother's hand and sobbing was emerging into a conscious experience in the moment with me. Her grief broke through as guilt was exposed. She sat up, still crying. I reminded her that I had tissues next to the couch. She didn't move. Then I said that she obviously did not deserve to use my tissues because she was so bad. This must have registered because she immediately reached out for a tissue. She would take my comfort when I acknowledged the guilt that she had harbored for so long.

Before she left that session, I said I was glad we had reached this point. Ms. R. said, "I am too." This was a major acknowledgment for her. I then told her that I had wondered if she would give me a sharp verbal slap as she had in the past when I made our work explicit. I said that instead she had been able to take me in, to take in my help and to begin to acknowledge it. I was speaking to Ms. R. about critical new achievements that were signs of her moving into the depressive position (Klein, 1940). Ms. R. was beginning to tolerate the vulnerability of needing and loving after her traumatic past. She was beginning to integrate herself by integrating her love and hate for a primal internal object and its transference representative, as found in me, her analyst.

Not long after this session, Ms. R. was able to fall asleep during another therapy session. Her sleep was quite peaceful. Her ability to relax to such a degree in my presence was quite new. Her ability to feel good enough to sleep was not resistance but rather was a new phase of trust. As Ms. R. slept, I experienced the most harmonious and musical kinds of feelings stirring within me. I felt a tenderness from her, sensing the induction of baby feelings within my lips and fingertips. Ms. R. was finally letting me emotionally hold her, and thus letting me feel the baby within her. As she did so, we had progressed past the stage in which she dreamed I wouldn't trust her to hold my baby, which seemed to have a projective identification of her own fears of being held. Yet, Ms. R. could only fully surrender to being held in an unconscious state.

Following this session, Ms. R. returned to her distancing maneuvers, but these maneuvers were less rigid. Despite all the backlash reactions, due to her fears of closeness with me, Ms. R. was yielding to new capacities for relatedness as they developed within her. She became more able to talk to me, rather than to lecture at me in a monologue. She began to allow an exchange, a real conversation between us. She no longer walled me off and talked at me in a detached manner on any consistent basis.

One day, following the session in which her mourning process opened up, she told me that she had missed her mother again, but that it no longer hurt so much. She also let me know several months later that she was crying a lot. She cried with and for people now, not just in isolation. She began to feel her attachments to her friends and colleagues much more strongly.

After she returned from her own vacation, she wrote me a letter. She was able not only to write it, but also to read it to me, respectful now of the boundaries of the session, and of the work that these boundaries allowed us to do together. Her letter to me was quite a contrast to the journal she had read to me after our separation during my summer vacation. Although she began the letter with her usual distancing tactics, saying that she would have to leave therapy for financial reasons, she revealed a great deal of her hidden affection for me. This letter, like her tears, seemed to be part of a mourning process. I had become an object that she was addressing, not just a mirroring audience used to applaud her performance or an idealized mother with which she yearned to merge. Pathological mourning (in which she remained arrested in an attachment to a symbiotic mother and a sadistic narcissistic father, or father-mother of separation) was changing into true developmental mourning, seen in many different forms. The developmental mourning involved object-related grief, which could be felt. As she became capable of containing guilt, I needed to emotionally hold Ms. R. (Winnicott, 1971) within the psychic state of grieving her guilt. This allowed her to increase her capacity to contain guilt.

Through the structural work that had been done within the therapeutic Object Relationship (Grunes, 1984), Ms. R. had come to refine raw aggression into grief affects, which allowed her to contain and process her inner experience, and thus to make developmental advances in self-integration and individuation. As grief became tolerable, the developmental process proceeded, in which her internal objects were transformed, as she gradually formed loving connections to each of them. Her hated and loved symbiotic mother began to transform into a person she could talk to, through her engagement with me, her analyst, and through her letting go of the original silent mother as she grieved the loss prompted by her guilt toward that silent mother, as well as the loss of that mother's death itself. This relationship with me became a real Object Relationship in which interaction and dialogue became possible, whereas words and the symbolic communication of separate individuals had been absent with her real mother.

Ms. R.'s internal sadistic father, who used words only as accusations and demands for submission, was being transformed as well. Now Ms. R. could begin to talk to me. As mourning opened the psychic space for contact,[3] Ms. R. could use words for communication, and a dialectic developed between us, as it began to develop in her internal world. She could speak to the mother and father figures now who she so loved and hated. In parallel with this, her relationship with her still living father significantly improved, and she began to feel empathy for him.

I told Ms. R. of the tenderness I had felt as she slept peacefully through that one session. I can only guess that again my bringing to awareness the hints of intimacy between us embarrassed her, and she seemed compelled to attack me in response and to devalue the meaning of my message. I was aware that I was authentically conveying my experience with her, but the tenderness in my message seemed to evoke shame in her. She put me down and called me egocentric for presuming to read her messages in her unconscious state. D.W. Winnicott might have defended her response, saying that she needed to destroy my interpretations because I was being too omnipotent by making them. Yet, my experience with Ms. R. during this silent session of tenderness, of a peaceful sleep that seemed to allow her to be held in my metaphorical arms, allowed me to reach out to Ms. R. when she began to reveal her anxieties to me and to ask me if I thought she was a monster. I had gained access to the tender part of her and my ability to sustain connection with this tender part of her allowed my relationship with Ms. R. to transform. She responded by openly expressing her doubts about herself, which she had never been able to do before.

As I could reflect the goodness in her, she could show a new conscious concern and responsibility about her actual behavior and its effect on others. She was truly entering the depressive position now, the Kleinian position in which acknowledgment of one's own aggression (her hate for her mother, expressed in her grief) allows for a growing capacity for concern (Winnicott, 1965). The psychic space for reflection, and for the sustained connection with me that was necessary to consciously reflect, had been opened up by the mourning process. She had begun the grieving of her aggression and the grieving of her loss, and through such grieving had been able to reconnect with her primary love (see Balint, 1965).

Conclusion

Ms. R.'s new capacity for interpersonal dialogue seemed reflective of a new internal dialectic that was evolving within her as psychic space allowed for the opening up of mourning, and mourning in turn allowed for the opening up of psychic space. Ms. R.'s dialogue with me was continually being internalized so that a verbal-level dialectic could be internalized where once there was only a nonverbal mother-child dialogue. The internalizing of such a dialectic had been allowing a more flexible psychic structure to take form.

During the treatment stage following the therapy just described, Ms. R. asked me if she is "bad," and I could ask her about her concern. She began to tolerate my questions. She began to respond with discussion, reflection, and dialogue that showed the development of capacities for mutuality in relationships—all part of the depressive position and becoming an interpreting subject (Ogden, 1986). Ms. R. could now receive interpretations, beginning to see them as varying perspectives on meaning.

Formerly, Ms. R. intensely defended her fear of being bad with protests about what a good person she was. This had aroused critical feelings in me. In later work, Ms. R. was responsive and open to consideration of her intrapsychic conflict. This allowed me to feel much more positively to her, and she had been able to express gratitude toward me, a significant sign of self-integration, as Melanie Klein's writings (1957) help us understand. She told me that I've never stopped caring about her. However, she has also declared many times, as in the past, "You're not big on praise."

In response, I told her that she hid the best parts of her so that I couldn't respond to them. I was now able to tell her that as frightened as she'd been of her own aggression, she was even more frightened of her tenderness. She listened when I said this, now allowing the space between us for reflection, discussion, and communion, as we struggled together with her self-sabotaging tendencies to withdraw or attack.

The analyst's object survival led to the refining and neutralizing of archaic aggression, which was particularly profound due to developmental trauma. Object survival opened up the capacities for psychic space and interpersonal dialectics. The opening of such dialectics, along with the containment and tolerance for dysphoric grief affects (and for the depressive fantasies that accompanied those affects, related to the destruction of the object), allowed for a developmental mourning process.

This developmental mourning process is based on the dialectic of self and other within the internal world, and the negotiation of feelings of guilt and loss in relation to the object. The opening of an interpersonal dialectic allowed for the opening of an intrapsychic dialectic, and thus for mourning. Mourning, in turn, allowed for increasing degrees of sustained dialogue and for increasing degrees of self and object differentiation, as well as for increasing degrees of psychic space (where psychic conflict can be sustained), and for analytic space, where a holding environment could increasingly develop its interpersonal dialectic.

Ms. R.'s mother was not there in early development to support separation through mirroring, dialogue, and responsive interaction. Neither was the father a constructive agent for the daughter's separation. As the father became actively abusive, he began to maliciously undercut any needs of the daughter, including primary needs for separation, and for her to be loved for herself so that separation could be based on connection. As mourning of the "good mother" took place, the analyst supported this process by providing a holding environment for the mourning, and by facilitating moves toward separation that were formerly opposed.

In the case of Ms. R., mourning led to dialogue, and dialogue began to lead to deeper and deeper levels of mourning. In this way, Ms. R.'s capacities to love have been expanded, and her defensive hatred and archaic rage reactions were modified.

Notes

1 This behavior of being above the other, and above one's own needs, can be described in terms of Melanie Klein's manic defense or as a manifestation of a schizoid-grandiose self.
2 The preceding year she had gotten pregnant by the man with whom she lived and wished to leave. This resulted in her having to get an abortion, which was the ninth abortion of her lifetime. She seemed to have been acting out her wish for symbiosis repeatedly through pregnancies that she would then have to abort since, in reality, she was not at all ready to be a mother, and she was apparently seeking a symbiotic union with her own mother through the pregnancies.
3 Psychic space is also called "potential space" by Ogden (1986), who draws on D.W. Winnicott's ideas on the importance of a dialectical relation between psychic fantasy and psychic reality.

THE CASE OF DAVID: ON THE COUCH FOR SIXTY MINUTES, NINE YEARS OF ONCE-A-WEEK TREATMENT

Originally published in 2005, *American Journal of Psychoanalysis* 65(2):103–134.

Prior Treatment and Adult History

David had been in psychoanalytic treatment many times before coming to see me at the age of 42. In his early 20s, he had been in four-times-a-week treatment with a male analyst for five years. During this early analysis, David continually felt frustrated, bored, and blocked in self-expression. He could not seem to get past his blocks, and his sessions were full of complaints and verbalized intentions to leave, which seem to have been countered by the analyst's responding with interpretations that never seemed to ring true to David and did not seem to have had a psychic impact. Eventually, the analyst left David, leaving his practice for other career plans. David was left feeling very angry and very disillusioned with the idea of receiving any genuine psychotherapeutic help.

David had been angry for a long time in this analysis, but for a long time, had protected the analyst from his anger. When he did finally express his anger, it was mostly in terms of threats to leave the analysis and in terms of emotionally detached protests that he was required to attend four sessions a week. When the analyst made interpretations, they were perceived by David as arguments to keep him coming four times a week and to keep him coming to treatment. A power struggle ensued, ending with the analyst's announcing that he was leaving. Years later, during his third year of treatment with me, David woke up to all his rage at this analyst, crying out: "Why the hell was he trying to convince me to stay when he was planning the whole time to leave himself?"

At the time of the actual treatment, David's anger was repressed and was defended against with obsessional defenses that caused him to lack connection to his affects (and to the internal objects related to those affects). Consequently, he was apathetic and monotone in his expressions and was perpetually doubting everything in his life. David often spoke as if nothing seemed to really matter or to mean anything. A major exception to this was his relationship with his children. Also, David was disturbed by sexual conflicts related to a marriage that he experienced as growing increasingly dead.

David's entrapment in his own apathetic detachment made the whole world look gray to him. David would doubt any potential feeling, need, desire, or hunger. His capacity to love was truncated. In fact, he sexualized a great deal of feeling but split-off sexual impulses from any core self-desire. In his perpetually detached state, David had powerful libidinal urges that he did not know how to negotiate. This was at least partially the result of his having tried to control things by playing a good boy role with his wife, as he had with his mother while keeping all his built-up resentments locked inside (as he had with his former analyst). At 16, he had felt intensely involved with a girlfriend (his first love) but had let her leave him and go abroad without any conscious experience of loss, grief, or anger. He had passively accepted her final adieu with the anesthetizing words, "We'll always be together in spirit."

This girlfriend later went off and joined a cult. Only after opening up to his grief in treatment with me could he articulate questions he never asked her then, such as "Why did you leave?" "What are you looking for in this cult?" "How are you?" "Do you care about me?" "Why did you leave me?" and also failed to make the simple statement that only later he could really feel: "I miss you!"

Dull, gray, and feeling apathetic about everything, David proceeded to get married to a female biologist. He was not sure that he felt strongly connected to his wife but married because he thought there was something wrong with him because he would leave every woman whom he had dated, after a fairly short period, always feeling disappointment. David had externalized his disappointments, thinking they must be related to the woman he had just dated. He kept hurting each woman in order not to feel trapped in a connection that at first seemed potentially alive—at least in terms of an initial sexual desire—but which very quickly became dead and dried up for him. As each connection dried up it blended in with his general feeling of gray, colorless boredom, which was accompanied by constant obsessions, ambivalent thinking, not feeling, and disconnected feelings.

In order to avoid being like his father, who left his mother (when he was one) and every other woman, ending up alone, isolated, and alcoholic, he decided he had to stick with a relationship whether he liked it or not, whether he felt trapped or not. He willed himself to dismiss his own disappointment with the female biologist he was dating, defensively fleeing from conflict, while complying and submitting to the relationship as he had earlier submitted to his mother. He willed himself to stay with Cindy, the biologist, despite what he experienced as the loss of fun and sexual desire, and even of an alive feeling connection that he had formerly felt.

David did not want to be alone. He wanted to have children. So he did. He had three children whom he loved dearly. Nevertheless, only for fleeting instances could he regain any desire to be with his wife. He stayed in a marriage that he began to resent more and more. He wrote a letter to the woman he had had once dated. The letter was full of romantic longings of an infatuated and/or in-love nature. Unconscious of his motives, he managed to leave the letter where his wife could see it, never sending it. This precipitated a marital crisis that made him seek more psychotherapeutic treatment.

Over a period of many more years, David saw one analyst after another, just as he had dated and left women. As with the women, he experienced a repeated sense of disappointment, feeling a loss of alive desire with the analysts just as he had lost sexual desire with the women. Several analysts saw him two times a week, refusing to see him less than that. One analyst had been provocative and seemed slightly off the wall to him, while obviously trying to engage David. When, as usual, he began to feel nothing was really happening, he told the analyst that he was going to cut down to once a week. The analyst said that he could not go along with this. Consequently, David said that meant he would not be seeing him anymore. David saw another analyst twice a week, even though reluctant to do so. He liked this man, but just after a year of treatment, the analyst died.

One more attempt at analysis was even more frustrating. David went to see a well-known senior analyst who had a reputation for being insightful about primitive things, even though his background was as a classical analyst. David became dubious quite quickly, as he sensed a deadness in the analyst, who may have been depressed at the time. David thought to himself, but did not dare say out loud: "What is wrong with you? All you can say is, 'We're finding things out about your mother!' How can you be so dull and detached? How did you get your reputation as a sharp, on-the-mark analyst? How could you have gotten that reputation when you're not even here?" David left politely after sticking it out dutifully for one year, never feeling authentically responded to. He never expressed any of the thoughts he was having about the analyst. He left feeling fed up with all analysts and thinking that neither analysis nor psychotherapy had anything of value to offer him.

David stayed out of psychological treatment as long as he could. However, he was constantly angry at his wife and aroused by other women who would briefly kindle sexual desire and a feeling of sexual intimacy that he lacked with his wife. Every sexual interest turned into another woman making demands on him that he could not meet. He felt damned if he did and damned if he did not about staying in his marriage or leaving it and, even more poignantly, about staying in life or just walking through it in a gray apathy. With time, his obsessional doubting intensified. Also, his fear of losing his children intensified as he thought about divorce. He felt disconnected and ambivalent about everything. His body could temporarily make him feel alive when he engaged in a new sensual or sexual fling, or sometimes he could feel awakened by dance or by female massage therapists.

However, the brief interludes of arousal quickly died out. With his negative opinion of psychoanalysts and psychotherapists, he might never have tried treatment again if he were not faced with a professional crisis as well. He was being forced to give talks on his research studies at well-known universities in order to work toward tenure at his university. He started to have anxiety attacks and panic attacks right before going up to the podium to speak. At one time, the anxiety was so gripping that when it was his turn he quickly backed away with the excuse that he was not feeling well. Afterward, scared that he would become so inhibited that he could not speak at all—which would risk his opportunity to achieve tenure or even to continue his research and teaching—he decided he would have to give in and seek the aid of a psychoanalyst again, even though he saw no results from his past attempts at treatment.

He then came to consult with me, with a definite agenda to just deal with his public speaking symptom. Otherwise, he feared he would waste more time and money and would build up more resentment and dissatisfaction as he faced disappointment and meaninglessness again.

The Beginning of the Current Treatment

Despite all of the clinical experiences that made him quick to doubt any hopes for an alive treatment, David had developed capacities in his former treatments to reflect on himself and his behavior. Although such self-reflection was mixed in with compulsive and defensive obsessional thinking and doubting, which chopped up his thinking and prevented him from having any depth of feeling, which colored his perception of his life gray, this potential for free association and self-reflection within a potential spontaneous, authentic self was clearly in evidence. David's years with analysts had given him some sense that he needed to take time to think things out with the analyst. He could obliterate any positive thought he had with a negative one, yet he was clearly prepared to stick things out for a while and try to think things out. He also became less protective of me than he had been of his former analysts.

Perhaps this was because I am a woman and did not evoke the father and stepfather transferences that related to men who had left him and who would be fantasized to leave him any minute. He had much more anger toward his mother than toward his father and stepfather, even though he was compelled to suppress the anger to protect his mother who had been the one parent who never left him. However, he was not unconscious of his anger at his mother. Consequently, David was more conscious of his anger with women, particularly in relation to his wife, although even this anger was numbed out when he first came to treatment in his state of perpetual doubt.

In relation to the transference, David showed no anger at first, only distrust. With his monologues of obsessional doubting, David would speak generally of distrusting the work with analysts, asking how, if I was not going to be "real" with him and tell him about myself, he could feel open and real with me. Over time, he progressed to more personal complaints and distrust about me. He mentioned that he had heard my approach was not empathic enough. He had heard from someone who once left therapy angry at me that I had not helped her. He said he believed that someone like him needed a lot of empathy and he did not think I could offer it. I registered the unconscious transference of a mother with a dried-up breast—probably a mother who was actually emotionally withdrawn from him. I refrained from making any interpretations, let alone transference interpretations, for many years of treatment, until his separation mourning allowed for a therapeutic alliance and differentiated neurotic transferences.

At this early time in treatment (first and second year) I accepted all David's distrust, doubting, and disappointment. Later, he asked to lie down on the couch. In D.W. Winnicott's (1971) sense of object survival, I survived. I had not abandoned David, nor retaliated against him. Nor did I make interpretations that would feel to him like retaliations. I did, however, finally make one critical transference resistance interpretation that proved to be critical to opening up the treatment and deepening the work.

Transference Resistance

As I listened to more and more statements about why David believed our work was meaningless and would be fruitless, I began to hear another theme. It was the theme of his mother having constructed theories about him. In fact, contriving her view of David from her theories, David's mother would make interpretations about his feelings. She would presume that she knew about feelings of his that he was not sharing. These interpretations felt like intrusions to David, which was a good reason for me not to make interpretations except occasionally or after time.

David's mother would propose that he was angry and would tell him he should express his anger to her. Of course, he was angry, but how could he admit it to a mother who seemed to be playing the role of being a "good mother," a mother who had progressive educational theories about him and what he wanted? Therefore, to express his anger, David withdrew further when his mother would make her demands on him to "produce" the anger. Secretly, he knew if he ever did express it, she would get terribly hurt and might strike out at him. She might humiliate him by telling him he had to come over and be spanked for being bad.

One day, when he was accused of being bad, he refused to come for a spanking and ran away. His mother got hysterical and helplessly broke down and cried. As he told this to me, he concluded that his mother was really quite fragile and that if she could not humiliate him and make him feel helpless and small, she had to feel her own helplessness, misery, and despair. But the mother he wrestled with now, represented in his internal world as an internal object, had theories about herself being a progressive mother who could hear her child's anger.

David spoke to me about these associations and memories related to his mother. I began to realize that when he spoke of distrusting me because he thought I would just want to prove my theories by using him as a guinea pig, that I was the direct target of one aspect of his negative mother transference. It was a critical aspect of the negative mother transference that acted as a transference resistance in treatment, one which all his previous analysts had failed to pick up. I was realizing that David remained behind a defensive wall in all his treatments because of the failure of the analysts to pick up and interpret this transference resistance, making his self-fulfilling prophesy that nothing was happening come true.

So I made my first transference interpretation to him by saying in quite simple terms that he seemed to fear that I was constantly preoccupied with trying to fit him into my mold, i.e., into my theories and theoretical model. I thought he was thinking, I told him, that I was constantly fitting all he had to say into a theoretical mold that was inside my mind. I cited that he had questioned whether I would stick him into a Kleinian mode or a Freudian mode, but in my case, he assumed all he said was being put rapidly into a category of theory in my mind so that I would lack any empathy in the sense of being able to feel his subjective experience of things. In my walled-off mind of theory, I could not possibly feel what he might feel and understand his perspective. Instead, I would be too preoccupied with fitting him into the theoretical niches in my mind.

This transference interpretation seemed to immediately wake David up. He had been totally convinced that this molding of him into a theoretical model in my mind was absolutely going on at all times. To hear me formulate his transference fantasy—which we both knew related back to his mother, who narcissistically did relate to him through the image of her own theory of him—allowed David to see that I was not actually in the box he had been putting me into (in his theory making about me). He seemed to open up his body and breath freely for the first time at this point. He seemed to stick his neck out of a defensive shell. He actually looked at me! Not the way he looked at me when he had been demanding that I tell him about myself to make the situation an equal one so he could open up to me. Now, he looked at me with a relief at having taken the first step out of his internal psychic prison.

It was soon after this that he requested to lie down on the couch, after I explained that he might be freer to have spontaneous thoughts and feelings this way, particularly if any of those thoughts and feelings pertained to me.

Transitional Object Stage of Treatment and Separation-Individuation Mourning, Still 60 Minutes, Once A Week

At this stage in the treatment, David needed me to be a subjective object (Winnicott, 1971), that is, one who could be there to help him feel and affirm his own subjective experience without showing any needs of my own as a separate person with my own subjectivity. Heinz Kohut's idea of a selfobject relates to the subjective object as D.W. Winnicott first conceptualized it. In this role, I could provide the necessary attunement for David to tolerate the powerful affect states of an arrested developmental separation process, called abandonment depression affects by James Masterson (1976, 1981, 2000).

However, David only had the affects of the later stages of this painful separation process. He never experienced himself in a void or vacuum. He was capable of feeling the beginning stages of object loss in terms of depression. However, his depression was defended against by emotional detachment, narcissistic devaluation, a chronic sense of angry aloneness, and distancing toward the object, both from his analyst as an external object and from his internal objects. Part object projections were placed on idealized women whom he was attracted to, and the negative part other such as the analyst or his wife object projections were put onto his wife and, at times, onto me.

Within this state of emotional detachment and distancing, David defended against unconscious and dissociated rage that was part and parcel of his chronic depression, which also had obsessional features of doubting everything. David seemed to doubt everything because he could not feel connections through alive affect states. Without his feelings, all was gray and all was fairly hypothetical to him, which had been his general attitude toward clinical treatment. All was speculative and subject to negation, which made for an air of pessimism, often accompanied by David's mild contemptuous derision of himself and others. Yet, he could love his children and have temporary infatuations with women. His love for his children was a strong and consistent anchor for him throughout his daily life, helping to sustain him despite his mental sea of doubt. David could project onto his children all the vulnerable and alive qualities of his own self that had become so buried. He could actually resonate with the reality of these qualities as expressed within his children's authentic natures.

David also maintained an alive sensuality that would come to birth anew each time he met a woman who triggered his particular images of attractive women. His infatuations with these women would die pretty quickly, however, because in not having completed his own separation process and in not having mourned the losses in his life (related to his father and an early girlfriend), David was limited in his relatedness. Before any new developmental growth could occur, David had to experience primal levels of anger, at the level of narcissistic rage and separation trauma rage, which he could only experience, conceptualize, and process within the safety of a holding environment in treatment. This rage began to emerge, along with the grief of related object loss, as the analyst successfully maintained the position of a subjective object in treatment. From this position, as his analyst, I could empathize—both verbally and silently (viscerally as well)—with his subjective states and the memories and associations attached to those states.

At this stage, David also needed me to be aware of the off-target part object transferences (good mother/bad mother, bad father) that were projected onto others outside—with the bad mother being projected onto his wife and sometimes the bad father onto me—without having me offer symbolic level transference interpretations. David needed me to help him connect with symbiotic longings that had been cut off when he lost his father at one and then when he lost his first girlfriend at 16. His wife had become the displacement for the aversively experienced separation, while the 16-year-old girlfriend, whom he had never mourned, still played an unconscious role for him as an early symbiotic "good" mother, which he then displaced onto assorted women to whom he was erotically attracted.

David was able to feel conscious loss related to his 16-year-old girlfriend for the first time in his Object Relations treatment with me. Processing the grief of this loss—which later would be seen to relate back even farther, to the loss of his father as a nurturing and sensually affectionate other at one—allowed David to resume the psychic development. Such development had been arrested when he could not tolerate feeling the loss of his girlfriend, which recapitulated the traumatic loss of his father. When his father left the household, David was left with a mother who was out of touch with her body and her feelings. In fact, David's mother may have carried her own pathological mourning state with the symptomatic reactivity of a numbed-out body. As a one-year-old child, David felt her body tensions and her compensatory mental hyperactivity, as his mother continued to react to object losses related to her primary family by dissociation and disconnection.

The split mother transference, from the primal time of psychic arrest during the separation-individuation period, was manifested through David's polarized views of his 16-year-old girlfriend versus his wife, while the negative father transference, coming from a later stage, at nine years old, was the first layer of transference resistance after the projection of the narcissistic mother full of theories. The analysis became a comfortable Winnicottian holding environment for David to feel his feelings. I was a self or subjective object who could feel with David his own feelings, without imposing any experience of my own. Nevertheless, when there was any disruption in this subjective object containment (related to Bion's idea of the therapeutic container), I became experienced as the negative father, the intimidating contemptuous judge whose judgments would bring some feared humiliation.

Distancing: Defending Against the Connecting That Would Come at the Point of Loss

David's distancing from me was the way he negotiated my existence before he could become more separate and could truly connect through the developmental mourning process at the separation-individuation stage level. Essentially, I could serve as a split-off part of him, but not yet an object in my own right. I was neither loved nor hated. I was either part of the environment (like the air; see Balint, 1968) or the negative (part object) father, who was feared as a detached, demanding, and contemptuous judge. Yet David's distancing alternated with feeling his need for connection, which would prompt feelings of loss that had been both dissociated and repressed for a lifetime.

David had a lot of anger at his wife, onto whom he projected his externalized bad object (mother/father), and who later would receive a more differentiated negative mother transference projection. David projected the bad object onto his wife and distanced from her as he distanced from me in the treatment situation. However, as the rage, grief, and loss of his early separation trauma mourning were experienced and processed, David became increasingly capable of looking at his projections and transference projections in relation to his wife. He was able then to associate to his automatic negative reactions to his wife, so that he could see his reactions in the light of memories of the reactions to his mother that he had suppressed and repressed to comply with the demands of her narcissistic character for such compliance.

Each time he could tolerate the affects of rage, grief, and loss, David was able to more clearly remember and differentiate the attacking mother, the withholding mother, and the mother whom he experienced as disrupting his boundaries. He also remembered the mother whom he experienced as seductive and possessive and whom, he concluded, had unconsciously wanted him to be her lover. In addition, he discovered, through the connection of affect and memory related to his projections, the subjectively experienced unemphatic mother who offered pseudo forms of empathy and the demanding and needy mother who would turn into the critical mother of attack.

The Appearance of the Bad Object in Dreams and of the Eroticized Bad Object, the "Demon-lover"

David had repetitive dreams of being chased by Nazis. He tried to escape but was only able to survive by lying down in the street and playing dead. David's associations to this dream were links back to memories of being literally chased by bullies from school or of being bullied into a masochistic submission to psychic torture and humiliation by a counselor at a camp he attended in his adolescence. Then there were also associations back to his primary objects, his parents. He recalled his father sticking his tongue in his mouth to supposedly demonstrate to him how to kiss. He remembers how repulsed he was by his father's violation of his boundaries, which took place in various ways from the age of nine when his father would attempt to engage him in arm wrestling only to have his father cause him physical pain as he supposedly played.

David's first memories of his father were all intense, humiliating, and painful experiences where he suffered at the hands of male authorities or male bullies at school. As he recalled the memories, he felt an anger rise up from within. He was not consciously aware of any erotic aspect. Yet, the memories of his father were tinged with yearnings for closeness that turned into pain, a pain that had a physical and sometimes a sensual intensity that left him feeling seductively provoked and then betrayed.

Then memories of his mother emerged as well, in relation to boundary violations. Sadistic humiliation and a mode of narcissism in the mother were expressed as hostile seduction. David recalled being chased around and threatened with spankings that did not physically hurt but made him feel small and humiliated.

He remembered his mother intruding on his autonomy by insisting he carry an umbrella when it was not raining. He also had fantasies of her treating him as an object that she possessed and whom she could attempt to seduce, as when he imagined her saying to him as a three-year-old, running around without clothes, "Oh what a cute little penis!" The mother was also seen as careless and incapable of containing him. He had a dream of her washing him in a sink and then the sink dropping so that he would be shattered and killed.

I interpreted his sleeping difficulties at this time as a fear that his wife would pick up a knife and stab him in the middle of the night. My interpretation was related to his unconscious guilt over his anger and aggression toward his wife, which he had been expressing in critical comments. He feared retaliation from her, both as his wife and as the transference figure standing for his mother, whom he had retaliated against in the past by distancing and passivity, but whom he now felt rage toward as he confronted his memories and dreams.

As David freed his anger, he felt more alive, rather than being imprisoned in a passive and reactive false self that distanced rather than allowing contact and connection with others. He unconsciously experienced the new aliveness, however, as a mixed blessing, because he had gotten the definite impression from his mother that she could not tolerate his anger, even though she went through a contrived exercise of asking him for it. David's mother's own narcissistic image of herself as a mother prompted her to ask him to confide his angry feelings. But he knew this was a trap and he withheld all his feelings. His fears of his wife stabbing him with a knife seemed to go back to his mother, who wished to hit him and who he could unconsciously imagine would attack him for his escaping her grasp and for all his mental retaliations experienced in thinking hostile thoughts about his wife, who also represented his mother in his unconscious.

It can be seen that David's dream of playing dead in relation to surviving the murderous approach of the Nazis could be a symbolic play by his unconscious on his playing dead with his mother. By withdrawing his emotional self from contact and by displaying a passive-aggressive demeanor that had retaliatory impulses behind it, he tried to emotionally survive. He was forced to distance when he could not separate from his mother or separate in the present from his wife.

David began to consciously feel his retaliatory impulses in the form of rage and anger; he no longer had to stay in a passive reactive position. Gradually, he began to face his image of the bad object mother that he projected onto his wife and gain his self-agency as he owned his feelings. He could then face both his wife and his internal mother. His re-owning consciously his formerly unconscious anger allowed him to feel a new freedom and autonomy. His anger opened the doorway to discovering his sense of grief at having lost the early good mother whom he loved to the bad mother who, like his father, found ways to intimidate him and to seductively provoke him.

David's sense of grief was to become the main theme in later dreams that he had in the two months before the analyst's vacation. He dreamt of a cat he missed that had died three years earlier, and he dreamed of his dead father, who had died of alcoholism. He had associations to an old friend and a recent friend who had both hung themselves.

His sadness was palpable in recalling this, as was his sadness and agonizing grief when he began to speak of the severe disillusionment of many of his most prized and cherished fantasy wishes, such as the fantasy of his wife becoming a more slender woman, more appealing to him. David yielded to his grief, with tears choking up in him. And he sobbed profusely in thinking of how he felt he could not let go of the fantasy of being with another woman, one who would be the new representative for his first two girlfriends who had left him and would, at a deeper level, be an incarnation of his early (one-year-old) father's sensuality and affection.

Separation Mourning Allows for Observing Ego Development and Self-Reflection

The mourning process allowed David to self-integrate and separate from the internal object enough that it could be experienced by David on a symbolic level, clarifying his projections and distortions in the marriage situation. David no longer needed to be reactive. Through the conscious processing of the abandonment depression affect states and the separation loss mourning, his inner self became a true self having its own natural developmental evolution. This opened up psychic space and interpersonal transitional space. It also allowed him to have an observing ego perspective in relation to his fears, wishes, and intrapsychic conflicts. He now could open himself to the true external other and form good enough internal object psychic representations and structure. With good enough internal object psychic structure he had objective observing ego perspectives, separate from any superego operations, and his superego operations also became more benign and less persecutory, allowing for increasing degrees of self-reflection.

The Forming of a Therapeutic Alliance and a
Therapeutic Object Relationship

As I interpreted the negative father transference, David no longer externalized this in the treatment situation as a transference resistance through projection and projective identification. Consequently, he and I could now work together differently, as allies, forming the traditional psychotherapeutic alliance for analytic work. With symbolic representations that could be understood in their displacement modes from the past to the present, David could become, in Thomas Ogden's terms, an interpreting subject, and I could become a whole object (both loved and hated) or separate other with whom David could engage in interactive dialogues, integrating affective and cognitive levels of interpersonal experience.

David's internal psychic dialectic developed along with observing ego development and self-reflection. So, for the first time, David could tolerate and be aware of psychic conflict. He even became exquisitely aware of when he could contain the affect states related to two sides of a psychic conflict at once and when he could not. David could now relate to the ambivalence of love and hate for a whole object, without resorting to externalization as he had to when he was merged with or in opposition to his internal objects. Now, he could form a therapeutic Object Relationship (Grunes, 1984).

As this new evolution of relationship in the treatment evolved, so did a developmentally progressive "love affair with the world," as in Mahler's (1975) description of the practicing period in the developing separation stage toddler, prior to rapprochement. However, David would regress from this outward focus, which was to include a new curiosity and interest in the actual personality of the analyst, after the pain of new grief, related to a new oedipal level form of disillusionment (as opposed to separation grief). Then he would temporarily return to his old distancing defenses with his accompanying tendency to devalue the other, the treatment, his marriage, his life, and his own capacities to find fulfillment in life.

His old ambivalent mode of doubting and its accompanying angry and frustrated depression would temporarily return. However, although he regressed to old defenses, his new and solid psychic structure (internalized good enough Object Relations) now allowed him to analyze the situation in a self-reflective manner. He and I could now talk about David's former distancing, detachment, and devaluation as a defensive operation in which he reflexively had attempted to protect himself from an internal father, whom he experienced as a retaliating and spoiling object.

We began to confront together his new level of fears, different from the earlier abandonment fears from the separation period. Now, he had fears of success, fears of castration, and fears of sexual betrayal, reactive to old betrayals that he would enact in identification with the aggressor. These new fears would be defended against with the old defenses, but they were operating at a level of separation and whole object perception and of ambivalence characteristic of the oedipal era, rather than the precedipal. He would act out the transference resistance of withdrawing from his father, or from me as a displacement for the father. His father could have knocked him down with an arrogant and contemptuous attitude characteristic of the father's envy.

David could now associate to memories of his father's demonic and demon-lover attitude (contemptuous aggression mixed with sadistic seduction and eroticism). Prior to separation phase mourning, David's withdrawals from the world and success could be seen as a precedipal fear of his mother withdrawing her emotional contact when he left her to individuate and failed to support her narcissistic defenses by mirroring her. Now, his withdrawals, following a more differentiated form of professional success and success in his marriage, could be seen to be reactive to his unconscious, aggressive impulses felt toward his father and feared as coming from his father in competitive retaliation.

Therapeutic Alliance and Beginning Transference Analysis

Being newly aware of his internal objects, David was now able to join me in analyzing his former negative transferences. He could now visualize and thus symbolize the view of his mother intruding on his boundaries, as well as his view of his father terrorizing him with seductions and frustrations, such as sticking his tongue in David's mouth on the pretext of teaching him how to kiss girls. He could also now conceptualize the father who asked him to read articles and report to him, instilling in David a fear of being unprepared to talk before an audience, an audience unconsciously presumed to be an omnipotent and contemptuous father judge.

Another result of David's adequate separation through the mourning process was his new ability to psychically and emotionally surrender to all his feelings and much more of his internal life than formerly while lying on the couch in his treatment sessions. He now confessed, as if it has been a long-term shame-ridden secret, that he actually felt relaxed with me and psychically held by me. He reached this disclosure to me by analyzing a defensive thought he had, which he could be separate enough to observe with a new level of observing ego and self-reflection.

As an interpreting subject, he knew that his thoughts were thoughts and his feelings were feelings. He no longer just reacted to a thought or feeling as if it is a concrete reality imposed on him by an external other. He formerly engaged in much projective identification of this sort. Now, he could have the thought on the couch while with me, "I don't want to give her the satisfaction of letting her [me, the analyst] know that I feel relaxed here." He could report this to me as soon as he is aware of thinking such a thought. This shared thought then became part of a chain of thoughts that constituted a psychoanalytic free association process.

Through the mourning process, David found a new sense of agency. After many years of once-a-week mourning work, David could actively question himself as to why he did not want to give me the satisfaction of knowing his newfound comfort with me. He thus engaged in internal psychic dialectic and simultaneously in interpersonal dialectic, or dialogue, as he shared his internal thinking with me. In questioning himself, along with me as the witness and confidante, a role related to me being a separate other and no longer just a subjective object (or self object), he realized how reflexive his former distancing withdrawal reactions to me were. He also realized how this reactivity was so reflective of his defensive withdrawals from his wife.

Thus, David engaged in the therapeutic process, not just the content, as a subject for analytic discussion. In the words of Thomas Ogden, he could see aspects of the process as "analytic subjects" in the transitional space between the analyst and the patient.

This is related to Wilfred Bion's views on reverie. This phenomenon is also related to D.W. Winnicott's (1971) discussion of object survival in relation to the analyst and patient. As the analyst survives the patient's primitive aggression, (i.e., the bad object transference acting out of primitive rage affects), the patient can for the first time view the analyst as an external other rather than as a subjective object or fantasy self extension. As David processed his analytic associations with me, in particular, his thought of not wanting to give me the satisfaction of knowing his comfort with me, he was also linking his former distancing reactivity—which would have dictated that he did not share with me his sense of being held by me—with a differentiated maternal transference. This differentiated mother view was a neurotic level transference, as opposed to the earlier characterological level transference enactment (see Masterson, 2000), which stemmed from separation-individuation trauma and psychic arrest. In other words, differentiated transference is based on transference projection as opposed to projective identification.

In linking his defensive thought in relation to me with a mother transference, David recalled continually believing that he had to distance himself from his mother so that she would not possess him and control him as her own exclusive narcissistic object. He feared, in reaction to actual experiences with his mother, that if he shared any authentic part of himself with his mother, she would impose her theories on him. Then she would have been defining him rather than allowing him to define himself through his own self-initiated self-expression. David then gave further meaning to his associations by linking his defensive behavior with his wife with that which he had assumed he was compelled to enact with his mother, and which he felt an urge to enact with me at the moment before his newfound reflective thought. He said to me that he played the "same game" with his wife as he had with his mother. He explained that he had always acted with a distancing defense so that he would not fall back into a compliant position with his wife where he could not feel his own feeling states—especially the feeling states related to anger and aggression that were an important part of providing him with his own unique experience of subjectivity.

Having successfully engaged in such an analytic process with me, David now articulated for the first time his vision of analysis as a journey. He furthermore stated that he saw analysis as a journey of "hope." Also for the first time, he now articulated that he wishes to join what he calls the "club" of dental surgeons in his profession. For the first time, he saw being in a club of shared intentions with other professionals as a way of helping people and giving meaning to his own life. David communicated to me that he wanted to belong rather than be an outside skeptic—because now, for the first time, he authentically felt like a type of medical benefactor as a dental surgeon, as he came to believe in the process he was engaged in with me in psychoanalytic psychotherapy.

At an earlier time, David spoke to me in a deadened and depressed state. At that time, he had referred to thinking about me without revealing if he was actually having a fantasy about me or just having general thoughts. He spoke in generalizations. He spoke as if he were going through some rote demonstration to an analyst of knowing that he could speak of having sexual fantasies about the analyst to the analyst. He did this without revealing anything specific about his fantasies. It was all a vague report.

Repression and the Fall

David had a dream in which he started to have associations to me on a very conscious and rational level. For example, he had a woman in his dream who was the director of a psychoanalytic training institute. As he mentioned this, I laughed slightly, recognizing the veiled reference to me that his unconscious was making as he associated the woman in the dream to this other female director. His response to my slight laugh was to say, "Oh. You're the director of a psychoanalytic institute too, aren't you?"

Interestingly enough, in this same dream in which I (mother/father) appeared symbolized in a displacement figure, David had a smashing fall. He fell underground, and the ground sealed over him with cement. I responded to his telling me this with an interpretation that brought together the two parts of the dream.

I told David that he only seemed able to have very rational and surface-level thoughts about me as a professional person in the dream. I said that whatever unconscious wishes, fantasies, or feelings he had about me seemed to be buried under his mind's repressive defenses, which were metaphorically displayed in the dream by his whole body being buried under cement. I also suggested that the fact that he fell in the dream seemed to relate to some formerly dissociated and now repressed trauma that was being relived in the dream, and that may have to do with why it was too threatening to be more engaged with me and with thoughts and feelings about me on a conscious level. Perhaps he was afraid of reexperiencing the repressed trauma with me. To want to know more about me than superficial things on a professional and public level could be feared unconsciously as dangerous, depending on whom I represented and what he feared would be the consequence of opening up to me on a deeper level.

In response, David associated the fall in the dream as being related to a sexual rejection. He later associated it to being dropped as an infant—another dream—and being stabbed with verbal attacks from his father during latency and then attacked by a male authority in a drug treatment program during adolescence—then abandoned and betrayed by girlfriends. His unconscious condensed the infant fall (being emotionally dropped by mother when father leaves), the latency and adolescent "stabbing" verbal attacks, and then being sexually seduced and dropped by girlfriends as a young adult man, with an overall theme of sexual rejection (from the infant body, through the adolescent and adult sexual body). Significantly, in the course of the same session, David said that he would be afraid to ask me a question because he anticipated that I would refuse to answer it (thinking of stereotypic analytic technique). I responded by interpreting that if I did not answer a question he asked, he would experience me as sexually rejecting him.

Distancing, Interpretation, and Surrender:
The Opening of the Core Loving Self

In the session following the one after this dream, David returned to his old distancing defenses. He detached, ruminated with obsessional doubt, and closed off his affect life in an extreme way that resembled his old self, prior to the separation-individuation mourning process. All seemed gray and dreary to him again about life and psychotherapy.

As his analyst, I struggled within myself about whether to bring up how much he was limiting what could happen in treatment by continuing to come only once a week (albeit for 60 minutes). I interpreted that he seemed to be enacting in this session the dream of the last session. I said that he was sounding and acting like his whole vital and bodily being, the being within him of feelings and passions and desires, was buried under cement. I said that his obsessional defenses and the wall of repression that they reinforce seemed to be dominating the session, suggesting to me that if he wished to be dug out of the buried psychic state, he needed to have the leverage to counteract these defenses, and with only one time a week for his treatment, I did not see us having that leverage. I added that I hesitated to say this to him, because in the past, whenever I had mentioned the possibility of his coming even one more time a week, he seemed either to not hear me, to dismiss me, or to forget that I said any such thing. However, I continued, for me not to say anything would be to not do my job, so I reluctantly ventured forth again and took the plunge.

David listened and responded thoughtfully. He said that this time he would seriously consider what I said and recommended. His initial reaction in the next session was to return to the old mode of distancing to avoid psychic conflict. He said that if my recommendation was to come more often, he thought it would be best to leave treatment altogether because I seemed to be saying that one time a week was not enough. However, even as he said this, his unconscious brought up the other side of the conflict that was not being stated as a conflict. This was to be the session where he opened up his long-buried core self, the core self that held his potential for loving. As he talked about leaving, his buried longings to love and be loved erupted into the affect color of the moment more fully than ever before. As he acted like the detached father who left him and his mother in his infancy and many times afterward, he began to remember his father in a whole new way, seeing for the first time behind and beyond the surface layers.

From Distancing to Surrendering to the Core Loving Self through Developmental Mourning Grief (Depressive Position): Critical Psychic Transformation through Mourning in Session in the Eighth Year of Treatment

The session began with David saying, "I'm thinking of quitting if your recommendation is to come more often. Maybe I need to seal off under cement, just as my dream portrayed a part of me doing. Maybe I need to do that now to keep safe, basically to cut off, if you say the treatment may need more time weekly for us to have clinical leverage. I can't even imagine coming more often and spending more money! It's too much already. I only imagine losing, not gaining, from coming more often. I don't really believe that anybody can help me. I've been feeling miserable, which I've heard is a sign that treatment is working. I don't want to feel miserable, and I think that continuing to come will only make me more miserable." Then his tone changed, opening to feeling: "I feel sad." He started to cry. He reached for the tissues. He said he felt like somewhere, way back, he was made to feel like he was being stabbed in the heart and ripped apart—crying and hurting—going increasingly into that wounded place within.

I suggested that he might be feeling the feelings that were intolerable to him at one year old when his father left the family home and left his mother. Since the feelings were intolerable then, from a traumatic separation, he might believe that stopping and consciously feeling them with me now would be intolerable and that leaving treatment seemed far preferable. However, I pointed out that he was feeling the feelings now, a deep grief, and he was surviving.

David's grief brought him back to an image of his son (who was nine years old) being exquisitely vulnerable. He said he thought of himself as a nine-year-old and of how vulnerable he must have been in relation to his father. David could not remember his vulnerability in terms of when his father actually left the family, when he was one year old, although David agreed with me that he may have been forced to feel his mother's broken heart as a heart-stabbed feeling state that he was feeling now as thoughts of his father rose to consciousness.

David said that he felt a heart-wrenching pain of hurt and grief, related to being a nine-year-old in a vulnerable body who was actively attacked by his physically stronger father. He told me that his father would purposely hurt him when he would give him a bear hug, or he would squeeze his hand so tightly that it would hurt. He also told me that his father would intrude on him by saying he wanted to show him how to tongue kiss with girls and would actually stick his tongue in David's mouth. This made David feel nauseous. This experience was like the feeling he felt when he thought of coming to psychoanalytic treatment twice a week and seeing me more often. He would be too vulnerable to being hurt and would be left more miserable than he already felt, as he had been feeling lately (while I was away on a week's vacation).

But then his tears of physical and emotional hurt in relation to a bullying father turned to other memories of his father. First, however, he spoke of dreams in which he was always chased by Nazis and left for dead, pretending to be dead even though he was not dead. David said that he had to play dead, and I said that he had to really kill off a vital part of himself to act dead, the emotional part of him. David cried as I said this. Then, when he said that he had so many dreams of Nazis chasing him and of barely escaping, he said he felt dead inside. He wondered if such things had actually happened to him in a past life.

I said that whether it had happened in a past life or not, I would see that this feeling state of being ripped apart in his heart and trying to deaden himself to avoid the pain, as well as to avoid attack, could also be a metaphor for how he had felt as a one-year-old, when his father left abruptly and he was left with a mother who felt like she had been stabbed by her husband and by his leaving.

He agreed, saying he thought that his guilt (the "fall" in the other dream) reaction in relation to his father was a defensive protecting of himself from remembering his father's (childhood father) actual sadism. David said that he had always felt guilty, as if he had committed murder, which made the attacks on him in his dreams seem like symbolic retaliations (from his childhood superego). He confessed that he had always felt like he had killed his father by not totally taking care of him, which was what his father demanded of him by his own self-destructive behavior when his father was an aging alcoholic. Instead of being trapped by his father's impossible demands, David had worked hard to train himself to set limits with his father. He then told his father, "I'll see you, but you can't live with me. You have to take care of yourself." His father did not take care of himself. He drank himself to death and died. David said that he always wondered if he could have saved his father by taking care of him. But he also knew he could not have done it.

As he spoke, David opened up his internal emotional life more fully. He began to surrender to a deep, but secretly held and buried, grief. He sobbed and sobbed with the tears and anguish of grief-stricken longing and regret. He finally said, for the first time, at the child (and infant) level of feeling from which he felt it, "But I also loved my father. He could be mean and hurt me, but he also had some wonderful qualities" (a phrase he would repeat word for word in relation to his wife as his love could not open toward her). David cried and sobbed deeply, fully, and with articulate verbal communication. "Only now are these qualities coming back to me. I forgot them and I forgot my love for him. Maybe I even forgot him and his love. Maybe that's why I can't really love my wife, which is what she keeps saying. Maybe I had to find this love for my father before I could love again. Maybe my problems with my wife are not as much about her as I thought. Maybe I had to feel this pain, this pain of this physical scarring, of this ripping apart heart pain, to remember and to feel the love and the longing for him."

At this poignant moment, I, as his analyst, had to say it was time to go. I said it as if a matter of fact, but inside I felt my own emotional reluctance. However, I knew we had reached the critical psychic point we needed to reach for David to be able to renew his early capacity to love and to therefore lead a more fulfilling life.

On the way out, David smiled at me and seemed to be laughing at himself, perhaps acknowledging by this that he was really in treatment, and a therapeutic Object Relationship. As he smiled, he seemed to be admitting to me and to himself that he was not really on the verge of leaving treatment. Maybe we both realized at that moment that his thinking of leaving at this point was significant. Such thinking on his part reflected his main mode of distancing defense, which had formerly caused so much dissociation from himself. He would naturally go back to such a defense, as the other side of his ambivalence and psychic conflict about being in relationships in general was emerging through the treatment relationship. He distanced just at the point when he feared and yet desired to surrender to a deeply buried and emerging old love for his father, a love which he needed to expand his capacity to love in the present.

Perhaps in threatening to leave the analyst, he was retaliating toward all those who he had needed and loved, who had betrayed him by leaving him in abrupt and noncommunicative ways that, in his own words, denied his existence. All these traumatic separations had registered on his unconscious as abandonments and so he would abandon me and his analysis.

Confirming such a hypothesis was his behavior right after opening his emotional soul in this session—not only to himself, but also to me. On the way out of the office, he left his coat on one of my chairs, something he had never done before. I told him. He smiled as he picked up his coat. Perhaps he was leaving a piece of himself behind to stay with me. But perhaps, also, he was abandoning a part of himself as he had felt abandoned. Or, more to the point, he could have been demonstrating to me that he was not going to leave me then, by leaving a part of himself with me, showing by his behavior that he was involved with me and our work together, despite what his words from his conscious thoughts said and would say, as his distancing defense continued to play itself out.

Ironically, his behavior then demonstrated the other side of his conflict, that of leaving a part of himself with me. His distancing defense spoke again through behavior as he forgot to tell me that he would be away the following week. When he became conscious of this unconscious distancing move, he immediately called me, consciously wanting not to have his session. He called and asked if he could reschedule. I offered him an alternative session time.

When David came into the next session, he said that he felt a shift that week. "I've been taking care of myself rather than being self-destructive. I'm feeling that my life is better. I finally decided to re-decorate my office after 10 years. But I'm also realizing that I fear that my wounds will never heal. I guess that's why I think of leaving treatment and don't want to come in more frequently."

I said to him, "You never put it that way before." He continued, "When I was going down this block to your uptown office, I was remembering a relationship I had with a woman on this block. I was in my 20s. Remembering it now, I feel grief and regret. I'm so much more aware of my feelings than ever, but so much of what I feel now is grief and regret."

David returned to the obsessive doubt that cognitively shielded him from his grief and sadness. He said, "I ask myself what I'm really getting here, especially if it just means feeling these painful feelings. Why am I here?" I didn't say anything.

David continued, "I feel that I was dropped, psychically and emotionally dropped. I'm thinking of my father now. I guess I want to be held." (He was dropped by his father when he left his mother when David was one, and he was emotionally dropped, perhaps, by his mother at this point, when her husband left. The father who had held him as an infant left and became the father of his latency stage [nine years] who "stabbed" him with verbal attacks and repulsive and/or painful bodily intrusions.)

I said, "Maybe you want me to hold you, but fear I'll drop you."

David responded, "It's hard to imagine you holding me."

I said, "Maybe not as you are now, but as you were when you were very small and very young."

He answered, "I started thinking of my father, and then I thought of him attacking me with words."

I said, "You may be able to recall the later memories of being verbally attacked, but such memories, which are cognitively accessible, may reflect [screen memories] an earlier body memory of being dropped, from the time of your infancy." I continued, "You got in touch with the love for your father last week. You wanted to be held by the father you loved, but then you expect to be dropped and attacked."

David responded, "No wonder I can't imagine you helping me." (Especially if "helping" means "holding" him.)

I ended the session by saying, "How can you expect your wounds to heal when you expect to continually be dropped and attacked? This has been your perception of the entire world." David agreed and was reflecting on what I just said as I added, "It's time to go for this week."

The Analyst Comes Alive as an Object

When do analysands become curious? When do they become curious about the "other" in all relationships and relatedness in their lives? The critical turning point seems to be when they become curious about the analyst. David illustrates this very well.

In one session, following separation-individuation modes of mourning, David commented, with a new level of self-reflection, that he was aware that he did not really consider the needs of the other and the personality of the other enough, as he was so self-absorbed. At this point, he had become aware that he had often seen his wife through the veil and screen of defensive projections. As soon as David reflected on himself in this way, I took the opportunity to say that I did not think he related to me as a separate person, but more as someone to tune into his experience with him, without conveying any sense of me as a separate other. David understood what I meant. Interestingly, it was after this that he brought in the dream about the fall under cement in which he associated to a woman who represented me, being the director of a psychoanalytic institute. He had then some very rational and superficial associations to me, only touching on the level of my professional position, not venturing further into the terrain of what I meant to him unconsciously, or into any view of me as a unique personality.

After David opened to the deeply buried love for his father, a primal object of love and desire in his life, this changed dramatically. For the first time, he expressed openly curious thoughts about who I was as a person and revealed observations he was beginning to make about me. There was an alive and joyous affect that provided an avenue for the clear articulation in his speech as he declared that he did not know much about me but did wonder about me. He exclaimed that he wondered if I had children, but did observe that I was someone who liked colors and who he knew liked to dance (I had mentioned this). He added that he knew I liked to write books, and since I founded and ran an institute, he thought that I was quite ambitious. I seemed to have a vividness for him now that I had lacked before! Although he did not sound as if he felt sexual when he spoke, he might have felt sensual. He also spoke of how he experienced me in the treatment, saying that I seemed smart, and he said, "It's not just what you say, it's what you don't say!" He said, "You've been extremely respectful of my boundaries, which is really important for me."

David's observations about me were quite in contrast to the way he had referred to me in a detached and pretty disinterested manner earlier on, in the first years of weekly treatment. However, now David was viewing me through experience and a new developmentally achieved level of curiosity (through the developmental mourning process) rather than through projection and detached stereotypic fantasizing. He spoke of me with a passionate aliveness and this opened the colorful parts of him as he spoke of my dressing in colors. As love could come alive through truly experiencing the other (as an external object, rather than as a projection of an internal object), so could creativity (see Kavaler-Adler, 1996/2014) on the love-creativity dialectic as characteristic of psychic health). In the same session that David spoke of me in this new alive manner, he also revealed an emerging passion to create an integrated theory about his work as a dental surgeon, for the first time experiencing this work as being an involvement with individual people who have interesting and unique personalities.

He thought of creating his own theories as a composer composes music, which significantly differed from his early associations to any theory making since the thought of it had been tied up in the projection of a mother who used him narcissistically to fit into his theories. As David spoke of being creative by constructing his own theories, I responded with an affirming enthusiasm, which was what I genuinely felt. There was such an excitement in his coming alive like this.

Perhaps my response could at least be partially described by James Masterson's clinical theory of "communicate matching," meaning that the therapist/analyst responds with a level of interest comparable to that which the patient is exhibiting, the kind of "love affair with the world" of Margaret Mahler's practicing period in toddlers that extends into the rapprochement era when toddlers bring their newfound interests in the world back to their mothers. By meeting David with my enthusiasm, which I did naturally at the time, only thinking of Masterson later, I was affirming the reality of the world to David as a mother of the rapprochement era should, as I became alive as an object but still was needed to reflect his experience as his own unique separate experience, following the mourning of separation.

The Wife Comes Alive, and So Does David's Capacity for Psychic Conflict and Compassion

As the analyst came alive in David's consciousness and internal world, so did his wife come alive as a more vivid personality, rather than being seen through the veil of projections of bad object images (dissociated part objects related back to the mother and father). His wife became a three-dimensional character now as he spoke of her to me, whereas formerly she had been flat (the "witch mother," the "needy mother," the "inadequate mother," or the "judgmental mother"—all of whom were subliminally feared in the transference but experienced in off-target transferences or displacements in relation to the wife). He also became increasingly concerned about her and more empathic and compassionate toward her.

Whereas formerly David had spoken of his wife often in terms of a litany of complaints, now he spoke of trying to see beyond her particular foibles to the positive aspects of her that he even mentioned using the same phrase as for discovering the long-buried good father—as possessing some "wonderful qualities." He also became concerned that in his focusing on the things about her that annoyed him, he was encouraging his children to mock her for these things. He spoke of how unfair he felt it was of him to blame her for being who she was, and said he was trying not to do this anymore. He said that he was working very hard to be aware of his reactivity with her, to be aware of how he merged into her and just reacted automatically to things she did and said, without considering what was being triggered in him by her behavior. He said that it was fully about him when these automatic reactions were triggered, and he was trying to find out the meaning of these reactions with the help of treatment so that he would not inflict his old childhood problems on his wife. He spoke with a great feeling of caring and concern at this point.

Eventually, he said that he was succeeding at not blaming her for being who she was and that this had caused things to be much better between them. He said that they were actually having fun together now, having really great times together with their children as a family, and enjoying being alone together. He even said that they were having more sex now and were feeling a deeper connection with each other and within the sex than before. However, he added that even though his wife thought things were wonderful now, he could not help feeling that something was missing for him. He felt grief and some despair about this. He related missing something to holding on to the attachment with his old girlfriend at 16, and the one after that.

He spoke of wanting to hold on, crying as he spoke of the clinging feeling (the other side of the distancing defense), exclaiming, "I don't want to let go!" I brought David back farther in time than the old girlfriends, to the father who had been coming up in his dreams, whose loss went back to his infancy and symbolized to him the loss of a whole sensual and potentially sexual part of himself, especially when he was left with a mother who had been so disconnected from his body (being in a pathological mourning state). He had seen his wife as the desexualized mother, who was disconnected from her body. Now, he said that it was hard to sustain any view of his wife as sexual and that he continually experienced (now separate enough from his formerly unconscious experience to do so) how his perceptions were clouded by the return of the mother transference.

Since David had mourned enough to separate from his formerly unconscious transferences, just as he had mourned enough to separate from the internal mother whose blueprint lived inside of him from his childhood, he was able to separate from being consumed by any of his former part object identifications that had kept him a prisoner of dissociated self-states. With self-integration through mourning, he now could experience his different self perspectives on a symbolic level and not be consumed or possessed. With this new ability to conceptualize his self-experiences, he could speak freely, and without any need for encouragement on my part, of psychic conflict and of his difficulty holding on to both sides of a psychic conflict at once.

In one session, he articulated the analogy of the difficulty in feeling both sides of a conflict about identification in a sports event and in feeling two sides of a conflict concerning his wife. During a basketball game, he identified with the underdogs, and then, later in the game, with the former champions that were then the new underdogs. He said it was hard to feel for both at once. Likewise, he said that he found it difficult to stay open to loving and receptive feelings with his wife when he kept observing things about her that made him feel critical of her. He said that he kept closing off when he had critical thoughts and not sustaining the former love and intimacy they had shared. He was concerned that he could not feel love for her and also tolerate his critical thoughts without closing off emotionally. He said he was disillusioned that he could not solve this conflict, but he was aware that it was a conflict.

Disillusionments, Oedipal-Stage Mourning and Existential Grief, and the Opening of Memory

In a session in the ninth year of treatment, David declared, "the Israelis are getting murdered and the rest of us feel the burden of the grief. That doesn't negate the good things in the world, but the grief is really a weight." In the same session, David spoke of his personal grief in relation to the disillusionment of prized lifelong fantasies, hopes, and wishes. He combined thoughts of his personal disillusionments with thoughts of the general suffering in the world, feeling at one with humanity in that we all share the grief of life and its existential limits and disillusionments. He spoke of the Buddhist idea of life as the suffering of what is, and his grief feelings were palpable as he sobbed out his newfound observations.

As David stated his personal disillusionment, oedipal-stage grief, beyond the separation grief of abandonment depression spoken of earlier, arose along with the existential grief of life's limits and longings. He cried out to me and himself as witnesses that he felt forced to surrender his long-held and desperately cherished fantasies of having his wife's body and sexuality change, of having another woman who captured the sensuality of his early girlfriends, of having an omnipotent life span rather than the aging of his body he is aware of, and of having infinite choices instead of the necessity to give up so much to fully commit to his profession and his marriage. The volatile grief catharsis was followed by a session in which memories opened more clearly and fully than ever before. He recalled the details he formerly glossed over as he remembered the now defined betrayals and abandonments of his former girlfriends.

One memory was of his second girlfriend calling him from Europe in ecstasy, wanting him to be happy for her when she told him that she joined a cult and was never coming back. He recalled for the first time in sessions that he experienced a searing pain going through his entire body at the moment when he heard her words. Now, he spoke of betrayal and cried out to her the words he could never say back then when he dissociated from his feeling self to avoid the terrible agony of the abandonment void and repressed his thoughts about her. He had remembered in an earlier session that he went to bring her back from the cult with her brother and never asked her why she left, what she wanted, or if she thought of him; nor did he tell her that he missed her (feelings which he had dissociated and thoughts he had repressed). In this later session, he cried out angrily at her: "What about me? How can you treat me like I don't exist?"

Other betrayals came to mind as he cried out his formerly unvoiced rage at his former girlfriend. Associations led back to his father and his mother as well. He spoke with anger about seeing women walking with baby carriages, "proudly showing off their babies." He exclaimed that he could see his mother as one of them, and defined their behavior as narcissistic, as the possessive owning of their infants as self-image reflectors, rather than as separate human beings with unique needs. This sense of betrayal by his mother was joined with his father's form of abandonment betrayal and his later verbal attacks that were like knife stabs after his suffering of the original abandonment wound. This, combined with the betrayals of other male authorities (a lot of whom were former psychoanalysts), added up to fears of rejection that became a fear of sexual rejection when his unconscious mind had amalgamated it all as part and parcel of his early girlfriends' rejections. He then became the one inflicting rejection, when he identified with the aggressor and left women he dated later on, after his first two girlfriends and before his marriage.

He not only identified with the aggressor but also protected himself from triggering the whole abandonment trauma again by becoming disappointed and leaving the women, not giving them a chance to leave him. It had been easy to feel disappointment in any relationship because he no longer had possessed his full feeling self. He had dissociated his infant feeling self and had repressed later feelings and thoughts under the cement of his unconscious capacity for repression, with symptomatic evidence in his conscious despair and obsessive doubting. All this was his explanation for fearing more involvement with the analyst and with himself in treatment. Many of his memories of betrayal were of former male analysts who had offered a pseudo form of relationship, "which was just like what I had with my parents." He added that one had made him attend sessions four times a week for many years, taking his time and money and leaving him in a state of intensifying frustration. As he spoke of this, he felt his anger toward this former male analyst keenly and consciously. He was not only frustrated by a lack of authentic relationship or any clarification of his conflicts and symptoms but was also left by the analyst after the analyst had constantly given him reasons for staying in treatment when he wanted to leave. Naturally, with his infant past, he had experienced this leaving as an abandonment.

I said that there seemed to have been an impasse in this treatment and others because the analyst could not negotiate a countertransference related to not having been able to help him emerge as an authentic being beyond his former false self. I said that it was not enough to interpret transference or be aware of it, but that analysts needed to understand the need and process of developmental mourning and know how to allow it to emerge in interaction with transference analysis. David stated that he did not remember anything useful spoken about the transference by these former analysts. He said that maybe they were listening for the transference, but they never said anything, and they never invited him into awareness of the transference as he said I, his present analyst, had. I added that before that could be done, a critical developmental mourning process had to take place.

Despair Opening into Sadness and the Working through of Grief Sadness (and Regrets) to Arrive at an Integrated Self and a Commitment to Work and Marriage

In the sessions following David's existential grief suffering related to the disillusionment of his lifelong illusions and fantasies, and the sessions in which memories of betrayal opened up from this disillusionment, David returned reflexively to his former mode of unconscious distancing defense. He spoke with despair about life again but, significantly, not with the former sense of detachment. He spoke more angrily of how he kicked the wall next to his bed as a 10-year-old as if he was kicking the world for its being so disappointing. He spoke of the famous hippie, Abbey Hoffman, as an "out there crazy guy" who had tried to reinvent himself as an environmentalist and then had killed himself when he gave up on the world and decided that life sucked. He spoke again, naturally, about thoughts of leaving psychoanalytic therapy, because "what was the use of defining his conflicts when he still could not resolve them."

But as always in the pattern of evolution of the developmental mourning process and its distancing defenses, this angry, and formerly detached and cynical, despair opened its psychic veins to the renewed palpability of profound grief sadness. He reacted to growth-enhancing disillusionment with despair even though it was this disillusionment that was allowing him to accept the limits of life and his own personal mortality, which he now spoke about at length. And then the despair changed its affect color from anger to sadness. He was once again in a phase of mourning, and this would now allow him to touch the ability to make self-integrating commitments that he had formerly failed to reach—commitments within both his work and his marriage. He spoke of realizing that even though he always thought that he should have stuck with his interest in singing and made a career of it, rather than becoming a dental surgeon, he had recently found out how impossible such a lifestyle would have been for him, on speaking to a singer in a jazz club. He realized that he had built a specialty that he was interested in within his work.

Then the major challenge to commitment repeatedly arose, his reluctance to fully commit to his wife in marriage. But now, he could see the transferences that he projected, which made him pull back from her and feel that something critical, something sensual and sexual, was always missing. His wife had begun to accept him, compliment him, and see him in a much more positive light as he saw her more positively and resisted his old rejecting reactions. He cried out again in despair, "But I don't want to let go of you," implying that he could not let go of the memory of his first two girlfriends and of the fantasy of the erotically arousing woman that had been manufactured out of the cloth of this memory as it was repressed. He felt his clinging response, the other side of his distancing defense, and longed once more for the other woman. But he also felt that this longing to be somewhere else with someone else, and the feeling that he was betraying his first girlfriend by being with his wife, was keeping his own psyche split and divided. I made him aware that it went back farther than his first girlfriend, to the sensuous holding he had felt with his father in infancy.

He knew he needed a resolution. As we had the last session before my summer vacation, he proclaimed that he would be thinking about the therapy and about coming more often. He repeated his old way of thinking, that if he did not want to come more than once a week (at 60 minutes), maybe he had to leave. But this time, there was a new question mark in his comment. He questioned whether this was true. He questioned whether either there would be an alive process in treatment if he came more often and allowed his sexual feelings and wishes to come into the transference or if there would be a deadness if he remained at once a week. He was able to tread the high volatility of a high-wire perspective, the newfound mature and developmentally progressive perspective of ambivalence.

David smiled warmly at me as we ended for the summer, wishing me wholeheartedly a great summer! I responded warmly, simply saying, "Thank you, and you too." How different this moment was from an earlier one in the same session when he had protested that he might have some sadness about the summer break from me, but he would be quite glad to have the time and money he would gain, again speaking of the treatment situation as a losing proposition. It did not sound this way at the end of the session. Perhaps he had heard me after all when I said that he seemed to have no awareness that the feeling of depression he reported at the beginning of the session from the middle of the night before the session might have something to do with his unconscious reaction to losing me for the summer.

Dad as Demon-lover, Mom as Demon-lover

David had proclaimed in one session when his love for his father and the memories of his father were coming back to him, "I wanted to be close to my father, but in order to be close to him, I had to deny the whole dark side of him, which was a big part of him." In this statement, he captured the essences of how he had had to split himself to hold onto his father, with the consequence that his marriage and erotic fantasy life had been split, his views of women had been split, and he felt split and unfulfilled in any overt place or in any commitment he overtly made. Also, by splitting off the dark side of his father as he said, he had formed a part object demon-lover father that had inhabited his internal world and had obstructed his ability to remember and connect with the loving side of his father in adulthood. He also suffered the guilt of not caring for his father when he was old in an exaggerated and unconscious way that had made him have the psychic fall he portrayed in his earlier dream. He was always ready to fall into guilt and was continually guilty in his marriage.

His mother also had a repressed demon-lover side as he recalled her emotionally seductive behavior with him and proclaimed that she unconsciously had wanted him to be her lover. He had two part object parents as demon-lover figures in his internal world, and this had kept his own feeling self locked up and dissociated as a dark and unknown terrain. As the demon-lover parents came to light, he could own the fullness of his feeling states and therefore of his authentic multi-feeling self. He had become whole in treatment and left for the summer with the ability to feel and speak of two sides of a psychic conflict at once, and to be fully born into the depressive position's fruitful geography of conscious and rich ambivalence.

CHAPTER 7

"MY GRADUATION IS MY MOTHER'S FUNERAL": TRANSFORMATION FROM THE PARANOID-SCHIZOID POSITION TO THE DEPRESSIVE POSITION IN FEAR OF SUCCESS, AND THE ROLE OF THE INTERNAL SABOTEUR

Originally published in 2006, *International Forum of Psychoanalysis* 15(2):117–130.

Introduction

Sigmund Freud first addressed the fear of success in his 1916 paper (later published in the Standard Edition in 1957), "Those Wrecked by Success." In this paper, Freud distinguished between an external satisfaction that is seen on a manifest level as the prize of success that consummates ambition and an "internal frustration" (Freud, 1916, p. 317). The internal frustration "wrecks" the experience of success, so that what was desired is no longer desirable once it is achieved. In speaking of the internal frustration that stymies, spoils, and undermines success, Freud did not distinguish between neurotic guilt and existential guilt. In fact, such a consideration did not emerge in psychoanalytic thinking until Melanie Klein used clinical findings to distinguish between the phenomenology of the paranoid-schizoid and depressive positions. Once one is aware of the contrast between these two phenomenological psychic positions, one can distinguish between neurotic guilt, in which fears of retaliation predominate, and the existential guilt that manifests as grief when made conscious. In existential grief, actual remorse and compassion for a whole and separate other can be felt.

These distinctions allow us to see the developmental progression in a case of fear of success and its resolution. Without these distinctions, Freud left us with a globalizing oedipal level view of unconscious guilt. He did not address the issue of existential guilt, yet he uses the word "remorse" loosely, which implied existential guilt as opposed to neurotic guilt. In fact, in his descriptions of Lady Macbeth in "Those Wrecked by Success," he used the word "remorse" twice:

She who had seemed so remorseless seems to have been borne down by remorse. (Freud, 1916, p. 319)
What, however, these motives can have been which in so short a space of time could turn the hesitating, ambitious man into an unbridled tyrant, and his steely-hearted instigator into a sick woman gnawed by remorse. (Freud, 1916, p. 323)

Yet, when Freud actually assigned a motive to Lady Macbeth's enactment of unconscious guilt in her sleep-walking, obsessive cleaning rituals—after her cold-blooded murder of Duncan, through the instigated acts of her husband—it appeared that the guilt he was citing was not related to the existential guilt of remorse at all, but rather to the neurotic guilt related to a conviction that she had been punished, perhaps retaliated against by God or the gods. Freud concluded that this is Lady Macbeth's childless state, which followed after her partnership in murder that causes her to be driven mad with guilt. In other words, he implied that her guilt relates to her unconsciously believing that her childless state is the result of a punishing act of retaliation by a higher power. Therefore, according to Freud, it was the conviction that she had been punished in a retaliatory manner for her crime that undid her sanity and plunged her into guilt to the point of suicidal despair, as when she cried in Shakespeare's **Macbeth**, as quoted by Freud (1916), "All the perfumes of Arabia will not sweeten this little hand" (p. 324).

In citing Lady Macbeth's unconscious guilt as being related to the realization of her childless state after her crime, while also using the word "remorse" to describe the nature of her guilt, Freud (1916) conflated neurotic and existential guilt, also conflating two psychological states of mind, which became differentiated in the writings of Melanie Klein. For in Klein's profound discovery of the contrasts in psychic functioning between the paranoid-schizoid and depressive positions, she allowed for the distinction between the terror of retaliation, which appears as neurotic guilt within the paranoid-schizoid position, and true existential guilt, which is subjectively experienced as remorse, as well as regret. It is based upon this distinction that the unconscious motivation for fear of success can be examined, as I will do in the case of Sandra.

When we see that there is a developmental journey in those with a fear of success that evolves from the terror of retaliation in the paranoid-schizoid position to the anguish of existential guilt and remorse in the depressive position, we can see how Klein's view of mourning (1940) and my own view of developmental mourning are essential to understand the transformations within varying gradients of the fear of success and its ultimate incomplete, but ever-evolving, resolution. It is also important to note that existential guilt is a grief that encompasses object loss within it so that the route through mourning is a definitive one. Grief, related to existential guilt and remorse, is also an affect state, so it has a visceral body experience related to it, although it can have symbolic associations related to cognitive representations. Thus, existential guilt as grief is a natural phenomenon, as opposed to neurotic guilt, which is constructed through cognition employed in the service of defensive operations.

The case I will present in this study will illustrate an analysand's fear of success in relation to a terror of retaliation that bypasses the oedipal level, and which is initially experienced as a psychic fantasy of a preœdipal nature. The psychic fantasy was enacted on a visceral level within the woman's body. As the female analysand underwent Object Relations psychoanalysis, she moved from this terror of retaliation for success to an ability to achieve success. In so doing, she had to suffer depressive-position pain. The woman's developmental experience was a natural evolution of the pain of loss and regret, which interacts with true compassion and concern (Winnicott, 1963, 1963) for the other. I speak of such compassion, which has the grief of regret and object loss within it, as existential guilt.

The route to such compassion, once faced with the grief of existential guilt, is a mourning process, which has a natural organic course of developmental evolution. To describe this process, I use the term developmental mourning (Kavaler-Adler, 1991a, 1992a, 1993a/2013, 1993b, 1996/2014, 1998, 2000, 2003a, 2003b, 2004, 2005a, 2005b). Through the process of developmental mourning, the female analysand to be presented can be seen to navigate through progressive stages of separation-individuation highlighted in the transference dynamics and in the therapeutic Object Relationship itself (Grunes, 1984). In doing so, she relinquished paranoid fantasies of annihilation and retaliation that initially haunted her in the form of mother-father part-object attackers that were visceral as well as psychic in nature, and which could appear as vampires, cannibals, or her own "killer rage." As will be seen, the analysand was able to evolve through mourning into a separate and related self, acquiring a unique, individual, and ambitious voice that could finally bring her the success she had hungered for.

Yet, in doing so, she felt the grief of leaving her mother behind and, in Klein's terms, suffered and endured the guilt and loss of the depressive-position despair. Sandra paid this price in order to move ahead and "go for" her success. In doing so, she had to endure unconscious visceral punishments, which were followed in more advanced treatment by "black moods." Both the visceral punishments and the black moods appeared on the clinical scene as backlash reactions. These reactions after any success brought her past her mother in her accomplishments in life and differentiated her from her mother's identity.

Fear of Success in Sandra

Sandra entered into an eight-and-a-half-year Object Relations psychoanalysis by saying, "If I were to be out there like you, I'm afraid they would destroy me." After a critical mourning and separation-individuation process in treatment, she made the contrasting statement: "My graduation is my mother's funeral." Her earlier statement expressed the experience of "fear of success" in the paranoid-schizoid position in which the internal demonic "saboteur" was active, a saboteur that enacted a split-off part of the self that was merged with a hostile and inhibiting introject of the parent. The later statement, made after self-integration and separation-individuation in her analysis, reflected the depressive position experience of fear of success. By discussing Sandra's case, I will elaborate on the developmental journey that transforms the fear of success from an unconscious sabotaging enactment to a psychological state of compassion in relation to rivals, while still being able to claim one's rightful success in the world.

When Sandra entered her treatment with me, she experienced herself as being inside a numb, frozen, and paralyzed body, in which she felt like she had a metal rod between her head and her feet, as opposed to an alive feminine body. In this numbed state, she split-off and projected her hunger, envy, and impulses (part-self and part-objects fused through psychologically undigested affects), as all those developmentally arrested in the paranoid-schizoid state of mind do. Consequently, she was continually in terror from her externalized part-self and part-others she projected out, experiencing them as threatening her from outside. Any needs or demands from others colored those others in her mind as voracious psychic vampires.

Sandra's own hunger felt insatiable in her disconnected state in relation to her body at that time. She went from two to five psychoanalytic sessions a week, yet craved "eight" sessions, which she related to wishing she could have eight hotdogs when she ate one hotdog on the way to one session. Projecting her own hunger outside onto others—as well as the oral envy that accompanied this hunger owing to her feeling of extreme inadequacy within herself at that time—resulted in her being in a psychological state of siege in which she was constantly threatened by the needs of others. She could, however, re-own her own needs to the extent that she could focus them on the analyst in a transference that could be described as an idealizing transference (Kohut, 1971). The idealizing transference seemed particularly obvious as she tried to rid herself of her insatiable hunger, envy, and ambition by merging in with the analyst.

Sandra said to me in the beginning, "I feel you, like I hear the way you hear, and see the way you see." She spoke of seeing through my eyes, and of me writing in her mind when she found her way to reading some of my books. Sandra seemed to be expressing a wish to be her own idealized self, but her conscious sense of herself was just the opposite. At first, she had described herself as a numb person, but the frustration of this numbness also caused her numb feeling to alternate with the feeling of a "killer rage." She felt helpless and impotent in the face of her own killer rage at this time, and in the face of her envious and voracious projections onto others. Yet within the sanctity of the therapeutic Object Relationship (Grunes, 1984), where she could live psychologically within her idealizing transference connection with the analyst, she found an oasis, and it was here that the latent and dissociated self began to emerge, a self that had been arrested owing to separation-individuation trauma in her preœdipal years, as well as in the years following.

Initially, however, Sandra's terror of being "out there" made any ambition, desire, or wish for recognition on her part too dangerous. Her initial solution was to live through the analyst, not only by imagining herself as seeing through my eyes and feeling through me but also in her wishes to vicariously experience success in the world through my success. She explicitly stated to me that she would get extremely excited in thinking of me giving a professional presentation or in my assuming any position of authority or stardom in the world. Sandra said that she felt hot inside with excitement and expansiveness when she thought of me before an audience. This became extremely interesting later in treatment when her own ambition to be a motivational speaker arose. At this earlier time, however, she spoke with an intense feeling of "wanting to be there" when I emerged into public view with my own presentations, and she would imagine that I was becoming ever more developed in my communication with the world and my expression of my talents.

Sandra's Internal Mother

Sandra's internal mother, as internalized from childhood, was reflexively engaged in an unconscious tug of war over Sandra's capacities for success because success implied separation from her mother, and Sandra's mother had always reacted in quite a hostile manner to her moves toward separation. Sandra's internal mother compelled Sandra, as her first child, to be either an idealized extension of herself or the bad child who contained her mother's split-off dark side, with all its unacknowledged and unassimilated aggression. When in the state of her mother's bad self, Sandra felt heavy, gloomy, dirty, dull, numb, and serious. In Sandra's mind, it was a contrast to who I was—her transferential mother. To get out of this state, while still enmeshed in psychic symbiosis with the childhood mother who had become a fused symbiotic internal object, Sandra could move toward achievements in the world, such as making good grades at school. Through this outward achievement, Sandra could gratify her mother's narcissistic wishes, given the frustration of her mother's own arrested state, because she felt a constant pressure to achieve.

There was another message from Sandra's mother as well. Any achievement also threatened to evoke Sandra's mother's dissociated envy, and Sandra would experience this threat in projections of her internal envious mother onto others. Any step on Sandra's part toward having her own voice, opinions, and accomplishments, was followed by terror, grief, loss, a collapsing of self-confidence, and paranoia about being assaulted or killed. This created her backlash reactions of somatic and visceral aspects. She would feel choked, suffocated, and repulsed. She would become nauseous from choking back a vomiting anger and a sense of poison within her. Alternately, Sandra could return to the visceral sense of an empty pipe within her or deadness and numbness. As her affect life came alive, however, through the separation and mourning process, she also had backlash reactions of boiling hot rage, as if she were on fire. Eventually, she would face her feelings of object loss. She would face her grief, disillusionment, and sadness.

Despite these painful backlashes, however, Sandra's developmental strivings to be out there in the world persisted and flourished into a culminating triumph throughout her treatment. As she became increasingly aware of formerly dissociated affect states, she began to acknowledge her envy, greed, hunger, and insatiable cravings. Instead of just being a victim of the projected internal mother, she became an agent of her own envious and murderous wishes as she hungered to have what I, as the other, had. As long as I represented an idealized extension of her self, she could feel enlivened and restored by my success in the world, for she was to me as her mother was to her. But she too, like her internal mother, had wishes for being the center of things.

Therefore, although she could momentarily be thrilled as a part of me, relishing my accomplishments in the world as if they were her own, she would in the next moment have a backlash reaction from her dissociated envy, lust for fame, power, and distinction in the world. So at one time, she could feel sincere admiration for me. For example, she would see me present some of my work before an audience, related to her interest in psychology, and would exclaim: "Your presentation was just marvelous! There is something in you developing. It's just getting better and better. I guess I feel warm inside now"; and "I don't know how it happened but I feel excited." Yet, at other times, she would feel envy: "I envy your vision. I want it for myself."

Sandra's vicarious experience of my success in being out in the world was obviously intense and extremely visceral, which suggests the early level of its psychic origin, as in her feeling hot and excited in her body when expressing her response to a professional presentation of mine. Her envy, therefore, could be just as intense and visceral. This could explain why, when Sandra projected envy onto others, they often would take on the powerful and sensual form of a vampire. The projection of a vampire contained a highly visceral oral erotic hunger, from primal infant development.

As Sandra progressed from wanting to be a part of me and wanting to be merged with me as her idealized object (and self-extension), she began to want a higher form of identification. With some progress in separation, she could say: "I want to be like a musician who takes in from you and then uses it for myself. I want to become myself but can take in and learn from you." She began to feel that she could take me in as a model and psychically digest me, rather than remaining a part of me. As she moved in this direction, Sandra still felt elated after a presentation of mine. Afterward, however, she experienced a feeling of loneliness, when suddenly she was overwhelmed by the awareness of being a separate being. As self and object images separated in her internal world, which she experienced consciously through remembering a dream of her body separating from her mother's body, she became developmentally and psychically separate. Consequently, being a part of me no longer worked for her.

Then Sandra's anxiety about the conflict of wanting to be out there, and yet fearing exposure and hate from others, returned to her in a new way. As her observing ego developed through mourning, allowing her to reflect on her own anxiety, Sandra said, "I'm so happy for you when you're out there, for your joy and excitement. But I'm not there yet. Will I get there?"

Despite her hesitation and fear, and her concern about her own capacities, Sandra began to feel a desire for, rather than a dread of, taking risks to be out in the world. She began to create her own performances, presentations, and successes. On her developmental journey, however, Sandra felt both states of paralysis and states of conscious envy. In a state of helplessness and paralysis, thrown back onto the inadequate self that feels like it lacks agency without the support of a mother (she spoke of grandiose pride on top of a helpless inadequate part), she cried with grief over her despair. She had risked being out there and then collapsed. I interpreted the psychological bind she was in owing to the separation trauma she carried with her, and she was deeply relieved. I said:

> You feel helpless because you're in a psychological bind in your mind. You fear being out there because you're afraid of being hated, resented, and envied, but you simultaneously fear staying in the cocoon or shell that you felt you lived in originally because you no longer could stand to

feel empty, detached, and numb. When you withdraw now, you're aware of feeling isolated and alone.

Another way in which Sandra attempted to deal with this bind was to try to raise herself up from the helpless state by a defensive manic triumph in relation to me, as if triumphing over me (as a transferential mother and model) would raise her up. She told me in one session in her second year of treatment, "I'm going to have a large apartment and a concierge, and you'll be in this little office." She laughed with conscious contempt at this mental triumph and said, "I want diamonds and pearls now." By the time she was able to say this to me, she did not need me to interpret it. She interpreted it herself: "I can't believe that I can be so open about my envy and contempt now."

In this session, she progressed from urgent wishes for a bigger apartment to a feeling of missing me and wanting to continue our journey into her internal world, wishing for the riches within. The symbolic gifts from her relationship with me became more important in the transition of the session, and she relinquished the immediacy of the wish for a concrete achievement of attaining a new and bigger apartment. But, overall, she was becoming increasingly conscious of her wish to shine in her own right. She articulated this in the third year of treatment: "I no longer want to be fused with you. I want to have my own voice now." Such a wish expressed her developmental progression from wanting to be an extension of the idealized me—a state of psychic symbiosis in which she lived happily in a vicarious relation to me—to a later state of a differentiated self-identity, with individuation, connection, separation, and relatedness.

The Split-Off Saboteur or Antilibidinal Ego Opposing Separation

In addition to an aggressive internal mother—who used Sandra as an extension of herself and as a split-off part of herself, housing the mother's projections of aggression, depression, and hunger—Sandra had a specific form of a hostile internal and sabotaging object within her. This part-object mother was explicitly retaliatory in reaction to Sandra's natural and organic developmental moves toward separation. This reactive and retaliatory mother operated side by side with a good mother who nurtured her. Sandra projected the good mother onto me when she was in the early years of her treatment and was in an idealizing transference. The good mother of the past, who became internalized, would read Sandra wonderful fairy tales and tell her fascinating stories about her own life. All this made it easy for Sandra to listen in a highly receptive way to me in my relating to her and in my interpretations.

This was almost as if she were drinking in my words. I represented a good mother whom she felt merged with in her infancy, before separation needs threatened her mother and resulted in a traumatic disruption of bonding, along with the negative internal saboteur that she developed from this trauma.

The mother's primitive aspects were noted by Sandra. The specific pattern of her mother's attacks on her for separation, however, became more conscious and apparent as critical memories arose through Sandra's associations while on the couch. Two particularly vivid memories seemed to explain the phenomenology of Sandra's internal saboteur in relation to her moves toward being out in the world and claiming success. The first memory was of being five years old and coming back home to her mother with a candy that a neighbor had given her. Sandra remembered her mother exploding into a rage, grabbing the candy from her, and then throwing it into the fireplace.

The second memory was of being in high school and going out to a disco. Sandra recalled with deep humiliation and shame—which later would evolve into her own rage—that her mother came after her, found her in the disco, pulled her outside, turned around, and slapped her hard upon her face, in front of other teenagers who were in front of the disco. Her mother did not say anything, but it was clear to Sandra that her mother did not want her going away from home and socializing with boys. This was only a follow-up to her not wanting Sandra to socialize with neighbors when she was five years old.

Furthermore, even beyond these specific remembered incidents, Sandra recalled that her mother had a generally punitive and restrictive attitude toward her that prevented her from playing with other children when she was young (even though her mother could leave her to go back to work when she was six). She got the message loud and clear that she was not supposed to have any friends apart from her mother. Even her father could be a threat. Although the father had some affection for her when she was very little, he felt on the outside of the exclusive orbit that Sandra's mother kept with her first child, Sandra. This resulted in Sandra's father's rejection of Sandra in favor of treating her younger sister as special, a sister who was born when Sandra was six years old. Sandra's father also became hostile in attitude toward Sandra. He would push her away with insults, reprimands, or contemptuous assessments of her. Once, when he saw her perform on a girls' volleyball team in high school, he told her that she "just didn't have it."

The combination of Sandra's mother's hostile and visceral rebuffs during her childhood, and her father's verbal ones, could be seen to have formed the internal sabotaging object (part-object, with part of mother and father combined) within Sandra's psyche, in both its repressed and split-off and dissociated aspects. However, the mother's visceral-level attacks were most obvious at first when

Sandra was still psychically in the paranoid-schizoid position when regressing on the couch, prior to her developmental journey through mourning and separation-individuation in treatment. One form this took for Sandra in the beginning of treatment was that she would lie on the couch and have fantasies of stabbing herself in the heart or stomach. There was, however, an even more dramatic form of sabotaging attack from her internal object that was exclusively visceral in nature, beyond the symbolized fantasy of a visceral attack.

Recapitulation of Early Infant Illness through the Articulation of the Internal Saboteur

In the first and second years of treatment, Sandra recalled a critical trauma from her infancy that occurred prior to her separation-individuation stage trauma and its later age levels of separation trauma. It was unclear how much she could actually remember since it had occurred when she was so young, and how much was repeatedly described to her by her mother. Perhaps most of it was described to her, but early trauma often does remain in memory in a way in which other experiences of such an early time would naturally be forgotten.

The trauma that Sandra described was of having gotten ill as a baby, and of being brought by her mother to the hospital in her native land in Holland. Her mother had apparently had to leave her alone in the hospital. But then her mother was told by the doctors to come and get her child. They told Sandra's mother that her little girl was going to die, and recommended that the mother take her child home so she could die at home. On the way home by train, Sandra's mother was in a state of despair, crying incessantly, while holding her baby daughter on her lap.

As the mother held her baby girl, her baby began to spit up and vomit. By that point, her mother was in a state of apathy. She assumed the doctors were correct and that she would lose her daughter imminently to death. So she just sat and let her daughter vomit over and over again onto her blouse and skirt. This seems to have been what saved Sandra, for as she vomited on her mother's lap, she must have spit out all the toxins related to her illness. Being with her mother again must have re-established a maternal bond for Sandra that she seems to have needed to allow her body to react in its own defense. It seems that she healed herself by vomiting up the poison that was within her, which was perhaps also the poison of fear of having been wrenched away from the presence of her mother while in the hospital.

On the couch, Sandra associated one day to a blue blouse I was wearing, remembering the blue color of her mother's blouse, when she was held on the mother's lap, while on the train ride home from the hospital, and vomited on her mother's blouse. Could this have been actual memory as opposed to her mother's recollection? Perhaps yes, because Sandra must have been overcome by the sensory stimuli at that time. In addition to associating the color of my blouse (that of her idealized transferential mother) with the blue blouse of her mother at a time when being reunited with her mother saved her life, Sandra also dreamed of a part of herself in a blue blouse. She associated to a spiritual aura linked in her mind with the blue color, and with the nature of that part of herself that appeared in her dream. Certainly, it must have seemed highly spiritual to her to be saved from "heaven" by being in her mother's lap again.

The Inverse Use of Sandra's Infant Illness Experience by Her Adult Unconscious

As Sandra's analyst, I began to notice that there were many times during the first two years of treatment (perhaps unconsciously corresponding to her first two years of life) when Sandra would simulate choking, coughing, and vomiting when on the couch. The vomiting began to appear to be like a visceral event that had unconscious messages in it. As I witnessed Sandra reliving the infant illness, I began to realize that the timing of the events was unconsciously programmed. I interpreted this when I could see what the unconscious program was. I came to believe that it was a program of reaction to a preœdipal conflict around separation needs and strivings that was evidenced by Sandra, both in her analysis and in all her life activities.

Sandra had reacted through body symptoms to her internal mother's assault on her developmental separation needs all her life. She had also reacted to forced separations from her mother through her body, having often become sick when her mother had become sick. She became sick when she needed her mother, while her mother was in the hospital unavailable to her. Once sick, she could join her mother in the hospital. When an adult, Sandra reacted to the two sides of her separation conflict through physical bulimia. Once she put a boundary between herself and her mother by coming to this country and leaving her homeland, she transformed the physical bulimia into the behavioral symptom of compulsive shopping. Once Sandra entered psychoanalytic treatment, however, she evidenced a psychological form of bulimia, in having reactions within the transference of throwing up the transferential mother who triggered off the internal mother who opposed her separation. Alternatively, she had cravings to swallow the analyst whole as in her fantasies of having eight sessions with me as if they were eight hotdogs. With Sandra's lifelong tendencies to have somatic and visceral symptoms in reaction to her unconscious conflicts, it was interesting to see how the visceral transformed into the psychological within the treatment process.

Earlier reactions to success in the world or, in Sandra's words, to being "out there," would trigger Sandra's identifications with an internal mother who became enraged by her moves to separate and be out in the world, away from the exclusive orbit of her relationship with her mother. The conflict between Sandra's developmental needs to separate from this mother, and her regressed needs to cling to her by identifying with her, would be enacted within Sandra's body as visceral reactions that had bulimic simulations. Sandra would feel nauseous and feel like vomiting on the couch. Later in treatment, however, after a profoundly powerful developmental mourning process, Sandra would manifest an internal backlash from her internal mother through emotional reactions rather than body reactions, either of a visceral or somatic nature. So instead of feeling nauseous with the urge to vomit, Sandra would speak of "black moods" that would envelop her right after any success in the world, each success having symbolic separation meanings.

Sometimes this would happen in the middle of the night. Then Sandra would speak with some anguish in her analytic session the next day of how she went to sleep feeling really good after risking speaking up in a class in graduate school, or after presenting work in a group, and then describe how she woke up feeling horrible, feeling, as she described it, in "a black mood." She would exclaim: "Nothing happened on the outside." I would then interpret to her that her childhood separation conflict was unconsciously being triggered again by her success in the world the day before. Within her black mood would be painful emotions connected with an internal rage, and the black mood would also manifest as the reliving of verbal level assaults from her later childhood and adolescence.

In addition to the emotional state of the black mood that recapitulated her mother's rage affect at critical points of her separating as a child, Sandra would have the experience of verbal attacks that re-enacted her father's verbal abuse of her during her childhood, and particularly during her adolescence. In essence, there was a combined negative mother-father bad object within her internal world that spoke to her through emotional states and internalized verbal assaults.

When she became conscious of the verbal assaults within the affect state of rage, as well as of its associated pain, she would begin to have differentiated memories of her father attacking her self-esteem with verbal comments. One memory was of her father attending a volleyball match when she was on a volleyball team in high school. Instead of applauding her and appreciating her courage in being on a team and competing, her father sadistically commented, "You don't have it." At that time, Sandra could not have known that this kind of attack on her came from an alcoholic father who was suffering from his own decline in life and much frustrated ambition. She began to feel a hatred for her father that came back in these black moods, where her being "out there" in the world, before an audience, competing, was looked upon with scorn by her father. Similarly, she suffered from repressed rage and hatred when her father attacked her developing femininity and womanhood in her adolescence by chopping off all her hair after she had gotten a then-stylish Jane Fonda hairdo at the hairdresser.

As Sandra's hatred toward her father became conscious, she was able to move toward the grief of losing an earlier father who had shown affection toward her. She became able to forgive her father as she came to forgive and appreciate her mother through the course of her developmental mourning process in treatment. The latent love that lay behind her rage and hatred emerged into a powerful current of love toward the analyst in the transference, a love that was quite different from her earlier idealizing of the analyst, from the time when her affect self had still been in a sealed-off and split-off state.

Sandra's Subjective Experience of her Developmental Mourning Process

Sandra's earlier projections of others outside destroying her for daring to be "out there" in the world transformed to a grief-laden existential guilt as she imagined her mother being left behind as she separated and became successful in the world. It was in the middle of a developmental mourning process, which had both object loss (abandonment depression; Masterson 1976, 1981) and the grief of guilt in it (Klein's depressive position; Klein, 1940), that Sandra said, "I'll become more successful and my poor mother will be left behind, after giving everything to me." This statement came quite a bit earlier than her statement "My graduation is my mother's funeral," which was said later, at a time when she was accepting her success more but still carrying the fear of killing her mother off with each success. The first statement was said when Sandra was continually having backlash reactions after success. But as she proceeded to grieve, and found within her grief a discovery of the love for the mother she had cut off from, she became increasingly able to tolerate her guilt on a conscious level. Through grieving, she ceased to have continual and severe backlash reactions.

Sandra's guilt extended beyond a defensive reaction to her rage, which early in treatment was experienced viscerally as a sensation of knife-stabbing attacks in both her heart and her hip. She also had ceased to have impulses to actually stab herself while lying on the couch, but these sensory phantasies signaled both her internal mother's retaliatory attacks on her for her moves toward separation and her own attacks of hate toward her internal mother for not letting her go. Sandra became increasingly conscious of her hate in treatment, speaking in visceral terms of affect experience, saying "A virus has gotten into my heart and if I don't slow down I'll have a heart attack." As she slowed down to feel her hate, it melted into anger and then into love. But to get to the love, she had to consciously own her guilt over her hate toward her mother and family. As she became increasingly conscious of her guilt, she could cease to act it out viscerally in her body.

As Sandra accepted her hate, she also opened the door to her love. She experienced the melting of her cold defensive hate from formerly unconscious rage. She described this psychological phenomenon in the visceral terms of body metaphor, saying as she cried deeply on the couch, "a stone in my heart has dissolved." Sandra surrendered to her grief over her hate. She began to feel the longings for her mother that lay behind her hate and behind the defensive wall of frozen hate that had sealed her off from her own heart core and the love from her heart.

Sandra began to surrender to a primal longing for her mother as she existed in the present as an external other. Feelings of grief and sadness had led to this more differentiated longing for her mother, and consequentially the pain of a frustrated or traumatized child transformed into the adult compassionate pain of conscious regret. She could now encounter her external mother in the present and appreciate her, saying "My mother never lost her spirit. I brought her cakes, flowers, and spiritual tapes on Mother's Day, and she smiled with love and warmth."

Even though it was neurotic and defensive guilt that made Sandra feel that her autonomy was a crime, and which had made her feel like stabbing herself in the heart in the body locus where her love for her mother had turned to hate, it was an existential guilt that made her feel she was responsible for pulling away from her mother throughout her adult life, and even now, in the present, during the third year of her psychoanalytic treatment. As she turned her existential guilt into grief, Sandra was becoming increasingly independent of her mother on a deep emotional level, and now could choose to have a relationship with her that would not impede her own growth and her capacities to be "out there," engaging with others in the world with all the creative talents that were emerging with her grieving and "letting go" process.

Sandra focused on the visceral pain in her psychoanalytic sessions and its psychological transformations. The stabbing transformed into the emotional pain of fearing that her mother would die before she could speak to her, before she could learn how to communicate with her, before she could learn how to say, "I miss you." Sandra sobbed as she felt the sadness of longing for her mother, longing to forgive and surrender after so many years of withholding herself, and of being mechanical with her mother. Even more profoundly, the visceral stabbing pain opened up into a longing to be able to say things to her father as well, to reach him before his death, to have a father, to say, "I miss you." Sandra cried with a new form of grief as she proceeded past the rage she had come to express toward the father of her past. She had felt her rage and her hurt in treatment, and now she could miss the potential father, or father representative, later experienced in a male mentor, with whom she could have a better experience.

As Sandra sobbed and sobbed on the couch about her grief in missing her mother, she said that the stone in her heart was dissolving and that she felt better after every session in which she opened to her deep crying. She then said, "It felt like I hit rock bottom the last time. It felt like something cracked inside of me as I cried, and now I'm walking around with pain in my heart. I realize I sort of killed off everybody in a way. I had this denial that I needed anyone. I tried to put the hunger into concrete things like food and shopping. I really want to call my mother and talk to her now."

Sandra continued her grieving process, with its psychic and developmental transformations.

She said:

I felt some virus got into my heart, but maybe that's because my heart is not as frozen as before. I need to cry and cry and cry. It feels like the pain is going away as I cry.... I feel really sad, like someone really died. I never went through such sadness in my life. It's hard to believe that nothing happened on the outside. It feels like both my parents died. This sadness and heaviness seems endless, like there are endless layers on the inside of me, really endless. It's such a difficult thing to go through psychoanalysis. I don't where I'll end up. It gets deeper and deeper. Maybe there's something psychotic and then what is it? Who is the other person inside of me? That's what it feels like, like there's another person coming out, a person inside sitting with face in her hands, sitting with such sadness, sadness. I cannot lift my head and look at the world. It seems endless, like penance. I guess I want to break everything in myself. I never know when I come here what I will talk about, what will come up. I really don't know who I am anymore. It's related to all these sadnesses I never felt before in my whole life.... Before I didn't know the difference between the inside and outside. Maybe my asking is bringing two images of myself together. On the positive side it feels like an ocean cave today. I really like getting into these places. It feels like the source of something. It feels so connected—my God!

At this point, I said to Sandra, "I think you're saying that there is a way of experiencing things now that is like experiencing God." To this Sandra replied:

> I think that's true. It's like experiencing an energy—very wonderful! It makes me feel very safe in happiness and sadness. I don't know how that whole thing happened. I feel the shift today. But when the reconnection happens, all of a sudden it's getting connected to a greater source, a channel … I've been changed, like; before, my energy and frequency was so low and now everything is tingling, like sparks or something I'm feeling, like joyful! This is something. Divine!

As soon as Sandra said this, she had a brief backlash reaction, indicating the old paranoid-schizoid position fear of success. She said, "I hope I didn't demolish anyone in my class at school. I'm afraid I'll antagonize everyone against me when I speak up. It was safer to be mute like before." The success in class was linked then in her association process with her wish to have me exclusively and to have the teacher of the class exclusively. Unconsciously, she was wishing to re-establish an early exclusive bond with her mother, but then she had to risk the wrath of her father in response. In identification with the envious father within her, she questioned whether any of her feeling expression had been authentic, and with the air of her father's contemptuous disdain and disregard for her, she wondered whether she was faking all her feelings just to be special to me.

As Sandra continued in this grief-defense process, along with her transference-defense process, she was also experiencing the forward and backward movements of a developmental separation-individuation process, with its continuing backlash reactions related to the reliving of the separation trauma of the past, as well as the trauma of having an internal father who attacked her for connection as well as for separation. Yet the compulsive retaliation from the internal parents that had formed the psychic structure of her antilibidinal ego became progressively less powerful for her as her mourning process continued to open her core self (felt as a "heart center") to her innate capacity to love. She articulated the trenchant power of the conflict as it played itself out, out in the world, as well as within her mind and body. She said, "I'm really out there. I'm really out there, and I feel I'm going to die. It just feels like I can't go on crying and crying. I want to get away from the feeling. I'm doing something wrong, crying and sobbing." I responded to this, "You're crying now because you believe that you're a bad child for coming out on your own. This crying of guilt feels different than the crying of pure loss and love."

Sandra looked to the therapeutic Object Relationship with me for comfort and expressed her transferential wishes quite openly and consciously: "I just feel like I want you to be my mom and I will be the child. I'd like to hug and kiss you like I hugged and kissed my mother when I loved her." Sandra was now able to express her core object longings in words, without acting out by displacing them onto food or things she would buy in whirlwinds of compulsive shopping as she once did. She sought safety in the maternal transference as she experienced her internal bad mother (the mother of separation and the contemptuous and rejecting father) as attacking her again from within. At one moment, she faced her existential guilt and remorse. Then she did not need to seek safety in a haven with me. Then in the next moment, she faced the old internal attack; she faced the return of the old bad objects and the old self-feeling state. She was, however, vulnerable to this feeling on a conscious level, and could begin to define and understand it.

Sandra was no longer cold, frozen, numb, and sealed-off. She was now experiencing all parts of herself and all parts of her internal world. She could therefore be conscious of her core developmental separation conflict. She could observe it rather than be internally possessed by it as she once had been. In the process, her sense of her interior world changed and she felt "an ocean cave," and "a low key depth" within her. She still, however, experienced the residue of the split-off self, with its hostile "bad object" attacks on her self as it emerged through self-expression into the world. Sandra allowed herself to surrender not only to her tears of grief, as she longed for the "good" internal mother, who she was afraid she had killed off when trying to escape from the "bad" mother who was internalized in a state of hostility toward her separation and individuation process. She also surrendered to the organic developmental thrust within her toward her own emerging personality in the world.

The Dream of Sandra's Body Separating Out From her Mother's Body

As psychoanalysts, we can observe both the internal and external world developments that signify to us that true psychological transformation is taking place. Looking at the internal world through psychic fantasies, and through fantasies within dreams, can present us with evidence of the psychic changes taking place, as well as illustrating transference and defense processes. In the case of Sandra, one particular dream vividly displayed her developmental progression and psychological transformation. It also seemed significant that, as Sandra was so sensitive to psychological phenomena on a visceral level, the dream should be a dream about her body, and that it should simultaneously serve as a paradigm for her developmental journey, as she progressed in separation and also in fuller and deeper experiences in the depressive position. Entering more fully into the depressive position, Sandra could feel and interpret her own internal experience, enlarging her general sense of interiority.

The dream I refer to was simple, direct, and vivid in nature. In the midst of' journey of sadness and longings, and following her freedom from repressing or dissociating her hate and blocking off her healthy self-asserting aggression, Sandra dreamt that her body separated out from her mother's body. This dream in itself would have meant less had it not been followed by a psychoanalytic session in which the transference-countertransference dynamics allowed both Sandra and I to experience the psychological reality testified to by the dream. It was in the same session in which Sandra reported this dream to me that I, for the first time, had a totally different affect and self-state experience from that of Sandra when with her.

At the end of the session, Sandra spoke of feeling a wonderful flow of sensuality and elation through her entire being. She asked me whether I was feeling it with her as I had for years felt feelings with her. In fact, I had not long ago detected her hunger, fear, and longings as she had felt them in sessions through my own body and feeling states. Not long before, I had also felt on a visceral level the sensation of my lungs opening in a session as Sandra had felt herself expand through her lungs opening. Yet, in this session, following her dream about her body separating out from the body of her mother, I felt feelings contrasting with those Sandra was having.

As Sandra felt fluid with joy and excitement, I felt slightly depressed. Although this reaction on my part could, of course, just have been related to a personal state of feeling within myself, it seemed more likely that it had meaning in terms of Sandra's internal world and its transformation. Perhaps I was experiencing being the sad and depressed child that Sandra had felt like when her mother was in a manic state of contrived joy. Or perhaps I was just having my own separate experience of feelings she was at that point leaving behind. Even if the feelings were only attributable to my own feeling state at that time, the fact that I felt such distinct feelings from Sandra was a new evolution in our work together. This seemed to signify that her separation from her mother on an intrapsychic level was now resulting in a boundary between us that was not being crossed by Sandra's projections into me, as in the very real psychic transmission within projective identification. Perhaps she was leaving me behind as her transferential mother, and I would have to fend for myself, without being with her. If so, this meant that Sandra was no longer being held back from her own journey by fears that her mother would die, even though she would continue to have thoughts about her mother's death with each new achievement and success.

Graduation and the Survival of Two Mothers

It was in Sandra's fifth year of treatment that she completed a course of graduate school training in literary and psychological studies that would allow her to graduate and to forge out into the world in a new professional role, a role that she hoped would lead to her dream of becoming a motivational speaker. By the end of this fifth year of psychoanalysis, Sandra had navigated through the deepest and darkest terrors of her internal world and had faced the depths of her sadness and separation-individuation grief. She had also faced the depressive-position pain related to her existential grief as it came to consciousness through regrets.

One particular regret had been that related to having cut off and frozen out her mother, who was now in her life again, as she had followed her to this country. At one moment of anguish, having vividly recalled the events of her almost fatal infant illness, Sandra cried out, "How could I have done that to my mother who saved my life when I was a baby?" She also cried out about her regret that she had left her own son at home in her country with her mother, and then with her ex-husband's family when she had left her native country. She sobbed as she exclaimed, "How could he have lived without a mother!" as she became acutely conscious of her own primal yearnings for repairing and continuing a connection with her own mother, whom she had come to accept, love, and have compassion for.

Part of Sandra's depressive-position grieving process, within her overall developmental mourning process, consisted of learning how deeply her heart could open to love channeling through the sadness of grief whenever she managed to contain her aggressive impulses. This included containing her compulsive urges to retaliate against her now almost adult son who came to join her in the United States, and who was hostile and provocative in his behavior toward her for a long time. When Sandra contained powerful aggressive and retaliatory impulses, she could feel the pain of her own early traumas and deprivations. She could also begin to have conscious memories and psychic fantasies that gave meaning to what compelled these impulses. In the process of containing and defining her aggressive impulses, Sandra moved from identifying herself as a criminal with "killer rage" to identifying herself with such pacifist social reformers as Martin Luther King and Mahatma Gandhi.

This depressive-position mourning, combined with the mourning of loss related to separation trauma and separation needs, all contributed to a developmental mourning process that allowed Sandra to reach her dream of authentic and colorful self-expression at the time of her graduation. Prior to this self-defining celebration of her selfhood and adulthood, Sandra suffered from the fear of her ambition brewing in her, combined with the guilt that she always attached to her ambition. This guilt had both neurotic and existential elements, and illustrated a developmental advance from the paranoid terror of the paranoid-schizoid position, a position in which she had lived prior to her developmental mourning process in treatment.

Sandra declared almost defiantly, while lying on the couch prior to her upcoming graduation, "My graduation is my mother's funeral!" As she spoke, there was more of a sense of challenge and preserved personal motivation in her declaration than in the past, when she had made another depressive position statement, "I'll go on and succeed and my poor mother, who gave everything to me, will be left behind with nothing." Now, Sandra was not turning back. She owned responsibility for her guilt consciously, but she was ready to move ahead without the usual intimidation and post-achievement backlash.

On the night of Sandra's graduation, she was asked to give a speech as she collected her certificate and its degree. Instead of being terrified at this prospect, she rose to the occasion with excitement. She did, however, suffer some anxiety and apprehension beforehand, fearing she would lose her sense of self or her voice. But once up on stage, Sandra scintillated and sparkled. She was not even inhibited by the fact that her mother was in the audience. She spoke to the graduation assembly with an air of spontaneous joy, tempered with a dignified sense of genuine accomplishment. Her humor emerged as well, and she spoke in turn to each of her professors with a personal and direct attitude, combined with professional strength and an identification with her new field and her new career. She gained much applause on this occasion, but what was most striking was her ability to shine forth in front of her mother.

Sandra was, in fact, able to accept the mixture of her mother's congratulations and pride in her with her mother's remaining narcissistic attitude, for Sandra's mother could not resist telling her that Sandra reminded her of herself when she was young. She said that she thought of herself as the vibrant one who won applause and had never seen her daughter in that view before. Sandra noted her mother's reluctance to share the stage before the audience of life with her, but she was not at all stymied by this aspect of her mother's response, nor was she guilt-ridden because of it. She told me in her analysis that, in spite of her mother's narcissistic comment, she could tell that her mother was glowing with pride in her daughter's accomplishment, and she also perceived her mother's gratitude for Sandra's rapprochement with her. They had bonded significantly before this event. So Sandra came to see that her mother could not only survive her success but could also benefit from it. All this, tested out now in a critical moment of reality, allowed her to feel confident about her future and her talents.

In the analyst's office, a parallel process took place with her transferential mother. As her analyst, I played this part, and Sandra could see that I was surviving her success as well. She could see that I would go on with my own life and my own successes, and she relinquished her formerly grandiose view that my life would end along with her mother's when she was capable of leaving me, which she did do, with an appropriate and organic "graduation," a termination from treatment three and a half years later. Sandra had to admit that her graduation was not her mother's funeral, and any unconscious wish she had had to knock her mother and her transferential mother off the stage as competitors was tempered by her deeply felt relief that we had survived her accomplishment and had survived any unconscious murder that this accomplishment had represented to her beforehand.

Later Conclusion

The case of Sandra illustrates developmental progression in treatment that resolves the fear of success and allows Sandra's unique self to be born (as split-off parts are owned and integrated). Sandra individuates and finds her voice and her ambition, for example, the ambition to be a mother and a motivational speaker. This developmental progression is very different than Heinz Kohut's proposed dual tract of narcissism separate from Object Relations.

One sees in this case a mourning process that organically navigates through the multiple stages within separation-individuation, simultaneously integrating split-off parts of the self, including the aggression within the 'internal saboteur' or 'antilibidinal ego' (Fairbairn, 1952). Once this aggression has been owned and experienced as motivated from within, after an identification with the parent as the aggressor has been resolved through separation, the terror of a retaliatory attack upon one's success is greatly reduced. Further, the fear of such an attack is progressively conceptualized in psychic fantasy, as opposed to remaining somatic and visceral in manifestation.

The guilt within Sandra that created an unconscious or dissociated dynamic of internal attack from an internal sabotaging object (actually a part-object) was lessened and even obviated. Mourning and separation allowed for the owning of aggression and the lessening of its projection onto the parental displacement as a retaliatory object. Then true regret was felt, allowing for success to simultaneously be allowed.

Two of Sandra's fantasies highlighted the early as opposed to the latter stages of her development through the mourning and analysis within treatment. The first implied a paranoid-schizoid position state of siege in which part-object others haunted and threatened her. Sandra implied that vampires and cannibals, manifestations of her own oral envy, would kill her the minute she put herself out onto the stage of the world, let alone that she sought success once out there. Just being recognized and given attention threatened Sandra with the fear of being murdered.

When beginning treatment, she said, "I feel that if I was out there like you, people would want to destroy me." Let's look at this quote from the analysand, as opposed to her later statement, which came at the end of treatment when she was claiming her success: "My graduation is my mother's funeral." A Kleinian perspective seems more useful than a Freudian one to understand the transition in psychic states that manifest in the later quote in comparison to the first quote. Through Klein's phenomenology of psychic change, the two statements can be understood.

However, Klein's idea of a persecutory internal object that could be innate in its origins needs to be tempered with Ronald Fairbairn's understanding of an internal object. From Fairbairn's perspective, the internalized primal external others (mother, parents, family) become merged with split-off parts of the self (see Ogden, 1986) to provide the dynamic of psychic assault that becomes the internal saboteur or antilibidinal ego (Fairbairn, 1952). This is how part-object introjects (not full symbolized others) acquire their visceral dynamic to become "internal objects" (see Ogden, 1986). Therefore, the threat upon which fear of success is motivated can be seen as an actual pathological psychic structure, beyond Freud's idea of drive or impulse, and even beyond Klein's idea of psychic "phantasy."

Nevertheless, Klein's view of internal objects as psychic phenomenon is also highly pertinent to a view of fear of success as it manifests in the subject discussed here—Sandra. For it is in this dream dreamed by Sandra that the developmental transformation is seen that obviates the threatening nature of the internal saboteur that forestalls success. When Sandra dreamed of her body separating from her mother's body, the fantasy was not a psychic structure initiating the agency of the self, but a phenomenon reflecting the evolving of the self and bringing it to consciousness through psychic fantasy. When Sandra dreamed of her body separating out from her mother's, the dream reflected the developmental dynamics as they played themselves out in the transference. In addition, the dream reflected developmental dynamics that transformed the nature of the transference from projective identification to the ability to perceive the transferential mother as other.

As Sandra ceased to enter into her through projective identification—the actual psychic affect state of Sandra's self—the analyst experienced this critical developmental transition symbolized in Sandra's dream by feeling a different psychic state than that felt by Sandra. This new phenomenon of different affect states in analyst and analysand contrasts with earlier transference-countertransference experience of the same feeling or affect state, from a time when projective identification was still operating, with its unconscious psychic transmission through the body of Sandra to the body of the analyst, related to Sandra's former lack of separation and differentiation.

Whether the terror and inhibition that unconsciously compel the symptomatology of fear of success is motivated by retaliation through unconscious attack (as would correspond to Freud's [1916] oedipal cases of "The Exceptions: Those Wrecked by Success") or the terror is of the nature of retaliation through abandonment and annihilating object loss, the paranoid-schizoid position state of mind may be operating. Sandra manifested both. It is only when she navigated through developmental mourning that she evolved past both forms of retaliatory terror. For at this point, symbolized by the dream of her body separating out from her mother's body—internal mother and transference mother—she entered Klein's higher-level position, the depressive position. Success was no longer equated with the retaliatory threat of either murderous attack or abandonment but was rather associated with the pain felt in a state of compassion for a separate other, which makes one fear hurting the other through success.

At this later point, regardless of the other's reaction, the primary preoccupation is with injury in the other, the other who is now truly other—as opposed to the other being perceived as a stereotypic retaliatory part-object as was symptomatic of the paranoid-schizoid position. The "it" has become a person as separation and self-integration allows the self to become a subjective person, with an internal life that Sandra related to as the "ocean cave" and "low key depth" of the world within her psyche, her "internal world." Sandra also became, in Ogden's words, an "interpreting subject," as she became a subjective self, aware of having an internal world, rather than automatically reacting as an object without subjectivity and self-agency. Once she was an interpreting subject, she was able to make some of her own interpretations about her psychological experience along with those of the analyst in treatment. This was all part and parcel of entering and enlarging her psychic state in the depressive position, originally described theoretically by Klein.

In feeling the pain of hurting the other through one's success, by making the other feel lacking or left behind, consciousness is involved, as differentiated from unconscious growth. Now Sandra, or any subject involved in this developmental journey through mourning, will feel loss and often regret. At the point at which Sandra was finally able to allow herself to achieve and own her success, she said, "My graduation is my mother's funeral." This was a statement of existential guilt, which involves the grief of loss when one leaves another behind or fears hurting the other. There is both concern (Winnicott, 1963, 1965) and grief in this statement and regret. There is, however, also a full conscious awareness in the affective suffering of grief that modifies or even dissipates unconscious sabotage of the self in its unique expression that we call "success."

Existential guilt therefore overcomes neurotic and unconscious guilt, and transpires into compassion and concern through the willing surrender to grief. This is the essence of Klein's depressive position and all that she began to speak about in "Mourning and its relation to manic depressive states" (1940), in which she realized that aggression, when made conscious through psychic fantasy, could be part and parcel of a normal, healthy, and developmentally evolving mourning process. This realization of Klein is clearly different from Freud's earlier view in "Mourning and Melancholia" (1917). Freud had divided the normal mourner, who engaged only in the pain of loss—supposedly free of inhibiting levels of unconscious aggression toward the love object—from the melancholic, whose unconscious aggression forestalled mourning. For Freud, the melancholic was not seen as being capable of bringing aggression to consciousness and owning it for its possible transformation. Without this transformation, aggression could not be brought into consciousness to become part of healthy mourning. Klein showed that this transformation was possible and therefore viewed mourning in a way that integrated the melancholic character and the "normal" mourner. In the case of Sandra presented here, the transformation described by Klein is seen and becomes the resolution for pathological levels of inhibition owing to a fear of success.

FROM NEUROTIC GUILT TO EXISTENTIAL GUILT AS GRIEF: THE ROAD TO INTERIORITY, AGENCY, AND COMPASSION THROUGH MOURNING; PART I

Originally published in 2006, *American Journal of Psychoanalysis* 66(3):239–260.

Theoretical Background for Case Presentation

Freud

Sigmund Freud (1915) initiated psychoanalytic interest in the psychological meaning of the mourning process in his paper, "Mourning and Melancholia." Yet his view of mourning at this time did not include the processing of aggression. In fact, aggression is seen in this paper only in its defensive form, in a "melancholic" individual who is so dominated by her aggression in its unconscious form that she remains paralyzed in a state of blocked or pathological mourning. She remains addicted to a hatred toward a lost other, which is turned defensively into a self blaming attack on the self. By contrast, Freud's supposedly healthy mourner is seen in a pure state of loss, without mention of aggressive dynamics. Freud speaks of the slow and painful detachment of the ego from the lost love object as if a visceral adhesion needed to be relinquished bit by bit, resulting in an excruciating pain related to object loss. This painful journey would be necessary to free any of us from dead and/or lost other so that new relationships with alive and present others could be formed. Freud implies more than describes the grief-ridden pain of any separation or loss.

Aggression, however, remains a subject only for the subject who can't detach him-or herself from the lost other who is encapsulated in Freud's image of the melancholic. It is the melancholic who is acknowledged to have hate toward the lost other, not just love. In fact, Freud's thesis implies that there is more hate than love, for as Fairbairn's (1952) addictive characterological ties to bad objects tells us, it is where there is more hate than love due to the actual aversiveness of the internal object that one is most trenchantly tied to the other. Separation supposedly fails when the other cannot be loved, because mourning necessary for separation requires more love than hate to proceed.

Freud's melancholics try to control their hate. They try to protect the lost object[1] who would supposedly represent the primal parental object on an unconscious level. They do so by turning the hate against themselves. The object must be protected as an internal object within one's internal world, especially when defensive idealization is substituted for a love that fails to be enough to preserve the goodness of the other inside of the self. Without enough love for a good internalization, and its representation, to be preserved within the psyche, mourning fails. A pathological attachment remains. Although Freud was the first Object Relations theorist, when he said, "The shadow of the object falls upon the ego" (1917), he was certainly not acquainted with the developmental vicissitudes of Object Relations treatment we know today.

Consequently, he saw limited help for the melancholic who was stuck in a state of pathological mourning. From his perspective, the melancholic might gain insight into how his or her hate for the other was being perpetually and unconsciously turned against the self for defensive purposes. However, whether the melancholic's aggression was turned toward the self or back outward against the other, Freud never articulated how hate could be resolved, or how love could be renewed. Consequently, the love for sustaining and developing relationships with those others who were present and alive in the melancholic's current life could not flow or evolve into motivation toward life within a field of external Object Relations.

Klein

Melanie Klein's (1940) paper on "Mourning and Its Relation to Manic Depressive States" totally transformed this psychoanalytic perspective. Perhaps written to extend Freud's studies on mourning, this paper by Klein tackles the subject of aggression in a whole new way, which leads to important developmental insights. It places aggression in the center of an alive and active mourning process, rather than outside of it, where it would remain split-off, as an obstacle to mourning and, thus, to a vital avenue to psychic change and evolving self expression.

Interestingly, in this paper Klein uses herself as the clinical subject, Mrs. A. Therefore, she is telling us the theoretical tale from the inside out. Practicing in London as a psychoanalyst, Mrs. Klein lost her adult son to death. She felt alone and paralyzed. She was unable to cry in a way that would bring relief. She suffered from hallucinatory symptoms, such as imagining the ceiling to be coming down on her. She was unable to dream. She shied away from going out of her house to meet people and felt like generally withdrawing. She was in a state of shock. She held herself back from all friends, family members, companions, and colleagues. But Mrs. A. (Mrs. Klein) began to come out of her shell-shocked state when awakened through certain fantasies and dreams to a drama replete with her own aggression.

Melanie Klein dreamed scenarios of triumph over her dead and lost son. She unconsciously triumphed over her son because she remained alive. She also dreamed of hostile and envious attitudes in figures from her childhood that informed her of her own displaced hostility, as it arose in the form of contempt with hidden envy and was now focused on her dead son. Once Mrs. Klein could own her own hostile, competitive, envious, and contemptuous attitudes toward her son by consciously seeing how they emanated from her own being, and could see how such attitudes had unconsciously been perpetuated in the great stage of her internal world, she was able to let go. She was able to surrender, and thus mourn, grieve, and cry in a way that could bring true relief. With surrender to her grief, she could connect to her deeper self through the mourning process. She could connect to the core self from where tears of grief sadness flowed to the core of the self where love endows pain with the grief of sadness. In this way Mrs. Klein, ourselves, and the patient I call Helen in this essay become connected to the object of loss, who can now be preserved within the internal world so that the lost object can be relinquished in one's external world. Consequently, intrapsychic separation and redistribution of love onto current others can take place.

Kavaler-Adler on Developmental Mourning and Psychic Regret

The groundwork laid for understanding mourning as a critical psychological process by Sigmund Freud and Melanie Klein has helped me to construct my own theory of developmental mourning (see Kavaler-Adler 1992b, 1993a/2013, 1995, 1996/2014, 2000, 2003a, 2003b, 2004, 2005a, 2005b, 2006a). This theory extends into a second theory of psychic change and personality transformation, which occurs through the conscious experiencing of the profound guilt endowed experience of regret, which I call "psychic regret." Psychic regret is the experience of affectively alive and conscious grief in the face of the existential combination of guilt and loss. This loss is the loss of love or of the love object itself, in the face of one's own hostile aggression and its self sabotaging effects. The guilt that becomes grief might have neutotic aspects but also has an existential base that one can grasp through self-reflection, and such capacity for self-reflection develops fully through a mourning process that has its own developmental evolution.

In the words of Emily Dickinson, who mourned as much as she could on her own through her prolific poetic writings: "To scan a Ghost, is faint/ But grappling, conquers it" (in Dickinson, 1960, "'Tis So Appalling—It Exhilarates"). We are always haunted by our internal ghosts, which house our misdeeds toward others, as well as toward ourselves, within an internal world of our symbolized and presymbolic relationships. Once we can symbolize our misdeeds, we can know them and grapple with them. However, the capacity to symbolize the inchoate knowledge that at first may only exist in the visceral form of body tensions and mental pressures (compelling obsessive thinking) is often only arrived at through a mourning process that has a natural developmental pathway, based on that which I believe to have innate psychic predispositions.

Developmental mourning encompasses many affect avenues toward the pain of grief, and consequently toward the love-endowed grief that connects us to the old internal world relationships, while allowing us to let go of them at the same time so that we can move on to new and positive relationships in our current lives. Abandonment depression grief, such as described by James Masterson (1976, 1981, 2000), and separation grief, such as described by Margaret Mahler (Mahler et al., 1975), are prominent aspects of the overall developmental mourning process that I have described both theoretically and clinically in my writings.

Through a successful experience with an experienced psychoanalyst who is informed in terms of Object Relations theory and practice, the aversive affect states of body void experience due to abandonment trauma, as well as the primal rage related to that trauma, can be tolerated so that a good enough connection (see Winnciott, 1971, on the "good-enough" mother) can be tolerated—first with the analyst, as an external other, and then within the internal world, as an internalized relationship that is based on connecting with the steady presence of the external other in the form of the psychoanalyst. The following case of Helen can be seen as a case in point.

In reading the case that follows, readers can discover for themselves how a numbed-out psychic state, originating in infantile loss at a traumatic level, can transform into sophisticated symbolic capacities for interpersonal connection. They can learn how this proceeds through a mourning process that plays out its developmental blueprint as soon as the split-off rage, a form of raw archaic or primal aggression, related to the dissociated state of trauma, can be assimilated through tolerable levels of affect experience. It is the holding environment of psychoanalytic treatment (Winnicott, 1963) that contains this experience. Then containment is translated and transferred to the new "home within" (quote from

Helen) that is built through the containing therapeutic relationship into the psyche or self of the patient. Profound grief becomes tolerable after the archaic modes of rage are modified into the aggression of self agency. This happens through a natural developmental separation and self-integration process, which are all part and parcel of what Melanie Klein has called "the depressive position" and what Margaret Mahler has called "separation-individuation."

Melanie Klein spoke of a combination of loss and guilt in speaking about her view of the depressive position psychic (and self) state, which dynamically overlaps with a sequential series of linear developmental phases, as depicted by Mahler, when describing mothers and their two-year-old toddlers. Mahler observed the "low keyedness" of those toddlers with strong enough ego development due to the sustained and adequate presence of the mother during these phases. This low keyedness referred to a slightly depressed psychological state, which was evidence of the mature ego's capacity to tolerate the interpersonal yearning that is born out of tolerable object loss in the form of sadness. Those toddlers who were not lucky enough to have a mother's sustained and responsive presence throughout the years of self formation, from one to three years old, did not show the ego (or self) development necessary to reach a state of grief-stricken sadness and live consciously through it.

In the latter toddlers, the "terrible twos," universally evidenced in tantrums, were more eruptive and disrupted than in those toddlers who could reach, contain, and tolerate grief when the presence of the mother was temporarily absent. States of such affect that could not be tolerated and expressed in an object-related interpersonal atmosphere supposedly caused self splitting, resulting in dissociated self states with dramatic borderline and manic depressive features. Thus, the splitting and dissociation of the self can be seen through these studies to relate directly to the overwhelming nature of aggression within frustration, and at such an early time that aggression remains enacted either inside the body/mind or in behavior, so that the capacity for the symbolic assimilation of self experience is disrupted. This indicates why the disrupted toddler who grows up into an adult who seeks psychoanalytic treatment must have a strong and responsive connection with the psychoanalyst. With this connection in the holding environment of treatment, this hypothetical analysand can begin to assimilate dissociated and aggression-laden parts of the self. Consequently, the grief of object loss can be felt and processed, en route to more loving and, thus, positive new Object Relationships.

However, within grief related to object loss is often the guilt of existential despair in the face of a newly developing capacity for self-reflection. Once self integration evolves, along with separation-individuation, the self can look at itself and become aware of the guilt of one's own aggression in its hostile or relationship destructive form. Thus the grief of former object loss is poignantly mixed with the guilt of regret in relation to one's now conscious knowledge of how one hurts the one she/he loves. As Klein's depressive position indicates, the one one loves is now recognized as the one one often hates, and vice versa. Without a pure enemy to hate, entering Klein's depressive position, through mourning and self integration, one is faced with the profound pain of regret, which comes from an awareness that one is hurting the one one loves, as well as realizing that one is not truly loving oneself enough. One's own hostility, whether in thought or deed, becomes a constant haunting ghost in the private chamber of the mind, on both conscious and unconscious levels. To the extent that one can make the dilemma of this existential predicament conscious, one can face regret, and can then transform one's attitudes and behavior toward better relationships in the future. To consciously grapple with regret, as Emily Dickinson, our now acknowledged greatest American poet suggests, is the phenomenon that I have called "psychic regret." To be in a state of psychic regret is a psychological working through process.

In presenting the case of Helen, I show that this psychological working through process, which begins with developmental mourning and evolves into psychic regret, is a poignant and profound human journey that brings us face to face with our own internal worlds. As we face the world within, self agency and self reflection evolve and further develop into inferiority (as opposed to existing in a split-off body/mind state) and interpersonal compassion. Of course, intimacy, love, and creativity can then follow and evolve without significant disruption. I present the case of Helen to let the clinical situation and the voice of the analysand tell the developmental story. In doing so, I thank my theoretical mother, Mrs. Melanie Klein, for her brilliant insight, namely, that mourning is a critical and fundamental basis for the clinical and developmental processes, as they can grow up hand in hand.

Two Forms of Developmental Need Experienced as Crimes: Separation and Hunger

When Helen first entered an Object Relations psychoanalysis that was to move from two times to five times a week, she came in a confessional frame of mind. Burdened with all kinds of guilt, she wished to find a safe location in which to confess what she considered to be her "crimes." She said she identified with murderers and knew what it was like to be out of control of an overpowering rage that forced one into destructive and self-destructive action. Without any encouragement from my end, she told me that she wished to tell me every one of her "crimes," so that she could start anew, free of guilt and sin.

She began to tell me the stories. The major and most haunting crime was that of her early abandonment of a child. From the way that she first stated it as a terrible crime of abandonment and neglect, it was not yet clear how external circumstances had forced her to leave behind a child from a first marriage in her homeland, a European country. Wracked with the pain of guilt, she told me the story as if she were fully in control of everything and had maliciously chosen to commit some heinous act, an act that in her mind certainly was equivalent to murder. According to Helen, she had abandoned her mother. She had abandoned her father. She also had abandoned her sister and had left her stuck with the fallout of her parents' miserable sadomasochistic marriage. Then she had abandoned her ex-husband. And worst of all, she had abandoned a two-year-old boy, her very own child. From the couch she cried out, writhing with agony, "What will become of me? . . . Nobody will want me! . . . How could I have done such horrible things?"

Helen often saw others, particularly women, as vampires of bloodsucking hunger. Without the development of her own capacity to set boundaries, she felt like the prey of the bloodsucking female beast. This was a projection of Helen's that mirrored the bloodsucking needs of an unbounded and somewhat disembodied early mother. This was a mother that lived viscerally (often as nausea and headaches), not yet symbolically, in her internal world. Helen did not project this beast mother onto me on any conscious level. Instead, she maintained a secure splitting operation in which I lay on the idealized side of the split. Her idealization of me served many psychic purposes. One obvious one in the beginning was that by keeping me clean, morally pure, and as the embodiment of many envied talents (which reflected potentials of her own that she would later develop), I could serve for her as the ultimate omnipotent judge of her character. Through my judgment, she would reach her own purification.

The first step toward that on her psychic agenda was to confess her crimes. Then, when all was out in the open, Helen seemed to be hoping that I would hand out the sanctimonious dispensation that she so craved. Helen's hunger for judgment and forgiveness came from a level of object need for a primal mother who had nurtured her in infancy. Yet this same mother, who she experienced within her internal world as a bad mother, had also emotionally abandoned her when this childhood mother was frequently hospitalized for illness, as well as when her mother failed to allow her to separate in the normal developmental phases. Her mother resisted her separation, and therefore her internal mother psychically possessed her. At some unconscious psychic level, her mother became a witch that could be seen in her vampire projections.

As Helen's analyst, I listened, and I was able to feel intensely present with her. My presence offered her a degree of safe feeling, despite her agony and despite the paranoia she felt out in the world where she projected that which she named her "criminal part."

In the beginning, Helen's view of herself as a criminal colored all her self-designated crimes equally, no matter how minor any act might seem to an objective observer. She spoke with almost the same sense of terror and trepidation to me when she spoke of borrowing pens with colored ink from a schoolmate in elementary school, and then of not giving them back, as she did when she spoke of leaving her two-year-old child behind (with her mother) in her native land. She had similar terror when she spoke of stealing a pin cushion from a "five and dime" store. She was intensely mortified at the moment of her telling, finding her shame less totally annihilating with me than she might have found it with a priest or reverend, despite her Christian origins. Emotional survival seemed precarious to Helen at any such moment of mortification, and she marveled that she survived to come and confess again in the next session. Assigning me the imagined powers of a shaman, goddess, or Tibetan monk sustained Helen's faith that somehow her being with me in this act of self-flagellating revelation would vindicate her. As I understood Helen's "crimes" as attempts at separation from a possessive and often engulfing mother, and also as a desperate and hungry cry for mothering, Helen became less terrified of being judged as bad. Then we could question together the judgment she had against herself.

However, the judgment was still being enacted by a dissociated psychic structure with unconscious visceral and somatic dynamics. In Ronald Fairbairn's (1952) terms, this dissociated personally self-attacking psychic structure could be called an antilibidinal ego, for it attacks the ego for being basic psychological needs. In Jeffrey Seinfeld's terms (1989), it could be called an "antidependent self."

The Visceral and Psychic Experience of Identification with the Aggressor on the Couch

While Helen was recounting her crimes in the first year of treatment, she also had visceral and psychic manifestations of her antilibidinal ego's internal attack. She spoke of "lying here on the couch and stabbing myself with a knife." She also spoke of "taking an overdose and dying." Her body enacted this suicidal fantasy on the couch. She had visceral stabbing pains as she verbally attacked herself for all her "crimes," especially the crimes she enacted by separating from her mother and family, as well as the crime of leaving her child, who unconsciously could represent the earlier tie to her mother.

Then there was also the crime of her hunger, which she had formerly played out with actual acts of bulimia and which she played out in treatment on a psychological and visceral level. Helen hungered for more and more of the analyst, wishing to swallow her in the form of eight hotdogs before the session, which she said symbolized the eight sessions with me she wanted during the week when she could only have five sessions. But she was attacked for the crime of her own hunger by impulses to vomit that were reminiscent of the actual vomiting she had done when she was still living in her own country, and in her family home, with her mother and father. Helen also felt nausea. I speculated with her that her nausea and impulses to vomit were symptomatic reenactments of an infant illness she had suffered, which had caused her to be hospitalized with doctors who predicted she would die. My speculation brought memories back to Helen of her mother's reports from this time.

Only when the doctors sent her home with her despairing mother, she was told, did she vomit up the toxins and recover through being in the lap of her mother, re-forming the bond with her mother. Reliving the symptoms of this early infant illness would be an antilibidinal mode of self punishment, both for her insatiable hunger, which manifested in the transference, and for her crimes of moving toward separation from a mother who had punitive reactions to her attempts to separate as a child, as well as from a father who attacked her with accusations of guilt in a competitive and envious way. Along with her suicidal thoughts, Helen heard her depressed father's words of cynicism about life: "Everything ends anyway."

In relation to her "crime" of leaving her family and coming to America, Helen said, "Before I came to America my mother possessed me!" However, leaving the mother she could not adequately separate from, because of her mother's resistance to her moves toward separation, became manifest as an insatiable hunger for me in the transference. She punished herself for this hunger by imitating the former attacks of her parents, still operating within her as an antilibidinal ego attack in her internal world. This internal attack provoked terror within her of her own hunger. Helen feared her hunger would prevent her from ever getting away from me, just as she had feared she could never leave her mother. Her mother had actually punished Helen for having any friends other than her mother, and her mother had kept her in her exclusive possession until she began school. Helen spoke to me of her fear: "When you speak I feel like eating a steak. I'm afraid of my feelings for you. When I feel this hunger for you I'm afraid that only this will be important. I'm afraid nothing else will matter. I ate a hotdog before I came here. I felt like I could have eaten eight hotdogs."

When Helen lay on the couch and told me of fantasizing about lying there and stabbing herself in front of me, I associated to another patient of mine. I thought of Phillip, who early in his treatment had spoken of fantasies of "committing hara-kiri," the Japanese form of suicide, in response to the anguished hunger he felt for a father who would continually seduce him with the siren call of his emotional need, only to turn around and betray Phillip by a vicious verbal attack to push Phillip away. Phillip's father's attack would come just at the moment that Phillip would feel compelled to respond to the anguished and silent (and perhaps unconscious) call of his father's emotional need. Phillip's fantasy of stabbing himself in the manner of the Japanese ritual suicide was a mimicking of his father's stabbing verbal attack and was a visceral image of the intrapsychic event of feeling the impact of the attack. His identification with the aggressor was clearly drawn in his description to me as a continual antilibidinal ego attack (Fairbairn, 1952).

As with Helen, Phillip had converted his retaliatory rage at his parents into a state of self persecution and self blame. As all children are prone to do (Fairbairn, 1952), Helen and Phillip both protected their internal parents from their external and their internal aggression by blaming themselves. In this way, they psychically protected the image of each parent. Thus, they saw themselves as criminals as well as tortured victims when they had not yet gained their own sense of self agency. Their self agency could only develop through the affect journey of experiencing their separation from their parents, which for both Helen and Phillip involved a critical mourning process in psychoanalytic Object Relations treatment.

Understanding the Unconscious Compulsions Behind Helen's "Crimes"

Helen and I investigated the nature of her "crimes" together. We found that her greatest guilt about leaving her child with her mother in her homeland resulted from the extension of a year's trip to the United States, a trip that had been agreed on by her and her first husband. She decided to extend the trip when she found out that her husband was having an extramarital affair. Helen was glad to find an excuse to stay in the United States. She wanted to start school here in a profession different from the one she had achieved a professional degree in her country. She worked as a waitress meanwhile to make money, thinking that she would send for her son when she could.

For the first time since her teen years, while in the United States, Helen was free of an eating disorder, as her family remained far away from her, across an ocean. Desperate needs to separate from her mother, who could never allow her to physically or emotionally separate from her in earlier years, were finally being overtly expressed. For the first time, she felt free from her mother's needs (mostly narcissistic, for mirroring), and could shut out the haunting emotional blackmail that came from her mother. Sometimes this emotional blackmail could come from her father as well—even by phone and letter—across the ocean. For example, one day her father phoned her in a rage and accused her of killing her mother by not returning home, saying that Helen's mother was hospitalized for a heart attack because Helen abandoned her.

Despite such intense blasts of emotional blackmail, Helen stayed in the United States and worked long hours to avoid feeling guilty. By working hard to become a U.S. citizen and to go to graduate school in a new profession, Helen avoided thinking about all of her behaviors that she viewed as her "crimes," given her scapegoated "bad child" role in her family. She was compelled to defend herself against submission to her family through judgments toward them that mimicked the scapegoating judgments that had been projected onto her. She compulsively identified with the aggressor and thus reinforced the malignant power of her "antilibidinal ego." To defend against it she had cut off her feelings and froze herself into a cold and contemptuous attitude, but her hungry self spoke nonetheless through her body and her psychic fantasies on the couch.

Physical and Psychological Bulimia

In the United States, for the first time since her teen years, Helen could swallow food without feeling compelled to spit it up. During her teens, food had become for her some overly rich and yet poisonous mother that she hungered for, envied, and yet needed to get rid of, because she could not digest its overwhelming rich sweetness—just as she could not move forward with an adequate developmental separation. Helen noticed, however, that her eating problems, which used to involve buying rich cakes and pastries and then regurgitating, had been replaced by a compulsive urge to shop and spend money on clothes. The emotional separation from her mother had not been made, even though the physical one had. Still, the physical distance from her mother and father had allowed Helen to reduce her symptomatic behavior from her eating disorder to a compulsion to shop, which induced less shame than the eating disorder had.

Although she suffered conscious anguish and unconscious symptoms, not seeing her mother and father allowed Helen to focus on having a new life. In her new life, she felt quite disconnected from herself, and from her husband and child. She made some attempts to see her child, but her husband's family now had him.

They prevented her from seeing him. Not able to see him, Helen detached even more. Gradually she gave up any ideas she had to have her son come over to the states.

Helen wanted and needed to have her self first. She hoped to have a profession that was more suitable to her than the one she had studied for abroad. She wanted a life! Although her ex-husband's family did take her son from her mother, and then blocked any efforts Helen made to visit her son, even when Helen came to Europe, she also may have detached from the whole situation because of her guilt. She viewed herself as a criminal, or murderer, who was unfit to be a mother.

When I understood this with Helen, and helped her to put the pieces together, her guilt and the accompanying shame decreased enough for her to lie on the couch and have memories that she had earlier lost contact with. I understood that she had been driven to escape her family and not look back (for a while) by a powerful developmental arrest around separation needs and separation trauma. Also, I understood that her other "crimes," such as those of taking her schoolmate's pens or stealing hair pins from the five and dime store, were reactive to a powerful hunger, and to a derivative envy, provoked by an overly giving and overly intrusive and envious mother. She spoke to me of the intrusive side of her mother: "She asked me to tell her my secrets, and when I did she punished me for what I revealed. I felt tricked and seduced." The intrusive or engulfing mother stood side by side in her mind with the withdrawing mother, who would punish her for separation by withholding love. The memories that Helen revealed clearly substantiated my way of understanding her symptoms.

Memories

Two memories arose explicitly on a cognitive level. These memories stimulated intense rage reactions in Helen, transformed her general feeling of having an empty void within, instead of a sense of self, into alive affects. First came the memory of being five years old and returning to her apartment after going to visit a neighbor. She brought a candy back that her neighbor had given her. As soon as her mother saw the candy and realized where Helen had been, she grabbed the candy from Helen. Then Helen's mother flew into a violent rage and threw the candy dramatically into the fireplace. Helen was shocked by this monster that her mother had turned into. She felt numbed out, not daring to feel rage at that childhood time when her mother was the one so filled with rage. Helen's articulation of this memory revealed that shame, guilt, fear, and a general sense of being a bad girl began to color her formerly colorful world gray.

A second memory that revealed the nature of Helen's childhood mother's reactions to her having separate motivations or separate relationships occurred when Helen was in high school. One night she went to a disco, which was a very common activity for teenagers at that time. Her mother found out that she was there and came after her. When her mother found her, she smacked Helen very hard across her face. Helen was not only stunned and enraged but also deeply humiliated because her mother had slapped her in front of people. She felt ugly and her rage made her feel ugly. There was no one to talk to about the incident.

Helen's father was estranged from her, favoring her younger sister. He had become her worst enemy as he belittled her, criticized her, and condemned her. When Helen's father saw her dressing more like a woman when she was a teenager, he assaulted her femininity. In fact, he cut off her hair when she wore the stylish Jane Fonda hairdo of the time. When she enjoyed being a member of a sports activity in school, her father came to see her team play, only to ridicule her and to proclaim that she wasn't good enough to perform on the team. With an emotionally abusive father, who lacked any ability to understand her, Helen became all the more vulnerable to her dependence on her mother, and there was nowhere to turn when her mother attacked her.

Helen's mother had shown that she could not stand her daughter's growth when it involved making friends, having sexuality, or meeting boys. The meaning of the two memories of the mother's punishments for her moves toward others and thus toward separation from her is further illustrated by Helen's mother's general resistance to allowing Helen to have friends. Until Helen was six years old, before her sister was born and before her mother returned to work, Helen's mother would play all day alone with Helen. In fact, Helen never had playmates! This contributed to Helen's sense of being strange and alienated, if not outright "bad." She was quite alone later at school. Her mother encouraged this isolation by calling her the "serious" one, insisting that Helen think about her studies all of the time.

The Body Memory of Infant Sickness

Helen's internal world expressed itself through her body, often as a concretized visceral metaphor. Her body language implied reenactments of early illness that were not yet symbolized as conscious and differentiated memories. Other memories arose through Helen's body. A vicious cycle of reliving an early infant illness began to appear. Nausea and headaches had always been common somatic self attacks for Helen (antilibidinal ego attacks). Frequently, while lying on the couch, Helen would suffer these attacks. Often the aggressive impulses that lay behind these attacks would reveal themselves in associations and memories that occurred right before and after the attacks.

Helen's aggression appeared in these symptoms as her psyche (antilibidinal ego) inhibited a primal rage that was triggered whenever she was angry. Helen could not experience a more differentiated form of aggression until a separation process, at the level of affects and mourning, could be processed in treatment, having had her early separation process arrested during her toddler years. However, Helen's somatic attacks revealed more than repressed and dissociated repression. I speculate that they also revealed the reliving of many times that Helen had been hospitalized during her childhood when her mother was sick and hospitalized. I further speculate that these body symptoms were enactments of an even more deeply repressed early infant illness that had nearly led to Helen's death.

When Helen was still a baby, prior to the disruptions between her and her mother in relation to separation needs, she had been hospitalized for having a high fever. At first, when they came to the hospital, she was removed from her mother. But because the doctors thought that her situation was hopeless, they called her mother back. They told the mother that she should take the infant to let her die at home. Her mother was devastated, but some part of her never lost hope. She took Helen home on a train, the baby placed on her lap. All the way home, Helen vomited and vomited, soiling her mother's "pretty blue blouse," as Helen's mother recalled. When she saw me in a blue blouse, Helen remembered having been told that her mother wore a blue blouse at this time and connected my wearing this color with a spiritual emergence in me and in herself, as she dreamed of herself wearing the spiritual blue color. As a new spirituality emerged within her during her analytic sessions, as well as in her dreams, Helen had associations back to times in her childhood when her mother had been particularly loving toward her.

Helen's mother, as the story was told, felt too weak with despair to care about cleaning herself off when she was sent home with a baby girl whom the doctors expected to die. Consequently apathetic, she just held her baby and let her vomit repeatedly, crying tears on top of the baby's vomit. Helen's mother did not then realize that she was allowing baby Helen to vomit out the toxins of her infant illness, so that she could return to life and, ultimately, to health. In fact, it seems obvious in retrospect that Helen's mother was allowing Helen to emotionally reconnect with her as she held her in her lap.

It appears that the doctor's decision to send the baby home with her mother had saved the baby's life because the baby and her mother were reunited. It was also the reuniting that allowed infant Helen to spit up her venom, making the oral throat cavity a highly sensitized place for taking in everything associated with good mother and for spitting or crying out all associated with mother loss and with bad mother, such as the possessive vampire who haunted her in psychic fantasy (phantasy) as a demon-lover (see Kavaler-Adler, 1993a/2013, 1995, 1996/2014). This demon-lover mother, the vampire, threatened to provoke escape into a regressive merger with the mother of pre-separation infancy.

Now in psychoanalysis, Helen relived the infant illness on the couch. Despair blanketed her like death. Enveloped by despair, associated with the threat of death, Helen would cry out loud to the analyst, seen as a mother, that all seemed hopeless. Far beyond her more superficial symptoms of headache and nausea, Helen's double-edged psychic and physical despair created an annihilation anxiety of piercing dimensions. Each time Helen relived this sense of dying from a hopelessness and despair, which interacted with the helplessness of having her aggression split-off from her central self, she and I would find out a bit more about this infant illness from which she nearly literally died. How the psyche used the experience of the infant illness then became quite significant, because we began to realize that there was a timing to these reliving events on the couch. It was not just about her aggression in the abstract. It was about her traumatically frustrated separation needs.

The Antilibidinal Ego's Use of the Unconscious Infant Illness

As I witnessed the reliving of infant illness in Helen, I began to realize that the timing of the events was unconsciously programmed. I interpreted this when I could see what the unconscious program was. I came to believe that it was a program of reaction to a preœdipal conflict around separation needs and strivings that was evidenced by Helen, both in her analysis and in all her life activities. For example, when she graduated from a graduate school program while in treatment, she declared, "My graduation is my mother's funeral," referring both to her actual mother and to me as her transferential mother. Such dramatic guilt, promoting conflict over separation, had been reinforced repeatedly by the mother's resistance toward Helen's healthy separation strivings. Helen was forced to identify, on a primitive body level, with her mother's assaulting attitude toward her need to move through separation-individuation development, forming dissociated reactions within her as she moved forward in life. This was her preverbal level of identification with the aggressor, as her body felt like vomiting, or felt empty and depleted, and her mind expressed the emotional distress in painful and dark affect states, which could also be experienced in self-assaulting thoughts, reminiscent of her parents' verbal attacks on her.

Whenever Helen accomplished anything in her studies or her life, she would enter what she described as a "black mood." Then she would collapse into the helpless and traumatized state of an early infant falling into inertness and death. These retaliatory strikes from her own psyche against her separation process, through the success of coming out into the world with her own unique identity, were clearly a repetition of what she had experienced being done to her throughout her development. Helen had unconsciously, at this primal level, identified with her mother's attacks on her moves toward separation in order to hold onto her mother. She was holding onto her primal mother, the one she had experienced as saving her from death during her infancy. Holding on to this mother meant identifying with the mother who would not let her go during her many phases of separation need. Helen seemed to have formed a whole antilibidinal ego structure, attached to the rejecting object of the mother of the separation period (also a primitive or punitive superego), through her need to hold on to a mother who rejected her separation needs. Her mind somatized her identification with the early rejecting mother and her body gave preverbal and presymbolic voice to its manifestations.

Differentiation through Mourning and Separation

When Helen began to experience a conversion of her inward attack into an external attack, still motivated by identification with the aggressor, she began to have fantasies of slapping me hard as her mother had. This became eroticized as well so that the attachment and aggression became a conflictual and stimulating sadomasochistic event. But verbalization allowed Helen to reach a symbolic level of fantasy with this event, and she then could begin to consciously experience her own aggressive impulses. To do so she also had to feel the loss of the early good mother and to suffer a developmental mourning process (Kavaler-Adler, 1993a/2013, 1996/2014) at the level of preœdipal trauma and arrest.

The mourning of loss with separation opened many doors. Gradually, Helen began to enter the depressive position where all her polarized affect and self states could become intermingled and integrated. This led to Helen becoming increasingly articulate in her ability to know and communicate her feelings and thoughts and to differentiate between them. Differentiating her feelings and thoughts, knowing that they were feelings and thoughts, not just impulses compelling immediate action and reactivity, allowed Helen to differentiate her internal and external mothers, which related to past and present mothers. Helen's internal mother was profoundly stamped with the imprints of her childhood past.

Her external mother, a mother present in her current reality (having moved to America), was now capable of offering her a more adult connection. She could accept Helen more as she was today. The external mother, the mother who had followed her to the United States eventually, and who was now living in New York, showed her new acceptance of Helen in her success. Helen was able to invite her mother to her graduation from graduate school. Despite Helen's prediction that "My graduation is my mother's funeral," neither her real mother nor her transferential mother died when she graduated. We both were able to congratulate her. Her mother did overidentify a bit with Helen, trying to claim some of the radiance of Helen's day of triumph for herself when Helen rose to the occasion and made a speech at her graduation. Nevertheless, her mother was proud and excited for her and was accepting of her new professional identity.

Surrender—from Self Persecution to Regret: The Critical Separation-Individuation Process through the Grief of Mourning Loss and the Owning of Aggression

While Helen was stabbing herself on the inside and the outside within her psychic fantasy life on the couch, she illustrated that she was a captive of a pathological identification with the attacks of both her mother (mostly over separation issues) and her verbally assaultive father. In Fairbairn's (1952) language, she had formed an antilibidinal ego structure from the internalized bad parents. The aggressive attacks of her childhood were compulsively mimicked now in continuous self attacks. Her child self was attacked, in the form of the helpless and defensive "libidinal ego" (Fairbairn, 1952). The attacking antilibidinal part of herself was polarized against this child self, as it was identified with the hostile aggressive aspects of her parents.

Consequently, her own vulnerable and needy self was possessed by a sadomasochistic drama in a dissociated area of her psyche. In Fairbairn's language, the sadomasochism was being repeated continuously in a split-off area of the psyche. As this area of Helen's psyche was split-off from the central ego area that was in contact with the world, all the power of its aggression was unavailable for the central ego or self. Consequently, in the early stage of treatment, Helen lacked healthy assertive aggression that could endow her with the capacity for self agency. All this contributed to her feeling of being numbed out, as if a "metal rod is lodged inside of me, from my neck and down through my body and legs."

To have interpreted to Helen anything about her aggression at this early stage, particularly in terms of there being an intentional aggressive attack toward herself or others, which she often projected onto others, would have been a clinical error. She already told me that she felt like a murderer and spoke of consciousness of her "killer rage," but before the affect journey of the separation-individuation process she was to go through in treatment, she was unable to feel any agency or conscious intention in relation to her rage and her impulses.

Prior to the mourning and separation process, she had also felt victimized by her hunger. However, Helen was able to put this object hunger into her treatment so that she opened an idealizing transference attachment. This allowed her to surrender to the treatment and to the analyst as a transitional object (Winnicott, 1971), which allowed her to proceed on a developmental journey that she came to vividly describe as an affect journey in which helpless despair turned to grief. Through this grief that allowed for self integration, Helen could modify her feeling of being possessed by her split-off aggressive parts—as she had been possessed by her parents. She could then feel all her affect states, including conscious hate, loss, love, and longing. In this way, she increasingly became able to own her interior life. In Fairbairn's terms (1952), Helen was developing her central self area. In Klein's terms (1940), she was integrating her internal world.

After confessing all her "crimes" to me as her analyst and transitional object, Helen opened her need to me. Through needing me she came to find herself. In the beginning, she cried out to me, "I need you on the inside," as she also suffered experiencing her inside as an empty void within a metal rod. But the empty void was also a vacuum in which she experienced a voracious hunger as she relinquished her numbness and felt a connection to me, her analyst. When her hunger would disrupt the numbness of the void she would feel anguish to swallow me whole as she had swallowed sweet cakes in her active days of bulimia, when she still lived with her family in her homeland.

Helen had psychic fantasies along with this intense anguish of voracious hunger because her psychic needs for another, after an incomplete separation, had been turned to visceral form. Helen reported fantasies of speaking through my voice, seeing through my eyes, and having me write in her mind (as she read some of my books). She craved to merge with me in this psychic way because she saw me as having all the capacities and attributes that she needed to express herself out in the world. She imagined that if she were to "put herself out there," she would be destroyed. She projected her own envy and hunger onto others. Helen also experienced the actual envy and aggression from others as she had experienced the assault of these impulses from her mother and her father when she had threatened them with her separation and development. Consequently, Helen expressed intense wishes to face the world through an intense and intimate identification with me. In essence, she was also viewing me as possessing all of her own hidden potentials.

These potentials were not yet available to Helen to use because of her split-off aggression and because of her sealed-off vulnerable self. This vulnerable core self was obstructed from contact with the world by the very aggression she split-off, when it became a whole pathological antilibidinal ego, or self, as Fairbairn (1952) wrote about. Because Helen's aggression was being used against the expression of her self, and particularly of her needing self, she identified with the pathological self attack and felt like she actually saw herself stabbing herself while she lay on the couch in my office. In this state of sealed-off self attack, which blocked her from any healthy communication with the world, how could she help to feel like a murderer?

The child self in her had been murdered as her developmental process was disrupted at the time of separation, and now she had powerful backlash reactions of stabbing herself and losing her self-expressive abilities every time she attempted to separate or each time she started to succeed in the world in ways that threatened her internal mother with her separating from her. However, as Helen connected to me as an analyst through her fantasies of merging with me, she also allowed her affect states to begin to express themselves toward outside others. She could then begin to relinquish her projections of her internal parents onto these outside others. In Kavaler-Adler's words, a developmental mourning process was about to begin.

This is the end of Part I of this study. Part II will appear in the following chapter of this volume.

Notes

1 When I speak of the lost object being relinquished in the external world, as memory within the mourning process allows the lost object to be preserved symbolically in the internal world, I am not speaking of the sealed-off and dissociated internal world of Ronald Fairbairn but, rather, of the internal central ego of Fairbairn. This internal central ego is connected to the external world (not being sealed-off behind a schizoid dissociation barrier), and consequently, connections with external world others are sustained through the symbolic connection to past objects that have been relinquished as concrete objects. This central ego of Fairbairn overlaps with Melanie Klein's internal world, which interacts with external world relationships.

FROM NEUROTIC GUILT TO EXISTENTIAL GUILT AS GRIEF: THE ROAD TO INTERIORITY, AGENCY, AND COMPASSION THROUGH MOURNING; PART II

Originally published in 2006, *American Journal of Psychoanalysis* 66(4), 333–350.

Developmental Mourning

One day Helen cried out, "I feel like I have a virus in my heart and if I don't slow down I'm going to have a heart attack." The virus in her heart turned out to be her own hate, which she began to consciously experience as the cold hostile attitude she had turned against her family at the time when she fled her family and country and came to the United States. Helen's antilibidinal stabbing attacks—which took the form of mental accusations toward herself—concerning guilty crimes made her viscerally nauseous. They reflected the inward defensive turn of self-attack, however, that her hate toward her family took, as she unconsciously protected her family from attack by hating herself.

In the third year of treatment, such visceral attacks transformed. They transformed into the coldness of a defensive hate, a hate that she had employed to protect herself against her parents' guilt attacks, and that she used to hold herself together, while on her own, as she wasn't yet psychologically separated or individuated. In the third year of treatment, Helen's associations proposed that she now felt the core of this cold defensive attitude within her heart, where her lost loving attachments had been frozen off. After experiencing her hate as a visceral and somatic virus, through the conscious awareness that evolved in treatment, she was able to let go of her hate. For the first time, then, she could surrender to the grief of the loss she had created by compulsively pulling away from her family, and from her own child.

Consequently, through consciously connecting to her hate, Helen could yield to that which she had sealed-off inside of her beyond the dissociated coldness.

Lying on the couch, Helen cried and cried, and cried out: "I can't believe nothing's happening on the outside! I feel like my mother is dying, and my father too!" Sobbing and sobbing, Helen cried out that she was afraid her mother would die before she could tell her, "I miss you. I love you." She cried that she couldn't say it to her mother, and added that all that applied to her father too. This session of sobbing grief became the beginning of many months of sobbing out her grief.

After feeling the connection with her primal mother again through this grief pain, she cried out for her son as well. For the first time, she felt the anguish that her son must have felt when she left him: "How can a child live without its mother?" Helen turned her neurotic compulsion toward guilt accusation into the true empathic owning of her regret (third to fifth years of treatment). Also, as neurotic guilt changed to this existential guilt, felt through affects of grief and loss, she began to make the reparation that was possible in her life. She began to communicate with her ex-husband's family and began to send packages to her son, ultimately arranging for him to come to America to live with her and her new husband. Helen did this despite the resistances of her ex-husband's family, who had been trying to keep her away from her child for 14 years (her son was 16 when he first came to visit her). Originally, she had left her son with her mother, and then her ex-husband's family had insisted that her son live with her ex-husband, which prevented Helen from ever communicating with her son, and from bringing him to live with her in America before.

Now, as she faced her hate, and surrendered to the grief, sadness came with the new conscious awareness of this hate. She surrendered to the profound loss and longing coloring her grief. Suddenly she was free to pursue all the practical difficulties that she had to pursue to get her son back. Most importantly, she actually did so. Her son came to live with her permanently in New York, and despite much hostility that he persistently directed at her, she took responsibility for him. She worked at containing and processing her retaliatory rage, and at containing her attempts to communicate with her son and to receive his communications.

Nevertheless, every such success in her life brought its backlash, seemingly due to the unconscious programming Helen experienced from the time of traumatic separation conflict. The virus of hate returned for a while too, even after she felt good following her ability to face her grief. By facing her grief she had reconnected with her internal parents, as she reported experiencing them within her or as she projected them onto me as her analyst (her mother transference) or onto male authorities (her father transference).

Sometimes, the backlash from her internal parents' fear of her separation, often projected onto the transference, would come in the form of punishment fantasies enacted through her body on a visceral level. Her body would react to her visceral level of identification with the aggressor with body attacks, going into a visceral or somatic attack of illness. She would feel nauseous, and would then feel like vomiting, in the mode of expulsion that she had acted out physically when she had been bulimic. Now still psychically bulimic from her separation conflict, Helen would feel like vomiting, as if reliving the infant illness she had had when she reportedly had vomited herself back to health on her mother's lap as an infant. In fact, she seemed to be reliving the illness as a punishment for separation. She would, however, also be punishing herself for her oral cravings for me as her transferential object.

Helen seemed to unconsciously believe that her internal mother would be angry at her as she moved forward in her life by attaching herself to me. She told me on days when her love was free to emerge, "I feel so much love for you, like when I would love my mother so much when I was young. I think you would be a really good mother!" She would feel good then, and we would both feel a sense of warm closeness. Then an attack would come. I would interpret this to her as her internal mother's envy as she separated from her mother and made a transitional and therapeutic attachment to me. Ultimately, of course, Helen returned to her mother in a new positive adult relationship and left me in a gradual separation process.

As Helen became more aware of her own hate, related to rage toward the same parents that she loved, she wanted to know all about her aggression! She found herself associating to black women in her dreams as being the disowned aggressive parts of her. At that point in her treatment, following many stages of grief and mourning, I could interpret her returning void states feelings as expressing her hate. Earlier in treatment, this would have been a mistake. At the earlier time, I knew it was very important to see how her sense of being numbed out and in an internal void, which felt like having a metal rod stuck through her, was a reaction to the absence of an early mother that she had lost through a traumatic form of separation (closing herself off in order to leave and breaking the connection with her mother and others). Listening to her anguished associations, in the earlier part of treatment, such as her cries, "What will become of me?" I interpreted her early void feeling as an abandonment reaction. I believed that her actual victimization as a child had left her feeling helpless as an adult. To have talked to Helen about her own aggression at this earlier time in treatment (first two years) would have just made her turn all the more against herself in a masochistic attack, related to her identification with the abandoning parent who was also an aggressor.

However, once Helen had mourned considerably and had opened her sense of agency by reconnecting to her internal mother—as loss opened the old love behind the separation mother's rage and assault—she could use interpretations about her aggression to her advantage. When I told Helen of her return to the feeling of a void, which now actually was more of a thought than a visceral sensation, she was quite curious to know that this could now be a defensive reaction to disguise her hate, as she advanced forward in her life and was afraid of a renewed attack of her parents' hate. As Helen faced her hate and felt her loss, from the early traumatic loss, which allowed her to feel her capacity to love and need, Helen said, "The stone inside my heart has dissolved," in the third year of treatment.

The Development of an Inside and Helen's Newfound Interiority: The Two Selves

In the beginning, Helen spoke of "needing me on the inside." She could not then feel she had an inside without taking me in through my voice and presence, needing more than the symbolic content of my words. She wanted me to come inside of her and to warm her up, where the void was. As she mourned, and felt her internal states, making the formerly intolerable feelings of rage, loss, love, and longing tolerable through my presence in our therapeutic Object Relationship (Grunes, 1984), Helen began to speak of feeling her own inside, rather than of needing me on the inside of her to feel she had an inside. She was now a psychological, and thus symbolic, human being. At first, Helen spoke of having two selves. She said:

> You know, it always feels like I'm dealing with two people inside of me. One is cold, angry, and indifferent, and feels shut off, and the other can really feel and imagine how another person feels, and can really feel for the other's pain. I'm grateful I have another chance to deal with this thing I ran from 20 years ago, leaving my son and family. But this other side, this cold angry side wants to kill me for facing my guilt and for wishing to repair things.

She cried as she felt the antilibidinal side threaten her in a murderous way, a personified psychic structure replicated from the cold and envious attack of her internal parents. Helen's newly developing observing ego then responded back to the backlash of the old self with new concern and moral conscience. "I guess I'm going to see for myself what kind of person I am now that I've been able to arrange for my son to visit after all these years."

Helen felt a compassionate self growing within her through the mourning process. This was in spite of the retaliatory attack from her antilibidinal ego self, which was now an old self whose feelings could be consciously felt, rather than being acted out in a sealed-off and dissociated place. With more compassion for others, she had more compassion for herself. Consequently, Helen had vivid views of the part of her that could come to tolerate her regrets and to learn from them.

As her imagination came alive with her new consciousness, Helen visualized herself with her head in her hands, sobbing, grief-stricken, with all the sadness of her life emerging. The sadness of loss that Helen felt and visualized was also always accompanied by the sadness of guilt, and she would define more and more the existential grief in this guilt, as she defined and faced each of her regrets. Helen said, in her third year of treatment, "That's what it feels like, like there's another person coming out, a person inside sitting with face in her hands, sitting with such sadness, sadness. I cannot lift my head and look at the world. It seems endless, like penance. I guess I want to break everything in myself." As she saw herself this way, and felt her pain and the object love related to the pain, consciously, she also spoke of being able to be inside of herself and her body. She spoke of "finding a home within." She spoke of having an inside, rather than of being outside of herself, performing for the reflective feedback of others. She said, "I feel it on the inside. I was self-conscious when I was on the outside of myself."

Ultimately, Helen discovered her inside as an internal world, which she could visualize in psychic fantasy. She spoke of the image of an "ocean cave," suggesting that the internal world, which formerly appeared to her in the image of a void or empty metal pipe, was now experienced as a home within the ocean of her unconscious. It is commonly known among psychoanalysts that the unconscious is often seen in psychic fantasy as an ocean. Sometimes the ocean is threatening when the passions have been repressed and threaten to erupt as out-of-control impulses (Kavaler-Adler, 1992a).

As Helen faced her unconscious by re-owning her split-off and dissociated aggression, the image of a peaceful ocean came to her mind often in sessions. When she felt loving toward me in the transference, re-experiencing loving feelings toward her childhood mother, she would have the image of lying on the beach, beside the ocean, and would imagine the sun radiating down on her. She would say, "I'm heating up," as the sun would shine down on her in her mind. This sun was her image of her transferential mother's love and her own love toward me as her transferential mother. In her vivid visual fantasy ("phantasy") I was the sun mother radiating down on her. The image of an ocean cave, however, went a step further. It spoke of how she could live peacefully in her own unconscious and actually inhabit it as a home in which she lived within her own psychic space. The image of an ocean cave also suggests a peaceful and mellow habitation, where the cool ocean contained her and protected her from the threats of the outside world. In her own words, she had found "a home within." Helen's ocean cave also suggests the psychic capacity for interiority, or of having her own inner self space.

Individuation, Coming Out, in the Course of Separating

On some days, Helen felt her lungs opening up in a session. Following this, she was able to speak in a related and spontaneous way in her life. She was amazed that she could speak freely, without self-consciousness, with a feeling of being inside of her body and with a freedom from her former hypervigilant watchfulness of herself. This happened as she surrendered to the sadness within. Through this, she opened to authentic and present interpersonal contact, and to the new healthy psychic internalizations that would come from such contact. Helen's lungs opened in session, expressing the somatic symbolism of this "coming-out" process, entering a state of continuing identity in the world, with an individuated voice and a true and spontaneous self. Interestingly, I had visceral countertransference, as my lungs too had felt expanded in the session in which she felt her lungs open.

Countertransference

Sometimes, I would share such a resonance with Helen because it helped her feel that I was in tune with her as natural developmental evolutions came about. I consider the sharing of such visceral countertransference events in a totally different category from sharing personal self-disclosures in treatment. This sharing of my resonant reaction could be seen as falling under the category of what James Masterson (1976) has called the developmental function of "communicative matching." This function takes place between therapist and patient, as between mother and toddler, when the developmentally arrested patient is progressing in the separation process after the separation trauma has been faced repeatedly in the painful affects of the abandonment depression. Masterson speaks of the therapist providing a developmental function that the mother of the patient was unable to provide in infancy and childhood.

In contrast to my sharing of this visceral resonance as a way of providing developmental attunement, there was another visceral and affective countertransference event. In a session in which Helen reported a dream of her internal self and other images separating out, which is a novel developmental phenomenon described by Mahler, Pine, and Bergman (1975), I noticed that my feelings at that time did not match those of Helen. Helen reported, "I dreamed that my body and my mother's body separated from one another," at a time when she was in a major internal turmoil, and she didn't know why.

When I spoke to Helen about her guilt, she became more and more distraught. At other times, it was helpful to speak to her about her horrors and crimes as she saw them. In her group therapy (monthly mourning group) with me, she asked the group to hear her speak about her "crime" of neglect with her child, and to face her directly with her responsibility, and to not let her off the hook. Only when she reported the dream of her body separating out from her mother's body did I realize Helen's need for my validation of the internal developmental transformation that was taking place. Therefore, I intuitively at that time placed the interpretation of the developmental event before the psychodynamic conflict related to her guilt. A guilt interpretation was only helpful in this context when it could be joined with her backlash reaction to a new step in intrapsychic separation.

Since there was no external event that Helen was aware of creating such internal upheaval, her reporting of a dream was critical. Interestingly, however, it also made me aware of my conscious objective mode of countertransference affect. Helen assimilated the information about the development change as self and mother images became represented in her mind as two separate bodies. She was relinquishing her sense of having a merger between her body and mine. This was very upsetting for Helen, but once I interpreted it, she was much relieved. She began to feel a sense of joy, flow, visualization, and creativity open within her.

In contrast to other times, when I had felt feelings similar to those she felt and described, I felt quite differently. It was clear that the change in my feeling state relative to hers was related to Helen having gone through critical psychic steps of developmental separation through the deep grief affects of the mourning process. Instead of a flow of joy at the end of the session in which she felt such joy, I felt mildly depressed. I was feeling quite separate from her, and I thought this was related to her body and mine, as the symbolic transference mother separated out in her mind. I shared this connection with her and she said, "That's too bad. These feelings are so wonderful. I'm sorry you're not feeling them."

Dissolving the Antilibidinal Ego
and Opening Up Conscious Aggression:
Transforming Aggression into Self-Agency—from Guilt to Regret

Each time that Helen relived her self-sabotaging punishment for success, she did so at a level of new affective awareness that she had formerly lacked. A gradual process unfolded of the compulsive reenactment transforming into a consciously experienced reliving, with sharp affect awareness. This allowed Helen to wed her affective and cognitive experience and, thus, to more acutely differentiate the present from the past in her experience. This included differentiating the internal mother (or sometimes mother-father) object inside of her, which carried the blueprint of her past traumas, from the present-day external mother, sister, father, etc. The reliving at an affect level opened up psychic space for choice rather than compulsion so that Helen could feel all the affect dimensions of a developmental mourning process at the level of preœdipal loss and object connection disruption.

Such psychic and self evolution can also be described in terms of James Masterson's (1976, 1981, 2000) "abandonment depression," which includes primitive affect states of primal rage, void sensations, and cognitive blankness at the point at which any process of free association would stop, as well as connecting to all the natural affect states that open up in consciousness when the sensations of the affect block have been tolerated. In the case of Helen, I observed and experienced such affect states expressing themselves as feelings of loss, feelings of love, and longings for contact with the primal other, which often includes wishes to merge at a psychic fantasy level.

Ultimately, the commingled experience of love and loss was felt by Helen as grief affect, a tactile form of internal object contacting sadness. As an example, when Helen cried, "I need you on the inside," she was expressing an abandonment depression void experience at a level of differentiation where words could be found to express it. When she experienced memories in her body at an earlier time in treatment, which were so severe in visceral terms that she felt a metal rod was lodged between her head and her toes, she was at a less differentiated, more primitive level of amorphous affect, experienced in visceral and somatic terms.

Helen had many illnesses prior to treatment and a clear bill of health, without illness, as her mourning process was resolved in treatment. This affect-level reliving, with all its current transitional object connections in the treatment situation, and all the conscious connecting with internal objects, formerly enacted in the form of symptoms, illustrated the critical psychological shifts that appear to follow an innate developmental course. These shifts occurred in degrees of transformation. They can be described in terms of psychic relinquishments of the formerly split-off, and affectively sealed-off, pathological antilibidinal ego structure.

Observing Helen's progress, I propose that the relinquishment of old psychic structures results in the freeing-up of the aggressive forces and impulses, along with their internal world object attachments, that had been part of the psychic reenactment of the archaic antilibidinal structure. Observing Helen's progress, I witnessed her increasing consciousness and ownership of aggression. Simultaneously, and seemingly consequentially, I witnessed the natural development of her capacities for self-agency, self-articulation, self-reflection, observing ego reflection, boundary formation, and other so-called ego functions. Yet, also vivid in terms of this developmental progression that I witnessed in Helen was her newfound capacity for feeling, facing, and both intrapsychically and interpersonally negotiating that which I have defined as "psychic regret."

The Analysand's Expression of Regret and its Evolution into Compassion

Helen's movement into the psychic capacity for regret can be described from many angles and dimensions. I will describe four content forms that her regret took. Later, I will describe how her conscious containing and owning of formerly split-off aggressive dynamics, within herself, interacted with her capacity to feel and know regret as a powerful form of psychological anguish. The affect awareness in this form of a psychic anguish totally differentiates the experience of regret from that of a guilt compulsion prompted by an identification with the aggressor.

First, there was Helen's regret related to the leaving of her child at such a young age (about two). That which Helen had spoken about earlier with cries of despair, due to fears of having sinned in some unforgivable manner that would bring the worst of punishments (leading to her own self-punishing torture, as in inflicting the symptoms of her infant illness on herself again), was now—after the separation and mourning process in treatment—experienced as a grief-laden sense of regret. Rather than cries of fear broadcasting her terrors, such as "What will happen to me? No one will want me! I'll never have friends!" Helen now came from a place of concern for the other, maintaining and sustaining an object-related psychic bond that formerly had been disrupted by her aborted attempts at separation from a possessive mother. She spoke with a great depth of feeling for the pain of her child, who now lived as an adult in her American home, saying, on the couch, "How can a child live without a mother? Even though I left my child with my mother it isn't the same as having his real mother! I couldn't have endured what I put my child through!" Through such deeply felt affect levels of regret, Helen created actual acts of reparation, as when she brought her child to live with her in New York.

Another time of regret involved Helen's agonized feelings about having retaliated against her mother by punishing her with cold distancing behavior, with a general sense of disconnection from her mother's life, and with a warding-off of her mother's wish to be involved with her life. This was an externalized form of identification with the aggressor, as opposed to the internalized form in which she attacked and punished herself within through an antilibidinal ego structure. Helen felt this agony of regret when she remembered her infant illness and the role of her mother in rescuing her from the hospital and saving her life. "How could I be so cruel to my mother when she saved my life?" she cried out from the couch. I listened. She wept. I felt deeply close to her in her grief moments of vulnerability. My presence allowed her to feel what formerly had been too intolerable to feel. Gladys Foxe (2002) uses the term reciprocal resonance to describe this kind of intimate experience between analyst and analysand, which seems to apply to how close I felt to Helen and to how I felt, even at the beginning, that she was going to let me help her.

Helen's Growth and its Relationship to the Psychoanalytic Interpretation of Aggression in Klein's Depressive Position

Then there was my interpretation of Helen's "void" experience, which led to a new way of owning and transforming her aggression. In the beginning, Helen had experienced the visceral-level void experience as part of Masterson's abandonment depression. It would have been detrimental, therefore, at that point to make any interpretations about her aggression in relation to the void. I believe it would have made her feel blamed, like she was a bad child. At that earlier time, Helen needed my compassion for her void experience as a psychophysical reaction to the trauma of her mother's disconnection from her during childhood when she expressed separation needs. Her mother not only frustrated her but also had seemingly traumatized her by arresting her normal developmental process.

However, once Helen underwent the painful evolution of her developmental separation (by tolerating the abandonment depression affect states), she became an interpreting subject (Ogden, 1986) who could symbolically understand her own impulses and motivations. She then became capable of tolerating an internal aggression, which formerly had felt murderous, because she could begin to cognitively process her affect states and understood their meaning on a symbolic level. Consequently, with this developmental growth, I could interpret Helen's void experience in terms of her aggression so that she could move forward in her capacity to love and sustain connection with her internal mother.

At the moment in Helen's fifth year of treatment when I told her that her sense of void was related to her hate, as her awareness of her regrets was at its height, Helen appeared to feel immediately liberated. She had been addicted to the hate for her mother when it had been unconscious and dissociated into the split-off antilibidinal ego part of her psyche. When I spoke to Helen about her hate now, she reacted by offering a lot of fertile free associations, rather than with any traumatized disruption or withdrawal. She associated to dreams of black people, who she interpreted as representing her split-off aggressive (shadow) parts, which she began to re-own as she came to understand the projections in her dream. She also associated to a dream of merging with a twinlike (twinship transference) male other, through a purifying baptism in an ocean of water. This male other was with her so that she didn't feel afraid. She felt a sense of empathic understanding and attunement from the mere presence of the other, which she designed as a male counterpart in her dream. It was clear to me that she was at that time experiencing me, at a preconscious level, as an empathic presence, so that a transitional object transference took on the character of a twinship transference, one form of Heinz Kohut's (1971) idealizing transference.

Helen had projected the idealizing and twinship transferences onto me. Then in her dream life, she seemed to have converted me into a male figure to satisfy her heterosexual longings as a genitally developed woman at a conscious level. Her purification in the ocean of baptismal water seemed to be a metaphorical depiction of the interpretation process that was going on in treatment at that point, an interpretation process whose mutuality we shared.

Helen's associations to my interpretation of her void state as a somatic symptom of her dissociated hate touched on how much gratitude she could actually feel now toward this mother who she had been used to hating. This followed a profound positive transference state, different from Helen's earlier idealizing state. In this fifth year of positive transference, she felt loving feelings for me as a transferential mother figure, as she had felt when a child with her mother, before her alienation took place, when she left home and country in adulthood. From her transferential love for me in the developmental maternal transference, she now felt a renewed and reparative love for her actual mother. She reunited with her mother. Following experiences of gratitude toward me, as her transferential mother, she expressed much gratitude toward her actual mother. In fact, she spoke of how grateful she felt that her mother could receive her forgiveness when she now felt it, which assuaged former compulsions to retaliate as a way of punishing the mother of the past.

Helen also spoke about how she was developing the joy of giving within herself for the first time. She spoke of having such joy in my presence and of wanting to give that to others. She said:

> I have this feeling with you. It's not contrived. It's not manic—of peace and joy. Am I making this up? No! I'm feeling it right now! I want to rise above the negative stuff in others—like the complaints—envy—stabbing—I want

to give love because you've given it to me. I want to pass it on. I was where others were before. It's hard to overcome.

Then, she spoke of wishing to give something to someone every day now. She said:

> I hope I can hold on to this feeling inside for a long time to come. I think this is the greatest gift one person could give another person. It's a kind of joy—joy like you want to cry. It makes the world so different! Something has dramatically changed. Now I can have vision. Everything is in this flow—understanding, enlightenment, creativity, and love—everything is in it. I keep practicing and practicing. Coming here is a kind of spiritual practicing. ...

She added, "After going through my feelings of envy and aggression, the light comes out!"

Helen now said that her experience with me allowed her to remember having experienced love from an early mother, a mother who later became negatively colored by her separation trauma experiences. In uncovering this mother, Helen uncovered her own capacity to love. She spoke of seeing her mother on Mother's Day, and of giving her flowers, cake, and a whole set of "spiritual tapes." Her mother received these gifts graciously, with love, and Helen felt gratitude that her mother had "never lost her spirit." "She looked so beautiful on Mother's Day," Helen said. "She never lost her spirit! I am so grateful!" At the end of the session in which Helen told me this in analysis, she herself had a big, beautiful smile on her face. She said she felt like the sun was shining down on her, just like when she felt close to her mother in high school. Helen recalled how she had felt when she was intensely involved in loving her mother. She added that she had felt this way many times with me.

Breaking the Vicious Circle from Generation to Generation

The last experience of regret that I will mention is that of Helen's regret related to the retaliatory aggression that she couldn't help feeling when it was provoked by her son who now lived with her. Helen struggled intensely to contain and control her aggressive impulses toward her son, and she generally succeeded. However, the effort was monumental at times. It began to be less so as she could convert her aggressive impulses into feelings of sadness and compassionate grief for this son who she now truly loved, but also a son who caused her much pain—particularly when she would feel a retaliatory aggression toward him that she had felt toward her own mother. As Helen struggled to contain an inward sense of erupting rage, she baptized herself in the ocean of tears that would emerge as the sadness of regret penetrated her from her own, now more compassionate, psyche.

Helen spoke repeatedly of her struggle to contain the rage provoked by her son. Eventually, she spoke of combining this containment process with the sustaining of her memory of her former abandonment of her son whom she had left when he was such a small child. Helen's concentration on containment and connection in order to remain committed to her child brought her much regret in both affective and cognitive forms. As Helen mastered this process by relinking present and past realities that had formerly been disconnected (see Bion, 1963, "attacks on linking"), she began to realize that there were positive payoffs for her in doing so. She began to realize that when she contained her rage, and converted it to sadness, and then to the renewal of love, she could concentrate on her own work, reading, projects, and ambitions.

Helen found cognitive focus as she sustained a center of affect awareness within herself, giving her a central axis that reflected the enlarging of a central self or, in Fairbairn's (1952) words, a "central ego," free of split-off antilibidinal parts dominating her psychic terrain. Through concentration and focus, she found self-agency and self-articulation. All could be brought to the symbolic level now as she could concentrate and focus. For the first time in her life, Helen did not lose her memory and her intellectual abilities when she was emotionally upset. She could now feel frustrated and deprived, unfairly treated and extremely angry, full of conscious sadomasochistic fantasies of retaliation, without feeling overwhelmed by her affect, without feeling traumatic overload.

Resolving Integration of Love and Aggression Allows Relinquishment of the Identification with the Aggressor

The close link between aggression and love can be seen in an acute affect-level experience that Helen had in her fifth year of treatment, within a session, when she was feeling and processing much regret and, thus, integrating herself through integrating her love and hate. I listened as Helen spoke, and she continued by telling me that she interpreted this experience as her simultaneous wishes for connection and separation, wishes that she still experienced as being in conflict. She associated to her anger—the aggressive impulse—as being a sign of her need to make sure she could separate, even in the moment when she felt an ecstatic sense of merger. She then related this admixture of opposite desires conveyed through her own affect experience to another moment in treatment when she felt like the sun of mother love was shining down on her, making her body hot, while she almost immediately also felt a sense of nausea. She related the nausea to an angry impulse, again related to her need to preserve an escape exit for separation. She spoke of the mixture of love and hate in this regard, or the mixture of need for the love object and need to separate, illustrating her depressive position capacity to feel ambivalence at an acute affect level in relation to one other love object.

Breaking the Chain of Reenactment: The Difference between Psychic Regret Suffering and Masochistic Suffering

Regret is related to an internal psychic event. Regret therefore stands in contrast to the more commonly understood experience of bereavement, which is related to an external event, the actual death of a loved one. Regret involves both the loss of the other through losing the loving aspect of the connection when one's own hostile aggression intrudes on that connection and the grief of knowing the pain of that loss as a heartfelt visceral experience that goes beyond the defensive cognitive mechanisms of guilt.

I have written about this in *Mourning, Spirituality, and Psychic Change: A New Object Relations View of Psychoanalysis* (Kavaler-Adler, 2003a). I also wrote at that time of how Melanie Klein (1940, 1975) approached an understanding of Object Relations at the primal heart level when she wrote about the depressive position, which D.W. Winnicott ([1963] 1982) would have liked to call the position of concern (Gross-Kurth, 1988). Klein spoke of guilt and loss together as the crucial affect-level experience that changes the internal world within the depressive position. I add up guilt and loss and find the clinical phenomenon of regret, in which guilt is a heartfelt anguish, not a defensive mental operation.

The loss of love in regret either can be consciously suffered, resulting in psychic change toward psychic growth, or can be denied, repressed, dissociated, and generally blocked from awareness. If it is not consciously suffered, it will result in symptoms within one's own psychophysical being, and in destruction to external interpersonal relationships, particularly love relationships. Helen's case, as well as many others I have written about (Kavaler-Adler, 2003a, 2003b, 2004, 2005), illustrate how suffering regret consciously helps to develop one's capacity to love.

Helen's showing the tolerance for regret as the core experience of ambivalence within the depressive position allows for the analysand's own insights to emerge quite naturally from an intuitive level. Helen began to sense for herself what it is to suffer the existential grief of regret as part of suffering in the Buddhistic sense of all of life, of "what is." This suffering is organically based in the body, and it totally differs from masochistic suffering, which is a reactive self-punishing reenactment. Masochistic suffering is based on an ignorance of what one is suffering, the original events compelling reenactment remaining unconscious or dissociated. The suffering of regret is an existential suffering, a necessary suffering of what is, and it involves the containing of much aggression. Suffering the pain of hurting the one one loves, which is always part of the human condition of loving, is a necessary process in the course of becoming capable of truly appreciating the loved one and of truly developing a capacity to love that transcends one's own narcissism.

Helen learned that this form of suffering involved a sacrifice. As she learned this through containing her rage in the face of provocation from her adult child, she began to empathize with well-known representatives of civil disobedience and political nonviolence, such as Mahatma Gandhi and Martin Luther King. Whereas in the beginning of treatment she empathized with murderers, by the fifth year of treatment, when she had learned to suffer regret, and to gain the openness of her intuitive unconscious that this suffering brought, she quite naturally began to empathize with pacifists. Experiencing this with her has made me aware that what I am discovering about regret in clinical treatment has important messages for other spheres of social and political concern in the world.

In a paper on "Psychic Pain," in her collected papers, the neo-Kleinian Betty Joseph (1989) quotes Bion, who has written that "those who cannot suffer pain cannot suffer joy!" Betty Joseph, like Bion, understands that the suffering of pain, related to the longing for another, who one will love ambivalently, and will hurt, is an affect-level experience of Klein's depressive position. Helen articulated all of this in her personal experience within her analysis and was consequently able to overcome her compulsion to reenact the identification with the internal world aggressor that had promoted her symptomatology of masochistic self-attack, as opposed to conscious suffering that brings mourning and healing. It is this affect experience of mourning within the depressive position that allows one to find again the primal love so as to have a good enough object connection inside the psyche to allow for a symbolic level of knowing, experiencing, and communicating.

To move from protosymbolic experiences, which are often preverbal, and are visceral and behavioral (that which Wilfred Bion spoke of as a psyche filled with Beta elements), to symbolic level experiences (referred to by Bion in terms of Alpha elements in the psyche) is a journey of love and grief. It is our wish to love that makes us human. It is our longing for another and our highly aggressive conflicts around loving that force us to grow in the human psychic (and spiritual) struggle.

Klein and Bion understood this, and my analysand, Helen, came to experience this through the mourning process in her treatment, in which the role of containing aggression and tolerating the experience of regret became so fundamental.

On one day, Helen spoke of how painful it was to contain her aggression when it rose up as a powerful rage toward her child. On another day, she spoke of how Gandhi and Luther King felt this sense of physical pain that she felt when containing her rage for a purpose, a purpose based on love, whether love for humanity or love for her son. On a third day, Helen spoke of observing her son, for the first time, struggling with the pain and tears of containing a rage that was not immediately acted out. In the past, her son had acted out his rage continuously against her, and then with a girlfriend. Now, he became willing to feel pain. This was the same pain so familiar to Helen as she sacrificed her acts of overt rage and discharge for her son's benefit, and tolerated the internal impact of rage so that she could face the pain of regret over hating the one she also loved. Her son seemed to have unconsciously identified with his mother's process, transforming the generational family dynamic from identification with the aggressor to identification with the healer. It had been Helen's sacrifice, the mother's sacrifice, which brought about Helen's depressive position capacity to love and, thus, to also create her own self-expression. In doing so, she cultivated the creative self-expression, in turn, a young adult who had suffered early trauma in the form of early mother loss. Helen's sacrifice seemed to be interrupting the vicious circle of reenactment.

Feeling the "Letting-go"

This entire process resulted in Helen's being able to mourn at a whole new level. When she suffered the loss of a second husband, she was able to grieve repeatedly, lessening the attachment, viewing a clear conscious portrait of the mother and father transferences toward her husband, and seeing a clearer picture than ever of who her husband (of 10 years) had really been. Helen described her mourning process in developmental terms, as allowing her to now really feel the "letting-go," not just the longing for the lost other. The emphasis in her mourning process had shifted naturally, developmentally, toward a whole new level of accepting separation as a part of life, even when it meant feeling intense grief pain repeatedly in the course of the cycles of mourning.

With this natural developmental journey of mourning, Helen's sense of embodiment in her body grew dramatically. She described to me, and also vividly displayed, how she felt more and more like a woman. She began to desire men who were integrated at a higher level than her former husbands. She began to articulate an acute sense of longing for a man—not a man who was partly the father she had never had or one who was overwhelmingly the early mother of security that she yearned for, but a man who could uniquely be known and appreciated for himself. She felt a formerly latent femininity emerge. In this transition toward an adult sexuality, Helen also found men in her life who she could look to as more solid father figures, as well as men to be examples of a more masculine maturity.

Melanie Klein has written about the difference between manic and true reparation (Klein, 1940). Manic reparation is based on an urgent wish to have a quick fix, without going through the painful grief process that brings real possibilities for renewed love and real possibilities for reparative gestures and acts. True reparation is always imperfect. It involves accepting the faults and weaknesses within oneself and the other. Getting to true reparation is a slow process. It is the kind of process that Helen had undergone. The capacity to accept the slow process of true growth and true reparation is based on an ability to tolerate the intermingling of formerly polarized affect states that results in increasing degrees of refined and subtle affects.

Psychoanalytic theorists have, for the most part, not spoken of developmental growth in terms of affect experience and the developmental increments in affect tolerance and affect integration. Klein's view of the depressive position does allow us to speak in these terms. No one could articulate this developmental affect-level psychic growth process better than my analysand, Helen. The development of Object Relations, which includes the capacity to sustain a fully ambivalent, multicolored, and whole object view both of oneself and others, is an affect experience growth process. Through this affect-level growth process, a multitude of cognitive capacities and ego functions evolve. Helen understood this now, firsthand!

PART TWO:

DEVELOPMENTAL MOURNING AND EROTIC TRANSFERENCE

CHAPTER 10

MOURNING AND EROTIC TRANSFERENCE

Originally published in 1992, *International Journal of Psycho-Analysis*, *73*(3), 527-539.

In "Observations on Transference Love" (1915), Sigmund Freud speaks of erotic transference as both a resistance and a conduit for the deepest unconscious desires and conflicts to emerge. The two disparate courses that erotic transference can take oppose one another. To the degree that the erotic transference is a resistance, it fails to be a conduit for unconscious desires. When erotic transference is a conduit for unconscious desires, it allows those desires to be understood within the course of psychoanalytic treatment, reducing all forms of resistance.

Freud (1915) credits the attitude of the analyst: "keeping firm hold of the transference" (p. 166), but not succumbing to it, as well as the educative work done on the analytic process, as the two main factors in containing the resistance aspects of "transference love"; so that the infantile aspects of the love can emerge and be analyzed. Yet, his comments throughout the essay emphasize the continuing difficulty, and sometimes the impossibility, of modifying the resistance so that treatment can proceed, as in the case of "women of elemental passionateness" (Freud, 1915, p. 166). He sees it as likely that a woman will retaliate for the unrequited nature of her love by withdrawing all co-operation from treatment.

Perhaps Freud would have been more optimistic about the facility to use transference love, by terms of containing and transforming the resistance aspects of it, if he had taken another factor into account. I propose a third, and I believe a critical factor, in modifying erotic transference from a major transference resistance into an ongoing positive force in the treatment process. Mourning as a clinical process is the third factor that I propose.

Mourning was first acknowledged as a primary emotional process in Freud's (1917) *Mourning and Melancholia*. However, it was Melanie Klein who first saw mourning as the primary affective process underlying both developmental growth and clinical psychotherapeutic treatment. Klein's papers on the depressive

233

position dynamics, such as "Mourning and its Relation to Manic Depressive States" (1940), highlighted the potential clinical acumen to be gained by understanding the mourning process.

In the following case, I demonstrate how an attunement to object-related contact, within the course of psychoanalysis, allows a natural mourning process to unfold, thus contributing to an ongoing positive evolution of the use of erotic transference in treatment. The case also illustrates male transference love in relation to a female analyst, which was never discussed by Freud. My case is a case in point not only in demonstrating the role of mourning as a primary clinical phenomenon that affects the course of the erotic transference but also in demonstrating that the erotic transference is as primary in men with women analysts as it is with women analysands of male analysts.

My case study also returns to the notion of erotic transference as a primarily object-related phenomenon, as compared to the changed definition of the erotic transference offered by self-psychologists, such as Trop (1988). Trop refers to erotic transference as the emergence of a developmentally "curtailed" need for "mirroring of the sexual self" (p. 281). In the case I am presenting, it can clearly be seen that the erotic transference was based on object-related yearnings that motivated the expression of repressed areas in the analysand's personality. It was this expression of the repressed phenomena, connected to the object-related yearnings, which allowed the analysand to become a sexual being. As the analyst, I did not mirror this man's sexuality, but merely received and understood his feelings.

The Case of Mr. L.

Mr. L. came to analysis in his late 20s, after many disappointing relationships with women. He was working in a mediocre job and was frustrated by his wish to be an artist. He had friends but was generally detached emotionally. His main reason for seeking out treatment was to understand why he could not successfully relate to women, particularly on a romantic basis. He tended to become involved with distant and rejecting women, who at first were sexually seductive.

Mr. L.'s disconnection from all his feelings, and in particular from his sexual feelings, made him unable to initiate sexual involvement. Therefore, he was drawn to women who actively seduced him, but all relationships with such women were short-lived. Once he was conquered, the women he chose tended to withdraw from him, even though he would try to hold on by attempting to please them in various ways, canceling out his actual reactions. Many other women, who he associated with as good friends, would not entertain the idea of dating him or seeing him as a boyfriend. They did not view him as a sexual man, and he was deeply discouraged by this, although he remained detached from his pain until he became engaged in his psychoanalysis.

Mr. L. was interested in working with a woman analyst, and this seems related to his motivation to seek treatment as a way of dealing with his lack of sustained romantic relationships. He began treatment on a twice-a-week basis, but quickly moved into three-times-a-week, and then into four-times-a-week treatment. The course of his analysis extended over a six-year period.

The Mourning Process

Mr. L.'s analysis involved many stages of mourning. I will outline the overall movement from mourning of a precedipal object, to the capacity to allow a latent erotic transference to emerge. I will then outline the mourning of the oedipal object that took place with the blossoming of the erotic transference. Next, I will discuss the mourning process that allowed the erotic transference to become a transitional vehicle toward erotic relations with an available external object, as the erotic desires for the analyst were resolved. I will comment on the potential resistance aspects of the erotic transference that were resolved through varying stages of mourning. I will also comment on the need for conscious mourning of object loss, as opposed to a compensatory mode of narcissistic mirroring that can be used as a defense against feeling such loss. I will highlight how the mourning of the precedipal object allows the erotic transference to be tolerated, and used as a mode of exploration, rather than being resistantly manipulated by the analysand.

Mourning of the Precedipal Object

Early on in Mr. L.'s treatment, his yearning for a precedipal mother was first felt by me and by Mr. L. himself, as it appeared both in memories and in the transference. One memory of a painful separation from a male friend at latency appeared to be both a screen memory of early yearnings toward the precedipal mother, as well as being a poignant object attachment and object loss in its own right. Mr. L. remembered lying in a dug-out hole in the dirt of the wilderness at the time when he lived in Nebraska. He and his friend, Richard, would fantasize together that the remains of a building they found in their private wilderness were the foot of a giant castle. This was their land of enchantment.

It was a romantic world where friendship and adolescent homosexual love could bloom. The height of their mutual enthrallment arose one quiet summer afternoon, when they lay side by side, and also half on top of one another, inside their dug-out hole, a hole dug out of the dirt and the leaves. They didn't speak. They were blissfully at peace. Perhaps at that moment, Mr. L. felt a sublime feeling that he had always yearned for, a sublime feeling that he may never have quite attained in infancy, with a mother who was full of tension and depression. His mother was remembered as hard. Although Mr. L.'s warm, soft, and tender body contact with his male friend could have had aspects of some early breast that was more yielding than the remembered mother, it is also likely that his tranquil contact with his friend could have been the fulfillment of a yearning that had long been aroused and frustrated by his early mother.[1]

Mr. L.'s earliest memories of his childhood involved frustrating scenes between himself and his parents. He remembered his parents telling him as soon as he learned to talk that he must stop, hold his breath, and not say anything unless what he wished to express was truly important. Such directives threw Mr. L., still a toddler, into a tailspin. His urge to speak felt like a gasp that was pushed back into him. His words got all contorted inside. All spontaneous gestures and voice felt arrested. He was stunned and stuck. His excitement to convey his feelings was crushed. He felt as if he was forced literally to swallow his words. Deep body tensions were set up at this time that made withdrawal backward and inward into himself a reflexive reaction.

Given all this tension about expressing himself in words, it is no wonder that the happiest time of his life was remembered by Mr. L. as this time of tranquil silence as he lay comfortably, in body contact with his best friend. When he was then forced away from his friend by the same parents who forced his voice away from him, he felt internally desecrated. His parents were having trouble in their marriage, and with an abrupt attempt at resolution, they decided to leave town and move to New York. There was no discussion with the children.

Before Mr. L. knew what was happening, he was sitting in the back of his family car, peering mournfully out of the back window. He had never said "good-bye." The last time he and his friend Richard were together they hadn't discussed it. Nobody said anything. They got into some ridiculous fight over nothing. Now he might never see him again. Nor would Mr. L. see the other friends that he had made in Nebraska. He felt depleted, defeated, dead inside.

Only later in his analysis did Mr. L. mourn the loss of his friend Richard, and the loss of the kind of quiet contentment that he had so treasured during those few precious moments, those few and precious days. As his grief-laden sadness emerged, alternating with the angry protest against his parents that he had never made at that childhood time, his potential tenderness was born, and it touched his analyst. He embroidered his memories with the feeling of tender love, which felt belated now in the present. Although on the couch, Mr. L. let me know that tears arose, tears formerly blocked and suffocated. I felt him in his tender tear-filled sadness, and he felt me feeling him, so a Winnicottian (1971) atmosphere of holding was engendered from which mourning could continue, as so many poignant times in his childhood were yet to be remembered.

Mourning his friend, who galvanized psychic yearnings for a good precedipal object, was just the beginning of Mr. L.'s mourning in treatment. It was this mourning, and the need for the analyst which it opened up, that helped Mr. L. to reveal repressed memories of childhood shame.

Mr. L. also mourned for parts of himself, child parts of him that had been injured and left behind. He remembered shame-ridden experiences of paternal castration. One memory of being punished and spanked particularly stood out. There was another memory of his father going into a rage and slapping him across the face. Both memories brought back to him his sense of despair about ever being understood. His father was not interested in hearing what he had to say.

His father would never have listened nor understood that he stole some quarters from their next-door neighbors in California because it was his only way of expressing his misery, as well as his wish to retaliate against the parents who tore him away from his friend Richard and all the other friends in Nebraska. His parents united in their wish to punish him. He was seen as immoral, as a thief! He was forced to apologize to his neighbors in his parents' words. He couldn't even use his own words. He went through what felt like his trial and conviction in a numbed-out state—dejected, passively obedient. He saw himself as a piece of shit, as a cast-out turd.

He waited in his room as he was commanded by his father, not knowing what would happen next. Centuries seemed to go by. Then his father entered his room and commanded him to "Drop your pants!" His father spanked him on his bare behind, and never once looked him in the face. He submitted, and his self-hatred drowned out awareness of his hatred for his father. Later, he would act out this hatred and would do everything possible to disown his aggression since he associated his father with aggression. However, unconsciously he would identify with his father's detachment. Mr. L. commented on how, even at the height of his father's aggression toward him, in the midst of his own humiliation, his father seemed detached and uninvolved, seemingly doing what he thought he had to do. Mr. L. felt that he didn't even get the dignity of his father's personal sense of anger.

Mr. L. had repressed his reactions, not being able to tolerate the awareness of how lonely and unimportant he felt in the midst of his humiliating castration. In treatment, his hatred toward his parents, and particularly toward his father, came alive. So did his shame. He asked out loud the questions and protests that he could never have expressed at the time to his father. His secret superiority emerged as well, his belief that his father was contemptible. Yet he had always treated himself with contempt, repeating his father's behavior toward him.

He had dreams in which another man split-off from him or came inside of him. Sometimes he held dialogues with this other man. He realized that this other man was a part of him, another half. He had his father inside him, and there was nothing he could do about it. All he could do was make peace with his father, by understanding his father's pain and grieving now for both of them. His rage at his father spent, his feelings of shame and humiliation beginning to heal with the expression of his inner wounds and the expressions of his shit-flawed self-image, he could now make amends. Moving from the paranoid-schizoid to the depressive position, he was able to realize how much pain his father must have been in to have been so numbed out himself, to have been so frequently filled with rage, so indifferent to anything his son said or thought.

Forgiveness came as he felt empathy for the lonely soul within his father. He could see a whole picture now too, one that had eluded him as a child. He could see how his father was both emotionally rejected and dictated to by his mother. He could begin to see his mother's pain too, for she was jealous and lonely with a husband who was in love only with his work, and who frequently had affairs with his secretaries. The whole picture began to come together, and Mr. L. began to have two whole parents. Only in this way could his own self become whole.

Mr. L. was freed by his capacity to feel the chain of affects, from his anger to the narcissistic hurt within his shame, and to the loss within his sense of loneliness as he separated from his internal bad part-object parents. Grief followed anger and hurt. He could then feel his parents' pain within his own pain, without the threat of losing his own separate perspective. He would never get to communicate to them what he had felt, and his grief was partly for that. There would always be a rift between them.

Yet, as he communicated his pain to me, his analyst, he psychically healed the rift with his parents and grew to empathize with their pain. He grieved the loss of what they could never be to each other. Through grief, he allowed a tender sadness to emerge within him that was the route to contact with others. He could know and touch others now, and they could know and touch him. His painting became more tactile. The color of rebirth from his despair emerged. His barriers with me were analyzed and resolved, as he could let me feel him and could feel me in turn.

Dreams, as well as memories, revealed Mr. L.'s need to reconnect with good objects within him that had been blocked out of awareness by fears of feeling their loss, and by relations with dead and depriving internal objects that had been held on to when his good objects had been repressed. His sense of self had been depleted by the loss of these objects, and his attachment to bad objects, which seemed representative of his parents' detachment from his needs, prevented him from allowing good object contact in the present. In one dream, which manifested during the fourth year of treatment:

> Mr. L. emerged from a hut in the wilderness to find old friends who he had missed for many years. In relating the dream, he explained that he was warm and cozy in his hut, but he was all alone. It was as if he had found a cocoon in which to heal himself, as he was healing himself in treatment, but the cocoon could become not only a solitary place for recuperation, but also a place to hide, which might isolate him from others.
>
> In the dream, I, his analyst, appeared as a messenger to bring him out of his cocoon and into the forest where his lost friends were still waiting for him, after many years. There was snow all around. He saw trees that were cold and bare. He was blocked by one tree and tried to bang on it. He hit it again and again, but there was no response. Instead of moving on to find his friends, he got caught up in trying to get this cold, dark, tree to respond. The tree and others around were made of petrified wood. He finally gave up, concluding that "You can't get blood from a stone!" Having been caught up so long in trying to get a response from this stone tree, it had gotten darker and colder. There was snow all around.
>
> Finally, he found a bench in the wilderness on which all his friends lay piled up together under a blanket. In the dream, he realized that he almost came too late. They might have frozen to death. He might have lost them. But he discovered them just in time. He lifted the blanket off them, and his friends greeted him. They had kept warm by holding on to each other. He felt their warmth. Once having found them, they were free to go. He let them leave, grateful for the contact, and no longer holding them back from moving on with their lives. As they left, a bed appeared where the bench was, and a female friend of Mr. L.'s appeared on the bed. He wished for her affection and felt his attraction to her.

In Mr. L.'s associations to this dream, he said that at the point when he let his friends go, feeling the contact with them, and keeping their warmth within him, he felt his penis "strengthen." He related this strengthening of himself, within his penis, to an overall strengthening of his sense of self, but also particularly to his sexual self. His associations indicated that he connected his ability to let go of his friends, which allowed the discovery of a woman, to the strengthening of his penis. He understood that he was in danger of freezing his friends and killing them, which would have meant losing them forever, because he had frozen them in a moment of time within his memory in order to avoid losing them. He had put them under a blanket, or blanketed them with repression, because he wanted to hold on to them forever.

He remembered later that within the dream he had felt as if they had been pulled away from him when they had earlier left the hut he was in to find "greener pastures." This is how it had felt to him in his life. He never wanted to leave his childhood friends. They had left him to move on with their separate lives, and he had tried to hold on to them by repressing the memory of them and their warmth, trying to keep them frozen in time behind a blanketing wall of repression. In this way he remained alone, and he was not yet then ready to move on into a psychic place of sexual adequacy where he could relate to a woman.

This dream was a dream of significant mourning. It occurred a month after other dreams in which Mr. L. appeared furious at women who made him feel impotent. It occurred after incidents in life with women in which he felt that his penis could only stay hard if he was filled with cold rage. If he felt affectionate, he felt impotent. With this episode of mourning, just as with the episode of mourning his childhood male friend, his sense of self changed. Again, he allowed good internalizations to form within him by reuniting with warm friends from the past, no longer excluding their sense of warmth and love from his consciousness, nor any longer splitting them off in a seclusion that would turn them into cold "petrified trees."

He gave up on getting warmth from cold trees that seemed to represent a depriving early mother, as well as the distant women whom he had been drawn to, seemingly as a compulsive reenactment in relation to such a mother. He came to terms with the loss of his friends in his life, and in this way felt the sadness that emerged with his associations to the dream. This sadness helped him get past his anger, past his fury at women, and past the cold rage that had more recently opened up into such fury. The sadness helped him assimilate his memories and his good internal objects, and this allowed him in turn to open up to feelings toward his analyst that had been frozen in time as well.

Just as he found a woman on the bed in his dream, so too in his analysis he began to find the analyst as an oedipal level sexual object, now that his precedipal connections had been restored. Although from early on in treatment, Mr. L. could experience erotic feelings toward women in his life, he had kept these feelings split-off from contact with the analyst. He had alluded to wishes to be seen as attractive to the analyst and had feared being repulsive, but he had never felt the force of his own erotic passion. Earlier, he had strengthened his sense of self by restoring his childhood friend Richard to his consciousness, facing the never before faced grief of saying "good-bye."

This made Mr. L. more capable of containing his feelings, and he opened up to his feelings of shame and anger. Now, his ability to say "good-bye" to friends of his later (college) years—friends who, like Richard, also represented preœdipal needs for basic nurturance and affectionate contact—enabled him to acquire a strengthening of his "penis," i.e., of his basic sexual identity. This allowed him to contain erotic feelings, and to open up an erotic transference that had formerly remained latent. The girl he discovered on the bed in his dream became associated with his female analyst.

Erotic Transference

Up until the time of the mourning process described, Mr. L.'s erotic desires were fixated in sadomasochistic fantasies of being tied down by a woman, and of being made to submit to all kinds of sexually arousing tortures. His fantasies echoed Mr. L.'s passive submission to women in his life and to his female analyst. These fantasies were used for masturbation, which became a ritual of re-enacting an enslaved position that Mr. L. inhabited in relation to his mother. His enslaved position in relation to his mother was most chiefly characterized by his inability to say "no" every evening when his mother asked him to go into the kitchen and get her "her" ice cream.

One dream highlighted the deeper level of his humiliation. He dreamt that he was forced to sit naked at the dinner table by his mother. He shivered from the cold, felt mortified as others sat at the table for dinner, and when someone offered him a blanket to cover himself, his mother flew into a rage. Mr. L.'s associations revealed that he thought his mother was getting sexual stimulation from his nakedness, and that he felt exploited by her and uncared for. This view of himself as a sexual victim pressed for reenactment and could have become a resistance to opening up to contact with his analyst, and with his unconscious oedipal erotic desires, if significant mourning had not already allowed him to feel that he was strong enough, and sexual enough, to reveal his fantasies to me rather than to pull me into a covert form of acting out.

Generally, Mr. L. had eroticized his rage toward his mother, and had developed certain characterological patterns. He inverted himself into the role of the victim and controlled others by being controlled. His sexual fantasies, which he cherished and nurtured during his secret masturbation rituals, were filled with this role of erotic victimization. Sometimes one woman tied him up, sometimes three at a time.

One dream revealed his transference to me as one of these women who intimidated him and even terrified him. The woman in his dream was huge compared to him. He was forced to please her in all kinds of ways that substituted for any kind of sexual intercourse since his penis was too small. The dream revealed his secret terror. When he consciously constructed and controlled his sexual fantasies and sex play, he could turn the terror into erotic thrills. In his dream he didn't have that control, and much of his emotional withdrawal from me in the clinical situation could be understood in the light of his terrified inhibition and his hidden erotic longings.

With the mourning process proceeding, however, Mr. L. began to emerge from his guilt-and shame-ridden cocoon by sharing his masturbation fantasies and dreams with me. As he did so, his size dimensions in relation to mine became more proportionate in his fantasies and associations. His dreams began to reveal all kinds of phallic explosions, and often these dreams were wet dreams.

In one dream, there was a tidal wave of emotion coming in at both of us from the outside. It was clear that Mr. L. saw both of us as threatened by the breadth of his passion. His emotional longings had to be experienced full force, just like his phallic eruptions, in order that the two could come together. Mr. L. spoke of standing up to the tidal wave and facing the fear. He would face his passion now that he had me by his side.

As Mr. L.'s tidal wave of passion came out into the open, leaving the ocean of the unconscious, and coming out into the light of day, he wooed me fiercely. He constantly thought of "lines" to say to me as he entered my office, which he revealed with some degree of embarrassment, testing the waters. Over time, his shame diminished and his awakening sense of humor became more predominant.

Also, during this period, Mr. L. would constantly observe what I wore, waiting to see if I would wear a red dress. If I did, he hoped I wore it specially for him. He found everything I wore exciting! With his secret attraction to me no longer concealed, he opened up all the oedipal erotic desires that seemed to have been rebuffed during his childhood by his "cold tree" mother. His wish for me to wear a red dress, which he considered "sexy," became an ongoing motif in his daily speculations about whether I had dressed that morning with him in mind. Former dreams of being in a bed with a strange woman now turned into dreams of feeling loving and close, feeling that we were becoming integrated with one another.

This period brought dreams and fantasies of my lying beside him in bed, or of me suddenly appearing at his doorstep and coming inside his home to make love to him. He described waking in the morning and imagining me beside him. He wanted to feel the pressure of my body, our tenderness, our caressing. He imagined us sharing our secret flaws, bonding through the sharing of our shame, revealing the awkward areas in our bodies, evolving an exquisite attunement to each other's entire body surfaces.

The erotic feelings came up directly in our sessions. He exclaimed that he felt a full feeling coming up from his "gut and through his penis" while being with me in a session. When we discussed his coming four times a week to work with all the dreams and fantasies that were opening up, he felt a kind of sexual ecstasy, believing then that I really wanted him.

Mr. L. wanted me to yearn as intensely for him as he yearned for me. Once, upon meeting a young woman he was attracted to, he vividly described to me his pursuit of her, painting a scene for me that culminated in a sweet, sensual, and prolonged kiss. Not receiving the reaction he expected, he burst out in an uncharacteristic exclamation, which felt as if it was accompanied by the stamping of a foot: "God damn it, I want you to be jealous!" His mother always had been jealous of any girl that he showed interest in. In fact, she would have tantrum-like rages, stamping her feet. He resented this, as it had made him feel overwhelmed with guilt, but now he realized that he wanted me to be jealous.

Mourning the Oedipal Object

Since I had become so vividly painted as Mr. L.'s oedipal love, only disappointment and mourning could bring his transition into finding a true love who could be his own. A critical time of growth arrived during my summer vacation, leading to his last year of treatment, his sixth year. Mr. L. reported to me that after my departure, he had woken up in the mornings with the weight of grief that he had never known before. He felt a heavy sadness and wept. His sadness brought the full impact of his realization that I was never going to come to his home, to his bed. I would never be his.

Surrendering to this truth, he emerged from his cocoon in a radically new way. He felt a newfound sense of determination, a willingness to take risks. He joined a dating service, made a video of himself, and within three dates he had met the woman who would become his bride. As he began to date her and to know her, his painting showed his erotic joy, and the mournful colors of his past brightened. His romantic fantasies were replaced by romantic realities that were better than any fantasies could have predicted. His courtship with his fiancée was filled with surprises, gifts, tender concern, and caring.

On Valentine's Day, Mr. L. canceled one of his analytic sessions (for which he paid) to take his fiancée to a well-known elegant restaurant. In his words, he was determined "to give her royal treatment." It became clear that I had served as a transitional love object, who could be relinquished as I was internalized within him. When Mr. L. left treatment, he said, "You will be deep inside of me for the rest of my life!" But he also said, "You're no longer the focus of my erotic longings." As his treatment drew to a close, his fiancée was the one who empowered the female figures both in his fantasies and in his artwork. He was now working in an executive-level position and was also expressing himself in art. Primarily, at that time, he was preparing for a wedding and marriage. His mourning of his analyst was the last stage in an overall mourning process. This mourning process allowed him to open up the full force of his erotic feelings and fantasies, without being held back by shame, repressed anger, and despair as he had once been. It allowed him to feel more whole so that he might face his fear and contain his feelings.

In this way, Mr. L. could collaborate in analysis in order to understand his feelings rather than being compelled to re-enact his childhood oedipal wishes without self-reflection in treatment. He no longer needed to try to please me or play out the part of a sex slave, with the sexual aspects of the drama hidden. His transference love became a real love, in which he appreciated the real aspects of the relationship with the analyst, and by being open to contact with the analyst as he mourned his losses and opened to formerly blocked-off feelings, he could integrate her into a loving core within him, where he already had installed his childhood friends.

At one point in treatment, Mr. L. had resisted engaging in new relationships with women, as he wished to remain in an exclusive erotic relation with me, his analyst. However, he voluntarily brought this up for discussion in his analytic sessions and was able to prepare to mourn me by facing his resistance and letting go. When I left for my summer vacation, in Mr. L.'s sixth year of treatment, the grief he felt about having to say "good-bye" to me as an erotic love object came with the growing realization that I could become an internal object within him that could make him more secure, but I could not be a real external lover. This gradually enlarging awareness allowed him to let go of me, as he had of his childhood friends, and to move toward a woman who could truly be available to him as a lover and as a wife.

Because Mr. L. had been able to use his analyst as a transitional object, he could choose a wife who was warm, loving, caring, and related in a way that his former girlfriends had never been. As he mourned childhood friends, let go of negative internal parents, and grieved for the parents who had hurt him, he could take in more good internalizations of the analyst. Then, in time, he became able to grieve for the loss of his fantasy wishes toward the analyst. This allowed him to open up to a new relationship with a woman that could truly fulfill his needs as an adult man.

As Freud first said in his "Observations on Transference-Love" (1915), erotic transference can become the major mobilizing force in favor of this psychoanalytic treatment. However, Mr. L.'s willingness to enter erotic transference in an overt way, and his later willingness to surrender to it, were both facilitated by the mourning of object loss and object disappointment. Without such mourning, Mr. L. might have ended up sitting forever in the "transference glow." In a case reported by Gould (1989), just such a situation was described:

> While some of his good feeling may be a reality-based reaction to feeling good and gratitude for the improvements in his life, the uncritical glow I think, also bespeaks, in addition, a transferential halo. I suspect that his current transference resistance may be in his pleasure of basking in the limited intimacy of the therapeutic situation. He can enjoy psychological and emotional closeness that is time-limited each session and in which concurrent physical intimacy with its attendant anxieties is not possible. (p. 64)

In a discussion of Gould's case, I (Kavaler, 1989a) point out how Gould's analysand's resistance was related to a failure to mourn the regrets of his past. I speculate that his transference resistance, which was also an erotic transference resistance, was reinforced by defenses against the feelings of grief related to the guilt of his own rejections of intimacy with women in his life, with roots in the original mother-son situation.

Gould's analysand's resistance to grieving can be contrasted with that of Mr. L., who was able consciously to confront his resistance to giving up the fantasy of an exclusive bond with the analyst as he was able to feel the grief of regret related to his rejections and distancing in relation to women in his past. This allowed him to tolerate the attendant anxieties of intimacy in his life, which Gould states her analysand, Mr. M, still could not do. In Mr. L.'s case, his developing capacity to grieve in his treatment, beginning with his grieving the preœdipal object, allowed him to remember and grieve each former relationship with women in his life. Mr. L. mourned his own part in creating distance with women who aroused erotic desires in him after he experienced the anger toward these women for their own distancing. Both the anger and the sadness of regret were parts of his mourning process.

Gould's (1989) analysand had not yet mourned and faced his losses, many of which had been promoted by his own aggression. He was, therefore, not able to say "good-bye" and to accept the limits of reality that dictated that he needed to move on to a real erotic relationship with an available woman. Gould's analysand's perpetuation of the erotic transference tie to his female analyst seems to be a good example of what Freud cautioned about in relation to the resistance aspects of the transference love. The analyst's abstinence alone did not dissolve Mr. L.'s resistances. The analysand's mourning was essential, and I, as the analyst, needed to be aware of the defenses against this mourning, particularly defenses that served to deny guilt and regret.

In Mr. L.'s case, guilt and regret were faced and felt many times during the course of his treatment. He felt regret about never having said "good-bye" to Richard. He felt guilt and regret about his fight with Richard before he left. He felt guilt and regret about not having been able to let go of his friends and not having respected their needs and their freedom. He felt guilt about all the times he had held back from women and from me, his analyst. He felt regret about all the times he had held back in retaliation against his parents, even though he knew that they had hurt him. He got past such retaliation by grieving the losses that came with his hostile behavior, and at one point said, "Just because my father doesn't call me for my birthday doesn't mean I have to hold back from him. I don't have to continue to act like he does."

The mourning of one's own aggression, and the specific mourning of the oedipal object within the depressive position, is a basic developmental understanding within Kleinian theory. Mr. L.'s feeling of regret is an essential aspect of mourning, related to the owning of aggression as part of the process that leads to the healing power of tolerated loss, and to the self integration process that comes through mourning within the context of the holding aspect of the transference (Modell, 1976). Feeling regret is essential in Kleinian theory in order that reparation to the object can be made, to both the internal and external object. The mourning of loss, in terms of grieving regret for times when potential love and connection was destroyed by distancing behaviors, is critical for resolving neurotic longings for an incestuous object.

The Negative Transference and Mr. L.'s Aggression

The analysand's destructiveness was expressed in a passive-aggressive manner, as withholding himself from contact with the analyst. This was dealt with on a continuing, session-by-session basis, in terms of resistance to connection. The destructiveness also appeared in fantasy form, rather than in enactment. The analysand's sexual fantasies were of a sadomasochistic nature in which he controlled the sadist through masochistic submission. All this was related to a relationship with an internal mother within him. Through the avenue of confronting resistance to contact and connection, interpretations could be made about the sadomasochistic scenes being played out, and about both the aggressive and erotic nature of the wishes behind them. With this neurotic patient, the object-related strivings were always in preconscious if not conscious awareness, and the resistance interpretations were enough to make Mr. L. aware of his desires and his fears of his desires. His sense of shame was resolved through his connection with early memories so that he did not block resistance interpretations due to shame.

The mourning that took place in the treatment allowed Mr. L. to resolve his aggression into healthy self assertion, which was expressed increasingly within the therapeutic Object Relationship, and also in other relationships in his life. During the course of the analysis, I, as the analyst, would experience the withheld negative transference and its underlying aggression in terms of feeling sleepy. However, when I confronted Mr. L. with the point at which he had pulled back he was able to respond in a manner that was reparative to object connection and facilitative to the analysis.

Object Relations Versus Self-Psychology

Erotic transference is primarily an object related phenomenon. It is the transferential expression of the most intense mode of desire for the object. It is a psychophysical state of desire, as shown in the case of Mr. L. who needed to feel like a full sexual subject, the owner of sexual passions. In its full form, erotic transference expresses the most passionate combination of genital cravings for the other, combined with deep longings for tenderness and the reparative gift of love. A separate other is its prime target, and psychic fantasy charts the route to that target.

Yet, in 1988, Jeffrey L. Trop redefined erotic transference in terms of his self psychological view of development and psychic structure. In an article entitled, "Erotic And Eroticized Transference: A Self-Psychological Perspective," he writes: "I describe this as an erotic transference in that the developmental need is for mirroring of the sexual self" (p. 281). His definition places the patient he addresses in that paper in the role of a sexual object, not of a sexual subject. Also, he speaks about a need for an oedipal self object arising in the transference, totally negating the desired object as a separate other. His definition of erotic transference seems to limit his treatment and to set up a schema that opposes the full-blown emergence of unconscious erotic desire.

In his 1988 article, Trop writes of a female patient in terms of his definition, stating that her erotic attraction to men in her life is related to the revival of a "developmental longing for a protective, involved, and alive father to compensate and protect her from her undermining experience with her mother" (p. 277). Trop believes that, due to a mother who always stole her father's attention from her, this woman's healthy desire to exhibit herself, and to feel that she was attractive to a man, had been cut off and defended against. Trop writes: "What she had not acquired during her development was confidence in her own capacity to elicit aliveness and responsiveness in others" (p. 278).

Up to this point in his article, Trop has dealt with his patient more as a sexual object than as a sexual subject. According to Trop's definition of erotic transference as the need for mirroring of the sexual self, a self psychologist might actually attempt to provide a positive mirroring reflection for such a patient, which would keep the patient in the position of the object of the mirror, denying her as a sexual subject with passions of her own.

Worse, using his definition, a self-psychologist might use such mirroring as a narcissistic compensation that would block the erotic passion from emerging. To offer mirroring of the self in the face of sealed-off erotic desire only creates a narcissistic compensation that never can replace the kind of object-related eroticism that one feels when the sadness of object loss opens up renewed love and desire. Such narcissistic compensation defends against object loss, and thus defends against the very fundamental object-related growth process that can only come through mourning.

However, Trop himself does not succumb to any such facile notion of mirroring, and he appropriately deals with his patient's shame. He helps his patient to see that she finds the exhibition of herself shameful due to the early injury following her father's repeated attraction to her. He does not, however, deal with the repressed exhibitionistic wishes behind the inhibition concerning self-exhibition. Further, he does not deal with any conflicts over repressed sexual passions, passions which may have gone underground when the patient's father hurt her by turning away from her to attend to her mother. He deals with the narcissistic aspect of the patient's view of herself in her father's eyes, without delving into the fantasy level of her expectation of a man's lack of response to her.

Nor does Trop deal with his patient's conflicts about successfully arousing men, as opposed to the perhaps safer consequences of being rejected. He is appropriately related to his patient's concerns as he addresses his patient's shame about the exhibition of herself, but he is not yet dealing with her conflicts over her erotic desires.

Trop's definition of erotic transference seems to be restraining him as he then moves gingerly into the area of erotic desire. Trop (1988) writes that when he interpreted his patient's inhibitions in relation to self-exhibitionism to the father's past behavior, as well as attributing to both parents' behavior the related problems she had in primarily attracting pseudo-confident men, interpreting that she was too inhibited to initiate interaction—his patient began to develop sexual feelings for him, her analyst (p. 279). This could be the emergence of a potentially powerful erotic transference as a major conduit for the deepest unconscious desires, but then Trop interprets:

> The therapist conceptualized the patient's erotic feelings as being fueled by a revived need to consolidate her own femininity by evoking a mirroring response from him. This constellation of hopes for a responsive man had been repeatedly fractured by her father's withdrawal from her. (p. 279)

Trop thus isolates a self issue, and neglects all the object-related conflicts related to wishes for the most intense mode of object connection, the erotic connection. Trop writes:

> The therapist communicated to her that her fantasies about him helped her delineate a vision for herself as a woman with a responsive and admiring man. It helped her to consolidate a feeling that a man would be able to appreciate her and that she would be capable of pleasing a man. (p. 279)

This leads to the patient talking about her fear of exposure in a social situation, but then the beginning-to-bud erotic transference seems to be averted. Trop writes:

> She began to go to social events and dances and gained more confidence. She still felt attracted to the therapist, but said that she knew her life had to continue and preferred to keep these feelings to the side. (p. 279)

Reading this, it appears that erotic transference never flowered with Trop's exclusive focus on the self, and the patient therefore never mourned the loss of the therapist as a fantasy love. It appears that she merely displaced her feelings onto others, putting a whole erotic part of herself aside, i.e. splitting it off, in order to put feelings for the therapist aside. How much self-integration was actually achieved in this case then becomes questionable.

Trop's definition of erotic transference, as related to the wish to have the self mirrored, neglected the patient as a sexual subject with deep erotic passion, and his treatment minimizes the patient as a sexual subject, although some discussion of sexual fantasies in the transference is alluded to. Explicitly, he refers only to the female patient's wishes to have warm interludes with the therapist and to hold hands (p. 279). This leaves the reader in the dark as to how deep a level of erotic desire was reached in the treatment situation. One could conclude that the emergence of explicit eroticism was minimal and that this accounts for the patient's relative lack of difficulty in turning away from erotic desires in the transference to external sexual relations. The lack of difficulty suggests displacement rather than the kind of resolution that can come from grief and mourning in which a deeply erotic part of the self becomes integrated into the central self, and thus becomes interpersonally connected to others.

The lack of such in-depth resolution is also suggested by the patient's choice of a future sexual companion or date. The chosen male is noted by Trop to be different from past object choices in terms of being shy and kind rather than being pseudo-confident. Although this choice may indeed be a change for the better as Trop suggests, the choice of a shy and kind man may also imply that the patient backs off from initiating a sexual relationship with a man who is less shy and possibly more erotic and passionate. One might even conjecture that the new object choice is in line with choosing a male similar to the analyst for whom the erotic transference was aborted by displacement rather than being fully developed and thus necessarily mourned. This could be another form of living in the transference glow as in the case of Gould (1989).

At the end of his 1988 paper, Trop expresses the opinion that the oedipal wishes described in the transference need not be renounced (p. 282-283). He states that they can be "consolidated and integrated" (p. 283) without renouncing them. He then goes on to add that these erotic wishes for the oedipal object can be "reality tested and mourned but will not necessarily dissolve at the end of therapy" (p. 283). This is the first time Trop mentions mourning, and his belief that the wishes need not be renounced suggests that he does not seriously consider mourning. To mourn is to feel object loss, even if only of a fantasy object, and there is renunciation necessarily involved.

In the case of Mr. L., addressed in this paper, it is clear that Mr. L. did renounce the analyst as an erotic oedipal object in order to open up to a full erotic relationship with another woman. However, he did not need to renounce me as a real internalized object, someone who had been with him for six years and had emotionally held him and related to him. He renounced the oedipal erotic parent aspect of me, the fantasy part of me, the transferential part of me, but not me as a real object. This explains why renunciation could be tolerated. It was not traumatic. The evidence of this is that Mr. L. felt deeply sad about letting go of me as a fantasy lover, rather than feeling enraged, paranoid, empty, or fragmented.

It is not comprehensible to me how Trop can assume that mourning of the oedipal transference object takes place without any renunciation. Perhaps it is the impossibility of such a mode of mourning that explains why Trop only mentions the word "mourning," and does not indicate any of the mourning process as actually having occurred in his case example of treatment.

Perhaps Trop intends to say that mourning involves the sustaining of a fantasy of the analyst as an erotic love object in one's internal world, even once the fantasy is finally recognized as a fantasy. Such a fantasy may continue to enrich the inner life of the patient once treatment ends, even if the disillusionment of recognizing that the fantasy cannot become a reality is acknowledged with grief. However, in the case of Mr. L., it can be seen that the patient was able to have a rich and passionate fantasy life that accompanied his real sexual life at the end of treatment, and this fantasy life was totally focused on his fiancée at this point, not on the analyst. If Mr. L. had needed to continue to fantasize about the analyst while sexually relating to his fiancée, his erotic life may have been attenuated.

Overall, Trop's case represents the work with an analysand who is still in the paranoid-schizoid position. As Ogden (1986) has pointed out, within the paranoid-schizoid position the self lacks a sense of subjectivity and is experienced as an object. Trop's treatment reflects his regard for his analysand as an object, not as a sexual subject. He never moves into the depressive position. To do so, he would need to go through the negative reaction to his mirroring, not just assume that mirroring has only positive effects. The threat of being possessed by the mirror always leads to negative transference, and it is only through the negotiation of this negative transference that the subjectivity of the self in the depressive position can be reached. Trop's use of mirroring can defend against the negative reaction to the object, and thus can defend against the emergence of the self through the unsealing of unconscious erotic passions.

Summary

This article proposes that the clinical mourning process is a critical factor in transforming an aggressively-laden erotic transference, and its potential for use as resistance, into a conscious erotic transference that progressively mobilizes the psychoanalytic treatment process. A psychoanalytic case is used to illustrate that the mourning of the precedipal object allows an erotic transference to emerge into consciousness in treatment. The case also demonstrates that erotic transference takes the form not only of desiring but also of mourning the oedipal level object. The case serves as a case in point in illustrating that erotic transference appears in cases in which female analysts treat male analysands. Further, it illustrates that erotic transference remains a primarily object-related phenomenon as opposed to being a merely narcissistic phenomenon. Finally, it illustrates the course of working through the erotic transference in an analytic treatment in which the therapeutic Object Relationship facilitates mourning.

Notes

1 The relationship between the two boys can also be seen as a normal homosexual love that is a developmental move toward adolescence. However, in terms of the building of a psychic structure, it is most helpful to see it in terms of the tender attachment to a preœdipal object that precedes the attachment to an erotically desired object, the latter object being generally classified in terms of psychic structure formation as an oedipal object.

CHAPTER 11

LESBIAN HOMOEROTIC TRANSFERENCE IN DIALECTIC WITH DEVELOPMENTAL MOURNING: ON THE WAY TO SYMBOLISM FROM THE PROTOSYMBOLIC

Originally published in 2003, *Psychoanalytic Psychology (Divison 39 journal)* 20(1):131–152.

In "Observations on Transference Love," Sigmund Freud (1915) spoke of the erotic as both a resistance and a conduit for the deepest unconscious desires and conflicts to emerge. The two courses that erotic transference can take may be said to oppose one another. To the degree that the erotic transference is a resistance, it fails to be a conduit for unconscious desires. To the degree that erotic transference is a conduit within the course of psychoanalytic treatment, it reduces all forms of resistance.

Freud credited the attitude of the analyst "keeping a firm hold of the transference" (Freud, 1915, p. 166), but not succumbing to it, as the main factor in containing the resistance aspects of "transference love" so that the infantile aspects of the love can emerge and be analyzed. Yet, his comments throughout the same paper emphasized the continuing difficulty, and sometimes the impossibility, of modifying the resistance so that treatment can proceed, as in the case of "women of elemental passions" (p. 166). Such women, he believed, are likely to retaliate for the unrequited nature of their love by withdrawing all cooperation from treatment.

Perhaps Freud would have been more optimistic about the facility to use transference love, through containing and transforming the resistance aspects of it, if he had taken another factor into account. I propose such a third and, I believe, as critical a factor in modifying the erotic transference from a major transference resistance into an ongoing positive force in the treatment process. Mourning as a clinical process is the third factor that I propose.

Mourning was first acknowledged as a primary emotional process by Freud (1917) in "Mourning and Melancholia." However, it was Melanie Klein who first saw mourning as a primary affective process underlying both developmental growth and clinical psychotherapeutic treatment. Her papers on the "depressive position" dynamics, such as "Mourning and Its Relation to Manic Depressive States" (Klein, 1940), highlight the potential clinical insight to be gained by understanding the mourning process.

The case described here demonstrates how an attunement to object-related contact, within the course of psychoanalysis, allows a natural mourning process to unfold, thus contributing to an ongoing positive evolution in the use of erotic transference in treatment. To understand the interaction of the erotic transference and the developmental mourning process, it is necessary to view erotic desires not merely as drive impulses, but also as expressions of object-related desires, with a full range of oedipal and precedipal dimensions.

The psychic fantasies that emerge within the erotic transference can in this context be seen to chart a developmental course, crystallizing the intense and multitextured object-related desires. Symbolizing these desires inevitably leads to loss and grief, as symbolization is a developmental separation process (Kavaler-Adler, 1992a, 1993a/2013, 1996/2014). It is through the mourning of this loss and grief that psychic structure transformation becomes possible (as opposed to the "symbolic equation"; Segal, 1986). Without this mourning process evolution, erotic transference can act as a resistance to psychic change, as Freud first warned in 1915.

"Potential space" (Ogden, 1986; Winnicott, 1971), or psychic space, opens as developmental mourning evolves out of the normal disillusionment created by the symbolic expression of erotic desires. There is a gradual relinquishing of the old object constellations that bind oedipal and precedipal object longings within the framework of historically formed character structure. Where Fairbairn (1952) spoke of letting go of the bad object, I speak of letting go of the erotically desired oedipal object through symbolizing desire and tolerating the affects of loss and grief that the inevitable disillusionment of desire demands.

Symbolization, connecting to the affective engagement with longing and loss, culminates in the capacity for new external Object Relations—external in the sense that they exist beyond the internal world where the cherished oedipal object or objects prevail. The oedipal object then is not simply renounced, but relinquished with a transformational flourish, leading to renewed and evolving Object Relations engagement with the external world. This process does not simply involve saying good-bye to an incestuous object and hello to a non-incestuous object, for such an exchange would not transform the initial psychic structure. Rather, it consists of relinquishing internal world ties while transferring affective links to these objects—through symbolized psychic fantasies, onto new external objects with whom true intimacy can be achieved—intimacy at an adult level, colored and enhanced by the richness of childhood oedipal wishes.

Such a journey is necessary for healthy heterosexual and healthy homosexual maturity to evolve. Homosexual erotic transference has the same power and intensity as heterosexual erotic transference. Like heterosexual erotic transference, homosexual erotic transference is multilayered and multitextured with differentiated oedipal desire genital intensities interacting with precedipal hungers. The oedipal love object always causes the projections of an early breast mother as well as the more differentiated oedipal object.

Homoerotic transference occurs with heterosexual, homosexual, and bisexual analysands. It is, therefore, of particular interest to study the nature of the erotic transference with homosexual and bisexual analysands in relation to a heterosexual analyst. Such cases, permitting us to see that the journey from protosymbolic enactment in the course of psychoanalytic regression to symbolic expression, punctuated by the affects and memories of mourning, offer a unique perspective on a developmental progression that also occurs in heterosexual analysands. The heterosexual can discover the homosexual energies in full Object Relations analysis, just as the homosexual can discover heterosexual energies in extensive analysis. The common denominator is mourning as a developmental process (Kavaler-Adler, 1993a/2013, 1996/2014).

The case vignette I describe here, from a longer case study, highlights the journey of mourning as a developmental process. The subject is a lesbian woman who was in treatment with me, a female heterosexual analyst. In this treatment situation, the intensity of the analysand's erotic transference held the potential of blossoming into a symbolic level where mourning could occur only through the transition of protosymbolic enactments expressed in the form of wooing and courting the analyst.

When I speak of the protosymbolic expression of erotic transference, I mean sensory and visceral experiences, with powerful pressures for behavioral enactment, but with little representational form in the patient's internal world or secondary process. By symbolic expression, I refer to vivid verbal descriptions of psychic fantasy constructed from differentiated whole object characters. The individual's vivid verbal descriptions gradually separate out from impulsive visceral and somatic reactions, gradually becoming an adequate container of transference longings in treatment sessions, without enactments by phone or concrete gifts (with unanalyzed motives) of the undefined visceral impulses outside the perimeter of analytic sessions.

"Pauline" was a middle-aged woman who had been living in a lesbian relationship for 12 years when she entered treatment. She was formerly married to a man for many years and left the former marriage due to the abusive behavior of her husband, as well as her interest in other men and women as romantic partners.

She was a highly intelligent and intellectual woman of strong academic interests, who had been a university professor, at the graduate level, for 16 years. She had a child from her former marriage who was grown and who lived in another state.

One of Pauline's presenting problems when beginning psychoanalysis with me was that of compulsions to fantasize about having affairs with women other than her long-term partner and extreme terrors that she would act on these fantasies and lose the love and security of her lesbian marriage. She also was hidden behind the facade of a butch pseudomasculine identity when she began treatment. She dressed in a masculine manner and believed that she was "in disguise," so that others would not suspect her extreme emotional vulnerability. It was during treatment that she came to discard her masculine mode of dress and to dress and groom herself in a distinctly feminine manner. She came to re-own the feminine side of herself so that she could integrate her masculine and feminine attributes in a true self that was vulnerable, receptive, and aggressive in a much less stereotyped manner than had been her practice.

The first three years of thrice-weekly analysis for Pauline involved an intense mourning process, which transformed the nature of her transference expressions, particularly her erotic transference expressions. To describe the varying forms of developmental evolution that open up naturally in an Object Relations psychoanalytic treatment, I call the mourning process a developmental mourning process (see Kavaler-Adler, 1993a/2013, 1996/2014). Such a developmental evolution involves the integration of self through abandonment depression mourning related to preœdipal separation-individuation loss and trauma, grief for narcissistic wounds, grief for unrequited love with its oedipal disillusionments, mourning of actual object loss (as in the parents' death), depressive position existential mourning of grief related to hurting the love object, and mourning of depressive pain related to the relinquishment of omnipotence and the acceptance of existential limits.

These modes of mourning characterized the developmental process in this analysand. Pauline's developmental mourning continued throughout her fourth and fifth years of treatment, but the first three years of mourning and its working through allowed significant transformations to become highlighted and defined during the fourth year.

Although traditionally, erotic transference has been viewed as a defense against remembering, I believe that from an Object Relations perspective, erotic transference provides a transitional object experience for the analysand. As such, it offers an avenue to consciousness for the deepest desires and conflicts of the internal world. In addition, erotic transference helps access memory despite inhibiting it by functioning as a protective screen against experiencing the links to differentiated recall. Why can erotic transference function in this seemingly contradictory manner? The most intense erotic desires always originate from early infant experience, as well as from every level of precedipal and oedipal experience, and from all that experience derived from both the precedipal and oedipal levels whose influence continues into adolescence and adulthood. Whether the erotic transference is a defense against or an avenue to the unconscious depends on its reaching the symbolic level of felt and then spoken psychic fantasy.

However, for this erotic transference to be contained and then transformed from the protosymbolic sensory and visceral level to a symbolic level of differentiated psychic fantasy and differentiated affects of love, lust, aggression, and tenderness, the developmental mourning process is essential. I first demonstrated this in "Mourning and Erotic Transference" (Kavaler-Adler, 1992a), describing the treatment of a male analysand. What I present here is an excerpt from a more recent case, in which I focus on the critical role of mourning and erotic transference in a lesbian woman.

Pauline's Erotic and Homoerotic Transference

From the onset of treatment, Pauline's erotic transference was front stage and center, and Pauline herself was aware that from the beginning I was an object of her desire. Through the emergence and expression of erotic transference in treatment, Pauline gained insight into her primal yearnings for her mother that could compel her into perpetual enactments in her life, sabotaging her attempts to commit to a long-term, intimate relationship. But she was only able to relinquish the compulsion to enact this erotic transference in her outside life through behavior that was potentially sabotaging to herself and her long-term monogamous and committed love relationship with a female partner after she surrendered to repeated cycles of developmental mourning. In the process of this surrender, she let go of her primal mother and father.

With developmental mourning, she opened up psychic space in which she could develop a new relationship with me as a transitional object. Then, using this relationship as a base, she was able to develop new psychic internalizations that could be carried to other relationships.

From the beginning of treatment, Pauline experienced me as her artist muse, a form of mother-muse-lover. Her mother had in fact been an artist. Pauline both wished and feared that I would become her "demon-lover" (Kavaler-Adler, 1993a/2013, 1996/2014), the dark and powerfully erotic side of this mother-muse-lover trinity. When she first asked to be in treatment with me, she expected me to attract her and repel her simultaneously, just as her mother had. I embodied the transference displacement of her oedipal fantasy mother, just as many other women had for her, particularly women writers and artists—both gay and straight—with whom she had fantasized having affairs.

Pauline presented herself as agonizing over what she considered to be her sinful betrayal, not in her behavior but in her thoughts, of her steady live-in lover and partner, whom she "loved more than life itself." Pauline tread her course in her own words, like a "hamster on a wheel," always turning her head toward some new female attraction, having let go of the idea of having male lovers following her divorce from her husband and prior to her long-term lesbian relationship. She reported experiencing her attraction to me as an "ocean of longing." This feeling was accompanied by repulsion and terror at entering a hopeless land of endless and unfulfilled desire, where she would suffer once again the agony of intense abandonment and self-annihilation, which for her were integral components of unrequited love.

Entering my office, she had in her head the whole script of an anticipated romance based on sexualized needs for an early maternal responsiveness, as well as on profound and frustrated oedipal desires, placed and displaced onto a woman. This script, which became a fantasy blueprint for her agenda within the psychoanalytic situation, had been developed and rewritten within her mind over several decades, the result of multiple forays and mishaps in matters of the heart. I fit vividly into Pauline's category of artist-muse-lover as I possessed, according to her, an "erotic intellect" and a flamboyant personal style and language. I also fit into the category of artist—her mother's category, which made me a muse, because I had written two books and many articles about women writers and artists. So I presented a convenient target for her projections of (the muse-goddess-artist) an idealized fantasy of her mother as a narcissistic extension of herself. Pauline could cling to her fantasy ideal mother to buttress her own inadequate sense of self. Her higher level romantic desires overlapped with her precedipal hungers for a self-extension perceived as being outside of herself.

I became the target both for Pauline's self needs and her instinctual oral and genital desires. I also became a target for her projections of the dark side of that role, as the erotic demon-lover, similar to Fairbairn's (1952) exciting and rejecting object. One of Pauline's initial fantasies of me was that I would stab her in the vagina with a knife while she was on the couch. I certainly was at first the phallic mother for her, reflected in her initial fears of my interpretations. Only erratically, with some trust in me developing during the first year of treatment, could Pauline take in and digest my interpretations.

Initially threatened by them, she needed to understand their connection to her fantasies of me as a dangerous phallic mother. Pauline later told me that when I sat in a certain high-backed chair, I had seemed like this awesome, omnipotent judge. She was too intimidated by this image of me to tell me how she felt at this time. Gradually, she could experience the deep emotional connection between her internal phallic mother and its projection onto me by mourning her disillusionments in the transference. This mourning process brought Pauline's memories of her mother's cutting rejections and threatened abandonments alive in the moment.

But this lay ahead. During this early treatment stage, Pauline was quite emphatic in expressing her wish to turn the tables on me, placing me in the same vulnerable position of need and desire she so feared being in herself. She wanted me to want her from a helpless position of out-of-control desire. And she split-off and projected onto me her own unconscious internal infant and child psychic states, which evolved into the open format of analysis through her expression of erotic transference fantasies whose meaning became increasingly clear with each phase of mourning during treatment. In the beginning of treatment, I felt the power of her affect in a highly visceral and sensory form, as described by her own phrase as an "ocean of longing." She idealized me. In one of her dreams during this period, I appeared as a huge, female icon, floating high above her in the air, and then descending to her bed within a theater used for grand operas and stage productions, where she found herself. In this same dream, I had long flowing hair and wore a colorful silk gown. I also had an erect penis, despite my exaggerated female attire and my role as an icon.

Pauline's goddess image of me was accompanied by paranoid thoughts. She broadcast her general sense of distrust in the beginning of treatment via her description of the scene in another dream, which followed the other, and which directly preceded her first consultation with me. In this other dream, she unzipped her chest, gave me her heart, and then experienced the terrible sense of a black hole of unrequited love, which she fantasized as having the huge enormity of the grand canyon.

Despite the terror that she exhibited during our first sessions, Pauline gradually began to trust me. This initial trust allowed her to share with me her first erotic transference fantasies. She was a brave soul from the start, and her courage extended to an acute curiosity about her own internal life. So she shared these fantasies as they arose during our sessions, along with intense feelings within her body, suggesting layers of unsymbolized somatic expressions of her most profound desires (protosymbolic) that accompanied the symbolic level of her fantasies and associations. On the level of conscious fantasy, she reported visions of having an affair with me in my office, where she would order me: "spread your legs," and would "take your pearl in my mouth, drown in your come, and then wrap you in a blanket and feed you."

This fantasy also included a negative oedipal triangle, which revealed itself in her free associations to the fantasy. Pauline imagined meeting my husband after he banged on my office door, entering my office in an enraged state (one form of primal scene fantasy). She imagined engaging in an open skirmish with him as he jealously "defended his territory." Another frequent fantasy, with a multitude of variations, was of her being an audience of one, watching while a man—sometimes my husband—made love to me. In this fantasy, she cheered me on to orgasms as my male lover forced me into a state of submission by beating me—which she imagined I would love—or merely penetrated me, as I surrendered to him in a state of passionate and hungry lust, from a passive receptive position. She also imagined herself as the male lover, or as the other woman in a "ménage à trois" with a male lover who appealed to both of us, providing each of us with pleasure.

Pauline revealed many levels of erotic fantasy during treatment. At first, she longed to make love to me as one woman to another, wishing me to be in the more vulnerable and receptive position, while she was in the more active phallic role. Later, during the third year of treatment, Pauline went through a phase of picturing me as a phallic woman, as in her dream reported earlier, who penetrated her with my penis. This fantasy interacted with her father transference projections onto me, and with the full emergence of her identifications with her father as the seductive male among women, the "cock of the walk." Still later, during the fourth year, she imagined a triadic relationship, in which, in her male persona, she and another "man" penetrated me, or, conversely, in her female persona, she was penetrated by me in my male persona and by another man in the same scene. The man was anonymous in the scene of her being penetrated along with me, but when she was the one penetrating me along with another man, her fantasy would sometimes portray this other man as my husband.

Ultimately, Pauline reported an orgasm fantasy of being ravished anally by a group of male father figures, which she had reported within the first year of treatment, changing during the fifth year of treatment into the fantasy of highly mutual and erotic intercourse with such father figures, with diminished sadomasochistic dynamics.

At times, throughout the first three years of her treatment in particular, Pauline also expressed her erotic negative transference in sadomasochistic wishes to throw me against the wall and "fuck" me then and there in the treatment room. I interpreted the connection between her wish for love through anal submission and her wish to have me submit to her as she had me do in her fantasy of 'throwing me against the wall and fucking' me. However, at the moment of rage and desire, I could not interpret this. It had to be "strike when the iron is cold," as Fred Pine (1985) speaks of when addressing clinical work with those of primary developmental trauma and developmental arrest. At the moment of rage and desire, the compulsive urge toward exhibitionism was at its height. Only when Pauline was feeling loss and was therefore more in contact with her inner self could I ask her to define her anger, bringing the protosymbolic exhibitionism to a symbolic level. The intensity of both her rage and desire was at such moments palpable. Nevertheless, over time, her ability to entertain interpretations about the transference implications of these and other fantasies developed as she worked through her mourning process.

Although Pauline could express these psychic fantasies to me verbally during the first three years of treatment, she still had great difficulty coping with the highly visceral body experiences that accompanied her report of these fantasies to me. Sometimes, Pauline stopped in the midst of describing such a fantasy, cutting off her verbal level of functioning, because she became overwhelmingly dizzy or felt suffocated as she literally felt as if she were choking on her emotions. Then, feeling it impossible to breathe lying down, she would sit up to feel she could breathe. She could not say the words of love to me at this earlier time, during the first two years of treatment. She could say the words of love by her third year when she had mourned her primal mother loss, from preœdipal separation-individuation stage trauma, and could differentiate her feelings, her thoughts, me, and her internal mother.

Thus, her somatic discomfort lessened, and she felt the freedom to articulate her desires as she found the words to express her love and her wishes to be loved. She could say the words later, relieved of the former pain and of the tremendous backlash reactions of guilt and despair that came when she associated to fears of having betrayed her real-life lover by declaring her (transferential) love for me. When I interpreted Pauline's guilt and fear, it helped. Pauline's guilt could turn to concern as she realized, with my help, that she was afraid of hurting her lover as she had been hurt by her mother's rejections. Pauline could then differentiate her transference love from her love for her real-life partner.

Pauline was still unconscious of the incestuous nature of her longings for me and the guilt and shame they invoked. Yet, during this period when the verbalization of her feelings was first becoming possible, during her second and third years of treatment, she would often leave her psychoanalytic session overwhelmed. Frequently unable to complete her sentences, she left at the end of a session only to discover that she often could not sustain the connection with me until the next session without calling me beforehand in a state of terror and despair at how she thought she had offended me. I interpreted Pauline's fears of me, as her transferential mother, retaliating. I also emphasized, however, Pauline's genuine desire to connect with me at a very primal level and her fear of losing that connection as she had lost her mother. This calmed her.

Only later could true reparation be made when she let go of me as her transferential mother and surrendered to the vivid experience of loss in developmental mourning. Her visceral intrusions and disruptions, as well as her guilt-ridden backlashes, changed as she traversed the stages of developmental mourning. This transition is encapsulated during the first three years of treatment in her using and then relinquishing a concrete romantic gift—a gift that condensed her longings in an inchoate, preverbal, and protosymbolic form.

From the Protosymbolic to the Symbolic: Giving the Romantic Gift

In the beginning of treatment, Pauline attempted to enact a fantasized love affair, which she imagined taking place between us, by sending me beautiful, long-stemmed red roses. Even after discussing with me her impulse to send them, she felt compelled at times to actually act it out. There were also many other times when she thought she would send them and restrained herself, but the impulse to call the flower shop was powerfully acute. On the occasions when she did send this romantic gift, she wanted the beauty of the flowers to speak their own symbolism. She reported that she imagined them opening to me with a full color and redolence that possibly represented the way she felt her mind and body opening to me. So, in this action, as in her fantasies, Pauline was able to play a masculine and a feminine role. In courting me by sending flowers, she enacted her male persona, while in symbolizing her body opening to me through the opening of the blooming roses, she enacted her female persona. Pauline said, later, during her fourth and fifth years of analysis, that when she sent me flowers she was regressing to an early psychic place, a child's place, where words never adequately expressed feelings. Only an image or symbolic gift could.

It was through the mourning process that Pauline was able to move beyond the enactment of wooing me through actually sending flowers to using the flowers as a symbolic expression of her own feelings. Increasingly, she began to verbalize her flowering feelings. As psychic space opened within her, Pauline felt her feelings toward me while in the room with me at a level that grew increasingly tolerable for her. Through mourning a lifetime of losses, her psychic fantasies became better containers for her feelings, felt subjectively as unrequited love. In this process, Pauline opened to her primal longings for the first time. She offered them to me verbally. For example, she reported, "I want you so much right now" or "I'm feeling this feeling in my vagina, wanting you." It was only at this point that she could describe her erotic transference fantasies without splitting them off into compulsive activities and obsessional thinking outside the sessions.

It was important for me to receive these expressions of Pauline's feelings without interpreting at the time. She needed to feel that both her love and her aggression could be accepted by me. In Winnicott's terms, she needed to see I could "survive" her impulses and passions. She needed to know I heard her, and was not rejecting her as she expected me to in her anticipatory script of unrequited love and repetition of the traumatic experience with her mother. However, because I was not responding to her expressions of love as a lover, she experienced me as rejecting her oedipal wishes, which had served, in part, as a defense against precedipal rejection. Such disappointments, experienced at tolerable levels in treatment, led Pauline to a tolerance of loss and with its painful grief affect, evolving into an overall mourning process.

It was only at this stage of treatment that Pauline began to reveal the deeper longings that were now becoming differentiated from the diffuse ocean of desire within her. She expressed the heartfelt yearnings that had formerly been split-off and projected onto the "other." She was able to own and articulate the wish to sit in my lap and for me to stroke her hair, as well as the wish to be held and comforted at my breast like an infant. Such moments of courageous revelation spoke volumes about the tender child within, but these wishes also revealed a dark side, resonating to the most primal terrors of the muse mother turned demonic. For example, when Pauline announced her core wish to inhabit a special place in my vagina, through phallic penetration (which would result in her living inside of my womb), the underbelly of her fantasy flipped dramatically into her consciousness. She reported a black, swirling terror erupting from within, a vortex comprised of an infinity of darkness. This was the visual representation of what she experienced as the impinging threat of her being suffocated and lost inside my womb, as it turned into an infinite black hole.

The fantasy flipped to the dark side, repeatedly, each time I failed to instantly reciprocate her feelings. If I did not express feelings akin to her own (twinship transference), I became the sadistically withholding mother of "unrequited love." But with the container of the holding environment of psychoanalytic treatment, Pauline could feel rage and disappointment, ultimately surrendering to the grief of loss that opened a rebirth of connection to her inner self, her internal world, and to others in her interpersonal world.

Glimpses of Developmental Mourning in Treatment

If mourning helps to create a safe analytic space to contain erotic transference in treatment, disappointments in erotic transference wishes also open up grief and mourning. Cycles of mourning and erotic transference interact. As they do, psychic fantasies become more refined and verbal, a new capacity for digesting transference interpretations emerges, and the nature of the erotic fantasies evolves from sadomasochistic to mutually interpenetrating dimensions.

Pauline showed all these trends as she navigated the many forms of mourning during analysis. With each transference disillusionment, she relived an experience of unrequited love. When she first felt unlovable and unwanted by me because in her mind I was not playing the role of the lover in her transference script, she experienced primitive abandonment and annihilation terrors. These terrors originated when she was three years old (perhaps even earlier), after her mother, angry at Pauline's father, threatened to leave him and therefore threatened to leave Pauline and her entire family. After recovering from the black hole sense of self-dissolution, Pauline was able, aided by my support and presence, during her second year of treatment, to recall her mother's dramatic displays of threatening departure—signaled by her putting on red lipstick.

This memory led to other memories of her mother periodically withdrawing to bed, leaving her feeling emotionally abandoned and devastated. She remembered her mother's punitive cold rages whenever Pauline expressed either implicitly or explicitly her own needs. And she recalled now, too, her mother's total withdrawal when Pauline was 14 years old and first experienced erotic feelings for other females. The mother's extreme emotional withdrawal at this time was a retaliatory reaction to her daughter not fitting into the mother's beliefs concerning what she thought her daughter should be, as the mother wished to gratify her own narcissism.

Pauline's sexual interest in girls and women threatened her mother's whole image system that supported her mother's narcissistic defenses. Feeling narcissistically affronted by Pauline being herself, which involved feeling attracted to females at camp, Pauline's mother withdrew all her warmth and proceeded vindictively to punish Pauline through her own form of narcissistic injury. Recalling this led Pauline to remember many incidents in which she had suffered narcissistic injury because of her mother's behavior. Her mother's favored weapons were contempt and sarcastic ridicule. More than once during Pauline's childhood and adolescence, the mother had slapped the daughter when she dared to disagree with or express anger at her.

At other times, Pauline's transference disillusionments in relation to the analyst, which she experienced as unrequited love, brought up memories of acute and traumatic loss triggered by rejections from women who served as mother displacements. These other muse goddess experiences (occurring prior to my taking that projected role in the transference) ranged from a latency and teenage love for a girlfriend, to many rejections by straight women who were threatened by her intensity when she claimed that she wanted to be friends only, and to her rejection by a bisexual woman, when Pauline was in her early 30s. This last rejection occurred after Pauline had been married for many years to the husband that she soon separated from after this attempted affair. At this stage of her life, Pauline saw the artistic woman she was enamored with as potentially offering her the only chance to give and receive love, especially with a female. When such a hope was harshly repudiated, she fell apart, but with the support of her previous psychotherapy, she established a lesbian identity and connected with a lesbian community.

Specifically, Pauline was able to form a deep love attachment to a woman prior to her analysis with me, and with this growing and developing lesbian relationship, she was supported in her attempts to assume an identification with other lesbians that she discovered in New York. Nevertheless, each of her losses still demanded grieving, which Pauline, with increasing depth, plunged into during our analysis. She mourned all her maternal abandonments and unrequited love affairs with women and then the grief of losing men as intimate and sexual partners. In addition, she mourned the split-off needy and dependent child part of her, as she reconnected with it through re-owning what she had projected onto me in her erotic fantasies.

A dream brought up an opportunity for interpreting her fear of her own needs. Pauline dreamed of throwing fish endlessly back into a boat. She associated this endless and fruitless task with trying to meet my needs. I interpreted her seeing me as an insatiable mother whose needs and demands overwhelmed her. However, I also interpreted that she was projecting her own overwhelming needs and demands into me as a transferential mother. She got angry. I was interfering with her script of repeating rage at an overly demanding, narcissistic mother. After her anger, she found insight and began to understand my interpretations. She acknowledged her understanding by saying that she was afraid she would be too much for me. I then interpreted that her mother had seemed to experience Pauline as too much for her, leaving her feeling hopeless about having any needs at all. Seeing her needs as my needs, I continued, was a way of defending against her hopelessness and the related anxiety.

Following this, Pauline mourned the latent feminine side of her personality that had been split-off as well when she assumed a masculine persona in the world. Femininity and helpless dependence had been associated in her mind, so to not seem too needy, she had rejected her feminine side. As she regained the split-off parts of her psyche, such as her potential feminine self, Pauline felt more whole and better equipped to deal with other forms of mourning.

In order for Pauline to regain the split-off feminine part of herself, I needed to interpret a whole line of projective identification. Through projective identification, Pauline had mentally "put into" me her identity as a woman. She saw me as being her feminine self on a protosymbolic level or on the level of the paranoid-schizoid position. On the level of the depressive position, where she could experience symbolic meanings, she saw me as representing her feminine self or identity. I addressed this with her, after the point of interpreting her distaste for feminine identity within herself as when she associated such femininity with neediness and helpless dependence on a narcissistic mother.

It was clear that her view of her defensive disowning of a feminine identity was ego syntonic. The dialog between us went something like this: I said that she was using me as her disowned feminine self. By being absorbed in me, and all my feminine attributes, including my mode of dressing, she was avoiding her own need for a female identity and for the development of a potential authentic feminine side of her personality. I said this was a problem. She retorted: "That's the solution." She said she was quite content to use me as her feminine self. I reiterated that that was "the problem." She laughed and replied: "No! That's the solution!"

However, as Pauline entered the depressive position more and more through the mourning process, nature took its course, and she decided that she had needs for a feminine part of herself that she had denied. She realized that she wanted to be seen as beautiful, not just as handsome. Her lover balked at her wish to wear a dress and more feminine clothing in general. However, she was able to express to her lover the pain of always being in the position of the adoring lover who worshipped the beauty of the other woman. She exclaimed that she wanted to be seen as beautiful, even if she did not have the same form of beauty as her mother. She began to wear a brooch of her mother's and other items of jewelry that her mother might have worn. She could only do this when she had consciously processed her rage at her mother's rejections and thus could forgive her mother and re-own a wish to identify with her, while also retaining her lesbian object choice and her separate identity as a woman who could erotically love and adore other women.

The Depressive Position

The other forms of mourning seen in Pauline's process, as a form of therapeutic action in developmental terms, fall within Melanie Klein's depressive position—the mourning of guilt and loss related to hurting the person we love, as well as the grief of accepting the losses that come with acknowledging existential limits and our mortality. The latter was often experienced by Pauline as the relinquishment of certain aspects of heterosexual love and life. Pauline experienced the depressive pain in the transference with me. She felt the grief of regret after angry, negative transference projections, in which she accused me of being her cold, abandoning mother, or the "medusa, Gorgon head" mother of frigid rejection in her teenage years. At this time, Pauline first indirectly revealed to her mother that she was homosexual by being attracted to girls at camp, which was reported to her mother by the camp director.

Now, Pauline yearned to repair her former relationship with her mother through her relationship with me. She tried to regain the sense of love she had formerly felt for her mother, prior to her mother's emotional withdrawal when Pauline was 14 years old and had revealed her lesbian proclivities. She sought to regain the love connection to her mother by relinquishing the defenses against the grief and loss she felt in having lost her mother, opening areas of psychic receptivity by accepting sadness and longing. She also faced a formerly unconscious guilt that followed her paranoid rage.

After experiencing many cycles of mother loss and disruptions between us in the transitional Object Relationship, followed by reparation and a renewed love born out of her deep grief of mournful sadness, Pauline opened to new modes of interpersonal dialectic with me. She opened, too, to the dialectical understanding of self and other contained in my transference interpretations. In Thomas Ogden's (1986) words, she became by the fourth year of treatment an interpreting subject, with the capacity to reflect on her own experience from a more separate and dialectical perspective and to take in my interpretations as gifts of insight to digest and use. She had previously experienced such interpretations as assaults on her wishes to merge directly with me through sensory and visceral erotic overtures, as she had indeed attempted to do during the earlier stages of treatment. But in this fourth year, Pauline reported that she felt sad about "giving up the fantasy of being your lover" in her own mind. What led to this point was Pauline's relinquishment of her protosymbolic activity of sending me roses and calling me outside the perimeter of an analytic session. She had used the roses and calls as an attempt to repair what she experienced as a break between us during a session, at times when she would accuse me of being cold and rejecting, just like her mother.

Pauline's increasing use of her own symbolic fantasies to contain her affect, rather than employing them in an attempt to seduce me into an enactment of a wish for sexual merger with an idealized artist mother, was shown in how she greeted me on my return from a vacation during the fourth year of treatment. Her vivid words depicted me as a separate and erotically desired lover. But her meaning this time was clearly metaphorical and symbolical. She visualized entering me, upon my return, as a man penetrates a woman, but also as a woman penetrates a woman, "with your beautiful vulva and clitoris opening like a flower, glowing, radiant, and receptive." She then expressed her joy in being with me in reality in a session in a sublimated way, surrendering her former attitude of pressuring me into responding to her erotic love overtures. Mourning disillusionments of the idealized mother in the transference, mourning unrequited love, and mourning the grief of hostile encounters with her internal cold mother, frequently projected onto me, all led to this point.

An Example of Mourning through Reparative Dialogue Following Depressive Grief

How does the transference in this treatment expose the painful regret, highlighted in Melanie Klein's theory, of hurting the one you love? Pauline spoke to me through this aspect of her transference. Her own words illuminate how the process works. "It was so heartbreaking after I left that other session, when I got so cold, I felt like all the warmth in the world was gone, like those days when my mother withdrew to her bed and it felt like the sun never would come out. That's why I had to call you afterward!" The yearning for reconnection to a loving bond with me was conscious at this point, but her fears of me retaliating were less conscious. Pauline acknowledged her own aggression, but could only see her fears of my aggression after her longing for a renewed bond of love was validated.

In these remarks, Pauline was exploring why she had called me after a session during which she was angry and accusatory toward me, just before I left for summer vacation. She was terrified I would leave without her being able to make reparations to me. She had tried to coerce me into apologizing to her during that session, for something I had allegedly done during the previous session. After she left my office following this session, she grew concerned that she had hurt me. She had never seen herself as cold and accusatory—that had been primarily her experience of her mother whenever her mother was angry. But each time Pauline experienced the pain of her regret after expressing anger at me, she increasingly realized that she could act in the same cold, sarcastic, and accusatory manner as her mother. This realization was partly prompted by my comments about her behavior, as I attempted to respond without submitting to her coercion.

It was extremely difficult for Pauline to perceive her own coldness, because, as she observed, it hadn't been part of her self-concept. Pauline found it painful to understand that she could be cold like her mother. Yet, she did (and does) know that she had hurt me and, once hit by the pain of this awareness, her sense of regret, as well as her fear of abandonment, compelled her to repair her connection with me as quickly as possible by apologizing. She imagined that I must have been bitterly disappointed in her, and personally hurt because, after all I had done for her, she had acted so ungratefully. Pauline's regret seemed to express genuine concern for me at this point, not merely a defensive fear of retaliation from me as the feared maternal object. Both this and her ability to reflect on her own self-concept in terms of how aggressive parts of herself (modeled on her mother) were left out of this self-concept signified that she was operating more within the depressive position than she had been formerly. Pauline was reflecting rather than reacting, increasingly over time, as she mourned her real childhood experiences with her mother, as well as her wishes inscribed in psychic fantasy. She began to see herself as well as her mother from a more separate and objective position.

She could not wait to tell me of these insights and to see my face and to hear my voice again. She was terrified that she had killed off all the warmth between us and all the warmth in me. She said that she was afraid I would never again show her approval or the warmth in my eyes or the warmth of my smile. In fact, she feared that I would never smile at her again. She feared I would freeze up and turn into the Gorgon's head, the head of Medusa—the image of the cold stone-faced mother she had seen at the dinner table when she was 14 years old.

Unlike earlier in her childhood, when Pauline turned 14 years old, she reciprocated her mother's rage. The ensuing cold war was bitter. Fearing that she would never regain her warm mother, Pauline fell into despair. Her relationship with her mother seemed over forever! Despite her own anger, she felt terribly guilty at seeing her mother's accusatory stare; she believed that she had stabbed her mother with her anger. This belief, however, was mixed in with the feeling that her mother had stabbed her. Perhaps to defend herself against total loss of love, Pauline transformed the terror of being stabbed in the heart to the castration of being stabbed in her vagina. This displacement captured her mother's rejection of her sexuality. When she entered treatment, she feared that I would stab her in her vagina.

When I answered the phone during a session (a rare exception), Pauline experienced my action as if I had stabbed her, mistakenly believing that I was giving her less time than other patients, as if I had abandoned her. She came to the next session prepared to defend herself. But when she became aware of her cold and accusatory manner, and of her coercive insistence on receiving an apology from me, which cut off rather than facilitated communication and contact, she felt bereft with the depressive pain of regret. She felt she would die if she could not repair things and remembered back to the 14-year-old girl who had thoughts of killing herself. Like then, all the warmth had gone out of the world. Therefore, when she started to feel responsible for her part in precipitating the coldness she was experiencing, Pauline started to grieve. This followed my interpreting her coldness as a part of her she could not own because it was too much like her mother's coldness.

Pauline's grief hit her with the force of a huge weight, and she experienced a sadness that seemed infinitely thick and heavy. This sadness was a symptom of her love and need for the transferential mother and was as well grief and regret related to the real analyst she had hurt, which in her fantasy was a crime. Once discussing such a precipitating incident or action, we sought out together what I had actually done and not done. We also defined her own exaggerated fantasy of annihilating all my love for her by her retaliation. As she remembered her mother's behavior toward her when she was 14 years old, Pauline began to see how she was reliving her past with me. She became aware of how she had never fully mourned her grief over the loss of her relationship with her mother. But Pauline's regret over attacking me in the present was also real. She felt better when she was able to cry deep tears of sadness while with me—tears of regret and remorse. In doing so, Pauline began rebuilding the loving connection with me inside of herself—going back to the love in infancy with her mother—as I stayed present and empathized with her pain.

Pauline had not injured me the way she fantasized, but she had frustrated me by closing off any emotional connection to me, departing from me coldly before my summer vacation. She felt compelled to repair her connection to me before we actually separated. In apologizing, she needed to understand that her fantasy of keenly hurting me was, in part, a projection on to me of her mother's very real hurt and of her own pain when she was 14 years old. When Pauline said that she feared she deeply wounded me, I interpreted her fear of her own retaliatory impulse to get back at me as she could never get back at her mother, both because of her fear and because of her guilt. My interpretation helped her to become more in touch with how her aggressive impulses always brought up a devastating sense of mother loss.

All this sorting out of the past and present—of me as separate from her mother, and of her striking out to hurt, and of her retaliating when she was feeling hurt— was part of Pauline's mourning process. Her mourning involved processing the depressive pain and her fantasies of hurting the ones she loved—me as well as the internal mother I represented. Pauline's mother seemed to come alive in the room with us as Pauline mourned the loss of love her anger created.

Within this period of mourning, a dialectic developed between us in which I was able to freely apologize for an angry moment in which I seemed cold to her. My apology helped her to reconsider how I then appeared to her. She exclaimed that she had to remember that I had never previously acted coldly with her, even though she expected me to respond that way in response to the cold manner in which she expressed her anger toward me. Prior to my apology, she had attacked herself for her coldness toward me, not only mentally, but somatically, stabbing herself viscerally in her own heart. After my apology she was able to associate to her somatic symptom and to realize that the anger she turned inward played a part in creating the symptom. As she said, "I couldn't forgive myself for getting cold toward you," I interpreted her somatic symptom as self-punishment for her rage, as she feared she had not sufficiently repaired her hurtful attack on me.

Although I chose to apologize to Pauline for speaking to her with some anger, the content of what I had been saying at that moment was important. I had been speaking of her projection onto me of her cold mother whenever I was not feeling her pain as mine, prompted by her wish that I be completely inside her pain with her. My apology for the touch of annoyance in my tone, which she accurately picked up as I interpreted her projection and the powerful longing for intimacy behind it, allowed Pauline to receive me as a loving presence through my reparative gesture. Consequently, Pauline began to show more self-reflective understanding of my interpretation than previously. In addition, her reception of my reparative gesture allowed Pauline to forgive herself. But this explanation leaves out one step in Pauline's process: She needed to mourn the loss of love that she had felt as she opened herself to receiving my apology. She did this by yielding to a deep sadness, combined with a sense of her own hurt, which yielded to a renewal of loving feelings toward me. I knew as she cried in response to my apology that she was receiving me and my apology as a whole constellation, which could be sustained as a psychic reparative element within.

Such incidents occurred repeatedly in the interpersonal sphere of her mourning process. Both my apology, which acknowledged my role in provoking her anger (even though the anger was already there from the past), and my sharing my own reactions seem to have helped Pauline surrender to her natural developmental mourning process, and to thus surrender the paranoid stance that she would regress into within the transference. She needed feedback from me as a real, present, and differentiated other in order to lessen her paranoid fears and to understand the nature of her paranoid expectations with their self-fulfilling prophesy script. Pauline could gradually differentiate me, as well as others who became mother displacements, from the true mother of her past who had genuinely betrayed her due to her mother's limitations.

Pauline's reception of my apology psychically interacted with the pain of her own regret about attacking me. This was repeated many times, permitting Pauline to move from the protosymbolic level of somatic and interpersonal enactment to interpersonal communication. My apology allowed her to listen as I interpreted her coldness as a reaction to her disappointed fantasy of my being fully inside her pain with her, not simply feeling empathy to her pain from a separate position. Given our dialogue, and her own processing of depressive pain she felt (pain containing grief and guilt), Pauline now understood the symbolic communication in my interpretation and so could associate freely to it on a symbolic level.

Through our dialogue, Pauline came to understand the nature of her implicit, lifelong definition of love as being inside the other's pain. She formed this belief through her history of merging with her mother's pain as a way of reaching and loving her mother after her mother had withdrawn from Pauline. This understanding opened up the floodgates of earlier memories. Pauline vividly recalled how she sat in her mother's bedroom, listening to silence, which was finally broken by a storm of tears from her mother. Now she realized how her mother had withdrawn into emotional paralysis many times throughout her childhood, controlling all those around her in her family who felt punished by the silent and guilt-provoking accusations in her cold martyrdom. In the face of her mother's punitive coldness, Pauline would lose all sense of her own agency.

Pauline now realized how she had relived this period many times in the transference with me. She had tried to cross the gap created by her mother's despair either through erotic overtures or angry accusations, both of which caused her much guilt and self-punishment until she understood the scenes she was reliving. Once Pauline remembered this terrible time when "all the sun had gone out of the world," she could grieve the loss of her mother's love.

Countertransference and the Analyst as the Container for Developmental Mourning

In his article, "In Love and Lust in Erotic Transference," Glen O. Gabbard (1994) quoted Freud (1915) on "forecasting grave consequences for gratifying the patient's sexual and romantic longings" (p. 386). Sexual enactment forecloses memory. Yet, as Gabbard (1994) articulated, Freud encouraged actual marriage between analysts and patients. He was inclined to concretize the longings by recommending marriage, not yet really believing that tendencies toward erotic enactment could transition into verbal symbolism for analytic work. Freud was concerned with finding memories rather than repeating unconsciously driven behavior, yet he did not see how an analyst could serve to facilitate the expression of erotic feeling through words and verbal communication. The expression of powerful feelings in the treatment room was not distinguished from action.

I have found in my clinical work that with a focus on feelings that are intensely erotic, but which have another side of feared loss of the love object, an analyst can contain powerful affect states in the service of developmental mourning, resulting in memory rather than enactment. Can an analyst feel pleasure in this process and still serve as an adequate container for this developmental mourning process to unfold? I would say, "yes," particularly after my experience working with Pauline and her intense homoerotic transference. Melanie Klein's theory of development helps me to conceptualize this and to fill in gaps in Freud's view.

Freud lacked a developmental view of affect process although he had a developmental view of libidinal drive conflict and fixation. Melanie Klein's view of psychic movement from the paranoid-schizoid to the depressive position allowed for an affect focus that has a developmental evolution. Following from her thinking, I speak of developmental mourning, which requires the analyst to serve as a container for powerful affect states in the patient as a means for progress in developmental affect terms.

Gabbard (1992) spoke of a case in which the erotic transference served mainly as a resistance. But he used interpretation to allow symbolization to unfold and to articulate the enacted sexual fantasies that went on through subtle power dynamics between analyst and analysand in the session. He spoke of unwittingly encouraging a sadistic attack, which gratified the analysand's wish for erotic masochistic submission by repeating interpretations in a forceful and penetrating way when the analysand resisted reflecting on his interpretations and resisted even hearing them. Then he interpreted his own countertransference interplay with the patient.

Although intense grief for a lost paternal object emerged in Gabbard's treatment, he did not focus on the mourning process in the treatment per se. He did not see himself as a psychic container for grief affect as I do in reviewing the case of Pauline, as well as in reviewing the case of a male analysand in an intense erotic transference (Kavaler-Adler, 1992a). Gabbard astutely noted the erotic transference as a resistance, but his focus was entirely upon interpretation by the analyst. This is where we differ, because, following Klein's view of developmental movements toward increasing forays into the depressive position, I focus on a developmental mourning process as the major route to transforming erotic enactments into symbolic erotic fantasies. I see these erotic fantasies as carrying deeply repressed affect states, which can become alive as a dialogue for psychoanalytic work. Because Gabbard did not focus on mourning, he did not emphasize the affective aliveness that moves the erotic transference into a developmental process. My Object Relations viewpoint, which emphasizes the critical developmental role of mourning for psychic change, presents a different view of therapeutic action from that of classical theory, and it is in this respect that my view of the treatment process seems to differ somewhat from Gabbard's.

My clinical experience suggests that interpretation would not have been enough in the case of Pauline. Pauline needed me to provide a developmental function as a psychic container for her powerful erotic and grief states. I would speak of the "container" both in terms of D.W. Winnicott's holding environment and in terms of Winnifred Bion's (1959, 1970/1988) view of the analyst as an active processor of all kinds of preverbal experience when in the room with a patient. When an erotic transference has a primary preœdipal origin, as in the case of Pauline, despite the evolution of the erotic transference into oedipal dynamics, the role of the analyst as a container for developmental mourning becomes essential in my opinion, along with the use of interpretation. The analyst needs to tolerate, contain, and bring to a symbolic level of understanding through his or her own affect experience in the session all the intense arousal of the analysand, especially when erotic intensity is mixed in with abandonment depression rage, void sensation, and a particularly powerful form of grief sadness. This allows for potential protosymbolic enactment to move to a level of symbolism, interpersonal communication, memory, and to the opening of psychic space for new and whole object internalizations.

Perhaps reflective of the distinction between my way of viewing the process and that of Gabbard, Gabbard speaks of love being harder for an analyst to accept than sexual desires. This has not been the case for me, and was not in the case of Pauline. My technique involved a capacity to breathe deeply and to open my whole psychophysical being to the reception of feelings of love and intimacy that Pauline needed to express. This technique could be seen as a countertransference reaction, but I believe it evolved naturally as I sensed the developmental process from my analysand on an affective level. My main goal was to help Pauline communicate. Whatever pleasure I felt in Pauline's expression of her feelings and of her fantasies about me (so idealized in the beginning) was in the background as I focused on allowing Pauline the full psychophysical expression of her feelings and wishes. This may not have been true at all times, but was true as a general rule.

As Pauline expressed the feelings she felt so deeply in the moment, she was able to re-own split-off parts of herself by tolerating the intense affect and by verbalizing the longings related to that affect. My capacity to allow this full affective emergence encouraged Pauline to surrender her tendencies to enact sexual overtures with wooing behavior, such as in the form of sending flowers, and encouraged her to tell me her sexual fantasies as they were repeated in states of both rage and desire. Pauline was able to feel the loss of the idealized primal object and of the romantic oedipal love object as she opened to memories of rejection and unrequited love with her mother and with other women. Being allowed to express her deep loving as well as erotic thoughts allowed Pauline to surrender to her dependent longings and to recall tender memories of her mother from when she was very young.

Unlike Gabbard, I found the love in these wishes and fantasies to be quite moving. I felt a tenderness that was pleasurable, and I could allow Pauline's experience, while needing only to interpret the link back to the precious few memories of her mother's tenderness toward her. I did not resist making such interpretations, but there were times in which I did not in order to avoid aborting

Pauline's very personal sense of experience with me. Some might say that I was engaging in a countertransference enactment as I allowed myself to feel the full range of tenderness that was emerging in Pauline in the here-and-now moment, but the developmental process that unfolded testifies to the therapeutic action involved in my psychic holding and containing.

Burch (1996) differs from Gabbard in speaking of finding the hidden erotic desires behind a more benignly presented love transference. With Pauline, such desires were often out in the open, although she would close them off when she feared she was betraying her actual female lesbian lover and feared losing her real-life love relationship. Burch (1996) emphasized the difficulties of the analyst in tolerating the emerging reliving of "the erotic-romantic aspects of the early mother-daughter relationship" (p. 475). Burch stated that there is a neglect of the female analyst and female patient experience of this mother-daughter romance in its sexual form in the literature. I found this mother-daughter romance to be there from the beginning with Pauline, but it was always expressed with a great deal of conflict, as Pauline started out predominantly in a paranoid-schizoid psychic state in which she was terrified of an attack from me following her open expression of desire for me. She feared being stabbed in her vagina (and later in her heart).

Pauline felt safer when she could encapsulate her longings to love me and to be loved by me in her scripted sexual fantasies. I did not need to do anything to stimulate such fantasy. I had no reciprocal countertransference fantasies, although I felt a general body excitement when Pauline expressed deep loving tenderness combined with erotic sexual desire. As Pauline differentiated through repeated cycles of mourning, in terms of loss, trauma, narcissistic injury, and regret over not being able to care more for her parents when they were old, the body feelings she could arouse in me became more distinct. Toward the end of her treatment (fifth year), I was aware of a distinct vaginal contraction in me as she expressed a fantasy, at an oedipal erotic level, of taking me over to a bed and making love to me. This had never happened earlier in treatment, when I had experienced a general body excitement.

Also interesting, throughout the treatment I never experienced homosexual erotic fantasies. I was curious as to whether I would. But I discovered that on a level of conscious cognitive fantasy, I still had ideation that was heterosexual, rather than homosexual in nature, despite my body sensations. Consequently, I did not experience what Gabbard's (1994) female colleague, in consultation with him on her countertransference, experienced in his article on erotic countertransference. Gabbard's consultation supervisee actively fantasized a romance with her male patient. She anticipated the excitement of the breakdown of boundaries, the reversal of the power dynamics in a sexual surrender to her patient. She relinquished this fantasy when her patient started to actively fantasize sexual love-making with her, allowing his repressed sexual desires to be expressed symbolically in the transference.

My patient, Pauline, had active sexual ideation in the beginning, even when she was in a position of enactment through active wooing behavior. I received her feelings, opened myself to contain them, even focusing on deep breathing that allowed me to take in the impact of the affect in my body. Yet I never had homosexual fantasies on a cognitive and ideational level. My sexual fantasies remained heterosexual (unlike Joyce McDougall's [1998] homoerotic love memories, recognized in her countertransference in an analysis, which she speaks of in *The Many Faces of Eros*). On the other hand, I did feel narcissistic gratification in some of Pauline's expressions of fascination with me as an erotic and sexual figure. However, any pleasure I may have taken in her response to me was always modified, and increasingly so by my interest in helping Pauline mourn her transference love so she could invest both her love and sexuality in a real-life relationship.

I, therefore, began to interpret Pauline's wishes toward me as wishes toward her mother, rather than just receiving them and containing them within the context of a holding environment. Once I was taken over by some anxiety that I had delayed interpreting and I began to interpret her maternal transference wishes a little too abruptly. Pauline reacted with shock and rage at this point. As I continued to make transference interpretations, Pauline's rage became an angry dynamic that she articulated. She told me that she felt I was taking something away from her. She told me that she feared she was just going to reexperience the sense of unrequited love, felt as a traumatic level, that she had felt when she tried to approach heterosexual women with her loving adoration of them during her 20s. Pauline then recalled the devastating rejection she had suffered at the hands of a bisexual woman that led to a deep depression and to the breakup of her marriage to a man. As she remembered the shocks of rejection she felt in response to this bisexual woman's seductive behavior, followed by belittling and distancing comments, she collapsed in the grief of emotional despair. For the first time, then, Pauline tolerated the anguish of loss that she needed to feel whole again.

Ultimately, Pauline's rage with me led to another phase of an active grieving process, in which the displacement of desire for her mother to another woman had brought renewed trauma. In my presence, with the containing of the session structure, and with my capacity to be with her in her pain, Pauline was able to actively mourn and to let go of the dejected self-image she had carried with her from this traumatic experience. Letting go of this allowed her to lose 70lbs in weight (which she kept off) and to re-own a feminine side of herself that she would have felt too vulnerable to own before.

In contrast to Gabbard (1992) saying that he deflected his male patient's experiences of love, I generally stayed directly with Pauline's expressions of love to me. However, I felt I had resisted relating these loving feelings, so filled with sexual desire, back to the longings for the mother. I believe that Pauline's mother's rejection of her in adolescence, due to her homosexual interests, had resulted in such a traumatic experience of abandonment and self-annihilation that Pauline lived in a constant fear in the transference that she would lose her basic and core maternal object. I came to understand increasingly how Pauline feared that her anger and desire would alienate me forever. Pauline was intensely vulnerable and needed a great deal of reassurance. When I was not sensitive to Pauline's need for such reassurance, I became the cold, abandoning mother.

Surrendering the Projected Fantasy of an Omnipotent Bisexual Muse Mother and the Re-owning of the Feminine Self

In *The Bonds of Love*, Jessica Benjamin (1988) spoke of the need for recognition of self through recognition of desire. If this desire, which emanates from a core true self and its spontaneous gesture (Winnicott, 1971), is not received by the parent, the desire must be split-off or repressed, and it frequently gets projected into another. Pauline's core homoerotic sexual desire was not only not received or acknowledged in her adolescence, but it was also devastatingly rejected and denied. This could not have been anything less than traumatic, similar to Melanie Klein speaking of the child's trauma if reparative gestures toward the mother are not received by the real mother (see "Envy and Gratitude," Klein, 1957/1975a). When one's own desire is not validated, as stated by Benjamin, it is frequently hidden behind an identification with a man who is seen as a legitimate source of desire. This was true in Pauline's case. Pauline identified with her father as the parent who expressed open erotic desire, and whose behavior expressed his erotic desire as part of his identity, while her mother's eroticism was constantly disowned and expressed indirectly through her narcissism.

When Pauline saw me as a transferential figure of both erotic desire (a female goddess with a penis) and as a muse offering creative and narcissistic modes of inspiration, she was combining her parents, as she saw them, in a combined transferential image. The transferential muse mother combined with the phallic desire of the father is symbolized by a female creature, with flowing long hair and flowing long gowns, who possesses a penis. Such a picture appears to be an archetypical combination, as well as a kind of intrapsychic psychic fantasy phenomenon, seen as innate and axiomatic by Melanie Klein (1940).

As previously stated, Klein had noted, in her clinical work with play therapy with children, that mommy is perceived as having daddy's penis inside of her body, before mommy and daddy are differentiated as two separate human beings. At the level of intrapsychic conflict that Pauline regressed to in her analysis, her internal parent was a combined mother-father, or mother with a penis of father inside of her. I have shown how Pauline's mourning process changed this internal constellation, so that I became a differentiated female figure. Her fantasy that she possessed a penis with which to penetrate me changed as well. Although defensively holding onto the illusion of having a penis, when Pauline surrendered to the loss of the mother as an idealized figure and faced the traumas, injuries, and disappointments that her actual relationship with her mother had entailed, she could re-own her feminine genitals as a conscious part of her constitution. She did so after having a dream in which she viewed me as walking away with her female genitals, lodged in a glass case for protection. She had given her feminine side away to me, as symbolized by the female genitals in the case and, after the anxiety aroused in the dream, she wanted to reclaim her feminine side.

Facing the loss and the disillusionment related to her mother throughout the course of treatment allowed her to do this. Pauline no longer had to give everything up to her transferential mother to protect her from her anger and from her wishes to separate. Pauline proceeded to dress in a totally different style of dress. She began wearing female suits and dresses and wearing more feminine shoes. She grew her hair into a flowing style, where it had formerly been short and chopped off and clipped. She began wearing jewelry and earrings.

Pauline sustained this new manner of dress, often alternating dresses with feminine pants suits. Her new identity appeared consistent and firmly routed in identifications with her real mother as she remembered her, and with me as her transferential mother. She could now have her desire, while owning female, rather than male genitals. She could more playfully entertain the illusion of having a penis now, without desperately needing to be an extension of a mother who is seen as a goddess who has everything, including a penis, and without having to be a phallic woman. As Burch (1996) has noted, lesbian women often have the benefits of a healthy fluidity in gender identity capacities, not only a pathological side. This was true for Pauline. As she became more solidly identified with female receptivity, female softness, and female desire, Pauline also retained a sense of phallic penetration in her intellectual pursuits and in her professional work as a teacher.

Burch (1996) has stated how rare it is in the literature to see any studies of erotic feelings in the transference in a female analysand with a female analyst. I have many female patients expressing such feelings, both heterosexual and homosexual patients. This case of the interaction of mourning with the full acknowledgment and symbolization of sexual feelings in a female analysand with a female analyst is all-the-more important in light of what Burch has cited as a lack of such discussions in the literature.

Burch also speaks of a mother-daughter romance that continues beyond the preœdipal period and which can interact with an oedipal romance with a father figure for a little girl. This can be seen in the case of Pauline. During the fifth year of treatment, she developed a powerful oedipal transference to a male colleague who she saw as a father figure. She had conscious fantasies of wishing to marry him and distinct erotic fantasies of having sex with him that interacted with her transformed masturbation fantasy, in which submission to men becomes a mutually pleasurable heterosexual intercourse. Yet, at the same time, she retained erotic longings for me that she felt she had to give up. These longings became displaced into a female friend, and were as intense as ever in their homoerotic nature, despite her heterosexual longings.

Pauline went through an extremely anguished mourning process in her fifth year of treatment to face the loss of her illusion that she could marry the man she had a romantic crush on. At the same time, Pauline had to face the loss of having a romance with a particular woman in her life. She had to face loss as unrequited love, but in a gentler form than earlier because, despite being a lesbian, this woman did not have the same oedipal-level erotic desire for Pauline that she felt toward the woman. Pauline also needed to relinquish her wishes to act out a love affair with this woman due to her commitment to her long-term female lover, whom she still loved "more than life itself." Having developed a capacity to contain, face, and process the anguish of grief, within her developmental mourning process in treatment, Pauline was able to mourn much more on her own during the termination phase of treatment and in the year following that termination.

When we met again in a consultation, Pauline shared how she had tolerated the intense depressive feelings of loss and grief related to this last mourning process. Tolerating the grief allowed her to reflect on her life. She came to terms with relinquishing the chance to act out a heterosexual love affair at this time in her life, and she sublimated her wishes for men. This allowed Pauline to work with a male mentor in her professional work, and to thus grow from a mutually gratifying learning process between her and this male mentor. She also had to relinquish wishes for a new female love, which we analyzed as being, in part, a wish to displace longings for an erotic connection with me that now had to come to a definite end.

Pauline faced her losses and reinvested in her lesbian marriage of 16 years. She accepted a more feminine identity within a broader bisexual identity and a commitment to a lesbian relationship. She continued to feel the grief of surrendering her fantasy of emotionally merging with an idealized mother-lover who would serve as her inspirational muse as well as her erotic lover. In surrendering the enactment of such wishes, she was left with the pain of loss, but she was able to find new ways of using her creative resources in her work as she faced this loss. She was able to re-own her own capacities to inspire herself and to enjoy erotic fantasies that could be part of her actual sex life with her lover, but which could not be fulfilled in reality. Simultaneously, she reopened areas of poetry and creative imagination within herself.

My acceptance of her erotic wishes toward me helped Pauline to be less conflicted about these wishes, less scared of driving women away when she had such wishes toward them. As Burch (1996) has suggested, if I were not to accept these wishes from the analysand, I would be repeating the mother's shame-inducing withdrawals from her to the extent that I failed to be open to the expression of such wishes at any one time. I would become the rejecting mother whom she pictured as a cold, stone goddess, self-contained, with a penis, but not showing warmth, interest, or engagement with her. Sometimes Pauline would see me as this cold mother at times of separations when she was particularly sensitive. But her later fantasies of our reuniting and having our bodies open to each other suggested a happier resolution of her separation anxieties.

To the degree that I could accept the full expression of Pauline's erotic longings, she avoided being retraumatized and came to accept these desires, in both their oedipal and precedipal dimensions. It was important that I acknowledged her adult homoerotic nature and not just see the expression of her wishes as a regression, in keeping with Burch's (1996) comments. The wishes behind these fantasies could still be analyzed by Pauline and me together. For example, we analyzed how her fantasy of falling in love with and marrying her male colleague was a wish for a closeness with her father that she had never had, when her sister was her father's favorite and she remained in a special sadomasochistic connection with her mother.

CHAPTER 12

EROTIC TRANSFERENCE:
A JOURNEY TO PASSION AND SYMBOLIZATION

Originally published in 2014, *MindConsiliums* 14(1):19–43.

I have always worked with erotic transference. Such work came to me naturally, perhaps because I always believed, as Freud did, that the erotic transference could be the primary vehicle for having the deepest conflicts in the psyche to emerge. Freud, however, often saw erotic transference as a resistance, whereas I most frequently see it as a transitional Object Relationship.

Fairbairn (1952) spoke of letting go of the bad object. I speak of letting go of the erotically desired oedipal object through symbolizing desire and tolerating the affects of loss and grief that the inevitable disillusionment of desire demands. Symbolization—which I define as connecting words to affective engagement, particularly with longing and loss—culminates in the capacity for new external Object Relations. Relationships are external in the sense that they exist beyond the internal world where the cherished objects prevail. The oedipal object then—like the precedipal object that precedes it—is not simply renounced, but relinquished with a transformational flourish, leading to renewed and evolving Object Relations engagement with the external world.

This process does not simply involve saying good-bye to an incestuous object and hello to a non-incestuous object, for such an exchange would not transform initial psychic structure. Rather, it consists of relinquishing internal world ties while transferring affective links from internal objects onto external objects through symbolized psychic fantasies. With the new external objects, true intimacy can be achieved—intimacy at an adult level, colored and enhanced by the richness of childhood oedipal wishes.

Although traditionally erotic transference has been viewed as a defense against remembering, I believe that from an Object Relations perspective, erotic transference provides a transitional object experience for the analysand. As such, it offers an avenue to consciousness for the deepest desires and conflicts of the internal world. In addition, erotic transference helps access memory as long as it is felt and not enacted. The most intense erotic desires always originate from early infant experience, as well as from every level of precedipal, oedipal, and post oedipal experience. Whether the erotic transference is a defense against, or an avenue to, the unconscious depends on its reaching the symbolic level of felt and then spoken psychic fantasy. This symbolic level is based on affect links that often stem back to primal experience, sometimes to precedipal abandonment trauma, and in more neurotic cases back to primal loss at later levels of development. I explain this in my article on "Lesbian Homoerotic Transference in Dialectic with Developmental Mourning: On the Way to Symbolism from the Protosymbolic":

> When I speak of the protosymbolic expression of erotic transference, I mean sensory and visceral experiences, with powerful pressures for behavioral enactment, but with little representational form in the patient's internal world.... By symbolic expression I refer to vivid verbal descriptions of psychic fantasy constructed from differentiated whole object characters.... The individual's vivid verbal descriptions gradually separate out from impulsive, visceral, and somatic reactions. Such verbal descriptions become an adequate container for transference longings in treatment sessions, without enactments by phone, concrete gifts, or undefined visceral impulses outside the perimeter of the analytic sessions. (Kavaler-Adler, 2003b, p. 159)

The attitude of the psychoanalyst is extremely important in promoting the clinical and developmental use of erotic transference, as opposed to becoming mired in erotic transference as a resistance, which can also promote countertransference resistances. The analyst's attitude must be an open attitude in which she demonstrates a receptive and welcoming holding environment, where all levels of erotic sensation and erotic desire can be expressed through words. If there is any attitude of resistance on the analyst's part, the patient will sense it. Then the patient's yielding to the natural flow of erotic desire will be impinged on.

Sometimes, the words that go with erotic transference are filled with the sensation of the libidinal urges in a physical way, which could convert them into hysterical body symptoms or psychosomatic problems, if inhibited rather than encouraged by the analyst's attitude. Especially with those not so secure at the oedipal level, the urge to express deep erotic urges and desires will be felt much more on a full sensory level, and erotic impulses can be seen as mere eroticization of primal needs for a loving connection.

Erotic transference is best worked with on the couch, where the analyst can have the best attitude for receiving the affective expression of the patient, and for integrating thoughts about their experiences. When early erotic cravings are mixed in with precedipal hungers, the analyst can use the freedom behind the couch to process intense sensory experiences. Also, on the couch, the patient can express him or herself most freely, diminishing shame, or allowing shame to be spoken about. In some cases, however, erotic transference can be worked with sitting up.

Sometimes, the mourning of loss relates back to precedipal hungers as well as to oedipal desires. After sadomasochistic expressions of eroticism from a disrupted precedipal connection, psychoanalytic treatment can allow for a transformation from eroticized submission or domination into emotional surrender to the mourning of early object loss. This, in turn, allows for the creation of new "good-enough object internalization," and consequently increases the patient's capacities for mutuality and intimacy.

Clinical Example: Leonard

With a neurotic man who I will call Leonard, I listened to him admit that he was trying not to think of me when he was having sex with his wife, because he didn't want to have to talk about his fantasies with me. He referred to wishes to be loved by me as being associated with his loving, but somewhat seductive mother. He would openly speak about feeling attracted to me, but tried to avoid full consciousness of his fantasies. He openly acknowledged the transferential link back to his mother as he spoke of his attraction to me.

Leonard also spoke of his experience of closeness to his mother in childhood, which naturally made the loss of his mother, when she died, extremely painful. He spoke of missing his mother every day of his life, and surrendered to the profound depth of his grief in my office. This carried over to intense grief for two siblings who had died, and to grief for losing the connection to his entire family as he married, had children, and grew increasingly successful in his career, which transformed his whole belief system into one in conflict with his family's views. As he separated from his family through developing his own beliefs and his own achievements in the world, Leonard felt the painful anguish of losing a feeling of intimacy with his family. In treatment with me he would sit and grieve both the literal and metaphoric separation from his family, and he would feel the anguish of those actually lost to him through death.

One day, in the middle of all this, Leonard said, "I'm distracted by your boots." He smiled. He said he was always trying not to be distracted by my sexuality, and he admitted he was cutting off thoughts about me when having sex with his wife. But he said he couldn't stop looking at my tall black boots, with their pattern leather design over leather. Leonard then declared that he could see me as a dominatrix, and he could imagine himself kissing my boots and submitting to me, to be in the embrace of my power, to be loved by the "goddess."

Through his willingness to share these fantasies, we could finally get to his wish to return to a position with his mother where he would feel safe and powerful through her, rather than having to put himself out in the world and risk sharing his own original beliefs with others. This would keep him safely in the "cult" of his family where he could ward off feelings of loss. The other side of this was his wanting to individuate more, and he was presenting at professional conferences for the first time. Through all this, Leonard began to acknowledge that he was blocking a natural process from happening when he cut off his thoughts about me during sex. He said he would now try to be open to those thoughts and risk sharing them with me so that we could understand more about his desires and fears.

This led to Leonard telling me that the sadomasochistic fantasy of submission to me as a dominatrix was actually a cover fantasy defending him against a more basic desire to kiss me and make love to me with great pleasure. He said he had let himself have this fantasy when making love to his wife. However, in being in the room with me and telling it to me, he felt his fear of falling deeply in love with me and of then feeling intense frustration even more than he felt then, because he knew we couldn't really make love. My role as a transitional object can be seen as this statement then led Leonard to loving memories of his mother and her warmth, which opened Leonard to another phase of mourning the loss of his mother, to whom he knew he had been very special. He could then work more with his intense conflict of wanting to be a little boy again with his mother, and wishing to act that out with me.

Leonard knew that his wish to act out being a loved little boy with me was his attempt to deny his mother's death. He knew such wishes were in conflict with wanting to be a fully grown man with me and with his wife. However, being fully a man meant experiencing the frustrations of his wife's lack of warmth. It meant conscious suffering of his wife's frequent emotional unavailability, which contrasted with his more emotionally related mother. With me, his female analyst, Leonard could feel a warm communication, and also appreciate the boundaries that would protect him from being overwhelmed by frustration and from being unfaithful to his wife. As Leonard spoke of his desire for me, he increasingly surrendered to mourning the loss of his mother. He experienced anger as well as sadness in mourning his mother. She had been both seductive and stimulating toward his sexuality, as well as being angry and disapproving toward his developing sexuality.

I felt more affect overall with Leonard and other oedipal level men than I did when I first treated a man I will refer to as Lewis. Even when Lewis was having fantasies of me showing up at his house to become his lover—and even when he spoke of fantasies of us becoming intimate lovers who would be familiar with each other's body oddities and idiosyncrasies—I felt his tenderness without feeling the level of love and loss I was now feeling with Leonard.

Homoerotic Transference in Heterosexual Woman

With the homoerotic desires of the heterosexual woman that are expressed in relation to a female analyst, it is interesting that these can emerge in an analysis as a negative oedipal dynamic prior to the full heterosexual transference emerging with men and father figures in the world outside the treatment room. The later phases of the homoerotic transference also generally emerge during the precedipal developmental mourning process, in which primal separation from the early mother ensues (see Kavaler-Adler, 2003a) and serves certain transitional stage and transitional object functions.

With June, a heterosexual woman with an important transitional stage period of homoerotic treatment, there was an initial phase of sadomasochistic fantasies related to a demon-lover figure that captured the hardness and domination of her actual father. Images of this demon-lover father figure were mixed in with June's erotic desires, including desires to be whipped that came out through watching pornography. Following this very contrived fantasizing, June shared her more natural erotic desires, which evolved through a homoerotic transference on the way to heterosexual transferences, often called a negative oedipal period. At first, this involved her attraction to me, her female analyst, her wishes to be intensely close to me, and then her wish to be a man making love to me. First June spoke of her attraction to me and to all female bodies through me: "There's something Latin about you. You're really out there with your sexuality. You're not like other therapists who seem so drab and dull. The way you dress is so colorful and you really show your legs!" There was a merger with me in this sexual attraction, a somewhat undifferentiated state of experiencing her sexuality through me. Dream: "I'm not sure if it was you or me, but someone had their dress up over their head." This dream expressed June's wish and fear that sex could get out of control.

June went from revulsion with the female body—stemming back to memories of her father's sexually assaulting comments to her mother when he was drunk—to great attraction for the female body. She began to intensely desire me. For a while, June found herself looking at female bodies and found them more attractive than the male body. This would change. She said she didn't want to offend me so she didn't tell me that she knew when she looked at female bodies she was thinking of me. June imagined me encouraging her sexuality in the world, in contrast to her mother's and father's repetitive assaults on her sexuality. She pictured me saying, "Get out there and go dancing!"

June said she imagined making love to women in magazines, or possessing women she might see on the street. She knew these were displacements from me, but in her words, she didn't want to "disrespect me." But then June admitted her erotic desires for me directly to me, saying, "The erotic transference may be the best part of analysis. I always resisted it." June and I analyzed a sleepiness she began to feel on the couch in sessions as her wish to make love to me as a woman, and also as her wish to be a man with an erection making love to me.

Even after June moved toward heterosexual fantasies, she still had an intense homoerotic desire to be close to me, with sex merely as a vehicle to the closeness and tenderness. She said, "Wouldn't it be great if we were two gay women? Then we could have a special love together that would be even more special than the love between a man and a woman. I like to fantasize that my love for you could be made even more special if we could be together as two gay women." In the third year of treatment, June felt deeply touched by me. She cried and said she experienced such joy that she felt like she had an endless flow of love going through her. I asked if it was sexual, and she said "Oh yes, sexual, very sexual! I feel my whole body open up and tingle when I hear you speak."

The body excitement of June operated at a protosymolic level until she put it into words following the analyst's question about sexual feelings. A big part of the psychoanalyst's job when working with erotic transference is to bring the protosymbolic body experience to the symbolic level through the transference. It is the developmental mourning process that I have written about in all my books and articles that allows this transition to take place. June had undergone progressive cycles of this developmental mourning, so that sensory and visceral experience could be brought to the symbolic level of articulated psychic fantasy, and the affects of sadness, anger, rage, love, and tenderness became differentiated object related experience along the path of developmental mourning. I showed this in many of my cases, including that of the male patient, Mr. L., in "Mourning and Erotic Transference," (see Kavaler-Adler, 1992a).

Mourning and Erotic Transference in the Male Oedipal Patient

Another male patient who illustrated the interaction of erotic transference and mourning (Kavaler-Adler, 2003a), I call Phillip. Phillip imagined coming to his sessions as dates with me, musing before each session at that time about what underwear to wear, as if I would be seeing it during sex on a date. From the couch, he said to me, "If you would just give me what I want, I wouldn't have to get so involved with all these women who drive me crazy."

Phillip's wish to have a date and sex with me immediately led back to memories of sexual interest in his mother as a little boy. Phillip remembered his eight-year-old curiosity about his mother's body as his mother spread her legs while wearing a bathing suit at a swimming pool. This led back to the transference with me, where he imagined seeing my legs spread open, first as a little boy, and then becoming a man who could make love to me as he fantasized approaching me. Phillip, like Leonard, who was also dealing with oedipal level wishes and conflicts, quickly moved from erotic transference desires with me back to memories of their mothers, and vice versa. For these neurotic men, the mother remains the original erotic object, and associations to the erotic transference with me have always led right back to the mother. By contrast, with the man at a precedipal level, I, as the analyst, need to be more primarily a transitional erotic object through which the patient can first develop to a level of mutuality in truly erotic relatedness over a sustained period of time.

Aggression in Erotic Transference

Then there's the aggression in the erotic transference. Ellen said several times to me: "I want to throw you against the wall and fuck you!" She conjured up images of me being beaten by my husband on a vacation, within her fantasies of me reaching ecstatic sexual orgasms. For Ellen, her anger was often filled with eroticization during the course of the intensity of her homoerotic transference.

Countertransference Work within Erotic Transference Work

Also in the case of Ellen that I will describe more fully later, conscious levels of countertransference became guides in the treatment. For example, I felt, intuitively, the visceral awareness that it was helpful to Ellen when I opened my breathing while she was trying to express highly vulnerable feelings while on the couch during the earlier phases of her treatment. This helped me become an adequate psychic container for Ellen when she was in a state of acute vulnerability on the couch, needing to express her deep hunger for me and her desire for me, both mixed up in longings that she attempted to put into words as they pulsated through her heart and emerged as visceral throbbing in her vagina. As I opened my own breathing, Ellen found enough psychic space to contain the body pulsation of her desires as she wished to transform such body desires into words of love and tenderness. Through the expanding of my breathing, Ellen found enough psychic space to articulate her body sensations and visceral level affects as words of yearning, even though in her first dream she had pictured me stabbing her in her vagina with the rejection of unrequited love.

Also in relation to countertransference, I found that I had an effusion of overall body warmth with Ellen in her earlier phases of a precedipal eroticized transference, which transformed into differentiated clitoral sensations as she psychologically advanced in treatment to a differentiated oedipal stage with the erotic transference proper, through her developmental mourning process. Despite these body sensations, I was interested to find out that I never had homosexual psychic fantasies. My fantasies continued throughout Ellen's analysis to pertain to men—even when stimulated by Ellen's passions. This did not, however, interfere with my engaging with Ellen at whatever level of hunger or desire she evolved to.

Loss in Erotic Transference

Lewis converted his past hurt and rage into love and forgiveness for his internal parents. Then he could find good internal objects in his dreams. In one dream, he found warm friends who allow him to relinquish his masochistic attachment to his internal cold mother, that part of his childhood mother who appears like a petrified tree in his dream, someone so walled off that he can never reach her. He was able to both find and let go of his friends. This enabled Lewis to keep his friends within his psyche as symbolic internalizations. In the letting go, Lewis found his phallic power. Then his erotic transference emerged in the internal world through dreams, as well as emerging in the external world through his treatment. Lewis said that at the point when he let his friends go, feeling the contact with them and keeping their warmth within him, he felt his penis "strengthen." From an Object Relations perspective, this made a lot of sense. Lewis demonstrated that as external Object Relations are internalized and sustained through connecting to the symbolic connections in dreams, phallic and self potency are both enhanced. Lewis related this strengthening of himself within his penis to an overall strengthening of his sense of self, but also particularly to his sexual self (see Kavaler-Adler, 1992).

Lewis's earlier erections were only supported by cold resentments toward women. It occurred after incidents in life with women in which he felt that his penis could only stay hard if he was filled with cold rage, but this body part potency did not enhance his potency as a person. If Lewis had felt affectionate he had felt impotent (see Kavaler-Adler, 1992; Kavaler-Adler, 2006a, p. 110). This all changed with a progressive mourning process in treatment that allowed Lewis to develop into a man. One memory of a painful separation from a female friend at latency appeared to be both a screen memory of early yearnings toward the prœdipal mother, as well as being a poignant object attachment and object loss in its own right. Lewis remembered lying in a dug-out hole in the dirt of the wilderness when he lived in Nebraska. He and his friend, Richard, would fantasize together that the remains of a building they found in their private wilderness was the foot of a giant castle. This was their land of enchantment.

Within his analysis, Lewis mourned the loss of his childhood friend, and the loss of the kind of quiet contentment that he had so treasured during those few precious moments, those few and precious days. Mourning his friend, who galvanized psychic yearnings for a good prœdipal object, was just the beginning of Lewis's mourning in treatment. It was this mourning, and the need for the analyst which it opened up, that helped Lewis to reveal repressed memories of childhood shame. Lewis mourned for parts of himself, child parts of him that had been injured and left behind. He remembered shame-ridden experiences of paternal castration.

One memory of being punished and spanked particularly stood out. There was another memory of his father going into a rage and slapping him across the face. Both memories brought back to him his sense of despair about ever being understood. His father was not interested in hearing what he had to say. All Lewis could do was make peace with his father, by understanding his father's pain and grieving now for both of them. His rage at his father spent, his feelings of shame and humiliation beginning to heal with the expression of his inner wounds and the expressions of his shit-flawed self-image, he could now make amends.

Lewis was freed by his capacity to feel the chain of affects, from his anger to the narcissistic hurt within his shame, to the loss within his sense of loneliness as he separated from his internal bad part-object parents. Grief followed anger and hurt. He could then feel his parents' pain with his own pain, without the threat of losing his own separate perspective. He would never get to communicate to them what he had felt, and his grief was partly for that. There would always be a rift between them.

Dreams, as well as memories, revealed Lewis's need to reconnect with good objects within him that had blocked out of awareness by fears of feeling their loss, and by relations with dead and depriving internal objects that had been held on to when his good objects had been repressed. Lewis allowed good internalizations to form within him by reuniting with warm friends from the past in his dreams. Lewis no longer excluded himself from his friends' sense of warmth and love, as he had in the past by repressing his friends' introjects out of consciousness and defending against warmth. Through this, Lewis progressed to psychic integration. He no longer split-off from others in order to preserve a regressive attachment to a petrified tree person who would reject him, having always before recreated the bad object nature of his mother within his internal world. Formerly, Lewis had run after distant women who were like his mother. After mourning, he was drawn toward a warm, lovely, sexual young woman who he fully engaged with and eventually married. The sadness in letting go of his friends had helped him get past anger to love.

Early in treatment, Lewis had strengthened his sense of self by restoring his childhood friend Richard to his consciousness, facing the never before faced grief of saying "good-bye." This made Lewis more capable of containing his feelings. He then opened up to his feelings of shame and of anger, resolving anger toward both his parents. Lewis became more masculine through forgiving his father, which allowed him to sustain an internal loving tie with his father as a male figure in his psyche. Along with resolving anger and the related shame, Lewis' ability to say "good-bye" to his internal college friends allowed him to open psychic space and to thus contain erotic feelings. Through mourning the loss in separating from his internal object friends, Lewis opened to an erotic transference that had formerly been latent. The girl he discovered in a bed in a dream became associated with the female analyst.

Specific Differentiated Heterosexual Erotic Transference in Lewis

Up until the time of the mourning process described, Lewis' erotic desires were fixated in sadomasochistic fantasies of being tied down by a woman, and of being made to submit to all kinds of sexually arousing tortures. His fantasies echoed Lewis' passive submission to women in his life and to his female analyst. These fantasies were used for masturbation, which became a ritual of re-enacting an enslaved position that Lewis inhabited in relation to his mother. He could never say "no" to getting his mother her ice cream each night, and later he became passive aggressive and controlled others through masochistic submission in his fantasies. The mother's use of Lewis for her own sexual arousal was in a dream. His mother got enraged in the dream when someone gave Lewis a blanket to put over his naked body when he was exposed at the dinner table.

We can see the interplay between mourning and resistance in Lewis' erotic transference. Lewis' view of himself as a sexual victim pressed for reenactment. This could have become a resistance to opening up to contact with me, his analyst, and resistance to his unconscious oedipal erotic desires emerging. However, with significant mourning, Lewis felt he was strong enough to tolerate his sexual passions as they emerged in dreams that symbolized his erotic transference. Lewis began to reveal his fantasies to me, rather than persisting in covert forms of acting out where he would control others by being controlled, as in his sexual fantasies.

Originally, Lewis had to be his mother's slave and try to pleasure her. He couldn't say "no." He would try instead to be stimulated by his enslavement and submission to his mother. In the beginning dreams of analysis, Lewis was a small figure with a tiny penis, who was with huge women. Then, as Lewis mourned, his body grew more proportionate to the woman in his dreams and fantasies, who he began to identify as me within his transference view of me.

When Lewis' passion opened up, there was a dream of a tidal wave of emotion coming toward both of us from the ocean. Lewis' erotic passion threatened him and me in his transference dream. In the dream, he was afraid his ocean of erotic passion for me (in the transference) would overwhelm both of us. "His emotional longings had to be experienced full force, just like his phallic eruptions, in order for the two to come together. ... As the tidal wave of passion came out into the open, leaving the ocean of the unconscious and coming out into the light of day, Lewis wooed me fiercely" (p. 112, Kavaler-Adler, 2006a, also Kavaler-Adler, 1992a). He thought of "lines" to say to me. His sense of humor awakened, and he integrated it into his painting. If I would wear a red dress, he imagined I wore it especially for him. He found everything I wore exciting!

Lewis' sexual attraction to me in the transference revealed all the oedipal erotic desires that seem to have been rebuffed during his childhood by his mother. In his dream of a petrified tree, we see the symbolic mother who is cold, hard, and immured against receiving warmth and love. This petrified tree can be seen to represent the coldness in his childhood mother, and in all the women he had dated as an adult who had rejected him, at the time prior to mourning in treatment, when he himself had felt cold, blocked, and thus impotent.

Lewis' dreams chartered his erotic transference evolution for Lewis. Formerly, his dreams had him in bed with a strange woman, reflecting his earlier transference with me, his female analyst. As Lewis mourned and opened his heart to me as a transitional other (mother), his dreams began to express love and closeness.

Lewis desired the erotic intimacy he imagined in the transference. This period brought fantasies of my lying beside him in bed, or of me suddenly appearing at his doorstep and coming inside his home to make love to him. He wanted to feel the pressure of my body, our tenderness, our caressing. He imagined us sharing our secret flaws together, bonding through the sharing of our shame, revealing (from shame to pride) the awkward areas of our bodies evolving in exquisite attunement to each other's entire body surface (Kavaler-Adler, 1992a; 2006a).

The erotic feelings came up directly in our sessions. Lewis exclaimed that he had felt a full feeling coming up from his "gut and through his penis," while being with me in a session, on the couch. When I suggested four, rather than three, sessions a week for his analysis, Lewis went into a sexual ecstasy. He interpreted my clinical suggestion as though I was a lover revealing how much I wanted him.

Since I had become so vividly painted as Lewis' oedipal love, only disillusionment through mourning could bring his transition into finding a true love who could be his own. A critical time of growth arrived during my summer vacation, leading to his last year of treatment, his seventh year. Lewis reported to me that after my departure he had woken up in the mornings with the weight of grief that he had never known before. He felt a heavy sadness and wept. His sadness brought the full impact of his realization that I was never going to come to his home, to his bed. I would never be his.

Surrendering to this truth, Lewis emerged from his cocoon in a radically new way. He felt a newfound sense of determination, a willingness to take risks. He joined a dating service, made a video of himself, and within three dates he had met the woman who would become his bride. As he began to date her and to know her, Lewis' painting showed his erotic joy, and the mournful coldness of his past brightened. His romantic fantasies were replaced by romantic realities that were better than any fantasies he could have predicted. His courtship with his fiancé was filled with surprises, gifts, tender concern, and caring (see Kavaler-Adler, 1992a, 2006a).

On Valentine's Day, Lewis canceled one of his analytic sessions (for which he paid) to take his fiancé to a well-known elegant restaurant. In his words, he was determined to give her the royal treatment. It became clear that I had served as a transitional love object, who could be relinquished as I was internalized within him. When Lewis left treatment, he said, "You will be deep inside of me for the rest of my life!" However, he also said, "you're no longer the focus of my erotic longings."

Because Lewis had been able to use his analyst as a transitional object, he could choose a wife who was warm, loving, caring, and related in a way that his former girlfriends had never been. As he mourned childhood friends, let go of negative internal parents, and grieved for the parents who had hurt him, he could take in more good internalizations of the analyst. Then, in time, he became able to grieve for the loss of his fantasy wishes toward the analyst. This allowed him to open up to a new relationship with a woman that could truly fulfill his needs as an adult man.

Lesbian Homoerotic Transference

Ellen could only relinquish acting out of the erotic transference in her outside life, with all its self sabotaging devastation, when she surrendered to her repeated cycles of developmental mourning. Through her organic affect experience in mourning, Ellen released old internal object ties and then her analyst became a transitional object, allowing her to gain new psychological internalizations that could be invested in her current outside relationships. I was her muse demon in the transference, but I also was a stable other to whom she could express all her feelings, so that she could finally have someone to express all her levels of love and sexuality to.

In expressing her love to me, Ellen spoke of "an ocean of longing." However, the other side of the ocean of longing was the dark, Grand Canyon abyss, or the feared ocean of black swirling fluids emanating from her emotional vortex within the psychic area lacking loving internalizations. In the transference, Ellen could allow consciousness of the agony of all her life's experiences of unrequited love, but then she feared endless unfulfilled desire. Ellen feared that she would again suffer the agony of intense abandonment, accompanied by terrors of self annihilation. These terrors were all integral components of Ellen's psychic state in relation to unrequited love, since her unrequited love for her mother stemmed from the earliest stages of development.

Ellen had come into treatment with a script of an anticipated romance based on sexualization of both preœdipal and oedipal levels of her childhood. She knew I had written well known books about women artists and writers, so she put me in the category of being like her mother, who was an artist. This was part of what made her crave me and yearn for me. She came into treatment fearing I would stab her in her vagina, and in her heart. She had never recovered from the emotional stabbing of her mother's rejection when she was 14, and was reported to be having crushes on women at camp by the camp director. Her mother took her out of camp and froze her out, sitting like a "medusa" mother, in cold stony silence at dinner.

All Ellen's wishes were captured in her early dreams, as well as her fears. In her first dream, I was a female goddess icon, the unconscious muse demon, who floated down from above in an opera house. I came from high above her and then descended onto her bed. I had long flowing hair and wore a colorful silk gown. Significantly, in terms of her own bisexual wishes, I also had an erect penis. I was mother-father-lover combined, as the muse demon figure of preœdipal developmental arrest always is, like Melanie Klein's mother-father psychic fantasy that precedes any experience of a differentiated mother and father. For Melanie Klein, the father is inside the mother in infancy, and thus Ellen's dream emerged with the father's penis in her goddess muse mother's body, who was me, the analyst, in the transference.

In another dream at the beginning of treatment, Ellen unzipped her chest. She handed me her heart with a sense of dread—fearing that her heart will be stabbed by me as she had felt with her mother and with many other women in her adolescent and young adult years who she had fallen in love with. She feared being lost in a Grand Canyon of emptiness after giving up all her love and desire to me.

In the first year of treatment, Ellen's language was somewhat contrived, and her fantasies were like elegantly crafted unconscious scripts. Ellen spoke of "spreading my legs" and of "taking my pearl," and she didn't neglect to speak of the wish to "drown in my come" after she penetrated me and gave me an orgasm. The language was explicit. I felt some overall sexual body feeling, which later became more body-specific as she reached the oedipal phase. The countertransference in my body showed the difference in the developmental level. In the beginning, Ellen's erotic longings disguised her split-off infant longings for nurturance, which she unconsciously displaced onto me through projection in her fantasies. She imagined herself wrapping me in a blanket after sex with me. She spoke of holding me as if she was speaking of holding her own child self. It can be seen here to what degree Ellen's adult erotic desires were overlaid with infant longings for nurturance and mothering, as I, as her love object, came to represent her split-off infant self.

I also represented Ellen's latent feminine wishes, and if I as the analyst were not open to hearing these explicitly eroticized desires, I would be blocking the unconscious flow of her developmental longings. I would be blocking the emergence of her split-off and repressed infant self that needs to grow up and become a receptive feminine self in adult form.

Ellen's erotic transference was also accompanied by dreams of oedipal competitions with my husband or of other triadic relations where she would join me in being penetrated by my husband. Other times she would be an extension of my husband, joining him in penetrating me. She could be versatile and playful in her fantasies before she had to face the loss of not actually being both genders at once. She spoke of an open skirmish with my husband, while my husband "jealously defended his territory." In other fantasies, she would be an audience in the background while I had sex with my husband, and she would be cheering me on to an orgasm.

Then, in the third year of treatment, I became the phallic woman, as in Ellen's early dream, and I would be felt to penetrate her. This is when she was beginning to accept her more receptive and feminine side, after much grief and mourning, as she recalled the narcissistic injuries and rejections of her mother and other women. In the fourth year, she had fantasies of being penetrated by me and a male persona, so she could experience both her desires for her oedipal mother and oedipal father and also for experiencing a new gender identification as a woman. Symbolic level associations evolved as she went from sending me long stem roses to telling me her feelings. Her fantasies also went from sadomasochistic scenes with a group of men ravishing her to mutually interactive sex. Simultaneously in transference fantasies with me in her fifth year, after a vacation, she imagined re-joining me by speaking of my body opening to her "with my vulva opening to her as a radiant, glowing, flower." She was beginning to imagine true surrender rather than dominance and submission. She, through the mourning process, had become a woman and was no longer secretly an infant in a woman's body.

As Ellen expressed her feelings and fantasies directly to me in the moment, our transitional Object Relations analytic bond provided a critical avenue of converting the defensive function of erotic transference into the curative function of integrating with an external Object Relationship. Gradually, over time, Ellen saw how the sharing of her fantasies allowed her to get to the raw body sensations and emotional feelings behind the fantasies. Such sharing helped Ellen come out of a sealed-off state in her mind, where her fantasies have been masturbatory, often distancing her from being present in her life and with the woman she loves. As she shared her fantasies of me with me, and as she opened her heart and vagina in a concert of object desires, Ellen gained access to an external Object Relationship with me. Consequently, she could become increasingly present with others, and most particularly with her female lover with whom she has a deep and abiding marriage, filled with both friendship and love for 17 years.

Working with erotic transference also means working with aggression as well as negative transference. Sometimes the aggression is eroticized as when Ellen would scream in her sessions, "I want to throw you against the wall and fuck you!" when she was angry at me. To interpret this, I had to strike when the iron was cold, not when it was hot (Pine, 1985), because at the moment of intensity Ellen had regressed and was not hearing my words at a symbolic level. Later, she could hear about the feeling of disappointment or rejection that was behind her rage, and she could have linking associations back to memories of how hurt and rejected she had felt by her mother and other women.

The best time to interpret with Ellen was when she felt loss, relinquishing with heavy grief the aspired-to loves of her past. At times of grief, tolerating loss, and contacting her potential renewal of love, through the tolerance of loss, Ellen could hear me speak about her motives and her experiences because she was in touch with her internal self and was not defensively stuck in her focus on me as an object of her projections and projective identification. In Melanie Klein's terms, she was in a more depressive position state of mind, rather than a paranoid-schizoid state of mind (Klein, 1940).

As Ellen worked through mourning her memories from the past, she could hear transference interpretations. Then it was time to move from being a container for her deepest psychophysical expressions of love, hunger, and vaginal desire, and to begin to interpret how her feelings toward me extended back to her mother, as they were part of an erotic mother transference. When I first began interpreting this, Ellen did experience it with shock and with a feeling of rejection. She expressed much rage toward me, such as when I told her that her wanting to hug me was a wish for a mother's hug. Even though she did reveal her more vulnerable child self to me when on the couch, wishing to be in my lap and have me stroke her hair, she responded with shock and rage when I first began to interpret her mother transference.

She wanted me as a muse and lover, which had to be addressed as a major defense, although it had earlier developmental transference implications. Ellen's aggression could be contained in the treatment. Then her grief could be felt and processed so that she could move on in her life by bringing her more conscious loving self fully into her relationship with her external life lover, her lesbian lover. Her oedipal longings then also emerged toward men as father figures, which was later interpreted.

During the first years of treatment, Ellen had "great difficulty" coping with the highly visceral body experiences that accompanied her report of her sexual fantasies. She would become dizzy or suffocated, choking on highly vulnerable emotions of love and tenderness. Sometimes she had to sit up when lying on the couch, just to breathe, because too much intense emotion was coming up at once. As Ellen opened to her breathing, I would also breathe in, intuitively sensing that this would allow Ellen potential psychic space to spontaneously say the words of love after experiencing the anguish of her three year old separation trauma. As she could feel and simultaneously express her feelings in words, her somatic discomfort lessened. Then she could have her desires increasingly contained in differentiated words. Ellen said later, during her fourth and fifth years of analysis, that when she sent me flowers, she was regressing to an early psychic place, a child place where words never adequately expressed feelings. Only an image or symbolic gift could.

Ellen had to bring her erotic fantasy level into conjunction with her sensory arousal on the couch when she described her love for me. She enacted the love by sending me long stem roses from a flower shop, and within this enactment was a seduction meant to ward off her feared retaliatory mother's aggression. Her mother had always been offended by her feelings and had turned cold as Medusa toward her when she found out about Ellen's homosexual leanings during her teen years. As Ellen proceeded through her developmental mourning process in treatment, I was able to interpret the symbolic messages in the earlier enactment of sending me long stem roses from the flower shop. She agreed enthusiastically when I said that she could be both a man in being the agent of courting me with flowers and a woman in her identification with the flowers as representing the feminine vaginal core opening. She totally agreed with my interpretation at a time when she had advanced to being aware of her own interpretations and motives, being able to verbally express her one-to-one intimate desire for me as love object, without the former oedipal transference triangles she had in her sexual fantasies.

Through mourning a lifetime of losses with me as a psychic container for her sitting behind the psychoanalytic couch, Ellen's own psychic fantasies became better containers for her feelings that had formerly been repressed with the pain of unrequited love. In the mourning process, Ellen opened to her primal longings for the first time and offered them to me verbally.

On the couch, Ellen would express deep sensory hunger and desire: "I want you so much right now. … I'm feeling this feeling in my vagina, wanting you." It would be very much in the moment, not hidden behind a defensive screen of sexualized fantasies in which the hunger and yearnings would be hidden by her actions as if in a movie script. Now, especially by the third year, she was truly present. As I opened my breath, Ellen risked more vulnerability. Only when she could express these feelings directly could she describe her erotic transference fantasies without splitting them off into compulsive activities and obsessive thinking outside the sessions.

Early on, when she was still in the idealizing erotic transference, with me as her idealized muse mother, Ellen needed me to receive her instinctual cravings and her affect yearnings. I was a Wilfred Bionian psychic container, not yet interpreting, but processing what I felt so I could interpret later. It was important for me to receive these expressions of Ellen's feelings without interpreting them at the time. She needed to feel that both her love and her aggression could be accepted by me. In D.W. Winnicott's sense (Winnicott, 1971), she needed to know I survived her impulses and passions, just as Lewis needed to know that I could help him survive his passions as they emerged from his unconscious as an "ocean," similar to Ellen's "ocean of longing."

I contained and survived Ellen's passions, but her negative transference emerged in interaction with her erotic transference because, as her analyst, I had to inevitably disappoint her as I was not responding to her expressions of love as a lover (p. 165). Consequently, she experienced me as rejecting her oedipal wishes, which had in part served as a defense against preœdipal rejection. Such disappointments expressed at tolerable levels in treatment led Ellen to tolerate loss by tolerating painful grief affect as she evolved into an overall mourning process.

Through feeling the pain of loss and traumatic rejection, Ellen could also articulate fantasies that showed the double-edged sides of her primal cravings to merge with me and to have erotic desire be the fuel toward this preœdipal merger. This was captured in the fantasy she articulated to me on the couch of wishing to inhabit a special place in my vagina, which she would get to through her phallic penetration of me, still imagining herself, as she had imagined me in her dream, to have a penis. However, the fantasy flipped to the underbelly of unconscious fear as she then imaged a vortex of black swirling fluids inside of me, like the Grand Canyon, that would swallow her up. Ellen's double-edged desire and conflicting fear resonated with the same erotic wish versus terror scenario in one of my male patient's fantasies, Phillip. Phillip imagined entering me through sexual penetration of my vagina, seeking then to be in my womb, only to end up lost in this railway tunnel that becomes a labyrinth of endless avenues to nowhere, one form of vagina dentata fantasy.

Ellen's fantasy desire flipped to the dark side each time I failed to instantly reciprocate her wishes. But her conscious protests could be more clearly understood through the vivid illustration of her unconscious fantasy as it emerged into her consciousness through her free associations on the couch, echoing a beginning treatment dream of being trapped in the waters underneath a swimming pool in her health club.

If I did not express feelings akin to her own, I became the sadistically withholding mother of unrequited love. But with the container of the holding environment of psychoanalytic treatment, Ellen could feel her rage and disappointment, and could ultimately surrender to the grief of loss that allowed her to be reborn through connecting with her inner self, her internal world, and to others in her interpersonal world.

Mourning helps to create a safe analytic space to contain the erotic transference in treatment. Simultaneously, disappointments in erotic transference wishes also open up cycles of grief and mourning, and cycles of mourning and erotic transference interact interacting (see Kavaler-Adler 2003b). The working through of erotic transference fantasies involves a natural evolution of mourning in which sadomasochistic fantasies transform into mutually interpenetrating dimensions that are truly erotic. With each transference disillusionment, Ellen relived the experience of unrequited love and mourned the related self and object loss. Consequently, she regained, through mourning, parts of herself that had been formerly trapped in old psychic attachments.

During the third year of treatment, Ellen became more whole and thus more able to deal with all kinds of mourning. She ultimately processed bereavement mourning for both her dead parents, which involved her regrets that she couldn't have been there more for them due to her anger. Then forgiveness came. Ellen also had mourned the loss of self in her narcissistic injuries incited by her mother and by other women as well as by her male husband of former years. Ellen mourned her separation losses with each break in the connection with me in treatment, whether due to actual gaps in treatment and vacations or due to her anger that pushed me away. She did all the levels of developmental mourning, as she separated, differentiated, and found her way to creating her own unique, somewhat bisexual identity. In addition, she processed the grief of bereavement.

Ellen processed her oedipal level mourning in relation to me in the transference and to a male mentor that she fell in love with for some time, fantasizing that he would marry her. As Ellen mourned and became someone who knew she was making interpretations, she also viewed my interpretations very differently than in the beginning of treatment when she had been so vulnerable to experiencing interpretations as rejections. She came to poetically describe my interpretations as "gifts of insight," and became a full psychoanalytic companion on the analytic journey.

In the fourth year of treatment, Ellen decided that she had to relinquish the belief that she could really be my lover. She could then do the oedipal level mourning. She said, "I feel sad about giving up the fantasy of being your lover." She relinquished the fantasy but did not renounce the oedipal object in the way Freud speaks of. She mourned and lessened the reality of this fantasy for herself. The mourning allowed for surrendering and relinquishing, rather than some kind of forced cognitive renunciation or submission to reality. Ellen relinquished her protosymbolic action of sending me roses. She began to express her flowering feelings for me. She reached a symbolic level through the mourning. Her erotic desires became thoughts with feelings, not actions or delusional beliefs.

Ellen's words became alive to her with all the nuances of core heartfelt affect combined with erotic desire. Words became authentically integrated with feeling level reality, the reality of the true internal self. Both metaphor and symbolism came alive. Ellen's words came into poetic form in the spontaneity of the moment, the moment that can only be felt by the true inner feeling self: The eroticism was no longer sexualization, but rather authentic desire that joins the heart and the mind in words that contain the body sensation so that it does not have to be enacted to be felt.

After a separation with me in her fourth year of treatment, three times a week, she could greet me upon my return with the following words echoing authentic erotic desire, without any coercive script that she is trying to force me into as in her first years of treatment. Ellen said: "I see myself entering your open vagina with your beautiful vulva and clitoris opening like a flower, glowing, radiant, and receptive." See how different this language is from the earlier language of "drowning in my come," and "taking my pearl." The words were now spontaneous, in the moment of feeling, no longer contrived or stereotypic in any way. There were no longer any euphemisms for vulva and clitoris like "pearl." Now my sexual body was all out there in Ellen's mind, living, evocative, inviting, and no longer in any way confined to a script. This was all part of the movement from the protosymbolic to the symbolic level that began with her feeling compelled to actually send me long stem roses from the florist.

Ellen mourned the disillusionments with her idealized mother. She mourned the self loss that she had repressed when constantly, through her life, she had been confronted with unrequited love. She mourned by feeling her grief related to hostile attacks on me, as she projected her cold internal mother onto me. This resulted in her arriving at the point of true, sublimated, symbolic level interpenetration. She then could accept her separateness, and her ability to re-connect in an authentic way, as mutuality and symbolic communication have emerged beyond sadomasochism, just as in the case of Lewis.

THE THERAPEUTIC ACTION OF WORKING WITH EROTIC TRANSFERENCE: AN OBJECT RELATIONS VIEW OF CLINICAL EXPERIENCE: DIFFERENTIATING THEORY FROM CLASSICAL AND RELATIONAL VIEWPOINTS

Originally presented on March 2019 at the ORI's Annual Conference on Erotic Transference.

In "Observations on Transference Love," Sigmund Freud (1915) speaks of erotic transference as both a resistance, and as a conduit for the deepest unconscious desires and conflicts to emerge. The two disparate courses that erotic transference can take oppose one another. To the degree that the erotic transference is a resistance, it fails to be a conduit for unconscious desires. When erotic transference is a conduit for unconscious desires, it allows those desires to be understood within the course of psychoanalytic treatment, reducing all forms of resistance.

Freud (1915) credits the attitude of the analyst: "keeping a firm hold of the transference" (p. 166), but not succumbing to it, as well as the educative work done on the analytic process, as the two main factors in containing the resistance aspects of "transference love"; so that the infantile aspects of the love can emerge and be analyzed. Yet, Freud's comments throughout the essay emphasize the continuing difficulty, and sometimes the impossibility, of modifying the resistance so that treatment can proceed, as in the case of "women of elemental passionateness" (p. 166).

He sees it as likely that a woman will retaliate for the unrequited nature of her love by withdrawing all co-operation from treatment. He does not distinguish borderline and neurotic cases but does imply that the borderline nature of the "women of elemental passionateness" is the most resistant to using erotic desire on a symbolic level, where fantasies can be spoken and not enacted. We can say with Freud that with a woman, or man of borderline level elemental passionateness, therapeutic action with erotic impulses—as opposed to fantasies—is limited because dissociated aspects of the Self are enacted and not remembered. This would be an entryway into distinguishing eroticized part object transference from whole object erotic transference, the latter being seen through our clinical work as the conduit to repressed unconscious desires that Freud spoke of.

A developmental perspective, which accounts for the different psychic structure of borderline and neurotic patients, or for the difference between those developmentally arrested, and stuck in the paranoid-schizoid position, and those who can be engaged on the more advanced developmental level of the depressive position, allows a fundamentally different perspective on the potential therapeutic action of work with erotic transference. In fact, we might observe that Freud could have been more optimistic about the facility to use erotic transference love, in terms of containing and transforming the resistant aspects of it, if he had taken another factor into account.

I propose mourning as a critical clinical factor in modifying the erotic transference from a major transference resistance into an ongoing positive force in the treatment process. Mourning as a clinical process, articulated in my theoretical term developmental mourning, is the critical clinical factor that I propose for allowing the therapeutic action of erotic transference work. Also along with mourning is the transitional erotic object role of the analyst, when a developmental perspective is maintained.

Mourning was first acknowledged as a primary emotional process in Freud's (1917) "Mourning and Melancholia." However, it was Melanie Klein who first saw mourning as a primary affective process, underlying both developmental growth and clinical psychotherapeutic treatment. Klein's papers on the depressive position, such as "Mourning and its Relation to Manic Depressive States" (1940), highlight the potential clinical acumen to be gained by understanding the mourning process.

The cases to be described here demonstrate how an attunement to object-related contact, within the course of psychoanalysis, allows a natural mourning process to unfold, thus contributing to an ongoing positive evolution in the use of erotic transference in treatment. To understand the interaction of the erotic transference and the developmental mourning process, it is necessary to view erotic desires with a full range of oedipal and precedipal dimensions. The psychic fantasies that emerge within erotic transferences can in this context be seen to chart a developmental course, crystallizing the intense and multitextured object-related desires. Symbolizing these desires inevitably leads to loss and grief, as symbolization is a developmental separation process (Kavaler-Adler, 1992a, 1993a/2013, 1996/2014). It is through the mourning of this loss and grief that psychic structure transformation becomes possible (as opposed to the "symbolic equation"; Segal, 1986). Without this mourning process evolution, erotic transference can act as a resistance to psychic change, as Freud first warned in 1915.

"Potential space" (Ogden, 1986; Winnicott, 1971) within the therapeutic environment, and psychic space and psychic dialectic within the internal world, both open as developmental mourning evolves out of the normal disillusionment created by the symbolic expression of erotic desires (Kavaler-Adler, 1992a, 1993a/2016, 2004, 2006). There is a gradual relinquishing of the old object constellation that binds oedipal and prœdipal object longings within the framework of historically formed character structure. Whereas Fairbairn (1952) spoke of letting go of the bad object, I speak of letting go of the erotically desired oedipal object through symbolizing desire, and through experiencing the affects of loss and grief that the inevitable disillusionment of desire demands.

Connecting with the affective engagement with longing and loss, through symbolization, culminates in the capacity for new external Object Relations—external in the sense that they exist beyond the internal world where the cherished oedipal objects prevail. The oedipal object then is not simply renounced, but relinquished through grief, leading to renewed and evolving Object Relations engagement with the external world. This process does not simply involve saying good-bye to an incestuous object and hello to a non-incestuous object, for such an exchange would not transform initial psychic structure, nor provide meaning for the developmental journey. Rather, it consists of relinquishing internal world ties while transferring affective links to these objects—through symbolized psychic fantasies, onto new external objects with whom true intimacy can be achieved. I speak of intimacy at an adult level, which is colored and enhanced by the richness of childhood oedipal wishes.

Such a journey is necessary for healthy heterosexual and healthy homosexual maturity to evolve. Homosexual erotic transference has the same power and intensity as heterosexual erotic transference. Like heterosexual erotic transference, homosexual erotic transference is multilayered and multitextured, with differentiated oedipal desire genital intensities interacting with prœdipal hungers. The oedipal level object always causes the projections of an early beast mother, as well as the more differentiated oedipal object. Homoerotic transference occurs with heterosexual, homosexual, and bisexual analysands. It is, therefore, of particular interest to study the nature of the erotic transference with homosexual and bisexual analysands in relation to a heterosexual analyst.

Such cases permit us to see the journey from protosymbolic enactment, in the course of psychoanalytic regression, to symbolic expression that can be transformed through the affects and memories of mourning. Therefore, studying case material of gay individuals offers a unique perspective on a developmental progression that also occurs in heterosexual analysands. The heterosexual can discover the homosexual energies in full Object Relations analysis, just as the homosexual can discover heterosexual energies in the extensive analysis. The common denominator is mourning as a developmental process (Kavaler-Adler, 1993/2013b, 1996/2014, 2003a, 2003b, 2013).

In some of the case vignettes to be described here, the intensity of the analysand's erotic transference held the potential of blossoming into a symbolic level. However, it was through the developmental mourning progression in treatment that the transition was made from protosymbolic enactments of wooing and courting the analyst into the poetic expression of psychic fantasies related to the analyst, which then carried over into romantic engagement with realistic lovers outside of the treatment arena. In these cases, the transitional object function of the analyst, as an erotic object, is particularly highlighted. In more distinctly neurotic cases, the transitional object function is less necessary, as the analysand can participate in immediate free associations that recall memories of the primal parental objects, and in the case of two men to be described, of the oedipal mother.

In all these case studies—some of which have had longer case evolution in former publications—I return to thinking of erotic transference as a primarily object related phenomenon. This contrasts with an article by Trop (1988), a self psychologist, who changed the object related definition of erotic transference for his own clinical perspective. Trop refers to erotic transference as the emergence of a developmentally "curtailed" need for "mirroring of the sexual self" (p. 281).

In my cases, it is clear that the erotic transference is based on object-related yearnings that motivate the expression of repressed areas in the anaysand's personality. It was this expression of the repressed phenomena, connected to the object-related yearnings, which allowed the analysand to become a sexual being within the full context of whole object intimate love relations. As the analyst, I did not mirror the patient's sexuality, but merely received and understood the feelings. This is how my Object Relations perspective differs from self psychology, just as it differs from the classical ego psychology position in which erotic transference is always viewed primarily as resistance.

I also differ in my views from those in the relational school of psychoanalysis, which will be dealt with at the end of my paper. This will involve a discussion of the use of conscious countertransference from an Object Relations perspective, as opposed to from a relational perspective.

Developmental View of Erotic Transference Work and the Analyst as a Transitional Erotic Object

In an article of mine in the *International Journal of Psychoanalysis* (Kavaler-Adler, 1992a), entitled "Mourning and Erotic Transference," I wrote about the psychoanalytic Object Relations journey from the preœdipal mourning and healing process, to the oedipal level erotic transference. This was a true whole object erotic transference, not an eroticized part object transference, as the regression to preœdipal level memories, fantasies, longings, guilt, rage, losses, and forgiveness allowed for a developmental mourning process. The developmental mourning process moved the analysand toward whole object erotic desires, which evolved fully within the transference with myself, a female psychoanalyst.

Mourning within the treatment took place on both the earlier preœdipal level, and later on the oedipal level, when the relinquishment of the analyst as an erotic and romantic love object took place. The mourning of the parents in the preœdipal phase, and the mourning of a latency age friend, who inspired both romantic and loving feelings, all led toward the emergence of a full fledged whole object erotic transference. The mourning of the parents involved a great deal of anger, rage, and shame, but later evolved into forgiveness and compassion. The mourning for the lost latency age male friend—who he was pulled away from when his parents decided to move the family to another state—came back through the poetic experience of memories, as well as through the anger at the parents who provoked his sense of loss and abandonment. I will quote from my earlier description in the article "Mourning and Erotic Transference" (Kaveler-Adler, 1992) as it relates to this patient's mourning of loss (I will call the patient Paul here):

One memory of a painful separation from a male friend at latency appeared to be both a screen memory of early yearnings toward the preœdipal mother, as well as being a poignant object attachment and object loss in its own right. Paul remembered lying in a dug-out hole in the dirt of the wilderness at the time when he lived in a mid-Western state. He and his friend, Richard, would fantasize together that the remains of a building they found in their private wilderness was the foot of a giant castle. This was their land of enchantment.

It was a romantic world where friendship and adolescent homosexual love could bloom. The height of their mutual enthrallment arose one quiet summer afternoon, when they lay side by side, and also half on top of one another, inside their dug-out hole, a hole dug out of the direct and the leaves. They didn't speak. They were blissfully at peace. Perhaps at that moment, Paul felt a sublime feeling that he had always yearned for, a sublime feeling that he may never have quite attained in infancy, with a mother who was full of tension and depression. His mother was remembered as hard, and dreams depicted her as a hard stone-like wood tree, or as a seductive, emotionally unavailable, figure. Although Paul's warm, soft, and tender body contact with his male friend could have had aspects of some early breast that was more yielding than the remembered mother, it is also likely that his tranquil contact with his friend could have been the fulfillment of a yearning that had long been aroused and frustrated by his early mother.

Paul's earliest memories of his childhood involved frustrating scenes between himself and his parents. He remembered his parents telling him as soon as he learned to talk that he must stop, hold his breath, and not say anything unless what he wished to express was truly important. Such directives threw Paul, as a toddler, into a tailspin. His urge to speak felt like a gasp that was pushed back into him. His words got all contorted inside. All spontaneous gestures and voice felt arrested. He was stunned and stuck. His excitement to convey his feelings was crushed. He felt as if he was literally forced to swallow his own words. Deep body tensions were set up at this time that made withdrawal backward and inward into himself a reflexive reaction.

Given all this tension about expressing himself in words, it is no wonder that the happiest time of his life was remembered by Paul as this time of tranquil silence as he lay comfortably in body contact with his best friend. When he was then forced away from his friend by the same parents who forced his voice away from him, he felt internally desecrated.

Only later in his analysis did Paul mourn the loss of his friend Richard, and the loss of the kind of quiet contentment that he had so treasured during those few precious moments, those few and precious days. As his grief-laden sadness emerged, alternating with the angry protest against his parents that he had never made during childhood. Paul's potential tenderness was born. This tenderness touched me, as his analyst. He embroidered his memories with the feeling of tender love felt belatedly now in the present. Although on the couch, Paul let me know that tears arose, tears formerly blocked and suffocated. I felt him in his tender tear-filled sadness, and he felt me feeling him, so that a Winnicottian (1971) atmosphere of holding was engendered, from which mourning could continue, as so many poignant times in his childhood were yet to be remembered.

Dreams, as well as memories, emerged during his developmental mourning, and it was at the end of one particular dream that the analyst first became a desired oedipal erotic object. At the end of this dream, in which he rediscovered the warmth of friends who resided within his internal world, Paul transitioned to oedipal dynamics, from the preœdipal.

Finally, Paul found a bench in the wilderness on which all his friends lay piled up together under a blanket. In the dream, he realized that he almost arrived too late. His friends might have frozen to death. Paul might have lost them. He discovered them just in time. He lifted the blanket off them, and his friends greeted him. They kept warm by holding on to each other. He felt their warmth. Once having found them they were free to go. He let them leave, grateful for the contact, and no longer holding them back from moving on with their lives. As they left, a bed appeared where the bench was, and a female friend of Paul's appeared on the bed. He wished for her affection and felt his attraction to her.

In Paul's associations to this dream, he said that at the point when he let his friends go, feeling the contact with them, and keeping their warmth within him, he felt his penis "strengthen." He related this strengthening of himself, within his penis, to an overall strengthening of his sense of self, but also particularly to his sexual self. His associations indicated that he connected his ability to let go of his friends—which allowed the discovery of a woman—to the strengthening of his penis. He understood that he was in danger of freezing his friends and killing them, which would have meant losing them forever because he had frozen them in a moment of time within his memory in order to avoid losing them. He had put them under a blanket, or blanketed them with repression, because he wanted to hold on to them forever.

Just as he found a woman on the bed in his dream, so too in his analysis he began to find the analyst, as an oedipal level sexual object, now that his preœdipal connections had been restored. Although from early on in treatment, Paul could experience erotic feelings toward women in his life, he had kept these feelings split-off from contact with the analyst. He had alluded to wishes to be seen as attractive to the analyst and had feared being repulsive, but he had never felt the force of his own erotic passion. Earlier, he had strengthened his sense of self by restoring his childhood friend Richard to his consciousness, facing the never before faced grief of saying "good-bye."

This made Paul more capable of containing his feelings, and he opened up to his feelings of shame and anger. Now, his ability to say "good-bye" to friends of his later, college, years—friends who, like Richard, also represented preœdipal needs for basic nurturance and affectionate contact—enabled him to acquire a strengthening of his "penis," i.e., of his basic sexual identity. This allowed him to contain erotic feelings, and to open up an erotic transference that had formerly remained latent. The girl he discovered on the bed in his dream became associated with his female analyst.

Paul's Erotic Transference

Up until the time of the mourning process just described, Paul's erotic desires were fixated in sadomasochistic fantasies of being tied down by a woman, and of being made to submit to all kinds of sexually arousing tortures. His fantasies echoed Paul's passive submission to women in his life and to his female analyst. These fantasies were used for masturbation, which became a ritual of re-enacting an enslaved position that Paul inhabited in relation to his mother. His enslaved position in relation to his mother was most chiefly characterized by his inability to say "no" every evening when his mother asked him to go into the kitchen and get "her" ice cream.

One dream highlighted the deeper level of his humiliation. He dreamt that he was forced to sit naked at the dinner table by his mother. He shivered from the cold, felt mortified, as others sat at the table for dinner. Then when someone offered him a blanket to cover himself his mother flew into a rage. Paul's associations revealed that he thought his mother was getting sexual stimulation from his nakedness, and that he felt exploited by her and uncared for. This view of himself as a sexual victim pressed for reenactment, and could have become a resistance to opening up to contact with his analyst, and with his unconsciously oedipal erotic desires. However, significant mourning had allowed Paul to feel that he was strong enough, and sexual enough, to reveal his fantasies to me, rather than to pull me into a covert form of acting out.

Generally, Paul had eroticized his rage toward his mother, and had developed certain characterological patterns. He inverted himself into the role of the victim and controlled others by being controlled. His sexual fantasies, which he cherished and nurtured during his secret masturbation rituals, were filled with this role of erotic victimization. Sometimes one woman tied him up, sometimes three at a time.

Another dream revealed his transference to me as one of these women who intimidated him and even terrified him. The woman in the dream was huge compared to him. He was forced to please her in all kinds of ways that substituted for any kind of sexual intercourse since his penis was too small. The dream revealed his secret terror. When he consciously constructed and controlled his sexual fantasies and sex play, he could turn the terror into erotic thrills. In his dream, he didn't have that control, and much of his emotional withdrawal from me in the clinical situation could be understood in the light of his terrified inhibition and his hidden erotic longings.

With the mourning process proceeding, however, Paul began to emerge from his guilt and shame-ridden cocoon by sharing his masturbation fantasies and dreams with me. As he did so, his size dimensions in relation to mine became more proportionate to his fantasies and associations. His dreams began to reveal all kinds of phallic explosions, and often these dreams were wet dreams.

In one dream, there was a tidal wave of emotion coming in on us from the outside. His emotional longings had to be experienced full force, just like his phallic eruptions, in order that the two could come together. Paul spoke of standing up to the tidal wave and facing the fear. He would face his passion now that he had me by his side.

As Paul's tidal wave of passion came out into the open, leaving the ocean of the unconscious, and coming out into the light of day, he wooed me fiercely. He constantly thought of "lines" to say to me as he entered my office, which he revealed with some degree of embarrassment, testing the waters. Over time, his shame diminished, and his awakening sense of humor became more predominant.

Also during this period, Paul would constantly observe what I wore, waiting to see if I would wear a red dress. If I did, he hoped I wore it specially for him. He found everything I wore exciting! With his secret attraction to me no longer concealed, he opened up all the oedipal erotic desires that seemed to have been rebuffed during his childhood by his "cold tree" mother. His wish for me to wear a red dress, which he considered "sexy," became an ongoing motif in his daily speculations about whether I had dressed that morning with him in mind. Former dreams of being in a bed with a strange woman now turned into dreams of feeling loving and close, feeling that we were becoming intimate with one another.

This period brought dreams and fantasies of me lying beside him in bed, or of me suddenly appearing at his doorstep, and of me coming inside his home to make love to him. He described waking in the morning and imagining me beside him. He wanted to feel the pressure of my body, our tenderness, our caressing. He imagined us sharing our secret flaws together, bonding through the sharing of our shame, revealing the awkward areas in our bodies, evolving an exquisite attunement to each other's entire body surfaces.

The erotic feelings came up directly in our sessions. Paul exclaimed that he felt a full feeling coming up from his "gut and through his penis" while being with me in a session. When we discussed his coming four times a week to work with all the dreams and fantasies that were opening up that ere opening up, Paul felt a kind of sexual ecstasy, believing then that I really wanted him.

Paul wanted me to yearn as intensely for him as he yearned for me. Once upon meeting a young woman he was attracted to, he vividly described to me his pursuit of her, painting a scene for me, which culminated in a sweet, sexual, and prolonged kiss. Not receiving the reaction he expected, he burst out in an uncharacteristic exclamation, which felt as if it was accompanied by the stamping of a foot: "God damn it, I want you to be jealous!" His mother always had been jealous of any girl that he showed interest in. In fact, she would have tantrum-like rages, stamping her feet. He resented this, as it had made him feel overwhelmed with guilt, but now he realized that he wanted me to be jealous.

Mourning the Oedipal Object

Since I had become so vividly painted as Paul's oedipal love, only disappointment and mourning could bring his transition into finding a true love who could be his own. A critical time of growth arrived during my summer vacation, leading to his last year of treatment, his seventh year. Paul reported to me that after my departure, he had woken up in the mornings with the weight of grief that he had never known before. He felt a heavy sadness and wept. His sadness brought the full impact of his realization that I was never going to come to his home, to his bed. I would never be his.

Surrendering to this truth, he emerged from his cocoon in a radical new way. He felt a newfound sense of determination, a willingness to take risks. He joined a dating service, made a video of himself, and within three dates he had met he woman who would become his bride. As he began to date her and to know her, his painting showed his erotic joy, and the mournful colors of his past brightened. His romantic fantasies were replaced by romantic realities that were better than any fantasies could have predicted. His courtship with his fiancé was filled with surprises, gifts, and tender concern and caring.

On Valentine's Day, Paul cancelled one of his analytic sessions (for which he paid) to take his fiancé to a well-known elegant restaurant. In his words, he was determined "to give her royal treatment." It became clear that I had served as a transitional love object, who could be relinquished as I was internalized within him. When Paul later left treatment, he said, "You will be deep inside of me for the rest of my life!" but he also said, "You're no longer the focus of my erotic longings." As his treatment drew to a close, his fiancé was the one who empowered the female figures both in his fantasies and in his artwork. He was now working in an executive-level position in his job, and was also expressing himself in art.

Primarily, at that time, Paul was preparing for a wedding and marriage. His mourning of his analyst was the last stage in an overall developmental mourning process (Kavaler-Adler, 1993a/2013, 1996/2014, 1995, 2004, 2003a, 2003b, 2006a, 2006b, 2013). This mourning process allowed him to open up the full force of his erotic feelings and fantasies, without being held back by shame, repressed anger, and despair as he had once been. It allowed him to feel more whole so that he might face his fear and contain his feelings.

In this way, Paul could collaborate in analysis in order to understand his feelings, rather than being compelled to re-enact his childhood oedipal wishes without self-reflection in treatment. He no longer needed to try to please me or play out the part of a sex slave, with the sexual aspects of the drama hidden. His transference love became a real love, in which he appreciated the real aspects of the relationship with the analyst. Also, by being open to contact with the analyst, myself, he was able to mourn his losses. He opened to formerly blocked-off feelings, which he could integrate into a loving core within him, where he had already installed his childhood friends.

At one point in treatment, Paul had resisted engaging in new relationships with women, as he wished to remain in an exclusive erotic relationship with me. However, he voluntarily brought this up for discussion in his analytic sessions and was able to prepare to mourn me by facing his resistance and letting go. When I left for my summer vacation, in Paul's seventh year of treatment, the grief he felt about having to say "good-bye" to me as an erotic love object came with the growing realization that I could become an internal object within him, which would make him more secure. However, I could not be his real external lover. This gradually enlarging awareness allowed him to let go of me, as he had of his childhood friends, and to move toward a woman who could truly be available to him as a lover and as a wife.

Because Paul had been able to use his analyst as a transitional object, he could choose a wife who was warm, loving, caring, and related, in a way that his former girlfriends had never been. As Paul mourned his childhood friends, let go of negative internal parents, and grieved for the parents who had hurt him, he could take in more good internalizations of the analyst. This allowed him to open up to a new relationship with a woman that could truly fulfill his needs as an adult man.

As Freud first said in his "Observations on Transference-Love" (1915), it is possible for the erotic transference to become the major mobilizing force in favor of this psychoanalytic treatment. However, Paul's willingness to enter the erotic transference in an overt way, and his later willingness to surrender to it, were both facilitated by the mourning of object loss and object disappointment.

Without such mourning, Paul might have ended up sitting forever in the transference glow. In a case reported by Gould (1989), just such a situation was described:

> While some of his feeling may be a reality-based reaction to feeling good and gratitude for the improvements in his life, the uncritical glow I think, also bespeaks, in addition, a transferential halo. I suspect that his current transference resistance may be in his pleasure of basking in the limited intimacy of the therapeutic situation. He can enjoy psychological and emotional closeness that is time-limited each session, and in which concurrent physical intimacy with its attendant anxieties is not possible.

In a discussion of Gould's case (Kavaler, 1989a), I point out how Gould's analysand's resistance might have been related to a failure to mourn the regrets of his past. I speculate that his transference resistance, which was also an erotic transference resistance, was reinforced by defenses against feelings of grief, which would come in relation to the losses due to his own rejections of intimacy with women in his life. Such self sabotaging rejections shad roots in the original mother-son situation, since Gould's patient had to distance to avoid his mother's control and entrapment.

Gould's analysand's resistance to grieving can be contrasted with that of Paul, who was able to consciously confront his resistance to giving up the fantasy of an exclusive bond with the analyst. Paul was able to feel the grief of regret related to his rejections and distancing in relation to women in his past. This allowed him to tolerate the attendant anxieties of intimacy in his life, which Gould states her analysand, Mr. M., still could not do. In Paul's case, his developing capacity to grieve in his treatment, beginning with his grieving the precedipal object, allowed him to remember and grieve each former relationship with women in his life. Paul mourned his own part in creating distance with women who aroused erotic desires in him after he experienced his anger toward these women or their own distancing. Both the anger and the sadness of regret were parts of his mourning process.

Developmental Mourning Journey
in the Lesbian Homoerotic Transference

Karen could only relinquish acting out her erotic transference in her life, with all its self sabotaging devastation when she surrendered to the progressive cycles of developmental mourning within her psychoanalytic Object Relations treatment, where her transference with myself, her female analyst, was particularly intense. It was through Karen's organic affect experience, within the developmental context of mourning, that Karen was able to release old internal object ties so that her analyst could become a transitional object, allowing her to gain new psychological internalizations that could be invested in her current outside relationships.

From the beginning of treatment, I was Karen's muse and demon, or muse demon, within the transference. However, I was also a stable other who she could express all her feelings to. Consequently, Karen could finally have someone to express her many levels of love and sexuality to. In expressing her love to me, Karen spoke of an "ocean of longing." However, the other side of the ocean of longing was the dark, Grand Canyon abyss, or the feared ocean of black swirling fluids emanating from her emotional vortex, within the malnourished psychic area that lacked loving internalizations. In the transference, Karen could allow consciousness of the agony of all her life's experiences of unrequited love, but then she feared endless unfulfilled desire. Karen feared that she would again suffer the agony of intense abandonment, accompanied by terrors of self annihilation. These terrors were all integral components of Karen's psychic state in relation to unrequited love, since her unrequited love for her mother stemmed from the earliest stages of development.

Karen had come into treatment with a script of an anticipated romance based on the sexualization of both preœdipal and oedipal levels of her childhood. She knew I had written well-known books about women artists and writers, so she mentally put me in the category of being like her mother, who was an artist. This was part of what made her crave me and yearn for me. She came into treatment fearing I would stab her in her vagina and in her heart. She had never recovered from the emotional stabbing of her mother's rejection when she was 14 that was precipitated by the report of a summer camp director about her having crushes on women counselors at the camp. Her mother had reacted to the report by immediately withdrawing Karen from the camp. Then, her mother had sat frozen with rage at the home dinner table, sitting like a Medusa mother in Karen's mind, as her mother's cold stony silence at dinner pierced into her.

Both Karen's intense wishes and her morbid terrors were captured within her dreams. In her first dream, I was a female goddess icon—the unconscious muse demon—who floated on her own from above, within the realm of an ornate opera house. I came from high above her, and then I descended into her bed. I had long flowing hair and wore a colorful silk gown. Significantly—in terms of Karen's own bisexual wishes—the dream figure of me that Karen created also had an erect penis. I was the fantasy mother-father-lover, all combined. Like Melanie Klein's mother-father psychic fantasy, which precedes any experience of a differentiated mother and father, I was the muse/demon figure of the archaic preœdipal period, possibly tied into a developmental arrest, due to the failings of her early mother and mothering environment.

In another dream at the beginning of treatment, Karen unzipped her chest. She handed me her heart with a sense of dread, all the time fearing that her heart will be stabbed by me, just as she had felt with her mother, and then with the many other women in both her adolescent and adult years with whom she had fallen in love with. She had to begin to face the empty void within her, which remained after all the adored women rejected her. In relation to me, her female analyst, she feared she would be lost in a Grand Canyon of emptiness, after giving up all her love and desire to me.

In the first year of treatment, Karen's language was somewhat contrived, and her fantasies were like elegantly crafted unconscious scripts. Karen spoke of "spreading my legs" and of "taking my pearl," and she didn't neglect to speak of the wish to "drown in my come" after she penetrated me and gave me an orgasm. The language was explicit. I feel some overall sexual body feeling, which later becomes more body-specific as she reaches the oedipal phase. The countertransference in my body showed the difference in the developmental level. In the beginning, Karen's erotic longings disguised her split of infant longings for nurturance, which she unconsciously displaced onto me through projection in her fantasies. She imagined herself wrapping me in a blanket after sex with me. She spoke of holding me as if she was speaking of holding her own child self. It could be seen here to what degree Karen's adult erotic desires were overlaid with infant longings for nurturance and mothering, as I, as her love object, came to represent her split-off infant self.

I also represented Karen's latent feminine wishes. If, as Karen's analyst, I was not open to hearing these explicitly eroticized desires, I would be blocking the unconscious flow of her developmental longings. I would be blocking the emergence of her split-off and repressed infant self, which needed to grow up and become a receptive feminine self in adult form.

Karen's erotic transference was also accompanied by dreams of oedipal competitions with my husband, or of other triadic relations, where she would join me in being penetrated by my husband. Other times, she would be an extension of my husband, joining him in penetrating me. She could be versatile and playful in her fantasies before she had to face the loss of the fantasy of being both genders at once. Karen spoke of an open skirmish with my husband, while my husband "jealously defended his territory." In other fantasies, she would be an audience in the background, while I had sex with my husband. In her fantasy, she would be cheering me on to have an orgasm.

Then, in the third year of treatment, I became the phallic woman, as in Karen's early dream. Then, I would be felt to penetrate her. This was when Karen was beginning to accept her more receptive and feminine side, after much grief and mourning in which she recalled the narcissistic injuries and rejections of her mother, and of other women.

In the fourth year of treatment, Karen had fantasies of being penetrated by me and a male persona. In this way, she could experience both her desires for her oedipal mother and oedipal father, and could also experience a new gender identification as a woman. Symbolic level associations evolved as she went from sending me long stem roses to telling me her feelings about wanting to send me long red stem roses. Karen's fantasies also developmentally traveled from sexual fantasies of a group of men ravishing her, to fantasies of mutually interactive sex. Simultaneously, in transference fantasies with me in her fifth year, after a vacation, she imagined re-joining me by speaking of my body opening to her "with my vulva opening to her as radiant, glowing flower." Karen was beginning to imagine true surrender rather than dominance and submission. Through the developmental mourning process, she had become a woman. She was no longer secretly an infant in a woman's body.

As Karen expressed her feelings and fantasies directly to me in the moment, our transitional Object Relations analytic bond provided a critical avenue of converting the defensive function of erotic transference into the curative function of integrating with an external Object Relationship. Gradually, over time, Karen saw how the sharing of her fantasies allows her to, not only get to the raw body sensations behind the fantasies, but also to the emotional feelings behind the fantasies. This indicated that she was traveling a developmental route of self and internal world object development, and not just defensively operating out of an eroticization of potential affects within the transference.

By sharing her emerging erotic fantasies, Karen came out of a sealed-off state, or out of a closed system, within her mind. She traveled beyond her earlier mental state, where fantasies were only masturbatory, as they had been when she was distancing form being present in her life with the woman whom she had committed to within a primary love relationship. As Karen shared her fantasies of me with me, and as she opened her heart and vagina in a concert of object desires, Karen gained access to an external Object Relationship with me. Consequently, she could become increasingly present with others, and most particularly with her female lover, with whom she had had a deep and abiding marriage, a marriage that had been filled with both friendship and love for over 17 years.

Aggression and Negative Transference

Working with the erotic transference also means working with aggression, as well as with negative transference. Sometimes, the aggression is eroticized, as when Karen would scream in her sessions: "I want to throw you against the wall and fuck you!" when she was angry at me. To interpret this, I had to strike when the iron was cold, not when it was hot (Pine, 1985), because, at the moment of aggressive intensity, Karen had regressed. Consequently, she was not hearing my words at a symbolic level. Later, Karen could hear about the feeling of disappointment or rejection that was behind her rage. Then, she could have linking associations back to memories of how hurt and rejected she had felt by her mother, and by other women.

The best time to interpret with Karen was when she felt loss, relinquishing with heavy grief the aspired to loves of her past. At times of grief, tolerating loss, and contacting her potential renewal of love through the tolerance of loss, Karen could hear me speak about her motives, and about her experiences. At those times, Karen was in touch with her internal self, and was not defensively stuck in her focus on me as an object of her projections and projective identification. In Melanie Klein's terms, she was in a depressive position state of mind, rather than in a paranoid-schizoid state of mind (Klein, 1940).

As Karen worked through mourning her memories from the past, she could hear transference interpretations. Then, it was time for me to move from being a container for her deepest psychophysical expressions of love, hunger, and vaginal desire, to the interpretation of how her feelings toward me extended back to her mother, and were part of an erotic mother transference.

When I first began interpreting this, Karen did experience it with shock and with a feeling of rejection. She expressed much rage toward me, such as when I told her that her wanting to hug me was a wish for a mother's hug. Even though she did reveal her more vulnerable child self to me when on the couch, wishing to be in my lap, and wishing to have me stroke her hair, Karen responded with shock and rage when I first began to interpret her mother transference. She wanted to have me as a muse and lover, which had to be addressed as major manic defenses, although such transferences had earlier developmental transference implications. Karen's aggression could be contained in the treatment. Then her grief could be felt and processed so that she could move on in her life. She began to bring her more conscious loving self fully into her relationship with her external life love, her lesbian lover. Her oedipal longings then also emerged toward men as father figures, which was later interpreted.

Chapter 13

Opening Potential Space

During the first years of treatment, Karen had had "great difficulty" coping with the highly visceral body experiences that accompanied her reports of her sexual fantasies. In fact, as she spoke of more of the early tender loving fantasies, she would become dizzy or suffocated, choking on highly vulnerable emotions of love and tenderness. Sometimes she had to sit up when lying on the couch, just to breathe because too much intense emotion was coming up at once.

As Karen opened to her breathing, I would also breathe in, intuitively sensing that this would allow Karen potential psychic space to spontaneously say the words of love after experiencing the anguish of her three year old separation trauma. Gradually, Karen could feel, and simultaneously express, her feelings in words. So, her somatic discomfort lessened. Then she could have her desires increasingly contained in differentiated words.

Karen said later, during her fourth and fifth years of analysis, that when she sent me flowers, she was regressing to an early psychic place, a child's place where words never adequately expressed feelings. Only an image or symbolic gift could express her feelings.

Karen had to bring her erotic fantasy level into conjunction with her sensory arousal on the couch when she described her love for me. She enacted the love by sending me long stem roses from a flower shop, and within this enactment was a seduction meant to ward off her feared retaliatory mother's aggression. Karen's mother had always been offended by her feelings, and had turned cold as Medusa toward her when she found out about Karen's homosexual leanings during her teen years. As Karen proceeded through her developmental mourning process in treatment, I was able to interpret the symbolic messages in the earlier enactment of sending me long stem roses from the flower shop. Karen agreed enthusiastically when I said that she could be both a man in being the agent of courting me with flowers, and could also be a woman in her identification with the flowers as representing the feminine vaginal core opening. She totally agreed with my interpretation at a time when she had advanced to being aware of her own interpretations and motives, now being able to verbally express her one to one intimate desire for me as a love object, without the former oedipal transference triangles she had in her sexual fantasies.

Through mourning a lifetime of losses with me as a psychic container for her sitting behind the psychoanalytic couch, Karen's own psychic fantasies became better containers for her feelings that had formerly been repressed with the pain of unrequited love. In the mourning process, Karen opened to her primal longings for the first time, and she offered them to me verbally.

On the couch, Karen would express deep sensory hunger and desire: "I want you so much right now. ... I'm feeling this feeling in my vagina, wanting you." It would be very much in the moment, not hidden behind a defensive screen of sexualized fantasies in which the hunger and yearnings would be hidden by her actions, as if in a movie script. Now, especially by the third year, she was truly present. As I opened my breath, Karen risked more vulnerability. Only when she could express these feelings directly could she describe her erotic transference fantasies without splitting them off into compulsive activities and obsessive thinking outside the sessions.

Early on, when she was still in the idealizing erotic transference, with me as her idealized muse mother, Karen needed me to receive her instinctual cravings, and her affect yearnings. I was a Wilfred Bionian psychic container (Bion, 1970/1988), not yet interpreting, but processing what I felt so I could interpret later. It was important for me to receive these expressions of Karen's feelings without interpreting at that time. Karen needed to feel that both her love and her aggression could be accepted by me. In D.W. Winnicott's sense (Winnicott, 1971), she needed to know I survived her impulses and passions, just as Paul needed to know that I could help him survive his passions as they emerged from his unconscious as an "ocean," similar to Karen's "ocean of longing."

I contained and survived Karen's passions, but her negative transference emerged in interaction with her erotic transference, because, as her analyst, I had to inevitably disappoint her as I was not responding to her expressions of love as a lover. Consequently, she experienced me as rejecting her oedipal wishes, which had in part served as a defense against precedipal rejection. Such disappointments, expressed at tolerable levels in treatment, led Karen to tolerate loss by tolerating painful grief affect, as she evolved into an overall mourning process.

Through feeling the pain of loss and traumatic rejection, Karen could also articulate fantasies that showed the double edge sides of her primal cravings to merge with me, and to have erotic desire be the fuel toward this precedipal merger. This is captured in the fantasy she articulated to me of wishing to inhabit a special place in my vagina, which she would get to through her phallic penetration of me. She was still imagining me to have a penis, as in her dream of me floating down from above in a large vault ceiling Opera House. However, the fantasy flipped to the underbelly of unconscious fear as she then imagined a vortex of black swirling fluids inside of me—like the Grand Canyon—that would swallow me up. Karen's double-edged desire, as well as her conflicting fear, resonated with the same erotic wish versus terror scenario, in one of my male patient's fantasies.

In fact, Phillip (see Kavaler-Adler 2003a) imagined entering me through sexual penetration of my vagina. He unconsciously longed to enter my womb, but the longing flipped to the dark side of the associated terror. Once in my womb, Phillip pictured becoming lost and entrapped in a railway tunnel, which morphs into a labyrinth of endless avenues to nowhere: obviously one form of vagina dentata fantasy.

Karen's fantasy of desire for me as a womb (part object) mother flipped to the dark side each time I failed to instantly reciprocate her wishes. However, her conscious protests could be more clearly understood through the vivid illustration of her unconscious fantasy, as it emerged into consciousness through her free associations on the couch—echoing a beginning treatment dream of being trapped in the waters underneath a swimming pool.

If I didn't mirror her desire with my own, thus failing to be the fantasy lover, I would automatically become the sadistic withholding mother of "unrequited love." Nevertheless, with the container of the holding environment of psychoanalytic treatment, Karen could feel her rage and disappointment. Then, she could ultimately surrender to the grief of loss that allowed her to be reborn through connecting with her inner self, with her internal world, and with those external others in her interpersonal world.

The developmental evolution of mourning in psychoanalytic treatment helps to create a safe analytic space to contain the erotic transference in treatment. Simultaneously, disappointments in erotic transference wishes also open up progressive cycles of grief and mourning. Subsequently, these cycles of developmental mourning work, and erotic transference work, interact (Kavaler-Adler, 2003a). The working through of erotic transference fantasies involves a natural evolution of mourning, in which sadomasochistic fantasies transform into mutually interpenetrating dimensions, which are truly erotic.

With each transference disillusionment, Karen relived the experience of unrequited love, and mourned the related self and object loss. Consequently, it was through mourning that she regained parts of herself that had formerly been trapped in old psychic attachments (see Fairbairn, 1952).

During the third year of treatment, Karen became more whole, and thus became more able to deal with all kinds of mourning. She ultimately processed bereavement mourning for both her dead parents. This involved Karen's regrets that she couldn't have been there more for her aging parents, due to her unresolved anger. However, with mourning her losses, and expressing her rage in treatment, and defining her anger, a natural state of forgiveness opened up in Karen, toward her parents. Karen had mourned the loss from the disruption of her developing self, when assaulted by her mother's narcissistic attacks and abandonments. She also faced the rage she felt toward other women, and toward a former male husband of hers, with whom she had lost parts of herself.

In treatment, Karen could mourn the separation losses that she carried with her, which were consciously relived within her transference. She felt rage, hurt, and loss each time there was a loss in the connection with me—whether due to actual gaps in treatment related to vacations that separated us—or due to her own anger, which she often expressed by pushing me away and creating the loss of engagement.

Karen processed all the levels of developmental mourning. She separated, differentiated, and found her way to creating her own unique, bisexual identity. In addition, Karen processed the grief of bereavement, since the death of her parents had occurred.

In addition to separation loss and bereavement loss, Karen processed her oedipal level mourning in relation to me within the transference. Then, she processed the mourning of a male mentor who had served as an oedipal love object. She found herself fantasizing that her male mentor would marry her. As Karen mourned, and as she became someone who knew she was making interpretations, Karen also began to view my interpretations quite differently than earlier in treatment. Before, she had found interpretations from me, as her analyst, to feel like rejections only. But later, she began to value the insight she gained through interpretations. In fact, she began to describe my interpretations as "gifts of insight." She became a full psychoanalytic companion on the analytic developmental journey.

A highly significant treatment phenomena, in terms of developmental progress toward the depressive position capacity to symbolize, is shown in the concrete protosymbolic action of giving a romantic gift, versus the evolution toward expressing love and desire in symbolic terms. In a journal article (Kavaler-Adler 2003b), I laser focus on this critical example of progression within erotic transference, as the journey from eroticization of affect to true erotic desire, which is combined with heartfelt love, evolves. Karen relinquished her protosymbolic action of sending me beautiful long-stem red roses from a flower shop. She reached a symbolic level though mourning, and consequently began to express her flowering "red rose" type feelings for me in words. Her erotic desires became thoughts with feelings, as opposed to either actions or delusional beliefs of consummating love with me.

Karen's words became alive to her with all the nuances of core heartfelt affect, which became combined with erotic desire. In fact, Karen's words became authentically integrated with feeling level reality, the reality of the true internal self. Both metaphor and symbolism came alive. Karen's word came into poetic form in the spontaneity of the moment, the moment that can only be felt by the true internal feeling self. The eroticism was no longer sexualization, but rather became authentic desire, which joined the heart and the mind in words. And further, such words served as symbolic mental containers for all the erotic body sensations. Consequently, the erotic desire and transference did not have to be enacted to be felt.

The developmental evolution was seen in the fourth year of Karen's treatment, after she was separated from me during my vacation. Karen greeted me upon my return with the following words, which resonated with authentic erotic desire, without being compelled to try and seduce me with a contrived script, as she had done in her first years of treatment. Karen said: "I see myself entering your open vagina with your beautiful vulva and clitoris opening like a flower, glowing, radiant and receptive." We can see how different this language was than Karen's earlier language of "drowning in my come," and "taking my pearl." The words were now spontaneous, in the moment of feeling, no longer being contrived in a stereotypic way. Also significant is that there were no longer any euphemisms for vulva and clitoris like "pearl."

In this culminating phase of Karen's treatment, my sexual body was all out there in Karen's mind: living, evocative, inviting, and no longer visualized through the confines of a mental script. This was all part of the movement from the protosymbolic to the symbolic level, which began with Karen experiencing great compulsion to actually send me long stem roses from the florist. Hanna Segal was the first to theorize about those arrested in the protosymbolic in her writing on the symbolic equation (Segal, 1986). When Karen could relinquish sending me concrete roses, and could speak of her flowering feelings and flowering image of my feminine body, she had transitioned to full symbolic expression.

As the depressive position mourning process evolved, Karen mourned the disillusionment with her idealized mother. She mourned the self loss that she had repressed when constantly, through her life, she had been confronted with unrequited love. Karen mourned by feeling her grief related to hostile attacks on me, as she had formerly projected her cold internal mother onto me, as well as also experiencing some of my actual coldness, as well as her own. The therapeutic action of psychoanalytic Object Relations work with erotic transference results in Karen arriving at the point of true, sublimated, symbolic level interpenetration with me, her analyst, and within herself, as she developed the capacity for psychic dialectic. Karen came to accept her separateness, and her ability to re-connect in an authentic way, as mutuality and symbolic communication have emerged beyond sadomasochism, just as in the case of Paul.

Since Karen and Paul were able to access their erotic transference desires, I did not need to have these desires for them, while they were repressed, as Gabbard (1992, 1994) writes about a supervisee having felt for her patient in her countertransference. Nor did I have homoerotic fantasies as a response to the homoerotic transference of my patient, as Joyce McDougall writes of having in her book, ***The Many Faces of Eros*** (1998). Throughout the treatment with Karen, I only conceptualized heterosexual fantasies, but I did feel erotic arousal in one session late in her analysis, when Karen was fully at the oedipal level of development, as well as having her mature adult homosexuality.

The Oedipal Male Neurotic's Erotic Transference Dynamics

With a neurotic man, who I will call Leonard, I listened to him admit that he was trying not to think of me when he was having sex with his wife, because he didn't want to have to talk about his fantasies with me. He referred to wishes to be loved by me as being associated with his loving, but somewhat seductive mother. He would openly speak about feeling attracted to me, but tried to avoid full consciousness of his fantasies. He openly acknowledged the transferential link back to his mother, as he spoke of his attraction to me. Leonard also spoke of his experience of closeness to his mother in childhood, which naturally made the loss of his mother, when she died, extremely painful. He spoke of missing his mother every day of his life. He surrendered to the profound depth of his grief as he lay on the couch. This carried over to intense grief for a sibling who had died, and to grief for losing the connection to his entire family as he grew increasingly successful in his career.

Leonard's vivid and enduring success transformed his whole belief system into one of conflict with his family's views. As he separated from his family through developing his own beliefs and his own achievements in the world, Leonard felt the painful anguish of losing a feeling of intimacy with his family. In treatment with me, he would grieve both the literal and metaphoric separation from his family. He would also feel the anguish of those actually lost to him through death. One day, in the middle of all this, Leonard said: "I'm distracted by your boots." He smiled. He said he was always trying not to be distracted by my sexuality, and he admitted he was cutting off thoughts about me when having sex with his wife. But he said he couldn't stop looking at my tall black boots, with their patent leather design over leather. Leonard then declared that he could see me as a dominatrix, and he could imagine himself kissing my boots and submitting to me, to be in the embrace of my power, to be loved by the "goddess."

Through his willingness to share these fantasies, we could finally get to his wish to return to a position with his mother, where he would feel safe and powerful through her, rather than having to put himself out in the world, and having to risk sharing his own original beliefs with others. This would keep him safely in the "cult" of his family, where he would ward off feelings of loss. The other side of this was his wanting to individuate more, and he was giving professional presentations at his corporate job for the first time. Through all this, Leonard began to acknowledge that he was blocking a natural process form happening, when he cut off his thoughts about me during sex. He said he would now try to be open to those thoughts, and risk sharing them with them, so that we could understand more about his desires and fears.

This led to Leonard telling me that the sadomasochistic fantasy of submission to me as a dominatrix was actually a cover fantasy, defending him against a more basic desire to kiss me and to make love to me with great pleasure. He said he had let himself have this fantasy when making love to his wife, but that in being in the room with me, and telling the fantasy to me, he felt his fear of falling deeply in love with me, and of then feeling intense frustration, even more than he felt now, because he knew we couldn't really make love. My role as a transitional object can be seen as this statement then led Leonard to loving memories of his mother and of her warmth. This opened Leonard to another phase of mourning the loss of his mother to whom he knew he had been very special. He could then work more with his intense conflict of wanting to be a little boy again with his mother, and wishing to act that out with me.

Leonard knew that his wish to act out being a loved little boy with me was his attempt to deny his mother's death. He knew such wishes were in conflict with wanting to be a fully grown man with me. as well as with his wife. However, being a grown man meant experiencing the frustrations of his wife's lack of warmth. It meant conscious suffering of his wife's frequent emotional unavailability, which contrasted with his more emotionally related mother. With me, his female analyst, Leonard could feel a warm communication, and also appreciate the boundaries that would protect him from being overwhelmed by frustration, and from being unfaithful to his wife. As Leonard spoke of his desire for me, he increasingly surrendered to mourning the loss of his mother. He experienced anger as well as sadness in mourning his mother. Leonard's mother had been both seductive and stimulating toward his developing sexuality, while simultaneously being angry and disapproving toward his developing sexuality.

I felt more affect with Leonard, and with other oedipal level men, than I had when I first treated Paul. Even when Paul was having fantasies of me showing up at his house to become his lover—and even when he spoke of fantasies of us becoming intimate lovers, who would be familiar with each other's body oddities and idiosyncrasies—I had felt his tenderness, without feeling the level of love and loss I was now feeling with Leonard. But also, with the oedipal men, I was aware that their desire for me would quickly lead to psychoanalytic associations back to memories of their mothers. Phillip for example, imagined seeing my legs as a direct lead in to a memory of seeing his mother with her legs spread open in a bathing suit, when he was eight years old. He imagined entering my vagina and then my womb through the space between my legs. However, he was clear in his knowledge that these were early little boy yearnings toward his childhood mother. I was not needed as a transitional erotic object with Leonard and Phillip as I was developmentally so needed by Paul. Yet, for all three men, their erotic thoughts about me led to a meaningful developmental mourning process that helped each to self integrate and individuate, while also offering them insight into their unconscious wishes and fears.

This link between the erotic desires and the transitional object role—and between erotic desires and transference repetitions leading to meaningful self integrative mourning—distinguishes the therapeutic action of these Object Relations treatments from classical cases. The theoretical interpretation of classical analytic cases, and from ego psychological cases, would tend to emphasize erotic transferential thoughts as being resistance and defense. The differences between these Object Relations perspectives and relational school cases will be touched on in the summary.

Homoerotic Transference in Heterosexual Women

Burch (1996) has written about the rare case in the literature of a female analyst and a female patient, in relation to erotic transference. In the case of Karen, I wrote about the lesbian female patient with the female analyst. I also have written about cases of homoerotic transference in heterosexual women whom I have worked with. I will share one case today.

It is interesting that a heterosexual woman's homoerotic desires for a female analyst can emerge in an analysis as a negative oedipal dynamic, prior to the full heterosexual transference emerging with men and father figures in the world outside the treatment room. This phase of homoerotic transference also generally emerges during the precedipal developmental mourning process in which primal separation from the early mother ensues (Kavaler-Adler, 2003a). The homoerotic attraction can serve certain transitional object functions.

As I have written about in my 2003 book, ***Mourning, Spirituality, and Psychic Change: A New Object Relations View of Psychoanalysis***, the heterosexual woman that I named June passed through an important transitional stage period of homoerotic transference. Prior to this phase, there had been a phase of sadomasochistic fantasies, related to a demon-lover figure, who symbolized the hardness and domination of her actual father. Images of this demon-lover figure were mixed in with June's erotic desires, including desires to be whipped, which she experienced after her husband introduced her to some pornography.

Following June's very contrived fantasizing about being masochistically submissive to a sadistic male who dominated by whipping her, June began to open to more natural, and less contrived fantasies related to her erotic, rather than eroticized desires. These homoerotic fantasies manifested in the transference, on the way to her later heterosexual desires. Such a phase of homoerotic desires is often called a negative oedipal period, when viewed in a Freudian framework, but such labeling doesn't account for the transitional object function of the psychoanalyst who is of the same gender. It also doesn't account for the depth of desire, as well as love, that can be felt in this context.

June had intense wishes to be emotionally close to me, which were accompanied by her physical attraction to me, and ultimately by her wishes to make love to me. At first, June spoke of her attraction to me, and to all female bodies that she saw as representing my body. She said to me at this transitional stage: "There's something Latin about you. You're really out there with your sexuality. You're not like other therapists who seem so drab and dull. The way you dress is so colorful, and you really show your legs!" There was a partial merger with me in this sexual attraction. June was beginning to experience her sexuality through imagining my embodied being, and both identifying with it and desiring it. She told me about a dream that she thought of as related to both me and her, not differentiating who was who. She said: "I'm not sure if it was you or me, but someone had their dress up over their head." This dream also expressed June's two sided wish and fear that sex could get out of control.

June progressed from revulsion with the female body—stemming back to memories of her father's sexually assaulting comments to her mother when he was drunk—to great attraction to the female body. This is when June began to speak of intensely desiring me. She told me that she found herself looking at female bodies, and finding them more attractive than the male body. This would later change, but at this time I was the center of her homoerotic desire, and I served as a transitional object—not just as a transference object. At this time, June could give life to her desires by focusing them on me, and by communicating them to me. This allowed June to symbolize her desires, and the body impulses related to such desires. Through such symbolic communication, she contained her desires.

It became very personal and intimate as she spoke to me, saying: "I didn't want to offend you, so I didn't tell you that when I looked at all these female bodies, and found them fascinating, I was thinking of you." June then told me that she imagined me encouraging her sexuality in the world. She said that this was in contrast to her mother's and father's continuous assaults upon her developing sexuality. She pictured me saying: "Get out there and go dancing!"

June's own expressions here were indicative of the transitional role I played as both an object of desire, and as an alter ego who could lend her the inspiration of my own sexuality and of my own life energy. In fact, I was a positive muse figure, in contrast to the demon-lover muse figure of her father and the devalued feminine, sexual victim figure, of her mother.

Also at this stage in her eight-and-a-half-year treatment—around the third year—June told me that she imagined making love to women in magazines, as well as imagining the erotic possession of women on the street. She said that she knew these women were just stand-ins for me in her mind, but in her words, she didn't want to "disrespect me," so she displaced her desires. However, as June became emboldened by telling me of these fantasy attractions, she also began to admit her erotic desires that were directly focused on me. In fact, she proclaimed: "The erotic transference may be the best part of analysis. I always resisted it." It was at this time that June and I analyzed a sleepiness she began to feel on the couch, in her sessions, as her desire to make love to me as a woman, and also as her wish to be a man with an erection, who was making love to me.

Even after June moved toward heterosexual fantasies, she still had an intense homoerotic desire to be close to me, with sex merely as a vehicle for the closeness and tenderness. She said: "Wouldn't it be great if we were two gay women? Then we could have a special love together that would be even more special than the love between a man and a woman. I like to fantasize that my love for you could be made even more special if we could be together as two gay women." As we moved into through the third and fourth years of treatment, June said she felt deeply touched by me. In fact, she cried deeply, and said that she experienced such joy that she felt like she had an endless flow of love going through her. I asked if it was sexual, and she said "Oh yes, sexual, very sexual! I feel my whole body open up and tingle when I hear you speak."

June's body excitement operated at a protosymbolic level until she put it into words, which she did after I asked her about sexual feelings. This can be done both through the transference, and through the therapeutic Object Relationship, which has a transitional object trajectory. The developmental mourning process, which I have described in so much of my work, is a psychological avenue for this transition, as the relinquishment of the old forms of eroticized attachment make way for the higher level erotic attachment, as part object experience transforms into whole object experience.

June's psychological journey can be seen as progressive cycles of such developmental mourning affect, accompanied by the progressive developmental symbolizing of experience (more full case Kavaler-Adler, 2003a, 2006). These cycles become phases of developmental mourning, in which sensory and visceral experience can be brought to the symbolic level of articulated psychic fantasy. The affects of sadness and grief, anger and rage, and of love and tenderness, become differentiated object related experience, along the path of developmental mourning. I have published many cases that illustrate this, including important cases that pertain to male analysands, such as the case of Paul described here, and the case of Phillip described in "Mourning, Spirituality and Psychic Change..." (Kavaler-Adler, 1992c, 2003a).

Contrast with the Theory of Erotic Transference Work Described by Relational Psychoanalysts

I will compare my views about working for therapeutic action with erotic transference with the relational approach described in a clinical article by Dr. Jody Davis (1994) and with some of the commentary on the Davis paper by Dr. Irwin Hoffman (1998). The clinical article appeared in the **Psychoanalytic Dialogues** journal and is entitled: "Love in the Afternoon" (Davis, 1994). I am choosing to discuss this paper because it has been used in the world of relational psychoanalysis education as a model for doing work with erotic transference. I will not be comparing my approach with other relational theorists. Also, I will say that a case vignette with erotic transference by Dr. Galit Atlas in a book authored by her and Dr. Lewis Aron, **Dramatic Dialogues**, seems closer to my viewpoint of Object Relations erotic transference work than does the case by Jody Davis, which has been lauded as a prominent example of a paradigmatic shift in theory making (Kuhn's [1962] critical mass change that suddenly revolutionizes old paradigms of theoretical thought).

To begin with, Jody Davis claims that she is focusing on her patient's adult sexuality without referring to childhood repetitions or developmental avenues toward psychic change. In the cases I have discussed of "Mourning and Erotic Transference" and "Lesbian Homoerotic Transference," the male heterosexual patient and the female homosexual and bisexual patient were developing their adult sexuality during the later phases of treatment, but their unconscious transference dynamics were all rooted in childhood, as in the other cases I discuss in this paper as well.

Dr. Davis is dealing with oedipal level transference, which may give bloom to the blossoms of adult sexual desire. However, in my psychoanalytic view, she is certainly not just a woman to her patient. She is a transferential mother, as she herself attests to when she compares her countertransference sexual attraction to her male patient with the erotic feelings she presumes the patient's mother may have held for him but did not openly express. Through such an analogy, Davis then gives herself permission to express her erotic attraction to her patient. She implies that this is her way to challenge her patient to face his developing sexuality.

I would respond to this rationale for her clinical disclosure with a brief report of a former female patient of mine, who came into treatment after a profound and dramatic countertransference acting out of erotic desires by an older male psychoanalyst. In that case, the male analyst's open declarations of erotic desire for the female analysand actually created a massive psychological block within the young woman analysand. Following the male analyst's declaration of his desire for her, the female analysand became totally inhibited in the expression of any sexual desire for her male analyst. In relation to this, Dr. Davis's confession of desire for her male analysand seemed to demand a reciprocal declaration of desire for her by her male analysand, rather than allowing for a free flow of unconscious thoughts, feelings, and fantasies from her male analysand.

So it appears in the case of Dr. Davis, that even if her patient wasn't threatened by the open expression of her own desire for him, or by a demand for a reciprocal response, the analysand will no longer be psychologically situated in a free analytic process, where she can initiate the session through that which emerges from within her or his internal world, and from her or his unconscious dimensions of that internal world. I propose that even if inhibition, withdrawal, or merely resistance don't result in blocking the patient, the analysis will still become skewed toward reflecting the internal world of the psychoanalyst, and toward the unconscious of that analyst, as opposed to being an evolution of the patient's mind in treatment—with all the body feeling that the mind's evolution in treatment may entail.

In his discussion of Davis's paper, Dr. Irwin Hoffman is enthralled by the "poetic" nature of Jody Davis' descriptions. I would reply to this enthrallment by stating that the primary poetry that we should be concerned with as psychoanalysts is that coming from the patient rather than that coming from the analyst. In the cases that evolved and blossomed within my practice of working with erotic transference, beautiful and romantic poetry often emerged from the analysand, or patient, as the patient's erotic desires emerged into consciousness. Plenty of examples of this could be seen in the cases of Mr. L. and Pauline in my journal articles of "Mourning and Erotic Transference" (Kavaler-Adler, 1992a) and "Lesbian Homoerotic Transference in Dialectic with Developmental Mourning..." (Kavaler-Adler, 2003b), or in the case of June in my book, "Mourning, Spirituality ad Psychic Change..." (Kavaler-Adler 2003a).

The psychoanalyst's poetry can be motivated by the patient's romantic oedipal transference, which generally involves the patient sustaining an idealized transference of the analyst. In my opinion, the psychoanalyst needs to take care to not be distracted from a clinical focus on the patient's unconscious conflicts around her/his sexuality, and from the patient's conflicts around the integration of love and sexuality that constellate within the core impulses of erotic desire. The analyst needs to sustain a focus on the emotional Object Relations that extend beyond silent or hidden fantasies all along the way.

Further, in relation to Dr. Irwin Hoffman's declaration that Jody Davis is illustrating how relational analysis is curing the classical analytic situation of its arthritic technique, I have much to say. In reading Hoffman's discussion, Hoffman appears to be trumpeting out his declaration that in traditional analysis the analyst is "dead," while the patient exposes vulnerable erotic desires. One can't miss Hoffman's angry retaliatory attitude within such statements. Hoffman practically declares the analytic situation to be a sexual abuse crime scene when he declares that the analyst is "dead" in his/her body when the patient is risking the vulnerability of exposing alive desire for the analyst.

There are several problems with Hoffman's declaration in my opinion. First, Hoffman is assuming that the analyst is emotionally dead, just because the analyst is listening to the patient, and is trying to understand the meaning of what the patient is saying. Hoffman appears to not believe that analytic listening is an alive activity, an activity that is alive in both the body and mind of the psychoanalyst. I would propose that it is generally when the analyst is narcissistic that her/his limitations in listening to the "other" would require open confessions of her/his feelings and fantasies to keep the analyst feeling awake and alive. It is quite a dramatic and provocative statement by a psychoanalyst to propose that when analysts are silent that proves that they are dead inside. This seems to be the assumption behind Hoffman's viewpoint, as expressed in his discussion of the Jody Davis paper.

Obviously, I disagree with Hoffman. I know that when I listen to the erotic feelings, thoughts, fantasies, and dreams of a patient, I feel the full impact of their desires in my whole body/mind psychophysical being. However, my goal is to understand the underlying symbolic meaning of the patient's wishes, fears, and conflicts, so that patients can become increasingly free to express love and intimacy within the realm of the potential erotic relations in their life in the world. I am working actively in my mind to do this, while also understanding where the patients are coming from by feeling the projected aspects of their desires as I feel and temporarily introject them to be able to analyze the patient. If I were emotionally dead in the treatment room, I couldn't do any of this, nor could I have written about the erotic transferences of my patients as I have done repeatedly in articles and book chapters.

I am an Object Relations analyst, so I add my awareness of my internal world into the equation of processing the internal experience of the patient/analysand. In this way, I consciously define for myself, and for the patient (now or later), what is being deflected or projected ("put into") into me, from the patient. All of this psychological processing ("processing of projective identifications," Bion's "alpha function") creates an active, resiliently alive process, which accompanies the traditional role of the analyst listening for transference/resistance/defense material, and is absolutely necessary to help the patient construct their authentic awareness, and for the defining differentiation of the patient's potential subjective experience, and for the overall evolution of a "true self" (Winnicott, 1960).

Consequently, the psychoanalyst is far from "dead," but is, on the contrary, an evolving container and processor of the patient's potential subjectivity, and of the extension of subjectivity within the moment, into an evolving authentic, integrated, differentiated, separated, and existentially true being, rather than being compulsively shaped into a contrived image self.

Therefore, regarding Hoffman's accusations of deadness, I would say that it is only the analyst who is compelled to disclose her/his own erotic desires and fantasies, related to the patient, who might be suffering from internal deadness. I propose that it is the analyst who carries a degree of deadness into the treatment room who is the one more apt to rationalize self disclosure—particularly of erotic desire—as being in the service of the patient.

Conclusion
Mourning to Contain the Erotic Transference, as Opposed to Eroticized Enactment

When the affects of developmental mourning, and the memories and symbolization that can come from the subjective experience of these affects in the treatment room, emerge and are expressed, the psychoanalytic clinician sees a developmental journey toward true erotic desire and true erotic transference. This is in contrast to seeing an eroticized enactment, which wards off the deepest/unconscious childhood need (dependence) in the patient. As seen in many of my writings on erotic transference, and particularly in the cases of Mr. L. (Kavaler-Adler, 1992a) and Pauline (Kavaler-Adler, 2003b) as well as Laura (Kavaler-Adler, 2003a), which correspond to the cases in this paper of Paul and Karen, we see the developmental mourning process evolve within clinical work.

It has been demonstrated in case vignettes—related to my published cases— that this developmental mourning process allows for the ultimate containment of the deepest erotic desires. In parallel with this development, there is an organic evolution of a capacity: to love, to create, to feel concern and compassion, and for agency, for interiority, and for a growing capacity for psychic dialectic between the parts of oneself. Without the developmental evolution of developmental mourning, the patient can remain stuck in perpetual splitting, continuously resulting in polarized and dissociated beta elements in an undifferentiated and unintegrated psyche.

Once contained in the therapist/patient dyad, constituting a holding environment, the patient's erotic desires—as well as aggressive impulses—can be symbolized in dreams, fantasies, and words. Such desires—with their earlier precedent of oral cravings—can then be understood and analyzed by the psychoanalyst; as demonstrated in Karen's transition from sending large vases of red stem roses to the female analyst, to the time when she could put the feelings represented in the concrete roses into the symbolic language of poetic words. A poetic evolution of erotic desires was seen in this case. Such clinical transition, with developmental evolution, becomes possible as the analyst plays the role of a transitional erotic object, as I did for Paul and Karen, as well as Leonard and Phillip. It can also be seen evidenced in these case vignettes, which have longer descriptions in my published books and journal articles, that eroticized enactments are transformed into full emotional poetry through the developmental avenue of the mourning process in treatment, related to primal level losses.

I propose that it is the mourning process that plays the most significant affective role in the transition from the protosymbolic enactments to the symbolic level mentalized communications. Without the Object Relations therapeutic action of a developmental mourning process (Kavaler-Adler, 1992c, 1993a/2013, 1995, 1996/2014, 2003a, 2003b, 2004, 2005b, 2006a, 2007c, 2018), the eroticized protosymbolic enactments could have derailed the treatment away from psychoanalytic work. This is not accounted for by classical analysts or ego psychologists.

PART THREE:

OTHER CLINICAL TECHNIQUE PAPERS

AN OBJECT RELATIONS APPROACH TO DREAMS: FROM PROTOSYMBOLIC TO SYMBOLIC, IN DREAM CONTENT AND WITHIN THE THERAPEUTIC OBJECT RELATIONSHIP

Originally published in 2015, *MindConsiliums* 15(11):1–27.

The content and process of Object Relations work with dreams can be considered in terms of developmental progressions, from dissociation and body disconnection to body connection and self integration in relation to whole object representations. The growth from body disconnection to body connection can be seen in the content of dreams and can be seen to follow a parallel developmental path to that of sustained connection within the therapeutic Object Relationship (Grunes, 1984). Further, there are parallel developmental paths seen through dreamwork and treatment, in relation to symbolism vs. protosymbolism, whole object representations vs. dynamic internal part objects, as well as growth from patient enactments in therapeutic sessions, in which dreams are presented—to associative dialectics between patient and analyst.

Once the associative dialectic can be established within the dreamwork, the patient has achieved the depressive position level of an interpreting subject (Ogden, 1986), which encompasses self-reflective capacities and observing ego capacities. As we look at these developmental progressions through dream content and therapeutic dream process, we need to consider the opening of potential space (Ogden, 1986) along with the analyst's object survival of primitive aggression. We need to consider the development of self and object intrapsychic dialectic, which allows for a critical developmental mourning process to proceed, as opposed to fused and sadomasochistic constellations of self and object. We need also to consider the development of the capacity for concern (Winnicott, 1963), which is another avenue of growth as whole Object Relations develop through successful mourning and self integration, thus allowing for the subjectivity of the other, as well as for the subjectivity of the self, to flower.

Unlike the classical model of psychoanalysis, the Object Relations analyst is less concerned with discovering latent meanings and unconscious instinctual wishes within dreams, but more in engaging with the analysand's basic capacity for entertaining meaning at all. The analysand's attacks on linking (Bion, 1959) between self and other, self and analyst, and between mind and body, inside and outside, past and present, love and eroticism, initiative and aggression—are all actively engaged by the Object Relations analyst through the therapeutic Object Relationship.

Such a focus precedes interpretation of intrapsychic conflict but does not exclude it. The emphasis on metabolizing splitting and projective identification, as it is experienced within the room with the analysand, and processed as observation or as induced countertransference, is related to the degree to which a patient manifests the psychic structure of the paranoid-schizoid position as opposed to that of the depressive position (Klein, 1948). Manic defenses (Klein, 1935) against depressive anxieties are also a primary focus. For those with more neurotic characters, who are more centrally located in the depressive position, intrapsychic conflict and latent meaning are an important focus.

For the Object Relations analyst, however, the therapeutic Object Relationship, and its holding and integrative functions, is attended to throughout, and regressions from symbolic association to protosymbolic enactments is engaged through relational interpretations that are posed as parallel phenomena with that being communicated through dream and thematic content in regards to the intrapsychic domain with its transference phenomena. This presentation will focus more fully on borderline patients than on neurotics.

Case of Ms. P.

In the case of Ms. P., the dreams chart the patient's journey from the external view of her own affect states to the inner experience of subjective affect and object connection, leading to a profound developmental mourning process. Object survival of primitive rage is addressed in the transference to the analyst, placed in the role of the bad object, and was critical in this case.

Dreams of holocausts and nuclear explosions externalized the archaic rage from preœdipal trauma, combined with later trauma from the loss of the mother to death at the age of nine, and the trauma of the father's sexual molestation as well as physical emotional abuse. Following dreams of such externalized explosions, in which the rage is symbolized as a part object, cut off from object connection, the patient presented a dream to the analyst that had more differentiated figures and relationships. But again, the internal affect was split-off and deflected outward, however, not now into the environment, but into the transference object.

Ms. P. dreamed of the analyst as a mother with an infant in her arms. She gave the infant to a nurse or nanny, and the patient was not allowed to hold the baby. The patient's response to the dream was to react, rather than to associate. She cried, "You didn't trust me to hold the baby!" There was no potential space for dialogue between patient and analyst here, and no room for internal psychic space that would allow for self-reflection. There was no interpreting subject in this patient to see that there was symbolic meaning in the dream. She only reacted as if being impinged on in a victimized way by the analyst's distrust—in terms of the analyst not letting the patient, in the dream, hold her baby (the baby probably being symbolic of the part of her that does want to surrender to the analyst). The potential meaning was foreclosed by the reaction, rather than opened through affect-object and conceptual links that occur in free association. We find Hanna Segal's symbolic equation, the thing in itself (Segal, 1957). This foreclosure of psychic and analytic space is seen then to parallel in the dream content the externalization of body and emotional experience, cutting off links to potential subjectivity and to having an "inside."

After the analyst gave the baby to the nanny, rather than to the patient, there was a scene in the dream where the analyst's husband's car was crashed into by a truck. Ms. P. seemed to be placing her reaction to the analyst's distrust outside of herself. The disowned internal reaction came back at her as a murderous impulse. But she herself evaded this murderous attack by creating a dream in which the analyst's husband was crashed into. This could be seen as an attack on the analyst indirectly, but also it preserved the analyst and killed off the husband, who could be seen as a father figure. She could be killing off her own father to preserve the transferential mother, the long-lost mother who died during her childhood and who was eliminating the abusive father. Her rage was used as a weapon against this father. In this way, Ms. P. avoided feeling her rage toward her transferential mother, who she wished to maintain as a symbiotic self extension, who was unambivalently loved.

Following this dream, Ms. P. expressed a conscious rage toward the analyst. As she split the good symbiotic mother, who held the infant, and the mother of separation who became colored by the demonic father, she experienced deep hatred for me as the preœdipal bad object in the transference. She screamed at me about how I "won't do me one little favor!" after I said "no" to her request to change her session time because it was raining. She accused me of being a "classical analyst who charges her for missed sessions," basically cursing me and displaying her suffering, while demanding an explanation from me, the analyst, for her refusal of a request for an alternate session time. She also threatened to leave treatment.

When her rage subsided, I said to her that those who accuse others are often feeling guilty themselves. Ms. P. sounded very curious about this comment, allowing space for dialogue for the first time in the session, after the urgency of her rage. She asked, as opposed to proclaiming and accusing, "What do you think I feel guilty about?" I said, "We can get to it," thinking that Ms. P. may have been harboring guilt over her mother's death. After this session, in which I survived Ms. P.'s rage in Winnicott's sense of suffering the expression of the rage, without retaliation or abandonment, object related contact could be established at the end of her session, after the Fairbairnian "exorcism" of the bad object in the rage.

Ms. P. had another dream. She brought this dream into our session in a very different manner than ever previously. She presented four parts of the dream, in clear detail, in a tone of curiosity and interest, so markedly different from her reactive expressions of victimization in earlier dreams. Now, there was potential space, and for the first time, Ms. P. began to associate and to allow analytic space for a dialectic, paralleling a freeing up of intrapsychic dialectic from sadomasochistic impingements that had blocked symbolism and dialectic.

Ms. P. described four scenes. The first was a scene of her dead mother coming down to her, from above. She reached out her hand to her and was sobbing and sobbing in the dream (expressing the potential mourning that as yet has not been done). The second scene was of her being in the bedroom of her childhood home, where she lived with her father after her mother's death. She was on the bed with her girlfriend and was sucking her girlfriend's breasts. She began to become sexually aroused, and just at that point, a man started to enter the room. She jumped up and hid under the bed.

The third scene in the dream was of a black boy delivering food to a white man. When reporting this scene, she had transference associations. She said that the white man was me, the analyst, but she said that I was Ronald Reagan in the dream. She said the black delivery boy was her. She commented that the black boy was delivering fast food and she hated fast food (unlike the slow food of breastfeeding). She wondered out loud why I was paying her in the dream, since she usually paid me, and she wondered why I was paying her so much. It seemed to her that I was paying her far more than the food was worth. She sounded perplexed but was operating on a conceptual and symbolic level—apparently unblocked by the expression of rage in the last session (Kernberg speaks of defending against symbolic capacities that are developmentally established)—rather than reacting as if impinged on. She reported one last scene in the dream, where there was someone on a bicycle riding away from her, and she couldn't identify him or remember who he was.

She then left the room for me to enter a dialogue with her about the dream. She curled up in a fetal position on the couch. She didn't have any more thoughts about the dream, but she wondered about the third part in which I was the Ronald Reagan figure giving her, the black boy, money. I said that I had some thoughts about that part of the dream, and Ms. P. responded rather than reacted. She maintained the potential analytic space between us. She invited me into her psychic space with a tone of curiosity. I asked, "Do you want me to tell you what I'm thinking?" She said, "Yes, I really want to know." So, I plunged in and said, "You think you are paying me so much, giving and giving to me and I am taking and taking, but in your unconscious, as expressed in the dream, you seem to feel just the opposite. Your feeling seems to be that I am giving and giving to you and you are using me up, just like you feel you used up your mother and killed her." Ms. P. erupted with an agonizing cry at this point, screaming and gyrating, saying: "It's true! I did it! I did it! It's true! I did it! She loved me so much and I hated her. I wanted a younger mother! Then I got my sister-in-law when my mother died! But I wanted my mother! I killed her. I don't love her the way she loved me: I killed her! I did it! She used to do so much for me! I just took it and took it all from her!"

For the first time, Ms. P. gave vent to expressions of grief for the loss of her mother. This was following the transferential rage of the last session, and the sobbing scene in the first part of this new dream, in which she gave symbolic representation to the grieving that she had not yet been able to do in reality. She sobbed and cried in this session, saying how her mother had called her a special name that nobody else called her—mourning her loss by expressing how much she missed her mother. At the end of the session, she let me reach out to her without spoiling and destroying me as she usually did. I said I was glad we had gotten to this point and she agreed. I remarked that she had not responded with her usual verbal sarcastic slaps, and had validated her ability at that point to take me in, to not spit me up or repulse me. She sustained the contact until she left the session.

In the next session, Ms. P. regressed from the symbolic level of this dialectical dream interpretation and engendered mourning process to a protosymbolic sensory level. She fell asleep and slept peacefully throughout the session. While she slept, I felt the relaxation in her sleep, and experienced it as a beginning regression to an early symbiosis, prior to the traumatic separation of her mother's death, which came in a relationship with a mother who could never separate from the symbiotic tie between her and her daughter while alive. This mother could never say "no" to anyone, including her husband and her daughter. Consequently, her death came as a dramatic and traumatic disruption, rather than as any tolerable separation. There had been no preparation for it. Ms. P. experienced her mother's death as a cataclysm, as sudden, acute, and murderous in its cutting off intensity and its abandonment of Ms. P. to her father. This was true despite the fact that the mother had been in the process of dying from cancer for at least a year.

As Ms. P. slept in the session following the acute opening of her developmental grieving process, a symbiotic mode of relationships was experienced between her and myself. I felt it in the induced countertransference, based on her projective identification. I felt a sensory kind of communion with Ms. P. through baby feelings induced in my lips and fingertips, a phenomenon I have not felt before or since. During this session, while Ms. P. slept, I also felt like I heard a kind of musical lullaby in the background. Ms. P. slept throughout the session, and when the session was over, she responded naturally to my saying it was time to go, waking like a sleepy child, and then able to let go of me as formerly she had not been able to do at the end of the session time.

Case of Ms. R.

In the case of Ms. R., another developmental progression, in Object Relations terms, can be seen both in the content of dreams and in the process around the use of the dreams in sessions. Ms. R.'s initial dreams (during the first months of treatment) were expressions of disconnection from her body as well as from others. Within the therapy session, this was reflected by a state of detachment, alternating with an extreme vulnerability. In her vulnerable state, she responded to empathy for her inner experience, which was filled with a sense of shame. But her backlash reaction to receiving an empathic response to her vulnerability was to kill meaning with me through clichés and sarcasm. One such cliché was that I might be selling her snake oil with my suave empathic manner. This destruction of the links that create object connections disrupted the growth of love and meaning, and such destruction of love and meaning is seen in parallel with the original disconnection in the body.

The intersection of dream content and the process of sessions in which a dream is presented could be seen in Ms. R.'s first dream. She described herself as the observer in this dream, excluded and outside. She aligned herself with the central ego (Fairbairn, 1952), which stood outside of the sadomasochistic psychic structure she carried with her, in which victim and aggressor part objects displayed themselves.

In this first dream, Ms. R. was an observer, an outsider, watching a group of people in the ocean who were attempting to scuba dive. She was off in some exotic environment, far from home, far from her vulnerable emotional center. She was emotionally sealed-off. In such a position, she spoke with the tour guide, who she agreed could have been me, the analyst. The guide told her that the swimmers were using the wrong scuba diving equipment. Instead of fins, they had baggies on their hands and feet, so that they were unable to either swim or to feel their way underwater. They were numbed out and sealed-off from contact, which put them in great jeopardy with the elements under the water.

As Ms. R. related this dream to me, she displayed the same kind of numbness, detachment, and disconnection that she represented in the dream by the swimmers with baggies. She couldn't connect with any of the feelings in the dream. She was the outsider, or else the person whose senses were sealed-off by plastic baggies. She was numbed off from contact with the ocean of feeling around her and with other swimmers. The guide in the dream could not only be me but could also be a projection of the detached and eviscerated shell of her ego core, Fairbairn's (1952) central ego part of her. In the session in which she reported the dream, Ms. R. was blank, unrelated, numb to all feeling. By choosing to be on the outside as an observer, she avoided feeling helplessly excluded by others, Klein's (1940) manic stance. But she paid the price of her position of omnipotence. She lost all feeling and she was, therefore, crippled like the swimmers with baggies on their hands, instead of fins to swim with.

My main approach to contact with Ms. R. in this session was to tell her that the detachment in the dream was shown in her disconnection from me and herself in this session. She was numbed out, as if she was an eye watching outside her body. The more she kept away from all the feelings within herself, the more she unconsciously feared all feelings as threatening assaults from an overwhelming ocean. In her view, she had no fins to get through this ocean of feeling. Feelings were foreign to her as she warded them off. As she warded me off, she detached herself so as not to be touched, while other times showing herself to be intensely vulnerable to my sensing her internal experience. As I made the connections for her between her detachment in the session and her numbed out state in the dream, with her body warding off feelings with baggies split away from the mental eye in her that observed as an outsider, she began to experience some of her detachment and distancing.

Due to her level of disconnection (at the early time), she was not able to be present at a symbolic level. She could not have associations to a dream. She could not join me in a mutual association process. Her experience was sensory in a negative sense, which meant that sensation was lacking and replaced by numbness and void, related to isolation. Ms. R. appeared to be warding off the sealed-off self in which an ocean of feeling was tied up with internal persecutory and victim counterparts, reflecting a developmental arrest in which a sadomasochistic psychic structure presided. This also demonstrated a deficit in self-and-object dialectic for psychic structure. Such lack of dialectic at first arrested potential mourning.

At this time, Ms. R. reacted to the dream rather than responding to it. She became "it." Rather than be in a symbolic dialogue with it, she was in a semi-merged state with it. Through projective identifications, she projected herself into the dream and resisted contact with the dream as a separate other. She failed to be an interpreting subject, who could see her interpretations and associations as feelings and thoughts that had symbolic meaning. In parallel with this lack of observing ego and interpreting subject capacity was her failure to experience a sense of agency outside the dream. She was merely an outsider in relation to the other characters in the dream. She was living in it, through projective identification, and it was living inside of her. There was no potential space. Split-off parts of her, components of a sealed-off core self, appeared to perpetuate her frozen state. The dream was as follows:

> Women were struggling on a lake of ice, trying to hold on to mountains of ice (ice breasts) in order to not drown in the ocean that was expanding as it consumed the ice melting within it. The ocean threatened to swallow all the women up. The women continued to cling to the ice, struggling to survive. Watching these alter-ego women, Ms. R. remained detached. Ms. R. said she knew it was a hopeless situation, so she didn't even bother to struggle. In the dream, she knew she was going to drown and die.

Ms. R. enacted her role as a distant observer in the session in which she presented her dream to me. Although she didn't have associations that suggested a symbolic engagement with the meaning of the dream, she could discuss her feeling reaction in the dream, a feeling of hopelessness and doom. One way of interpreting her feeling is as a psychic fantasy of persecutory anxiety reaching the pitch of annihilation anxiety or Winnicott's (1965) degree of "unthinkable anxiety." This is a pre-symbolic or protosymbolic ("beta elements" in Bion's language) experience.

In response to the feeling sense of the dream, I opened the avenue to entering her internal world, as it existed in the dream, through understanding the feeling expressed by Ms. R. I responded to her in relation to her entrapment with her own internal closed system, within her psychic structure. The dream fantasy captured the internal threat. As I addressed the threat, the terror of contact with me as a transference figure, and as an "other" outside of her closed system, I was offering her a new Object Relationship. My explanation was both related to her state of being trapped in her own psychic structure and in the distant place she was in the session, from which she was impervious to loving and needing, and could not take in my presence and its potential internalizations.

My explanation was also allegorical. I helped Ms. R. to see that this dream illustrated why she desperately needed to avoid contact with me, maintaining the position of an observer. I told Ms. R. that the dream revealed her fear that she was coming close to a dismal fate. I began to focus with Ms. R. on the use of the dream. If we see the women who are struggling as a composite split-off part of her, a part warded off, we see the child victim in her, frozen out of contact by an "ice breast" mother. With an ice breast mother, she has no mother to support her sense of self, and feelings become an overwhelming ocean that she expects to drown in. Ms. R. knew at an unconscious level that she would drown if there was nobody there to help her contain and process her feelings, her oceanic unconscious.

A critical stage of mourning within treatment helped Ms. R. to own split-off parts and to enter a level of symbolic free association, in which intrapsychic conflicts related to shame, guilt, and envy could be dealt with. A full blown oedipal state merged, and Ms. R. owned her capacity to love and to create. Through the grieving of her lost father, her inadequate internal mother, and the parts of the self that had been split-off due to the trauma of her childhood experience, Ms. R. both developed and re-owned her capacities to love and to create. She connected to longings for a former love, as well as to jealousy for the man's current girlfriend, who formerly was experienced as a precedipal mother to be envied. She connected more directly to her creative work than ever before, as the compulsion to create, which was tied into an addiction to her internal demon-lover, was relinquished.

Through the grief process, Ms. R. turned compulsion to free creative motivation and connected to her work as she connected to the deeper core of ambivalent love within her. She then overcame blocks and resistances that stood as obstacles to connecting to her work, these blocks and resistances relating to disowned shame, guilt, and envy. These obstacles became avenues to connecting with her internal self and its capacity to love her internal objects, and thus to sit down readily to connect with her creative work. She claimed that she could never before sit down so readily to her work, and engage with it. Having mourned the shame of needing the parental objects of her past, she could now need these internal objects as symbolized introjects within her internal world, and thus she could need her creative work, and express the needs through symbolic themes. Her ultimate creative writing theme, at the end of treatment, was of the melting of a frozen off self (placed in the climate of Alaska), and the yielding to affection and love.

Ms. R.'s dreams showed this developmental progression both in content and in dreamwork. She had a dream later in treatment (end of second year) of cuddling with a teenage boy in a romantic atmosphere, in which she also saw her male object as vulnerable, rather than as omnipotent. The male character in the dream was prone to embarrassment, reflecting a mild residue of her own shame, but now was integrated with the affection and capacity to love that such mild vulnerability allows. The dreamwork had been transformed by the mourning process into a depressive position symbolic free association process. No longer was Ms. R. in a state of detachment in her sessions, where she had to rely on me, her analyst, to initiate feeling state responses to her dreams through the engaging with her psychic structure and the confrontation of the enacted disconnection in both the treatment session and in the dream content.

As mourning and separation proceeded, she became capable of initiating all her dream association processes, becoming prolific in her symbolic metaphors, relating now to highly differentiated subjected feeling states. Such connection with symbolized subjective states allowed Ms. R. to differentiate male and female genders, and the dialectics of affection and romance between the genders. She owned and developed the formerly devalued female part of her, and it grew up to engage with masculine and vulnerable figures, symbolizing the whole object masculine side of her own internal world and of her personality.

Dreams and Dreamwork with Ms. K.

Ms. K. had been in treatment three times a week for almost two years. She was a 25-year-old woman writer, formerly an Academic Scholar. When Ms. K. first came into treatment, she was in a constant rage. She was full of accusations, full of emotional blackmail, and terrified behind her aggressive attitude. Her early dreams reflected the state of disconnection she was living in, as her narcissistic character defense of constant achievement and success was not holding up. The rejection of her first novel drove her crazy. In the first sessions, she proclaimed with absolute and adamant seriousness: "I have to be famous!" She claimed she was a victim of her parents' projections and expectations, but seemed to find some relief when I didn't agree with her, as I said she would have to find out about her own projections.

In one of her earliest dreams, Ms. K. was outside herself, disconnected from both her body and from the characters of her internal world, who emerged as part objects, part objects engaged in sadomasochistic scenes she obsessively watched on a pornography cable T.V. channel. She would watch such T.V. as one way of forestalling an internal sense of an engulfing emptiness and darkness.

The first dream was simply that of a man beating a woman. Ms. K. was a witness to this but was outside the scene. She thought in the dream that if she could steal this film of the man beating the woman, she would be cured. But she was too intimidated to steal the film when she was told not to take it.

At this early time in treatment, Ms. K. was unable to have symbolic associations to the dream, in contrast to her later prolific manner of association. At that time, she merely reacted similarly to Ms. P. and Ms. R. in the beginning of treatment. Being outside the internal world scene, she was outside also of her symbolic capacities, lacking the three dimensions, not only of whole objects in her dreams, but also of symbol, symbolized, and her own alpha function agency as an interpreting subject. Her reaction to this dream was an exclamation that she could have taken the film. She said that she could have found out what was wrong with her. Later sessions showed that the "film" was not only a kind of schizoid barrier within her that mimicked the pornography film she watched on T.V. but was also a symbolic screen memory of an adolescent for a trauma. The trauma was that of oral rape, which occurred when she was 12, and the sealed-off view of self perpetually carried this trauma and pressed her toward violent reenactments.

Another dream from her first months in treatment again displayed the state of disconnection she was in, living outside her body and being sealed-off from the vulnerable and needy part of herself. The dream took place in a writing colony, but it was supposed to be a medical school. The women studying at the medical school all had their uteruses in plastic bags hanging on the wall. She again was on the outside as an observer, but the women were also outside their bodies, looking at their insides from outside. As Ms. K. described the dream, she did associate from uterus to fetus, which related to an interpretation I had made of her feeling about herself that was continually projected into images of snails and protosymbolic sensory experiences of snails. Ms. K. had been preoccupied with snails from the beginning of her treatment. She was obsessed with snails. Initially, when feeling like she was falling apart, after the narcissistic injury of her book rejection, she had psychotic delusions of living in her own secret world, where she was the king of the snails. She then saw snails in a lamp in my office and saw snails all over. When I said the snails might be like her self in fetus form, she reacted with a powerful affirmation: "Yes! Yes! Yes!" she cried, with her usual intensity and drama.

At the time of this dream of women with their uteruses in plastic bags hanging from the wall, suggesting that they had dissected themselves for personal inspection and study, Ms. K. immediately thought of characters outside uteruses as fetuses. But she was able to remain at this time on the level of such a symbolic association. She became flooded with snail sensations and visions, conjuring up the snail as a fetus and the fetus as a snail. The sense of a body part, which defined a core feminine part of the self as being sealed-off in plastic suggested an eerie sensation of schizoid barriers, excluding the feminine part of the self from connection with the rest of the body self. To view the excluded and numbed out feminine part as a fetus suggested a total primitive self excluded from the body it was to reside in. It suggested abortion and the merging of levels of sexual trauma and primal abandonment trauma.

Although Ms. K. could be prolifically verbal and symbolic at times, she remained numbed as if she was shielded in plastic. Another dream of being behind glass mirrored the disconnection from the world and from the body connection to that world. This dream became a prologue to an intense sequence of sessions in which oral rape symbols and memories were finally deciphered. Progressions to the symbolic level were quickly reacted to with a backlash to the sensory implosion of the protosymbolic level of the paranoid-schizoid position, in which persecutory anxieties dominated Ms. K.'s psyche.

During her initial days in therapy, Ms. K. had been a psychic bulimic, taking me in whole, spitting me out, and getting nauseous in her first session because of the conflict between taking me in and splitting me up. Gradually, she was able to take me in and sustain some connection, digesting slightly, but the urge to orally expel me was overwhelmingly compulsive. When Ms. K.'s sensory level snail preoccupation began, therefore, to transform into a symbolic key to an oral rape trauma, Ms. K.'s capacity to let me be with her as an ally was quite new and alluring. At the moment she grasped the image of the snail in a totally novel way, as the combined image of her lips and the male rapist's penis on which her lips were forced, a whole mystery yielded its story. Darkness had turned to light through this deciphering of the snail symbol, just as other dreams of hers suggested, when dark places turned into bright open and sun-drenched apartments.

Ms. K. and I shared a feeling of ecstasy as this deciphering of her snail hieroglyphics unlocked the mystery of her personal Rosetta Stone. The collaborative effort at this time was given representation in a dream where I was seen as a fellow academic scholar entering a haunted house with her, searching for ghosts (as in Dickinson, 1960, "to scan a ghost is faint, but grappling conquers it").

Yet, her regression from this parallel growth in symbolic capacity, free associative capacity, and the sustaining of a therapeutic alliance, quickly collapsed into a protosymbolic level of enactment. Ms. K. began to act like I was the demon-lover rapist, forcing her to submit to experiencing the pain and memory of the rape, forcing her to remember the inner scream that was choked within her, the kiss forced into her, and the penis forced into her mouth. Since it all took place by the ocean, I wondered if she had hallucinated herself into the state of a snail on the beach at the moment when her mouth was forced into fellatio, when she felt like a "screaming cloud of pestilence" erupting without release. She said that she had been thinking of snails the whole time, and might she not have traveled outside of her body, dissociating enough to feel on the outside looking in, or sealing off behind a film of plastic, like a disconnected uterus or fetus lying on the beach or hanging on a wall.

Back and forth we traveled from the protosymbolic to symbolic level, and back again, and then forward to new symbolism as memories begin to come alive in a more differentiated form. She remembered standing in a hallway, being carried over a shoulder, with a hand over her mouth so that all the screams inside imploded within her. She felt like she was clinging to an electrically charged fence, eruptions of electrical charge battering her from within, beating her down from within.

Soon after this entrance into the symbolic level digestion of memory, in between sessions, Ms. K. lost me, and when alone trying to write, words and images converted back to protosymbolic body sensations. Since the creative act, just like an analytic session, had become the scene of enactment, of going into the dark cave or black hole, from which she never would return, her attempt to sit down in a room alone retraumatized her. Ms. K. explained that she had lost me when telling me about this, telling of the snails that began to swim in her mouth, erupting from symbolic containment into protosymbolic sensory impingement—engulfing her and terrifying her.

Following this, Ms. K. had a dream of snakes and of holding onto a snake, not being able to let it go. Dreams of dinosaurs evoking her oral rage, and of snakes evoking her terrors of phallic penetration, seemed to be part object images of dissociated body feelings, just like that of the snail. At the paranoid-schizoid level of the dream, where persecutory terrors predominated, she remained more reactive than reflective, yet she had a moment of reflection as she asked: "Why couldn't I let go of the snake? I could have let go of it. I kept holding on to it." Would Ronald Fairbairn's view of holding on to the bad object to control it be appropriate here? Perhaps we can see the snake as an essential part of her own body self, also merged with a bad part object, which she couldn't relinquish like an externalized uterus or fetus? Rodents expressed rage in her dream. Snakes may have expressed erotic intensities without subjective passion, as they seem to have done in the poetry of Emily Dickinson (see Kavaler-Adler, 1993). Ms. K. clung to the split-off intensities that invaded her and controlled her when she could not integrate them and experience her own subjective desire. While dreaming of snakes and imagining snails, the oral rape memories were accompanied by her fear of me as the demon-lover snake, the snake that suggested her own insatiability as she lived in a sealed-off state, prior to critical mourning. Snakes, snails, and dinosaurs are also split-off erotic intensities without subjective passion, as seen through the work of Emily Dickinson and other women writers I've written about in *The Compulsion to Create* (Kavaler-Adler, 1993a/2013), who are obsessed with a demon-lover and who have no adequate inner container to tolerate their own subjective desire.

As Ms. K. began to grieve the anguish of the rape, she reverted back to a defensive enactment of the protosymbolic level. She said the rapist had forced her to work so hard in her analytic sessions to recover from the rape. The rapist had forced her to need me and treatment. I was then perceived as having too much power because she had revealed her secrets to me. I could control her like her father, forcing her to submit (later in treatment, she spoke of wanting to be forced, and the fear of freedom when she was not forced). She exclaimed that I was coming on top of her, reflecting incestuous desires, terrors in relation to her father's phallic sexuality. The snake dream showed that she was clinging to the snake that could both bite and strangle her. This biting snake was a part of her, a part of her that she had felt and expressed toward her sister in childhood. She had torn up her sister's room, reminiscent of Klein's tearing up the breast, and she had felt her teeth tingling from the fantastic urge to bite her sister's nose off.

Ms. K. had several dreams of being in a writing colony that was about to be invaded by Nazis. Nazis represented the hostile part of Ms. K.'s psyche that demanded she work 10 times harder than she was ever working. As she put it, in her family everybody had to keep working. If anyone stopped working, it was a terrifying threat to everyone else in the family, because it meant someone had a need, and nobody could deal with their own needs so they couldn't stand the exposure of the needs of another. Ms. K. said that rather than feel neglected when everyone else was working, she had worked twice as hard as everyone else. This had brought her many overt awards. But the compulsion to work and to create in her creative work drove her into a state of manic frenzy, alternating with despair, which she and I often spoke about as the Red Shoes Syndrome.

At the time of studying at Oxford, she had broken down into a state of debilitating despair. She found academic scholars at Oxford to represent a world of what she described as a Nazi standard of excellence. She claimed to be persecuted by a Nazi part of her that demanded more and more from her to the point that she would work night and day on a project. Then, when the project was over, she would fall apart. She would feel eviscerated, emptied out, and like she was falling down endlessly into darkness. Yet, just as she held onto the snake in a dream, so too did she hold onto the Nazi in her. It was her demon-lover, and when she was not worn out from her manic flights into the compulsion to create, she would turn her demon-lover back into the inspiring muse that initiated the whole cycle again. In the transference, I appeared as the Nazi demon-lover in her analysis. She said that she came to see me because I was tough, rather than being a hand holder. But she then became frightened that I was a "ruthless academic." Along with this, she thanked me for having "de-fanged" her.

In the first dream of the Nazis invading the writing colony, Ms. K. was still merged with her muse-demon-lover. She was still possessed by her manic states. She was still losing her connection with me as a good object, which resulted in her becoming overwhelmed by compulsions to create herself into a star through her work, in order to ward off the darkness and ugliness she felt within, which had been symbolized by her snakes, her big grey and dripping snails surrounded by floods of mucous and semen, and her dinosaurs. The dreams reflected the engulfment by her dark inner world and its bad part objects, as it reflected engulfment by her own rage. The Nazis were coming to the oasis she found in the writing colony. The writing colony allowed her expression for her deepest desires, as she expressed her inner life in her novels, but it was also vulnerable to the onslaught of her inner Nazis. These Nazis demanded that she write for some purpose of excellence or achievement that took her away from her internal self.

In the first dream of Nazis invading the writing colony, she was overwhelmed by the threat of the Nazi invasion. She clung to her girlfriend, who was also at the writing colony, wanting her to pack and escape with her. She handed the novel she was writing to her girlfriend. It was an offer of a gift of herself that which she felt was her very essence, and her girlfriend looked away. Instantly, the room they were in became filled with rats, which was related to rodents, which was Ms. K.'s term for Rhodes Scholars. Ms. K. was then surrounded by rats and threatened by the Nazis invading. She felt alone with the rats and the Nazis, abandoned by her girlfriend.

When Ms. K. reported this dream, she was still at a protosymbolic level or in the paranoid-schizoid position, where she reacted rather than associated. However, I gave her some of my own associations, which she was able to take in and respond to. She reacted by saying that she always had vile animals and Nazis in her dreams. She proclaimed that they live inside of her. I said that the rats coming out seemed to express the rage she felt when her girlfriend was indifferent to her book. She agreed and was then able to say in response that she was left all alone because of her rape and injury.

She said she felt paralyzed, as though her girlfriend's rejection of the book was a total rejection of her. This left her surrounded by rats, Nazis, and darkness. In the session, she was enacting the paralysis and helplessness of the rage turned inward so that her symbolic capacities had to be inspired by my own associations. This tendency of hers to rely on my associations changed dramatically as she slowed down in treatment and began to connect with me so that a successful developmental mourning process could begin. However, at this time, my associations related to her rage in the dream helped her to connect to her blocked state of paralysis operating within the session in which the dream was presented.

When Ms. K. next dreamed of a writing colony, with the theme of the invading Nazis, she was in a very different place. During the interim between these dreams, Ms. K. had learned how to slow down from the whirling dervish dance of the Red Shoes. She had gone from rage and terror to deep states of sadness. She had become increasingly able to let me be with her and to directly express her need for me to me. This had given her the containing space to internalize me, and despite all her backlash reactions in which she returned to a helpless despair and self hating anguish, she had been able to feel the grief of the core object loss within her. As she allowed me to be with her and to contact her grief, she was able bit by bit to mourn and to internalize our being together, building in the psychic structure to contain and process mourning from within. This modified the sadomasochistic aspects of her psychic structure, allowing her to experience her erotic fantasies, such as a man beating a woman, without her living it out in her life. The mourning process is a separation process, which allowed her to separate from the Nazi part of her.

Therefore, her next dream about Nazis invading her oasis writing colony reflected quite a different self state. Already we have seen in the progressive sequence of her dreams, throughout the psychoanalytic Object Relations process, Ms. K.'s transformation from being outside of herself, outside of her body, and an outsider in her internal world, into being a subjective character within her internal world. Her dreams now gave life to her subjective experience. Even in the dream where her rage was split-off and placed outside of her in the image of rats, she was still in the dream, no longer looking on from the outside. In the later dream of the writing colony and Nazis, which came in the second year of treatment, Ms. K. was not only within herself and her own subjective states, but was able to associate to states of initiative and agency that had grown within her through the internalization of our therapeutic Object Relationship. There was more desire in this dream than persecutory fears.

She at first wanted to leave the writing colony to travel on a vacation and invited her girlfriend to go with her. Her girlfriend was disinterested, but rather than feel abandoned or enraged, she told her girlfriend that the Nazis were coming. She and her friend started to pack to leave. Then Ms. K. realized that she was going to have to go on her own. She left a book given to her by her father, ***Anna Karenina***, and then realized that she didn't need it.

Ms. K. did not wait for me to say anything about the dream. She began to comment on the sense of initiative she felt in the dreams. She remarked that she did not feel helplessly dependent on her girlfriend to go with her, nor on her father. She could let go of her father's book, as well as his philosophy of life. She gained a sense of self agency, and leaving the writing colony became colored by the pleasure of travel. She was no longer overwhelmed by the persecutory anxieties related to the Nazi part of her. The Nazis appeared less as a threat in this dream, and more as something she used for her own purposes, to convince her girlfriend to leave the writing colony to travel. She had separated from her internal Nazis and her mother-sister figure seen in her girlfriend. Her girlfriend's indifference to her didn't cause an externalized rage rejection as in the rats and rodents of the last dream. She contained her emotional reaction and had the subjective experience of initiative and choice.

A dream following this one showed Ms. K.'s developmental growth into a capacity for concern, as guilt and loss were felt and understood between us in the therapeutic mourning process. She was now able to have a dialogue with parts of herself that were formerly split-off and disowned.

In this dream, Ms. K. came into the place where she was employed in a political job and another girl who worked there was depressed and envious. The girl said to Ms. K., "You're lucky! You have your writing. I only have this job." Ms. K. tried to listen to the girl's distress and led her out into the sunlight where she could listen to her better. She felt compassion for her. She tried to understand her. She comforted her.

In her association to this dream, Ms. K. said that she felt concerned for this girl, who she could see as a part of herself. She felt inadequate when she didn't sustain a sense of what she had, and in this dream, one part of herself was reminding her that she had something special. She was able to empathize with the part of herself that felt inadequate rather than to have contempt for it. She was separating from the inadequate part of herself rather than using a manic grandiose defense against it. She was owning what she truly has, as symbolized by her writing, rather than trying to be a star to avoid feeling the darkness within her.

Ms. K.'s associations particularly focused on her ability to lead this other girl from the darkness into the light, reflecting how Ms. K.'s internal world darkness had changed. Whereas she used to feel an endless engulfing darkness, like the void of a black hole, she now had a differentiated darkness where she was in the darkness of her work environment or in the memory of waiting in a dark apartment for her mother to come home. She now had a contained and boundaried darkness, like a vagina with limits, as opposed to a vampire biting mouth or the illusion of the no limit vagina seen in demon-lover fantasies of women writers (Kavaler-Adler, 1993a/2013, 1995).

Subsequently, after more than one and a half years of treatment, Ms. K. dreamed a dream that highlighted the manic theme of her compulsion to create (Kavaler-Adler, 1993 a/2013), the myth of the Red Shoes. In this dream, she was the smallest child in a play. The following is Ms. K.'s description of the dream:

> I was playing the youngest child in a play with other girls (sister?). There was this Don Juan figure (father). The mother, who was like you, wanted to have sex with the man. But he had this young mistress like person with him. It was suspenseful in the dream, like a murder mystery. My mother had on really red shoes—like in the *Wizard of Oz*. She put on the shoes to get the man. Oh! The dance of the Red Shoes! You had them on—You, monster!

Ms. K. stopped after reporting this dream. I asked her why she stopped and didn't respond to her dream. She said she wanted me to tell her what it means. I told her we can find out what it means together if she told me her thoughts. I also saw that her taking this passive role was also an enactment of the child position in the session that was symbolized in the dream. No longer was she enacting being a rape victim as she had in sessions at the time of her early dream of a man beating a woman. Now, she was enacting the role of a child in the session, in which she presented a dream in which she was in the child role.

Ms. K. was able to respond to my invitation for her and I to collaborate on an association process, which illustrated the level of interpersonal and intrapsychic dialectic she had reached.

Ms. K.: "I think the mother in the dream is eroticized—related to my mother getting this grant to write a book. I connect success and sex. Now that she got this grant, she's in a position to have sex with a man. ... The dream puts me in the position of being the youngest child in the play. I don't want to play it anymore. I want to be an adult!"

Analyst: "Why do you have to be in this child role?"

Ms. K.: "Because she's going to leave me for this man. Yea! She has red slippers on. But she's like the more adult part of me. I think. Woof! Woof! [Animal sounds.]"

Analyst: "Can't you put that into English?"

Ms. K.: "I feel scared—upset—longing and fear."

Analyst: "I think it has to do with your going away next week."

Ms. K.: "Yes! You're a monster! I also feel rejected, angry, and mad. I feel mad at the New Yorker!"

Analyst: "You feel left by the New Yorker too, as well as by your mother, who's going away with her grant."

Ms. K.: "The New Yorker has gone from a great opportunity to a nightmare."

Analyst: "You're going away and you feel like everyone is leaving you."

Ms. K.: "[Whimpering] That car you hear screeching. That's what I feel like. I feel mad!"

Analyst: "You get mad when you're scared. Separation is hard for you and you're saying good-bye to me for a whole week. We won't see each other three times next week."

Ms. K.: "What do I do?"

Analyst: "You can feel it and talk about it, while you're here with me, rather than letting it hit you when you're alone.

Ms. K.: "My family is leaving me for success—my mother and my sister too."

Analyst: "You turn the pain of losing them into the image of yourself as a failure. You go into your hall of negative mirrors to avoid the feeling of loss, when you can't wear the red shoes and see yourself as a star."

Ms. K.: "I envy them. Are these real feelings about being a failure or a defense?"

I then took us back to the dream, since the dream was speaking to this question, about the red shoes as a compulsion to create, as a manic defense against the fear of loss and abandonment that Ms. K. was feeling throughout the session. However, I made the mistake of making an oedipal interpretation that went nowhere. We then returned to the underlying theme of losing mother, which led to both the leaving of me in the transference and the leaving of me as representing the whole therapeutic Object Relationship (see Grunes, 1984).

Analyst: "In the dream, your mother has success and sex. You're a child. She can have the man, but also the man has a younger mistress who is probably you. You're in competition with her and you don't want to deal with it, so you stay in the 'part' of a child, just like you regress here into child language. But you've also created a mother, who doesn't feel sexual without the Red Shoes of success images and star roles. She has to have a manic form of success to feel sexual."

Ms. K.: "Last night my mother was listening to me on the phone—trying to help me. I got off the phone and thought, 'This isn't helpful! I am rehearsing all my anxieties for my mother!'"

Analyst: "You're rehearsing before your mother just like you're rehearsing in the dream. You're acting out a part, like being in a play."

Ms. K.: "[Responding vehemently and enthusiastically] Yes! My performance is talking about my anxieties these days!" [Seeing the link between performing for mother, in the session and in the dream, Ms. K. brings our discussion back to the red shoes image in the dream.] "There were two pieces of shoes next to each other. One pair had a buckle over the in-step and the other was plain. My mother had one pair of shoes and you had the other."

Analyst: "So which shoes did she have and which did I have?"

Ms. K.: "[Changing the subject] I can't remember! I saw this woman at the airport when I landed. I imagined that she had been away at school. She was being picked up by her mother. I just looked at her and thought that she made me feel like something's missing from my life. I imagined this woman was surrounded by love and affection. I imagined her life wasn't hard."

Instead of responding to her movement into object related longings for love, and to the sense of losing her mother, or having never had her ideal fantasy mother, I brought her back to the dream image of the red shoes, returning to her pathological mode of manic defense. She followed me, and then we got back to the theme of love and loss in the session. The therapeutic Object Relationship gave her a context for her feelings of loss in separating from me, her analyst, and her transferential mother.

Analyst: "With the red shoes on, you don't have to work hard! They do all the work."

Ms. K.: "I want a pair of them!"

Analyst: "You sure do! The only problem is they kill you at the end."

Ms. K.: "They do not! I like them! [She acts like a cute child here and starts making animal sounds, [Greer!']"

But I had imposed my red shoes myth on her dream and her symbolism. My red shoes myth is about the manic compulsion to create a dance of death—substituting the narcissistic intensity and image of creative work for real sexual desire, which risks love and loss. My red shoes lead the woman who wears them to her death, as she marries the internal god muse demon, who keeps driving her to narcissistic achievement. However, Ms. K.'s red shoes may be different. They symbolize manic success, and success as sex substitute or as a prerequisite to getting a sex object, without risking sexual desire. However, since she also related her red shoes to the magic shoes given by the good fairy godmother in the *Wizard of Oz*, they were also associated with magically returning home to mother, without any effort. Dorothy's magic shoes brought her back to her home in Kansas.

The underlying theme of the session was of wanting her mother and losing her—wanting the good mother who would give her the gift of the red shoes, and the fear of losing her mother to her mother's addiction to the red shoes, and to a false and magical form of sexuality in relation to the man. Ms. K. was not ready for my oedipal interpretation about her retreating into childhood to avoid competition with her mother. For although she may have been the young mistress of her Don Juan father in the dream, she wasn't—couldn't—compete with a mother for this Don Juan man because she wanted her mother more than she wanted the man.

Her longings for her mother, and her abandonment fears, were dominant. Also, the Don Juan man was not a separate whole male figure. She was not jealous but envious. The man was a narcissistic extension of her mother (phallic-narcissistic, or Melanie Klein's man inside of mother), not a fully differentiated whole other. The conflict was not yet an oedipal one, but one over separation. She wanted her mother to stay tied to her, and yet she needed to let her mother go so that she could separate, and have her own success in the world, and her own sexuality.

The session in which the dream was presented ended on the note of loss and separation. After Ms. K. said that she wanted the red shoes, and made more animal noises after I say the red shoe leads to death, I asked her if she could translate her sounds into the language of an adult. She made an angry "Greer!" sound again, and then I interpreted her wish to stay a child.

Analyst: "Maybe you want to be little like the littlest child in the play in order to avoid having big feelings—Maybe your feelings feel too big!"

Ms. K.: "They are! I'm sad!!"

Analyst: "It's good you can feel it now. Then you can stay connected to me this week."

Ms. K.: "[Repeats] I'm sad!!"

It's time to go, and she looks at me sadly as she leaves. She waves good-bye to me like a little kid and says "I'll miss you!"

Ms. K. had gone from mad to sad. We had gotten to the sense of loss underlying the session. She was able to contain the sadness by sharing it with me at the end. This helped to lessen the need for her manic defense compulsion, in which she drove herself to assume the image of the red shoes success star, in which she possessed a man as a part object as a sign of the narcissistic intensity of the creative mystique.

The theme of her mother leaving her in the dream was brought full circle to her leaving me as her transferential mother and grieving the separation at the end of the session. This allowed her to tolerate loss during the week when away. When she began to obsess about herself by a failure, she thought back to my telling her of how her negative hall of mirrors, failure images were used to ward off the feeling of loss, just as the red shoes success images were. She was able then, on her own, to identify who she was longing for, from her past, at that moment when she assumed the negative mystique of failure and became narcissistically preoccupied.

This dream of the red shoes demonstrates that Ms. K. had developed to a level of body connection in which it was only her differentiated feminine sexuality that had a manic disconnected life of its own. Ms. K. was now in herself but was still a child in the dream, an outsider to her adult feminine body. But to own it, she had to tolerate separating from her mother and feeling the loss of separation. In the therapeutic Object Relationship with me, she was able to tolerate this as our relationship supported her capacity to feel both her rage and her sadness bit by bit, in tolerable doses. The increasing connection with me through these feelings, and the increasing internalization process, allowed Ms. K. to be increasingly in herself, and therefore to separate enough from her thoughts and feelings to own them as thoughts and feelings and to create symbols and associations out of them, instead of being trapped in them. She had become an interpreting subject.

The last dream of Ms. K.'s I will discuss occurred within the second year of treatment. It followed the red shoes dream and was an interesting contrast to it. In this dream, however, Ms. K. cut off her desire by returning to a position of narcissism and envy. She saw her girlfriend with her boyfriend in the dream and thought that she envied her because her boyfriend was thin. The man she was attracted to was heavy. She again, as in the last dream of the red shoes, envied a woman for having a man who was a narcissistic self extension. In this dream, Ms. K. retreated from her intense object related sexual desire to the position of envy for the mother and the man inside of her mother's body, the idealized phallus as an extension of the mother.

Ms. K. quickly responded to her own dream at this time. She did not hold back as she had when reporting the red shoes dream, taking a child position. She quickly initiated her own association and interpretation process. Her interpretation of the dream was that she had killed off her own sexual desire and the man who was the object of that desire with her envy. She analyzed her own spoiling process and we talked about her fear of wanting an available man and her fear of being wanted. She then was able to speak of her defensive distancing, through criticism of the man, and in this case of his weight, at any time when she begins to feel loses to him. She was now experiencing and analyzing her own psychic conflict and her own ambivalence, particularly her ambivalence about moving into sustained Object Relations, with all its threats of love and loss.

Conclusion

In all these patient dream sequences, we see the movement form body disconnection, psychic dissociation, and depersonalization to connection and self integration through the therapeutic Object Relationship. Interpretations of disconnection versus contact are made throughout, both in relation to the dream content and to the process around the dream experience in the session. Parallel movement is seen in body connection, self integration, sustained good enough relations and internalizations in the therapeutic Object Relationship, and in the capacity or symbolic association as opposed to enactment, projective expulsion and protosymbolic sensory experience, rather than symbolically represented experience. The capacity for creating and sustaining meaning grows along with the capacity for concern. Attacks on linking and meaning are seen in conjunction with body/mind dissociations and body disconnection and are modified as the mind/body splits are experienced and analyzed in the context of the therapeutic Object Relationship.

CHAPTER 15

NIGHTMARES AND OBJECT RELATIONS THEORY

Originally published in 1987 in Kellerman, H. (Ed.), *The nightmares: Psychological and biological foundations,* 33–57. Columbia University Press.

Beyond REM states, and deep into the phenomenological world of horrors, like a Disney World planet or a Twilight Zone paradox, we sink into the precedipal world of vulnerability in our sleep. Stripped of our daily ego orientation, what creatures do we find there? Where do they come from?

What is the world like for the Kleinian infant—still poised at the stage of paranoid anxiety, milk poisoned by envy and greed; which is felt, however, with projective twist as retaliation from without. Is this a land we revisit in our sleep?

And what about Ronald Fairbairn's world of black masses and exorcism, where repressed bad objects plot their malign and cancerous plots? Here are our inner Heathcliffs, Iagos, and Richard IIIs—each a synthesis of parental failures, abuse, and frustrations. As we cling to our inner ghosts in Fairbairn's endopsychic world, do we never know it so well as in our sleep? Why Hamlet would rather choose death than the alternative: "perchance to dream."

Following Fairbairn comes Harry Guntrip, who so vividly paints the devouring rage of the schizoid pain. There is no battle of good and evil in his world, just more and more hunger! It's a draining, consuming, vacuum-cleaner sucking of insatiable hunger that can never be fed in the isolated turret where our precedipal, schizoid part resides-cutoff from contact, secluded in the frequent concentration-camp motif of our dreams. The hunger the split-off true self, the baby closed off in a steel draw, cries unheard except in nightmare dreams and poetic explosions. In *Ariel*, Sylvia Plath describes her craving self as "The vivid tulips" that "eat my oxygen":

The tulips should be behind bars like dangerous animals;
They are opening like the mouth of some great African cat.
(Plath, 1961, pp. 11–12)

D.W. Winnicott and Michael Balint continue to define this internal world that dances forth in our dreams, but they look more from the outside. The external view brings us the trauma of the "Basic Fault," which leaves a perpetual crack in the self. It also brings us the baby who can't make it past the transitional stage and the transitional phenomena to authenticity, aliveness, mature dependence-as well as the baby who is stuck in the trap of identification and fusion, remaining undifferentiated and unintegrated. Parental neglect is assumed when "good enough" mother and transitional teddy bears are lacking. Yet, the internal objects are never drawn with the phenomenological pen. Rather, for both Winnicott and Balint, they are implied.

Despite differences among the Object Relations theorists, however, all the authors mentioned here (Klein, Fairbairn, Guntrip, Winnicott, and Balint) were addressing an era that predates the intrapsychic-conflict states of a cohesive and separate self. Unlike Freud, they hypothesized about the prœdipal era without reluctance. In doing so, they were closer to "such stuff as dreams are made on" than the master of dream analysis. This is particularly true when it comes to the nightmare, for in the nightmare experience the most primitive parts of a person erupt.

In their *Preliminary Study of the Personality of the Nightmare Sufferer*, Hartmann et al. (1981) suggest that the people who most frequently experience nightmares tend to be more schizoid than not. They lack sturdy, sustained ties with other people, i.e., ties with real external objects. Often insomniac as well, chronic nightmare sufferers tend to be depressive-position failures, who find ambivalence, loss, guilt, and mourning intolerable. They tend to return time and again to the paranoid-schizoid dilemma. In their world, annihilation of the self is a constant threat. The internalized ideal object is assaulted along with the ideal self; and stemming from the extreme schizoid split, the bad objects are very bad indeed. The struggle to preserve the ideal object, which has not yet been modified to the less omnipotent form of the vulnerable good object (and thus has not yet been accompanied by a modified bad object) arouses a constant retaliatory strike force from the contrasting malevolence of the bad object world. The oedipal and latency-age superego has not yet been formed. Horatio's Renaissance age of reason has not yet been reached. The middle ages continually strike back like Hamlet's ghost, and Hamlet can only cry: "There are more things in heaven and earth, Horatio, / than are dreamt of in your philosophy."

Nightmares and Psychotherapy

Within the psychotherapy process, the nightmare can play a special role. Even when a patient is not in the class of chronic nightmare sufferers, it is a poignant time in treatment when nightmare experiences, as well as memories, begin to emerge with some frequency. It is a time of increasing vulnerability for the patient, and it can be a time of increasing contact between the patient and psychotherapist. The therapy can be approaching fruition at this time. Yet, there are additional reasons for seeing emerging nightmares as a critical clinical development. For some of these reasons, we need merely look back to Ronald Fairbairn and Melanie Klein.

Fairbairn's Psychotherapy

Ronald Fairbairn (1952) was explicit in proclaiming the internal world of Object Relations to be a competitive arena in which tenacious ties to bad internal objects continuously subtract from external object-relational bonds. Following from his thinking, the major goal of psychoanalysis is to release the patient from inner ghosts, so that his innate strivings toward Object Relations could merge into the external world of interpersonal relations. In essence, the patient could only come alive, and be present in the world of living, through release from inner-world bondage. Clinging to past and primary parental object ties, the patient would be in constant battle with the therapist to oppose exorcism and release. This was the more true the sicker the patient, for the ties being clung to in the internal world were those particularly derived from bad early life experiences, where frustration and abuse predominated over good, interpersonally contactful experience.

For Fairbairn, real parents are internalized as inner objects only when they are bad, good parents being internalized only as secondary phenomena that work to ameliorate the effects of bad objects within the inner world. Thus, good parents do not have the phenomenological reality that the bad parents have when they are transposed into internal objects; and therefore, they are not sufficient to release the child from bad object cathexis. The child is thus destined to remain half-buried within the interior world unless some outside champion appears on the scene. Borrowing from the Catholic church, Fairbairn declared the psychoanalyst-psychotherapist to be the modern version of an exorcist. He was sometimes to evolve into the patient's champion-although admittedly the odds were against him. In this Fairbairnian scenario, the psychotherapist is both model and wrestler in his role as exorcist. He is the good-object model in the outside world, which can tantalize with goodness, as the internal bad parental objects tantalize with badness. His main asset in this tantalizing role of "model" is in offering "real contact," which Fairbairn believed was the primary goal of the patient's object striving, as opposed to Freud's pleasure-striving, ego-libido. In his alternate role as wrestler, the psychotherapist attempts to wrestle against the patient's resistances. The more the patient clutches his internal bad objects to his breast, the more the therapist strides against the negative transference (the transference projection of the bad objects onto the therapist), with sword-like interpretations, aimed at cutting through the imprisoning internal object bonds. He persists to induce the patient into relinquishing his hold on his internal phantoms. Thus, in his role as wrestler, the Fairbairnian therapist also plays exorcist, although his incantations are cast in psychoanalytic phrases. If the therapist triumphs, malignant inner formations are dispersed, while becoming the spurious ghosts that are devoid of power. The patient is then set free.

In the midst of this wrestling match, the Fairbairnian therapist does battle against intrapsychic defensive processes that guard the static inner world. Repression and splitting are terms that Fairbairn uses interactively, and clearly his meaning for such defenses extends beyond what was termed repression by Freud. Fairbairn is addressing a basic recalcitrance in the psychic system that is preœdipal in origin, extending back to the first year of life, when the pristine ego was first split asunder. In Fairbairn's system, secondary repression is carried out by an already repressed antilibidinal ego, against the libidinal ego and its cathected exciting bad object.

The Crux of Fairbairn's Theory in Terms of Bad Objects

Therefore, in Fairbairn's view, splitting and repression can only be overcome by the release of the bad objects (exciting and rejecting objects). Only when these internal bad objects are released can arrested development advance because only then can the ego parts (libidinal and antilibidinal egos) that were split-off and repressed with them be reintegrated into the central ego, or into what Heinz Kohut (1977) has more recently called the nuclear self. In Fairbairn's vie, once this reintegration has taken place, growth through external contact can begin to advance. The central ego can then transverse the transitional stage, from relating through identification (prolonged intrapsychic merger with repressed bad object residues) to relating as a differentiated self; a self that has graduated from total dependence to mature dependence, which entails mutual interdependence with external object figures. This is a schematic explanation of Fairbairn's developmental process, and it illustrates how defensive repression and splitting are used in the service of developmental arrest. Critical to further development of self, therefore, are renewed Object Relations with the external world. The self (Fairbairn's central ego) can only grow through Object Relations in Fairbairn's system, as is true for the theories of Klein (1975), Guntrip (1969), Winnicott (1965, 1971), Balint (1968), and all other object relationists. In the more current developmental language of Margaret Mahler (Mahler et al., 1975), we would say that the arrests in the separation-individuation phases of development (see Balint's **Basic Fault**) could only be overcome by contact with a good external object. This object could precipitate a mourning process whereby good and bad self parts, and good and bad object parts, could be integrated into a cohesive self structure and a cohesive object structure, which are differentiated from each other. In order for this to occur, the bad experiences from the past need to be consciously experienced, along with the closed-off painful effects that originally caused such experiences to be split-off from the conscious nuclear self, or to be repressed out of awareness.

The Importance of Fairbairn's View as Applied to Nightmares

Going back to Fairbairn, then, it can be seen why the release of bad objects is so central to basic intrapsychic structural change. In addition, the nightmare experience becomes critical as a part of psychotherapeutic treatment insofar as it serves as an avenue of escape for the repressed bad objects. When these bad objects are brought into awareness, a transition is made from a closed internal system into a conscious self that is an open system, open to developmental process through contact with the external object world.

Nightmares and Melanie Klein's Theory

In Melanie Klein's (1975) work, a slightly different inner-world struggle emerges and provides us with a different sense of the nightmare's importance. A Kleinian child is not struggling with repressed bad objects that come from bad experiences with real parents. The Kleinian child is struggling with his own badness, in terms of innate death-instinct energy, which manifests itself intrapsychically as "a priori" malevolent images: attacking breasts, intruding penises, and sadomasochistic parental intercourse scenes. However, these images are only initially persecutory in nature. Once one transverses the avenue from the paranoid-schizoid position to the depressive position, one begins to sense bad objects as having been spoiled by one's own aggression. Then remorse is felt—sadness, loss, and guilt—and yearnings for reparation come in reaction to the awareness of how one's own envy and greed destroy the good objects within the self. The task for the evolving Kleinian infant is not, then, the release of bad objects (as it would be for a Fairbairnian child). Rather the task involves the affective reality of feeling good objects (from good real parents) as spoiled, then tolerating the guilt and loss of this psychic reality, and then working through the mourning process. Intrapsychic change comes from "letting go" of our blocked depression and solidifying connections with one's own internal objects.

What role does the nightmare play in this process? When having a nightmare, we return to the persecutory anxiety of the paranoid-schizoid position in which the very fabric of the self is felt to be threatened. We regress from fears of object loss to a more basic terror in which our self (or Klein's ego) is threatened with annihilation. In nightmares, concern, caring, empathy, and guilt in relation to others are all temporarily lost. We lose the tenuous developmental achievements of the depressive position. In our nightmares, we return to a position in which others are persecutory unless they are omnipotent and ideal. We care not for them. We are totally preoccupied with self-protection because we feel as we did prior to various states of self-integration when we could easily dissolve or be wiped out of existence. We are totally helpless without an omnipotent other on which to depend. Along with the threat of annihilation from the outside, there are additional threats from the inside, coming from yearnings for merger with the omnipotent ideal object. These yearnings threaten us with death by dissolution. Our basic needs are a threat too because needing can cause homicidal wrath from our own inner bad objects.

Given this regression to paranoid-schizoid conflicts, the Kleinian developmental task (also the analytic task) cannot be accomplished through mere conscious experience of the nightmare—as it could be in Fairbairn's system where the release of bad objects is a primary goal. However, the return to the paranoid-schizoid position, within the nightmare, can be used therapeutically to get back to the deepest fears of self-annihilation-fears that can continually undermine depressive-position processes of love, integration, reparation, and differentiation. By returning to a stage prior to advanced structural change, we glimpse the basic blocks to personality change. Only when free of intense persecutory anxiety can we tolerate guilt, loss, and the accompanying despair that are essential and perennial components of the mourning process. Only then can the psychoanalytic treatment process proceed.

Clinical Material

Nightmares and Object Relations Working through

The following nightmare was presented by a patient in analysis during an early phase of her treatment:

> My mother appeared before me, with a cold, regal manner of detachment. She almost looked like a statue, because she was so frigid and stoney. She told me that she had something to announce to me. I felt shaky, and very small, especially standing in front of her. Even though she was sitting down, she seemed to tower above me. I think I was a very tiny child. I was scared to listen to her, as she pronounced, with accentuated definity that she had decided to die. I heard myself scream wildly, then, raging, almost like an animal. I was screaming, screeching, crying. The more upset I got, the more detached my mother got. It was awful. I felt so needy, and like I was going mad … I woke up still screaming, and thrashing around in my bed.

In this nightmare, the basic Object Relations constellations can be seen and addressed. It appears that the bad object part of the mother (real or fantasy, according to interpretation) was internalized, and projected out as a persecutory figure. C., the patient, re-experienced a very familiar position of victimization in relation to her mother—a painfully helpless position of total dependence. The patient's early childhood fear that her mother would die was turned into a harsh reality, and the mother became an active persecutory figure through her frigid promise of abandonment.

We can see in this nightmare the basic Object Relations that characterized the internal psychic structure of the patient and the Object Relations that characterized the transference projections within the therapeutic relationship as well as the modus operandi for this patient's current external Object Relations. These are all additional perspectives to that of the historical parent-child relationship that had become internalized, and each relationship constellation reflects the internalized parent-child Object Relations unit.

For instance, as treatment progressed, the patient was able to experience, more and more, that she herself was the cold, regal, and, detached figure, who bitterly and matter-of-factly dismissed life. She was her own internal bad object, her nightmare mother. It was the coldness. the contempt, and the air of triumph that walled her off from her sorrow, as Melanie Klein so clearly describes in her portrayal of manic controls defending against depressive despair-guilt and loss. Within the nightmare, the anxiety over guilt and loss seemed to be dealt with by denial and by manic triumph over the needy, hurting part of herself. Inside of her, she had both the mother part and the child part: and one was sadistically controlling the other, as Fairbairn's antilibidinal ego part would control the libidinal ego. In this way, the grief and loss of the child were not experienced so long as her conscious identification was with the hard, cold, withdrawn, and triumphant bad mother in her, or with her antilibidinal ego. However, the nightmare had reawakened the anguish of the child, and her pain and loss could no longer be denied. Experiencing the cold mother part of her, in connection with the hurting child, brought a melting surrender and sorrow. Rage, hurt, and love were expressed as part of a lengthy mourning process. Grief and remorse emerged as the aggressive mother part was felt. The hurting child could not be denied, and the sense of self-injury brought compassion along with remorse. Internal reparation could then be made. In this sense, a Kleinian unfolding took place. Mourning brought a renewed capacity for love, creativity, and object connection through need and love rather than through omnipotent denial and domination.

While this took place internally, parallel processes took place within the analytic relationship, and within the ongoing primary external relationship. Within the transference relationship, in treatment, the tendency had been for the patient to project out, through projective identification, the part of her that was like her internalized bad mother, i.e., cold, withdrawn, and withholding. When she experienced the therapist as being this bad object, she would withdraw and not speak. However, at other times, she would project out the helpless child onto the therapist, disowning her own needs, and her own hunger for the abandoning object. Then, she would portray her contempt and triumph more openly, and aggressive attacks on the analyst would take place.

While this alternating projective identification process took place in treatment, it simultaneously occurred in her relationship with her boyfriend. She would periodically freeze him out with her contempt, viewing him as the devalued child part of her. She would then see him as a helpless, needy, "dependent schmuck." When she herself became the demanding child, he would be experienced as a rejecting parent, distancing from her, who would not accept her love.

Fairbairn and Klein in Relation to Illustrative Nightmare

Fairbairn would view the internalized rejecting parent as a highly cathected sadistic object who must be clung to at any cost despite the masochistic submission required for continued attachment. If this unhealthy, indigestible internal object could be exorcised through the nightmare, the task of "releasing repressed bad objects" could be done. However, it would seem that Fairbairn would view the nightmare merely as a prelude to a whole working-through process of attachment and relinquishment of attachment to the bad internal object, as experienced within the transference relationship.

For Klein, the cold, impassive mother would be a bad internal object, created in the patient's own infantile fantasy. The patient's own aggression is primary in this, the bad object being constructed by her own destructive drive wishes. Thus, the nightmare could be seen by Klein as a way of formulating, for the patient, her manic defenses against the feelings of guilt and remorse, related to the sense of recognizing one's self as a rejecting mother, or as a demanding and aggressively clinging child. The nightmare expresses the paranoid-schizoid position view of the mother as a persecutory figure. Yet, in Klein's view, the road to health lies in re-owning the aggression that has been projected out in the paranoid position (the death instinct deflected outward). Re-owning one's aggression means consciously identifying with the projected bad object and re-introjecting it, along with experiencing the painful effects that come with awareness in the depressive position that one's own aggression has hurt and damaged the object. In this nightmare, the child might be seen as damaging the mother by turning her into a withdrawing figure through her own oral wishes to destroy and annihilate with greed and envy. Through envy and greed, the real good mother (external mothers being good in Klein's theory) has been spoiled and made bad by the child's hungry ravings. Envy of the good object turns it bad and depletes it through sucking and screaming that devour. Greed is the accomplice of envy. In turning mother bad, the patient can also be seen to become the bad mother as she is internalized through introjection in the depressive position. As the treatment process unfolds, the patient may be confronted with her omnipotent manic control, as portrayed in the nightmare's mother figure. Interpreting this would hopefully, lead to the patient's experiencing her own coldness, control, contempt, and devaluing attitude of triumph. Experiencing this means re-owning the aggression involved in such control, through the affective awareness of guilt and the pain of loss. The sense of loss and guilt is due to the damaging of the patient's internal object, in terms of turning it bad, and turning it against the self. The depressive working through of the guilt and loss involved constitutes the ongoing mourning process of treatment.

Object Relations work with Nightmares in Response to the Patient's Subject Point of View

The role of the nightmare in working through Object Relations can be seen again as we look at some clinical cases in which an initial nightmare is re-experienced quite differently at a later stage of treatment. In the case of J., an earlier nightmare of a monster mother became a later experience of the insatiable monster from within. The nightmare was as follows:

> I was sitting with my father, outside, in a field. We sat talking. The day was beautiful. But suddenly, the air began to darken and thicken. I heard a noise and looked behind me. A huge-mouthed monster emerged from behind us. I clung urgently to my father and screamed for him to protect me from the monster. He didn't respond. He sat limp and seemingly powerless … The monster began encroaching on us both … but before it did, I woke up, crying for help, and sighed with relief that it wasn't really happening.

When this nightmare was first reported by the J., her associations were to the devouring needs of her mother, which had overwhelmed and smothered her at a time when she was left to live with her mother, after her parents' divorce. Her mother was the monster, who had consumed her and prevented her from having any sense of self. She merely reflected her mother's grandiose image and complied with her needs. She always waited for her father to rescue her from her mother's grasp, but he never did. He seemed impotent in relation to her mother's treatment of her, and for all the years that she remained living with her mother (before college), her father withdrew from her life.

Over the years, as J.'s treatment progressed, she moved from this earlier position as the victim of her internal bad mother, and her interpretation of the nightmare changed as well. She brought up the nightmare again, quite spontaneously, saying. "Do you remember that dream I had about the monster that my father wouldn't protect me from? I used to think the monster was my mother, but now I think it was me. I think it was my hunger. I'm always hungry, no matter how much I get. I always want more."

She made this comment at a point in her treatment when she was beginning to "own" her insatiable cravings-for food, sex, and power. She had other anxiety dreams and nightmares at this time. Some were of holocaust explosions as her rage also surfaced. Others were of "savages" attacking her, which reflected her hungry and impulsive cravings and her envy and greed. She also had a nightmare of a "wimpy, dependent, clingy girl," who was being cut, beaten, and bruised by a man. She herself appeared in the nightmare as a friend, who was merely an observer. Yet, in her associations, she was able to own the disowned victim part of her, as well as the disowned sadistic bad object. More and more at this time—and in all the nightmares she mentioned—J. was able to own the bad object part of her that she had formerly interpreted as her mother. Thus, the working through of the Object Relations issues in treatment can be seen in terms of the patient's changing associations to nightmares and anxiety dreams. The changes reflected major growth in separation-individuation and the working through of abandonment depression effects.

A similar process was reflected in the reinterpretation of an early nightmare by another patient, L., who had a nightmare that went as follows:

> I was at a restaurant with a whole group of friends. There were all kinds of food on the table. My boyfriend began to tell a story about a dog that ate a cat in front of him. He laughs and says that he's afraid if he goes to sleep he'll be eaten up. I get terrified, but nobody else seems scared, and this increases my anxiety. Then, I look at the food on the table and see all kinds of strange fish that look like they're beginning to move. Snails, shrimp, lobsters start to look like they're coming alive again. I suddenly feel alone and shivery. The food seems to be getting bigger. Claws, fangs, and teeth start to come out of the food and move toward me ... I wake up startled and find myself shaking.

L.'s initial associations to this nightmare involve memories of hearing her father tell tales, during her childhood, of food that ate and devoured little children. Her anxieties in reaction to the nightmare are all related to fears of being devoured.

Then, several years later in her treatment (following increasing separation, through mourning and loss, similar to the case of J.), L. began to talk of her own greed and her own craving to devour everything around her. No longer was she the victim of bad objects: she had re-owned the bad object qualities. Recalling the earlier nightmare she was able to identify with the food and saw the dream, now, in terms of her own voracious hanger.

Nightmares of Traps, Suffocation, and Concentration Camps

At certain points in psychoanalytic treatment, it is not uncommon for patients to dream of being trapped, suffocated, or imprisoned. Fairbairn refers to the channel of transition in maturational development, from the stage of infantile dependence, where identification is the main mode of relation to objects, to that of mature dependence, in which differentiation has been achieved. Fairbairn does not use Margaret Mahler's phrase, "separation-individuation," but basically he talks about the same thing. Speaking of this channel of transition, Fairbairn notes that patients tend to have dreams that depict the developmental journey. They might dream of crossing a channel. They might dream of falling and drowning in the channel. They might dream of flying over the channel. However, if they feel stuck, and are unable to break out of the infantile mode of identification, they might very well dream of being trapped or imprisoned.

Borderline patients, in particular, who are stuck in the trap of identification and merger and who are unable to differentiate and individuate, often have anxiety dreams and nightmares that reflect entrapment or suffocation. Sometimes they dream of concentration camp images.

Harry Guntrip writes, prolifically, about schizoid patients who relate at an infantile level of identification, and who therefore have a constant life-death, need-fear dilemma, concerning wishes to stay in the womb of security in this regressed state of identification, which turns into a dread of imprisonment and suffocation in the womb. He believes that the "regressed ego" within us all woos us back to a secure objectless womb, deep within our interior world. However, if we succumb to the sirens of security we end up trapped, shut-in, and depersonalized. The fear is as intense as the wish.

A former patient, whose character reflected the undifferentiated schizoid dynamics described by Fairbairn and Guntrip (Guntrip's passive ego identification), had a typical nightmare of entrapment: "I was in your closet. All your clothes were hanging down on me. It was dark, and I had a hard time breathing..."

The sense of suffocation woke her up, and she retained the sense of being smothered, of choking. In the dream, there are no Object Relations. There are no persecutory bad objects. However, it is an Object Relations nightmare, and it is a transference nightmare. Since the closet described is the analyst's closet, the implication is that the patient is trapped inside the analyst's body. Perhaps she is inside the analyst's womb, which would be in keeping with the Guntrip regressed ego's yearning to withdraw to a hallucinated prenatal atmosphere of security. However, the process of entrapment in the womb is also one of developmental arrest, as Fairbairn describes. Since she relates through identification and not as a differentiated self, entrapment is inevitable. It so happens that this patient's nightmare, of being in the therapist's closet, came at a time in treatment when an idealizing transference was turning into a negative or devaluing transference.

During the idealization phase, the patient wished to swallow the envied and admired analyst. She introjected aspects of her, and overall she related through identification. As is common with schizoid patients, when actually with me, she had difficulty relating; but when away from me, she would have incessant conversations with me in her head, trying to express her deepest dreams to me in my absence. As treatment continued, more contact occurred, in which, on and off (Guntrip's "in and out" solution), she could share her thoughts. Also, instead of being blocked and withdrawn, she showed more open hostility and contempt. The idealized object was being more openly experienced as the bad object, and the fears in relation to the bad object were of being trapped. Thus, having wished to swallow the analyst, she now saw the analyst as swallowing her, as holding onto her in a regressive symbiosis that bound her to the analyst as her mother continued to bind her. Yet the nightmare does not indicate any active control or persecution on the part of the analyst. Nor does it indicate any active merger or regression into the interior world. The patient is just there, inside the analyst, among the analyst's things. She is there and doesn't know how she got there. She just knows that she can't breathe well. Has she yearned for withdrawal into this womb-world, as Guntrip suggests, causing her own trauma of being shut away from life? Is she the reluctant victim of a mother who keeps her from moving across the transitional channel to differentiation? Does she withdraw to get away from the mother, or is she withdrawing to stay within the mother? According to Guntrip, the good object will always turn bad, at the schizoid level of the human condition in which passive ego identification leads to suffocation. The more schizoid the person, the more he will turn to further withdrawal to escape the sense of entrapment, rather than struggling through the transitional channel of separation-individuation to differentiation and mature object relatedness. This patient's nightmare suggests the passive withdrawal of a schizoid ego, where the shut-in situation is experienced from the view of a victim. For Fairbairn, however, the patient is always an active participant, clinging aggressively to the bad object to avoid object loss and resulting ego loss or death.

Several other patients show similar nightmare themes of entrapment and suffocation. One woman dreamed of bursting out of her mother's home. She felt an explosive urge to break out of the loneliness. In the nightmare, the mother's house was experienced as suffocating "isolation." Being in mother, then, became being shut away from life. Another female patient dreamed of being back in her mother's house. The house was rocking from side to side, and she tried to stand in the center of it, to balance it. The theme of suffocation emerges more subtly here, as she takes great pains to open the window so that she can breathe better.

Following along with the nightmare theme of entrapment, we come to nightmares that are reported in terms of concentration camp images. One quite schizoid patient reported a nightmare in which she was under the vigilant observation of a concentration camp guard. She is thinking of escaping but is frozen, more from futility than fear. She looks at the male guard, who points his rifle at her, and she thinks how hopeless any escape is. She starts walking, thinking that she should be running toward the gate. She wakes up still with the hovering sense of futility and despair. She knows she must be terrified, but she can't feel it. She just feels hopeless.

Another patient reports a multifaceted dream in which one scene involves being in a concentration camp. It is the same patient who dreamed of an oral monster, and of needing to open the windows so that she could breathe in her mother's house. In this dream, which comes later in treatment, she and her boyfriend enter a room in a dark house, and suddenly they are concentration camp victims. They are emaciated and look near to death. Yet, just as suddenly as they are trapped in this demise, equally suddenly they get free by walking into the next room of the house. Then they return to normal health and appearance. There seems to be a magical quality of omnipotent denial in this dream that liberates it from the terror of a nightmare. Yet, it also seems a sign of self-growth, in that the helpless entrapment in the earlier nightmares is no longer felt; instead, there is a sense that one can determine one's fate. The patient is less of a passive victim and more in control. As reported earlier, this patient (J.) was able to cross the channel of separation-individuation increasingly in her analysis and was then able to own the oral aggressive bad object as part of herself. In doing so, she owns her aggression. In a nightmare that occurred most recently, this same patient speaks of a monster coming up the stairs to kill her. She is with her friends, and she cries for help, asking them to tell her what to do. She is aware that the monster is coming upstairs to murder her, and she is terrified. However, in this nightmare, she also is aware that she is in control of the monster. Her associations to the nightmare make it clear that she experiences the monster to be her own aggression, particularly her murderous rage that she can turn inward upon herself. Directly following the session in which she reported the nightmare, she became sick. She felt choked up with a sore throat and felt that she couldn't breathe well. She said that she experienced her sickness as her controlling the monster, turning it inward upon herself. Even though she was identified with the passive victim, who became sick from the monster, she was now also identified with the aggressive victimizer, the persecutory bad object or the antilibidinal ego (internal saboteur). The patient's ability to feel in control of the monster indicated the self-growth that had come with differentiation and the increasing owning of her aggression.

The concentration camp motif, in nightmares, can sometimes reflect a clear conflict over crossing the channel from identification and merger to the side on which differentiation and separation wait. Then the dream is no longer just of entrapment but also of the entire need-fear dilemma described by Guntrip.

The patient who dreamed that her mother was threatening to die later in treatment had the following nightmare:

> I found myself in this strange place. First, I was inside this house, but somehow I knew that if I went into the bathroom I would be put into a hot oven and be put to death. I was able to walk outside the house, and when I did I saw this whole free area, with the blue sky above, but all around the free area was this iron gate. Seeing that I was locked in all around, I thought of trying to escape. But then I saw that on the gates, which were surrounding everything, were these huge Chinese bulldogs that snarled and roared. They had big claws and huge teeth. I knew that if I tried to escape over the gate, I could be torn apart by the Chinese bulldogs. Yet, there was no other way out, and I knew if I stayed I'd have to go back into the house, and eventually into the oven ... I was terrified, but I knew I would have to try to climb the gates, and to get over them. My only chance was to get past the murderous bulldogs.... Yet, it looked like either way, I was going to die. Then, I woke up.

In this nightmare, there seems to be a schizoid "damned if you do, and damned if you don't" dilemma (no way out of the symbiosis), There is a threat of death by burning, which seems to represent returning to the suffocating womb, and suffering the shut-in schizoid fate of death by regression. Then there is the alternative threat by persecution from the bestial guards of the gate, which can be seen as the antilibidinal ego, turned in against the libidinal ego that needs to escape to the outside world of differentiation and outside Object Relations. In Fairbairn's terms, the libidinal ego is trapped in a repressed isolation, away from outside relatedness, by the aggressive antilibidinal ego, which is fused with the animalistic persecution of the rejecting bad parental objects (Chinese bulldogs). However, the regressive pull toward the inner house, within the gate, can be best understood in Harry Guntrip's terms as the frightened, weak ego that wishes to recede into the security of the objectless womb, away from the persecutory antilibidinal ego and its cathected bad object of the internal object world, and also away from potential outside persecutors (outside the gate or outside the self). Yet, the lure of the womb also carries the threat of the shut-in schizoid depersonalization, isolation, and entrapment. The prospect of death in an oven can be seen as the loss of ego consciousness, which is the fate of the ego that withdraws from all objects, both external and internal. In this dream, going into the bathroom is experienced as being forced into a hot oven. Guntrip speaks of the suicidal wish to stick one's head in an oven as a reflection of the yearning to regress into the womb for security.

Guntrip's Concept of the "Regressed Ego" as Applied to Nightmares

Deeper than fears of entrapment by either external or internal objects (or by the antilibidinal ego) are fears of the void within, of a deeper inward regression to a featureless place where no objects exist. Patients who give up their internal bad objects can be left with the terror of being isolated, depersonalized, and empty since they anticipate being left in an objectless state. One patient, who appeared to be operating at a high level of functioning, revealed an inner borderline void within a highly structured personality system. Despite her successful work and social life, she seemed unable to sustain an intimate relationship. It was through a nightmare that the hidden intrapsychic element of a psychic void was most clearly shown, hinting at an answer to the confusing mystery of this woman's character. Although as she grew up this patient had received auxiliary mothering from many of her mother's friends and friends' mothers (which was her way of escaping from an unavailable mother), she still retained an empty hole at her center. Many sophisticated psychic structures were built up through her extrafamilial relationships, but the inner void remained, only to emerge much later in a nightmare. Her younger brother had remained at home with her mother. When in treatment, she dreamed the following dream:

> My brother and I were together. The house was deserted for a long time. Then it seemed like the floor opened up and swallowed my brother up, and he was never heard of again.

Guntrip raises the idea of an objectless state, which Fairbairn conceived as impossible. For Fairbairn, no ego (or self) part could exist without an object part attached to it in the inner world. The central ego part had the attached ideal object. The antilibidinal ego had the attached rejecting bad object. The libidinal ego had its exciting bad object. Winnicott (1971) also indicated that there could be no ego without an object by stating that there could be no baby without a nursing mother. Michael Balint (1968) speaks of the primary love that evolves as a harmonious interpenetrating mix-up between self and object. He vehemently disputes and reputes the idea of primary narcissism, since it suggests an objectless state. Guntrip, however, believed differently, and in speaking about a regressed passive ego he theorized that a hidden heart of the self had withdrawn into hiding and was existing in an essentially objectless state. The fantasy of regression into a womb or of part of the baby self being put into cold storage for rebirth at a better time were fantasies volunteered by patients who were particularly schizoid in nature, patients prone to withdraw out of fear. However, withdrawal threatened isolation and ego-depersonalization, so the objectless regression was also a rendezvous with psychic death. Given this ultimate dread, the most terrifying fate Guntrip could imagine for the human ego is shown in nightmares of empty voids.

Sometimes patients with highly developed characters can reach down to the deepest schizoid dread in nightmares. Yet, the same patient can also touch on Guntrip's higher levels of bad Object Relations, both at the level of persecutory anxiety and at the level of depressive anxieties about moral accusers.

One young female patient has had a repeated nightmare in which she and her family are on a boat. It is dark, and they are in the middle of a black sea. The ice below them suddenly begins to break, and their boat begins to sink.

The patient reported this nightmare in association with her fears of closeness. It arose as she spoke of an intense, visceral "No!" which would come up in her just as she was about to yield to a man and to fulfill her wishes for merger. Even though the dream itself is not devoid of objects, the schizoid fear of engulfment in an objectless void is suggested. She speaks of her terror within the nightmare experience in terms of the ice breaking beneath her and of the black sea threatening to wash over the boat (self) that supported her. There is some suggestion of self-dissolution, but the main emphasis is on the devouring and engulfing black void, or black darkness. To yield herself, to let the ice break, would mean some psychic smothering, psychic annihilation. To let the ice break seems to mean to let her icy defenses of manic contempt and control be relinquished. Yet, if she yields to intimacy, she is afraid that her wishes for merger will bring annihilation and psychic death.

Also the fact that it is a black sea that surrounds her, and not just a black void, suggests that letting the ice break will result in death by drowning, which could refer to the endless tears that she is afraid she will cry if she relinquishes her icy false self-contempt and plunges into the depressive-position affects of guilt and loss. In this last respect, the nightmare anxieties suggest a higher level of development than the schizoid level. They suggest depressive-level anxieties. In deferring to Melanie Klein, Guntrip mentions her depressive and paranoid positions as psychic levels that supersede his schizoid level in terms of being higher levels of consciousness and development. He divides Klein's paranoid-schizoid position into two levels, with the fear of persecutory objects being at a higher level than the schizoid fear of emptiness and depersonalization. At the even higher depressive level, he sees the main anxiety being experienced in relation to moral accusers, bad objects who arouse a sense of guilt over aggression.

In the patient just mentioned, all three levels can be seen operating. The nightmare of the black sea suggests mainly schizoid-level fears. In other nightmares, her depressive anxieties are clearer, in terms of fears of moral accusation. In one nightmare, she felt an acute sensation of a whirling light coming toward her and accusing her of something horrible. Then she had a dream in which a Chinese woman threatened to sue her.

In and out of the web of accusatory dreams and nightmares, the same woman has dreams of persecutory bad objects in the form of sadistic sexual abusers. In one particular nightmare, she dreams that a policeman, dressed in an official uniform, is feeding her tuna fish, and simultaneously he is torturing her with a sadistic-flavored tone of triumph. As he jams tuna fish into her little-girl mouth, he reiterates: "You asked for tuna fish, well here's tuna fish!" The patient's associations to this last dream were to forced fellatio and her grandmother's sadistic and abusive attitudes toward her as a child. Yet, she had converted her persecutor into a man, and she didn't know why. She actively suspects her grandmother of having sexually abused her as a child. She has a fantasy that her grandmother forced her to have oral sex with an adult man when she was a very little girl. Now, her anger at men becomes connected with the persecution in the nightmare.

Psychic Levels: Adult and Child Nightmares in the Same Patient

As can be seen, nightmares can reflect all levels of Object Relations conflict, and of Object Relations fears. No patient is exclusively at any one level. In psychoanalytic treatment as adults, some patients have nightmares that reflect and recall earlier childhood nightmares. Patient S. had two nightmares in treatment that brought back earlier nightmares and earlier fears of persecution by bad objects. Initially, she dreamed that her mother was saying some cryptic message, over the telephone, about a penis. Then she was given the telephone, and she dropped it at the point where someone whispered three things that sounded like P. and penises. After reporting this nightmare, S. recalled a childhood nightmare that she had dreamed of many times before. It was about a phallic man who crept in through her window, expanded and inflated, and then crept around her childhood apartment. She cried, piercingly, for help, but no one seemed to hear her, even though both her parents were there. Her father sat "benignly" in a living-room chair, with his newspaper in front of his face. As S. ran from her bedroom and into the living room, screaming, her father turned casually toward her and said, "Having fun, honey?" Her mother continued to iron at her ironing board.

These nightmares are particularly interesting in light of the fact that this patient too has suspicions of childhood sexual abuse. She has headaches that can suddenly open up into dissociative states in which she feels like a tiny three-year-old girl, and has flashing images of her father coming toward her and sticking his penis inside of her. When she allows these flashes she quickly seals them off and represses them again. She seems to feel flooded with guilt for thinking such thoughts about her father.

S. also had a more recent nightmare that recalled another one from childhood. In the current nightmares, she was out jogging with her kitten, her kitten running beside her:

> I started running faster and faster. I was taking these long dance leaps. It felt wonderful! But then I saw this sharp turn at the end of the path. At each side of the turn I could fall a mile if my foot slipped two feet of ground at the turn. I got scared that I was going so fast that 1 would miss. I told myself I was being melodramatic. I told myself I could put my foot wherever I wanted. Then I missed the two-foot cement spot, and began falling. I couldn't believe it! I told myself that I just had to grab the railing, and then I would be okay. I said to myself, "There's no way you can die out here, when you're running!" Then I tried to grab the railing, and I missed. I kept falling … I woke up feeling this awful sense of horror.

When S. recalled this nightmare, I asked her if the sense of terror in the nightmare reminded her of anything. In response, she told me of a childhood nightmare, which had the same feeling in it:

> I and my parents were taken prisoner by a man, in the home we lived in when I was a child. The man wore a handkerchief over his face, and carried a rifle. When a neon sign lit up on one of our hearts, it meant that that person was going next. Both my parents were killed, and then the light lit up on my heart. I was going to be killed next. Then I woke up crying, with the same sense of terror as in the recent nightmare.

Harris (1960) wrote about the nature of falling dreams and attacking dreams as reflecting different levels of Object Relations, as well as reflecting different types of mothers (abandoning versus intrusive mothers). He believed that falling dreams reflect a more primitive level of relating in which one particular mothering person has not yet been cathected. He had a sample of patients who generally would have falling dreams and another sample that would generally have attacking dreams. My patient, S., had experienced both forms of nightmares, and it is not clear whether abandoning and/or intrusive aspects of the mother are related to the nightmares. However, the sense of terror in the nightmares remains equally intense, whether in falling or being attacked. The sense of impending self-annihilation is prominent in both.

Summary

Object Relations theorists focus on preœdipal fears and conflicts. It is in nightmares that this preœdipal world is most vividly able to emerge. The inner world that reveals itself is one of paranoid and schizoid anxieties, in which persecution and entrapment by bad objects threaten to annihilate a fragile and unformed ego or self. It is a world illustrated by Melanie Klein, Ronald Fairbairn, and Harry Guntrip in their particular views of the internal world of pathological object ties.

Clinical examples of nightmares are analyzed from different theoretical viewpoints as well as in terms of the working through of Object Relations dynamics in treatment. The important role of aggression in Object Relations psychoanalysis is demonstrated, as presented through patients' associations and responses. The importance of the separation-individuation process is emphasized in terms of the re-owning of nightmare aggression that is initially experienced as bad object persecution.

Particular nightmare motifs-traps, suffocation, and concentration camps are seen to be representative of schizoid-level anxieties in relation to an internal bad object world. Deeper schizoid anxieties (as described by Guntrip) are alluded to by nightmares of emptiness or black voids. The question is raised whether an inner regression can take place, beyond internal objects, to an objectless state, given nightmares of such character.

Nightmares are also reflective of varying levels of preœdipal anxieties. They remind us that fears of self-loss or lost ego-relatedness can occur in terms of schizoid fears of disintegration, disappearance, or entrapment, as well as in terms of paranoid fears of persecutors or depressive fears of moral accusers. In addition, defenses against depressive-position anxieties of guilt and loss can be shown in nightmares in which manic triumph, control, and contempt appear through sadistic bad object figures. Also, child terrors can be seen to reappear at adult levels of experience in differing nightmare themes, where the basic effective impact is not altered. Finally, nightmares seem to be indispensable experiences that provide entry to the deepest aspects of Object Relations development.

TREATING PATIENTS WITH JEALOUSY

Originally published as "Chapter 11: Treating patients with jealousy" in 2018, in O'Neil, M.K., & Akhtar, S. (Eds.), *Jealousy: Developmental, Cultural, and Clinical Realms.* Routledge.

Is jealousy really a green-eyed monster? Under what psychological conditions does jealousy become a personified monster? Under what conditions is it just a very intense instinctual and affective feeling experience that can be talked about, contained in symbolic psychic fantasy, and be understood? Under what conditions are jealousy not only a green-eyed monster, but a monster that enacts murder, as in Shakespeare's play *Othello*, and in the Verdi opera version of that play, "Otello?" How did Iago know how to push Othello's buttons, to turn a civilized man into a murderer? What role can we play as psychoanalytic clinicians in transforming potential destructive aggression, in the form of the green-eyed monster of jealousy, into the more benign experience of symbolized hostile fantasy, where self-reflection can be employed to tame the monster? How is jealousy different from envy? How is jealousy more primitive, and protosymbolic rather than symbolic, when primal envy is perpetuated by a primal developmental split in the psyche (precedipal developmental arrest or Michael Balint's [1968] "basic fault")? These are the questions I enter this chapter with. As I continue, I hope to address some of them.

Shakespeare's Othello

The viscerally acute and terrifying drama portrayed in Shakespeare's *Othello*, despite being fiction, is mythic in portraying the potential corruption of the human soul by the green-eyed monster of jealousy. Othello is from Venice, which is east of England, and his military commitment is in Cyprus, which is further east. So, from the Shakespearian Englishman's point of view, these lands might be considered less civilized. Yet, Othello is supposed to be a military man who has reached the highest ranks of society through his military feats. He is welcomed at the level of aristocracy, and in fact was welcomed in the home of Desdemona's father, who is a nobleman. It is there that Desdemona heard Othello's vivid tales of adventures and triumphs over strange creatures like cannibals, and was drawn to him as both a hero and a raconteur.

Othello has much reverence from varying levels of society in Venice. Yet, it is the ordinary military man, Iago, who is to bring him down, and turn him into a murderous villain toward a young bride who was presumed to be the most innocent of creatures, inciting the unconscious, and perhaps archetypical green-eyed monster part of Othello. And by the way, it is Iago himself who first speaks of jealousy as a green-eyed monster. Iago declares to Othello, "O, beware, my lord, of jealousy! It is the green-eyed monster which doth mock the meat it feeds on ... Good heaven, the souls of all my tribe defend from jealousy!" (Shakespeare, 1942, p. 1115).

It is also an ordinary military man, Cassio—although a man promoted in rank by Othello himself and who is the reason for Iago's intense envy/jealousy—who is to become the specter of tyranny in Othello's eyes. This can only occur when Iago succeeds at awakening the green-eyed monster from the personal unconscious of Othello, and perhaps from the Jungian collective unconscious depths inside of Othello. In fact, Iago sashays around Othello with a cunning art of dropping innuendoes and implications. Iago's hints of marital wrongdoing escalate—but only in Othello's mind—into a full-blown case of betrayal by Desdemona. The full-blown case implied by Iago advances his innuendos of Desdemona having taken Cassio as her lover. However, such implied—not spoken—accusations come so soon after Desdemona's marriage to Othello that the fallacious case—building only in Othello's mind—defies all reason. What makes Iago such a successful demon, and what makes Othello so vulnerable to his demonology?

First, we have the insidious art of Iago as he proposes implications. He is cunning and armored with salacious gestures, which are crafted to confuse and perplex Othello beyond all rational thought. Second, we have Iago's brilliant, though demonic, psychological acumen. Iago not only mocks and mimics the salacious gestures that are by implication reflections of Desdemona's womanly wiles with Cassio. He manages to provide Othello with ocular proof of betrayal, with the supposed concrete evidence of betrayal seen in Cassio possessing Desdemona's handkerchief. Iago also mocks a conscience for himself! He pretends—again, through the most subtle of hints—that he is distraught by his own accusations toward Cassio.

Performing his evil art "to a t" before Othello, Iago stops to repent his own suspicion of Cassio before Othello. He hesitates to advance to a full-blown accusation. He implies that these kinds of dangerous thoughts of another man's or woman's guilt must not be thought nor voiced lightly. He does a dance of undoing himself with doubt that only the devil himself would envy. He is a master of planting the seed of jealousy in Othello's mind, and then of letting it grow to full fruition—but only there, in Othello's mind—not in any overt way being fully formed as an accusation by himself. In this artful manner, Iago portrays, even for himself perhaps, his own mock innocence. He performs a dance of reluctance. Iago states, "In the mean-time, Let me be thought too busy in my fear I am—And hold he free, I do beseech your honor" (Shakespeare, 1942, p. 1116). And Othello, in response, in his own mind, thinks, "This fellow [Iago] is of exceeding honesty" (p. 1115).

So, there we have Iago. But what of Othello's vulnerability? What makes Othello such a fertile target for Iago's Machiavellian maneuvers? Of course, like Icarus, Othello has a long way to fall (the bigger they are, the harder they fall). Othello had been elevated to an aristocratic status by military feats and triumphs, and not by any pre-ordained category of birth, the latter being generally a characteristic precedent for aristocratic aura in his own society (Venice/mock England). This in itself leaves Othello vulnerable. In fact, Othello was a Black Moor in a brutally racial society in Venice/mock England in 1604, the early 15th century. Africans in that region were usually musicians or entertainers at that time. Since Othello was being sent to fight a war in Cyprus, a land further east than Venice is to England, he could probably have been accepted to have a noble military status. However, such status may only have been viable as long as Othello was being used to fight those considered to be the "primitives over there"—as long as his status only reigned in the no-man's far-off land of Cyprus.

Beyond all this sociology, what can we infer might have been the preparation for the disaster of the green-eyed monster of jealousy in Othello's mind? Did Othello secretly believe that he was unsuited for the lofty status to which he had arisen? Did he secretly feel like a fraud? Did he secretly believe that he was unworthy of all he had earned, not only in terms of status, but particularly in terms of winning Desdemona to consent to be his wife, especially when she was willing to be disowned by her father to marry him?

If so, could Othello's lack of self-worth stem back to primal trauma in Othello's precedipal childhood, which would inevitably compound oedipal stage jealousy in his psyche? Did Othello suffer early mother loss that would evoke primal envy in an intense pre-symbolic form, and thus could compel his psyche into a particularly violent form of oedipal level jealousy—as the triad of mother, father, and child follows the earlier primal attachment dyad with mother? Did Othello suffer maternal abandonment, in addition to the usual oedipal child's sense of betrayal, when he can't marry mommy or have mommy all to himself?

As readers of Shakespeare, we can never answer these questions, since we have no history of Othello's life or childhood. Yet, such questions have psychological conundrums related to early splitting and dissociation and related to primal narcissistic injury, annihilation anxiety, and developmental arrest. Such psychological phenomena may hide under courageous valor, and even under a spirit of generosity, which may survive without requiring a false grandiose self-exterior. In fact, Othello was never seen as a figure of arrogance, narcissistic false pride, and contempt. It is quite possible that Othello was primarily authentic, but nevertheless, he could have believed himself to be a fraud. This would make him highly vulnerable—vulnerable to all deceptions that challenge his self-confidence—and vulnerable to jealousy in particular.

In jealousy, there is always the haunting belief that the rival for the conquest of a dame is actually the more worthy one. For jealousy to have its full sway of tyranny, however, that belief must remain unconscious. The mind of the one obsessed with the tyranny of jealous rage is fundamentally plagued with fears of an unbearable loss. In the mind of Othello, if he were deranged with an obsessive fear of a primal loss at the level of maternal abandonment in infancy or toddlerhood, the only way of stamping out the murderous offense of betrayal is to murder the one who is believed to have committed the betrayal—in this case, Desdemona. Yet, in responding to the betrayal that is unconsciously interpreted as murder, the prized and desperately needed loved one must be murdered, and so ironically (unconscious irony), the man creates his own dreaded loss and actually repeats his own probable maternal abandonment (whether emotional or actual). We see then the denouement of a Greek tragedy. We see the self-fulfilling prophesy becoming fatal self-sabotage, as the rejection of self-abandonment is provoked unchecked by the authority of a reality related ego/self (Fairbairn's central ego, 1952).

Perhaps we can even relate this to suicide bombing today. However, suicide bombing seems more related to primal level envy, which perpetually destroys those identified as "other." This contrasts with the higher-level murderous hate in jealousy. In oedipal level jealousy, there are three whole object figures, who are also differentiated in terms of gender characteristics, as well as in terms of other personality characteristics.[1]

Differentiating Jealousy from Envy

Following Freud's view of jealousy as a competitive dynamic in the oedipal triad of two parents and a child, Melanie Klein (1957) spoke of how such jealousy had a narrative distinct from that of envy. This narrative of jealousy is separate from the narrative of relentless, perpetuated destruction toward the needed other in the oral stage level of envy where one always self-sabotages by "biting the hand that feeds you." Klein points out that in jealousy, there is love involved, not just hate, whereas in oral envy, the narrative is of compulsion to destroy what the other has because, at that level, all is polarized in a primal split of: "He has it. I don't."

So, with no dialectic in the binary, only polarization, one can only want to destroy with hate what the other has that you think you can never have. However, in jealousy, there is love because the object of desire is loved. This is despite there being trenchant hate directed at the rival. Further, the man (or woman) possessed by jealousy threatens to possess the loved third other, threatening to deprive the subject of all that is loved and desired in the third party, the desired object. Subjectivity is only experienced in the oedipal level depressive position, and not in the oral level paranoid-schizoid position dynamics. So, the narrative of true jealousy, as opposed to envy, encompasses love, as well as subjectivity, along with the hate of destructive and perhaps murderous intent.

Jealousy also always involves three differentiated personalities and is not like envy, which is reductive to one wanting what a second undifferentiated part object other has. With envy, not having what the part object other has is experienced as a severe narcissistic insult, or as the devaluation, and spoiling, of the self as object. Envy contrasts with the jealousy of a higher-level self as a subject who can eventually develop depressive guilt and grief, which leads to concern (Winnicott, 1964) and empathy.

However, Klein also implies that when one has unresolved, un-symbolized, and uninterpreted envy, the oedipal stage dynamic of jealousy is poisoned by the more primitive envy. So the precedipal stage dynamics, and the paranoid-schizoid position psychodynamics of each individual, effects the nature of the unconscious, as well as conscious, experience of jealousy, even when the oedipal stage triadic constellation of human relationship is reached. Especially in patients who have precedipal trauma and developmental arrest, oedipal level jealousy is often enacted in a highly undifferentiated and highly polarized form, which can extend to the act of murder. Those who have a good-enough level of contact and connection with mother during the precedipal phases, particularly during the separation-individuation phases, can internalize relatedness and attunement to a significant degree. In this way, primal trauma and psychic developmental arrest are avoided, despite primal disruptions and disappointments.

With such adequate internalization (Mahler et al., 1975; Masterson 1976, 1981), development of the subjective self, and the internal psychic structure of relationships and dialogue, and all forms of psychic dialectic and self-reflection can develop. The capacity to mourn object loss also develops, since loss is then at a tolerable level of grief affect, and can be processed by a psychic structured ego. Thus, what I have termed developmental mourning (Kavaler-Adler, 1992a, 1993a/2013, 1995, 1996/2014, 2003a, 2003b, 2004, 2005b, 2006a, 2007c, 2013b, 2014b) can emerge organically, from the affect on whole object connections within the internal world (mostly repressed). Consequently, the subjective self evolves throughout life, with an open system in which love and creativity can continually emerge from a sufficiently integrated self.[2] Jealousy can then become symbolized and contained internally through symbolization. Then it can be processed as murderous fantasy, or as a hungry desire to have what the other has in a third person, a differentiated, and loved other/lover. Thus, contained as murder in psychic fantasy, actual fatal murder does not have to be committed!

Clinical Vignette: 1

Primitive Envy Misnamed Jealousy

Every time I attempted to speak to Vivien of her problems with her boyfriend, which she would parade before me, she would lash out instantaneously with a sharp, enraged, and vulgar attack: "You're just an envious bitch!" That would be the end of it. There would be no discussion of what she or I thought was going on with her and her boyfriend. She implied that I would be out to make critical attacking judgments on what she and her boyfriend had, but she never actually said this. She warded off any projected and feared judgments by assaulting me with "You're an envious bitch!" Sometimes she would throw in, "My boyfriend thinks you're a dog! You're just jealous because no man would ever look at you!" (Hardly my experience, but reality was irrelevant.) When I once suggested she might be envious of a niece of her boyfriend's who was getting a lot of attention and gifts when graduating from high school, she erupted with accusatory rage (no reflective thought possible when her own sense of narcissistic injury and insult was aroused), exclaiming, "I got all the attention from all my teachers and family when I graduated. Everyone said I was brilliant, and my older sister cried non-stop at my graduation because nobody gave her any attention when she graduated! I know what 'jealousy' is!"

Then Vivien continued her assault on me: "You're just jealous because nobody ever went to your graduation, and you didn't have any boyfriends in high school." Vivien said this without any knowledge of my life. She didn't even posit her paranoid theories as "probably." To Vivien, her view of me was a fact because she chose to say it. "And," she continued to spit and spout, "and now you're old and no man would look at you!" "And," she ejected again, expelling her venom to get rid of the rage and self-hate inside of her, "You think you're a doctor just because you're a Ph.D.," which was said with belittling, sarcastic, mocking slurs. "You're not a doctorrrrrrrr. You're just a bitch!"

This woman had had a mother who would exclude her from any interactions with her father. But even more, on the gross level of the envious family dynamics, her mother would sit on her father's lap in front of her, and would exhibit her body intimacy with the patient's father, while proclaiming, to her daughter, "I'm really good in bed! I'm the one who won your father!" Given this behavior on Vivien's mother's part, it is easy to see the birth of the cumulative trauma of exclusion and humiliation that led Vivien to ram her relationship with her boyfriend down my throat, while simultaneously warding off any comments I could make to help her with problems in that relationship. It was as if I only wanted to tear what she had to shreds because I didn't have it.

Vivien assumed in me (or projected) the primal oral envy that Melanie Klein (1957) and Otto Kernberg (1975) talk about repeatedly. Yet, Vivien often flung out the word "jealousy" in her interactions with me. She would play the role of her mother and put me in the position of the excluded and inferior child she had felt herself to be when she had been faced with her mother's farcical displays of superiority. There were no differentiated people involved in Vivien's spit-out canon ball blasting comments. This didn't mean that Vivien couldn't be capable of seeing people as more differentiated at other times, reaching toward whole object and subjective self-experience. However, the minute her envy and profound shame were triggered, just as it had been when her mother practically undressed and had sex in front of her with her father, she would instantly regress to the pre-symbolic paranoid-schizoid level of psychic reactivity rather than sustaining any capacity for reflective thought.

Sometimes, an analytic comment of mine would provoke this. Vivien would experience any analytic comment as pointing out a lack in herself. Consequently, Vivien would fight to the death to annihilate me as a separate presence at that point. Since she could not digest my words at a symbolic level of meaning, she would polarize her internal part objects—now projected out onto me—in an envious display. Her envious attack would masquerade as jealousy in the way she used language. She would imply that I was jealous of her having her boyfriend, as her mother had taunted her into extreme states of envious hungry craving for her father. She might use the word "jealousy," but then would say I was an envious bitch, revealing her own state of unconscious envy. Vivien had to deny her hunger at any cost, as if it proved a lack in herself. She conveniently externalized and placed all her starving envy into me. Although she implied jealousy, I would hardly have been able to be jealous of her having her boyfriend, given the problems she told me about in that relationship.

It seemed that Vivien was repeating, through her projections, her primal envy. Yet, there was also jealousy. Vivien had been deprived of her father's attention by her mother, which probably made her jealous of her mother for having her father. Yet primal oral envy could take over the psychological realm of jealousy. Then, Vivien's jealousy could be intensified by hard-core starving hunger, impulses to destroy whatever I, the other, had. This was not just a compulsion to destroy a differentiated woman who she saw as having the attraction of another man or of men (as characteristic of oedipal dynamics). Vivien seemed to want to destroy me for having anything at all, at times when I was the bad object for her. It was as if unconsciously Vivien was saying, "if I can't have your breast, neither can you!"

Vivien knew I had a husband, which was the only thing she knew about my life. She would devalue this at a total level of destructive spoiling (Klein, 1957) by reducing my marriage to: "You have to bring home the money, Susan, or your husband will leave you. You better bring home the money, Susan!" Vivien always said this in a mocking sarcastic voice, as if spitting out the venom, similar to what her mother often done to her. Earlier in the treatment, Vivien had used the word "venom" to describe her mother's attacks. She said she had been the target of this kind of assault from her mother throughout her life.

Given this, I could not use any of my analytic skills with Vivien. Despite having told me about her history with her mother, Vivien would protect her mother's image, and displace her retaliatory rage attacks onto me. In this place of split-off rage, she did not operate on a symbolic level. Absolutely no analytic comments could be made about how Vivien was repeating what her mother had done to her by doing it to me. Vivien would cut me off at the pass. She would override my words so that potential meaning was aborted. Then, she wouldn't shut up until I was silent. Although there were more times in between these kinds of envious assaults, as she psychologically grew and developed her external life, there could be no alteration of this envious retaliatory reenactment with me, which eventually became only with me, as she sustained her outside life and relationships in a much better way. Her primal envy remained evident. Her envy of me for having a Ph.D., husband (or male tango partners attracted to me—I don't think she knew this), or books and publications, could never be felt as a differentiated jealousy where she actually verbalized the value of what I had or verbalized any real distinguishing characteristics of whom and what I had. Vivien reduced all to part object stereotypes.

I experienced being with Vivien in her hungry envious place as if I was constantly being reduced to absurdity. Nevertheless, increasing developmental growth and internalization of the therapeutic relationship have seemed to space out the time between those envious attacks. More transitional space developed in between these seizure-like states of paranoid rage, which I see as related to envy, as well as to primal hunger for a better object.

At what level can jealousy be played with? At what point can guilt over betrayal become modified into spontaneous play and real concern? At what point can jealous rivalry be thought about, rather than being enacted, and thus be played with (Winnicott, 1971)? In the case of Helen, below, we see a pre-disposition to jealousy, which sets her up to be suspicious. Her own self worth becomes the issue in working this through and helping her value herself as a woman that could actually inspire jealousy in another woman.

Clinical Vignette: 2

True Jealousy (As Opposed to Envy)

Helen had never had a long-term, truly committed boyfriend. She never formerly had a boyfriend with whom she lived, nor one with whom she could share intellectual interests and creative activities. When she found a man she could have this with, she began to imagine that he would be lured away by some other woman, who would seem more interesting and less boring than she. Helen could set up a self-fulfilling prophecy with this mindset and was, therefore, in danger of pushing her boyfriend away.

Whenever she shared with her boyfriend her fears about one woman or another being her rival for her boyfriend's attraction, her boyfriend would dismiss her thoughts as her own neurotic fantasies. He would not engage with her in any speculations about actually wanting to be involved with another woman. Then, one summer, her boyfriend stayed for a few weeks with Helen's family, at their country home, and Helen's two sisters were there. Her younger sister, who was always envious of what Helen had, tried to copy everything she did, and then would parade her hyper-valued imitation before Helen's boyfriend. In fact, Helen's younger sister would read books that Helen liked. Then she would compete with Helen by discussing the meaning of these books with Helen's boyfriend. Even though Helen's sister was far less sophisticated in her intellectual discussions than Helen was, Helen felt she was faced with a rival in her younger sister for her boyfriend's attraction and affection. What was envy of Helen in the psyche of her younger sister became jealousy in Helen toward her younger envious sister, who she then experienced as a rival for her deeply-valued boyfriend.

Helen's sister only wanted to have whatever Helen had, and to destroy Helen's enjoyment of what she had, as in envy. However, Helen actually valued her boyfriend (the third in the jealous dyad) and so love was involved. This was clearly characteristic of jealousy, as opposed to the hate and murderous destructiveness, seen in envy. Eventually, Helen talked to her boyfriend about her feelings, having contained them enough to speak about them with symbolic meaning in her three times a week psychoanalysis (later four times a week). As usual, her boyfriend was initially ready to dismiss her suspicions, but Helen fought to articulate how seriously hurt she was by him joining her younger sister in all these discussions and activities that mimicked her own interests. Her boyfriend listened then and began to judiciously distance himself from Helen's sister.

Helen, in turn, began to value her boyfriend more and to be less suspicious of him. Someone who never had the background of oedipal level jealousy with her father and mother that Helen had might have been less likely to have the ongoing jealous suspicions that Helen had. This relates back to how Helen took pride in thinking herself an oedipal victor in relation to her mother. She had always thought her father found her company more enjoyable than that of her mother. Given her own wish to be a victor of the man's love in a love triangle, Helen could easily be vulnerable to feeling that another woman—even her sister—would lord it over her, and leave her in the dust, with the male prize. Her mind was set up for this level of haunting jealous suspicion that poisoned her love life.

Helen was able to contain her instinctual impulses and affective feelings in the situation, to keep them contained in fantasy, and to talk about them in her analysis, and eventually with her boyfriend. Eventually, Helen could even play with her own preoccupations with jealousy when she spoke to me in analysis, lessening the despair behind her fears and gradually came to sustain internal world whole Object Relations for longer periods of time.

Clinical Vignette: 3

In the Transference: On the Couch, A Man

Leonard was an oedipal level neurotic, who had been in psychoanalytic psychotherapy with me for several years. He was capable of seeing me as a symbolic transference figure, having attained representational parental introjects in his internal world—as opposed to those who can only act things out with the therapist since they have not formed symbolic representational forms of their parental objects.[3] Leonard could therefore contain his affect life in symbolic fantasies, which he could convey to me with words. His transference fantasies revealed his oedipal stage jealousy and also his Kleinian depressive position capacities to feel and process existential guilt, as opposed to paranoid-schizoid position level persecution with urges toward retaliatory enactment. Therefore, Leonard could feel and mentally process the grief of loss. This was in contrast to somebody who is psychologically operating in Melanie Klein's (1957) paranoid-schizoid position, who cannot contain guilt but suffers persecution with powerful instinctual urges toward retaliatory enactment.

Leonard was aware of his jealous feelings and desires. For example, when he saw my husband bringing me a café latte at my office before his session, Leonard suspected the man he saw was my husband. Then, Leonard would have fantasies of what kind of husband my husband was for me. He would be glad that my husband seemed to be taking care of me, but he would also be conscious of feeling jealous about the relationship he imagined between myself and my husband. This would remind him of things he experienced with his parents in childhood. However, he would also imagine the other side of the oedipal triangle. He would think of my husband being jealous of him, whenever he would share intimate and sexual thoughts about me. He would fear a rivalry with my husband, in which he would feel small and inferior, or a rivalry in which my husband would feel inadequate, due to the degree of intimacy he shared with me. In many ways, Leonard had been an oedipal victor with his mother and father. In fact, his mother would share her confidences, feelings, and dreams with him when she could not speak about such things with her husband, Leonard's father.

Leonard was seen as the sensitive one by his mother. However, this left him vulnerable to not being seen as being as much of a man as his father. His mother would use Leonard to express all her anger toward her husband, and then she would be purged of her rage, so that when her husband returned home, she was friendly and even solicitous to him. This would provoke feelings of betrayal and jealousy in Leonard. He would be angry at his mother for treating him as so special during the day, and then catering to his father at night, having rid herself of her anger by expressing it to Leonard. Instead of just feeling used by his mother, he would feel betrayed, due to his oedipal level of unconscious fantasy.

Leonard would also be provoked into sexual interest toward his mother by his mother when she would seem to intentionally undress with her bedroom door open so that he could see her bare breasts. Then, when his mother succeeded in provoking him into looking at her, she would turn everything around on him, by glaring at him and saying, "What are you looking at?" He felt tricked by his mother's seduction and then humiliated by his mother's guilt-provoking accusatory attacks. However, later, in analysis, he also wondered why his mother needed him to be aroused by her, especially when she would walk around the house in fairly sheer nightgowns at night. When young, he had been stimulated to think about his mother's sexual relationship with his father. Then, he would feel jealous, but he would also feel convinced that his father was jealous of him when his father would get punitive, arrogant, and harsh toward him, challenging him to be a man, as if his father was facing a rival for his bride.

All this made Leonard angry at both his parents, but he often masochistically turned his anger into guilt, and self-condemnation, blaming himself to avoid feeling alone and threatened by hate toward his parents. Leonard would protect the image of his parents by telling himself that he was bad for peeking looks at his mother's body or for thinking that he was the superior sensitive man in the triad of father and son relationship with his mother. Leonard would imagine taking his "punishment" of being put down with sarcastic and contemptuous comments by his father, which implied that he wasn't a "real man." When his mother turned all her attention to his father at night, Leonard would also feel that he was being seen as the inferior man by his mother, thinking that his sensitive and empathic understanding of his mother's feelings only made him more feminine in his mother's eyes, and therefore in his own.

In the extreme dynamic of this triadic oedipal relationship, he would feel castrated by both his parents. Then, he would identify with their aggression by condemning and castrating himself in his own mind. As he belittled himself internally, he would feel more vulnerable to jealousy toward his father in relation to his mother, and toward his mother in relation to his father. He felt like a third wheel, losing the feeling of being the special son to his mother or his father.

In the transference, Leonard would imagine me at the window, with no blouse on, baring my breasts at the window, as if he would see my bare breasts as he came toward my office. He would seek erotic stimulation to make him feel not only instinctually stimulated, but also psychologically puffed up to feel like a man, a man who was capable of being attracted to his transferential mother on an adult sexual level. Leonard would also feel guilt. He would try not to look at me if I wore a summer dress, in which there was any hint of cleavage showing. He was, however, able to talk about all this in his psychoanalytic therapy sessions, and he became less anxious about telling me his thoughts. Gradually, Leonard's persecutory guilt lessened, and we could have a playful conversation.[4]

Leonard's existential guilt (as opposed to his neurotic guilt), in relation to jealousy, would be seen when he feared he would provoke his wife into jealousy. Leonard also feared provoking the husband of the woman he was flirting with into jealousy. He would feel that he couldn't have enough intimacy and sexual desire with his wife. So, he would turn to the affections of a former professor, who shared his needs, despite her own marital status. He and this professor would share their mutual attraction on the phone, mostly thoughts of sexual acts and confessions of love and desire.

In the back of Leonard's mind was always the fear that he would provoke his wife into jealous rages, and that she would then divorce him. He feared such retaliation in the paranoid-schizoid psychic position, but he also felt actual existential grief within guilt, since he loved his wife and didn't want to hurt her. Further, he had fears of humiliating castrations from his professor's husband, which would interact with Leonard's fears and jealousies related to my husband. Both my husband and the female professor's husband became transference father figures in Leonard's mind.

Sometimes, Leonard would imagine that God was punishing him for his psychological and enacted transgressions by creating new losses in his life. He had early-life sibling loss and remained very vulnerable to deep feelings of grief as new losses brought associations to his old primal losses up in his mind. He tried to ward this off by avoiding thoughts of sexual interest or desire with me in the transference, or by not facing consciousness of the depth of pain he felt with new losses that always encompassed the old losses. In a sense, God became the castrating and punishing father who was jealous of his erotic relationships with women, as his father had been experienced in relation to his erotic desires and sexual curiosity to his mother.

As Leonard spoke about all his provocations of jealousy in others, and also became less resistant to talk about his jealousy of others who he saw as rivals, some of whom were rivals for me in the transference, he became more accepting of all his feelings. As guilt and fear turned to play and empathic understanding of the frustrations and conflicts he was dealing with, Leonard was able to increasingly relax about the impact of the triangles with men and women that existed in his life. He gradually stood up to his wife when she was provoked into jealousy, and he found that she actually became kinder and more attentive to him, although she was initially upset. His wife also stopped asking him about his analysis with a woman analyst in a perpetually intrusive and disapproving way.

Further, his own jealousy became increasingly tolerable as he could put the emotion into words. Then, he could have all his feelings, so that the dangerous aggressive instincts that accompany jealousy (even in those at the oedipal level) would not threaten his psyche and his relationship. Leonard also accepted that he had once punched a guy who he caught having a sexual affair with his wife when he and his wife were very young (decades ago). With self-reflection, Leonard decided that he was entitled to take a swing at the guy, when he found him in his own house, in the middle of some sexual episode with his wife. As he came to accept his own jealousy, he became less frightened of retaliation in relation to his possible provocations of jealousy in others.

Then, Leonard's existential guilt could be felt and processed as just being human feelings. Leonard began to value that he could feel grief with poignant acuteness, even when losses were related to things he may have done to hurt the ones he loved, rather than to major bereavements that he had suffered. His actual bereavements were much more monumental, due to the tragic level of loss involved, and particularly the sibling loss. Gradually, Leonard began to see that this capacity to feel and tolerate guilt made him more of a man (and not just his mother's sensitive son). This, in turn, lessened his taunting and castrating attacks on himself in his internal world. He became less jealous of himself as the sensitive son in his internal world. He became less identified with his father in his father's jealousy toward him since he was separating from a father who defined manhood most differently.

Leonard became less afraid of provoking jealousy in others and became increasingly free. Our playful interchanges in subsequent analytic sessions were a testimony to this. In a period before "play" in his psychoanalysis was possible, Leonard had had so much painful grief, as well as angry resistance to sharing. He had suffered so much self-hate. But now we played! I said, "You are so much more spontaneous!" Smiling as he got up from the couch at the session's end, he said, "That's what I come here for." This spontaneity came after a long period of time in which he was questioning, "What am I here for?"

Clinical Vignette: 4

In the Transference: A Case of a Woman Who Could Express Jealousy Dramas in Fantasies in Analysis

Amy came into psychoanalytic treatment (three times a week) with a full-blown homoerotic transference toward me, her female analyst (Kavaler-Adler 2003a, 2003b). She had adopted a lesbian lifestyle years ago, after having been married to a man earlier on. Her attraction to the analyst became multidimensional in all kinds of playful scenes of triadic jealousy. Sometimes she would play the masculine role in these sexual scenes, and sometimes she would be identified with me in the feminine role. However, there was always an oedipal triangle, despite all her bisexual modes of expression, with altering gender identities, and altering sex object choice.

Some of Amy's fantasies were of having a sexual affair with me in my office. She said that she would "take my pearl in her mouth," "drown in my come," and then would "wrap me up in a blanket afterward," holding me tenderly. Aside from the fact that she saw me as representing her, up to then unconscious, child-self, as I regressed into the state of a tender child, wrapped a blanket, Amy also had the oedipal triangle, in which my husband was imagined banging on the outside of my office door, as my husband came to jealously "defend his territory!"

Amy obviously projected her own jealous rivalry toward my husband onto the fantasy figure of my husband. She also attempted to disown her own jealousy by becoming, in her fantasy, part of the sex scene between me and my husband, that which traditionally would be seen as the primal scene, with the parental couple in the internal world having sex in front of her. When I went away for a vacation, Amy told me of her imaginings about my vacation when I returned. She said she imagined me and my husband having sex in a hotel, where I would get excited to the point of orgasm by my husband beating me. She said she imagined that I loved being beaten, and imagined me reaching the heights of sexual excitement and ecstasy through surrendering to this erotic beating. She then imagined that she was in the background the whole time, watching the sexual scene, while she cheered me on to my orgasms.

So, she managed to avoid feeling excluded from the parental couple; she imagined other scenarios in which she and I were being penetrated by a man side by side, one after the other, so she avoided jealousy and exclusion in this way. She was then in the feminine receptive role along with me. Other times, she was in her masculine side, and somewhat in a false masculine persona. She herself later referred to this as her "false self." But she felt the erotic masculine sensations that she also felt in her real life, with her female lover, as she pictured strapping on a dildo and penetrating me. In this fantasy, Amy had my husband being the one on the outside, in the position of exclusion and jealousy.

When Amy did feel conscious jealousy, she would feel like exploding with rage, and she would speak of her fantasy wish: "Throw you against the wall and fuck you!" She remembered a scene of accidentally going into her parents' bedroom when they failed to close their door during sex. Afterward, everyone in the family was mortified with embarrassment and shame, staring down at their plates at the dinner table and not being able to look at each other. Nobody could speak about these sexual things in her family, even though there was so much sexualized enactment going on in her family all the time. With all this enactment, someone was always excluded.

One of Amy's most anguished early memories was of being three years old and being caught in a terrifying trap, in between the conflict between her parents, when her father returned home after an extramarital affair. Her father's sexual affairs were frequent, and Amy's mother was the most aggrandized of victims of her husband's exclusion. In this three-year-old's memory, Amy ran downstairs to open the door for her father, who was banging persistently on a door that had been locked with a new lock that he couldn't open. Her mother screamed at Amy from upstairs, "If you open that door, I will kill you!" Her father screamed, over and over, "Open the door!" Three-year-old little Amy was paralyzed, and she ran toward the door, and then ran away from it, as her mother screamed again: "If you open that door, I will kill you!"

Amy's mother's jealousy, and Amy's mother's betrayals, pervaded the household as Amy grew up. Naturally, Amy got some relief from the traumatizing effect of these scenes by eroticizing them. She would create triadic sexual scenarios in fantasy, and then in transference fantasy, where she could be in control by creating the fantasy. By making herself the audience in a scene of passionate love-making between myself and my husband, she managed to include herself and avoid her own jealousy. By being my lover, in her mind, and having my husband banging on the door from the outside, the way her father had banged on the door that night when she was three, Amy became the one in control. In her fantasy, Amy had my husband in the helpless position of jealous rage and frustrated sexual desire—implying also frustrated cravings for maternal nurturance from the preœdipal level. In this way, Amy could avoid conscious jealousy and all the threats of overwhelming feeling that came with it.

Later in treatment, Amy would have to feel this emotional need behind sexual desire more consciously. She had a dream where she associated to my needs being overwhelming, as she threw one eel after another over the side of a boat. However, when I interpreted that these eels also represented her own needs being felt as overwhelming to her, she had to admit to the conscious state of need, after having been defensive in response to my interpretation. Once she consciously began to own her needs, she had a chance for the child part of her, which she felt through loss and mourning of injuries and losses—to grow up. She then had her full feminine side organically emerge, as well as a natural (not false self) masculine side that wanted to develop. Amy began to own and integrate all the parts of herself that had been partially repressed and projected, as well as having been often dissociated.

Jealousy could be owned and tolerated in symbolic fantasy, when mourning of childhood losses (Kavaler-Adler, 1992a, 1993a/2013, 1996/2014, 2003a, 2003b, 2007c), such as emotional abandonment by her mother, could be felt with the support of the analyst and the analytic holding environment (Winnicott, 1965). This helped Amy to be able to commit to her long-term lesbian lover. This occurred even though Amy became conscious of desires for male penetration and male love in the later stages of her analysis, when oedipal desire, conflict, and jealousies became felt, and her feminine self emerged in full desire to surrender to male love and male phallic penetration.

In her own words, Amy no longer felt like "a hamster on a wheel" who was always drawn away from her lover to wanting emotional and erotic affairs with others. She became more present with her lover, as all parts of herself could be accepted by her, and by her lover and long-term partner. In fact, throughout her analysis, Amy had feared that she was betraying her lover by having fantasies of making love to me, and by actually calling flower shops to send me long-stemmed roses until she could put these gifts of love into words at a symbolic level.

In the middle of enjoying fantasies of love-making with me in her mind, Amy would stop and express anger about being lulled into such desires by analysis. She would fear that she was betraying her lover, and feared her lover would become highly enraged and jealous if she knew. One day, she confessed to her lover that she had actually sent me long-stemmed red roses, which was what she used to send her lover. She was extremely relieved when her lover understood that these kinds of things could take place in analysis. Amy had feared the wrath of her monumentally jealous and retaliatory mother. But she was met with a much different response. The Greek tragedy in her mind did not play itself out in a triad of jealous competition between her external world lover and her transference mother/lover (her female analyst). Seeing this, Amy could begin to relax.

Gradually, Amy began to enjoy the feminine side of her development. She stood up to her lover when her lover questioned why she wanted to dress differently. Her lover was shocked when Amy was considering wearing a dress. Ultimately, Amy decided to wear elegant pantsuits, with a touch of jewelry. As Amy's fears of jealousy within herself and within others lessened, she was able to articulate her needs and desires in words. Then, her need for powerful erotic fantasies in analysis lessened. Very significantly, her sex life with her lover/partner improved.

Clinical Vignette: 5

Simon: The Man Who Was Haunted by Jealous Thoughts

Simon said his relationship with Rachel was different than any relationship with women in his past. He felt more exposed to being truly known by Rachel, unlike with former girlfriends. He felt challenged with Rachel because of the intense periods of sustained intimacy with heights of sexual passion. Yet, somehow Simon continued to experience Rachel as a mystery, despite how many facts she shared about her life. Also, with Rachel, Simon was haunted by fears that had never plagued him before. In fact, in the past, he had been the one to cheat in a relationship, and he never thought of it as a betrayal at the time. He was shocked when his former girlfriend's jealousy resulted in a break up of a relationship of several years.

Now, with Rachel, Simon could not stop imagining that Rachel was with another man. He tried to deny to himself how deeply threatened he felt by such fears. In fact, it took much time for him to admit to himself that he actually felt haunted on a continuing basis by the fear that Rachel was with another man. Symptomatically, when Simon called Rachel on his cell phone, and she wasn't immediately available, he would begin to "freak out." Instantly, if Rachel did not answer the call and say "Simon," he would start to imagine that she was out on a date with another man, or that she was in bed with another man.

In his therapy sessions, Simon assured me that he never had such suspicious thoughts before about another woman. He said that it was something about Rachel that unnerved him. He wondered whether it was a combination of her deeply emotional and sexual availability that made him feel ongoing terror about losing her. However, Simon's terror of losing Rachel was often overwhelmed by his sense of enraged, and very self-righteous, aggression toward her. In fact, Simon explained this by interpreting her possible betrayal of their monogamous contract as a deliberate attempt to traumatize him, taking advantage of his revealing his sensitive nature to Rachel.

Where Simon's suspicions originated was only partially apparent to Simon. He referred to Rachel having kept one secret from him at the beginning of their relationship. But could such a small transgression really arouse his constant state of haunted terror and exquisitely sensitive vulnerability? Simon asked this of himself. How could he be almost feeling like he was losing his mind, simply over suspicious thoughts about Rachel's commitment to him? He could not believe it himself—how haunted he was by suspicions that Rachel was with another man. He brought this one shred of rational reason for suspicion into the consulting room and shared his thoughts while lying on the couch in his psychoanalytic therapy session. He would repeat this shred of rational reasoned suspicion over and over again, as he obsessed about why he could not trust Rachel, and why this led to him being distant from the woman with who he said he was most passionately in love.

So, we talked about Rachel's resistance to his interrogation of her about things in the beginning of their relationship. They had already decided to commit themselves to each other, and he assumed that she was being honest in saying she had not dated anyone else since that time. But then Rachel casually mentioned that she had gone on a date with a medical doctor on a certain date, which Simon quickly calculated was after he and Rachel had met and decided to get serious (meaning exclusively dating each other, to each of them). Simon went into a tailspin. He kept checking the date over and over again in his mind, and then he asked Rachel if she was sure she hadn't seen anyone but him after a certain date, prior to that when they had a serious conversation about commitment. Rachel stuck to her story of absolute exclusivity with him. Simon reacted by feeling like he was losing his mind.

Eventually, Rachel admitted that she had gone on one single date then because the guy looked so handsome in the picture she saw of him through an online dating service. She admitted that his lucrative income had also attracted her. Rachel defended herself by saying that she had been feeling very insecure about managing her life on the income she had. She said she just couldn't resist going on one date with this guy to check him out, even though she immediately decided to stay fully committed to Simon, as soon as she actually spent an evening with this other guy.

But this did not appease Simon's fears about Rachel's loyalty to him at all! In fact, his fear increased. After all, he tortured himself with obsessional thoughts because he had caught Rachel in a lie, even after he had committed himself to her, and even after she had proclaimed her commitment to him. Simon couldn't forget this one incident, even though it was right at the beginning of their relationship when they had just begun talking about seriously being together, way before they had even considered moving in together. Simon could not stop having the disturbing and perseverating thought: "If she lied once she could lie again?" and the accompanying thoughts: "Is she with another man now? Is she looking for a better catch, someone cuter, smarter, or richer?" He thought he was being rational since he had caught her in a lie about being with another man. Yet, the intense haunting nature of his jealousy obsession suggested—even to him—that he might be "a little nuts," because ever since that early time, Rachel had shown herself to be totally committed to the exclusive monogamy of their agreed-upon relationship.

Not knowing about how he might be unconsciously projecting his own wandering ways nor appreciating how Rachel might serve as a transference representative of a figure from his past left Simon in the dark, continuously crying out in therapy, "Why can't I forget this thing? It's killing me!" He found himself being more distant from Rachel than ever. He feared he would destroy the whole relationship, especially the most intimate sexual and emotional sharing that he and Rachel had shared.

In analysis, Simon was to learn that Rachel indeed represented a transference figure, in fact, the ultimate transference figure: his mother. Disturbing memories began coming back to him. One particular traumatic memory reared its head. When he was in his latency years, his mother—who was a fairly well-known actress before her marriage to his father—had run away from the family. She had left him and his younger sister all alone with a father who was emotionally detached and very rarely at home. In fact, when he and his sister weren't in school, they were often in the care of young teenage babysitters, with whom they felt quite insecure. Years later, one of the former babysitters, whom he met when away at a university, told him that his father had been seduced by his run-away mother into living half the time with her and also serving as her agent so she could try to get back into show business. That was disturbing enough to hear, but then the former babysitter told him that his father would talk about how his wife resented ever having left show business to become a mother. Simon was devastated when he heard this, even though he was then of college-age and no longer home longing for a mother who left him.

As his psychoanalyst, I said to Simon that it made sense that with such a traumatic experience of abandonment by his mother, he might have trouble trusting women. I also said that the fact that his mother's feelings had been building up to the point of running away to New York City to a hotel and leaving the family, also would make a case in his mind for suspicions about the underlying motives of women. After all, Simon learned that women who might on the surface be "playing their role" well—the role of devotion to caring for another, or others—might secretly be harboring desires to depart and to get rid of those who they supposedly care about, or those that they are caring for. Simon said that "yes," he could see that that all made sense. However, Simon didn't really "get it" on an emotional level. After all, to his conscious mind, Rachel seemed nothing like his mother, and to his conscious mind, he was "over all that," about his mother leaving him and his sister behind, to go back into show business in New York. To his conscious mind, all that was irrelevant to his current state since it was years ago.

Then, something came alive in the transference with me that made Simon think again. He began to fail to show up for sessions. He actually began to forget a lot of his sessions and hadn't even thought of setting a reminder alert on his phone so that he wouldn't forget. He was vague and distant in his sessions. When I tried to explore his unconscious "forgetting," he got defensive. He said that he forgot a lot of things, not just his therapy sessions. He was forgetting things for years. I suggested that forgetting things was a way of forgetting things that are too painful to remember, like the inconstancy of women, which he generally interpreted as betrayal and abandonment. Suddenly, Simon turned his accusing tone and accusing looks (not seen fully while on the couch) on me. He said that he thought I had ulterior motives in charging for the sessions that he forgot and didn't show up for. He never had a problem with the understood commitment that he would pay for his session times before, even if he couldn't attend, especially when he didn't ask for rescheduling for his missed sessions ahead of time.

Now—and it did seem sudden to me—Simon began to wonder if I really took pleasure in his not showing up so that I could earn money for sessions I did not have to work in. He even went on to say that, "no woman could be trusted!" He suddenly launched into suspicion of me even though he intellectually knew that I had been the one trying to reach him by phone and email when he wouldn't be showing for his session times. In contrast to me enjoying his absences so I could get paid for no work done, I had spent the sessions wondering how to reach him, and wondering what was going on with him.

Intellectually, Simon knew this, but emotionally, he needed an opportunity to see me as the betraying woman. Unconsciously, he may have needed to distrust me, so he could work out his trouble trusting women. He was becoming very afraid of being alone for the rest of his life. He was afraid he would not be able to sustain love for any woman, due to his deep distrust of women, despite his intellectual excuses for his mother and Rachel. We were still in the process of understanding Simon's distrust of me, and therefore understanding his fear of trusting women. The hurt and pain that Simon suffered as a child, when he was rejected by his mother—at least rejected in terms of being cared for daily by her—was beginning to surface.

Some of Simon's pain was related to how disturbing to him it was to have so much anger at his mother, as well as having so much anger toward me and Rachel. He was remembering an agony that he had repressed for a lifetime. When his mother left the family home and left him, he was forced to close off his internal subjective experience, in order to psychologically survive. Simon had had no choice but to repress his anger and rage. He had to cooperate with the program his mother and father had set up because he was totally dependent on them for his survival. And for psychic survival, he had to repress the intensity of his feeling. He had to go along with the program then and now he felt like he was being forced to go along with the program of attending sessions regularly in analysis. So, we looked at how trapped he felt and how angry that made him toward me. Outside of the transference, he knew it was his choice to attend therapy sessions or not. Yet, he was re-living the time of his mother's rejection of the care for him and his sister. It was inevitable that he should feel like rebelling against my program, of setting time frames. But under the rage about being forced to go wherever his parents wanted him to go was Simon's deep hurt about being rejected by his one and only mother. He felt too hurt to just feel anger and self-righteous rage. He carried a deep wound of narcissistic injury, which was part of what set him up to be so overtaken by jealousy. Unconsciously—for a lifetime—he had always doubted that he could be truly wanted! Just like Othello, he may have doubted he was okay, underneath his surface functioning in the world.

Conclusion

In this contribution, I have shared case examples of those who have triadic oedipal stage jealousy at a symbolized level, in contrast to those with enactments of primal envy. Jealousy can be worked with analytically, i.e., by means of interpretation of the unconscious. Those stuck in enactments of primal (oral) envy are primarily stuck in the paranoid-schizoid position, where differentiated whole object jealousy is not yet on the horizon, and where symbolization of such affect states of envy and jealousy is not developed. I have also shared the dilemma of a patient who has suffered unresolved oedipal stage jealousy, with possible underlying precedipal merger wishes as well, in the mind of a psychoanalyst.

Although the focus of this chapter was on jealousy, and not on the mourning process necessary to resolve the neurotic self-sabotage involved when jealousy remains unconscious, the clinical necessity for mourning as a developmental process has been indicated in each case. My longer clinical cases on the developmental mourning process itself (Kavaler-Adler, 1992a, 1993a/2013, 1996/2014, 1995, 2000, 2003a, 2003b, 2004, 2005a, 2006a, 2007c, 2013, 2014b) can be read in my books and articles.

Martin Bergmann (1987), in his book, *The Anatomy of Loving*, speaks of the ubiquitous human fantasy that true love will somehow rid someone of their feelings of both envy and jealousy. Obviously, when people do not enter analysis, both their feelings of envy and jealousy and their belief that love could rid them of such feelings would remain predominantly unconscious. However, in psychoanalysis, we have the opportunity to bring these shame-ridden and guilt-laden feelings— as well as the never conceptualized unconscious beliefs attached to them—to consciousness. In this way, we both help our psychoanalytic patients, and we also grow to understand the predicaments of the human condition in greater depth.

In the same book, Bergmann refers to the danger of failed analysis, in which envy and jealousy are not addressed as human phenomenology, and where the normal human mourning for the loss of the oedipal love object is not undertaken by the patient. He references Freud (1916) speaking about patients who consider themselves to be the grandiose exceptions, who would presume to not have to face the mental prohibitions against incest, nor to have to face being jealous of rivals. These are those "oedipal victors" who can only see themselves as the objects of jealousy but not as those with jealousy within themselves.

I agree with both Freud and Martin Bergmann that nobody can sustain healthy development, and healthy and sustained intimate relationships, without facing the limitations of the human condition. The human condition requires that we mourn, with true grief affect, and with conscious awareness of what must be relinquished, to move on to adult human relations. To mourn, one must symbolize the original primal love objects and the old infantile or oedipal mode of relationship. The old mode of attachment needs to be let go of, while one relinquishes possessive wishes toward those objects, including "omnipotent" attempts to control those onto whom those primal jealous objects are projected.

We may retain our old symbiotic and oedipal relationship constellations in fantasy, but in analysis, we need to make unconscious fantasies conscious so that we don't persist in acting them out, rather than just enjoying the former experiences as symbolic level fantasies. In the end, we do have to move on to different forms of relatedness, in which separation-individuation loss is felt, and in which oedipal loss of the incest object is tolerated through mourning as well. Only then can we move on to seeing who we are truly with within the present, in the external world, outside the internal world scenarios that press unconsciously for repetition.

The journey of grief, mourning, and loss is a difficult one, particularly for those with failures in primal precedipal mothering, if only in the later periods of separation-individuation (Mahler et al, 1975). With those who have had more adequate mothering, and mother image internalization in the precedipal years, the oedipal stage relinquishment of an incestuous love object, and the relinquishment of the regressive oedipal rival object, which foments intense feelings of jealousy, are somewhat less difficult. This is true, since what I call normal developmental mourning (Kavaler-Adler, 1992a, 1993a/2013, 1996/2014, 1995, 2000, 2003a, 2003b, 2004, 2005b, 2006a, 2007c, 2013, 2014b), in these developmentally higher-level cases, is not compounded by the patient needing to navigate the traumatic void, rage, and unsymbolized grief of the abandonment depression (Masterson 1976, 1981) that is consequent to primal developmental arrest. The abandonment depression is, after all, primal object loss due to the disruption of good enough mothering and the self-cohesion of "going-on-being" (Winnicott 1965, 1971).

Nevertheless, we all need to mourn and relinquish the old relationship constellations. We need to mourn both those with bad object attachments (Fairbairn, 1952) and those with over-stimulating but yet adequate oedipal stage attachments. The technique of interpretation in psychoanalysis remains our main tool to help people understand what they are carrying with them from the past, which needs to be understood (forgiven) and somewhat relinquished to move on. There is a danger in neglecting the interpretation process, which seems characteristic of some modern schools of thought. This has been clearly stated by the Object Relations theorist, Frank Summers (interview of Summers by Kavaler-Adler, and interview of Kavaler-Adler by Summers, 1997, The Newsletter of Division 39, plus personal communication, and also books, 1999, 2013), as well as by myself and other Object Relations theorists.

Notes

[1] See Kavaler-Adler (1993a/2013) for a view of jealousy in Charlotte Bronte's (1853) novel, *Villette*, versus primal envy in Emily Bronte's (1847) ***Wuthering Heights***.

[2] See Kavaler-Adler (2014a) on "Love-Creativity Dialectic."

[3] See Masterson (1981) on "Transference Acting Out."

[4] See Winnicott (1971) on "The Capacity for Play" in this regard.

CHAPTER 17

FEAR OF INTIMACY

Originally published as the "Fear of intimacy" chapter in
Akhtar (Ed.) (2014). *Fear: A Dark Shadow Across Our Lifespan*
(pp. 85–121). Karnac.

The fear of intimacy can relate to primal annihilation terrors or higher level fears of object loss and loss of love. The terror of losing any differentiated subjective self and its autonomy, or any primitive sense of existing at all, or of killing off the part object mother-other with one's basic states of emotional need, are seen in character disorders. Higher level fears of retaliatory aggression, and of one's own aggression killing off the object, as well as fears of grief-laden loss, and fears of overwhelming longings for the love of a loving other who can also withhold love and thus create the pain of unrequited love—all can be seen in oedipal level neurotic conditions (those already living a lot of the time in Melanie Klein's depressive position).

To break down some of the preœdipal terrors (Winnicott's "unthinkable anxieties"), as well as the higher level inhibitions that all together give us a picture of the fear of intimacy, I will have two sections of this chapter. The first section will outline the concepts of major British and American Object Relations theorists who speak in their own particular ways of the developmental arrests due to primal trauma, and of the higher level intrapsychic dilemmas and conflicts that forestall intimacy in relationships. The second section will give clinical examples from my own psychoanalytic Object Relations private practice of almost 40 years.

Theories

Harry Guntrip: Schizoid Phenomena, Object-Relations, and the Self

Harry Guntrip's "in and out program" (Guntrip, 1969, p. 36) is based on a primal and regressive splitting related to developmental arrest in character disorders. One

403

is damned if one does, and damned if one doesn't, in terms of basic human needs to be connected to the other (Fairbairn, 1952), to avoid abandonment and self-dissolution, and to simultaneously be free of the other enough to have one's own autonomy. One's autonomy feels threatened by terrors of entrapment, suffocation, and/or claustrophobia, when there is no psychic space (related to the internalization of potential and transitional space between self and other) inside the internal world, due to the lack of internalization of a separate other (e.g., mother of separation) during the separation-individuation process.

To be "in" is to crave connection, but in the developmentally arrested individual, who had not separated and self-integrated and who has not internalized the whole other (one who is, in Melanie Klein's terms, stuck in the paranoid-schizoid position), there is no connection of a subjective self with another subjective self, i.e., no interpersonal relationship. There is only concrete merger. Such concrete merger lacks the relief of relating to the other psychologically as someone represented by words, images, and symbolic meanings. Also, in concrete merger, one cannot differentiate if he/she is having thoughts and feelings about oneself or the other, as well as having no awareness about the subject of one's interpretations (see Ogden, 1986, on the interpreting subject). There is no dialogue, only a monologue in the mind related to reactive victimization, when the "harmonious" fictive merger breaks down. Then, the other is always perceived as enacting hostile impingements, intrusions, and active attacks.

So, there is no sustaining of contact within a connection through love and surviving through anger and hate. There is either merger that temporarily answers the primal human need for connection, which is the "in" part of the "in and out" solution, or there is the escape from the merger, through cutting off contact (abruptly if one is splitting and in the paranoid-schizoid position), which is the "out" part of the "in and out program" (Guntrip, 1969, p. 36).

The object and the dissociated self-parts that are attached to the bad and the idealized part objects are split due to the lack of integration of love and hate. One loves the symbiotic object that one has inside the internal world; the object from prior to the early precedipal trauma resulted from the failings of mothering attunement during separation and autonomy. One hates the separate other who evokes the traumatizing object of separation. The other is never an ambivalently loved and hated whole-object-other; and one cannot have anger within a sustained relationship with another, where the other can remain good enough to survive anger in one's mind, so that love could be renewed. As soon as anger is felt, it becomes hate, combined with a sense of betrayal and an accusation of abuse and victimization.

The other is no longer a good enough object to be accused and then loved again. The idealized object immediately becomes the hated bad object who must be totally spoiled, devalued, demonized, disowned, and left as soon as anger at the level of preœdipal rage and hate takes over. In other words, preœdipal separation-individuation stage trauma is re-lived and experienced again. One feels disappointed, outraged, and betrayed! Later, the same cycle of traumatic disappointment occurs after one attempts to merge with his/her symbolic pre-trauma mother, who is hoped to be the mother one never had. Now again, the new idealized object is devalued and becomes bad and demonized; and one relives being at the mercy of this bad object, which failed to negotiate attunement during separation.

Guntrip's schizoid compromise is when intimacy must be avoided in a relationship because of polarized fears of either entrapment or abandonment—in relation to a split internal object, which becomes whether idealized symbiotic mother or demonized bad object mother of separation. Consequently, one never offers his/her full self to the other. One is never present in full intimacy because parts of oneself must be dissociated and put out to others outside the relationship or displaced onto others, to avoid a full engagement, which feels like "putting one's eggs all in one basket." So, one keeps contact to a minimum (e.g., therapy only once a week) or avoids marriage in life, as well as in psychoanalysis. The compromise is to have some connection, because of a profound human need to have some contact and connection, while also avoiding the need for the other or responsibility for the needs of the other. In this way, one attempts to avoid feeling trapped and engulfed in the other's needs and being abandoned by the lack of adequate availability of the other for one's own needs.

Ronald Fairbairn: Psychoanalytic Studies of the Personality

Harry Guntrip derived his theories about the schizoid "in and out" solution and the "schizoid compromise" from Ronald Fairbairn's theories about the split self and Object Relationships that are incorporated within the psyche of anyone, but particularly of those who have primal failures in mothering in the first three years of life when the self is forming. Fairbairn (1952) speaks of how the infant and child, who yearns for and desperately needs an attachment to another human being, attaches to the bad object, which is traumatically frustrating in terms of the human need for contact with the primal mother, because one must have a connection in order to psychologically survive as a human being.

The bad object can derive from an abusive or/and abandoning mother (borderline), or a detached mother (schizoid), or from a false narcissistic mother, who demands that the child mold itself into the mother's narcissistic image and agenda for him/her. In all these cases, the child is deprived of the essential good mother contact and connection that could allow the child to move on and to relate to the father and others in the world. Without an adequate good mother relationship in infancy and throughout the transitional stage (in Winnicott's language; later called separation-individuation by Mahler), the child gets helplessly attached to the actual external primal mother, who fails to provide the contact and connection needed, and thus fails to help the child's growth. Then, the child (as well as the adult with the child still undeveloped within) becomes addicted to the bad mother. This addiction results in aggressive fights with the mother who was overly aggressive and abusive. One can also become addicted to a mother who is overly detached and withdrawn. This results in the internal world's early sadomasochistic dramas with the detached (schizoid) mother, who also enslaves the child as an extension of herself. Also, this early primal object can be the mother's false grandiose self-reflection of the child, or an attachment to the mother's image of herself, in order to avoid the conscious experiencing of the internal mother's deprivation.

Fairbairn writes of the child who is forced to relate through identifications rather than through the separate self-relatedness of emotional connection. This term of "relating through identifications" was picked up by Winnicott (1969) in his paper on "The use of the object or relating through identifications." The child who can't develop his or her own personality due to the lack of relatedness with a mother capable of being aware of the emotional needs and personality of the child, and who is then met with the failings of the father and others to relate, will be stuck in the position of relating only through being identified with the mother or with the image of the child created by her.

Inside the internal world of the child, there will be an undeveloped primal self craving to have contact and connection with the unavailable mother (see Fairbairn's concept of the libidinal ego attached internally to the tantalizing and seductive, but unavailable mother object), and split-off and dissociated from that will be the part of the self (the antilibidinal ego) that is attached to the rejecting part of the mother (the rejecting object). Both the libidinal ego and antilibidinal ego will be split-off in the internal world from any part of the primal innate self, called by Fairbairn the central ego. This central ego will be still in touch with others in the external world through the intellect, as in the schizoid personality, but not through relatedness and emotional connection, as these have traumatically failed during infancy and toddlerhood (the transitional stage or separation-individuation).

Then, the whole emotional life will be stuck in regressed attachments to the bad objects of the seductive and tantalizing types, and the bad objects of the rejecting objects. This will be a static drama in both the internal and the external world of the borderline character, as opposed to the totally sealed-off schizoids. This will be enacted in the external world as if every other person in the external world is the tantalizing object (the mother one never had), but then, inevitable disappointments take place, and the tantalizing object becomes the rejecting object. Therefore, the cycle of wishing for the object and being "in" is always inevitably followed by wanting to be "out."

The internal world repetition is continually replayed outside through projections onto external objects (as in borderline personalities) or is enacted in a sealed-off and dissociated schizoid internal world. Each reliving of the traumatic primal disappointment initiates a new cycle of craving for an exciting object that then switches into the rejecting object's abandonment and/or attacking abuse, which is another form of emotional abandonment.

D.W. Winnicott's Concepts Related to Fear of Intimacy

D.W. Winnicott's contributions to understanding the fear of intimacy are multiple. I will mention a few important concepts of Winnicott that are important to understand the fear of intimacy and the developmental theory that can be applied to clinical work. First, Winnicott (1960) spoke of the too omnipotent mother who impinges by substituting her gesture for the child's spontaneous gesture (Winnicott, 1963). This can be the mother who presumes to have knowledge of the child that interferes with the child discovering itself, or the too omnipotent psychoanalyst who interferes with the analysand (patient) discovering his own inner experiences as his/her own feelings and thoughts by showing too much knowledge of the patient with theoretical presumptions. This can be the mother who has her own narcissistic images of what she wants the child to be, and her own narcissistic agenda for the child's development along with this. Thus, the child becomes co-opted into acting as if he or she is the image of the parent; and any true impulses, feelings, and thoughts from the child's own individual being must be split-off, dissociated, and hidden or (in the higher-level neurotic or oedipal level individuals) it must be repressed. This narcissistic mother creates a false self in the child, which meets the mother's (and then usually the father's and siblings') images and agendas.

There is also the schizoid mother, who molds the child into the caretaking false self that Winnicott explicitly speaks of, while the true spontaneous impulses, feelings, and thoughts of the child and the later adult are dissociated and stifled before they can be expressed. Also, there is the too omnipotent aggressive borderline mother who opposes the spontaneous gesture of the child with her own attacking gesture. This results in the child submitting and later identifying with an overly aggressive dominance, or an overly passive submissiveness, both of which obviate contact and connection with another that could grow into intimacy.

Intimacy requires that one person gets to know the authentic self of the other and vice versa, in a mutual progression of getting to know who the other is, and a mutual willingness to reveal to the other who one is. This cannot happen without true self development in childhood, because authentic relatedness is obviated by the false self (Winnicott, 1960) enacting its coercive narcissistic performance, its borderline fight-and-flight, or its schizoid coercive caretaking. Also, the contact and connection with one's true self have been so arrested by a sealing-off and splitting off (or at a higher level—by the repression of authentic feelings and impulses), that one never reveals the self to the other. The other then never gets to know who one is, which is the essence of intimacy and interpersonal expression and responsiveness of back-and-forth intimate relations.

Other concepts of Winnicott (1965, 1971) that are so pertinent to understanding the fear or failure of intimacy are the following: the capacity to be alone, capacity for concern, object survival (of the mother and the Object Relations psychotherapist, in the face of the true self's most aggressive aspects), and the capacity for play. Also, there is the theory of potential or transitional space, a third area where intimate relatedness takes place—between the self and other that provides potential space (originally transitional space during a transitional stage that is developmentally related to Margaret Mahler's separation-individuation stage). In addition, there is the contrast between the mother as the mirror of the child's true self versus the mother as the narcissistic mirror. The narcissistic mirroring mother reflects back to the infant or child her own self, so the child cannot feel seen or known, which obviously obviates any hope that intimacy can take place with another.

Winnicott's (1958) capacity to be alone is a developmental understanding that one must be able to internalize a good enough maternal holding environment before one can be alone with oneself. This means that one must have a mother who can just be with oneself, as opposed to intruding on her needs or demands on the child. If one does not have the internalized maternal environment to develop the capacity to be alone, one cannot have intimacy. This is true since one must be able to be a separate other who can be alone with oneself in order to connect with an "other" as *other*, and not as a projection of a part of one's own psyche. In fact, the greater one's capacity to be alone, the greater is one's capacity to be with another, because one does not cling, intrude, or attempt to merge with the other.

One can tolerate the other only if he/she has a psychic space to be himself or herself. If one does not have the capacity to be alone, one will fear the needs of the other to be intimate, because this will feel like an intrusion on one's wish to merge or cling to the other for one's very survival (called the co-dependent in colloquial terms). The capacity for concern (Winnicott, 1963) develops as the mother (or therapist) allows the child (or patient) to experience tolerable guilt for its aggression along with an adequate dose of recognition for its good or loving aspects. This allows for guilt to turn into concern while guilt can be tolerated and not turn into hostile and retaliatory aggression or the disowning of responsibility in life (because of intolerable aggression).

Only through true concern for another can one be intimate. To not feel concern for who the other is, with all his/her individual desires and needs, results in using the other for one's own needs. This leads to exploitation of the other rather than in knowing the other and growing to know the other more, which is the essence of intimacy. When the mother has not offered the child the concern and empathy that results in developing concern and empathy in the child, the child will fear any prospect of intimacy (which would create vulnerability), since the other is feared as having a lack of concern. Then, one will exploit in order to use the other for survival needs, and through projections, will fear exploitation when the other might be looking for intimacy.

Winnicott's (1971) understanding of play is the capacity to imagine the other as a subjective other, rather than only seeing the other as a concrete object that one might try to manipulate. Imagination of the other is necessary for intimacy to take place, and intimacy will be feared if one cannot enjoy imagining the other. If one can imagine the other, one can play with the other, which will evoke joy in getting to know more about the other in intimacy, and thus will enjoy imagining more and more about the other. If the other just is "it" (not a subjective self, but a concrete thing), there will be no imagination in the mind that creates play and its accompanying spontaneous gesture in relatedness. The mother who mirrors her own image (or the image of her child created by her) will not reflect back to the child a recognition of who that child is, as a spontaneous being. This will create a fear in the child of the other molding him or her into the other's image, as opposed to being perceived and recognized as one attempts to reveal oneself in intimacy.

Margaret Mahler and Fear of Intimacy

Margaret Mahler's developmental theories from both her 1971 paper entitled "A study of the separation-individuation process and its possible application to borderline phenomena in the psychoanalytic situation" and her 1975 book on *Psychological Birth of the Human Infant* (co-authored with Fred Pine and Anni Bergman) pertain to the fear of intimacy and the defensive dynamics around the prospect or threat of intimacy. Mahler's paradigm of separation-individuation, based on mother-toddler observation, helps us to understand Guntrip's schizoid "in and out" dynamics (which are based on traumatic precedipal mother-child bond disruption). Mahler's theory also helps us to understand the dynamics of oedipal level conflicts over connection and separation in intimate relationships. Since at this higher level, primal splitting does not predominate, and the conflict over the desire for intimacy versus the fear of intimacy within connection can be felt. Mahler offers a perspective for both levels of split enactments around self-and-other connection-conflicts between yearnings for connection at the level of intimacy and fear of intimacy within connection that requires commitment.

The original mother-infant symbiosis that Mahler describes at the initiation of the infant's life (while she discarded her "autistic stage" that was an adaptation to a Freudian view of "primary narcissism" that doesn't hold up) is a stage of life that is continually yearned for. In neurotics, who make it through separation-individuation to the oedipal stage, the yearning may remain an unconscious fantasy with its accompanying wishes, that can be experienced consciously at the time of a normal experience of falling in love, but the fantasy and wish can be relinquished in these neurotics once a true intimacy develops, in which two separate individuals with distinct identities come to truly know each other.

However, for the person who was developmentally arrested during the separation-individuation phases (due to the failure of the mother to maintain sufficient attunement and emotional connection with the toddler of these stages), a perpetual addictive craving for the lost symbiotic mother will persist. The primal symbiotic mother (the Jungian "chthonic mother") will not just be yearned for but will be continually recreated in fantasy (as in James Masterson's 1981 "reunion fantasy"). This will undermine all attempts to sustain a state of connection with another, since the wish for a symbiotic reunion will constantly be traumatically disappointing, resulting in the other being experienced as the bad mother who failed during separation-individuation.

Such splitting at the point of disappointment will continually disrupt any relationship, as the perception of the other goes from being the idealized symbiotic mother to the bad mother of separation. So, the relationship is constantly disrupted before any true intimacy can evolve, an intimacy that would require two separate individuals coming to know, accept, and love each other. In fact, not only can someone with a primal traumatic disruption in the separation-individuation stages not sustain connection, but as the other becomes the bad object (mother), the split-off self-part related to the bad mother will also be the aggressive hating part of the self. Consequently, one's very identity as someone capable of love is lost.

In her 1971 paper, Mahler refers to the symbiotic era, which is developmentally prior to all the phases of separation-individuation, as the stage of dual unity. This is a concept used by D.W. Winnicott and by other British Object Relations theorists, such as Margaret Little. Michael Balint (1968) uses the term primary love for this early dual unity stage, in order to distinguish an Object Relations axiom of the primal need for connection (also Fairbairn's axiom) from the Freudian idea of the primary narcissism before longings for relations with the mother and others took place. Michael Balint opposed the idea of primary narcissism, a view that has been backed up by all infant research, including that of Mahler. Mahler relinquished her idea of a hypothetical primary autistic stage and revisited her view to make the symbiotic stage the most primal stage of human development. Emotional birth happens during the hatching of the separate self during separation-individuation, when the mother of separation is internalized, and a differentiated individual identity is formed.

Mahler (1971) also speaks of the coenesthetic feeling of being one with the other, which is created physically during symbiosis, and which is yearned for to acquire comfort later on. This coenesthetic feeling is more dramatically craved as a way of coming back to life in the toddler who is psychologically dropped by the unattuned and psychologically abandoning mother of the separation-individuation stages. The toddler who has tolerable levels of disruption of mothering presence and attunement during the separation-individuation stages will be capable of imaging the mother when she is temporarily unavailable. This child will be capable of tolerating the low keyedness or early child sadness related to feeling the loss of the mother, as long as the loss is temporary enough for the mother's image to be held onto and focused on by the toddler within his/her internal world. Managing this dilemma of temporality losing the mother is a sign of a successful internalization of the mother's presence during separation-individuation (differentiation, practicing, and rapprochement phases).

Such a healthy toddler will not have his/her psyche disrupted by overwhelming tantrum rage that can't be quieted but will have enough of a solid ego-self to be able to tolerate the affect of sadness, a primal mourning experience that Mahler calls low keyedness. Such a toddler will yearn for the mother but will not feel like he or she is falling apart. A toddler with an unintegrated mother image will instead be caught up in the frantic throws of desperate crying or perpetual tantrum rage. When this latter toddler grows up, he/she will try to hook into another to regain the blissful symbiotic phase of dual unity with the mother. However, when the symbiotic illusion fails because the other has separate and autonomous needs, there will be no internally sustained image of the other to have a sense of the other as good.

The other will become bad because there is no internal image of the mother of separation as a good-enough mother (Winnicott's term), who is physically (but not psychologically) absent and living a separate existence. So, true intimacy will fail because of the desperate attempt to control the other and to keep the other as part of the self or extension of one's own self, and it will undermine any relatedness through emotional contact and connecting communication. Instead of communication and interpenetrating mutual knowledge of each other as between two separate individuals who have a good-enough mother internalized, there will be rage at the other, now seeming to be a bad object.

The mother-other will then be experienced as having betrayed through not being the symbiotic other-half of one's self. The mother-other will be seen then as abandoning, abusing, or intruding and violating. So fear of intimacy in Mahler's paradigm is always related to a fear that the other will abandon one (if closeness and dependence are achieved) or will entrap and engulf one because of the needs of the other, who is experienced as foreign, intrusive, controlling, and possessive, when not the symbiotic other half. The mother, who tries to possess the child by attempting to keep the child in a state of symbiosis with her, will always create a powerful terror of intimacy. This is true because the adult with such a child inside of his/her internal world will be afraid of being taken over by the other, and will talk of wanting to get away all the time in analytic treatment (the patient can come to learn about a continuous obsession about escape, the escape fantasies). When the mother made a traumatic error on the other side—the side of abandonment—it can create constant fears of being left. The person with these abandonment fears may find a mate who is at first imagined to be the craved symbiotic other half, but who is actually someone with the escape fantasies that create an impasse with the suffocation and entrapment fantasies of the one who had the overly abandoning mother.

Theories of Melanie Klein and the Kleinians

Overlapping with Margaret Mahler's linear theory of separation and individuation in the developing self is the British theory of Melanie Klein, which focuses on self-integration as a normal primal splitting is assumed and becomes integrated with the healthy individual; while pathological arrests in splitting result in increasing fragmentation of the personality throughout a lifetime, unless clinical treatment allows for the integration of the split-off self-states and split-off internal objects. Such treatment always involves a mourning process of primal mother object loss (which becomes combined with object loss related to the father and with later losses).

In Klein's theory, there are two basic psychic positions that each have a whole constellation of anxieties, self-states, and defenses (see Kavaler-Adler 1993c), where each has its individual fears of self and other relationship in the world, and thus each psychic position has its own fear of intimacy. These two psychic positions can alternate in one's unconscious and conscious states so that there is more of a qualitative development from one position to the other without any absolute linear program as Mahler proposes. Yet, movement from the more primitive to the more advanced position does have a linear developmental progression, even though the more primitive state of perception is always returned to in states of anger, rage, trauma, and regression. One never totally leaves the earlier position. Modern Kleinians have more acknowledgment of the role of the actual mother, regardless of the actual position of the psyche achieved. The role of trauma has been more currently acknowledged than it was done by Klein herself, and it is seen as the fixation or arrest in the more primitive position.

The more primitive psychic position is called the paranoid-schizoid position. In the paranoid-schizoid position state of mind, one is reactive and experiences oneself as an "it" rather than as an "I." One is always a victim, since he/she is just reacting to others, and not feeling autonomy or self-initiating agency. In this position, one is not a subjective self, and others are just intruding enacting monster others or idealized others, with whom one merges and who do not have their own subjectivities (their own feelings and thoughts and opinions and fantasies).

One is either an idealized or devalued self or a grandiose or bad self. There is no in-between and there is no ambivalence. Thinking is black and white, and one is not aware of making interpretations. The world is a mixture of concrete phenomena. One part-object person enacts the primal sadomasochistic scenarios on another. The other retaliates. All can retaliate back and forth endlessly, mirroring the internal world dramas. One either adores and attempts merger with the other (breast or penis part object figure), or one protects against being killed or destroyed by the malevolent bad object other. The internal world of split idealized and bad objects is projected outside and is enacted against others to make them feel like the bad object enemies through projective identification or to make them feel like the idealized perfect omnipotent part object others.

The idealized object always turns into the bad persecutory other (persecutory breast from the oral stage or the persecutory anal object from the anal stage) as the inevitable disappointment takes place. One has to leave the idealized object that has turned bad to avoid being persecuted, and so one never loves and hates the same other. There is no such thing as a sustained relationship in this psychic position because the idealized projection object always turns bad.

Consequently, anger and aggression cannot be felt within the context of sustained love. The terrors of this psychic position are self-annihilation and self-destruction through abandonment and persecution. So a relationship with an idealized other that has a primitive narcissistic state of infatuation—as opposed to an oedipal level honeymoon—can never lead to true intimacy. To protect the self when the other turns bad, one must leave, escape and attack and kill the other to do so. Otherwise, one fears one's own extinction, and this extinction is annihilation, not just a death that would leave symbolic images and symbolic memories and symbolic effects of one's own existence behind with others in the world. This is a pre-symbolic position, so if one is persecuted and killed, one just disappears without a trace. One doesn't die and leave symbolic expressions of one's identity behind. To fear intimacy in this position is to fear being annihilated and disappeared by an alien other because nothing lasts.

Once one becomes angry at the idealized other with whom one craves merger, all is over. The hate in the anger wipes out the desirable image of the other, and there is no more love. There is no remembered history of the relationship. It becomes a phantom of a relationship that one was sucked into until one discovered the true betrayal and malevolence of the other. To leave or break up the merger relationship leaves no trace of a meaningful relationship. Without symbolic experience of one's own subjectivity and of the subjectivity of the other, there is no meaning. The past relationship that aroused a fantasy of love forever and a pseudo intimacy of merger becomes a lousy bum steer. Disillusionment within love cannot be tolerated. It is all over when the other turns bad until the same other (person) is once more resurrected as the projected idealized other.

This vicious cycle of idealization and devaluation, corresponding also to the "in and out" solution of Guntrip, can only change when the rage and hate that transpires during devaluation can be tolerated by the other, with sustained loving attunement. This can only happen with the psychoanalyst who creates a holding environment (Winnicott), and contains affects and hated split-off parts of the patient's self that are projected onto the other (Wilfred Bion). Only in the relationship with the psychoanalyst can the rage and hate related to transference disappointment, with consequent devaluation, be tolerated. When such aggression is tolerated and affectively contained, a more intimate connection with the patient and analyst results that can serve as a transitional relationship (Winnicott, 1953) to intimate relationships with outside others in the patient's life. Without this transitional therapeutic relationship, the vicious cycle of splitting the object into idealized and then demonized and devalued bad objects continues. So the pathological "in and out" solution of trying to merge with the object when it is idealized, and trying to escape contact with the object when it is devalued and demonized, perpetually continues.

In the more sophisticated psychological position, the depressive position, one experiences the subjectivity of the self, as one becomes aware one has thoughts, feelings, and needs. One is no longer just reacting to others. One has needs and desires. Most importantly, in terms of capacities for true object relationships and thus for intimacy, in the depressive position, one can sustain relationships because one can tolerate ambivalence. For example, loving and hating the same object, and having love survive the hate in anger, because one is also symbolic, and that allows communication about the meaning of one's anger so that it doesn't last forever, but can be relinquished while love renews and survives.

One can have conflicts over loving and hating one other person as one enters the depressive position. Hate never totally destroys love because the other is experienced as a subjective person, not as an "it." The other can have a separate point of view and have feelings and thoughts of her/his own. So, intimacy through communication becomes possible. Even in states of anger, the communication of one's reasons for one's anger, or one's reasons for one's hurt feelings, can result in feeling understood and understanding the other, if one can talk with the other/ lover about why one is angry. So, even at times of anger, relatedness is maintained. Consequently, intimacy can evolve as one gets to know oneself and the other one is with as anger is communicated.

The fears in this psychic position are of losing the other for whom one yearns rather than attempting to possess the other. Yearnings for the other can be tolerated, but one fears losing the other one loves and yearns for and desires, as subjectivity within sexual instincts turns into differentiated desires of the self toward the other. Instead of fearing self-extinction, one fears object loss or loss of the other who one loves, and one fears guilt for regretting one has hurt the one one loves. One also fears loss of love from the other, and fears disappointing the other, as well as fearing the actual literal loss of the other. Separation and breakups of relationships can be tolerated since the meaning of the relationship and its history is maintained, allowing one to wish to recreate it with another if one loses one love.

Masud Khan

In Masud Khan's (1972) article on "Dread of surrender to resourceless dependence in the analytic situation," Khan speaks of the terror of intimacy in people who have been overly possessed by mothers during the dual unity stage. He calls this the omnipotent symbiosis, in which one has been so extremely catered to that a regressive symbiosis is maintained far beyond its time, resulting in the failure of a normal expression of childhood aggression that would allow for the autonomous development of a separate self with its own agency. Khan likens the consequent demands to return to such an omnipotent symbiosis in the analytic situation to

Michael Balint's (1968) discussion of malignant regression versus a benign one, while in analytic treatment.

The patient of Balint's malignant regression demands that the analyst give them the relationship that they had in the regressive symbiosis, and even what they never had, as in the fantasy of a totally omnipotent symbiosis. The demands for the analyst to deliver this defend against feeling the horrors of regressing into dependence on another who is not fully controlled as an extension of the self. In the benign regression, the patient can feel the loss and grief of the wished-for omnipotent other, who would fully cater to the self, and who would not demand any autonomous functioning or self-agency. However, in malignant regression, the demands for the analyst to be the omnipotent symbiotic other persist.

Masud Khan points out, in relation to D.W. Winnicott's theory of true self development and the analyst's object survival of the most primitive rage in the patient, how critical it is for the analyst to allow the patient to risk the terrors of resourceless dependence in order to develop true self-agency—through aggressive demands and criticisms, and through rage toward the analyst for not providing what they never had. The analyst allows and meets the patient's accusations of the analyst's failure to be the fantasy mother-other, the fantasy mother who would never cease to be omnipotent and perfectly attuned. When the patient is allowed to express all the rage, which naturally and spontaneously emerges from within, true self development can begin again, even after its arrest after the dual unity or symbiotic stage. Khan (1972) writes:

> Hence the crucial task of the clinical situation and analytic relationship was for the analyst to present himself in his person vis-à-vis her with that authenticity of mutual rapport where she could register how he failed her and get angry about it, and how she failed him and be reparative in a genuine way. (p. 6)

Fear of intimacy at this level relates to a terror of being trapped in a profound dependency where one's aggression is cut off and/or stifled. It is a fear of being unable to have a voice as one's primal level of rage and aggression (which is at the core of developing an independent voice) and an independent self (with self-initiating agency) is obviated by the opposition to one's aggression. The analytic situation is the only place where primal aggression can be allowed without hostile retaliation or abandonment (Winnicott's object survival).

This is the Winnicottian holding environment, which also requires the containing and processing abilities of the analyst. Eventually, the patient learns to appreciate, understand and thus process and contain their own aggression.

The analyst's ability to tolerate and understand, at a symbolic level, the primal aggressive affect and complaints of the malignant regression, allows the patient to develop the capacity to process their aggression, and to thus communicate it symbolically in a relationship (from sarcasm to direct expression of anger). This also allows the patient to developmentally proceed to a level of grief, i.e., proceed to the mourning of the loss of the primal object as an external mother. Through grief, affects become more subtle and self-parts become integrated. Hate and love become symbolic anger and sustained communication.

This radically lessens the fear of intimacy, since intimacy can be tolerated when dependence does not leave one feeling resourceless, but rather allows one to communicate all that is felt. Anger, hate, and aggression do not have to be split-off or run away from by running from the relationship. Meeting the aggression of the patient also means setting limits and making the expression of aggression tolerable—by keeping it within an analytic frame as much as possible. Both Michael Balint and Masud Khan propose limit setting in clinical examples in order to transform the malignant regression into the benign regression.

Susan Kavaler-Adler: Theories of Developmental Mourning and the Demon-lover Complex

Fear of intimacy can be understood from the viewpoint of a failure to mourn the primal parental objects and to internalize them symbolically, and to thus psychologically benefit from the resources of relatedness that they provide, while simultaneously separating from them as external objects so that one can relate to others as truly differentiated others in the present. Kavaler-Adler's (1985, 1988b, 1989b, 1993a, 1993b, 1996/2014, 2003a, 2003b, 2005a, 2005b, 2006a, 2006b, 2007c, 2010, 2013) theory of developmental mourning deals with mourning as a primary developmental process, following the contributions of Melanie Klein (1940) in her article on "Mourning and its relation to manic depressive states" and following Klein's view of guilt and loss being an essential part of self-integration in the depressive position. Klein was the first to see mourning as a primary and fundamental clinical and developmental process.

Kavaler-Adler's theory of developmental mourning follows from Klein, but it also integrates aspects of Margaret Mahler on low keyedness, James Masterson on the abandonment depression, and D.W. Winnicott on object survival. Developmental mourning can proceed as long as one has attained whole-Object Relationships both within the external world and within the internal world. When developmental arrest due to failed preœdipal mothering traumatically occurs, mourning of the other as a separate and symbolized whole-object other cannot proceed. Then, splitting of the object becomes pathological and perpetual, resulting in the sealing-off of the internal affective self, or in the compulsive externalizing projection of the affective internal world, with its part-self and part-other constellations. As long as such splitting is perpetuated, no true intimacy can occur, because the other is looked to as an idealized symbiotic other half or is feared as a malevolent, persecutory, intrusive object, or is feared as an inadequate or dead object that would drain one of one's very life.

When developmental mourning of primal objects occurs from the early preœdipal time of separation-individuation and throughout life, aggressive affect states are being contained by a predominantly loving and attached self and other relationships in a symbolized form (see Kavaler-Adler, 1992-2013b). Then, there is more love than hate in mourning the losses of both primal figures and others throughout life, with whom one must separate. Anger and aggression yield to the affects and memories of grief. Sadness modifies hate into tolerable experiences of anger within loving relationships, and the pain of grief yields to love within loss and loss within love.

Increasingly then, disappointments and disillusionments within relationships can be tolerated, so that relationships can be sustained to the point that true intimacy can take place, where one person gets to know the other and vice versa. Mutuality occurs as one's own subjective experience can be conveyed to the other. The subjective experience of the other can be perceived, listened to, understood, and internalized. Internalization of affective relationships at the level of intimacy is part of a developmental mourning relationship that takes place throughout life.

With benign internalizations, the fear of intimacy lessens, since one does not fear that the other will destroy one's self, and one no longer fears one will damage or harm the other by just being one's full self. One's own unconscious aggression becomes more conscious and understandable, and thus increasingly less frightening. As one's own aggression becomes less frightening, so too does the aggression of the other, which is always partially perceived through the projections of one's own aggression, and through the projections of one's internal objects' aggression. One's internal objects' aggression gets modified as love trumps hate with the tolerance of anger and loss within the developmental mourning process.

Kavaler-Adler's demon-lover complex relates to the perpetuation of primal splitting that causes the idealized god-muse object to continuously turn into a bad object due to the repetition of primal separation-individuation trauma. However, in addition to the instant vicious cycle of the idealized object turning bad, there is the eroticization of the bad object, which results in the projected image and internal world experience of a demon-lover. Also, the Jungian concept of a demon-lover archetype can interact with the bad maternal-paternal object in early preœdipal childhood. This is related to a complex that results from failed mothering before the whole and subjective self is formed through whole object internalizations.

When the psyche is split and eroticized in this way, intimacy is terrifying because it threatens to be an experience of another destroying one, or co-opting one's self and identity, or of seducing and abandoning on the level of oral and anal sadism that has terrifying and nightmarish internal world images related to it (see Kavaler-Adler, 1985-2013b). One loses one's validity, self agency, and self identity in merging with the idealized god-muse figure, which is sought for a merger. This merger with the muse is experienced as transforming the muse into the diabolical demon-lover; it brings possession rather than transcendence. The longed for muse, from whom one seeks inspiration and transcendence, turns into the dominating demon-lover, an eroticized primal bad-trauma-object. The demon-lover then turns into the image of death as its dominating, raping, and eventually abandoning or murderous character emerges (Kavaler-Adler, 1993a, 1995, 1996/2014, 2000, 2003a).

Otto Kernberg: Love Relations

In his 1995 book on **Love Relations**, Otto Kernberg speaks of a gender divide in relation to the nature of conflicts (fears) of intimacy. Kernberg speaks of men having difficulty surrendering to commitment in marriage, while women have difficulty surrendering to sexual intimacy within marriage. In the section on clinical cases, the marriage between Judith and Allan illustrates such dynamics. Kernberg (1995) also speaks of the fear of receiving love or feeling love, which can be seen in the case of Paula (to follow), where such a fear interacts with a Fairbairnian concept of addiction to a bad internal object, and also with a terror of resourceless dependence, as spoken of by Masud Khan.

Salman Akhtar: Love and Its Discontents

In speaking of various psychological syndromes that interfere with falling in love and with sustaining love, as well as separateness, within long-term relationships, Salman Akhtar (1996) speaks of the varying developmental levels that interact in the inhibited and pathological modes of loving. Akhtar (1999) writes:

... the fact is that each of them [*each syndrome*] contains deficits and conflicts from various developmental levels. The inability to fall in love, for instance, might represent the lack of activation of early psychophysical eroticism through a satisfying symbiotic experience, and a defense against unconscious envy of the love object, and, at times, even a pronounced inhibition resulting from intense castration anxiety. Similarly, the inability to remain in love might emanate from a futile search for a transformational object, anxieties regarding fusion with the love object, and/or conflicts related to narcissism, aggression, and the Oedipus complex. (p. 94)

In his critique of Person's (1988) views, Akhtar (1999) writes:

She emphasized that brevity is an essential feature of passionate love. However, the capacity of the two partners for mature Object Relations helps them convert the flame of intense emotions into the steady glow of affectionate companionship. (p.78)

Clinical Cases

Leonard: Fear of Resourceless Dependence Obstructing Intimacy, an "In and Out" Schizoid Compromise in Treatment

Leonard demonstrates the precedipal level of fear of intimacy. In his own words, he intensely craved intimacy while also being intensely terrified of intimacy. However, through a developmental mourning process that reached back to his mother's death when young, and back further to infant and toddler trauma, Leonard found a marriage that gratified his sexual and emotional desires. He began to face his terrors to sustain the relationship. Prior to this evolving marital relationship, Leonard had been profoundly isolated. He self-medicated by having part object sexual relations with massage therapists, and dream and fantasy relations with his female analyst in a role of a sex slave, but he had been too frightened of rejection (related to unmourned loss) to risk a relationship with a whole-object woman. However, Leonard continued to fantasize about escaping from commitment. Sustained intimacy was terrifying, both because of the shame that made him fear being seen and known, and because of the terror of being back in the high chair (where he was helplessly controlled and abandoned)—to annihilation anxiety and a numbed out sense of being invisible.

Leonard, as an infant in a high chair, had to split-off from himself and had to look back at himself from across the room. His mother had left for an intolerable amount of time, traumatizing him, and (psychologically) almost wiping him out of existence. Resourceless dependence has to do with this level of terror. As with Masud Khan's patient, Leonard needed to express aggression all the time to feel any sense of power, when he felt so helpless inside. He had to say "no" to everything in his mind, and often in reality, to the point of devastating loss and self-sabotage.

Through the psychoanalytic process, Leonard made increasing progress toward true emotional intimacy, no longer just continuing to fill up the void with a hyper-sexuality and an overly sexualized romantic and then marital relationship. Yet, during the first few years of his Object Relations psychoanalysis, he would fend off any mutual rapport with the analyst. He would polarize himself and the analyst by distorting the analyst's statements, to maintain a stance of opposition in order to pathologically guard his fragile sense of autonomy. At times, he might have allowed a few moments of actual rapport, where he would surrender this oppositional mode of obstructing relatedness. However, he was sure to unconsciously time this so that it only occurred at the end of the session. Then he would immediately run out of the room (the "in and out" solution of Guntrip). This anal stage opposition, which reflected developmental arrest trauma during separation-individuation, came after an earlier period of symbiotic harmony in his relationship with the analyst.

This is symptomatic of Mahler's separation-individuation stage child who cannot imagine the mother enough to sustain a positive internalization of her, because the mother was too absent during the separation period when she was more present in an earlier symbiosis. Leonard's maternal abandonment was associated with the time he was left in a high chair for so long that he had to split-off from himself and see himself from across the room. In analysis, the couch became the high chair he feared being trapped in and imprisoned by, in a state of resourceless dependence, and he would always have escape fantasies along with his polarized oppositional enactments. When Leonard would surrender to the encounter, he could be sure he could escape the couch and the room at the end of the session.

Judith: A Higher Level of Conflict Over Intimacy, with Repression Rather than Primal Splitting

Judith's fear of intimacy involved an over-reactivity to statements by her husband that re-evoked insults and contemptuous attitudes and critical comments from her brother and parents in childhood. She feared her own anger and would avoid responding to her husband. Then she would turn her anger inwards and develop all kinds of visceral and somatic body tensions, knots in her stomach, back and leg pain, and also cramping in her feet. She would also attack herself with her anger turned inward, saying to herself that she was not as good as others in her academic community and inhibiting herself from speaking up and having a voice. This held her back at work, just as her reticence in her marriage or her long-delayed articulation of anger inhibited intimacy did.

In Kleinian terms, Judith demonstrated a depressive position conflict over anger, rather than paranoid-schizoid terror of outward retaliation, but they both interacted. In terms of fears of resourceless dependence, Judith feared humiliation that could extend to terrors of self annihilation. The childhood memories that re-emerged through psychoanalysis illustrated why. One memory was of being at a table in the kitchen of her childhood home, at four years old, while a doctor was attending to her wounds after her brother accidentally hit her with a baseball bat. In a state of extreme physical and emotional vulnerability, she was tortured by the doctor, the same doctor who was hired by her mother to save her and heal her. When she cried from the terrible pain as the doctor stitched up her wounds, the doctor screamed at her for crying. The doctor angrily told her to shut up as he flirted with her mother, and while both the doctor and her mother ignored her pain. No wonder Judith became terrified of anger, and of her potential internal rage, forcing her to continually repress her aggression so that she had to use distancing from intimacy in marriage to protect herself.

Also interfering with marital intimacy was Judith's fear of being defined by the other or molded into the image of the other rather than having her own autonomy of self-definition. She feared having her subjective experience being invisible to any other, and particularly with the partner of potential intimacy in marriage, her husband. Her parents had always defined her rather than hearing her. Judith was often called the sensitive one, as her mother fantasized about being Judith's confidant while exploiting Judith constantly. She was also defined by her parents as the fat one, or the too sensitive one, with all her vulnerability being seen as an imposition. If she walked down the street with her intrusive and sexualizing mother as a teenager, and her mother said to her that some older man was leering at her as a sex object, her own experience of feeling disgusted by her mother's comments was totally ignored. Judith's subjective state was denied. By denying her subjective state, Judith could be further defined by her mother—a mother who also felt free to barge into her bedroom at any moment and demand that Judith listen to her, regardless of what was going on with Judith.

When Judith's husband started to define her or mold her into his image by proclaiming her political beliefs, she would feel enraged, but the rage had been unconscious before her psychoanalytic psychotherapy. Now, the repressed rage appeared in dreams and sleepy feelings felt by the therapist. These rageful dreams would always disappear as soon as Judith could express her anger and understand it. Often, her rage would strike her the next day, and meanwhile, she was unaware of why she was distancing during sex, splitting off, and watching herself in the sexual act, rather than being able to emotionally surrender, even if her body had orgasms. Bringing Judith's awareness about her anger, while on the couch, helped her in communicating her anger to her husband and to relinquish control during sex, and surrender without being inhibited by an unconscious fear of submission.

Judith had many dreams in therapy. However, one stands out as a transformation of self through modification of repression. The dream described by Judith is as follows:

There was a tsunami, tidal waves of water heading toward me. But then suddenly the tidal waves of waters stopped and just stayed suspended in an archway around me, so that I wasn't in danger of being hurt or drowned. Also there were walls that had been holding the water in place that gradually fell away. Yet the waters remained static above and around me and I felt safe.

And Judith's associations to the dream were:

I was wondering why the walls could fall away and yet I could be safe and not be drowned by the raging waters. It felt like something could be let go of that was like a defensive wall that I needed before to survive. Now the walls could move away and I still survived and even felt safe. I think the raging waters are the multiple levels of my rage, my anger, and my sexual and erotic feelings too, all mixed together, but now no longer threatening to overwhelm me, despite the immense force of the waters. Somehow the waters are containing themselves now. I don't need rigid walls around me anymore, like the repressive wall barriers in my mind, or the wall of muscular obstruction that I experienced before in physical and emotional constipation.

When I was about six years old, I remember being terrified when I would be in the family car with my family, and we would drive through tunnels. I always feared the walls would come tumbling down on the side of the tunnel, and that we would be destroyed by the waters coming in and drowning us. My parents did comfort and reassure me when I had had this fear, unlike the times when they laughed at me for having nightmares, or ignored my pain at four when I was on the table being operated on by the doctor. Maybe I've revived their comfort as I let go of the rigid repressive walls that kept my anger at them silenced. I had also kept my love for my mother silent, since I feared my mother would manipulate me into some obligation to her if I expressed love to her. Here was another side of them when they were being parents. Also, my mother had been very tender and loving with my children when they were infants. Maybe that maternal love had been there for me very early on before the problems began.

This was the analyst's interpretation:

Yes, your dream seems to articulate a vision of the rigid defensive walls falling away since they are no longer needed. You seem to be unconsciously declaring that you can surrender now to your internal emotional life, without fearing that either your anger or your sexuality will be too much for you. As you allow your anger into consciousness, and we sort out all the different reasons for your anger, you have been freer to speak up distinctly and assertively to your husband, when you feel he doesn't hear you, or is trying to mold you into his image, or co-op you for his agenda and miss your subjective experience. Also, you can speak up quicker with your anger (in the moment), as the tidal waves of rage become moments of understandable anger that you can find words for, allowing you to surrender your rigid walls of opposition to your internal life. You have been able to speak up to me in your anger now too, with less fear of alienating me or of provoking alienation.

Other Examples of Fear of Intimacy
Related to the Various Theories

Carol: Attachment to a Bad Object

Carol held on to her internal bad object family by expressing their disapproving judgments against herself when she felt judged by her husband. Her turning against herself with a regressive attachment to the hostile attitudes of her bad objects, just when she needed understanding, was a manifestation of her fear of intimacy. Instead of speaking up to her husband at these times, so that he could understand her better, her (depressive position) fear of losing him caused her to self-attack using the very accusations that her family used against her in childhood. She called herself selfish for having her needs and wishes; a whiner and complainer; and "too angry" and aggressive.

Richard: "In and Out" Schizoid Compromise Solution and Developmental Mourning

Richard spoke of "time out of time," or "time out," and times of compulsive work. "Where is the third way of being?" he asked. Only in this third state of being, which he began to find in the analytic situation, could intimacy, as well as the true self spontaneity and mutuality needed for intimacy, become possible. This evolution toward allowing being, not just doing, is related to D.W. Winnicott's theories. Going into sleep to escape and not being able to get up in the morning, as well as his taking leaves of absence from work, and earlier from graduate school, were all part of the way Richard tried to create a "time out of time" or "time out" experience for himself, since he couldn't possibly tolerate the tension and anxiety of his defensive work mode, in which "doing" had dominated over all states of "being."

As a developmental mourning process began in treatment, Richard began to see the alternative state of spontaneous or quiescent being that he could allow himself, within the transitional and holding therapeutic environment and with the containing analyst. These moments of freedom (of being rather than doing) came gradually, and mostly at the end of Richard's double-sessions, as he was able to surrender to being in his body and feelings. First, his anger came. Then, his grief and loss. Then, the pain of longing for intimacy and commitment with his partner, who had temporarily threatened to leave him.

As Richard yielded to this pain in treatment, he realized that he carried anger that his mate could not rescue him. He confronted a helpless feeling about life turning against him after his transfer to junior high school. With this awareness, Richard's compulsion to work nonstop when back at his job began to yield to more freedom engaging emotionally and also to suspend work and let go. Consequently, he escaped into sleeping day and night or into perpetual vacations. He was able to express the huge "no" that he had been compulsively working against all his life. This "no" may have gone back to a two-year-old needing autonomy. However, the "no" became a bigger "no" toward life in general. Behind the "no" was the anger that he could no longer get his way through just being in his own narcissistic and instinctual self as he was in elementary school.

When in junior high school, his first girlfriend rejected him, and competition arose. Richard unconsciously gave up on relationships, fearing that they all would result in rejection. Then, in his 30s, Richard finally took a risk in having a relationship. He was pursued by a homosexual younger man, and he succumbed to a strong emotional need for this man, only slowly opening to sexual relations and often feeling resistant. This new relationship was threatened until he could find his repressed feelings, dreams, and memories in treatment.

Lying on the couch and discovering his repressed feelings and the fantasies, memories, dreams, and thoughts related to these feelings, which engender a developmental mourning process, Richard was gradually able to move past the emotional "in and out" schizoid solution or Guntrip's schizoid compromise. He began to stay in the relationship as he became capable of being more inside of himself. Instead of just being there for his boyfriend as a mentor, and instead of unconsciously wishing for his boyfriend to be his mother, or for his psychoanalyst to be a mother who could rescue him from life, Richard began to see that he could be his own mentor. However, this required him to sustain a connection with himself that allowed for empathy and compassion toward himself, instead of a severe judgmental view of himself, which perpetuated its own compulsive mode of negative thinking.

Surrendering control in analytic sessions was critical. He cried and sobbed on the couch, thus discovering the two-year-old child self within that wanted to kick, scream and cling to his mother. He learned that his saying "no" to life was a defensive demand for an oppositional autonomy when the challenge of risking true and authentic autonomy through saying "yes" was too frightening. As he sobbed out his pain of longing for his lost mother, when trying to reunite with his boyfriend after a separation, he realized that he was very angry. He then realized that he feared that consciousness of his anger would leave him all alone without anyone. He came to realize that the opposite was true. Richard's consciousness of his anger became part of moving toward more intimacy with his boyfriend and others. He began to sense that he was less alone. He gradually came to express his love. He also began to express his sexual desires, which had been greatly inhibited, causing a large rift between him and his boyfriend.

Phillip: Fear of Resourceless Dependence

The case of Phillip serves as another example of resourceless dependence in the fantasy of a patient who was in a transference regression while having achieved the depressive position and oedipal stage level of development. His dream-fantasy symbolized his fear, but also resolved it through an internal world that already housed a good-enough mother.

In the third year of his three times a week psychoanalytic treatment, Phillip had a rich and vivid fantasy of being a small infant, just placed on a bed by me, his transferential mother. In the fantasy, I left him on the bed and went into another room. In his fantasy, Phillip felt such intense rage that he thought his rage had gone after his mother and killed her. This expressed Phillip's abandonment terror within a depressive position psychic state. In this mature psychic state, as described by Melanie Klein, Phillip's core anxiety was not related to losing his self, nor was it the fear of another's angry retaliation, nor was it even a terror of the abandonment by the mother herself. Rather, it was the higher level terror of one's own rage when one is killing off the one he/she loves. Also, since he viewed himself as an infant, the one he loved as his internal mother in the outside world, his psychoanalyst, who was his transferential mother, was the one he felt totally dependent on when on the couch in a therapeutic regression. Nevertheless, instead of resourceless dependence, Phillip felt the power to kill off another with his rage.

Phillip also experienced the power of his sexuality. As Phillip evolved in his own fantasy, he said that when his mother came back into the room and picked his infant self up off the bed, he was not only relieved, but he was also suddenly gripped by seeing me, his transferential mother, as a demon-lover mother, because he felt his desire for me, making me sexual and thus evil. He found the power of his sexual desires in this fantasy along with the power of his aggression, and his capacity to symbolize these passions in psychic fantasy allowed him to no longer fear so much either the destruction of his aggression or his sexuality. This allowed him to commit to his wife much more fully, and to save his full erotic self for her as he was unable to do before.

In Phillip's words, the fantasy story had its fear of resourceless dependence plot and its own resolution. Phillip narrated his vivid fantasy to me with awareness of his maternal transference (I am using Phillip's exact unedited language):

> I see myself in a room as an infant. I see you in the room also. You're my mother. You're standing there in a black bra and black slip, holding me. You put me down on the double bed, where I can't roll off. Then you leave the room to go into the next room to get whatever dress you're going to put on. I'm lying on the bed and I don't know if you are going to come back or not. I can't tell if you're going to walk back into the room 20 seconds later or whether you'll walk out and I'll never see you again. Maybe you'll be dead. I am lying on the bed staring at the ceiling, and my neck doesn't even lift my head to see what's happening. My legs are these useless pieces of toy flesh. I can't move about on them. I want to speak and all that comes out is this inarticulate wail. I've got no power

at all to take care of myself (he's crying)—no power to feed myself—no power to say what I want and need—no power to move myself. I'm just like utterly and completely dependent on you. I don't want to feel all this stuff. You know I don't want to feel this vulnerable, needy, and powerless experience. I don't want to feel so dependent on someone who clearly doesn't have the judgment or love for me to not walk out of the room all the time. I can't take care of myself. I can't even walk. I don't speak. I can't even lift my head. I just feel this amazement seeing that all that is true—seeing that I'm completely powerless and dependent in that way. And you would walk out of his room, knowing what the implications are, and it fills me with this rage toward you—this feeling I could just crush you or strangle you—for failing me so acutely and so insensitively, as I see this force coming out of my little infant self, a force of rage leaving my heart and body, like in a third dimension—going off to accomplish its intent. I see it leaving me and going out the and this phantom that's left my body is gone. It's accomplished its mission and dissolved. What's left in its place is my knowledge that I've created the very thing I most feared. I truly am alone. There's nobody coming back for me.

All of a sudden I'm aware of birds singing, the breeze blowing, the curtains, and the sunlight coming back into the room. I realize I'm utterly alone. All of a sudden I wake up to the present moment. To the beauty of what's around them. It's wild! I was expecting that this phantom would go out and destroy you and I would be alone. This is what I had feared. Instead, all of a sudden I'm gurgling happily with birds singing. I'm alive to the moment—having released my rage and my fear. What do you know? OK, so now I'm on the bed, alive to the moment—a happy baby gurgling on the bed. You walk back into the room with a dress on a hanger. You say something affectionate. Everything's OK again. Then we start a new cycle. You put the dress on and then leave the room again, and once more I think, wait! Hold on! My legs don't work, and you're leaving me alone! (Kavaler-Adler, 2003a, pp. 182-183)

Paula: Resourceless Dependence Dream, the "Bathroom Memory," and the Pact with the Devil

Paula represents a case of preœdipal trauma compounded throughout childhood and causing a wall against intimacy. Paula revealed a resourceless dependence (Khan, 1972) dream related to developmental arrest due to trauma in the preœdipal infant-toddler period—in contrast with Phillip's symbolized phantasy of maternal transference abandonment, which exposed a transference regression to fear of a primal object loss. This contrast highlights the paranoid-schizoid self-annihilation terrors in Paula with the depressive position object loss fears in Phillip (who was regressing from the oedipal stage through his intrapsychic fantasy). This is Paula's dream:

> Paula is on the top of the staircases in a large house. The house is like her childhood home. She feels entrapped and imprisoned, in a state of aloneness and isolation. She finds herself trying to hold on to the wooden banisters, but she falls down all the flights of stairs. The wooden banisters all break and fall apart as she tries to grab them. She finds herself toppling downward and there is nothing to grab onto that would stop the fall. She is about to smash into a cold white marble floor that lies at the bottom of the crumbling wooden banister staircases.

I then interpreted to Paula that she was in a nightmare version of her childhood home that seemed to reflect her annihilation terror in the face of a detached and unavailable father who was never there to protect or support her, i.e., the wooden banisters. But even worse was her fate of falling onto an ice-cold marble breast mother. She fell onto this mother who could kill her rather than hold her, just when she sought support to stay above this cold marble mother from her father. Her parents were both paranoid-schizoid position part objects in this dream. The father was represented by wooden banisters that crumbled in the face of her dependent need, and which failed to support her. Her part object primal object (at the base) mother was a cold marble inert floor object. Due to Paula's dependent need for mother, the nightmare dream threatened murderous annihilation, as she seemed headed to smash into the cold floor, which was like the immured wall of a cold breast mother who could not hold or contain or nurture her. The dream was a nightmare because there was no resolution of primal self annihilation terrors. There was only the murderous and destructive ending of her core true self internal child being in the face of dependence on two part object and bad object parents.

Paula's dependence was thus the resourceless dependence that Masud Khan referred to. So naturally she had to fight any emotional dependence on the psychoanalyst or her husband, as this dependence would threaten to awaken the prœdipally arrested child within her. She had many memories of her mother threatening to murder her, or ignoring her presence and abandoning her. A memory came back to Paula that once again highlighted the endangered state of her childhood. Paula's nightmares of the archetypical terrors were interpreted in relation to her distancing and devaluing of the analytic process. Paula's own interpretations as she became an interpreting subject showed her growing ability to tolerate her rage so that she could symbolize her damned-if-you-do-and-damned-if-you-don't dilemma (need/fear dilemma) and to understand her unconscious pact with the devil (representing Fairbairn's addiction to the bad object).

The memory was of Paula running into a bathroom in the home of her teenage years (around 13) to escape her raging mother, who was screaming that Paula deserved to die and that she (her mother) would kill her. Paula remembered running into the bathroom to escape her mother, and then she remembered standing behind the bathroom door, crying out "I hate you!" to her mother, while she shivered and shook behind the door. Shivering from terror, Paula prayed that the lock of the bathroom door would hold. This wasn't the first time she was threatened with death by her mother.

When only four years old, her mother tried to trap her in her mother's lap. Her mother seduced her by offering to play with her mother's ear or to suck her thumb. The mother wanted to hold Paula for her own comfort. Paula felt imprisoned then, as she would experience lying on the couch analysis. At only four years old, Paula escaped her mother's grasp and ran out in the backyard where there were chickens that she liked to play with. Her mother's retaliatory response was to go after the chickens. Frantic with rage, Paula's mother grabbed the live chickens and put them into a bag. She then marched to the butcher to have the chickens beheaded and cooked. Paula was enlisted to march with her mother to the butcher. Her mother grabbed her by the hand and dragged her with her. When Paula cried and objected, her mother threatened: "I'll kill you too if you tell anyone about this!" That night, Paula's mother called her down to dinner in a voice that sickened Paula. There, on the dining room table, are the pet chickens, cut up and cooked. Paula didn't want to eat, but her father acted as if all was well, and her brother was in his usual dissociated and out-of-touch state. She had no choice but to eat the murdered pet chickens, and she felt the nausea until this day. Her own rage made her nauseous, but so did the unconscious re-living of being force-fed the murdered pet chickens.

Paula's problems with intimacy became obvious when one got in touch with Paula's internal world. Within this internal world, Paula was addicted (through primal attachment), to her malevolent, hated, and murderous mother. Lying on the couch, Paula became aware for herself that she could never allow herself to receive the sustained loving interest of a man. Recently, Paula had realized that she was sabotaging the interest of a man, who she dated and had sex with in the past, and who was trying to reconnect with her. She became aware that, like in other cases, she had interpreted his interest as purely sexual. She became aware that she never could believe that anyone was genuinely interested in her for herself, beyond sex.

In line with Otto Kernberg's (1995) discussion of those who cannot receive love, Paula forgot about an invitation to a special party, where she was supposed to meet her male friend's mother.

In her internal world, she maintained a pact with the devil, in which she could escape the murder of her primal maternal object if she stayed wedded to this voracious and rageful mother forever, by continuing to believe that she, Paula, was the rotten kid her mother accused her of being. Paula was addicted to her internal bad object and her bad object's view of her character (Fairbairn, 1952), so how could she ever think that someone would want her? She could understand a man's sexual hunger for her, which only made her interpret her position with the man as an exploited sex object position.

This position was comfortably familiar to her in her mind since she was an exploited child. However, to believe that she was wanted for herself was unthinkable since she never had that experience with her primal relationships. Therefore, she was stuck in a state of alienation from any intimacy, walled off against the intimate emotional state. In fact, she got out of bed and lay on the floor after having sex with one man because she feared imprisonment in the merger with the other (the merger her mother demanded of her when she wasn't threatening to murder Paula or wasn't actively abandoning her). Paula had to wall off from emotional contact to avoid re-living the resourceless dependence she has suffered from her mother (being force-fed the murdered pet chickens).

So, she lived in her head and only intellectually communicated with others. Or, she lived in her body in sex or yoga. But she could not experience an emotional connection that would allow for heartfelt intimate relations. So how could she believe she was wanted for herself? She forgot the men who might truly want her, just as she forgot therapy sessions she had had, in which she reached her more vulnerable feelings of need and longing for connection. All could become vague, abstract, or totally forgotten in her mind, despite briefly opening herself to her sadness and tears.

I would need to interpret her fear of remembering any authentic emotional connection in her treatment sessions, understanding how dangerous it was for her to remember our sessions, which would make her aware of her emotional needs. To sustain connection with the analyst would mean that she would feel the need for the analyst, who would put her in a position of possession, or would shame her for being, in her words, needy. By staying wed instead to the internal murderous mother (her pact with the devil), she walled off against the threat that she would be murdered by the external relationship with the analyst. She would need to become more aware of her fear of abandonment if she would sustain a connection with the analyst.

Gradually, Paula became aware of the other side of her damned-if-you-do-and-damned-if-you-don't position, the side of fearing being abandoned by the mother so that she would be in a totally isolated and thus unsustainable state. Forgetting the analyst and her analytic sessions, just like forgetting men who were seriously interested in her, was her unconscious way of controlling the abandonment. She would become the abandoning one, the one who was more in control (false self), rather than feeling the need for the other that would abandon her. In Wilfred Bion's (1989) terms, she would attack the links of relatedness in her mind to protect herself from the vulnerable position of emotional need that threatened to bring Khan's (1974) resourceless dependence. In Klein's (1940, 1946, 1957) terms, she used a manic defense to defend against the vulnerabilities of the depressive position.

By forgetting, Paula defensively opposed the developmental progression described by Mahler (1971) in her discussion of the child imaging the externally absent mother. Such imaging during the separation-individuation phases of development could keep a good mother alive and present psychologically, so as to build inside in the internal world the sustained image of a present mother, allowing her to go on being, in Winnicott's (1971) terms. By forgetting, Paula regressed to the paranoid-schizoid level of Klein (1975), where she continued to fear her own rage and the retaliatory rage of her mother, rather than to enter the more vulnerable state of the depressive position, where she would pine for the mother, and would thus feel a loss in her absence. The forgetting forestalled the whole developmental progression of mourning the primal mother, in order to separate and self-integrate, described in Kavaler-Adler's theory of developmental mourning.

Paula would relive her rage repeatedly but would resist the sadness and grief of feeling need for the other. However, Paula became aware of this in treatment, and gradually, she would acknowledge the sadness and tears she kept inside of her more often. Nevertheless, Paula still returned to her addiction to a demon mother who she eroticized when merged with the distant and absent father who lived as an internal object within her. This was her personal demon-lover theme and complex.

Only gradually could Paula relinquish the primal and profound ties to the internal bad object parents, and risk any need for the external object, the female psychoanalyst. Only as she became increasingly aware of how alone and isolated she felt inside (when not intellectually living in her head) could she tolerate feeling lonely and sharing this loneliness with the analyst. Only as the loneliness came up in dreams—where she was on the outside as the excluded one, or was misplacing or losing herself through losing major possessions such as her car or her house keys—could Paula admit that her attempts to escape relationships left her stuck in a fearful state of aloneness, without any emotionally needed intimacy.

Chapter 17

Return to Phillip: Capacity for Intimacy in Relation to a Whole Object Mother

By contrast, Phillip's internal mother was a whole object mother who left him for a few minutes, but who returned to nurture him, be affectionate, and contain him. She made sure he was safely placed on the bed before she left the room. He feared the loss of her, which he feared would leave him alone in a resourceless dependence, but instead, his rage showed he had a sense of self agency, intention, and empowerment even in the totally dependent infant state. He feared object loss, but not self-annihilation. In fact, Phillip symbolized the whole experience of a feared object loss all at a conscious fantasy level and thus worked out the fear as his mother returned.

Phillip saw that his rage could be survived by both him and his mother, and by both him and I in his state of maternal transference in his analysis, as well as in his marriage. This allowed Phillip to have erotic thoughts, without self-consciousness in his psychoanalysis, and in parallel to have erotic intimacy within his marriage. Phillip relinquished all his avenues of escape from monogamy once he saw that his relationships could survive his anger and aggression, and even his more unconscious precedipal infant rage. Even in the fantasy of infant dependence, he had the power of his rage and was not resourceless.

Phillip's fears of intimacy in marriage emerged in his transferential fantasies in treatment (see Kavaler-Adler, 2005). He feared that the female analyst would either be a traumatized mother who could be devastated by any honest reaction to her or a contemptuous father who could humiliate and ridicule him. He feared the analyst was secretly making contemptuous judgments of him that she didn't say overtly. He feared she would be devastated if he were critical of her rather than just generally devaluing the treatment for many years. When he evolved to a place where he experienced the analyst as truly understanding him and as providing, in his words, "a sustained holding presence" for him, it had to do with his being able to see that she was not the mother he dreamed of as a mother who drops her infant or shows him off to boost her narcissism in her inner insecure state. He also got there by realizing she was empathic to him over many years in a way that he finally was convinced distinguished her from the bad object contemptuous father he had carried in his internal world.

Now, he was more capable of intimacy than ever. However, in becoming so, he had to again confront his wife's fears of intimacy, which his wife still expressed by her projections onto him of a rejecting and irresponsible and excluding father. He had to face that his wife continued to set up with him the very abandonment that she feared by hostile rages, although she now apologized. He persisted in communicating to his wife that she could still speak to him in a scapegoating, demeaning, and dissociated manner. Phillip was continually faced with the difficulty of seeing how he could remain open to a relationship when his capacities for intimacy were closed off by his wife's attacks. Through his analysis and his Object Relations work of internalizing a more secure and containing relationship, he learned to assert himself and stay emotionally open rather than dissociating and closing off as he once did.

Return to Paula: Concluding with Early Trauma and Fear of Intimacy

The case of Paula, as formerly described, relates to Margaret Mahler's theory, in terms of the fear of possession by a borderline mother who wanted to pull her into a regressive symbiosis or to attack and abandon her. Paula was most conscious of her fears of entrapment with the female analyst, who quickly became the feared mother in the transference. She was less conscious of her terrors of abandonment and of yearning for the mother she never had than of wishing her mother would drop dead. In fact, Paula imagined her psychoanalyst as dropping dead when on vacation. She fantasized that if I dropped dead, she would be freed from any difficult choice about committing to or leaving therapy. She was less conscious of the need for me. This need was so traumatically frustrated in childhood that Paula had dissociated from her whole internal child core self and lived a whole life in an intellectual false self to avoid being aware of the primal and profound need in her for a mother.

Unlike Margaret Mahler's two-year-olds that can image the mother, and who consequently begin to keep the mother symbolically within the self when the mother is temporarily absent during separation-individuation, Paula could not image a mother that was emotionally absent even when physically present. She was left empty with a void inside where the primal connection with the mother should be. She had been numb when originally in psychoanalytic treatment. Then she became consciously enraged. Now she got to a feeling of sadness and tears in a "developmental mourning process" that continues through her analysis, as anger and rage now alternated with a feeling of need and longing.

However, Paula also regressed to cutting off, but much less than before. Her memories told of a mother who threatened to kill her at the age of four, and who later raged and attacked her until she picked up a knife at 15 and threatened to kill her mother. Then, her mother continued to emotionally attack Paula, only giving up the physical attacks. Her father was mostly absent. To be made aware of the need for her female analyst, every time she repeatedly thought of escaping prematurely from treatment, became part of the process of the treatment.

Mahler (1971, 1975) speaks of the double-headed monster of a traumatic separation-individuation period, where the borderline individual always ends up feeling damned if they do or damned if they don't. Paula had always kept more conscious of the side of this terror related to fear of engulfment and entrapment. She tried to be totally independent, through using her very fine intellect in a schizoid mode of false self-defensive self-sufficiency. She dissociated from her inner self where the vulnerable child and toddler self-remained sealed-off, walling off against feeling the agony of needing a mother who was never emotionally attuned or in touch with her.

The analyst was able to interpret this side of things once the affects of the abandonment depression mourning process (James Masterson) and the developmental mourning process had been felt. This involved feeling voids states, rage states, and ultimately deep grief and loss states. As dreams spoke of Paula symbolically losing herself by symbolically losing her car, or of being lost without any guidance or connection, Paula began to see that she was feeling as terrified of being alone as she was of being entrapped in the treatment and her marriage. She began to feel the true internal needing self that was her only avenue to connection and certainly to intimacy with another.

Paula could finally begin to feel the therapist feeling her. At first, she could not remember this when it happened. But gradually, she started to remember that there was someone there. After every session that would begin with how Paula resented the time and money spent for treatment, and with travel plans that were in part a plot to get away from psychoanalytic treatment, a transition began to occur. As the analyst pointed out Paula's unacknowledged need for the analyst and for the analytic process, which was evident in her dreams, Paula began to see it too. She also began to surrender to her inner pain in sessions, despite her fears of depending on anyone as she now needed to depend on the analyst.

Conclusion

In all these brief case vignettes, we see how there is a need-fear dilemma related to the human need for intimacy. We also see the many levels of fears related to surrendering to needing the other. The theories described initially are highlighted within the case examples. In this way, abstract concepts, such as resourceless dependency, the in and out solution, developmental mourning, the demon-lover complex, imaging the other to restore a coenesthetic experience in order to soothe the self, the depressive position versus the paranoid-schizoid position, addictive attachments to bad objects, and so on, can all come alive.

CHAPTER 18

TOLERABLE AND INTOLERABLE REGRET: CLINICAL TRANSFORMATION OF THE INTOLERABLE INTO THE TOLERABLE

Originally published in 2013, *The Anatomy of Regret: from Death Instinct to Reparation and Symbolization Through Vivid Clinical Cases* Karnac.

Intolerable Regret in the Mother and Validation for the Daughter

In classical psychoanalysis, we have been taught to not reassure patients. What does this mean? Why is this caution? My understanding of this caution has been that the patient needs to struggle with his/her conflicts over his own impulses, to find his/her own resolutions by consciously confronting impulses that formerly were unconscious or out of control. The analysand needs to have this process without any interference in it. Whatever the patient's struggle, he/she needs room for it. The patient needs the psychic space, analytic space, and transitional space to struggle with his/her own dilemmas. To not offer reassurance is thought of as allowing such space. Refraining from offering reassurance also allows patients to experience that the analyst is not afraid of their experience. When a psychoanalyst does reassure a patient (and this happens probably more often than we admit), it is mostly our countertransference enactment of a rescue fantasy. Perhaps getting the patient off the hook is a way of gratifying our own wish to restore our own inner harmony through a gesture that seems kind and compassionate at the time. Perhaps in this way, we attempt to create reparation for ourselves; reparation with our internal parent, through projecting that parental other onto the patient.

However, since the introduction of British Object Relations thinking, we have learned a few things about trauma and the early developmental arrests that can happen when trauma disrupts internalizations of "good enough" (Winnicott, 1974) Object Relations, developmental growth, and ongoing levels of psychic self-integration. When we look at an Object Relations psychoanalysis that aims to heal trauma, to give insight into trauma, and to not have trauma reduced to drive conflict, a whole new question confronts us about the difference between validation (validating not only psychic reality, but also real reality) and reassurance. If we, as psychoanalysts, mistake validation for reassurance, we may deprive the patient. So validation needs to be defined in terms of trauma, which by definition relates to actual reality and not to psychic reality, although psychic reality and psychic fantasy always interact with the concrete realities that are related to trauma.

Validation of trauma is critical in the healing of the self after trauma. Validation is also important in validating the dimensions of the trauma, as it repeats itself in compulsions and projective identifications in present life. The psychoanalyst needs to help the patient discover and validate her own trauma, and also needs to be an active source of validation at times. In addition, the psychoanalyst needs to help the patient find validation at its source—with the parents—whenever possible, or at least needs to not discourage the patient from seeking it with the original parents. However, at times, this can become a masochistic pursuit, which needs to be interpreted in terms of the parent who is incapable of tolerating the guilt and anguished sense of loss within the conscious experience of psychic regret.

When the parent is incapable of tolerating regret, and therefore of communicating validation of early traumatic events in the family, the analyst naturally becomes a primary source for the patient's validation. The analyst must also help the patient salvage her sense of reality in the face of the parent's denial of the traumatic events that have so impacted the patient's psyche and view of the world. The analyst needs to help the patient see the parent's incapacity to offer validation by helping her understand the psychic capacities needed to face the regret. This can help the patient differentiate from, and separate from, the parent, rather than remaining stuck in endless rage and retaliation, or stuck in endless Sisyphean cycles of efforts to extract the yearned-for validation from the parent— like Sisyphus endlessly pushing his boulder up the hill, only to have it fall again.

My own definition of validation, as it contrasts with reassurance, is that validation is an active and explicit acknowledgment to a patient of traumatic experience. It involves being a witness when the patient discovers the trauma through memory, free association, the interpretation of reenactments inside and outside the treatment, etc. The patient must discover the trauma at an affective level and have a gut feeling that the trauma occurred. However, this moment of affective realization can be forgotten all too quickly in the face of the psychic compulsions to protect the image of the parent. Therefore, witnessing the affective level disconnection becomes of critical concern, and it is the psychoanalyst who is there to be a witness in this way. To witness and verbally validate must be clearly distinguished from reassuring someone that they are good when they confront hostile or sexual impulses in themselves. To validate is not to reassure—it is to be a witness to what is, and to what has, held the patient back from living a new and healthy life in the present. The following case illustrates the critical role of validation in promoting psychic healing and psychic integration. In this particular case, the validation is of the parent's psychic arrest and of the parent's pathological intolerance for the conscious experience of guilt, intolerance for the psychic transformation of guilt into an affect-level experience of grief within regret.

A Vignette of the Case of Amy:
Validation of the Parent's Intolerance for Regret

Amy had discovered significant childhood trauma in seven years of psychoanalysis with me. She attended sessions two, three, and four times a week. She started treatment with no former psychotherapy experience. She made herself accessible to lying on the couch. The critical trauma discovered in this manner was that of Amy having been molested by her middle-aged alcoholic father when she was between the ages of four and six. Amy recalled her molestation through dreams, through masochistic experiences of abuse with sadistic and seductive men, and through her sense of being "held" psychically on the couch, which allowed Amy to free associate. Amy recalled that her mother had been a key player in the malevolence of the experience by neglecting to help or acknowledge that her small daughter was being visited each night in the dark by a drunken father. The mother failed to help her daughter by confronting the father or by acknowledging the event.

Instead, the mother added emotional abuse to sexual abuse by screaming with rage at her daughter when she would wash her off the next day, cleansing her of her own husband's ejaculatory fluids, which had been left as unwanted evidence overnight on her daughter's body. The day after each night's sexual intrusion, Amy's mother would assault little Amy with hostile epithets. She called her daughter a whore, a bitch, or scum. She blamed her small daughter for being a little seducer when she was obviously a small child and a helpless victim. The mother seems to have been in a jealous rage, discharging all the accumulated wrath she stored up toward a rejecting and alcoholic, philandering husband (older than she) on her small daughter.

Consequently, the usual oedipal stage dynamic played out an unconscious fury in this family. Much later in analysis, when Amy had come to terms with some of what happened and had gotten past her rage at her father, she spoke of the longings she had for her father, beyond the trauma. She spoke of feeling abandoned when her father "went back to her," left her bedroom in the middle of the night, and went back to her mother's room. And in most of Amy's romantic or dating relationships with men, she would end up feeling abandoned. There was one exception to this, in a long relationship that she was able to follow to its end, with her making the decision to part. But her tendency was to be drawn to men who would seduce and abandon.

The deeper abandonment, however, and its confounding with abuse, was to be found with her mother, the one who had actually been the better parent of her two. Her mother had left Amy to come and forge a path in America when Amy was eight. However, she allowed Amy's psychic survival by sending her a letter in which she said she missed Amy. She enclosed a dollar with the letter each week. Left with a cold and rigid aunt, Amy clung to these letters of reassurance, waiting to be reunited with her mother. Not having had enough of her mother, and yet unavoidably being so deeply attached to her as her one and only real parent, Amy suffered from the anguish of seeking acknowledgment from this mother for the horrors of sexual abuse that had been inflicted upon her by her father.

Amy's Psychic Turning Point in the Monthly Mourning/Therapy Group

After the discovery of herself in seven years of psychotherapy and psychoanalysis, Amy joined a monthly therapy group, which I run for four hours (with a break) on a Saturday, 10 months a year. This group focuses on each individual's mourning process within the group process. For years now, Amy had separated from her mother in all practical ways, living her life in New York while her mother lived in Miami, and working in her own chosen profession, which was not one suggested by her mother. Nevertheless, Amy's core emotional tie to her mother was still profound. To grieve her way out of this tie to a more individuated state, Amy would have to face a deep pain, a pain filled with the anguish and longing to reunite with her mother.

One Saturday during the group, Amy frantically related the tale of her sexual abuse to all the others in the group. When she reached the part of her tale that concerned her mother's unwillingness to hear anything she would say about her past and the experience of her father's molestation, she shared an angry, yet pleading longing for her mother to remember what had happened and to acknowledge it. She didn't accuse her mother as she spoke. She was not in her former rage about her mother's neglect of her fate, nor was she in her former rage about her mother's emotional abuse of her (the blaming, ridiculing, and humiliating of her when she had suffered the arousing intrusion and abandonment of her father).

In that moment, Amy let go of all the formulated accusations she might have directed like darts at her mother. She lay down her darts and arrows, and collapsed into the vulnerable longing of a child pleading for maternal love. The anguish of her cries was evident to all in the group as she disarmed herself and said, like a confused child, "Why won't she admit it? Why won't she remember it? Why can't she just acknowledge it happened? Even her dreams are saying it to her, but my mother won't listen!" At the height of the pain of her longing, I said to Amy, as her former analyst and group leader, "Your mother is incapable of focusing on the truth. If she were to acknowledge it, she would feel like she is a devil. She would see herself as all bad, and as all destructive. She can never admit it because she can't tolerate the guilt of regret without feeling annihilated by her own self-hate. She just isn't at a psychic level where she can bear it." At my words, a deep cry, a wail of pain, opened up from Amy's core being, where the internal infant self seemed to reside. A child's vulnerability transformed into an infant's longing. Yet she spoke words that revealed the meaning in her tortured cries, "I'll never get her back!"

Silence fell upon the group. The atmosphere opened to the poignant and universal longing that lay at the core of all our beings. "I'll never get her back," she cried again. There was a sense of feeling the internal psychic change in Amy happening right there in the moment! This pain of grief was the only road to true psychic separation for Amy, and in that moment, we all knew it. We all had our own core of pain to experience and transgress. Amy was suffering what is the essence of true grief. She had longed for reparation with her mother. Like all of us, she had fantasies of being close to her mother again. She had hoped that by speaking to her mother of her pain, of her knowledge of the past, of her little girl exploitation and trauma, her mother's caring would come out to meet her, bringing her together with her mother, as once she had felt as an infant. She had not blamed or accused her mother. She had let go of all of that to make her appeal. She tried over and over to find the right words. No words proved to be the right ones. There were no right words! There were only her words bouncing back at her. Her mother seemed to turn to stone!

As I spoke of her mother's incapacity to tolerate regret, which was related to her mother's more total incapacity to face what is, and what had been, as an overall mourning process, some realization was triggered in Amy that temporarily freed her and transformed her entire being into a cry for love. This was a cry for love combined with an anguished realization of disappointment, a cry that would pierce through the group membership like a wounded heart contracting into a final release of its agony: "I'll never get her back!"

In this therapeutic mourning group, I conduct a psychic visualization at the beginning of the group, a visualization in which breathing opens inner life. I ask all the members whether they can feel a connection to their heart. Some can and some can't. But in moments of grief, like the one Amy manifested, the heart is felt by all. I didn't have to explain more than I did. My confrontation about her mother's incapacity to feel regret was enough. I could explain it later. But now it wasn't necessary. The inner realization in Amy was complete. She was released as she let go and acknowledged for herself that she would never get her mother back. She gave herself her own validation, along with that which I and the group had given her. She could now witness her own fantasy of reparation and not be possessed by it. Her addictive need to cling to her mother was over. From now on she would deal as best as she could with her mother's demands on her to visit her or to call her, but she would no longer be as chained to her own need to initiate contact with her mother and hope for love and understanding. She could increasingly—with relapses—let go of her mother, because there were others to go to now that she was internally free of the pathological tie that bound her. She could feel the love and understanding from the group and me.

The Mother Who Reaches a Moment of Tolerance for Regret

Lisa had a different experience with her mother. It began with a psychic turning point that Lisa experienced in one particular session with me. This session was a moment of awakening for Lisa and me when our unconscious minds rose to the surface and met. Her courage to face her pain and my intuitive sense of her need at this time paved the way.

It was a late evening session in my uptown office in New York. It seemed dark that evening. The beginning of the session began like many others. Lisa seemed tortured in the silence, unable to speak, unable to begin. Something was building up inside of her, and her surface facial expression showed her unspoken rage at me for not rescuing her from what was within her. Her body showed tremors of tension that cried out, reminding us both of the traumatized child within her that threatened to break into consciousness. The tremor spoke of the internal child, a child crying for attention in an emotional vacuum, with her mother withdrawn from her. Yet, none of this was in Lisa's conscious awareness at the time—the child in the body was trapped by the mind that was forced to carry the memory, but which couldn't speak. I was only consciously aware of the tension, the waiting, wondering if she would find her way to words and feelings, wondering if it would be helpful for me to speak. Then suddenly, Lisa darted out of the room, saying by her action that she couldn't take it anymore. Lisa was angry again that I would get sleepy in the tense silence, where so much of her was pressuring from within a sealed-off emotional state, speaking only through the tension of its dissociation.

When she darted from the room and went out in the hall, I found myself leaving my office and going after her. I had developed an inner bond with her that compelled me, urged me to do it. With someone else, at another time, I might have sat there unmoved, feeling "enough already. Go! Leave me alone," as a countertransference response. But not in this case. I was outside my office, in the hall, standing by the banister of the stairs, while Lisa stood agonized and torn apart on the top of the stairs, leaning on, and beginning to bang against, the wall across from me. I watched while at first Lisa fought with herself, frantic with the pain and tension of indecision, seeking release, but terrified of losing control.

Turning a lifetime of rage inward against herself, Lisa began to bang against the unyielding cement wall, as all her life she had banged against the emotional wall put up by an unyielding mother, a mother who wouldn't let her penetrate her or enter her to have her own crying need heard and met. As she seemed about to bang her head against the wall—the head that had the mental instruments of torture operating on her, derived from unprocessed memories, which haunted her in the re-living of them—Lisa turned swiftly away instead! In a second, she had pivoted away from self-attack and entered into self-surrender. She bent over like a swan, yielding to her pain. She surrendered to the child within her that had needed to cry for decades, decades that could feel like centuries, when we were waiting together in the silence.

Lisa's surrender was complete for the first time. She could no longer run away. She let go and began to sob and sob! Her body convulsed within its cathartic release, and I gently suggested that she come inside my office again. Having chosen to let go of her opposition, Lisa followed me, still at the beginning of the sobbing that would bring years of agonized longing to the surface. Her need to purge herself, to wail until she could speak, already spoke its profundity through the body that had relented to letting the sobs pass through her entire being. As she sat back in a chair in my office, further from me than before, near the wall, half turned away from me toward the door, and half toward me, I sat with a new sense of peace inside, feeling we had arrived, no longer waiting. My silence was now filled with the sense of a deep emotional core of holding in my body, as if I was holding her body in my lap as she cried.

Eventually, I said the words to her that came with the feeling. I said without thinking, "Mommy, hold me. Please hold me, mommy." I spoke for the child within her. There was no effort. I knew she was inwardly responding. She did not have to speak to me. She continued to sob out her inner oceans and lakes of tears, tears from deep down, filled with sadness and longing, so different from earlier tears. I brought her the tissue box and handed her some tissues. Then I sat back down, tissue box in hand. We were deeply in communion now, and I was struck by how effortless it all was. The aggression that had caused so much resistance had temporarily left us, although it would certainly be experienced and understood at another time.

Describing the effortlessness of this session, as Lisa let go of her defensive controls and surrendered, brings back a memory of another time and place in my own life, when I discovered the abandon of total emotional and body surrender. I was at a therapy marathon in my early 20s. I had been crying for hours. It was in the middle of the night. Suddenly, a woman in the group expressed herself and opened up my entire being. I remember her exact words: "My mother came down hard on me, but my father always supported me." My chest and heart opened to the deepest wailing of grief, longing, and love. My tears poured out, but more viscerally prominent was the openness of my chest, so that I wailed like a baby, like a newborn infant just emerging from the womb. All my earlier crying had helped to open me up, but at that moment, when I heard the words from that woman that meant so much to me personally, I opened at a core level of body and being that cast my cries out to a volume and intensity that could touch all the other, 16 or so, people in the room.

How effortless it all seemed now, as I could release all the longings for the father who had died when I was ten. He had died and left me with an extremely critical mother, the one who "came down hard," as the woman said. The release of all my love and longing in a body surrender to all cries and sobs liberated me. This was the way into the present, into the now, into an eternal now that felt so peaceful, and which made me feel close with all around me as I could feel I was most truly myself. When a woman in the marathon group then spoke, saying directly and compassionately to me, "I feel your pain, Susan," I was able to turn to her and speak. In the midst of my release, I was totally in control, for the control was an authentic and centered control from within, not the defensive control of the mind that needs to be surrendered to in the now. All was effortless, just as at that time with Lisa. And these moments last. Even though mentally forgotten, these moments of complete contact and connection sustain us subliminally, and they come back. Once this happens, all is changed; and changed for the good.

For Lisa, her transforming moment allowed her to reach forward into the core of the mother who she had to confront in the present. She and her mother were to come face to face with love for each other, a love that they both had perhaps not known since Lisa's early infancy—prior to all the conflicts and traumas of the separation-individuation stages. It was through this encounter, the most tender of meetings, in a moment when her mother was tense with the conflict of whether to let go, that her mother's capacity for regret was momentarily—and perhaps eternally—realized. It was a moment that Amy, unlike Lisa, could never achieve with her mother. It is hard to say which mother—Amy's or Lisa's—was more damaged by their past. Yet, one mother (Lisa's) opened to a capacity for regret, and one (Amy's) did not!

Lisa's moment with her mother's transformation could be briefly related. It happened when Lisa's mother came to visit her and her siblings in New York, a unique event. Lisa's mother lived overseas in Eastern Europe. When she came to New York, it was a major event for Lisa, and her sisters and brothers, who lived in the city. Lisa played a main part in preparing activities and visits within the family for her mother. She had no idea how her mother would respond. Lisa had frequently felt abandoned by her mother, not only in childhood but throughout her adulthood. Her mother never called her—she always called her mother. She was also seeking something she could never find when she called. When she felt the icy chill of her mother's emotionally withdrawn state, and felt her mother's inability to listen, she either cried or raged from her intense disappointment.

Many times in her psychotherapy, Lisa related the devastated internal state within her that followed her attempts to reach her mother through phone calls. She also demonstrated her extreme sensitivity to not being listened to or to feeling like she was not being listened to in her transferential reactions with me in sessions. Lisa demanded intent attention at all times, no matter how silent she would be. This was quite understandable, given the extreme emotional detachment of her mother, which alternated with some capacity to listen and talk, as Lisa was able to open up more and to reach out more to locate her mother when she called. Yet the overall impression of Lisa's mother was that of an extremely depressed woman in emotional withdrawal, conveying an emotional emptiness to her daughter. So the event that I am about to report seemed almost like a small miracle when it came about.

Maybe the mother's meetings with her children, without the presence of her emotionally abusive husband, had been wearing down her resistances, and the thought of going back to the emotionally starved family and nation she came from was probably beginning to haunt and threaten her. The combustion of these varying factors began heating up Lisa's mother's emotional terrain, finally bringing her to an emotional precipice where true grief was a possibility. Just as she was approaching the pinnacle of the precipice, Lisa's mother hesitated, in conflict, tears behind the eyes, tears not yet cried. Her daughter saw her look. She recognized her own face in her mother's look, the one she had had most strikingly on the evening of the session in which she surrendered to my emotional holding and to her own need for relief.

Seeing the entire body of her mother tense with the internal censor humiliating her, and holding her back from release, Lisa looked directly into her mother's eyes, and whispered, "It's OK, Mom. It's OK to cry!" Her mother yielded and let go of her censorship, and abandoned herself to her tears of grief and yearning. Filled with the emotions she had resisted for a lifetime, Lisa's mother spoke from the depths of her heart, and directly to Lisa: "I hope your life is better than mine!" Lisa's mother clearly articulated this poignant remark in a new psychic state, one born in the moment. Lisa had been with her in her place of hesitation and need. This one phrase said by Lisa's mother spoke volumes about the grief of her life and about the buried love that had dissolved in an intolerable regret, which in this moment had transformed to a tolerable heartfelt regret. Tears came to my eyes as Lisa told me of this poignant moment.

An Intolerable Regret Becomes Tolerable

Lauren came into the writing group with a letter she had written to the group members. It seemed appropriate that she should read it because it was a writing group. The letter was lengthy. Someone in the group said it sounded suicidal, but it was meant to be an explanation for a comment that she had made that had hurt another group member. The letter seemed like a forced apology and an extensive explanation about what had caused her to react as she had. We all seemed to be witnessing a gross overreaction to the actual circumstance.

Lauren had told another woman in the group that she didn't care what her feelings were, and didn't care if she was changing and becoming more in touch with her feelings. Lauren said this with an edge of contempt in her voice, being, as she would later say, "cutting." She had been hurt by this other woman having called her a bully, and she was taking her pound of flesh in revenge. She hadn't killed anyone, but being faced with the impact of her comment on the other woman, she unconsciously felt that she had indeed committed a murder. Not being conscious of this belief, she defended against conscious knowing by evading full ownership of her aggression.

Unable to tolerate the guilt of her regret at the time of her comment, Lauren did not face the woman in the group and did not apologize in the group. Instead, she wrote Adrien an email in which she apologized for the comment that hurt Adrien but also externalized the blame on me, the group leader, rather than owning the regret. Something was still too intolerable to bear about owning her own guilt. Within the group, she read a letter she wrote, in which she spoke, with the lament of one wounded, of how miraculous it was that any of her own creativity even survived because of the annihilating emotional attacks of her father, as he particularly targeted her creative potential. Pressured by the unconscious force of a psychic fantasy, Lauren chose the role of a victim, defending herself, and pleading her cause at her own self-created trial, rather than merely owning regret and moving on. A potential existential guilt about the matter of what indeed had happened, in reality and in her own psychic reality, became a neurotic guilt, and therefore too exaggerated to bear. It was now the guilt of psychic fantasy murder, a guilt harbored in her unconscious domain. Triggering a latent and age-old psychic fantasy, Lauren's guilt turned to persecutory proportions. She retaliated by blaming and attacking me, the group leader, and also the therapist of the woman in the group, Adrien, who she felt attacked by in Adrien's comment about her acting like a bully. She decided to blame me because she also felt excluded from what she imagined to be a tête-à-tête about her going on in Adrien's therapy sessions. She was open about saying that she thought we talked about her together. In retaliation, she made sure to exclude me for a time being from her thoughts and her conversations with others in the groups.

Lauren gradually opened up to discussing her father transference with Adrien within another group with me, a mourning group, in which they were both members. She allowed Adrien to open her own pain to her about Lauren's rejection of her. She allowed Adrien to speak of her secret wishes to be friends, and of her secret affection for Lauren, who Adrien said reminded her of "the best part of her mother." Still, she left me out, punishing me for seeing her transgression against Adrien, and for seeming to be on her side. I examined my own reactions, and saw that I had felt favorable to Adrien when she had been rejected by Lauren with her comment about Adrien "chomping at the bit" and about Lauren not caring about her, just as Adrien had begun to open up more emotionally. I listened to Lauren as she became enraged at me in the mourning group, and said she didn't trust me, and that maybe all I was interested in was the money.

Eventually, my patience seemed to pay off, and Lauren began to speak about having a negative transference to me in the mourning group and said that she wished to begin to talk about it. However, when she attempted to talk about it in the group, she could not go past a certain point. She acknowledged that she had been angry at me since the incident with Adrien in the writing group. She said that she knew her anger at me had become mixed in with anger she had had for years with her mother and sister.

Yet, when she attempted to go into her feelings, she felt blocked in a way that was totally unusual for her, because Lauren was someone who could go deep into her affect states; after she could be totally expressive about her anger, her rage, and the sadness of her grief. Yet, she had a sister who had tried to have an exclusive relationship with her mother, moving in with the mother and excluding Lauren. Lauren was already conscious that her sister was trying to own her mother since she had never had her mother to herself in her earliest years, but Lauren had because Lauren was the oldest.

Lauren's anger at her sister for taking over her mother's life and excluding her certainly had played a big part in her anger at me for having therapy sessions with

Adrien—therapy sessions which made her feel excluded when she was in conflict with Adrien and heard my empathy for Adrien in the group. Now, in the mourning group, she couldn't actively express her anger at me, other than at a time when she went into a rage at me, accusing me of many things, which made her feel out of control. During the summer vacation from the group, Lauren called me for an individual consultation. She said that she thought she was inhibited in speaking about her anger at me and her negative transference because the other women in the group became her sister watching her and judging her.

I agreed to see Lauren for an individual consultation. She had been in groups with me for many years and rarely saw me individually. She knew, however, that she could see me individually if she wished to. She began the session with memories of the downtown office that she revisited for the consult, with memories of older writing groups she had been in with me, and of members who she remembered from these groups. On a one-to-one basis, she seemed fairly comfortable with me, despite her continuing apprehension about being with me in the mourning group. She told me that the group must conjure up transferential feelings toward her sister, which made her inhibited in revealing her feelings toward me in front of them. Lauren said that she had thought that her sister was trying to undo and take revenge against her for her own exclusive relationship with her mother, when she was alone with her mother up until the age of two, before her sister was born. I thought she might be right and told her so, impressed with her insights as usual.

The rapport between us over this kind of understanding allowed Lauren to go further, and to plunge into the heart of her anguish about herself and her own aggression. She said that her anger at me went back to the time of her conflict with Adrien in the writing group. She told me that she had felt that I was biased toward Adrien. She said that she had felt excluded. She also told me that she realized that she could be cutting and cold at times. I didn't say anything, knowing that she had been afraid of some condemning judgments being made by me in the group, particularly after she accused me of things.

In the group, she had said that she expected me to hate her. When I had asked if she thought I hated her right there and then, she replied, "Well, you couldn't feel too kindly toward me." Having voiced this fear of my aggression coming at her in a retaliatory judgment, she had apparently felt more comfortable owning her negative transference in the group, and she now had felt comfortable enough to come and see me individually. I hadn't acted out the retaliation she feared. I hadn't judged her. I hadn't condemned her, even when she may have been projecting her own condemnation of me, which had once erupted in a rage toward me in the group.

As I now listened in the individual consultation, Lauren seemed to feel free to continue. She was testing out that she could define her own aggression, without fearing that I would be defining it for her, and thus, in her psychic fantasy, condemning her as bad. Lauren did say that she could be cutting at times, expressing a cruelty that she did not like in herself. As she spoke, I could feel the psychic weight of Lauren's burden as she felt regretful about attacking another (even when she justified her lashing out in retaliation against Adrien's remark, which was injuring and mutilating to her, on a level of primal psychic unconscious fantasy). As I felt the heaviness of her psychic weight, I said, "I have the sense of some sadistic murder in the background, as if you really believe that by making your insulting remark to Adrien you really committed a murder." Lauren immediately and poignantly responded, "My mother always thought I committed a sadistic murder!"

Lauren released the weight of her psychic burden as she began to cry and to make the connections with her unconscious beliefs that she hadn't made before. As she could understand that her guilt had taken on the neurotic proportions of an age-old unconscious belief that she was a sadistic murderer—and as she saw this as her mother's projection of her own sadism, unable to bear the brunt of her own guilt and to consciously face it as a regret—Lauren felt free. She felt the pain and anguish of her own aggression, and the regret of the interpersonal losses that her aggression could create, but she could now clearly distinguish it from her fantasy that she was a murderer. She also could both see how her mother's projections onto her (and her own identification with them) had their origins in aspects of her mother's disowned her sadistic impulses. These disowned aspects of her mother included those when her mother had an exclusive relationship with one child, at the expense of the relationship with the other. With disowned parts of herself, the mother had also displayed passive-aggressiveness, which sometimes provoked her husband's overt sadism. Yet, as Lauren spoke about her mother, she was also able to forgive her, because she could see her own sadistic impulses, defined in cutting and her cold manner when angry.

In this way, Lauren was facing her existential guilt in the form of a conscious regret. She was differentiating her existential guilt from unconscious neurotic guilt based on a psychic fantasy of being a sadistic murderer. As her own psychic burden was thus relieved, Lauren was able to forgive the mother who had unconsciously encouraged her to be overburdened with guilt so as to escape from her own guilt. Lauren was immensely relieved by our discussion, and when she returned to the mourning group, she told the group about her session with me. It was interesting how she reported the session. She said that she had an "excellent" consult with me when she decided to discuss her negative transference with me. She said that even though it had actually been quite painful to confront her own murderess impulses, she had felt relieved.

I found it quite illustrative of how Lauren had moved into the depressive position in facing her transference with me, and that she was able to view the session as confronting her own murderess impulses. Once she was relieved to see the psychic fantasy of being a sadistic murderer in a conscious form, whatever she felt before as intolerable guilt became a tolerable regret, in which murderous impulses could be accepted within herself. This process allowed her to integrate a whole part of herself that her mother still perpetually disowned, unfortunately having done so at Lauren's expense. Owning her own regret now, Lauren made a point of saying in the group that our discussion about her mother's sadism had made her reflect on her mother's situation in her marriage and life, and had helped her to forgive her. She also said that she felt less forgiving of her sister, whose sadism she still felt being enacted on her, as she tried perpetually, in overt action, to possess their mother.

Conscious regret had allowed Lauren to move into a sustained depressive position state of mind, in relation to her negative transference with me. Now, she was interested in how her own aggression projected within the negative transference onto me rather than this aggression remaining an intolerable and overwhelming persecutory attacker from within. She still felt traumatized by her unconscious fantasy of being a murderer (and being stuck in the paranoid-schizoid position).

Lauren followed Melanie Klein's clinical phenomenology (separate from her metapsychology) by moving into self-integration as her split-off and repressed aggression became integrated and her depressive position capacity became a more sustained psychic position. However, it is D.W. Winnicott (1965) who informs us of how important the therapist is as the protector of the holding environment. In not retaliating against Lauren, I was able to preserve the holding environment. According to Winnicott's (1965, 1971) idea of "survival of the object," I as the therapist, could stand-in for the early mother, having "survived" by not retaliating and by not abandoning Lauren when she had expressed her raw aggression toward me (enraged accusations). I also purposely did not interpret Lauren's aggression when she projected it onto me (when she was operating in a paranoid-schizoid state of mind) rather than operating in a depressive position state of mind. To have done so would have felt like retaliation. Lauren was therefore able to come to move into the depressive position, where she could witness and reflect on her own aggression, and where she could own her own impulse to retaliate that she had expressed originally toward Adrien and then toward me (sister and mother). This kind of Winnicottian object survival is a key to psychic transformation in patients struggling with intolerable regret that is based on unconscious neurotic guilt, with its unconscious psychic fantasy base. Countertransference retaliation can sometimes prevent this psychic transformation that needs to take place. The transformation is from unconscious neurotic guilt to conscious existential guilt in the form of psychic and tolerable regret.

Following from Kleinian thought as well, we can see the developmental progression in Lauren from hostile and envious assaults to expressions of genuine gratitude. Expressions of gratitude renew an early potential for loving capacity within an authentic self-evolution, as this self-evolution takes place in terms of Object Relations development. In 1957, Melanie Klein published her paper on "Envy and Gratitude," a paper that had already been presented at a conference in the 1930s (Grosskurth, 1986). In this paper, Klein articulates the dialectical relationship between hostile aggression in its object-targeted instinctual form of envy and the development of the capacity for gratitude and its expression.

When instinctual envy remains unconscious, it can be a constant source of destructiveness in the form of spoiling both external and internal Object Relationships. When unconscious, it is often heard in the adult form of devaluing criticisms that create psychic distance from others, and which in their accumulation create an overall cycle of spoiling and disconnection from internal loving capacities. When unconscious envy is thus enacted, it serves as a polarized psychic state in relation to a depressive position stage of mind, a state of mind in which loving capacity can be enhanced and developed through the overt expression of gratitude. I would add that this expression of gratitude is, in itself, an expression of developmental achievement in terms of an achievement of separation-individuation and self-integration, which allows the "other" to be perceived as truly separate and to be perceived as a loving and "good enough" object to whom one can safely attach oneself, in terms of a "mature dependence" (Winnicott, 1971), without feeling threatened with retaliation or abandonment. In addition, the act of expressing gratitude directly to someone, and especially to a psychoanalyst, who also serves as a "good-enough" real object for internalization and as a transferential mother figure, allows for the internalization of a "good" interpersonal transaction that can become part of a new and better psychic structure within the psyche and the internal world.

All this can be seen in the case of Lauren, as she evolved in her mode of communication within the monthly mourning group experience, with the help of the one individual consultation. In the same group meeting in which she reported being so relieved and helped by the individual consultation with me, in which she viewed the psychic fantasy of her sadism behind her angry comments in group, Lauren evolved into a deeper affect experience of her gratitude. Toward the end of the group, she said with tears in her eyes, crying as she spoke, that I was "always here," and that I created an atmosphere of safety, in which she and all the others "could have our negative transferences."

451

The implication was that she, and the other members of the group, could all hate me if they needed to, and I would still be there, without retaliation or abandonment, thus loving them. In other words, they could hate me freely, and I would still love them, the essence of Winnicott's (1971) object survival. By saying this so spontaneously, with such deep contact with her interior self core (Winnicott's, 1960b, true self), Lauren was taking another developmental step forward and was looked at with admiration by other group members, who wished they could communicate from the depths of self feeling as Lauren did.

Lauren could evoke the truest example of Klein's "envy and gratitude" dialectic, as she contacted primal love through the expression of gratitude, after having expressed the most hostile envy and rage toward me. Her self-reflective awareness of her mother transference with me was obvious as she spoke of my being there for her and her transferential siblings (sisters). She contacted love through an awareness of loss and grief. She contacted love through a resolution of guilt into conscious regret. This conscious regret allowed awareness of wishes for reparation. Lauren could then reach out through reparative gestures toward me as the other who represented the primal object, as well as all the displaced objects upon which she had transferred her ambivalence toward her mother.

A Daughter's Regret toward Her Father
and Her Evolving Capacity for Spousal Love

Although Sharon's story has been written about, Sharon is in continuing evolution. Having entered into four psychoanalytic psychotherapy sessions a week, she had been engaged in a continuing depressive position working through process. Confronting psychic regret played a major part in Sharon's analysis, resulting in critical self-integration. This self-integration allowed Sharon to sustain a rather difficult marriage, and to enhance her capacities for mothering in relation to her two children. As she owned her aggression through a process of facing regrets, her son (now 13) became free to become himself and to connect to her second husband, gradually relinquishing a symbiotic and narcissistic mode of relating to his biological father.

Sharon's son was freed by Sharon's self-integration process because Sharon was no longer compelled to project out her disowned aggressive and inadequate parts (when she had formerly lacked self-agency) onto her son through projective identification, triggered by dissociative mechanisms. Her daughter (who was now six) remained free to develop as a separate person, greatly supported by the love and admiration of her father, Sharon's second husband. Sharon had already been in psychotherapeutic treatment when her daughter was born, although it was a preliminary stage of treatment, in which she had only attended sessions once a week. Sharon saw in her daughter a healthy vitality, self-assertion, and a capacity to play and to easily relate to others. She increased her psychotherapy sessions, which had become a more intensive psychoanalysis, to facilitate her daughter's growth as well as her own, and to deal with the difficulties in her second marriage. The former writings on Sharon spoke of many of the problems in her marriage. The following vignette on Sharon's treatment focuses on the poignant enlargement of her existential grief as it touches on her first consciousness of her former relationship with her now-deceased father.

In one session, Sharon had felt the pain of regret over her characterological self-righteousness. She realized this self-righteousness was another aspect of the defensive contempt she had spoken of many times in analyzing her relationship with her husband, friends, and acquaintances. We had spoken together of how she held onto her self-righteous attitudes, despite how destructive they were to her relationships, because it was a way of holding on to her mother. It was a way of identifying with her mother and having her mother through this identification when she couldn't have her through direct affect contact and interpersonal communication and connection. Her mother's affect self was walled-off behind narcissistic attitudes of martyrdom, contempt, and self-righteousness that hid intense shame and inadequacy, and a profound lack of self-agency. The mother could dissociate from her shame by inducing these feelings in Sharon and scapegoating Sharon. For Sharon, the only way out of feeling inadequate was to identify with her mother's false self, i.e., with her defensive narcissistic attitudes. In this way, Sharon could put herself above others and above her own needs, needs that had only lived in an arrested child self, sealed-off within her. Unconscious of it all, she had become an expert at condescension, even though appearing meek on the surface. She had become an expert in enacting Melanie Klein's manic defense, by which means she had warded off the grief of her own life losses and regrets. To consciously face her narcissistic defenses, as well as the schizoid ones of outward withdrawal and defensive self-sufficiency, Sharon had to take her attitudes one at a time.

After many psychic forays into Sharon's contempt, we came upon a related "animal," her self-righteousness. She realized that when she thought she was being open and confrontational with her husband, something she feared being, she would often provoke an angry tantrum in her husband. When we looked at Sharon's part in this—aside from her husband's defensive reaction to avoid seeing himself—we saw that she was actually speaking to her husband from a high-horse position of self-righteousness, which—without either of them being aware—provoked an immediate and reflexive tantrum rage in her husband. She was relieved that she played a part in these scenes, because her part she could change, and control, once aware of it.

So, we spoke about how she believed that self-righteousness gave her a sense of having her mother's power, rather than just being a victim of this power, as when it was aimed at her in sarcastic and ridiculing comments throughout her childhood. Having come to view her mother's extreme degree of actual powerlessness in relation to her position in the world, Sharon was now inclined to recognize that "my mother's only achievement was her self-righteousness." Sharon told me that she was realizing that her mother desperately needed the false pride that she had perpetually portrayed in her self-righteousness, but that she, Sharon, no longer needed it. She knew she was sabotaging her life by inhabiting the self-righteous frame of mind, and also knew that she had created a life that was worth living for: with her family, her new degrees of social life, her work as a professional, and her new success as a creative writer. She no longer wanted to isolate herself behind her own wall of a self-righteous attitude, but first, she had to see how this attitude was operating.

As we spoke of her character defense, Sharon increasingly realized how she unconsciously transmitted the same attitude in her mother that had so injured her own sense of worth and self-agency to others, alienating the very ones she said she wanted to be close to, especially her husband and her son. But from her internal child perspective to be self-righteous was to be the powerful part of her mother, to share in the power that as a child she had felt as monstrous and overwhelming, to be the sadist rather than the victim masochist. By letting go of her self-righteous attitude, of which she said, "it was all my mother had," she was saying "good-bye" to her mother. This had been the greater threat, to be all alone in the world, without a mother. No child could stand this, so being her mother's self-righteous narcissistic extension, as well as her scapegoated inadequate self, had been preferable. In saying "good-bye" to mom, Sharon was saying "hello" to new insights about the vulnerable position she had been in within her childhood family. That vulnerable position involved a relationship with her father that had long been buried in her unconscious and had only recently opened up. As the mourning process related to her father opened up, it brought the pain of what would have been an intolerable regret, a pain which now—with each phase of recognition—was becoming a tolerable anguish.

It was at the end of this session on self-righteousness that Sharon began to sense that I was sleepy. She felt me fading away a bit. She asked me if I was there. I said I was sleepy and would like to understand what it was about. Sharon said she thought I was bored with her, didn't want her around, and asked if she should leave the session early. I asked her why she assumed I was bored with her or didn't want her around, just because I had begun to feel sleepy. She said that it was obvious that if I was falling asleep, I was bored with her. I said it was not obvious, that this was only her interpretation of my motive for being sleepy. I said that many other interpretations could be made. I also said that something out of her awareness might play a part in my being sleepy at that particular time, aside from how much sleep I got the night before, since I hadn't been sleepy before she came. I said that I often recognized these kinds of sleepy states that felt like I was being pulled into some repressed area in a patient's unconscious mind, making me feel like I was being pressured by some unconscious pressure within them.

Sharon replied that it felt like a familiar place to her, to feel that I, like others, was really not there, like she wasn't interesting enough to listen to. She said that it had always felt in her family as if there were nobody really there, nobody listening to her or present with her, nobody who thought she was important. She said that that was how she felt with her father, especially after he was hospitalized when she was eight for depression, and he quit his job and withdrew increasingly from the world. I wondered if I wasn't being pressured into playing a role in her unconscious, internal world drama, by being made to feel like the half-asleep father who was so detached that he couldn't respond to her. Sharon "woke up" as I woke up, by saying this. Something seemed to dislodge itself from her unconscious at that moment. Sharon said that her unconscious might be making her feel like she was with her father again. She had always felt rejected by him because he was never "there." And that's how she was feeling with me, she said, like my sleepiness meant I was rejecting her.

The following session began with a whimper rather than a bang. Sharon said she had been feeling so much better lately—for the first time not having at least six things stored up in her mind that she was afraid to say to her husband (the transferential mother monster). It was new to feel that she could express herself and that she could feel pride and pleasure for the first time in completing a creative writing project. In fact, she said that she felt so much better, that she felt like she had nothing to say in the psychoanalytic session. I commented that when she had nothing to say, it was usually the beginning of something really important, because at that moment she was free of her pre-programmed agendas that served a defensive purpose in the session. After all, they were contrived from her head and didn't allow her to be in the moment and have free thoughts and feelings (free association). She was always puzzled when I said this, but she was seeing that it generally turned out to be true, that when she began by saying she had nothing to say, something new and important was about to emerge. Today was to be no exception.

Sharon began to let her thoughts come up more freely then, and one of her first thoughts was that she couldn't remember what had happened in the last session. I suggested that she might not want to remember that her father had come up in the last session after we talked about losing her mother if she were to give up her self-righteousness. She had clung to her self-righteous mother through identification because she was the only one there once her father started getting ill with depression. I reminded her of how she had felt when I had gotten sleepy. She then remembered and said, "I guess I didn't want to remember!" She had felt left with a mentally and emotionally absent father.

Sharon began to speak about being left with her monster mother when she rejected her father because he had become such an inadequate parent. She reiterated that he had been hospitalized when she was around eight years old. She said that this had followed her having lost her father by her pulling away from him and rejecting him at an earlier time. Her imagining in the last session that I was the father rejecting her seemed to be a projection of her rejection of her father, at least as Sharon was seeing it now.

Sharon began to try reconstructing the memories of her early life during the session. She said that since our earlier discussions of her father had brought out the painful memory of how he had actually been there for her when she was little and had loved her, she was now wondering when she had lost him. I said that some girls are loved by their fathers until they become adolescents and start to develop adult female sexual characteristics that threaten their fathers. Sharon replied, quite emphatically, that this was not the case with her. She said that her father had withdrawn from her much earlier, before the time when he went to the hospital. Now she was speaking of him having rejected her even though she had just referred to herself as a little girl rejecting him.

I asked her where her father was when she was three and her mother left her in the park alone with her brother, and then hit her for finding her way home again. She said that he must have been at work, but that at that time she might have felt that he would have wanted to protect her. She had repressed memories of her early childhood for many years, but she had uncovered in earlier sessions that her father had been close to her when she was little. She sensed now that her father had been more comfortable loving her when she could be held and cuddled and didn't have to be spoken to like a more separate person. But then she had discovered him to be such a woefully "inadequate parent" that she rejected him by mocking him, dismissing him, and turning her self-righteousness and contempt as weapons upon him. Unfortunately, that had meant that she was left all alone with her terrifying mother, the queen of contempt and self-righteousness, who called Sharon stupid, implied she was bad, and assaulted her with sarcastic comments.

Sharon now said that it all became about "who was hurting and rejecting who," back and forth between her and her father. She would coldly accuse her father of being inept, and he would reject her by being passive, silent, and withdrawn. "It got much worse after he was hospitalized and returned," she said. He just sat still and stared silently at her. She would become enraged and verbally attack him. Reflecting back on this time now, Sharon began to feel remorse. Her eyes filled with tears as she seemed to realize for the first time that "I never understood that he couldn't help it. I didn't know that he was cut off from himself and felt powerless to help himself. I was really cruel because I was so enraged that he was no longer there for me. I didn't realize that he couldn't help it. This is a really painful regret," she said as she recalled her coldness toward her father.

I spoke to Sharon's vulnerability within the feeling of regret and the memories of her own coldness that were being stirred, creating both a mental sense of guilt and a bodily sense of grief and loss. I said that she was dealing with both a neurotic sense of guilt and an existential guilt that had the grief of regret within it. I said that it was neurotic to blame herself now for something she was incapable of comprehending as a child or adolescent. I said that there was nobody there who could listen to her and help to see her father as a vulnerable being that existed beyond his being for the purpose to reject her. She was all alone with an intolerable sense of rejection by her father, being scapegoated by her mother, and feeling abandoned by her brother, who left home quite early for college. Sharon said that this was true, but she didn't think she had to choose to reject her father as she did. She was tearful as she said this. She regretted her cruelty toward her father, even though it was part of her youth, and not something she could reflect on from an adult position, as she could reflect now only after much therapy. I said that this was the existential guilt that she had actually rejected him and caused him much pain when he was already in a great deal of pain. It may be neurotic to exaggerate the guilt and to believe she could have acted and thought differently without any adult support or help, but nevertheless, the existential effect of her rejection was still there, and she could feel it now as she had developed the capacity to love someone separate from herself. Sharon responded by saying that she hated discovering this truth of her regret because it hurt so much.

In the following session, Sharon started by saying, "I'm impressed with my own abilities to dissociate. I don't remember what we talked about in the last session. I just know it was painful." Although she forgot what we had discussed, Sharon said that somehow she was feeling better. She said that she was feeling better with her husband, no longer obsessed with who was hurting who, and who was doing what to whom. I said that even though she wasn't remembering specifically that we had talked about her father in the last session, she was associating to the session by demonstrating that she was no longer acting out with her husband the pattern with her father of always obsessively calculating in her mind who was hurting who. It all came back to her then. She said that she realized that the session on her father had helped free her and release her. "It was a relief," she said, "but I don't want to go back there again today. Remembering how I rejected him, after he had been the one person who loved me early on, is too painful, although it is more tolerable than before."

PART FOUR

OBJECT RELATIONS PSYCHOANALYSIS AND GROUP THERAPY

CHAPTER 19

AN OBJECT RELATIONS VIEW OF
CREATIVE PROCESS AND GROUP PROCESS

Originally published in 1992, *Group* 16(1):47–58.

Abstract

This article describes a unique writing group experience. Members of the writing group undergo an intensive Object Relations working through process. They experience the individual dynamics of their internal editors. They work on conflicts over shame, guilt, and envy that reinforce hostile reactions of the internal editor. In this way, they resolve blocks to the creative process, produce writing, get feedback, give expression to the internal voice, and find the format or formats most appropriate for their unique modes of self-expression. They also help each other mourn the internal parents who constitute the internal editor composite. The mutual grieving process enlarges the inner space for creative self-expression. In sum, this article illustrates the interaction of group process with Object Relations intrapsychic process.

This long-term weekly writing group, which has met for four and a half years now, is a group in which each member presents regularly on a rotating basis. The presentations range from expressing feelings and associations that pertain to conflicts about wishes and resistances to writing, to the actual reading of a piece of work. Within this context, as the writing group leader, I facilitate awareness both about the writing process and about the interpersonal relations within the group that provides contact to engage with the overall creative process.

The *"Internal Editor"*

Utilizing Fairbairn's (1952) concepts of the "internal saboteur" and the "anti-libidinal ego," I help those who wish and yet hesitate to write to confront what I characterize as the "internal editor." The internal editor haunts the wouldbe writer by censoring that which he or she might wish to say before he/she can say it. The internal editor is a composite, derived from a multitude of parental introjects that prompt shame and guilt in the face of creative desire. The internal editor comes alive through transference, associations, and affectively laden memories that recreate the parental personas behind the internal editor persona. The repetitive intrapsychic pattern also comes alive in the pattern of interactions within the group. Transferences emerge and are repetitively worked through between myself and the members of the group and among the members of the group.

As the leader of a weekly writing group, I help group members to face the externalized form of the internal editor by presenting their work to other group members and thus risking exposure. Exposure brings projections of the internal editor onto others. Awareness of transference reactions brings forth feelings of anger, shame, guilt, and loss. When such feelings are understood and also shared by group members, the empathy in the group leads to the emergence of the internal editor's counterpart. This counterpart is a composite of loving and supportive figures who have constituted, in Winnicott's (1965) term, a "good-enough" internal parent. This is the internal parent who can hold the writer in a psychic embrace, allowing words and images to flow forth onto paper. As the presenter and the group members associate to the presentations within the writing group, they contact loving memories that open up conscious connections to the composite internal good parent.

For example, one group member brought in written accounts of dreams, narrative descriptions of houses, and narrative memories that helped her to reconnect to her love for her grandmother. It was this grandmother who gave her support against a mother who was rejecting and critical. Her internal editor reflected the rejecting criticism of her mother, but reconnecting with her grandmother through the sharing of her writing in the group allowed her to open a core of self-expression that could facilitate new strivings toward creative writing. The group members' associations to loving figures in their own past reinforced and enlarged this process. Their abilities to also analyze how her writing inhibitions related to a pattern of disconnection from this loving and self-expressive part of her also helped this woman to struggle in the face of the internal editor's self-criticism to grieve her injuries as well as her guilt. Only in this way could she develop her creative writing abilities when she herself doubted them so much!

As the group leader, I stay in contact with each group member's struggle, helping to bring each member's struggles into the forefront of the experiential moment at the time when that particular member presents. I also acknowledge the empathic contact and the interpretive contributions of others toward the presenter so as to facilitate the holding process in the group that leads to loving memories and associations. Each member of the group contributes to analyzing and interpreting the connections between the presenter's writing blocks and the ongoing struggle within the content and process of the writing itself. In this particular writing group, the majority of the members are psychoanalysts themselves, and all the members have had extensive psychotherapy, so there is a level of psychological sophistication that enhances the mutual contributions to an interpretive process.

Shame

To write is to risk exposure, and the writing group requires such exposure by requiring presentations. However, sometimes there are no presentations, but rather discussions of resistances. By requiring presentations, the writing group prompts the resistances to exposure, but the holding environment aspect of the group, based on the establishment of empathic ties, allows the resistances to be discussed and confronted. Resistances can generally be discussed in terms of fear of criticism, fear of inadequacy, fear of competitive triumphs by others, and embarrassment about one's own ambitiousness, which is often felt to be grandiose and presumptuous. Group members experience others in the group and/or the leader as being above them, beyond them—as others who do not have to struggle in the messy anal elements like they do. Their own confusion and self-doubt are felt as unique. Feelings of raw body exposure come up as nerves are touched through projections of feared judgments, which lead to humiliating memories. However, these humiliating memories can be shared, and then the text of the writing and the context of the group dynamics merge.

One woman in the group shared a short story that contained a most intensely mortifying view of herself during her adolescence. She experienced deep gratitude toward the other group members for understanding and accepting the part of herself that she had revealed in this story. The other group members responded out of their own personal understanding of what sharing such humiliating memories aroused in them. Each of them had revealed similar levels of shame in reading their written work and in talking about the inhibitions in their writing and their presentation of their writing to the world.

As can be seen, the sharing in the group allows the cross-fertilization of mutually inspiring associations. This allows self-stimulating interpersonal connections to generate deepening levels of reflective feedback. Increasing levels of intimacy are promoted as group members gain validation from one another.

Guilt

Another block on the road to in-depth self-expression is that of guilt. Guilt about taking time for oneself to be with oneself, to indulge in one's internal world, to write while alone, is a frequent theme among members of a writing group, and particularly among women. Guilt associations about not being available to nurture others resonate across the room, and the presenter expresses memories of guilt that are links in a chain back to early relationships that still exert a stranglehold. In discussing her difficulty taking time to write, one group member recalled memories of her adolescence in which she was made to feel intensely guilty for not wanting to stay home all the time with her mother, who was sick with a fatal illness. She spoke of how she went to a dance and was about to kiss a boy she felt extremely attracted to when she remembered her mother and abruptly pulled back. This woman recalled to the group: "I ran home, and then saw my mother extremely upset about my absence. My father gave me an accusatory look and said something like 'How can you do this to your mother?' I felt that he was accusing me of abandoning my mother just when she needed me the most."

As this woman recalled this memory, she linked it to her guilt about seeking personal pleasure in writing when there was always someone around who might seek her nurturance. As she made this link she not only was more able to take time to write, but she also incorporated her memory into writing she was doing on a book of memoirs. Throughout this woman's exploration, other group members related to their inability to leave others in their lives while they took time to write.

As this example shows, the articulation of the guilt memories lightens the burden on current relations and begins to allow the group member to write. The guilt, like the shame, becomes incorporated into the text of the writing.

Anger emerges and mobilizes creative motivation. This woman's anger at her mother of adolescence was expressed in the group, and expressing it freed her to feel her love. Feeling the love allowed her creative self-expression to flow. As Melanie Klein's theory (1940) informs us, love and creativity flow from the same place. This woman began to write of her loss of her mother, of her hurt, and ultimately she felt the sadness of her love.

The hurt and losses behind the anger can lead to persistent phases of mourning. Early loving connections are then remembered, and early parts of the self are integrated into the present and conscious sense of self. Deeper levels of material for writing are reached.

Another member of the psychotherapeutic writing group always felt paralyzed in relation to her wishes to write. Over the course of the years in group, a sequence of themes around anger and guilt were revealed, which freed up this woman's paralysis. Her anger at the group was transferential, and the nature of this transference became clear over time. This woman became aware of an anger that was defensive against loving feelings for early parental figures, such as a cherished grandmother. By being angry at the group, she was able to be angry at the mother of her past and to refine the love for her so that she could mourn. Just the expression of her anger to the group temporarily freed her so that she could write critical essays without fearing that the contempt in her anger would poison her essays. As long as she feared the nature of her own critical attitude toward those that she wrote about, she was paralyzed with guilt and could not write.

As she expressed her anger to the group, her anger was detoxified by the survival of the group members and myself. We survived because there was no retaliation. Rather there was a real interest in the nature of her anger and in how it related to her internal editor and in turn to her writing blocks. The group participated in exploring with this woman how her anger at us was not only anger at her projected mother, but also a transferential reflection of the contemptuous anger directed at her from her internal editor, an editor derived largely from an internalization of her grandmother. The group also helped this woman explore how her identification with her internal editor aggressor was a defense against her love for this internal editor figure, her cherished grand mother, toward whom she did not consciously wish to feel anger. Her anger was therefore displaced onto the group members, but this continued her guilt and thus her paralysis in relation to initiating writing that she said she longed to do.

When this member began to feel how her self-critical contempt was related to both shame about herself, and to guilt over the anger toward the grandmother with whom she chose to identify in an attitude of contempt, her self-contempt softened. Although she continued to express contempt toward herself for not being able to set time aside to write, and to have a backlash reaction of disgust toward her own writing after she had written it, she became much more quickly able to respond to feedback from the group about her self-contempt. She began to recognize her internal editor as being constructed from her grandmother's attitudes of contempt for others (not for her), an attitude with which she had come to identify. She listened more and more attentively as group members asked her about her feelings toward her grandmother. She began to recall memories of her grandmother's comments to her. She had already written essays on memories of her grandmother. Now, she recalled her love for her grandmother and recognized that she could love her without identifying with her bitter and cynical contempt. This awareness gradually freed this woman to be less critical of herself, and therefore less constricted by anger.

Expressing the anger to the group was the first step in freeing her love for her grandmother, and in differentiating herself from her grandmother. As she did this work with group members, she was able to own her motivation to write a bit more, a motivation she would disown by saying that she only did her writing because she was complying with homework assignments presented to her either from her profession or from the group. (We never actually gave her homework assignments, and our frustration of her wish to have them was important. However, suggestions for how she might follow up on her own motivation were sometimes given.) Each time this woman re-owned a piece of her own motivation to write, she would begin to make time to write again, would write, and would review past writing to see where she wanted to deepen or broaden her work.

It should be emphasized that behind this woman's anger was immense guilt. It became clear how each advance in this group member's written self-expression, which was the fulfillment of her deepest desires, was promptly followed by a backlash reaction. When paralyzed by this backlash, she began to say that she felt she didn't deserve the sense of intense pleasure she felt while writing. What this meant then became clear through this woman's associations, memories, and her transference reactions to others in the group.

Gradually this group member's guilt was felt by her and understood by both her and the group. Each time a piece of her guilt was dealt with, her loving connections with her internal parental objects became more fully established, as when she realized she felt guilty for being unable to take care of her mother in her old age. With such a realization, this woman could grieve for the loss of not having loved her mother enough to want to care for her. She began to face the pain of the guilt she felt for this, a guilt which had so paralyzed her, preventing her from writing. With the mourning, she began to feel disciplined from within. Gradually, she began to set aside time to write. Also, more and more frequently now, she writes in the subjective style in which she had always yearned to write. She is finding a form of creative self-expression that she felt had been denied to her as a child. The struggle continues.

Guilt about competitive feelings is another unconscious aspect of writing blocks that the group can help to make manifest. Often it is first expressed through anger. The reparative experience of having the anger and the competitive needs expressed can lead to increased freedom for the writer's inner voice. With a different group member, the anger emerged as a transferential response to the group leader. Ms. D. said she was angry at the group leader for not acknowledging her growth. She also felt hurt, and the anger seemed a manifest sign of narcissistic injury. Her guilt over competitive feelings was less manifest. However, after expressing her anger to me, the group leader, in the presence of the group, and with an empathic reception from the group members, who viewed her expression as healthy self-assertion, Ms. D. was able to begin to compete openly with the group leader. She chose a topic to write about that overlapped with an area of my writing. She actively began to disagree with my view and was supported by members of the group in expressing her differing opinions. When Ms. D. hesitated or backed down in expressing her differing views, two group members, in particular, challenged her. They interpreted her backing down as a submission to her internal mother, now in transferential form in relation to me. Ms. D. was told that she was submitting to her internal editor through her transference projection and transaction with me, the group leader. She began to emerge more and more with her views. She wrote a lengthy article in which she disagreed with those that held my opinions. For the first time, she proceeded to follow through on her article to submit it for publication. This beautifully written article became Ms. D.'s first actual publication after years of stopping just at the point of publication.

Envy and Fears of the Envy of Others

A major block to the richness of inner life that is required for creative efforts is that of unconscious envy. As the group leader, I sense the areas of inhibition in the writers within the group and often link them with interactions in the group that suggest envy and fears of envy.

Members of the group become aware of envy as they express feelings of shame about their own feared inadequacies. At one time, there was a mutual sharing of envious feelings toward each other by all the group members, following the communicating of much angry feeling. Some group members felt frustration and anger in response to their own wishes to be cared for by other group members. They began to understand that their wish for more attention from the others was related to their own envious feelings toward those from whom they demanded more. One woman saw how her anger at another's demands related to envy of the other woman's professional accomplishments.

Involved was much projective identification, in which a part of the self, which induces shame or guilt, is psychically put into another and is experienced as victimizing oneself through the other. This woman began to see how her envy was related to shame about her own internal demands that she felt she couldn't live up to. She was not happy with her own level of professional accomplishment. Through the group process, with its underlying mourning process, she was able to become aware that she had projected her inadequacy feelings onto the woman of whom she was envious. As she confessed her envy, others followed. One envied another's ability to be a creative writer. Another woman envied somebody else's ability to make interpretations. A fourth member envied another's lifestyle. The group came full circle with their sharing of their secret bastions of envy.

The envy that comes up between writing group members also relates to feared envy from internal others, from those very parental objects who have been incorporated into the psyche as harsh aspects of the internal editor. Fear of retaliatory attacks from envious others is often a roadblock standing between the potential of the writer and the actual performance of the writer. One of my psychotherapy patients who was a professional writer put it this way: "If I don't write I'll die, and if I do write I'll feel this voice inside me, threatening, 'Watch out!'"

In the writing group, the fear of self-expression due to projected and felt envy can be seen repeatedly. One member developed a powerful transference of her internal editor to me, the group leader. In her transference, she both resented my successes as a writer (also as a teacher, supervisor, analyst) and idealized me. She saw me as always being successful in my endeavors. When I raised the group fee, she was enraged and demanded that I be made a group member and that the group be a peer group. Other group members supported my status as leader. They inquired as to whether she was feeling envious of me.

Up to this point, the enraged group member, Ms. T, had been writing poems and short stories. She hated herself for not being able to write professional papers, papers like I wrote. She belittled her own writing, called it messy, confused, ridiculous, and useless. She had written about the shame-ridden images of herself that related to this backlash reaction against her own work, but she had not dealt with the envy that made her hide her work. As she felt compelled to hide her work from the world, she failed to explore how she could shape the work into a style that could compete in the world at large. After her outburst of rage at me for being the leader, Ms. T began painfully and honestly to face her envy, thanking the group members for helping her face it.

It was also important to Ms. T that I had asserted my legitimate claim to the position of leader by claiming my expertise in two areas: as an analyst who understood the Object Relations dynamics of the creative process and the interpersonal group process, and as a prolific writer who had worked through the phases of revision and critical reviews from publishers. My assertion was welcomed by Ms. T. She saw me as surviving her wrath. The scene of her enraged confrontations recurred as she challenged me as the leader when she wanted me to be able to change another group member's behavior. When I again survived her wrath and understood her feelings of envy, she was relieved. She began actively to help others in the group with their feelings of envy. She praised another member for confessing her envy to a third member. She said that this second member was "gutsy" for her confession.

As others were more openly expressive of their envy, Ms. T began to be more open about envious feelings toward me, and also began to reveal her idealized images of me. When she revealed her images of me, she began to move from resentment to amusement in recognizing how perfect she saw me, or how defective she viewed me in her defensive devaluation. Such insight into her own images allowed her to see two images of herself. She saw that she was most often projecting an idealized image onto me and was devaluing herself. To get past her self-devaluation, she had defensively devalued me. As she became conscious of this, she became increasingly free from her fears of exposing her writing to me and the group members.

She began to take in the praise of the group members for her writing. She also began to write more developed pieces. She moved from free associative writing in her personal journal to more explicit individual pieces that she shaped more incisively into the form of a poem or short story. She began to think consciously about the form of her writing, moving toward presenting her pieces out in the world. In the process, she took a short story writing class. As she developed her own area, she was less ashamed of not writing theoretical papers as I did and therefore less envious. Ms. T began to express her genuine admiration for my work, and she no longer felt she had to write like me. When the group decided to present professional papers together on a panel for a professional organization, she was able to write her own professional paper, which emphasized the phenomenology of creative process experience, rather than theoretical constructions. She was finding her own voice and was freeing up from masochistic self-constriction due to the contempt of her envious internal editor-the internal mother that she had internalized, identified with, and reacted to. Earlier in the group, she had exposed memories of her mother's hostile contempt toward her in a state of envy. Now she was able to see how she was reenacting her mother's aggression toward her in her aggression toward me.

The Mourning Process

Each link in the chain of roadblocks is also a potential link in self-expression. The very elements of shame, guilt, anger, and envy that impede creative writing when they are left unconscious or unshared become the elements of the creative tapestry as feelings and associations become conscious through interpersonal articulation. Each new articulation crystallizes interpersonal connections, and as these connections are made within the group in relation to external others, they are also made with those internal others inhabiting the internal psychic world. The process of engagement is mutually reinforcing, as internal links create external ones and vice versa. It is my thesis that *the affective process that integrates the internal and external connections into a sense of self that becomes creative writing is that of mourning.* Memories and moments of shame, guilt, and envy are felt with grief. There is grief in the sense of one's vulnerability, in the sense of one's pain, hurt, and the remorse behind guilt, and in one's helplessness in the face of one's own ambition and greed. This grief promotes a sense of love within loss and loss within love. The early ties of love are strengthened through acknowledging the limits one feels in the face of one's persistent difficulties. Such conscious acknowledgment comes about by working through the pain of guilt and its related sense of loss.

Melanie Klein (1940) was one advocate for such tenderness promoted by grief. The writing group exhibits a gradual and enlarging mourning process in all its Kleinian dimensions. Each group member's individual mourning process strengthens loving ties and brings a sense of inner richness, which in turn promotes motivation to express creatively. Also, there is the group resonance of this mourning process, a mesh of interweaving feeling associations across the interpersonal scope of the group. To touch and be touched becomes the loving sorrow of talent enraptured now in concern that Shakespeare captured in saying "Parting is such sweet sorrow." Mourning is such sweet sorrow, and creativity evolves with this affective backdrop.

The Writing Group's Mourning Process

I have stated that the underlying process that promotes the expression and integration of the inner voice is the mourning. I will now give an example from the group process.

Each member of the writing group goes through an Object Relations mourning process. It is the group process that promotes this mourning process. Each member of the group has faced their internal editor either by talking about their personal blocks in self-expression or by facing their projections onto other group members of the internal editor within them. In facing the internal editor, they face a composite of figures from the past to whom they are deeply attached. As they do so, there is an identification process between group members that allows one member to mourn in response to the mourning of the others.

During the first year of this four-year writing group, Ms. A was grieving for her son, who she learned was also a reflection of herself in relation to her internal mother. She was overly identified with her son, as she had been overly identified with her mother. The group helped her to separate from her son and to see how she could not speak directly about herself in the group. She began to feel compassion for her son in relation to some critical problems that he was going through. She began to see that he received the help he needed. At the same time, she began to speak more about her own frustrations. She began to let go of her son and to feel sad but relieved to relinquish him.

As Ms. A mourned and separated from her son, and also faced the anger toward her mother that had made her so angry at her son, she encouraged others in the group to let go of internal others who were holding them back from self-expression. Ms. S. began to face her love for her aunt, for her mother, and for her grandmother, grieving the loss of all of them. Ms. D. increasingly mourned her mother, the dying mother who had held her back by hating her for her beauty and growth during her adolescence. Ms. D. also began to contact the positive and supportive aspects of her father, whom she had stereotyped as a negative internal editor figure. As she began to recall the positive aspects of her father, her love diminished her hatred. Her anger could then be expressed with less guilt. Ms. D. could mourn and feel the recreation of connection with her internal parents as she felt her love for both of them. This allowed her to feel love toward other group members and for myself, the leader. She was increasingly open with her anger as she increased her love, and she became increasingly free to express her own voice in her writing. She then could express gratitude to others in the group by helping them freely express their feelings. Ms. D. became sensitively attuned to the mourning process within each other group member.

This group sensitivity to mourning created a holding environment of trust and caring that was crucial when another group member, Ms. N., was faced with a devastating series of losses. In her private practice as a therapist, Ms. N worked with a group of patients who were dying. She began to work with this group just following the death of her mother. In the course of the deathand-dying group, her father died. Then a majority of the members of the group died. Ms. N. began to have anxiety attacks. She brought these attacks into the group through her writing, and also through direct sharing of her fear. The group responded by helping Ms. N. to explore the gut-wrenching terror that she unconsciously felt behind her anxiety attacks. She was feeling that she was losing all her connections, and in reaction, she felt her sense of self dissolving. She looked to the group for support, and the members encouraged her to write piece after piece about the losses she was experiencing. As she did so, she began to tolerate her feelings of grief, but the writing itself was not enough to help her contain these feelings. It was only by bringing the writing into the group and reading it to the leader and to the other group members that she was able to cry with the kind of sadness that could help her contain her experience and to heal.

Her feelings were a potent force for the group. Each group member responded with feelings of their own about loss. Even if they didn't do so immediately, they did so when it was their turn to speak about themselves in the writing group process rotation. They also responded to Ms. N. with interpretations that helped her connect her grieving process and her growing creative process. Ms. N. responded with increasing gratitude that modified her envy, shame, and the guilt she had been feeling about her own neediness. The connections that the group helped Ms. N experience were between her grieving and her creativity, and between her love for her lost others and the creative flow of the inner voice that came from such love. These connections significantly contributed to Ms. N.'s being able to consolidate a new and healthier self than that which she had felt she had lost.

Ms. N.'s self-integration radiated outward to a new group integration. She became a formative force in reaching behind each person's defensive anger to their sense of loss and grief. The theme of mourning continued in the group, and the writing that evolved from it was becoming a connecting link between each group member and the others as each member read their writing to the group. The members cried as they read, and when they were crying, they began to open up in a multitude of ways. Comical aspects began to come up in their writing, as well as joy, incisive philosophical discussion, and theoretical commentary, and poignant and personal memoirs in which crystalline nuggets of their core selves could be communicated.

Reparation through Creativity

My thesis is that the reparation of the self comes about through mourning. Mourning is the essential affective process of self-integration that modifies the split-off parts of the self that serve as hostile parts of the internal editor. Mourning promotes creativity, but mourning can also be accomplished through the creative process. The ability to mourn through the creative process is dependent on establishing a good-enough primary object within the internal world. Without such good-enough object internalization, creative work displays compulsive reenactments characteristic of pathological mourning (see KavalerAdler, 1985, 1986, 1988a, 1989b, 1991a, 1991b).

The psychotherapeutic writing group helps its members develop and reinforce good object internalizations so that they become more capable of mourning through their creative work. Creative work that allows mourning is creative work that is ever-evolving in new self-expressive forms and new selfexpressive content.

Each member of this long-term writing group has shown a mode of mourning in her work. One woman in the group wrote memoirs of varying phases of loss and separation and reintegration within her life. Another member of the group focused extensively on a period of adolescent trauma. A third wrote memoirs of houses, relatives, and friends that were links in a chain of her individual character development. A fourth member wrote poetry and short stories that reflected all aspects of her painful separation process. In the following poem, this fourth member mourns the loss of her father, who died while she was still in the process of resolving her conflicting view of him within her internal world.

> Beneath a weary eye
> Last night late
> ate sawdust by candle light and cried
> wept in Venice for the ghost dragoons
> half lit dragged along the deep canal creaking sepulchre
> In ochre square from burnished iron balcony peered down
> my moonlit eye drifts along the steaming canal
> lost missed wanted
> forgotten which beginning
> sudden taken wanted waited
> regretted wantonly
> Come to me, Come to me
> In ochre square
> gray cut stone arches walking over steamy canal
> wastrel's daughter
> lean, binged on croquille
> "Can't get enough of these"
> lonely

March 4, 1990

Related to the internal father is the internal mother. In struggling to face the internal editor, each member of the group has dealt with mother. They continue to analyze how their internal editor is related to guilt toward the mother, and how it is related to identifications with hostile aspects of the mother. It is the connections in the group that have made it possible for them to do this. It is also the connections in the group that help each member connect with the original loving bond with mother, as they work to differentiate and separate from her more hostile qualities that have served to block their writing process.

One woman in the group became acutely aware of how much her ability to write from her feelings was related to her connections with myself, the group leader, and also with the other members of the group. She began to see how her transference to us as good mother figures allowed her to connect with deeply emotional parts of herself. Although she did not necessarily need to connect with these deep emotional parts for her professional writing, her ability to internalize the connections with the group and its leader was critical for her more personal writing—for the writing of poems, memoirs, and essays of a personal nature. As she began to internalize us, she was able to grieve the loss of her real mother, and to forgive herself for her anger toward her mother, examining the nature of her guilt toward her mother and the nature of the grudges she still held. This is helping resolve the anger and guilt.

As another woman becomes more open to her feelings and to letting in the feedback of the group members, psychic space can be seen to be opening up (Winnicott, 1971). The opening of this woman's personal psychic space is manifested in the opening of the "analytic space" (Ogden, 1986) in the group. This woman now allows all the group members to enter a dialogue with her and with the other members about the intrapsychic conflict that she is experiencing at that moment. Formerly, she foreclosed such space for dialogue and for the mutuality of analysis with an obsessional style of talking that walled others out. This style has been changing significantly, yielding to a vulnerability to interaction and to taking help from others.

Along with such a change in interpersonal relations manifested in the group has come a change in this woman's writing process. She is writing in a more personal style now, beginning to fulfill a long-held yearning for subjective self-expression that had formerly been hidden behind a more detached mode of academic writing. Her ability to write in this new way has been promoted by her ongoing mourning process within the writing group. As she has, bit by bit, allowed the emergence of grief that lies behind her anger and her guilt, she has opened inner psychic space and has won the support of other group members in facing the internal editor within her who has been most critical of her attempts to express her pain.

She is also learning that her attachment to her internal editor is continually fueled by a primary love for one particular mothering figure in her childhood whose love was always saturated with critical comments. Using the critical comments of her internal editor to stifle the pleasure of self-expression allows this woman to punish herself and to appease her guilt toward this early figure whose life was so lacking in pleasure. Although constructive criticism from the group is needed for her writing, this woman found it very hard to tolerate praise without criticism. Formerly, she had sought a severe and punitive form of criticism that would turn others into her internal editor and would defend her against her need to grieve the loss of her early attachments. To experience conscious grief means remembering lost love as sadness opens up within the cognitive context of memory. To grieve also means the process of integrating such love with the very real anger toward the same figures whom she loved so deeply.

The psychotherapeutic writing group serves as a holding environment as long as all kinds of feelings and needs can be expressed within it. Empathy and attunement allow loving connections to be formed. The loving connections within the self, and without, among group members and between the members and the group leader, help promote the capacity to mourn and to thus repair and integrate the self. Several of the group members, in addition to pursuing and presenting professional writing within the group, present writing that is more directly illustrative of their internal mourning process. The mourning process within the group and this more personal work also helps to open up their original thinking and creative integrations of thought and feeling in their professional papers and books. As mourning is done, the internal object and its ties to the self become better integrated, and so overall self integration is enhanced. Once this integration process progresses, the creative process, which is a process of relating to these internal world objects, becomes enriched. Creative motivation increasingly develops and becomes much more naturally sustained.

CHAPTER 20

ANATOMY OF REGRET AND REPARATION: RESOLUTION OF TRANSFERENCE RESISTANCES THROUGH THE COMBINED USE OF A WRITING AND CREATIVE PROCESS GROUP AND A MOURNING REGRETS GROUP

Originally published in 2000, Anatomy of regret and reparation: Resolution of transference resistances through the combined use of a writing and creative process group and a mourning regrets group, *Issues in Group Psychotherapy, Postgraduate Group Journal* 4(1).

Description of the Two Groups

During over 40 years of practice as a clinical psychologist and psychoanalyst, I have led writing groups. These groups focus on the overall creative process of each group member, which includes, but does not overly privilege, actual presentation and feedback on creative work. Each member speaks and/or presents work on a rotation basis. However, at points when conflicts or impasses emerge in the group, the interactive group process becomes highlighted, as opposed to serving as a background for the foreground focus of the individual psychic and creative process. When critical transference and transference resistance dynamics present themselves, interpersonal dynamics become the focus of the group, allowing projections and transferences to be sorted out. The resolution of conflicts, and the understanding of projections, and of *self* and *other* psychic structures, can then be applied to each group member's individual process, in relation to her or his creativity and creative project ambitions.

Within the course of resolving and understanding transference resistance, which emerges as a parallel dynamic to internal object or internal editor impasses to individual creative process, relinquishment of inhibiting old object ties unfolds into the affect evolution of the mourning process. For this reason, some who participate in these writing groups also choose to participate in my monthly therapeutic mourning group, where they can engage more fully with the depths of grief, loss, guilt, shame, and envy, all of which constitute affect constellations, with accompanying Object Relations conflicts. Blocked and unblocked aggression is understood in relation to defenses against object loss, which involves an interplay between grief sadness and depressive guilt sadness. The guilt sadness, so implicit in the relinquishing of formative object ties (Klein, 1940; Kavaler-Adler, 1993b, 1996/2014, 2003a, 2013, 2014a) is spoken of in the therapeutic mourning group, and sometimes in the writing groups as well, as the anguish of regret (Kavaler-Adler, 2004, 2013).

Unlike in the writing groups, where a rotation of presentation is employed, in the ongoing monthly therapeutic group (also called the Mourning Regrets Group), there is no individual rotation, but rather a full group process interaction, which begins with individual process within a structured meditative visualization. The opening of guided visualization involves a focus on breathing, combined with varying forms of free association. The guided visualization leads to a specific focus on allowing an other to emerge from each person's internal world, as if the person emerges through the breathing and body, rather than being directed from the group member's head. As the internal world person emerges (or sometimes a part of the self), each group member is asked to say what they need to say to this person and to wait for a response. Also, they are guided to speak gut feelings from their stomach, which brings up hunger and aggression, and to see if there is a heart connection, so that one can speak from one's heart to the internal person.

Each group member engages in an internal dialogue with the internal other or finds that such dialogue is blocked due to the lack of response of the other. All this is repeated with a meditative focus on a second person emerging from within, to be spoken to, while held in awareness, by looking directly at the internal other within the person's mind. Disconnections can become the focus, along with connections that may lead to grief, anger, rage, as well as to regret, forgiveness, and renewed love. Sometimes, the group member, with his/her eyes closed, cries during the meditative visualization, and often the deep grief and longings in the tears are shared in the group following the visualization.

The focus on the stomach brings encounters with anger, rage, hunger, and hate (sometimes manifesting as envy)—and also with deprivation, in relation to the internal other, who is often a parent, sibling, or an intimate relationship figure, such as current boyfriend or ex-husband. Group members find that the feelings in their heart are quite different than those in their stomach: as longings, loss, grief, and love are felt through the heart. If the heart feeling is blocked, this has psychodynamic significance. The stomach speaks in impulses, while the heart speaks in more refined affects. When the heart and stomach speak to each other, conflicts between love and hate often manifest. Then each participant can decide whether she/he wishes to take the internal other (the internal object that is based partly on a real past or present external object) into her/his heart or to leave them outside the boundaries of the heart and self.

When I ask each group member to open her/his eyes, the group opens space for each person to share their visualization, and the one who volunteers to share first begins the group. This focus on the individual in the group, by the group, allows for a great deal of empathy for the pain, longings, aspirations, conflicts, regrets, and grief of each group member. This leads to the group engaging with the old narratives of each person's life, and with transforming these old narratives into new ones. Old internal objects are relinquished, and new present external others are engaged with. New external connections are also internalized. New and healthier psychic structure develops, for healthier new modes of relationships.

As each person shares their meditative visualization, a group process emerges that engages the internal mourning process with communication in the moment, between group members. Over time, the relationships in the group evolve, and they create interactions that involve understanding and insight into each group member, and into how each person is subjectively experiencing and dealing with life. This monthly group exists for 29 years now. We never meet in July and August, but the four-hour group with the initial meditative visualization and a half-hour break for lunch is the ongoing format that has brought much in-depth engagement over the years. Members stay for varying lengths of time, as some leave after resolving some specific issues in their lives, but those who stay long term, benefit the most.

Description of Writing Group and Therapeutic Mourning Group Members

Both groups are open to adult women and men of all ages. The writing group described here had been meeting every other week, and had five (and sometimes more) members at the time. I call the writing groups creative process groups because, at times, they have had members who were pursuing other art forms, such as painting (Kavaler-Adler, 2000). A painter can bring slides of her paintings into the group, as one woman did, which can be shared in the same manner as other people's writing. A musician or actor could bring in a tape recording of her/ his work.

Nevertheless, at the time of this study, the writing and creative process group consisted of five writers, who were struggling with fiction, poetry, memoir writing, professional clinical writing, magazine writing, and fiction-memoir writing.

Sometimes they would share shorter pieces of free associative journal writing. I have also had people pursuing diary and letter writing, dissertation writing, and theoretical psychoanalytic writing, as well as clinical writing about psychotherapy and psychoanalysis. Sometimes writing group members have followed themes that were healing to them psychologically at the moment, such as writing a series of essays on their mother, father, grandmother, son, etc. In other words, my writing groups encompass both writing therapy and writing actively or professionally for trade publication. I can have professional writers and painters in the groups, along with beginning writers, who are at the point of just being able to write.

The two women who are at the center of this clinical narrative are both fiction and memoir writers. The woman I call Lillian was completing her first book, which was subsequently published. The other woman, who I call Adrian, had published one piece of memoir writing and was working on both fiction and memoir pieces at the beginning of this clinical story.

Looking into the Face of Medusa:
The Dramatic Clash between Two Articulate Ladies

Adrian and Lillian were members of both the every-other-week writing group and the monthly therapeutic Mourning Regrets Group. It was during the course of one writing group meeting that Lillian exclaimed that she had less and less interest in Adrian, and really had no concern for Adrian's new findings about herself. This came a year after Lillian and Adrian had an earlier clash that had been discussed, and which had only partially been resolved.

At that earlier time, Lillian said that Adrian had been "chomping at the bit" when she wished to speak about her view of the group process, sarcastically deriding the hunger behind Adrian's wish to have her turn in the group, and being critical of Adrian's self-expression, in asserting her own point of view of the group process. Adrian felt blamed for speaking up, just as she had felt in her family, and blamed at a point of making progress in being more direct about her anger, and about her needs.

This clash between Adrian and Lillian was now being revisited at a later time. The transference dynamics became clearer, as the clash between Lillian and Adrian re-occurred. This clash was confusing for the group members until the dynamics behind it could be defined. Lillian and Adrian had somewhat different views of how the group should be run, related to different interests, which were also tied in with transference reactions. Lillian wanted more psychological exploration, and Adrian wanted more focus on literary critiques of the individual writing projects presented in the group. Their negative reaction to each other's requests was influenced by each seeing the other as critical of the other's wishes. Lillian reacted to Adrian's critiques of people's writing in the group, and to her comment that she had been cautious in regard to commenting on Lillian's work. Adrian said that she believed Lillian didn't want critiques. She added that she had been afraid of Lillian's anger, which could be well articulated. This led to Lillian making a cutting comment, reminiscent to Adrian of the old one, in which she disdainfully replied that she had become increasingly less interested in Adrian. Adrian was hurt and was able to say so.

Lillian's disdain for Adrian came after Adrian had made progress in expressing her honest views of how others in the group could improve their work, which she had always done in a supportive and encouraging way, generally being very well received by other members of the group. But for Lillian, Adrian was now stereotyped as an editorial critic, who wouldn't accept and appreciate where people were at. Adrian replied, "I hold myself back from commenting on the writing." Lillian was insulted! Adrian said that she was afraid of Lillian's anger, and Lillian looked like she would like to explode. Lillian held herself back, but protested with obvious pain behind her protest, saying she had indeed been open to criticism of her work but was decidedly not interested in technical editing. Lillian continued, saying that she was in the group to receive feeling responses to her writing, which she believed she got from other members of the group, and particularly from me, the group leader, but not from Adrian.

"We don't all have to be the great writers you want us to be," Lillian stated to Adrian. Adrian replied, "This is why I'm cautious about giving you feedback. But I do admire you, and wish you could see my struggles and changes." Lillian threw back her most cutting comment then: "I find you less interesting than ever. I don't care about all your little changes that you say you're making." Tears immediately came to Adrian's eyes, and she took the risk of vulnerability even in the face of attack! "That really hurts me," she said. "You say I'm less interesting to you than ever now, now that I've been struggling to go to the other side of being in touch with my feelings, which is something I've always admired you for. Besides I also see you as my mother in this group, and now I'm afraid you'll leave me and the group. It's so easy for you to feel everything! It is a part of what I admire in you. I'm just beginning to get there, and it hurts me that you don't even see or care if I'm changing."

Lillian started to feel intensely guilty, which manifested at that point in more rage, expressed nonverbally now, in her withdrawal and facial attitude. Meanwhile, I felt rather sympathetic to Adrian, particularly because of the openness about her hurt, and about her wishes for understanding and interest (love) for Lillian. But in addition, I sensed my own countertransference bias toward her at this moment, just having come out of one of Adrian's individual therapy sessions. In fact, in that last individual session with Adrian, I had observed and felt a particular turning point in Adrian, a turning point toward awareness of the transference longings that had been inhibiting Adrian in her self-expression, particularly in her self-expression of anger. I knew the depths from which her admiration of Lillian's free capacity to express anger came from. I also knew the depths from which her fear of Lillian's anger came, and how conflicted she was when faced with Lillian as a transference mother. Adrian had projected her longing for love and support onto Lillian, defending against deep grief about losing love and support from her actual mother, due to her mother's death many years before.

Seeing a new state of openness in Adrian during her individual session and a new state of her insight into her defensive maneuvers, and knowing also how genuine her attempts to help other group members, with her tempered critique of where and how they were holding themselves back form fuller self-realization through writing, it was all too easy to defend her, while questioning Lillian's reactions. I began to say that it was clear that others in the group experienced Adrian's responses to their writing as helpful, which the members confirmed with their feedback right there and then. So I wondered out loud why Lillian found Adrian's comments so one-sided, critical, and demanding. In saying this to Lillian, I banked on the years I had spent working with Lillian in different writing groups I had conducted, and in the Saturday group (she had been a member of the therapy and Mourning Regrets Group, in the course of this writing group experience.)

Lillian and I had formed a therapeutic Object Relationship! Occasionally, she had some individual consultations. However, having been quite accusatory herself, Lillian was quick to feel accused just then, even by Adrian's vulnerable exposure of hurt, and even more so by my seeming favor for Adrian at that moment. Indeed, I knew I was feeling the sense of Adrian's pain at that moment. Also, having a countertransference reaction to Adrian as an individual patient made me think how unfair it seemed that just as she was becoming less inhibited, and was more fully expressing the full range of her feelings, she was rejected by Lillian. From experience, I also knew her vulnerability to fears of being envied and attacked. Given all this, I must have spoken with a heartfelt feeling for her plight that I lacked just then for Lillian (although in the past I had felt her internal struggles in groups, and she had generally felt me to be an ally). In fact, I became interpretive with Lillian, rather than responding to her growing hurt, which was still hidden and not exposed (in contrast to Adrian's exposure of hurt).

Lillian seemed to be fighting off that vulnerability to her own hurt with a defensive stance (Klein, 1940). Before directly interpreting anything, I asked Lillian a question that she experienced as an accusation, perhaps because of her vulnerability to feeling blamed and injured at that time when I understood Adrian's perspective. I asked, "Do you think you're caught up in a transference response to Adrian now?" Lillian remained cold, perhaps trying to appear indifferent, yet looking explosive. I continued, perhaps interpreting too much, rather than addressing the reason for Lillian's lack of receptivity: "The reason I ask if you're aware of a transference response is because you are seeing Adrian as all critical now, and are not seeing anything else about her."

Tense, cold, and irate, with the harsh chill of defensive indignation, Lillian shot back her answer like a dart: "I don't know about transference. How the hell would I know! That's your department! But I don't need to have a relationship with anyone I don't wish to have it with! Furthermore, I can't believe that Carol [another group member] said that I was resistant to feedback about my writing, when I've taken so much interest in her feedback, and actually re-shaped my work in response to things she's said. I also took feedback from Adrian, when she responded to the epilogue of my book."

Adrian responded then, allowing me to recede temporarily into the background. Adrian said:

> Lillian, when you gave me the epilogue to read and respond to, it was the only time you gave me work to read outside the group. I couldn't get the full flavor of the book without reading the whole thing, and you never let me read it, although you let Carol and Gerald read it. I was wary about responding to the pieces of it you read in the group because I know how sensitive you were about wanting the whole of it comprehended and responded to. I feared your anger, but I also thought it might be unfair to suggest anything about your technique, or the way you wrote, when only viewing small poetic pieces, without the whole narrative.

Lillian was not ready to yield yet. It was time to end the group, and I could feel the chill of her rage, could feel her wish to cut everyone off and escape. I felt quite uncomfortable ending the group at the appointed time for ending that particular day. However, I knew I needed to trust the process, and trust Lillian's capacities to regain her observing ego and her very astute capacities for self-reflection.

Nevertheless, I decided to call Lillian that evening, because I knew she felt unsupported by me. She may even have felt abandoned at the moment of her regression and transference dynamics. I imagined that she may have felt betrayed. When I called Lillian, it was clear that she wished to be abrupt and felt me as intrusive. I tried to appeal to her understanding of the writing group process. I said that she could discuss all her feelings and reactions in the next group. I said that she did not have to stay alone with them, as she appeared to do at the end of the group. I suggested that she was overwhelmed, and I could understand that in her anger she might be contemplating leaving the group, but, I said, I would hate to see her cut everyone off without communicating. I suggested that this group could, perhaps, be more receptive to her feelings than her family had been. She reared up, taking umbrage with my last comment, saying her family was fine! I felt intensely like an intruder.

I would never have called Lillian if I had had individual sessions set up with her. I tried to appeal to her observing ego, saying that her view of Adrian was one-sided when only seeing her as a critical and harsh judge and editor. I told Lillian that her view of Adrian was unusual for her because she was usually sensitive to all sides of people. I added the *coup de grace*: "That's why I think you're entrapped in a transference reaction." Lillian responded coolly, thanking me for the call, but saying that she was seriously considering leaving the group since she didn't want her writing to be subjected to Adrian's technical critiques. She said that she could get that from an editor, and said those critiques spoiled her experience of the group as a place for her to feel her work, and to feel others feeling it. I was struck by her still-stereotyped view of Adrian, reinforcing my conviction that she was unconsciously enacting a transference response. I said that we could talk about it all in the next group (two weeks later). I added that I would like to help her say what she wanted and need to say. Despite the frustration of this call and Lillian's ambivalence about receiving it, it was to be seen that she did take in what I said. Lillian began to use our talk in the call to sort things out.

Nevertheless, Lillian's anger was still the dominant communication at this time. I next learned from Adrian, in an individual session, that Lillian had been sending Adrian emails, in which she apologized for her cutting comments in group. Further, Lillian suggested to Adrian that they were both victims of the group format that I had constructed. I, therefore, fully expected to be the bad mother for Lillian in the next group.

Next Writing Group Meeting:
Reintegration of the Group through the Processing of Regret

Interestingly, Lillian had done a great deal of psychological work in the meantime. In fact, she came into the next writing group with a letter of remorse and regret, which she proceeded to read to the writing group. I suspended the usual rotation format to allow Lillian more time to be heard since it was critical to the whole group to work together through the group impasse, consequent to Lillian's perceptions of Adrian. Fortunately, every group member was willing to do this. Only Lillian was to become uncomfortable with having so much time to speak after she finished reading the prepared letter.

In her letter, Lillian responded to my question about her transference and demonstrated that she had now taken her reaction to Adrian quite seriously. She began to speak with a tone of grief, sadness, and remorse. She spelled out the nature of her conscious regret (see more on psychic regret in Kavaler-Adler, 2013) toward Adrian. Then she elaborated on her transference. We observed how psychic space opened up for each individual in the group, when Lillian could tolerate her own depressive position (Klein, 1940) affects of guilt and grief, along with opening herself—beyond her former manic defenses (attitude of contempt)—through her acknowledgment of her own regret. Lillian's acknowledgment of regret allowed her to speak about her transference response with grief and compassion for herself. Then she could show compassion for Adrian, and even for me. New interpersonal group mutuality that resulted from this allowed the group to provide a restored safe transitional space environment to its members, so they could test out their communicative skills in the group, now a transitional and transforming avenue to the world outside (the external world is beyond internal and transitional world space; and also the world of public readers—for writers). An internal dialectic within Lillian herself was now expanding into an external dialogue between Lillian and Adrian. This was consequently allowing reintegration within the whole group, as intimacy evolved through dialogues between Lillian and Adrian could be further developed through the therapeutic Mourning Regrets Group process.

We all heard Lillian say in her letter that she had bypassed the bounds of what was acceptable behavior to herself by her comments to Adrian during the last group. Lillian apologized and said that she could see that she had hurt Adrian by saying how uninterested she was in her. However, she said that she believed that Adrian's editorial view of the work in the group triggered off, for her, her reliving of her father's criticisms of her and her creativity, during all the years when she was growing up. Rather than remembering the pain, she relived it in the group, through relation to Adrian. Lillian further explained that she could not know she was experiencing transference, at first, because it was unconscious. However, with contemplation, she realized that she had to let in the truth and meaning of what I, as the group leader (and the psychoanalyst) was saying about that. She also showed some compassion for me, by saying that she had seen me work with the interaction of the individual writing and creative process, and the group interpersonal process, for many years, since she had participated in many of my writing groups.

Finally, Lillian revealed her own anguish and injury. She spoke of her father's continuous assaults against any form that her creativity would take, saying that it's a miracle that she could express herself at all after all that. Lillian then reminded us of her father's mental illness, which had developed along with his failure to succeed in his own art. She acknowledged the link between her reliving of the pain with her father, and her one-sided view of Adrian, with the transference projections that that entailed. Then Lillian proceeded to declare that she did not want her own writing critiqued in the manner that Adrian was establishing in the group. She also explained that hearing Carol join in with Adrian about her perceived lack of receptivity to criticism had contributed to her feeling less safe in the group. She said that she felt hurt by Carol, with whom she had shared so much.

Lillian said she has been thinking that it might be time for her to move on to another format for her writing, having been in my writing groups for 17 years, with a break of only a few years. She conjectured that she might need a class in playwriting, where her particular interest in that form of writing would be respected since now she was suspending poetry and memoir, and concentrating on playwriting.

Everyone listened very attentively as Lillian spoke. As always, she spoke with a great depth of feeling. She also had noticeably moved from a place of anger, which could have exploded into rage, into a more thoughtful and self-aware place. This self-aware place gained its containing tranquility; from her tolerance of grief and loss, and through the refinement of integrating grief affect with symbolic cognitive meaning, to the conscious ownership of regret and remorse (see more on existential guilt in Kavaler-Adler, 2004 & 2013). Lillian was confronting the potential loss precipitated by her own aggression, as she was also able to more clearly articulate the cause of her aggression, with her new level of self-awareness.

Object loss can be precipitated by one's own aggression (Kavaler-Adler, 2013). Therefore, feeling the grief of remorse and regret, as well as of loss, allows for the realization of psychic truth in the form of personal responsibility (Kavaler-Adler, 2004, 2013). Melanie Klein (1940) wrote of this evolution of the depressive position, as the affect transition from aggression to sadness, which defines self-integration, and allows for the enlarging of the capacity to love.

I have expanded on Klein's understanding of self-integration through the affect evolution and insight of the depressive position, by theorizing a developmental view of mourning. This view of mourning allows all clinicians, as well as others, to experience how grief is developmentally advanced by the experience of remorse and regret within guilt, as guilt accompanies the experience of loss (Kavaler-Adler, 1993a/2013, 1995, 1996/2014, 2006a, 2006b, 2013).

The Group Responds and Develops through Lillian's Creativity

When Lillian finished her self-expression, she would have been ready for others to begin their turns again, sharing writing in the writing group. However, I was clear that the group members needed to respond to her.

Gerald was the first to speak. He said that he was moved by the letter, but had the odd feeling that there was something kind of suicidal in it, as if Lillian had to kill herself off because of her guilt toward Adrian, and toward her father, because of the hate that she felt, even toward Carol. He chose this opportunity to say that he personally liked the group format as it was, had been very helped by it, and had been greatly helped by Adrian's commentary about his own writing, even to the point of transitioning into essays and short stories, from poetry.

Then Carol spoke, saying that she felt scared now of losing Lillian, who had become so important to her. Still, she said she felt she had to back up Adrian. Carol said that she had felt similarly to Adrian that Lillian was somewhat guarded about her work, and only wanted certain kinds of responses to it, but Lillian was not explicitly stating this. She said she would miss Lillian terribly if she left the group, and hoped she wouldn't. She said that she loved Lillian's work, and she felt Lillian was an enormously important and powerful presence in the group.

Another group member, Cynthia, remained rather quiet. However, she did comment that she felt the descent into death-like feelings that Lillian conveyed, as she reacted to Adrian's statement that she was afraid of Lillian's anger. Cynthia was aware that Lillian seemed to have experienced Adrian saying that she was afraid of Lillian's anger as an accusation that she, Lillian, was bad. Cynthia said she could relate to the depth of pain in Lillian's psychic descent, which she too had felt when she experienced herself as the subject of accusations.

Then Adrian spoke. She said that she really appreciated Lillian's apology and the struggle that Lillian was going through. However, she felt, because of her transference with Lillian, that her mother (transference mother) was threatening to abandon her. She said that this did not allow her to feel at all free to speak. Adrian continued, saying she thought that Lillian had tremendous power in the group. She even believed that if Lillian threatened to leave the group, she could get everyone else to do whatever she wanted them to do. She recalled other times when Lillian wanted the group to run in a particular way and had said so along with a threat of leaving.

As the group leader, I then pointed out that although we always discussed other options, the group format had remained pretty much the same. I added that Lillian, at one point, had wanted me to speak about my publishing and writing experiences, and this had clearly been overruled by the rest of the group, as it probably should have been. However, I added that whether Lillian stayed or terminated, she needed to take time to communicate with the group. I said that Lillian needed to sort out the decision in terms of her creative process needs versus conflict in the group so that she could understand her own motives. I asked, was Lillian thinking of leaving because of the projections and transferences within her, and in others in the group, that made her uncomfortable, and which demanded psychological work, or was she thinking of leaving due to creative process needs, such as to deal with playwriting?

Lillian then responded, saying first that she didn't really feel supported by anyone in the group except Cynthia. She said that she wished right then to feel held and that Cynthia was giving her that feeling by understanding the depth of her pain and anxiety. Everyone else, she thought, was making demands on her that she didn't think she could handle because she felt too exposed and vulnerable. She thought that she understood her part in the transferences, and wanted other people to also take responsibility for the group. It didn't all depend on her! She would stick with it for a while, and see how she felt in the group, but at the moment she didn't feel like exposing her work there.

This provoked some guilt among the group members. Adrian also felt an anger that she would deal with in her individual sessions, in terms of transference and associations, and defenses, before bringing it back into the group. Lillian also expressed a concern about what went on in my sessions with Adrian, since she was realizing that it was better not to have contact with group members outside the group. I said that Adrian might bring up things about the group during her individual sessions if they came from her associations, and she and I might then discuss her associations, in terms of who the group members represented to her, or what parts of her own self they represented. Sometimes, I said, when something came up related to the group, I would suggest to Adrian that she speak about it in the group.

Lillian was receptive to this answer. I was aware, however, that she had a valid concern about what might be said between Adrian and me in her individual sessions, especially since Lillian had no individual sessions of her own. She had some individual sessions with me many years ago, when she could afford such sessions. She had done some critical work then on her transference with me, which had helped her in the groups with me, and in her work within the groups, as well as in her life. She had told the group more recently, however, that since she experienced me as a mother, she would like to explore more in her transference with me. At times, she said, she felt the writers' group had interfered with her addressing these issues. This had influenced her decision to rejoin the monthly therapeutic Mourning Regrets Group.

The Next Stage in the Writing Group

A period of time followed in the group when Lillian held herself back, wanting to make clear that she was not this "mean person" that Adrian sometimes took her to be. She still flinched from Adrian's comment about fearing her anger, as if she took this to mean that Adrian saw her as an angry woman. It was a critical turning point when I could interpret to Adrian, in an individual session, that her fear of Lillian's anger was, at least in part, a fear of her own anger projected onto Lillian. Adrian responded powerfully to this interpretation and used it astutely in a group session with Lillian. She connected this phenomenon of her own projected anger with her own history in a way that was evocative for all of us, and which took Lillian off the hook for her transference projections. This allowed Lillian to move closer to Adrian, culminating in their rapprochement in the therapy and Mourning Regrets Group.

Then, during a writing group session, Lillian announced that she felt she had gotten an enormous amount from the group, and valued each person in it, but had decided, after continuing for a while, that she really needed a different format to work on her playwriting, and would have to leave this writing group. She maintained that she couldn't afford both kinds of writing groups.

Adrian responded by saying that she wished Lillian wouldn't leave, because she felt she had unfinished business with her, and the group was such an important format for her to work out conflicts with women. She said she had always felt frightened of competition with women, always fearing the envy and anger of other women, and also having a difficult time with her own envy. She said she really valued Lillian's incredible ability to articulate her feelings and also wanted to see the further development of Lillian's work. She told Lillian and the group, after a session in which I had interpreted her projection of anger, that it wasn't Lillian's anger she was afraid of, as she had thought. Instead, she discovered that it was her own anger she was afraid of! She said that she had repressed her anger her entire life. Not only wasn't her anger allowed in her family, but she had never dealt with her anger at her mother, resulting from the time when her parents had separated for a year, when she was nine years old.

Adrian went further with the history of her inhibitions in her aggression. She explained that she had protected her mother by pretending to be grown-up, saying to her mother, as they left her father and her home, "I'm glad to have it all behind me." As they packed up and left, however, Adrian was not at all glad to have it behind her. Adrian declared:

> I lied. I was furious! I held myself back, but I wanted to lash out at my
> mother and scream: 'Go back there and work this out!' I was giving up

my father, who I adored, and who had adored me, and was giving up my fairytale home, with all my adventures, and with my security. I didn't want to leave and go to some strange place in another state. At school I was excluded, because I was dressed in expensive clothes, and was forced to ride in a chauffeured limousine. I hated the school, the town, and my mother's misery there. My mother stayed up late, drinking. I wanted to lash out at my mother, and was terrified of how angry I was. My father had asked me if I wanted to live with him, and I had to shut myself up to protect my mother. He never forgave me! It was never the same, even when my parents got back together later. I never got my father back in the same way. He never got over feeling rejected. If I had been honest, and could have said what I felt, I would have said I wished to live with him. But that would have killed my mother, and I needed her more than anything. So there I was, pretending to be all together and grown-up, and 'supporting my mother,' while burying all my anger and my longing.

Then Adrian spoke of the longing that Lillian had profoundly felt when she read the letter to the group. She said, "Susan said the word 'longing' and Lillian sobbed out that grief. In my childhood, I had to bury all of it. No wonder I'm afraid of Lillian having all her feelings. I couldn't have any of my own. I wish you'd stay so we could work it out, Lillian. I've never had a chance to do that with a woman."

Lillian said that she was very moved by what Adrian said, and she could see the more vulnerable part of Adrian that was usually hidden. However, for herself, she didn't feel that she had any unfinished business. She believed she had dealt with who Adrian was to her, and she needed a group to focus on her playwriting, and couldn't afford to stay and pay for both writing groups. She also felt that it was healthy to move on from this particular form of writing group because she had been working in this way for years. However, she said she was going to rejoin the Mourning Regrets Group because she felt that she still had more to learn about her transference with me. Lillian said that the Mourning Regrets Group allowed for that kind of work in-depth. Adrian responded warmly at first, very relieved that she wouldn't lose Lillian altogether. Adrian said she was very happy that Lillian would be re-joining the therapeutic Mourning Regrets Group. Adrian said: "That's great! I'm really glad you're coming into mourning regrets." Later, in an individual session, Adrian expressed a more ambivalent reaction, saying she feared Lillian coming into the Mourning Regrets Group could spoil the group for her. She still had some fear of Lillian. Nevertheless, it was going to prove quite fortuitous for both Adrian and Lillian, and for the entire Mourning Regrets Group, that Lillian made the decision to re-enter that group. Lillian made a clear decision for herself that paid off for her and for others too.

Culminating Process in the Mourning Regrets Therapy Group

It was in one particular Mourning Regrets Group that an evolution of events allowed Adrian to hear Lillian in a whole new way. In this group, Adrian came to speak of gratitude and love that helped to open a vulnerable place in her heart.

In the second half of the four-hour Mourning Regrets Group, after the meditative visualization, Miriam told Adrian that she was hiding her power by acting so helpless. Miriam said that she knew it was a struggle for Adrian to express herself, but like herself at times, she believed Adrian was "not coming out with it" and was "pulling her punches." Adrian, at first, felt she was being misunderstood, and then suddenly did come out with it! She responded to Miriam by enumerating all the things she wanted in her life. She risked being open about her desires, instead of hiding them as she has all her life, even from herself. As Adrian listed her wishes, such as to be widely acclaimed as a novelist, re-marry, and give part of her business over to someone else, so that she would have more time to write, Miriam was impressed. The whole group thought it was great that Adrian knew what she wanted!

Lillian, however, had a different reaction. She said that even though Adrian felt competitive with her, and said she's afraid of envy, she wasn't as interested in the same things as Adrian. Lillian said she was happy to publish her work, but didn't believe that she was as interested in achievement as Adrian. She told Adrian that she wasn't competing in the same arena. Different things were important to her, like the time in the past that Adrian let down her guard in the Mourning Regrets Group, and said something really tender and appreciative of her. Lillian said she wanted to savor that moment and was really upset that the group leaders (I then had a co-leader) and the group intruded, and the moment was lost. However, Lillian said that in general Adrian didn't show that openness, so that when Adrian said she, Lillian, was so important to her, she couldn't relate to it. Generally, she felt pushed away by Adrian's attitudes, sarcasm, humor, criticalness, and rejections of what is said to her. She pointed out that even though Adrian said she could receive and take in what is said to her, including a recent comment by Miriam about her just made in the group, she did not show this. Instead, Lillian told Adrian, she was speaking as if negating everything said that might confront her with her own behavior. Lillian pointed out that Adrian overtly rejected Miriam by proclaiming that Miriam was misunderstanding her.

According to Lillian, even though Adrian proclaimed that she took in and remembered what she and Miriam and others said to her, she had no way of knowing this or feeling this. "What am I supposed to do, read your mind?" Lillian said to Adrian:

> You said in the writing group that I was so important to you, that I was some kind of mother for you. But that's not what I feel. I feel your harshness, your negations, and your critical judgments. I don't feel like engaging with you around your ambitions. That's not what's so important to me. I want to write, but I'm not so concerned with fantasies of fame and acclaim. What wins me is when you show the vulnerable part of you, as opposed to the ambitious part of you. When you said that sweet thing to me in the Mourning Regrets Group that time you won me! But then the moment was lost! And it was a moment. Then it all got covered over. When you said to me that you were scared of me, when I returned to this group, I wanted to be with you. I wanted to know what image you had in your mind of me. Who am I to you? What did that mean? But then you went back to hiding.

Now, as Lillian spoke, an incredible sweetness came into her voice. The nurturing, caring, loving part of her came alive as she vividly reached out toward Adrian. She also found Adrian hungry to hear what she had to say. However, Adrian said that she feared re-living with Lillian, as well as with Miriam, the shocked and traumatic feeling she had felt in boarding school, when suddenly all the girls turned against her, and she didn't know what it was about. She had stayed in her room, hidden away, because some girls had spread hideous rumors about her, as they seemed to be jealous when some boys had come to visit her, and not them. Lillian remembered that Adrian felt like any woman might turn on her, just when she was thinking all was fine! She felt out of control because she couldn't control how women would see her. She didn't know if other women would be envious, or if they would judge her for some reason she had no way of knowing about. But she said too that when Lillian spoke of that time when she (Adrian) had opened to her vulnerability and had said something tender to Lillian, she felt Lillian being there in a different way, in a way that reminded her of her mother, the good part, the best part of her mother.

Adrian said that she knew everything Lillian was saying to her about her defensiveness was true, but it was really hard to hear. She realized that she got a different response when she was vulnerable, but she found it really difficult to get to that part of herself. Lillian responded by saying that Adrian was capable of getting to her heart in a way that I spoke about in the visualizations, connecting to the heart. As Lillian spoke, recalling again Adrian's tender comment that had gotten lost, a comment that she remembered so well, from a Mourning Regrets Group two years earlier, Adrian suddenly said, "As you were speaking just a few moments ago, I had the thought that I'm not afraid of Lillian anymore." Lillian responded, "I knew that. Somehow I knew that."

Then Lillian said, with great tenderness, "I know it hurt you when I said I wasn't interested in you anymore in the writing group, but it was because of the way you hide the vulnerable part of you. I hardly ever get to see it." As she spoke of the two sides of Adrian and appealed to Adrian to show the heartfelt part of her more, Adrian was able to stay emotionally open for longer than ever before, in either group. As Lillian spoke sweetly to Adrian of how she kept things from others in her head and didn't reveal she was taking them in, appearing outwardly rejecting, I recalled my own sense of this with Adrian. I thought of all the times that I was surprised how much Adrian had taken in what I had said to her, and how she used it, because when I spoke Adrian often pushed me away. However, over time this had lessened, particularly in individual sessions, where she had become more open to me. I even ended up feeling at times like Adrian had been stealing my ideas from me rather than receiving and acknowledging them as coming from me. So often, as Lillian was saying, Adrian came out with sarcastic comments about me, and my interpretations in group, that pushed me away, as a person, even as she was quoting what I said as an analyst, and using it to understand herself.

This resonance with Lillian's comments made me feel much closer to Lillian than I had felt for a long time. The compassionate side of her was so strong when it came out that it made me forget she could also be cutting, as she had been at those critical times with Adrian. The loving part of Lillian was so powerful now that the whole group seemed deeply and intimately connected. There was a quiet and tranquil ease between Adrian and Lillian. Consequently, Adrian was noticeably more soft and yielding than usual. Then Adrian told Lillian that at times like this, Lilian reminded her of her mother, the most loving and tender part of her mother. Everyone in the group, as well as I, felt deeply touched.

Lillian responded by saying that Adrian needs to stay in touch with that inner place where she has her good parents. With reference to something said by me, she said that she agreed with me that we all need an inner connection with the good parents to be able to realize ourselves. She spoke of the movie ***The Buena Vista Social Club***, which Adrian and I had both seen. Lillian spoke of how a musician in the movie, in Cuba, fed and nurtured the religious statue in his home with food and drink, to feed the spirit that in turn nurtured him. She related this to nurturing the internal good parent object, by connecting to it through the heart, and spoke of her belief that all creativity and self-realization comes from this. She said, "Some people carry pictures of the Virgin Mary for the same reason," and laughed. Adrian was right with her now. Adrian said that she knew this, and thought that she should put up all her favorite pictures of the people she loved in the study, where she wanted to write.

A Return to Creativity through Mourning

The talk was coming back full circle to creativity and writing after resolving the interpersonal issues between Lillian and Adrian, and after the group descent into the areas of grief, remorse, regret, and the love that is renewed through grief sadness. Adrian said to Lillian and the group, "I know I need to stay in touch with that place inside of me where the love is, the goodness, the tender part of my mother. When I don't stay in touch with that place it's this huge battle, full of frustration, every time I try to write." It was clear that Adrian felt nurtured by Lillian, and that she could now symbolically take Lillian in. She could receive her through her words of observation, her interpretation of Adrian's need, and through her interpretation of Adrian's hidden capacities for contact. Adrian received Lillian's insight into the way her capacity for contact through vulnerability could be overridden by her conflicts over competitive impulses that could become a slightly alienating hostility.

In a later group, Adrian was able to expose her critical and rejecting thoughts in a benevolent and benign humor that shared the hidden hostility without enacting it. She remained aware, related, and even entertaining through this, as she listed the contemptuous and angry thoughts she had toward other women in the group during another Mourning Regrets Group meeting. She contained her aggression with loving warmth behind a lighter humor, lighter than the former sarcasm. Through her warmth and humor, Adrian demonstrated an observing ego capacity in relationship to hostile and/or competitive impulses, which formerly she was threatened by. Being able to contain her hostile wishes and impulses in humor and loving feelings, she became able to free psychic space for observing ego functions. She no longer was compelled (at least at this point) to turn against herself with a persecutory superego (Klein, 1957) or "antilibidinal ego" (Fairbairn, 1952) attack in order to unconsciously express her aggression, nor was she compelled to be paralyzed by the conflict around turning these impulses against others, which would inhibit her creativity and interpersonal relations.

With conscious ownership of her aggressive fantasies, Adrian could relate to others without fearing that she would destroy them (her mother). She contained her hostility, and neutralized it, through the loving feelings that she had now developed with the group members. Consequently, Adrian contained her hostile wishes in symbolic fantasies, and with the affect of loving warmth that accompanied her new and softer form of humor. Lillian's engagement with her helped her to this turning point, along with the intimate and intensive work on her defenses in individual sessions.

Lillian's Evolution

Lillian was freed up. She took space in another meeting of the Mourning Regrets Group, to speak of her wish to surrender to me. She said that one reason she returned to the Mourning Regrets Group was to deal with the nature of her attachment to me, and to who I represent to her, and have represented to her over the many years that she had been in my groups. As she spoke about wishing she could surrender to me, instead of holding herself back (as she was aware of doing), wishing she would surrender in the manner of another woman in the group, she opened up in a flood of sobs and cries of grief similar to the time when I mentioned her "longing," after she read her letter in the writing group. She cried at an orgasmic level. Then she said that she felt like she was experiencing me as her internal primal object and needed to be able to come close to me. "Otherwise," she said, "I know I'm missing out and sabotaging myself!"

Following this, Lillian and Adrian would sit together in the monthly Mourning Regrets Group. They giggled together, sitting next to the male group leader, and half flirting with him. Adrian acknowledged her competitive feelings toward Lillian and her envy and jealousy of her. They laughed and laughed! Several groups later, when Adrian was feeling distraught over a current failing on her father's part to show any affirmation of her as a woman—which reflected the earlier loss of her father's admiration at the time of her parents' separation—it was Lillian who quite spontaneously expressed her own admiration for Adrian, telling Adrian how beautiful she looked that day.

The Psychic Transition

In Kleinian terms, Lillian at first enacted a neurotic regression into the paranoid-schizoid position, from where she perceived Adrian as persecutory or assaultive. Lillian heard Adrian as expressing demands from some superior status. Lillian projected her own manic defense onto Adrian, lending to her own split-off contempt, with its air of defensive superiority. However, when Lillian began to mourn, she experienced the grief, sadness, and remorse consequent to her retaliatory attacks on Adrian (retaliatory against Adrian's projections of aggression onto Lillian). Lillian consciously suffered regret and remorse, in relation to the one cutting comment she made of Adrian.

Through such grief-laden regret and remorse, Lillian softened into a depressive position based psychic state of concern (see Winnicott, 1963; Klein, 1940; & Kavaler-Adler, 1992). This allowed psychic "potential space" (Winnicott, 1971) to open within herself, as well as in the transitional and interpersonal space between her and Lillian. As Lillian owned her own aggression, she moved from the paranoid-schizoid to the depressive position (Kavaler-Adler, 2000, 2003a, 2004, 2013). She did so through feeling the grief of hurting Adrian, who, at the unconscious level of primal Object Relations represented a father-mother whom she has hurt (Klein, 1940, 1957; Kavaler-Adler, 1993c, 1996/2014).

Feeling the grief, which followed surrendering to object loss and guilt, allowed Lillian to move toward a position of reparation as opposed to remaining in a position of persecution and retaliation. It was particularly at the point when Lillian could feel the regret of hurting another that she was able to surrender to grief and overtures of reparation (Kavaler-Adler, 2004, 2013). This allowed for mutuality, and a "capacity for concern" (Winnicott, 1963). Adrian and Lillian both re-owned their split-off parts. This furthered self-integration within each individual, and enhanced psychic healing and wholeness. The group process evolved. It continued to evolve from this.

An impasse in the group occurred, due to the paranoid reaction of Lillian, and due to Adrian's projection of her own anger onto Lillian. The resolution of this impasse came through Adrian's vulnerable communication of hurt and Lillian's ownership of guilt and grief. This allowed for a re-integration of the group in parallel with a re-integration in each group member, particularly the two members in psychic conflict and defense.

Unblocking Creative Motivation

Both Lillian and Adrian benefited, in a sustained way, from the group experiences that enable them to understand the nature of their own anger. They became increasingly free from the transference projections and displacements that had confused their perception of others, and which had motivated hostile reactions, and caused them to confuse the past with the present. Each group member was able to feel the loss of the parental objects, which they were protecting by repressing, and by displacing their anger. Others in the group, who could identify with their experience, benefited from their new understanding of their transference projections as well.

The Mourning Regrets Group moved forward, with the resolution between Lillian and Adrian. Through being in the group with Lillian and Adrian, others in the group could contact their rage, grief, and frustrated desires and longings, which were inhibited by old ties to primal parent figures. Evolving out of this new freedom, and new self-understanding, was a new and renewed capacity for pursuing creative work. Both Lillian and Adrian moved forward on writing projects, following through, and facing self-sabotaging tendencies that were prompted by negative internal editors, which were reflecting identifications with negative parts of their parents in their internal worlds. These internal editors had been projected outward in the interpersonal transference dynamics in the groups.

Lillian's Creative Progress

Specifically, Lillian was now able to own the ambition that she so long denied. This enabled her to bring a long-term writing project to full fruition despite extreme difficulties in the publishing process. Lillian had said that it was a miracle that she could create at all, given her battle against an internalized ("negative editor") father of childhood. She had been stuck before with an internalized father who had continually attacked her with hostile and belittling forms of criticism, for her self-expression. In the face of this and Lillian's self-sabotage of an entire career in another art form, it is Lillian's monumental achievement that she could now move through the act of writing, so smoothly, that she could finalize a complete book of poetry, memoir, and narrative, which resulted in her first major publication.

For many years, Lillian had been in writing groups with me, while also pursuing many forms of writing. She had switched from one form of writing to another, and had received feedback about the writing in the writing groups. In fact, she had opened up areas of mourning in herself, on her own, through reading her writing in the writing groups. She could open the pain of loss, and the anguish of longing, while reading to us in the group. As Lillian thus mourned, she consolidated the lyric of her self-expression in a book that spoke of her formative early life in terms of poetry and poetic narrative. She emerged with an expression of grief that would always renew love, and that crystallized a modern form of memoir. The memoir spoke deeply of her anguished and tormented love for a father, who had always felt compelled to damage himself, and the family he loved. In her writing, Lillian could speak of her hate. She could speak of her mother's love of mothering her daughters, and then having her mothering profoundly disrupted by the envious assaults of her husband, Lillian's father, who was suffering so much himself.

For the first time, Lillian navigated the rejections of publishing to find a publisher who believed in her work, and who was determined to publish it. However, her relationship with the publisher forced her into a repetition of some of the torments of growing up with her father. In the middle of the publishing process on her book, the publisher began to fall apart himself, just when she was depending on him for the birth of her work in the world. The publisher stopped being a friend and support and failed at maintaining professional boundaries.

Similar to her father, who fell apart repeatedly due to mental illness and resulting professional failure, the male publisher broke down due to a love affair in his life. The publisher lost the capacity to be aware of Lillian's professional needs. Lillian felt that her whole life was hanging in the balance because she had not followed through on former opportunities for success, and this seemed like her last chance to seize the day. Feeling dependent on the male publisher, Lillian was vulnerable to submitting to the publisher's demands for her to comfort him. Not infrequently, she was caught up in phone calls in which only a few minutes were spent discussing her book and its publication, and an hour was spent talking about the publisher's personal problems

Fortunately, Lillian was able to discuss this situation in the writing group. In the group, she received critical feedback about the inappropriateness of her publisher's behavior. She was given support to set limits for herself, and not to be pressed into service as this man's surrogate mother.

A critical turning point came in Lillian's ability to deal with this man came when Lillian re-experienced her anger toward her father in her transference associations with Adrian. Her rage toward her father could become freshly conscious when she experienced Adrian as the critical father who assaulted her creative efforts. In the meditative visualization during the Mourning Regrets Group, Lillian cried as she felt her deeper experience of longing for her father's love, which lay beneath the surface of her anger, and its transference expression with Adrian. During the meditative visualization, Lillian experienced herself as a "bleeding heart," a vulnerable heart part of her that was bleeding due to the agony of writing her father's love. Experiencing the anger with Adrian, which connected her to her yearning for her father, allowed Lillian to interpret and understand it when she felt the same anger at her father again. Then she could further recognize the negative father transference when she began to project it onto her male publisher.

Conclusion: Lillian

All this new understanding, through gaining insight in the group of her unconscious transference wishes and anger, allowed Lillian to set more adequate limits with her publisher than she was previously able to do. Owning the power of her anger, which brought self-agency, allowed Lillian to distinguish the effects of her past on her current inhibitions. This further allowed Lillian to demand to have her own needs met with the publisher for attention to her professional work. Then when the publication process was again delayed, Lillian spoke to the Mourning Regrets Group about the disturbing situation, not just to the writing group. The mourning regrets therapy and mourning group helped Lillian mourn the grief of past career disappointments, since carrying this disappointment within her, until then, had made Lillian vulnerable to being sucked into her publisher's inappropriate demands. Now Lillian could stand up to the publisher. She appropriately demanded that the publishing process proceed. With the help of the group, Lillian came to more clearly distinguish her need to stick with the present opportunity for her book's publication from self-sabotaging actions because they were repetitions of the past, where she would masochistically submit as if submitting to her father.

Making the distinction between the past and present, Lillian was now equipped to consciously work on the very real difficulties of her present situation. The group and I helped Lillian to see that her mother's masochistic submission stop her father need not result in her own submission to circumstances in the present due to a regressive identification. Specifically, we helped her understand that her self-sabotage in the past was different from her current attempt to negotiate a difficult situation with a man she was realistically dependent on for her circumscribed professional goals. Soon after her discussion of this issue in the Mourning Regrets Group, where Adrian, as well as the others, worked hard to respond empathically to her dilemma, Lillian announced in the group that her book was on the verge of publication. She stood up to the publisher over many critical editorial and publishing issues and was triumphant. The group applauded Lillian's creative process.

Conclusion: Adrian

Adrian's tendencies to be blocked or stuck in her creative work were also increasingly ameliorated by the work she did in the two groups. She continued in both for quite a while. As Adrian re-owned the power she had given up to Lillian, due to her transference projections, and due to difficulty facing the anger at her mother that lay behind her projections, she started writing on a more consistent basis. Furthermore, she developed the overall direction of her writing, as she followed her own internal emotional journey of mourning.

For the first time, Adrian became clear that she wanted to write a novel, not just a short story or play. Now the subject of the novel could emerge naturally, along with the freeing of her association process in treatment. She told us that she was going to write about an aunt who greatly influenced her emotional development as she grew up. In the past, she might have been overwhelmed by such a long-term ambition. Now, however, following an awareness of the projection process that psychically eviscerated her, she was able to engage in a psychic dialectic between her overall vision of the book and her natural mode of writing in spurts. Through the writing group and the therapeutic mourning group process, Adrian learned that her natural way of writing in spurts captured, and even expanded, a profound moment of experiencing which, in turn, gave birth to dialogue, visual imagery, character formation, and transformation through descriptive narrative.

In the writing group, Adrian began to read different pieces, which were reflective of moments that conveyed character portraiture. The group was impressed by her ability to capture the immediacy of the moment and the way in which this allowed her to give birth to colorful and vivid characters. They also observed Adrian's ability to subtly foreshadow interpersonal interactions through a moment of emotional immediacy, resulting in evocative images that could become full characters, or could be suspended in time as pivotal memories in the formation of a character. Lillian's view of Adrian as an overbearing critic disintegrated, and the same group that had heard Adrian speak about the critical importance of showing experience, rather than merely intellectually describing it, listened intently to Adrian's own experiments with this philosophy, as it lived through her own emotional life forming narrative.

Winnicott's (1971) "creativity of everyday life" blossomed in Adrian as "play" in her writing, as she spontaneously free-associated to her memories and emotional experiences in the writing group, as well as in her individual psychoanalysis. Reflective thought, following play, was implied, but purposely not stated, in her fiction writing. Such thought was expressed by her in the writing group. Each moment could live, and become a bead in the string that formed the necklace of the novel. This spontaneous flow of writing could become disrupted by inner compulsions when Adrian was once again feeling "possessed" by any unsymbolized psychic impulses, which had not yet been formulated in psychic fantasy form. Then she would feel blocked and ultimately would have to become conscious of unassimilated internal object personifications, such as that of a demon-lover, or a controlling mother. When her impulses and their internal object personifications were repressed, she felt depressed, because she was not in touch with her deeper self. She associated it to an early experience of constipation, when she was angry at her father, and could not allow herself to be conscious of the feeling (see Kavaler-Adler on the compulsion and blocking of creativity, 1993/2013, 1996/2014).

Another form that Adrian's creative progress took involved a new synthesis of her business and artistic abilities. Having suffered debt and financial strains running an advertising business—and having overcome all debt through re-owning her emotional power—she now considered a more lucrative business that could be beneficial artistically as well as financially. By now, she was bored with her advertising business and had thought of turning it over to her assistant. If she could do this, she could pursue the ownership of a theater company, since much of her advertising had been done for theaters. Overall, she hoped this would provide a better income and free up more time to write.

Adrian also had new motivation within the scope of her established advertising agency. She had choices now that she didn't have before, because whole new levels of motivation had been opened up. Although Adrian's potential contacts for initiating such a project had always been there, only after she dealt with her repression, displacement, and projection of her anger through the developmental mourning process (Kavaler-Adler, 1992a, 1993a/2013, 1995, 1996/2014, 2000, 2003a) could she feel the sustained motivation to write. Such motivation depended on unblocking the flow of Adrian's love, as in releasing her anger through psychic fantasies, which could serve as internal symbolic containers. Adrian's contact with her core loving self, which was continually dependent on her awareness of her aggression, allowed Adrian to prosper in her work: specifically, to pay off all her debts, to appeal to new clients, and to become increasingly successful financially, as her creativity deepened. Adrian's progress illustrated that she had mourned all the losses in her life in-depth, which included the primal mourning for her father and mother, and the death of a sibling. She had published one profound piece on mourning in a literary magazine.

Mourning loss allowed Adrian to mourn regret as well. She was now more able to grieve the losses promoted by her own defensive processes. She had been learning, through both her individual and group work, about how she blocked her deepest aspirations to create and write. She had been learning that she defensively blocked her capacity to love, by avoiding her anger, whenever she tried to protect her internal mother by protecting her external transference mothers. Finally, Adrian had learned how her repression and projection of her anger could cause her to convert her aggressive impulses into a cold and critical attitude, which hid her warmth toward others, and also blocked her own creativity when it was turned against herself.

CHAPTER 21

THE CULTURE OF THE MOURNING GROUP IN A CULTURE THAT OFTEN FAILS TO MOURN: EVOLUTION OF THEMES OF GRIEF AND REGRET RELATED TO PSYCHIC ANOREXIA AND SELF-DEPRIVATION

Originally published in 2020, *MindConsiliums* 20(8):1–15.

The American culture is known for its consumerism and manic results orientation. Americans are rarely perceived as having time for long-term emotional or psychological processes, let alone for a grief process that requires an internal personal focus over time. The culture as a group has just begun to learn about grief. Perhaps our first real venture into it was at the time of John Fitzgerald Kennedy's funeral. The horrific shock of Kennedy's assassination immobilized the country and gathered all us human souls together in groups with tears that could be, just for the moment, shared openly. How different this was than the gatherings in the street on VE day, after the triumphant victory of World War II when Americans kissed, danced, and hugged in the streets but would never have thought of crying in those same streets. How many years did it take us to have memorials for the Vietnam War where people thought of grieving together by the monuments? The Korean soldiers have still not been mourned as testified to in radio interviews by a few surviving Korean War G.I.s, just last summer (of 2003).

When Kennedy's son, John Junior, died another horrific death, by his own hand, after his father's death nearly 40 years before, Americans were just beginning to learn about grief. At that time, I was asked to appear as an expert on grief on a national television show on CNN, called "Both Sides: With Jesse Jackson."

Jesse Jackson interviewed three of us as experts on grief. It was clear that the show's theme reflected an awareness that the country that gathered in the streets to cry when John Fitzgerald Kennedy was shot would need to have a communal acknowledgment of grief when his song also tragically died. At the time of the television broadcast, we discussed anger within grief as well as grief itself. There was an acknowledgment that many citizens would be angry at John Kennedy Junior for the self-destructive and impulsive way that he drew the curtain on his own life. Unlike his father, who was shot by an assassin, John Kennedy Junior had insisted on flying his own plane despite predictions of dangerous weather conditions that caused a commercial airline to cancel its flight in the same direction. With Kennedy bravado and his own personal grandiosity, John Kennedy Junior had disregarded all warnings and had risked not only his life but also the lives of his wife and sister-in-law. The results were fatal as everyone knows. Such large-scale tragic negligence couldn't allow Americans to indulge in a grieving process in which loss was the sole and primary affect. The grief necessitated the inclusion of rage, not only about loss, but at the one lost, Kennedy junior himself. How could he have been so careless and self-absorbed? How could he have thought he would survive the fantastic threats of nature when lifelong professional pilots were called back in caution? Such questions intermingled with discussions of how grief encompasses aggression within grief, anger within loss, rage within sadness.

Jessie Jackson drew the interpenetrating comments of all three of us grief experts in different states, with her in another, as all spoke as if in one room. Despite a dark room around me, the conversation through my earphones brought connections between Jackson and us three grief consultants. We actually looked like we were in one room when our faces were flashed side by side on T.V., but how long would the observations we made, and questions we raised about the complexities of the mourning process, linger on in the minds of the general public who still expected grief to last no longer than a week or possibly a weekend?

In the Jewish religion, we have a week of Shiva, and in many cultures—the props of grief, such as wearing black clothing, are observed for at least a year. Yet the true complexities of grief, which resonate back to all the earlier losses and disappointments in our lives—stretching back before cognitive memory to infancy—are rarely anticipated. In this culture, the majority turn to anti-depressants instead. Those within this majority often perpetuate the cycle of blocked grief, altering their moods by medical edicts on prescription pads. A Prozac generation can hardly tolerate the successive cycles of grief, rage, anger, loss, and yearning that constitute the natural developmental evolution toward re-birth of self and renewed capacities for love, creativity, and intimacy.

Then we all were shocked into mutual grief by September 11, 2001. The date has the same infamy as the date of Pearl Harbor or D-Day, when we went "over there," landing on the beaches of Normandy. Possibly for the first time in New York, if not in American history, mammoth corporations acknowledged the need to grieve in the face of universal trauma. I joined others in the mental health field who were temporarily hired by a corporation to lead September 11th grief groups and to be available for counseling. The company that asked for us to volunteer actually seemed to understand that employees who might only consciously wish to go back to work would subconsciously be in shock when fellow workers, residing in the trade towers, had just been massively murdered. Bringing in mental health practitioners, American corporations seemed to be acknowledging, for the first time, that their employees needed to express their rage, their sadness, and their questions about how to grieve. We were there to tell such employees that whatever they thought and felt was O.K. There was no correct prescription for grieving the effects of traumatic loss. There was no exact way to deal with their children who expressed confusion and wondered why their parents did not want to take off and fly on a planned vacation. They needed to know that they could just listen to their children and could just talk about whatever horrible thoughts or memories come up. They wanted to say good-bye to their colleagues who they had worked with over years and wanted to say something with meaning to the parents of these lost colleagues. They got to express this in groups with psychoanalysts and psychotherapists like myself because corporations were willing for the first time to invite us into their doors. Trauma had hit the headlines enough to arouse interest about how to grieve its losses. Is our culture beginning to wake up to the mourning process despite this seeming preference for manic fixes and Prozac?

I do know that my monthly group has been a resource for many who can surrender to the realities of grief. For four hours once a month there are phases of grief experienced and shared and many mourn over years in the profound bonding that contains and nurtures them within. We originally called this monthly therapy group, "mourning regrets."

The Culture of the Mourning Group

From individual process to group process, from internal world to external world, from monologue to dialogue, the four-hour monthly Object Relations mourning group travels all the developmental avenues that evolve into self transformation. Pivotal moments of surrender to grief punctuate the movement toward psychic change. Loss and regret interact, and the aggression within loss (first spoken of by Melanie Klein in 1940, in her "Mourning and Its Relation to Manic Depressive States"), speaks in the present moment. This occurs first within the internal world in the group's initially psychic visualization and then within the external world within the group's interpersonal process. Within the group transferential projections and projective identifications also culminate their course into both group and individual awareness.

For the 10 years that the "mourning regrets" therapy group has been meeting, as the group leader, I always begin the group by conducting a guided psychic visualization. During this visualization, I ask all group members to close their eyes and breathe. I ask them to all themselves to let their thoughts come through freely into their mind and to keep breathing deeper as they see what they feel. I ask them to note any repetitive thoughts and then to see what the feelings are, both the more intense ones in the forefront of their awareness and the subtle ones in the background of their awareness. Then I invite them to enter the main part of the visualization, asking them to allow whoever comes to them in their mind to appear before them. I ask them to feel what they need to say to this person.

Still reminding the group members to breathe, I ask them to look directly at the person who arises in the internal world through the psychic visualization. I ask them to be aware of what they feel as they speak to the other. I then ask them to see if the other reacts or responds as they speak. I ask them to continue breathing deeper as they listen to what the other, within their internal world, has to say. I then ask them to experience what they feel as they respond back to the other. I often also ask them to see if they can feel a connection with their heart as they breathe, and ask if they want to say anything from their heart to the internal other in focus in the moment. I also ask what their stomach has to say to the person. Unlike the heart, the stomach speaks of anger, rage, and hunger when the heart speaks of love, loss, and yearning. At the end of visualizing this first person, who has freely arisen in their internal vision, I ask the group members to see if they want to keep the person in their heart or wish to put the person outside their heart. I then ask if they can let go of the person and say good-bye. I ask if they feel tensions related to resisting saying "good-bye." I ask them to open their breathing to these tensions, rather than fighting them, and to see what feelings open up within. Then as they welcome the tension, I ask them to breathe deeply again as they say "good-bye."

I then take this same psychic journey with the group as they keep their eyes closed and picture another person who arises within their internal world psyche. When they relinquish this second person I ask them to open their eyes, whenever they are ready, and I ask whoever wishes to start to share what they wish to share of their psychic visualizations with the group.

When someone begins to share their internal world experience they may take off into associations to confidential issues in their life, or they may relate their experiences to the ongoing interpersonal world they are in with the other group members. Those who open up tears of grief during the psychic visualization may begin to speak from the core internal center where the crying comes from. Someone may hand the grief-stricken speaker the communal box of tissues that rests on the back of the couch, where several members sit. The group listens intently to the first speaker. Generally, they respond to the content expressed by this person. Sometimes the group members don't respond to the speaker who shares their visualization and its message. If someone is passed over in this way by the group, and another member is responded to, I as the leader, might make a group intervention at this point. I might ask why the group is responding to one person as opposed to another, whereas my other interventions will be interpretations about any one individuals' mourning process, related to the content of what they share with the group or to the way they share it.

I also ask the group member who shares whether she or he wants feedback from the group about how they are coming across if the group has not been forthcoming in response. If they say "yes," the group will begin to share their withheld and tentative responses, which may include critical comments in addition to supportive or empathic ones.

The visualization lasts 30 to 40 minutes after the Saturday (once a month) group begins at noon. The follow-up from the sharing process then evolves for another hour and a half or an hour and 40 minutes, until we have our break for refreshments at 2:00 p.m. The group resumes at 2:20 p.m. or 2:25 p.m. Those who haven't spoken in the morning generally create a space for themselves to speak in the afternoon. Some members intentionally wait for the second half of the group to speak of deeply aroused feeling states and conflicts that they have been meditating on during the morning session, or which have been inspired by the morning session. Interpersonal conflicts, projections, and transferences often appear more clearly in this second group phase. Conflicts between members that make external the internal world conflicts over aggression often appear in this second group phase. The interaction between the feelings of grief and sadness within the mourning process, as well as aggression and defense within mourning, often play themselves out more openly in the second phase of the group's process (from 2:25 p.m. to 4:00 p.m.). We end promptly at 4:00 p.m.

The Individual Developmental Mourning Process within the Group

Beyond bereavement, developmental mourning is about the grieving of the loss of the primal object as it lives and haunts us within our internal worlds. The core of psychic change is the pivotal moment of surrendering to the pain of loss, surrendering to grief. The process of working with all the aggressive dynamics that block this is all part of the developmental mourning process. The grief of regret is the grief based on the psychological interaction and alchemy of loss and guilt. The grief transforms guilt through loss into the empathic promise of compassion or D.W. Winnicott's (1963) "capacity for concern."

In the case of Sharon, we can see this whole evolution through the process of one group session in which the macrocosm is seen in the microcosm. The group process witnesses and cultivates the developmental evolution that evolves at first through the internal world of one person within the group. First, there is the psychic visualization and then the sharing of that individual visualization with the group. There often follows a mild enactment of the pathological dynamics of the old internal self and object constellation played out in the safety of the group laboratory. The group processes this enactment, allowing a surrender to the pain of regret and compassion within the loss of the old self and its insistent tie to the primal mother (the punishing and depriving self in identification with the primal parent aggressor). Finally, each group member relinquishes the raging attack against the self, as the projected internal child self is re-owned and thus psychically integrated.

The culmination of this entire process is that the empathy between group members creates new and increasingly healthy identifications that can fill the internal void and build psychic structure. The old self-destructive identifications are gradually surrendered. The loss of the bond with the old mother can be experienced through displacements with a spouse. The gradual relinquishing of this bond is often punctuated by the agony and anguish of letting go. This allows sealed-off core self love to open and to transform into the longing felt at the moment of grief.

Sharon's Psychic Anorexia Evolves through the Group Process

Silence is felt for five minutes or so after I end the group's psychic visualization by asking everyone to open their eyes when ready. I have invited whoever wishes to start to speak. I have invited them to share their visualizations. Then Sharon, a group member who is generally quiet in the group begins to speak. She says:

> I don't usually speak, but I need to today! When Susan asked to see what colors come up with our feelings, I saw red and black, the colors of *rage*. I am filled with so much rage! That's why I'm generally silent here because I'm afraid that if I open my mouth, all my rage will erupt and I'll bite someone's head off! I'm filled with rage toward myself for how I spoiled my vacation for my family. I tried to blame my husband, but it's really me!

We were all having a great vacation over the holidays. My kids were doing great. I was getting along with my husband's parents.

Then on Sunday, our last day at the resort, my husband asked me if I wanted to go for a walk by myself. He offered to be with my daughter so I could be free to go. It was a gorgeous day and I was dying to go. It was such a great place to walk, up in the country. So I went. But as soon as I felt the pleasure of having time to myself and enjoying walking in the country, I had to create something to worry about to punish myself for having any pleasure. I started obsessing about having my husband's jacket with me, thinking that he would need it when I was gone and be angry with me. I worked myself up into such a state that when I got back I created a fight with my husband. I had to spoil everything. I can't tolerate having pleasure. I had convinced myself that he was angry at me for having his jacket, thinking he would want to punish me for going off and leaving him with my daughter. He had been generous and offered to baby sit for our daughter so that I could go. I never could have asked him! God knows I could never ask for anything I wanted myself! But even though he offered I was convinced that he resented it because I had to find a punishment for having anything I wanted.

The whole time I was on the walk, I kept focusing on the jacket, thinking that my husband would need it and would focus his resentment about me having a walk on my having taken his jacket. I made the whole thing up! Then I became so defensive, having created this argument with my husband in my head. I became so defensive that I actually created the fight I feared. My husband couldn't care less about his jacket, but he was upset about conflicts he was having with this mother. When he told me that he was upset I lashed out at him with utter contempt and self righteousness, telling him that I couldn't care less about his conflicts with his mother, telling him that that was all his problem, telling him to stop dumping his problems on me. Then he really was angry at me. I had created the whole thing!

I created the whole thing to punish myself for having pleasure, for having anything. I used to feel so much regret about my contempt but behind my contempt is my stoic self-righteousness about being superior to others because of my martyred attitudes that I can do without. I really get off on self-deprivation! The very thing that I hated in my mother is totally in me now! I can't even receive a present that my husband gives me. He just about gave up. In the past the group always heard about my husband raging at me. But now you can see how enraged a person I am!

It's all related to my need to deprive myself and to feel superior because I can deprive myself. I punish myself for having anything, and I punish anyone else for giving me anything.

It would be a torture for both my husband and myself when he would try to give me a present. I would be so cold, victimized and self righteous if he gave me something I didn't want, and if by *some miracle* he bought be something that I actually liked and wanted I would immediately squelch any pleasure in receiving the gift then. I would find some rationalization for why I really didn't need it. With therapy, this is the first year that I was actually able to take in my husband's and my children's celebration of my birthday. I used to torture everyone. I didn't realize how identified I was with the very thing in my mother that I hate! The last time I tried to give my mother a present, it was an invitation to come up against the wall of her dramatic and stoic martyrdom! I had gotten her a food processor, and the minute she opened it, she immediately said, 'Why don't you take it. I have one.'

I feel nauseous when I think of it. I want to throw up. Talk about bad food! I was fed a constant diet of my mother's self-deprivation, and I learned all too well how to turn a punitive attitude against myself, or against anyone else who dared to ever think of enjoying anything!

There is again a moment of silence in the group. Then Elaine says:

I'll take the risk of having my head cut off by Sharon. I think it's great that you're getting to all of this and you articulate it so well! I can really relate to it. It reminds me of a psychic visualization I once had in the group. In the visualization I was so filled with rage that I became King Kong knocking down buildings and destroying everything in sight. Then the scene switched and I was a two-year-old clinging to my mother, wanting my mommy. All this rage was just about wanting my mother.

It sounds like you attack your husband for giving anything to you because that's what your mother did to you. You are a child too, wanting your mommy, and so you take her in by being like her, when she won't let you take her in through having any feeling contact. Susan told me about how that works. You have said that the three-year-old in you once opened up in this group, before I came into it. Everyone said you were able to show the three-year-old in you who was emotionally abandoned and attacked by your mother. What would she say now when she sees you depriving yourself and scapegoating your husband, just like your mother scapegoated you?

Sharon is crying as she replies, feeling the grief of regret related to her own behavior:

> She'd say she doesn't want me to treat others like my mother treated her! She'd say that I'm silent in this group because I don't want to make anyone else here feel that horrible hurt of the three-year-old within me, the three-year-old who couldn't fight back. My internal three-year-old feels totally helpless—needing my mother, not having anyone to talk to. I was always being blamed by my mother for not being able to do things she wanted me to know things that she never taught me and which were way beyond me. I was always the bad one for my mother, and so I didn't deserve anything. I could only feel good if I deprived myself and felt self-righteous about it like she did. But then a lifetime of this has filled me with so much rage that I go around feeling like I could kill anyone who says anything to me.

Sharon turns to Nancy and says: "You got a shot of this today, from me. When you tried to talk to me in the waiting room, I turned cold on you, froze you out." And Nancy said, "I understood. You said you didn't like to talk before the group. I didn't feel attacked." (In the next monthly group, Sharon did openly express contempt and attacked Nancy in her attempt to explain her frustration and rage related to Nancy's "obsessionalism." Although Sharon is terrified of exposing this contemptuous part of her that wants to verbally bite everyone's head off, she is able to risk exposing it to the group when she is angry at Nancy. She finds out that she doesn't traumatize or kill anyone because Nancy is not a three-year-old. Nancy reacts with anger and an insulting retaliation that actually relieves Sharon, not being devastated. This relieves Sharon because she is afraid that she could devastate others onto whom she projects her vulnerable child self.)

Returning to the group meeting, Sharon says, at this time:

> You may not have felt attacked by me, but I felt ugly and mean when I said I didn't want to talk to you. I'm silent when I feel ugly with my mean and angry hate. Right now I just hate myself, but I know that the hate really goes back to my mother who screwed me up in the first place. I just regret like hell that I keep acting like her. I was always trying to be the total opposite to her. That's why I'm silent in here. I don't want to show the monster rage-aholic mother part of me. You guys only heard of the rage-

aholic part of my husband and saw me more as the victim. But it's time for me to fess up. I'm the rage-aholic hanging out in silence, hiding and trying to contain the monster inside of me. Anyone who is as self depriving as I am is filled with rage. Then we, deprivation addicts, feed ourselves with the attitudes of contempt and self-righteousness. Even as a child I could see that the only thing my mother had, in the midst of her mock saintly martyrdom, was her god damn self-righteousness!

Then Rachael said:

You sound so pained as you speak, so filled with grief and despair, but I think things will be getting better for you now because you are so filled with insight. You're so able to process your feelings and thoughts and see what your problems are!

Sharon responded (politely), "Thank you, but I don't seem to get anywhere with this insight. I have seen this all before. I think I'm getting better and then I'm right back in this place again!"

Then, as the group leader, I intervened:

Sharon you just demonstrated the very thing that you're complaining about, giving the polite platitude of a formal thank you to Rachael, and then proceeding to reject the gift in her words. This way, you rejected the gift of hope that Rachel was trying to offer you. Similarly, you reject your husband's gifts and his generous offer to babysit so that you can enjoy a walk and have some solitude, which you always say you are dying for.

Also you complain of being back in the same place, but the process of mourning and insight is always going back and forth. It's the process of all emotional growth. This culture has never understood how much time mourning takes. Actually it's a lifelong process. There is no growth and development in life without going back and forth in the grief and awareness of mourning, and in the return to the re-living of the old mode of relationship in the pathological mourning state. You can't just be there without regressing and having to work on the same issues again.

What makes you think that you don't have to be human like everyone else? You used to have the fantasy of the perfect people who you wanted to be like and also felt excluded by. But you secretly believe that you should be perfect. It's O.K. for everyone else to fall on their faces, but not you.

Chapter 21

Now Beverly joined the conversation:

> I can really relate to Sharon. In a session with Susan I remembered that when I was 12 I wanted to jump into the grave with my mother when my mother died. I hated her when she was alive, but even though she screamed at me, and threatened me, and scapegoated me, she was the only one who gave me any attention. So, naturally, I had to identify with her and had no sense of self when she died. My father had withdrawn a long time ago. I've been feeling so much rage toward him lately! The men in my life have to take all the rage and shit I felt toward him that I never got to express. That's part of why I'm having so many problems with my boyfriend now, especially after moving in with him. I keep wanting him to give me what both my mother and father didn't give me. It doesn't seem to matter sometimes how much I am aware of what I'm doing. I'm still doing it! What did help was when I actually felt the grief of longing to die with my mother, to jump into her grave, to be with her. Talk about self-deprivation, I was willing to deprive myself of my whole life just to be with her. When I realized that, I really did start to take my life more seriously and to do my artwork in a more creative way. I had my first exhibit in ages last year, after the message from that session with Susan about wanting to jump into my mother's grave—that really began to hit me!

Victoria was also motivated to talk:

> I know just what Sharon means about being attached to one's own self-deprivation. Just yesterday my boyfriend offered to help me with something. He was going to talk to the construction workers in my house for me about taking care of something. But instead of letting him help me, I began dictating to him what to say and how to say it. I just knew he would turn around and say, 'Do it yourself then,' and that's exactly what happened. I can't receive help or gifts either. It makes me feel out of control. I get back into control by refusing help and trying to do everything for myself. Then I feel burdened and angry. Then I don't feel like giving anything to anyone. I hide it. People actually think I'm generous, but secretly I know how withholding I really am.
>
> I'm just like my grandmother who was more of a mother to me than my mother. And just like her I secretly get off on thinking I'm better than others by not asking for anything for myself. My boyfriend wanted to take my grandmother to this party and she told him what time she had to

leave. He was a few minutes late, so she got in a cab and went by herself. He was totally puzzled and frustrated. He was only trying to help her so that he could have a good relationship with her for my sake. I'm sure she got off on showing him up and proving she didn't need anyone. She gets more out of that form of self-righteousness than out of accepting any human companionship or help. I'm the same way. I just know enough not to demonstrate it to the world. I've changed enough to live with a generous guy and to act generous even when I'm not inside, but I still get psychic feedings from attitudes of contempt and self-righteousness that are the pay off for self-deprivation, just like Sharon.

I have moments of grief and regret about it, especially when I drive my boyfriend away and everyone here knows that he's the best one I've had, including my ex-husband, but the addiction to those attitudes of being superior to others who show their needs is really powerful. Being above it can be a real high. When I'm in a state, I don't have to admit to myself that the hungry raging infant in me that I project onto everyone else is really starving inside of me!

The image of being superior is false food but sometimes it really feels like that's what's nurturing me. I think that the internal starvation shows up in this group when we do the psychic visualization. No matter how much I try to breathe deeply, and let go, I feel this deadness on the left side of my body. I have some real split in me. The right part of my body feels alive. But the left side feels dead, and I try to wake it up by letting the energy in my breath travel from my feet upwards, rather than downwards from my head. Of course it's in my head that all these fucked up attitudes and their addictions live.

Then Darlene:

As I've listened to everyone talk about self-deprivation and self-sabotage, I realize I have it too. I don't so much get off on depriving myself, but I don't seem to be able to promote myself whenever I have a conscious goal and have a conscious intention to succeed. I end up languishing. Eventually, I had to give up dancing and then I gave up writing even though I published a book. But ironically, I start having one success after another when I don't care, when I don't have any goal and when my creativity is involved with nurturing the performance of others. I've done fundraising for this organization, which I always had been scared to do. The organization has grown and when I was voted in as president I was able to find a way of creating a salary for myself. I don't want to go back to being poor, but now I don't seem hungry for the very things I longed for before, to be recognized as a dancer or writer. I can't seem to promote myself in these areas. I was just like you, Beverly, in the past. I too was so desperate to be seen and recognized, desperate for love really, that I would cry at auditions, just like Beverly who said she had cried at job interviews if she didn't get the job. I was also filled with shame about the neediness. Once I was desperate enough to think of sleeping with someone in the dance world to get a job. Looking back, it all seems strangely comical now. But at the time I was desperate.

Still I couldn't summon enough faith in myself to promote myself in a realistic manner. When Sharon brought up my book in another group I denied I cared about it anymore. It's true, just as Sharon had said that I stopped promoting it when my mother refused to read it. When I wrote it I was doing it for her approval. I did everything for her approval. Then when I didn't get it from her or from all the others onto whom I projected her I just gave up on my own goals. That's why it's so much easier to help others with their creative projects, ones that I am in a position to authorize, rather than to work on projects of my own that bring up the old craving for my mother's and father's approval.

My father was actively destructive to my creativity and my mother gave up hers, even though she had a tremendous talent as an actress and singer. I couldn't have what she couldn't have for herself, I couldn't win over the father figures in the dance world who I felt alienated from.

So depriving myself of success, even if I'm willing to do all the work of the creativity, felt like my fate. I didn't love the self-deprivation but I felt it was what I deserved. It was more comfortable than unconsciously believing that I was betraying my mother by any success out in the world. My mother martyred herself because she had to. When my father became mentally ill there was no other choice for her but to go to work at an ordinary nine to five job in order to support the family. And she did it without complaining. [Darlene is crying and sobbing as she says this.]

I'm the one who always complains, and my sister perpetually complains, but my mother never ever complained. She really seemed like a saint to me. She gave up any career to promote her enormous talent and I always thought she must resent it. But I eventually realized that my mother really wanted to be a mother! She was a really good mother [crying], and would have been a good mother if my father wasn't always disrupting everything with his rages and his active abuse of her. Lately I've come to forgive my mother. Just like Linda has said, I can't hold on to the old resentments when I really understand now what it feels like for her. And she'd reached out to me too now, even though she couldn't read my book. I also realize now that if she read it it would just open up too many old wounds. She's protecting herself by not remembering. She always loved my father, but even though he was so dependent on her he could never tell her. He tortured her and never expressed any gratitude to her for all she sacrificed. He never even told her he loved her.

I want my mother to know how grateful I am. I was able to tell her, over the phone and we both cried [crying as she says this]. She was a really good mother and she sacrificed for all of us. I still feel angry at my sister, and now I keep strict boundaries with her. I don't, let her know my feelings, although she does know I'm angry at her even though I won't express it to her. I don't want to share my feelings with my sister because my sister always fed off my feelings, allowing me to express all the feelings while she hid hers.

But with my mother, I no longer feel angry. I really have forgiven her. When I told her I was grateful I felt so much love for her. And when I saw her we could just look at each other and feel the love. We didn't even need words then. She called afterward and said she felt grateful. What did she feel grateful for? I didn't do that much. But she really took me in and I really took her in. When we did the psychic visualization I could connect with my mother in my heart and speak from my heart to her.

When Susan asked if we wanted to keep the person in our hearts when saying good-bye or put them outside our heart, I left my sister outside, but I took my mother into my heart. And my heart wasn't a bleeding heart then as it had been in relation to my father when I had him in the psychic visualization years ago. Now, with my mother my heart can feel full, not only with the sadness of grief that I've felt here many times, but also with the love that emerges out of the space opened by the sadness to my inner core. Just like with my husband this group has helped me to learn how to love. It's only through love that we can give up the self depriving state. I guess those who feel nurtured by me for their creative projects experience this through me now.

Susan, the group leader and analyst, responded:

Today's group seems to have evolved into a theme, a theme within the overall theme we share of the individual mourning process within the group. It seems like a theme of unconscious gratification through self-deprivation or through psychic anorexia. Nobody spoke more pointedly and succinctly and tragically to this theme than Emily Dickinson, who said, "The Banquet of Abstemiousness Defaces That of Wine." She also wrote, "Renunciation is a piercing virtue," at the point when she refused to marry the one man she loved and adored, her father's best friend, who proposed to her after her father and his wife were dead. "No" is the most exciting word in the English language, conflating the meaning of excitement and self-denial, perversely and paradoxically turning deprivation into its opposite, excitement! To have accepted the offer of marriage from the man she loved would have confronted her with realities of sex and marriage that—her poetry showed—she was terrified of.

This topic was not continued in the group, but more can be said to contrast the pathological mourning arrest of Emily Dickinson with the evolving developmental mourning process that Sharon and her fellow group members illustrated here. Instead of the real earthly thing that Emily Dickinson could have as a corporal being in a human body who could marry a mortal man, she chose to believe that she would have a far superior form of marriage in heaven, after her death. She believed that she would be rewarded for her stoic self-deprivation with the love of the father god figure who lived in her psyche as a demon-lover figure. Her fantasy god was actually her demon as he demonically drew her toward self-deprivation and death. She struggled to try to win the love of a grandiose godfather for whom she had to neglect the human size man, the man who actually proposed to her and would have offered her love in actual daily life on earth. By practicing psychic anorexia as her one and only true religion, Emily Dickinson developed and remained a prisoner of a demon-lover complex (as defined by Kavaler-Adler, 1993a/2013, 1996/2014, 2000, 2003).

Ending Summary

Sharon is using the mourning group to relinquish the pathological mourning state that she was fixated in when she first came to treatment with me 10 years ago, to deal with her own demon-lover complex. Sharon first came to see me, after reading my first of three books on mourning, *The Compulsion to Create.* She articulated to me at that time that by reading my book she had learned that she lived within an internal world of fantasy figures. These were figures of extreme and contrasting natures, either being demonic parents or perfect people (implying a psyche perpetually affected by the psychic splitting from precedipal trauma).

The mourning group has allowed Sharon to begin risking interactions with real external others, who she continually discovers to be quite different than her internal demons and angels. The group meeting reported here, in which Sharon speaks of her self-punishing rage and her psychic anorexia, is followed by a group meeting where she risks exposing as well as experiencing her anger and its defensive contempt. She risks creating conflicts over retaliatory aggression with another group member. In this group, she comes a long way from her lifelong pattern of schizoid seclusion and withdrawal. She steps beyond scapegoating her husband to encounters with fellow group members who can process her feelings and reactions with her. She sees in the next group that in contrast to her terrors of "biting" another's head off, the group member she judges with frustration and contempt does not die or become traumatized. The verbally assaulted woman merely gets angry and also begins to take a look at the content of Sharon's feedback about her own (obsessive) behavior, even though she is infuriated by the mode of Sharon's expression in her first attempt to bring the rage-aholic side of her out of the closet in the group.

The role of aggression within the mourning process becomes once more apparent in the laboratory of the mourning group! Melanie Klein (1940) certainly was right, when she went beyond Freud's (1917) "Mourning and Melancholia" and spoke of rage in psychic fantasy in her "Mourning and It's Relation to Manic Depressive States." She also spoke there of feelings of hate, contempt, and competition related to dreams and psychic fantasy that accompany all the grief and loss aspects of the mourning process. I would add that this is true whether or not the mourning process of the individual is related to actual bereavement or is related to the many, and lifelong, phases of mourning related to separation-individuation, the re-owning split-off parts, and the multiple phases of life long psychic development (see Kavaler-Adler, 1993b, 1995, 1996/2014, 2000, 2003a, 2003b, 2004).

COUNTERTRANSFERENCE, REGRET, AND AGGRESSION: DRAMA AND FREE ASSOCIATION IN AN OBJECT RELATIONS GROUP ENVIRONMENT

Originally presented at the ORI's Annual Conference and then published in 2020, Countertransference, regret, and aggression: Dramas and free associations in an Object Relations group environment, *MindConsiliums* 20(6):1–14.

Nancy had been in and out of individual psychotherapy with me. After much rage, devaluation, insults, and self-righteous assumptions about my moral shortcomings—which became tempered by her growing gratitude, love, and admiration, and by her willingness to view some of her own failings, including, for a brief moment, her own narcissism—Nancy had decided to terminate her individual therapy. She also decided to remain in my monthly four-hour mourning and therapy group, which she had been in for at least four years.

Never having terminated an individual therapy in a totally open way before, the termination process with me was experienced as quite an achievement by Nancy. She had openly owned all her hate and love of me and had seen her own growth. I had said she was less self-righteous and black and white in her thinking than before, although I certainly did see remnants of her former defensive splitting operations, where she tended to polarize everyone into good and bad mothers, to idealize herself on moral terms, and to devalue her creative capacities, with some secret contempt for mere mortal scribbling writers, like myself, hidden behind it. When she went out the door in our last individual session, she turned around and smiled in a glow of warmth, said she couldn't wait to see me in group, and said working with me had been "a pleasure."

Now here we were, back in the monthly Saturday group. This was after Nancy had left the last individual session in a glow of admiration, acknowledging her well-held secret that she had always enjoyed learning from how I intervened and engaged with different members in the group. She had also said that she and I shared a high and demonstrated intellect and that she would miss experiencing my intellect in our individual sessions but looked forward to experiencing my keen penetrating interpretations in group.

Now, we sat in a group several monthly groups later. Suddenly, a woman sitting next to Nancy in the group leaped up from beside her, ran across the room to a seat on the other side of the group, and said "I'm not going to stay next to that erupting volcano!" Eva said she had felt an erupting volcano of rage building up in Nancy, and that she wasn't going to just sit there and let her explode all over her. She also said that she felt terrified of Nancy because she was sitting there with her arms crossed across her chest like an imperious and imposing judge. Nancy responded at first with self-deprecating humor, by lifting her left arm and exposing the hanging plastic tag of a department store purchase in the underarm portion of her blouse. Nancy seemed embarrassed, but self-justifying, as if to say, "I'm not the mean critical judge that this woman sees, but rather an embarrassed woman who forgot to remove the store tags on the underarm of my blouse."

There was a momentary pause as the group members, somewhat nonplussed by the diversion to Nancy's underarm, tried to assimilate the twist of events. Eva, the woman who had leaped across the room to escape Nancy, and who had been sitting with a look of fear and intimidation in her eyes as she described the threatening judge across the room, won a few moments with the comic relief. But just then, Nancy leaped outward with the words of pointed accusation just as quickly as Eva had leaped across the room. She glared with the flush of rage roaring up her cheeks at Eva and declared, "You always act like a therapist in the group! You never reveal yourself!" This came after Nancy had earlier reacted to the way Eva spoke as if she was a snob, to which Eva had protested that she did speak differently because of her accent, a mere consequence of her immigrant status. At that moment Eva had still been composed, and she had defended herself in an outwardly cool demeanor. But that coolness evaporated as Nancy's visceral volcano was felt by Eva, and was felt so intensely that she leaped for her life across the room. Now with Nancy's pointed accusation, which seemed to have a whole indictment lying behind it, it was Eva's turn to erupt. Eva's eruption was one of wounded hurt and injury manifesting as a long sobbing scream, with gushes of terror and pain escalating out of her whole body. It seemed as if every one of the pores on Eva's body was screaming, crying, and sobbing.

I looked at the clock. It was time for our half-hour lunch break, in a four-hour group. It was my job to call the time-out break. At first, I felt like a reluctant referee, given the conflict that had just transpired. Sylvia suggested we take a little more time since things were so hot. In these few minutes, I believe that Nancy tried to reach out to Eva, and said that she wasn't the kind of person to hurt people, and she hoped she and Eva could work together on this. But Eva was still deep in her visible and palpable pain, for all to feel. She shook her head "no" as she continued gut-wrenching sobbing, her former childhood full of trauma leaking out of every pore. She managed to say, "It's too much!" She meant, "I can't respond to Nancy. It's too much." Then Nancy looked around the room for support, and defended herself by saying, "This is hard for me! Expressing anger is hard for me. And I can be overly aggressive sometimes. But I'm really an empathic person."

I felt the plea for support and did say to Eva, who was fairly new to the group, and had not known Nancy that long, "Yes. Nancy can be very empathic," but I was also aware that Nancy only wished to see herself as empathic, and had a hard time acknowledging the cold, enraged, judging part of her except when she turned it on herself. When she had turned it on me, she had always felt justified, and often self-righteously and indignantly so, but to be confronted with turning it on another group member was challenging her self-image of being the caring empathic friend to all her fellow group members, group members whom she had at one point seen as victims of me and my power in the group. To be exposed as the feared powerful judge before the whole world that existed in our psychotherapy group was leveled quite a tilt to Nancy's equilibrium.

Sylvia must have sensed it too, because she declared, more emphatically than I, "Yes. Nancy can be very empathic!" Then I had to call the lunch break. As everyone left the room for their brief and rushed lunch period, I sat with Eva, who was still doubled over with pain and injury and fear, quite a substantial contrast to the cool exterior that she had shown in the monthly group meetings up until this time.

The Afternoon

When everyone returned from lunch, Eva had moved to another location in the ring around of chairs in the room. She clearly had re-composed herself after her anguished expression of her vulnerability and need. The sense of an aftermath of conflict and a prologue to aggression emerging more openly in the group was in the air. Nancy began by saying, "I need to know if this will be resolved. I don't want to be in a group where this is going on."

I asked Nancy what she meant by being resolved. I added that perhaps she was being somewhat black and white by not realizing that Eva had just said she couldn't deal with things between them for now, not forever. I was indicating that this was all a process and that it didn't all have to be sorted out in one group session. Nancy would have none of this! She especially wouldn't have that I saw it as a positive development that the group members' conflicts and aggression toward each other were coming out into the open, so all group members could all learn about how we dealt with aggression.

Nancy then turned particularly and pointedly to me, and with the volcanic rage arising visibly in her declared, "I think there are too many people in the group!" This also came after another group member had gotten angry that Nancy had said to her in an accusatory tone that she was taking 20 minutes. Nancy wanted Cecilia to realize that she had been listening to her when she spoke in the morning, and wanted her to see her empathy for her. Instead, Cecilia threw back at her that whatever empathy she showed, it was lost when Nancy said in that accusatory tone, "You took 20 minutes!"

Nancy wasn't accustomed to receiving this kind of aggressive defense from a fellow group member. She had receded from the group members, but then turned angrily to me, with her comment, "I think there are too many people in the group!" Here would lie my regret, because as she pushed my buttons about the size of the group, a topic much discussed that had led to my setting a 10-person limit for a four-hour group, I lost my leadership role self-composure, and lashed out with my own angry retort. I said, "Nancy, that is such a red herring! It's not about the group size. This stuff happens inside of people when they are cutting parts of themselves off! It also happens outside in the world, where conflict within competition is rampant, so how can it not happen in here in the group?" Her bringing up the group size, after she had recently declared that she was "letting go of that issue," was searing into my own equilibrium. I therefore blurted out, "What planet do you come from Nancy? This is what goes on all over!"

Nancy controlled her wrath, but the control would leave from fight to flight later. She said, "That sounds critical." Then a new group member, who had been in another long-term psychoanalytic psychotherapy group, began to speak for Nancy. Helen turned to me, and said, "I certainly would feel criticized if that were said to me, 'What planet do you live on?'" Nancy felt somewhat supported by Helen, but what she didn't get was that Helen also had said that all this stuff about being polite in this group, and about each person having their time without conflict, was "bullshit!" It was Nancy who most of all wanted this polite paradise that provided a retreat for her from the outside world, the same kind of retreat she tried to establish with her boyfriend, where they nestled with each other, away from the cold cruel world. In fact, Nancy's original intention in coming to the group was to risk going out into the world, one day of a weekend a month, away from her boyfriend.

Yet, here was Nancy about to run for the hills as conflict arose, not only in the group, but between her and others. She wanted me to provide some mythic seclusion where all this didn't happen. She concluded that fewer people, or me being a better person, or me giving her some kind of support she wasn't overtly asking for, would extinguish this conflict, and would let her go back to her role of group member empathizer. But now it wasn't working. And I felt the tug, the pull, the silent enraged demand that I somehow rescue her, but I was not yet aware that she would actually leave the whole scene for good. I was under the mistaken impression that with all the years she had spent in the group, and after her decision to stay after friends of hers had left, and after her declarations to me of how she valued the group, and after her lauding my interventions in group, that she would stay and work on things over time. Yes, I believed we would all be working overtime—as the other members of the group continued to do after Nancy left.

The whole group was sensing that our work together was truly a process! I was wrong about Nancy being able to have this perspective when she was so upset. As Eva seconded me and said that it was a red herring, about how many members were in the group now, Nancy bristled even more. But then she shut down altogether when Cecilia said, "You may have been empathizing with me this morning, but then you said, 'You took 20 minutes!' Maybe you just need to sit with all this now!"

That was it! Nancy withdrew. I felt her withdrawal, her underlying pain. I did want to give her the chance to speak, since I had disrupted her with my defensive and angry comment about her living on another planet. I said as others started speaking about their internal struggles related to the earlier psychic visualization, "Nancy. Do you want to say anything?" She was quiet then, obviously feeling silenced after Cecilia told her to "Sit with it!" She was quiet, but that quiet in Nancy would be the quiet before either a storm or a withdrawal to avoid the storm. I felt helpless as Nancy shook her head "no," and said that she did not want to speak. I had acknowledged I had been critical toward her when Helen had confronted me with how critical I sounded. Nonetheless, I felt like Nancy had disappeared into some old kind of vacuum, like the one that she had withdrawn into continuously during the earlier part of her life—before therapy had awoken Nancy's awareness of her anger, her rage, her hunger, her need, and her losses. She had retreated as she had done so often in her life. Yet I didn't realize she wouldn't be back!

As the group ended that day, there was a feeling of things being unsettled, and I sensed fears of people losing control. I had been part of this atmosphere. Yet Eva was so relieved that I had been there during lunch to understand her pain and terror, and to hear her talk about the sister transference that had been ignited within her by Nancy. She began talking of this sister transference during the next group, and other groups. Eva was so relieved as she left the room, that she grabbed my hand and squeezed it, and kissed me on the forehead, before I could say, "Please put it into words." Just as she took me unaware like this, I saw Nancy had left the group room in my office and was headed out the front door of my office, beyond the waiting room. "What perfectly horrific timing," I thought.

I further thought that Nancy knew I never let her hug or kiss me. In individual therapy, I had asked Nancy to put her wishes to hug me into words, and this had allowed Nancy to have her full emotional surge of feeling come through her body, as well as coming into her eyes through tears. She then had said, "I love you!" That was a long time ago. Now, I became again, it seemed, the hated and self-involved mother that wasn't there for her! I felt the loss. I sensed her avoidant looks, as Nancy went through the outer door as if she were sneaking out the door. She appeared to be deliberately shrinking herself, as if to make herself invisible. I knew the rage was festering behind this attitude, but I didn't know I would never get to see her again. I would never get to help her work this all out or to even apologize to her for my "living on another planet" comment.

Eva had turned to me within the morning part of group. Cecilia defended herself with Nancy and then turned to me by email after the group to express her distress. Both these women would continue their work in group. Both would start to share with a whole new depth with the group, as they realized how angry they were and how terrified they were, each carrying a traumatized child self within each of them. I would work on this with them. The group would work with them, would listen, and ultimately respond.

But Nancy was gone, and I wouldn't know it until she sent an email to me and the group next month. She said good-bye to me in a cold cut-off tone in an email. She said she wouldn't consider coming into group or consulting with me individually. Apparently, my short email responses to her were experienced as intrusions. She coldly declared that she had no intention of speaking again in the group, even when I invited her to come to share her concerns. She said she had tried that and that I had been "aggressively critical!" She was removed, behind a wall of rage. There was no touching or contacting her. After all our work, I thought, after all the years of individual work and group work. Her cut-off was final!

Everyone else was to come in and continue the process. In the next group, I encouraged everyone to speak about their anger and disappointment with me for how I had responded to Nancy. They did, and I shared my experience and thoughts. The group felt really close together after this discussion, and in the next few groups there was enough trust to really open up interpersonal issues about aggression, and how the need to speak up after a lifetime of trauma could come out in aggressive ways that put each other off. There was room to talk also about how one group member had been holding on to a judgment about another that made her not like the other woman, and both women spoke.

Carol said that she was experiencing the discussion with the other woman group member, Cecilia, as reminiscent of her and her mother, each saying the other was putting their stuff onto the other. This led to sorting out who was angry at who. Both women got past the rage to a meaningful dialogue that included a group discussion of transferences, projections, and interpretations. I was very pleased with the group, and with my work in it then, but haunting me in the back of my mind was Nancy. That is why I had to write this paper. I had to write this paper to understand why I felt such a deep sense of regret as well as anger in relation to Nancy's abrupt departure and her refusal to speak to me. I had to see if there was anything I could have done differently that might have changed the outcome with Nancy. Nancy had been a group member for many years. Suddenly, she was gone. I want to understand. I want to understand my own regrets.

What Kind of Regret is this?

Where do I start with trying to understand my regret in relation to Nancy? Would I have been feeling such a heavy and profound sense of regret if she hadn't left? I don't know for sure. I am asking if my regret is real in the sense of existential grief about hurting the one you love. It is this kind of existential regret that Melanie Klein seemed to be speaking of when she described the combination of guilt and loss in the depressive position. Is this the kind of regret I have written about being felt by patients in describing regret as a fundamental part of a developmental mourning process in my book, *Anatomy of Regret*? Or is this regret of mine toward Nancy some kind of spurious item, where my regret is ultimately more of a narcissistic concern for my own loss in having Nancy leaving me in this abrupt way, undoing the heated-up warmth of her former individual therapy good-bye? Is it a more narcissistic regret about losing the chance to have Nancy and the other group members see me repair things with Nancy? After all, I was able to repair things in the rest of the group, after Nancy left, when the fears of aggression being out of control, and the fears of anger at me as the group leader, threatened to intimidate people or to cause others to leave. Could it be a combination of all these three things, narcissistic and humane, some jumbled up mixture with more things added into the mix as well?

What I do know is that I regret my comment about Nancy living on another planet, because it was hostile and critical, and must have been humiliating for Nancy. Helen had said it was as if I was telling Nancy she was an alien by proclaiming, "What planet do you live on?" But some part of me wants to defend myself and say, "But you were trying to make a point, that it's not just about the size of the group. The point being that these things happen in all groups, and that's part of what we're here for, to look at our enactments and understand where people are coming from, and to look at the projections and transferences behind all the anger, as in when Eva acknowledged she was experiencing Nancy as her bullying and humiliating and scapegoating sister."

Countertransference

If I have to defend myself, and that particular comment that everyone agreed had been hurtful, and which Nancy herself had declared to be "aggressively critical" in her retaliatory email, then did I genuinely feel regret at all? How could I be defending myself and also be truly grieving the loss of Nancy and her loss in feeling that I didn't care about her? And did I care if I could have been so callous at that moment just because I couldn't stand going through her complaints again about the size of the group, especially after Nancy said she was ready to let go of that gripe, and after I had put a limit on the group size that I felt was fair for a four-hour group? What was my heart feeling for Nancy in all this? Had I lost it all because she was demonizing me again, turning me all bad, and leaving me abruptly, with a cold shoulder and accusation on the way out the door? Couldn't I be beyond that, if I really cared deeply about her, if I really could love her, after all the time, and all the reparations between us?

I began to think not. I seem to have to acknowledge my resentment and regret about my own loss of face in all this, as I imagine Nancy glaring down on me as I wake from my sleep in the morning. Certainly, her ghost triggered a countertransference figure for me, and I didn't have to guess who it was for long. But I'm trying to get beyond this. I'm trying to see if I have at least a good kernel of genuine regret and existential grief in relation to Nancy. Don't I care that she is aching in her solitary rage, although I picture her being comforted and soothed by her boyfriend, a boyfriend who I envision as definitely not forgiving me?

I have pictured her in pain and find it hard to dismiss this thought from my mind. But I feel angry at her the minute I think, "Then why the hell don't you come in and talk about it, either with me or in the group? Why didn't you respond to my invitations to come in and express yourself rather than taking flight after your fight? Perhaps this is the best way you consciously and unconsciously can conceive to punish me! So why should I feel so bad for you then?" But I do, because a patient is a vulnerable and frightening thing, and I, more than any other perhaps, know the child in you. Or will you not come into therapy to talk about it out of mere spite because you resent that I would be paid for my time? What if I offered you a free session? But wouldn't that be masochistic of me after you twice refused either an individual or group session to communicate your concerns? Your retort was, "I have plenty of resources! I already tried to speak of my concerns and received no support from you! Good-bye!"

What a bitch! Why should I suffer grief, anguish and regret for your hurt, when you can't even come in again to tell me off? And do I really want you back, if you never let go of the size of the group issue, after you said you were letting go of it, and after I thought we could move into the heated things in the group without the diversion of this ongoing "red herring?" Eva agreed with me that the issue of the size of the group was a red herring. But that then most probably caused you to feel the group wouldn't be a safe place for you again! I can see how you see it. It seems so vivid to me how you must see it! I can't seem to let go of you! I can't help continuously seeing your point of view side by side with my own. I can't get rid of you! Why won't you come in and talk to me? Is it because I'm the bigger bitch who humiliated you with my "What planet do you live on?" comment when you were the vulnerable patient, and I was supposed to be in control?

I am writing all this so you will stop haunting me! Or am I writing this so I will stop being haunted by my regret that I couldn't control myself, and also by my resentment as well as by my regret, that all our years of work together seem evaporated? Or am I regretting that they are evaporated for you? Have I robbed you by turning you against me and forcing you into a position of hate again? So am I moving back and forth between my own paranoid-schizoid and depressive positions? Am I also—in the manner of Fairbairn's moral defense—turning all against myself to protect you and my image of you and my wanting to sustain love for you? Or am I the narcissistic bitch who is angry you wouldn't cooperate with me? Am I the bitch who just resented the hell out of you for rousing the others in a cry of rage against me, with your continuing rant about the size of the group?

Perhaps it is all of the above. This must be my mourning process, my developmental mourning process, by trying to digest the Nancy in my psyche and soul, my internal world ghost that always haunts me with the polarized view that I am addictively attached to, beating myself with the sides of your vision as if to repair things between us by trying to make your vision my own. But it never fits, damn it!

Regret as a Turning Point, the Transitional Pivot: Learning from Regret

(Melanie Klein's Reparation at Work, a Critical Phase of Developmental Mourning)

What do I truly regret? I truly regret the impulsive expression of my rage toward Nancy, which came out in the phrase, "What planet do you live on?" I believe this phrase did provoke someone who carried a great deal of shame within her from the past into a feeling of being aggressively shamed and humiliated. I would agree with the female group member who said that such words from me might be interpreted as implying that Nancy was somehow an alien in relation to others in our little group society.

No matter how judgmental and self-righteous Nancy was being in her judgments toward me and others in the group, such as Eva and Cecilia, I was not supposed to react impulsively like a group member was, nor even spontaneously like a group member who was allowed and encouraged to say whatever came to mind in the moment, because they were the patients. Even group members should be encouraged by the group leader to have some restraint, and some self-reflection as they speak, so that accusations like the one Nancy made toward Eva about acting only like a therapist in the group could be transformed into curiosity, questions that showed an interest in who the other group member was. But in the heat of a transferential moment, it is accepted for patients, and group members, to enact their anger, and then work along with the group and the leader to process this.

Nancy didn't give us any chance to do this with her, since she abruptly left and didn't stick around to hear that Eva was aware of her enactment of victimization in relation to her sister transference and real victimization in her childhood. I thought that Nancy was depriving herself by her withdrawal of so much, as she herself said how much she missed everyone, and left with a blind sense of her own victimization. However, I also realize that she left because she thought it was futile to convince me to reduce the size of the group so that she could be at her comfort level. Nancy, like all others, would need to stay with the discomfort of new things opening up for her in group, beyond her comfort level, but she clung to the size of the group as if it could keep her physically comfortable if the four-hour group could be reduced to, in her own words, "four or five people." She had cried as she longed for this fanaticized magical number of four or five people, who would, supposedly in her fantasy, share in some idealized harmonious journey together.

Of course, Nancy's fantasy of an ideal womb-like mini-group did not account for the practicalities of what I had to contend with as a group leader, who needed to have a certain number of people in the group to make it worth my while to work all day long on a Saturday once a month when I wouldn't have had my practice open at that time otherwise. And her fantasy didn't account for the fact that people left the group periodically, and sometimes a few at a time, and that there might not be any group left if I only took four or five into the group. But it was my job to access all this, not hers. She was entitled to be angry about me setting the parameters I saw as necessary and she was, in addition, entitled to her transferential rage toward me. Her retaliations against me for setting the group number limit, which she had referred to as "It's your way or the highway!" could have continued to be part of her therapy process, and could have been dealt with in the group as part of the group process if she had continued.

I resented her not letting this happen. But I also continue to regret that my assaultive phrase about her being from another planet came out as it did, stopping Nancy from bringing up once again that she did not approve of having so many in the group. Although I actually had a significant point about the issue of the group number being used as a "red herring" to divert me and the group from the more important issues of understanding how each person in the group was struggling with how to express and negotiate the communication and effect of their own aggression, I expressed my point as an "aggressive criticism," in other words, as retaliation against Nancy. I had emphatically declared that Nancy must come from another planet if she didn't know that aggression, and people being hurt by aggression, were part of life. In fact, it was a part of life that I hoped we could work together in the group to understand together as time went on.

From my point of view, the spontaneous expression of anger and injury in the group was a first step toward working with conflicts over aggression and over childhood narcissistic injury that still haunted us all in our internal worlds. In fact, that is what would transpire in the group, and that is why I said to Nancy that Eva would come around to dealing with their conflict even if Eva had said it was too much in this particular group. But apparently Nancy, obviously in retrospect, being so injured herself—although she was looking on the outside like the tough one, while Eva temporarily crumbled—could not have any long-range view. In fact, her rage must have triggered her despair that things could not be about meaningfully with change coming about. I presume Nancy regressed to an early childhood state of feeling in which her outside and inside worlds were dominated by a family that could never change.

Since I was not responding to Nancy's repeated rage about the group size by decreasing the group membership limit even more than I already had, could I have seemed like the immovable object to Nancy? In this way had I become, in her mind, an unchangeable and impenetrable object parent who refused to let her have any impact? "It's either your way or the highway!" she had once said. How very sad that Nancy would not stick around to see how she could have an impact on me—even though I didn't submit to her controlling, how I organized a group that I had created in my hard-won practice, and which I had worked with on monthly Saturdays for 18 years of my life!

But still, the regret is there. I feel sad about the loss of what could have been with Nancy if she had chosen to stay and work as a member of this special group. I feel sad about Nancy not being in the group as I go beyond my own countertransferential sadistic thoughts, to just feeling the loss of what could have been with Nancy. This would be my mourning process in relation to Nancy, but my regret is also a critical part of surrendering to the grief related to her loss. My regret dialogues with my retaliatory anger in my mind. I think of Nancy suffering after leaving the group with a double-sided response. I feel bad for her, and guilty about causing her injury. I see her sad child face in my mind, behind the more adult face she tried to maintain at the end of the last group she attended.

But I also feel angry sadism that resides within me as well as within her. I feel a sadism that wants Nancy to suffer and be tortured, just as I have been tortured after her leaving. I have been tortured because I can't continue the work and create a meaningful dialogue of understanding and resolution between us. It was this sadism, I am aware, that propelled me into my verbal attacking exclamatory question to begin with, "What planet do you live on?" This sadism does not seem to evaporate in the face of regret. However, my awareness of my regret is a pivotal point in my countertransferential mourning process. Through my conscious regret, I am learning how to contain my reactions and process them, as I continue to work with the monthly mourning and therapy group. Through all this, I become more capable of helping all the other group members work with and understand their own aggression as it emerges within this group!

Countertransference Regret and Facilitating the Group: Aggression and Transference Work as Part of the Group Developmental Mourning Process

The sharing of my countertransference regret with the group seems to have allowed the group to feel safe enough to risk openly dealing with their own aggression. My countertransference sharing took place in the group that met after Helen had said that the idea that we could be all be nice and polite if there were fewer group members was "bullshit." However, since Helen said this just at the moment when Nancy was just reacting to my "other planet" comment, Nancy didn't seem to get it at all! Helen seemed to think that Nancy didn't get that Helen thought Nancy's expectation for everyone to be continually polite and supportive of one another was what she, Helen, meant by "bullshit."

As Helen stated that Nancy may have had a whole different vision and agenda about what being in a therapy group was about, it paved the way for me to not only acknowledge my impulsive hostility toward Nancy but to also explain my angry motivation that lay behind it. I said, "This isn't an excuse for what I said or how I said it, but that's what pissed me off!" I meant that what pissed me off was Nancy's demand that everyone be well behaved, while she discounted her own accusatory behavior toward me and Eva since she thought her attacks were justified. I also referred to Nancy's assumption that if people in the group were angry and upset and competitive, it meant that I was the causal perpetrator of putting too many people into the group. Such an assumption by Nancy was what had ticked me off. Nancy's fallacious assumption about what the group was all about could put everyone in a straitjacket! But most of all Nancy may have wanted to put me in a straitjacket. This would be a way of punishing me, with the further punishment of a group rebellion and mutiny, which she might hope would provoke everyone into "abandoning ship!" This could be just my own paranoid countertransference, but there had been some evidence for this in Nancy's emails to other group members, where she got to point an enraged cold finger at me.

Fortunately for myself, the other members of the group, and all the new members coming in, things didn't go the way of Nancy's retaliatory impulse. In fact, instead the pendulum swung quite in the other direction. This occurred as I went to the hull of the group ship and began to take more control, beginning to guide us through the stormy waters of group aggression, as well as guiding everyone through the psychic visualization at the beginning of the group. This emerged naturally through the interactive process of me responding to the group's emotional evolution. I could see that themes of individual developmental mourning in the group could involve the angry and aggressive stages of mourning, as well as the grief-laden feelings of loss that would stimulate love and empathy between group members. Cecilia and Carol were to be the manifest couple in conflict in the group that allowed for a whole group engagement around aggression, hate, and transferential rage with underlying longings for nurturance and mothering.

The Paradigm Conflict of Cecilia and Carol

Cecilia had been taking a lot of time in the last group with Nancy, and also then in the two monthly three-and-a-half-hour Saturday groups afterward. Most of the group members were receptive to this since Cecilia was going through an extremely acute crisis, and was taking time to leave the crisis to come to the group and share the current trauma to get support. Cecilia took time to speak about the current trauma that had brought up a new heightened awareness of past traumas, which had directly threatened her very existence on an ongoing basis. Cecilia's description of all this could be hard to stay with. Some, in the group, could be more fully with her as she spoke than others. In the case of Carol, Carol as a group member questioned out loud in this third monthly group, after the last group with Nancy, why she was unable to feel empathy for Cecilia as she listened to her. Carol said, "Something is blocking my empathy and I want to know what it is."

Cecilia's response to Carol's comment was to declare that she had never liked Carol. Cecilia said that among other things that had caused her dislike of Carol was an incident that had occurred after group one day. Cecilia reported that she heard Carol speaking to someone on the phone before hanging up. She recalled the incident as Carol complaining that she had been sucked in by this person. According to Cecilia, in her frustration, Carol threw out some angry comments about the person on the phone that reflected derogatory judgments she made against someone who had wasted her time. Cecilia's reaction to Carol's angry judgments was not to understand why Carol needed to ventilate her frustration in this judgmental manner. Instead, Cecilia would make her own globalizing judgment against Carol. This Cecilia had kept to herself for some time, allowing her resentment against Carol to fester until she felt it was the right moment to reveal it in the group.

Now Cecilia came out with her secret resentment and made it public, which is what allowed the group process to work to detoxify Cecilia's judgments and Carol's judgments of each other. We were beginning to understand what Cecilia and Carol had triggered off in each other, from the sadomasochistic aspects of early relationships that they both carried with them within their internal worlds. Cecilia said that she didn't like Carol since the day of her comments about the unknown person on the phone. Cecilia said that she didn't want to associate with someone who had such contemptuous attitudes toward others and that this had made her wary of being in a group with Carol as well. Of course in all of this, Cecilia was being reactive, and might not have been fully aware of her own level of contempt manifesting toward Carol. When Cecilia told her reasons for not liking Carol, I remarked on Cecilia having made a globalizing judgment about Carol from only one incident, in which Carol was in a state of momentary intense anger and frustration toward someone, and was getting off her chest. My saying this helped Carol to express her point of view, which was also her way of justifying herself and being self-protective on her side, just as Cecilia was being self-protective on her own. Carol said, "If you judge me that way then I certainly don't want to share anything with you again, which I had done when I thought of you as a fellow group member."

As Cecilia and Carol each established their polarized platforms of defense and self-protection, Cecilia began to say that Carol was putting her own problems onto her, and Carol in turn began to say that Cecilia was putting her contempt onto her. This interpersonal stand-off then became a paradigm for each woman's internal world transferential conflicts. Carol made this explicit by saying, "This is exactly what goes on between me and my mother! We end up with our heels dug in, each saying that the other is putting their stuff on the other, each feeling blamed by the other for things that are the other's responsibility. My mother and I go through this all the time. My mother says I'm putting blame on her for my own problems and for my own projected judgments, and from saying I think mother was doing the same to me. Then we're stuck!"

I took this opportunity as the group leader to say that since Cecilia and Carol seemed to be in an impasse at the moment, it was time for the other members of the group to be invited in to say what they were, experiencing and thinking, during this two group member conflict. Larry spoke up first, and said that he had felt like Carol, felt that Cecilia could be contemptuous and judgmental. He said he had felt scolded by another group member, Sandra, and was sensitive to what he experienced as contemptuous judgments. Sandra was eager to begin the group process after the lunch break, and had turned to Larry and said, "Turn your cell phone off!" Larry said he felt like a child being scolded. He said as an adult he would like space to explain that he was on the phone with an urgent call. Instead, he felt judged by Sandra, so here were the themes of self-righteous contempt and accusation that had gone on between Nancy and Eva, which had led to Nancy's fight and flight reactions.

Sandra, Cecilia, and Carol were willing to work with these conflicts within the group. Consequently, there could be a different outcome than with Nancy. This time we didn't have to lose a group member. We didn't have to conclude that all this was due to the number of people in the room or due to the size of my office. We could see the internal world of each group member, with all their transferences manifesting in the external and transitional world of the therapy group.

After Larry spoke, Sandra said that she had thought he was rude because I had said it was time to start the group again, and he wouldn't put his cell phone away. Again, she had felt liked the wronged party, just as Larry did, and she got to express her viewpoint and to have her voice. Then Victor said that he had felt for Larry, Victor also believed that the way Sandra spoke to Larry had been more cold and domineering than it had to be. Victor shared that he thought that Sandra's tone might have made Larry feel like a little boy being shamed and humiliated by a mother's scolding.

The Vulnerable Child Emerges in the Next Group
After the Fight and Flight Reaction

The dialogues between these group members illustrate how rapid-fire negative judgments and projections can turn into communication and conversation. This evolving conversation had meaning for the whole group in terms of understanding these negative judgments and projections as defenses against a feared interpersonal affect contact that can potentially be transformed from disowned aggression, in the form of accusatory hostility, into empathic understanding and mutual surrender into curiosity about who the other is, also reducing the fear of not having one's own voice if one lets in the other.

This kind of transformation was even more dramatically experienced in the next monthly group as Sandra became the center of attention when she was in need of expressing a lot of anger related to every member of the group. I suggested that we go around the room, with Sandra saying what she was angry about to each person, which could lead to a dialectical exchange, reducing the polarization of angry rapid-fire judgments, as each person could speak back to Sandra in this way. Victor went first, but then Laura and Sandra became engaged in a negative transferential exchange that started to take over the group.

Laura was experiencing Sandra as a "scary mother" who was constantly critical and who couldn't be satisfied. Sandra was experiencing Laura as an incompetent child who wasn't worthy of being her peer. She told Laura that Laura wasn't willing to commit to attending group, every month, regularly, as she, Sandra had. Laura picked up that Sandra wished she would leave the group, and she began to fight to have her voice in the midst of Sandra's judgments. At one point, Victor looked at Laura and said, "I can see the terrified hurt child in you who feels she could not have a voice with her mother, the child who felt suffocated by the mother silencing her with her negative judgments." Tears came to Laura's eyes at this point. Laura really felt the pain of the agonized silenced child as she experienced Sandra as the "bad mother" who lived inside of her. Victor's empathy helped her open to her vulnerability and get past her silence. But then vulnerability turned to anger and she raised her voice and told Sandra off.

At that point, Sandra got up to run out of the room and leave the group. I stopped her. I closed the office door that she was opening, and asked Sandra to sit down so we could understand what was happening for her. I said that both Sandra and Laura were feeling like they were being silenced and suffocated by a rapid-fire judging and accusatory mother. I commented that throughout the group that day Sandra had heard everyone as being contemptuous, sarcastic, and critical, way beyond any of this contempt actually being expressed, and I referred particularly to Larry who she experienced as contemptuous. Then I said to Sandra, who was listening to me attentively, even when projecting negative judgments onto the group members, and making such judgments, "I think you have an internal contemptuous object mother you are projecting onto others, embellishing all that is said to you with the attitude of contempt."

Sandra listened. I then said that I thought she, Sandra, was feeling inside a lot like Laura had been feeling, as if she was being silenced and accused by a contemptuous, angry mother with rapid-fire judgments. However, I said, Sandra was enacting the mother's part, and I sensed that the intimidated child self was afraid to come out and be seen. As I spoke directly to Sandra at that moment, the child pain came into her eyes through tears that had just happened a few moments ago for Laura. I said that now we could feel her. I said that everything she had told us about the traumas in her life could mean so much more to us now since we could feel her.

There were a few moments of peaceful quiet while everyone in the group felt the vulnerable child self in Sandra emerge into the transitional and potential space of the Object Relations therapy group. We all felt Sandra and Sandra also felt us. Laura even reached out and said that she could feel Sandra now as "one of us" rather than as "Scary Sandra." This tranquility was about to be sabotaged by Sandra as she began to go back to her negative judgments, but I was able to stop her, just as she had trusted me enough to allow me to stop her from running out the door. I said that she had allowed us to be with her but was in danger of running back into her fight and flight behavior. I said, "If you had run out the door we couldn't have gotten to this!"

At this moment, Sandra was able to surrender her self-protective aggression, in the mode of identifying with her internal judgmental mother then. She let it go and allowed herself to stay with meaningful conversation and dialogue with me and with the group members. Then people listened, and she was able to speak of memories of her highly critical, rejecting, judgmental, and contemptuous mother then. She also spoke about meaningful memories of her father that had made her feel he joined forces with this mother, the same mother who had been internalized as her internal contemptuous mother, who could so easily have been anticipated in others, which then resulted in a self-fulfilling prophecy of provoking negative judgments at the moment that she made them.

Now people listened intently and empathetically to Sandra, including Laura, and Laura even said she felt a new commitment to the group because now she could see that we could get past the hostile exchanges that she and her mother had always had to the point of communication and empathy. The whole atmosphere was changed in the group as everyone listened to Laura because they could feel her. Sandra, in turn, demonstrated that she could feel the others. She spoke of how she had been listening to each one of them attentively for almost a year before she plunged in to speak at length about herself. Her capacity for attunement and listening to others was validated as she went around the room and said what she had retained of each person's struggles in life that were shared in the group. I underlined this validation by putting it explicitly into words.

The rest of the group that day was a free flow of mutually meaningful exchanges, and Sandra had people genuinely curious about her now. Now the group members could listen to Sandra, ask questions, and also understand her transferential dilemma. They could do so because each of them shared this transferential dilemma with Sandra in their own unique way. Consequently, each member learned from this group meeting about their own internal "bad object" parents. They also learned how they each had flight and fight impulses along with rationalizing attitudes toward their disappointing parents.

Conclusion:
Voices Being Heard, Transferences Being Dealt With, and Differentiation

All the transferences were emerging through this conflict, which was being contained in the group's holding environment. So now we could all work to understand it. We could work to understand how such conflict related to everyone's hunger for empathy, attention, and understanding, as well as to everyone's fear of the hostile and contemptuous judgments of others.

With this progress, the other group members began to chime in as well. Consequently, the whole group became engaged in expressing what fears they had of others' judgments. The group began expressing how difficult it was to trust that these difficult things could be given voice to, rather than being hidden and acted out in split-off ways outside the group, including by people dropping out as Nancy had. Before Helen had said that Nancy had been criticized by me in the last group she attended. However, she also said in the group afterward that Nancy seemed to have a different agenda of expectation for what the group was about, referring to what she thought was Nancy's expectation for everyone to be polite. Helen now came out and said, "This work is what I thought the group would be about, having all this intense stuff come out and be worked with. It's too bad that Nancy, who led the way with her own aggression, should not be here to benefit from what she began as the others are!"

I think Helen's words echoed a lot of what I had been feeling. Beyond my own regret about my critical comments toward Nancy in the last group she attended, was my underlying loss and grief related to not having had the chance to work with Nancy in the group at the level that I and the group were now working with aggression, in relation to the conflict between Sandra and Carol and between others in the group. Through the group process, a polarized opposition in the group, with Cecilia and Carol, and Sandra and Laura being enemies, was now transforming into the communicative dialogue of interactive human beings who were trying to understand and know each other. This could in turn lead to each group member in the room having their own individual internal capacity for psychic dialectic facilitated, as the external and internal worlds interacted, and empathy and compassion were created through dialogue.

REFERENCES

Akhtar, S. (1996). Love and its discontents: A concluding overview. In S. Akhtar, & S. Kramer (Eds.), Intimacy and infidelity: Separation-individuation perspectives (pp. 145–178). Karnac Books.

Akhtar, S. (1999). Inner torment: Living between conflict and fragmentation. Jason Aronson.

Akhtar, S. (Ed.) (2014). Fear: A dark shadow across our lifespan Karnac. Balint, M. (1965). Primary love and psychoanalytic technique. Butler & Tanner Ltd.

———— (1968).*The basic fault: Therapeutic aspects of aggression.* Brunner/Mazel.

Beebe, B., & Lachman, F.M. (1988). The contribution of mother-infant mutual influence to the origins of self and object representations. *Psychoanalytic Psychology, 5*(4), 309–337.

Benjamin, J. (1988). *The bonds of love: Psychoanalysis, feminism, and the problem of domination.* Pantheon Books.

Bergmann, M.S. (1987). *The anatomy of loving.* Columbia University Press.

Bion, W.R. (1959). Attacks on linking. *International Journal of Psychoanalysis, 40*, 308–315.

———— (1963). *Elements of psychoanalysis.* Karnac Books.

———— (1967). Attacks on linking. In *Second thoughts: Selected papers on psychoanalysis* (pp. 93–109). Elsevier.

———— (1970/1988). *Attention and interpretation.* Tavistock Publications.

Bowlby, J. (1963). *Pathological mourning and childhood mourning.* In R. Frankel (Ed.), Essential papers on object loss. NYU Press.

———— (1969). Attachment and loss, Vol. 1: Attachment. *Attachment and Loss.* Basic Books.

———— (1980). Attachment and loss, Vol. 3: Loss, Sadness and Depression. *Attachment and Loss.* Basic Books.

Brent, L., & Resch, R.C. (1987). A paradigm of infant-mother reciprocity: A reexamination of emotional refueling. *Psychoanalytic Psychology, 4*(1), 15–31.

Burch, B. (1996). Between women: The mother-daughter romance and homoerotic transference in psychotherapy. *Psychoanalytic Psychology, 13*, 475–494.

Davis, J.M. (1994). Love in the afternoon: a relational reconsideration of love and dread in the countertransference. *Psychoanalytic Dialogues, 4*(2), 153–170.

Dickinson, E. (Author), & Johnson, T.H. (Ed.) (1960). *The complete poems of Emily Dickinson*. Little, Brown, and Company.

Fairbairn, W.R.D. (1952). *Psychoanalytic studies of the personality*. Tavistock Publications.

Fonagy, P., Gergely, G., Jurist, E.L., & Target, M. (2000). *Affect regulation, mentalization, and the development of the self*. Other Press.

Freud, A. (1936). *The ego and its mechanisms of defense*. International Universities Press.

Freud, S. (1915). Observations on transference-love (Further recommendations on the technique of psycho-analysis III). *SE, XII*, 157–171.

———— (1916). Some character types met with in psycho-analytic work. *SE, XIV*, 309–333.

———— (1917). Mourning and melancholia. In *Collected Papers, IV* (pp. 30–59). Tavistock Publications.

———— (1957). Mourning and melancholia. In J. Strachey (Ed. & Trans.), *The standard edition of the complete psychological works of Sigmund Freud (SE), XIV* (pp. 237–258). Hogarth Press. (Original work published 1917)

Gabbard, G.O. (1992). Sexual excitement and countertransference love in the analyst. *Journal of the American Psychoanalytic Association, 42*, 1083–1106.

———— (1994). On love and lust in erotic transference. *Journal of the American Psychoanalytic Association, 42*, 513–531.

Gorkin, M. (1984). Narcissistic personality disorder and pathological mourning. *Contemporary Psychoanalysis, 20*(3), 400–420.

Gould, E. (1989). Perspectives on transference. *Psychoanalysis and Psychotherapy, VII*, 62–73.

Grunes, M. (1984). The therapeutic Object Relationship. *Psychoanalytic Review, 71*(1), 123–143.

Guntrip, H. (1969). *Schizoid phenomena, object-relations and the self*. International Universities Press.

Harris, I. (1960). Typical anxiety dreams and Object Relations. *International Journal of Psychoanalysis, 41*, 604–611.

Hartmann, E., Russ, D., Van der Kolk, B., Falke, R., & Oldfield, M. (1981). A preliminary study of the personality of the nightmare sufferer: Relationship to schizophrenia and creativity. *American Journal of Psychiatry, 138*(6), 794–797.

Hoffman, I.Z. (1998). Poetic transformations of erotic experience commentary on paper by Jody Messler Davies. *Psychoanalytic Dialogues, 8*(6), 791–804.

Horner, A. (2005). *Dealing with resistances in psychotherapy.* Jason Aronson.

Jacobson, E. (1964). *The self and the object world.* International Universities Press.

Joseph, B. (1989). Towards the experiencing of psychic pain. In M. Feldman, & E. Bott Spillius (Eds.), *Psychic equilibrium and psychic change: Selected papers of Betty Joseph* (pp. 87–98). Routledge.

Kavaler-Adler, S. (1985). Mirror mirror on the wall … *Journal of Comprehensive Psychotherapy, 5,* 1–38.

———. (1986). Lord of the mirrors and the demon lover. *American Journal of Psychoanalysis, 46*(4), 336–344.

——— (1989). Discussion of 'Perspectives on transference.' *Psychoanalysis and Psychotherapy,* Vol. VII, 80–84.

——— (1988a). Diane Arbus and the demon lover. *American Journal of Psychoanalysis, 48*(4), 366–370.

——— (1988b). Nightmares and Object Relations theory. In H. Kellerman (Ed.), *Nightmares: Biological and psychological foundations.* Columbia University Press.

——— (1989a). Discussion of 'Perspectives on transference.' *Psychoanalysis and Psychotherapy, VII,* 80–84.

——— (1989b). Anne Sexton and the daemon lover. *American Journal of Psychoanalysis, 49*(4), 105–114.

——— (1990). Charlotte Bronte and the feminine self. *American Journal of Psychoanalysis, 50,* 37–43.

——— (1991a). Emily Dickinson and the subject of seclusion. *American Journal of Psychoanalysis, 51*(1), 21–38.

——— (1991b). A theory of creative process reparation and its mode of failure: The case of Katherine Mansfield. *Psychoanalysis and Psychotherapy, 9*(2), 134–150.

——— (1992a). Mourning and erotic transference. *International Journal of Psychoanalysis, 73*(3), 527–539.

——— (1992b). The conflict and process theory of Melanie Klein. *American Journal of Psychoanalysis, 5*(3), 187–204.

——— (1992c). An Object Relations view of creative process and group process. *Group, 16* (1), 47–58.

——— (1993a/2013). *The compulsion to create: A psychoanalytic study of women artists.* Routledge. (Reprinted as *The compulsion to create: Women writers and their demon lovers,* by Other Press (2000), ORI Academic Press (2013).

———— (1993b). The conflict and process theory of Melanie Klein. *American Journal of Psychoanalysis, 53*(3), 187–204.

———— (1993c). Object Relations issues in the treatment of the precedipal character. *American Journal of Psychoanalysis, 53*(1), 19–34.

———— (1995). Opening up blocked mourning in the precedipal character. *American Journal of Psychoanalysis, 55*(2), 145–168.

———— (1996/2014). *The creative mystique: From red shoes frenzy to love and creativity.* Reprinted by ORI Academic Press (2014).

———— (1998). Vaginal core or vampire mouth: Visceral manifestation of envy in women: The protosymbolic politics of object relations. In N. Burke (Ed.), *Gender and envy* (pp. 221–240). Routledge.

———— (1999). Interview with Frank Summers. *Division Review* (The Newsletter of Division 39). The American Psychological Association.

———— (2000). The divine, the deviant and the diabolical. A journey through an artist's paintings during her participation in a creative process group: An evolution of "developmental mourning." *International Forum of Psychoanalysis, 9,* 97–111.

———— (2001, June). Anatomy of surrender. *Reportango, No. 31,* 27–29.

———— (2003a). *Mourning, spirituality and psychic change: a new object relations view of psychoanalysis.* Brunner-Routledge.

———— (2003b). Lesbian homoerotic transference in dialectic with developmental mourning: On the way to symbolism from the protosymbolic. *Psychoanalytic Psychology, 20,* 131–152.

———— (2004). Anatomy of regret: A developmental view of the depressive position and a critical turn toward love and creativity in the transforming schizoid personality. *American Journal of Psychoanalysis, 64,* 39–76.

———— (2005a). The case of David: Nine years on the couch for sixty minutes: Once a week. *American Journal of Psychoanalysis, 65,* 103–134.

———— (2005b). From benign mirror to demon lover: An object relations view of compulsion versus desire. *American Journal of Psychoanalysis, 65*(1), 31–52.

———— (2006a). From neurotic guilt to existential guilt as grief: The road to interiority, agency and compassion through mourning. Part 1. *American Journal of Psychoanalysis, 66,* 239–260.

———— (2006b). From neurotic guilt to existential guilt as grief: the road to interiority, agency, and compassion through mourning, Part II. *American Journal of Psychoanalysis, 66,* 333–350.

———— (2006c). "My graduation is my mother's funeral": Transformation from the paranoid-schizoid to the depressive position in fear of success, and the internal saboteur. *International Forum of Psychoanalysis, 15,* 117–130.

────── (2007a). Mourning and erotic transference. In J. Schaverien (Ed.), *Gender, countertransference, and erotic transference* (pp. 104–122). Routledge.

────── (2007b). Lesbian homoerotic transference in dialectic with developmental mourning: On the way to symbolism from the protosymbolic. In J. Schaverien (Ed.), *Gender, countertransference, and erotic transference* (pp. 157–183). Routledge.

────── (2007c). Pivotal moments of surrender to mourning the parental internal objects. *Psychoanalytic Review, 94*(5), 763–789.

────── (2010). Seduction, date rape, and aborted surrender. *International Forum of Psychoanalysis, 19*, 15–26.

────── (2013). *The anatomy of regret: From death instinct to reparation and symbolization in vivid case studies.* Karnac Books.

────── (2014a). *The Klein-Winnicott dialectic: Transformative new metapsychology and interactive clinical theory.* Karnac Books.

────── (2014b). Psychic structure and the capacity to mourn: Why narcissists cannot mourn. *MindConsiliums, 14*(1), 1–17.

────── (2014c). Erotic transference: A journey of passion and symbolization. *MindConsiliums, 14*(1), 19–43.

────── (2018). The beginning of heartache in character disorders: on the way to relatedness and Intimacy through primal affects and symbolization. *International Forum of Psychoanalysis, 27*(4), 207–218.

Kernberg, O. (1975). *Borderline Conditions and Pathological Narcissism.* Jason Aronson.

────── (1988). Object relations theory in clinical practice. *The Psychoanalytic Quarterly, 42*(4), 481–504.

────── (1995). *Love relations.* Yale University Press.

Khan, M. (1972). Dread of surrender to resourceless dependence in the analytic situation. *The International Journal of Psychoanalysis, 53*(2), 225–230.

────── (1974). *The privacy of the self.* International Universities Press.

Klein, M. (1940). Mourning and its relation to manic depressive states. *International Journal of Psycho–Analysis, 21*, 125–153.

────── (1946). Notes on some schizoid mechanisms. *International Journal of Psycho-Analysis, 1927*, 99–110.

────── (1957/1980). Envy and gratitude. In *Envy and gratitude and other works: 1946 to 1963.* Hogarth Press.

────── (1975). *Love, guilt, and reparation and other works, 1921–1945.* Hogarth Press.

Kohut, H. (1971). *The analysis of the self.* International Universities Press.

────── (1977). *The restoration of the self.* International Universities Press.

Kuhn, T. (1962). *The structure of scientific revolutions* (2nd ed.). University of Chicago Press.

Loewald, H. (1962). Internalization, separation, mourning, and the superego. *The Psychoanalytic Quarterly, 31*, 484–504.

Mahler, M. (1971). A study of the separation-individuation process—and its possible application to borderline phenomena in the psychoanalytic situation. *The Psychoanalytic Study of the Child, 26*, 403–424.

———— Pine, F., & Bergman, A. (1975). *The psychological birth of the human infant: Symbiosis and individuation*. Basic Books.

Masterson, J.F. (1976). *Psychotherapy of the borderline adult: A developmental approach*. Brunner/Mazel.

Masterson, J.F. (1981). *The narcissistic and borderline disorders: An integrated developmental approach*. Routledge.

———— (2000). *The personality disorders: A new look at the developmental self and object relations approach, theory, diagnosis, and treatment*. Zeig, Tucker & Theisen Inc.

McDougall, J. (1998). *The many faces of Eros*. W. W. Norton & Company.

Modell, A. (1975). A narcissistic defense against affects and the illusion of self-sufficiency. *International Journal of Psycho-Analysis, 56*, 275–282.

Modell, A. (1976). "The holding environment" and the therapeutic action of psychoanalysis. *Journal of the American Psychoanalysis, 24*, 285–308.

Ogden, T. (1986). *The matrix of the mind*. Jason Aronson.

———— (1992). The dialectically constituted/decentred subject of psychoanalysis. II. The contributions of Klein and Winnicott. *International Journal of Psychoanalysis, 73*, 63–626.

———— (1994). *Subjects of analysis*. Jason Aronson.

O'Neil, M.K., & Akhtar, S. (Eds.) (2018). *Jealousy: Developmental, cultural, and clinical realms*. Routledge.

Pine, F. (1985). *Developmental theory and clinical process*. Yale University Press.

Plath, S. (1961). *Ariel*. Harper & Row Publishers.

Pollock, G. (1975). Mourning and memorialization through music. *The Annual of Psychoanalysis, 3*, 423–436.

Rinsley, D.B. (1988). Fairbairn's "basic endopsychic situation" considered in terms of "classical" and "deficit" metapsychological models. *The Journal of the American Academy of Psychoanalysis, 16*(4), 461–477.

Schwartz–Salant, N. (1982). *Narcissism and character transformation*. Inner City Books.

Segal, H. (1952). A psychoanalytic approach to aesthetics. *International Journal of Psychoanalysis, 33*, 196–207.

————— (1957). Notes on symbol formation. *International Journal of Psychoanalysis*, *38*, 391–397.

————— (1975). *Introduction to the work of Melanie Klein.* Hogarth Press.

————— (1985). *The Work of Hanna Segal.* Jason Aronson.

————— (1986). Notes on symbol formation. *The work of Hanna Segal*, 49–65. Jason Aronson.

Seinfeld, J. (1989). *The bad object.* Jason Aronson.

Shakespeare, W. (1942). In W.A. Neilson, & C.J., Hill (Eds.) *The complete plays and poems of William Shakespeare: The New Cambridge Edition.* Houghton Mifflin Harcourt.

Shabad, P. (2001). *Despair and the return of hope, echoes of mourning in psychotherapy.* Jason Aronson.

Spitz, R.A. (Author), (1983). In R.N. Emde (Ed.) *Dialogues from infancy—Selected papers.* International Universities Press.

Steiner, J. (1993). *Psychic retreats.* Routledge.

Stern, D. (1985). *The interpersonal world of the infant.* Jason Aronson.

Stolorow, R.D., & Lachman, F.M. (1980). *Psychoanalysis of Developmental Arrests.* International Universities Press.

Strachey, J. (1934). The nature of the therapeutic action of psychoanalysis. *The International Journal of Psychoanalysis, 15*, 117–126.

Summers, F. (1999). *Transcendence of the self: An object relations model of psychoanalytic therapy.* Analytic Press.

Summers, F. (2013). *The psychoanalytic vision.* Routledge.

Trop, J. L. (1988). Erotic and eroticized transference: A self psychological perspective. *Psychoanalytic Psychology, 5,* 269–284

Tustin, F. (1990). *The protective shell in children and adults.* Karnac Books.

Winnicott, D.W. (1953). Transitional objects and transitional phenomena—a study of the first not me possession. *International Journal of Psychoanalysis, 34*, 89–97.

————— (1958). The capacity to be alone. *International Journal of Psychoanalysis, 39*, 416–420.

————— (1960). Ego distortion in terms of true and false self. In *The maturational processes and the facilitating environment: Studies in the theory of emotional development,* 140–152. Hogarth, 1965.

————— (1963). The development of the capacity for concern. *Bulletin of the Menninger Clinic, 27*, 167–176.

————— (1965). *The maturational processes and the facilitating environment: Studies in the theory of emotional development.* International Universities Press.

—————— (1969). The use of an object. *International Journal of Psycho-Analysis*, 50, 711–716.

—————— (1971). *Playing and reality*. Tavistock Publications.

—————— (1974). Fear of breakdown. *International Review of Psycho-Analysis, 1*, 103–107.

—————— (1982a). Ego distortion in terms of the true and false self. In *The maturational processes and the facilitating environment*, 140–152. (Original work published in 1960)

—————— (1982b). The development of the capacity for concern. In *The maturational processes and the facilitating environment*, in 73–82. International Universities Press. (Original work published 1963.)

—————— (1982c). *The maturational processes and the facilitating environment*. International Universities Press.

Wolfenstein, M. (1966). How is mourning possible? *Psychoanalytic Study of the Child, 21*, 93–123.